D1706620

Other University of California Press titles
by Richard G. Hovannisian

Armenia on the Road to Independence, 1918

The Republic of Armenia: Volume II:
From Versailles to London, 1919–1920

The Republic of Armenia: Volume III:
From London to Sèvres, February–August 1920

The Republic of Armenia: Volume IV:
Between Crescent and Sickle: Partition and Sovietization

The Republic of
ARMENIA

Volume I

Published under the auspices of the
NEAR EASTERN CENTER
University of California, Los Angeles

The Republic of
ARMENIA

VOLUME I

The First Year, 1918-1919

•

RICHARD G. HOVANNISIAN

UNIVERSITY OF CALIFORNIA PRESS

BERKELEY · LOS ANGELES · LONDON

University of California Press
Berkeley and Los Angeles, California
University of California Press, Ltd.
London, England
© 1971 by
The Regents of the University of California

Library of Congress Cataloging-in-Publication Data
(Revised for vols. 3–4)

Hovannisian, Richard G.
    The Republic of Armenia.
    (Bibliography: v.1, p. 479–518; v. 2, p. 531–572;   )
    Contents: v. 1. The first year, 1918–1919—v. 2. From Versailles to
London, 1919–1920—v. 3. From London to Sèvres, February–August, 1920
—v. 4. Between crescent and sickle: partition and sovietization.
    1. Armenia—History—Revolution, 1917–1920.
    I. Title.
    DS195.5.H56   956.6′2   72-129613
    ISBN 0-520-01984-9 (v. 1)
    ISBN 0-520-04186-0 (v. 2)
    ISBN 0-520-08803-4 (v. 3)
    ISBN 0-520-08804-2 (v. 4)

Printed in the United States of America
9 8 7 6 5 4

The paper used in this publication meets the minimum requirements of
American National Standard for Information Sciences—Permanence of Paper
for Printed Library Materials, ANSI Z39.48–1984. ⊗

To

KASPAR and **SIROON**
of KHARPERT

HOVAKIM and **KHENGENI**
of KARIN–ERZERUM

and
to

RAFFI, ARMEN, ANI, GARO
and all other children who
yearn from afar

Contents

Maps

Preface

For two and a half years, from the spring of 1918 to the winter of 1920, the Armenian people labored to lay the foundations of an independent state, the first such political entity in more than five hundred years. The obstacles were immense, perhaps insurmountable, but the nation, having suffered the unparalleled persecutions of 1915–1916, strove desperately to assure itself a collective future. Although independence was thrust upon the Armenians quite unexpectedly, they soon held it to be essential for self-preservation and regeneration.

Now, with the passage of a half century, it has become clear that the historical moment was unpropitious for enduring Armenian freedom. The opportunity had beckoned the Armenians too early, if measured by the experience of most peoples of Asia and Africa, or too late, if compared with that of the Balkan peoples. The fact that neither Nationalist Turkey nor Soviet Russia could countenance an independent Armenia on former Ottoman and Romanov territories, that the Allied Powers and the United States failed to effectuate their plans and pledges, and that the Armenians alone were too few and too weak to defend their country led to the collapse of the Republic of Armenia. The story of that republic, like the long history of the Armenian people, is characterized by an unequal, tragic struggle. The courageous efforts of the new state to defy hopeless odds evoke sympathy, but the historian is obliged to transcend sentiment in order to evaluate and set forth the complicated, often contradictory circumstances that rendered independence ephemeral.

My initial study, *Armenia on the Road to Independence, 1918,* was an attempt to integrate the numerous elements, domestic and external, national and international, which culminated in the emergence of the Republic of Armenia. The requisite research and the writing were challenging, for by its very nature the topic is extremely controversial, the facts often disguised, misrepresented, or undiscovered. Seeking history in a past shrouded in myth and distortion is a difficult, sometimes thankless pursuit. The widespread positive response to the book was therefore especially gratifying and indicated that my purpose, a balanced presentation of Armenia's road to independence, had been achieved.

Even as I undertook that project, it was evident that a history of the Republic of Armenia should follow. No meticulous investigation of this subject has yet been published even though primary papers, diplomatic correspondence, memoirs, and topical studies exist as source materials. It was my intent to write the history of the Republic in an additional volume, but, with the basic research completed and the outline formulated, it became apparent that a single tome could not treat the subject adequately. The story is many faceted, entails far-reaching ramifications, and remains much too clouded to permit condensation for the present. At the expense of putting aside a concise, straightforward account for the general reader, I have decided, therefore, to present a detailed, if not involved, history of the Republic of Armenia.

This volume, the first of three projected, focuses upon the establishment of the Republic and the immediate challenges it faced: the need to forge the apparatus of government, to persevere through a death-laden winter, to resolve the labyrinthine, enervating territorial disputes with Georgia and Azerbaijan, and to secure the active support of the Allied Powers and the Paris Peace Conference. On the Republic's first anniversary the fate of Armenia continued unsettled, not in small part as the result of the ambivalence and mutual suspicions of Great Britain, France, Italy, and the United States of America. In the meantime, the resistance movement took shape in Turkey and the Soviet regime consolidated in Russia. The second volume will cover the period from mid-1919 to mid-1920, with the further development of Armenia's domestic and foreign activities and the rising impact of Nationalist Turkey, Soviet Russia, and indigenous Communist groups in the Caucasus. By the second anniversary of the Republic, the Paris Peace Conference appeared at last to have taken a firm stand on Armenian independence, yet, on the other hand, the external and internal threats to the feeble state loomed ever greater. The third volume, spanning the second half of 1920, will integrate the various aspects of Armenia's frantic efforts to achieve a modus vivendi with Soviet Russia, to persuade the Allied and Associated Powers to enforce the Treaty of Sèvres, to rouse the League of Nations to action, and to withstand the carefully planned invasion by the Turkish Nationalist armies. Failure on all levels resulted in the loss of most historic Armenian lands to Mustafa Kemal's Turkey and in the Sovietization of the remaining small region.

Among the basic primary sources for this history are the records of the American Commission to Negotiate Peace at the Paris Peace Conference and the diplomatic correspondence of American and Allied officials in Turkey, the Caucasus, and Armenia. These documents, together with numerous other relevant papers, are deposited in the National Archives of the United States, particularly in Record Groups 59, 84, and 256 of the Legislative, Judicial, and Diplomatic Records Division. The British Imperial Archives, too, contain extensive materials on the events in the Middle East after World War I, with the records of the Cabinet Office, the War Office, and the Foreign Office foremost in importance. That Great Britain, more than any other Allied nation, was involved politically and militarily in the affairs of Armenia and the entire Caucasus during the immediate postwar period points up the significance of these papers. Beginning in 1952 the Turkish General Staff began publication, in serial form, of documents relating to the Nationalist movement and the "War of Independence." This valuable collection, entitled *Harb Tarihi Vesikaları Dergisi*, provides a broader perspective in evaluating Armeno-Turkish relations.

The Archives of the Delegation of the Republic of Armenia to the Paris Peace Conference served as one of the most comprehensive sources for this history. These voluminous papers, now integrated into the depositories of the Armenian Revolutionary Federation (Hai Heghapokhakan Dashnaktsutiun) in Boston, Massachusetts, include not only all delegation correspondence but also the files of Armenian diplomatic missions the world over, the memoranda of many non-Armenian groups in Paris, press clippings compiled from the major newspapers in the Caucasus, and, above all, true copies of thousands of documents that passed in and out of the Armenian Ministry of Foreign Affairs in Erevan. It is fortunate for the historian that these latter indispensable papers were forwarded to Paris by the Armenian government in 1919–1920 so that the Republic's delegation could keep abreast of the current state of affairs in Transcaucasia. The originals or copies of some of the documents are also preserved, along with other pertinent materials, in the Central State Historical Archives of the Armenian Soviet Socialist Republic, but utilization of these by foreign scholars is still very limited and closely regulated.

The memoir genre of writing has become noteworthy in making available many hitherto unknown details. In particular, recently published works of then-active Soviet and Turkish officials reveal for the first time the actual degree of Bolshevik-Nationalist collaboration vis-à-vis the Republic of Armenia. A recurring theme in the Turkish memoirs, especially those of the military leaders, is the trenchant opposition to the existence of a separate Armenian state, whether within or across the borders of the former Ottoman Empire. These memoirs, together with diplomatic papers and correspondence published by the Turkish and Soviet governments, aid the historian in assessing, confirming, or modifying the evidence submitted by Armenian writers that their country was the victim of a well-executed compact between Moscow and Ankara.

After the completion of this history of the Republic of Armenia, additional new information will undoubtedly come to light, providing future historians the opportunity to develop this study further and conceivably to revise or refute certain data I have accepted as valid and certain conclusions I have gradually and painstakingly drawn.

The use of numerous works written in the Cyrillic, Armenian, and modern Turkish scripts poses the inevitable problem of transliteration. Russian titles have been transliterated according to the Library of Congress system but with diacritical marks omitted and with several proper names excepted. Turkish proper names in the text have been spelled, not in keeping with the modified Latin alphabet currently in use, but as they were written in English during the first decades of this century: thus *Jevad*, not *Cevat*, and *Kiazim*, not *Kâzım*. The transliteration of Armenian titles is complicated by the difference between the modified orthography instituted in Soviet Armenia and the traditional orthography still used in Armenian works published abroad. Thus, were the transliteration key that has been employed by many European Armenologists adopted, the word for "denomination" might appear either as *haranvanout'yun* (Soviet publications) or *yaranouanout'iwn* (non-Soviet). To establish uniformity in rendering titles into the Latin alphabet, I have devised a key (p. 477) that has no diacritical marks and, while losing the letter to symbol equivalent in some cases, transliterates all words, whether in traditional or Soviet Armenian orthography, in a single form: thus "denomination" converts invariably into *haranvanutiun*.

In the text, the names of individuals are normally cited in full the first time they appear. The compiling of forenames has been a difficult assignment, as many sources, particularly those that refer to a person by military or other titles, do not list given names or even initials. But the long search that would allow me to revive more completely a forgotten Caucasian statesman or a British officer heretofore identified only by a common surname such as Stewart or Douglas has been rewarded in most instances by the ultimate discovery and the satisfaction of now introducing many of them into print. The names of several prominent Armenians are spelled as they were by the men themselves when they wrote in Western languages: thus *Boghos Nubar*, not *Poghos Nupar*. Armenian middle names were rare, although for legal purposes the Armenians of the Russian Empire had found it necessary to adopt the use of patronymics. With few exceptions, Armenian patronymics are not included in this study for they were used only in the Russian context and often altered the true name of the parent: thus Gevorg, the son of Hovhannes, would have to be rendered as *Gevorg Ivanovich* or even *Georgii Ivanovich*, rather than *Gevorg Hovhannesi*, the style now popular in Soviet Armenia. In the case of place-names, the form that generally prevailed during the period under consideration appears in the text: thus *Alexandropol*, not *Leninakan*, and *Constantinople*, not *Istanbul*. The sites that have been renamed in recent decades are shown in the glossary (p. 519), but not included are names that have undergone slight changes in preferred spelling, such as *Trebizond—Trabzon* or *Erivan—Erevan—Yerevan*.

The list of abbreviated titles that follows the preface contains frequently cited sources that require a special style of presentation in order to avoid excessive repetition or else possible confusion resulting from the use of more than one work by the same author. In the multivolume series in the list, the publication date of an individual volume is included the first time the volume is cited in the notes. If an abbreviated form is necessary in one chapter only, it is given there, not in the list. The translation of Armenian, Russian, and Turkish titles is provided in the bibliography. A comprehensive bibliography serving all parts of this study is planned for the final volume.

During the years that the research and writing were in progress, I received invaluable assistance from several quarters. It is a pleasure to acknowledge the services extended by the staffs of the libraries of the University of California, the Hoover Library and Institution at Stanford University, in Washington the Library of Congress and the National Archives, in London the Public Record Office and the Imperial War Museum, and in Erevan the Miasnikian State Library and the Academy of Sciences. I am thankful to Professor Rose Catherine Clifford (CSJ) of Mount St. Mary's College, to Arminé Garboushian, and to Vatché Bob Movel for their kind encouragement. Noël L. Diaz undertook the cartographer's difficult assignment of transforming my long-researched yet rough sketches into the useful and well-composed maps included in the text. Teresa R. Joseph fulfilled the duties of copy editor with admirable patience. I am very grateful to Marilyn A. Arshagouni who with keen eye and sharp wit followed the manuscript through its several drafts and to its final page proofs. To Professor G. E. von Grunebaum, Director of the Near Eastern Center of the University of California, Los Angeles, I am indebted for his steady support and especially for his unceasing dedication to the enhancement of Armenian studies and scholarship. The vision and the humanistic concern that are his engender deep admiration.

My father, Kaspar Hovannisian, was a continuous source of inspiration. The sole survivor of a large family that perished during the massacres of 1915, he began life anew in the United States but infused into that life a strong spiritual bond with his historic homeland. I am grieved that he passed on without the knowledge that this study had already been dedicated to him. And while the name of Vartiter Kotcholosian-Hovannisian does not appear on the title page, it must be stated that, even as she practiced the profession of medicine skillfully, her boundless love of history and of the land of Ararat has made her a constant companion in archives on three continents, in the meticulous process of rendering true and precise translations from several languages, and in the bittersweet experiences that have led to the completion of the first volume of *The Republic of Armenia*.

R. G. H.

Abbreviated Titles

Abeghian, "Mer harevannere" Art. Abeghian. "Menk ev mer harevannere," *Hairenik Amsagir*, VI (Dec., 1927–Oct., 1928), and VII (Nov., 1928–Jan., 1929). The volume numbers are not cited in the notes.

Adrbedjani pastatghtere [Republic of Armenia. Ministry of Foreign Affairs.] *Gaghtni pastatghtere: Adrbedjani davadrakan gordsuneutiunits mi edj.* Erevan, 1920.

Aharonian, *Sardarapatits Sevr* Avetis Aharonian. *Sardarapatits minchev Sevr ev Lozan (kaghakakan oragir).* Boston, 1943.

Armiano-gruzinskii konflikt [Armenian National Council of Baku] Bakinskii Armianskii Natsional'nyi Sovet. *Armiano-gruzinskii vooruzhennyi konflikt: Na osnovanii fakticheskikh dannykh i podlinnykh dokumentov.* Baku, 1919.

Banber Erevani Hamalsarani *Banber Erevani Hamalsarani: Hasarakakan gitutiunner [Vestnik Erevanskogo Universiteta].* Erevan, 1967——.

Banber Hayastani arkhivneri *Banber Hayastani arkhivneri [Vestnik arkhivov Armenii].* Publ. of Haikakan SSR Ministerneri Soveti arenter arkhivayin varchutiun. Erevan, 1962——.

Belen, *Türk Harbi* Turkey. Genelkurmay. *Birinci Cihan Harbinde Türk Harbi.* Prepared by General Fahri Belen. Ankara, 1964–1967. 5 vols.

xvii

Bor'ba v Azerbaidzhane

Bor'ba za pobedu Sovetskoi vlasti v Azerbaid-zhane, 1918–1920: Dokumenty i materialy. Publ. of Institut Istorii Partii TsK KP Azerbaidzhana–Filial IML pri TsK KPSS—Institut Istorii AN Azerbaidzhanskoi SSR—Arkhivnoe Upravlenie pri Sovete Ministrov Azerbaidzhanskoi SSR. Baku, 1967.

Bor'ba v Gruzii

Bor'ba za pobedu Sovetskoi vlasti v Gruzii: Dokumenty i materialy (1917–1921 gg.). Comp. by S. D. Beridze, A. M. Iovidze, S. V. Maglakelidze, Sh. K. Chkhetiia. Publ. of Akademiia Nauk Gruzinskoi SSR—Gruzinskii Filial Instituta Marksizma-Leninizma pri TsK KPSS—Arkhivnoe Upravlenie Gruzinskoi SSR. Tbilisi, 1958.

BRITAIN

GREAT BRITAIN. COMMITTEE OF IMPERIAL DEFENCE. HISTORICAL SECTION. *History of the Great War.*

Campaign in Mesopotamia

The Campaign in Mesopotamia, 1914–1918. Comp. by F. J. Moberly. London, 1923–1927. 4 vols.

Naval Operations

Naval Operations. Vol. V, by Henry Newbolt. London, 1931.

Operations in Macedonia

Military Operations: Macedonia. Comp. by Cyril Falls and A. F. Becke. London, 1933–1935. 2 vols.

Order of Battle

Order of Battle of Divisions. Comp. by A. F. Becke. London, 1933–1945. 4 pts. in 7 vols. Part 4 is entitled *Order of Battle: The Army Council, G.H.Q.s, Armies, and Corps, 1914–1918.*

BRITAIN, CAB

GREAT BRITAIN. CABINET OFFICE ARCHIVES. PUBLIC RECORD OFFICE (LONDON).

Cab 23

Class 23: *Cabinet Minutes* (especially War Cabinet, Cabinet Conclusions, Conference of Ministers, Conference of Ministers Conclusions of Meetings).

Cab 24

Class 24: *Cabinet Memoranda* (especially 'G' War Series, 'G.T.' Series, 'C.P.' Series, Eastern Reports, Foreign Countries Reports).

Cab 25	Class 25: *Supreme War Council (1917–1919).*
Cab 27	Class 27: *Committees: General* (especially Eastern Committee).
Cab 28	Class 28: *Allied War Conferences.*
Cab 29	Class 29: *International Conferences* (especially W.C.P. Series, British Empire Delegation, 'P' Series, A.J. Series).
Cab 44	Class 44: *Historical Section. Official War Histories: Compilations.*
Cab 45	Class 45: *Historical Section. Official War Histories: Correspondence and Papers.*
BRITAIN, FO	GREAT BRITAIN. FOREIGN OFFICE ARCHIVES. PUBLIC RECORD OFFICE.
FO 371	Class 371: *Political.* The class and volume numbers are followed by the document numbers, the file number, and the index number; for example, 371/3657, 3404/9846/512/58 represents Volume 3657, Documents 3404 and 9846, File 512 (Armenia), Index 58 (Caucasus).
FO 406	Class 406: *Confidential Print: Eastern Affairs, 1812–1946.*
FO 418	Class 418: *Russia and the Soviet Union, 1821–1954.*
FO 424	Class 424: *Turkey, 1841–1951.*
FO 608	Class 608: *Peace Conference, 1919–1920: Correspondence.* The volume number and the file numbers (three figures) are followed by the document numbers; for example, 608/78, 342/1/2/7948/10174 represents Volume 78, File 342/1/2 (Middle East, Armenia, Internal Situation), Documents 7948 and 10174.
BRITAIN, WO	GREAT BRITAIN, WAR OFFICE ARCHIVES. PUBLIC RECORD OFFICE.
WO 32	Class 32: *Registered Papers: General Series.*
WO 33	Class 33: *Reports and Miscellaneous Papers (1853–1939).*
WO 95	Class 95: *War Diaries, 1914–1922.*

WO 106

Class 106: *Directorates of Military Operations and Intelligence, 1870–1925.*

British Documents

Great Britain. Foreign Office. *Documents on British Foreign Policy, 1919–1939.* 1st ser. Ed. W. L. Woodward and Rohan Butler. Vols. I–IV. London, 1947–1952.

Denikin, *Ocherki smuty*

A. I. Denikin. *Ocherki russkoi smuty.* Paris and Berlin, [1921–1926]. 5 vols.

Djamalian, "Hai-vratsakan knjire"

Arshak Djamalian. "Hai-vratsakan knjire," *Hairenik Amsagir,* VI (April, 1928–Oct., 1928), and VII (Nov., 1928–April, 1929). The volume numbers are not cited in the notes.

Dokumenty i materialy

[Republic of Georgia]. *Dokumenty i materialy po vneshnei politike Zakavkaz'ia i Gruzii.* Tiflis, 1919.

Dokumenty SSSR

Ministerstvo Inostrannykh Del SSSR. *Dokumenty vneshnei politiki SSSR.* Vols. I–II. Moscow, 1957–1958.

General Andranik

General Andranik: Haikakan Arandzin Harvadsogh Zoramase. Transcribed by Eghishe Kadjuni. Boston, 1921.

Hayastani Komkusi patmutiun

Hayastani Komunistakan kusaktsutian patmutian urvagdser. Ed. Ds. P. Aghayan *et al.* Publ. of Institut Istorii Partii TsK Kompartii Armenii–Filial Instituta Marksizma-Leninizma pri TsK KPSS. Erevan, 1967.

Hovannisian, *Road to Independence*

Richard G. Hovannisian. *Armenia on the Road to Independence, 1918.* Berkeley and Los Angeles, 1967.

Istoriia Kompartii Azerbaidzhana

Istoriia Kommunisticheskoi partii Azerbaidzhana. Publ. of Institut Istorii Partii pri TsK KP Azerbaidzhana–Filial Instituta Marksizma-Leninizma pri TsK KPSS. Vol. I. Baku, 1958.

Istoriia Kompartii Gruzii

Ocherki istorii Kommunisticheskoi partii Gruzii. Ed. V. G. Esaishvili. Publ. of Institut Istorii Partii pri TsK KP Gruzii–Filial Instituta Marksizma-Leninizma pri TsK KPSS. Part 1. Tbilisi, 1957.

Iz arm-gruz otnoshenii

[Republic of Georgia.] *Iz istorii armiano-gruzinskikh otnoshenii, 1918 god.* Tiflis, 1919.

Kadishev, *Interventsiia v Zakavkaz'e*

A. B. Kadishev. *Interventsiia i grazhdanskaia voina v Zakavkaz'e.* Moscow, 1960.

Kandemir, *Karabekir*

Feridun Kandemir. *Kâzım Karabekir.* Istanbul, 1948.

Kandemir, *Kemal*

————. *Milli mücadele başlangıcında Mustafa Kemal, arkadaşları ve karşısındakiler.* Istanbul, [1964].

Karabekir, *İstiklâl Harbimiz*

Kâzım Karabekir. *İstiklâl Harbimiz.* Istanbul, 1960.

Karabekir, *Esasları*

————. *İstiklâl Harbimizin esasları.* Istanbul, 1957.

Kazemzadeh, *Transcaucasia*

Firuz Kazemzadeh. *The Struggle for Transcaucasia (1917–1921).* New York and Oxford, [1951].

Khatisian, *Hanrapetutian zargatsume*

Alexandre Khatisian, *Hayastani Hanrapetutian dsagumn u zargatsume.* Athens, 1930.

Khondkarian, "Opozitsian Hayastanum"

Arsham Khondkarian. "Opozitsian Hanrapetakan Hayastanum," *Vem,* I, nos. 1–2 (1933), and II, nos. 1–4 (1934). The year of publication is not cited in the notes.

Kompartiia Azerbaidzhana

Ocherki istorii Kommunisticheskoi partii Azerbaidzhana. Publ. of Institut Istorii Partii TsK KP Azerbaidzhana–Filial Instituta Marksizma-Leninizma pri TsK KPSS. Ed. M. S. Iskenderov *et al.* Baku, 1963.

Lenin, *Sochineniia*

V. I. Lenin: Polnoe sobranie sochinenii. Publ. of Institut Marksizma-Leninizma pri TsK KPSS. 5th ed. Moscow, 1958–1965. 55 vols.

Lepsius, *Deutschland und Armenien*

Johannes Lepsius, ed. *Deutschland und Armenien: Sammlung diplomatischer Aktenstücke.* Potsdam, 1919.

Miller, *Documents*

David Hunter Miller. *My Diary at the Conference at Paris: With Documents.* [New York, 1924–1926]. 22 vols.

Paris Peace Conference

United States. Department of State. *Papers Relating to the Foreign Relations of the United States, 1919: The Paris Peace Conference.* (Washington, D.C., 1942–1947), 13 vols.

Patma-banasirakan handes

Patma-banasirakan handes [Istoriko-filologicheskii zhurnal]. Publ. of Haikakan SSR

Gitutiunneri Akademia [Akademiia Nauk Armianskoi SSR]. Erevan, 1958——.

Rep. of Arm. Archives   Archives of the Republic of Armenia Delegation to the Paris Peace Conference (now integrated into the Archives of Hai Heghapokhakan Dashnaktsutiun, Boston, Massachusetts). The title of each individual file is given only the first time the file is cited in the notes.

Revoliutsion kocher   *Revoliutsion kocher ev trutsikner, 1902–1921.* Publ. of Institut Istorii Partii pri TsK KP Armenii—Armianskii Filial Instituta Marksizma-Leninizma pri TsK KPSS. Erevan, 1960.

Teghekagir   *Teghekagir: Hasarakakan gitutiunner [Izvestiia: Obshchestvennye nauki].* Publ. of Haikakan SSR Gitutiunneri Akademia [Akademiia Nauk Armianskoi SSR]. Erevan, 1940–1965. Since 1966, this journal has appeared under the title *Lraber hasarakakan gitutiunneri [Vestnik obshchestvennykh nauk].*

US ARCHIVES   UNITED STATES OF AMERICA. THE NATIONAL ARCHIVES (WASHINGTON, D.C.).

RG 59   Record Group 59: *General Records of the Department of State* (Decimal File, 1910–1929). Figures representing class and country precede the document numbers; for example, 861.00/715/2386 represents Internal Affairs, Russia, Documents 715 and 2386.

RG 84   Record Group 84: *The United States Foreign Service Posts of the Department of State.*

RG 256   Record Group 256: *Records of the American Commission to Negotiate Peace.* The citation form is the same as that used in RG 59.

Velikaia Oktiabr'skaia revoliutsiia   *Velikaia Oktiabr'skaia sotsialisticheskaia revoliutsiia i pobeda Sovetskoi vlasti v Armenii (sbornik dokumentov).* Ed. by A. N. Mnatsakanian, A. M. Akopian, G. M. Dallakian. Publ. of Armianskii Filial IML pri TsK KPSS—Institut Istorii Akademii Nauk Arm. SSR—Arkhivnyi Otdel MVD Arm. SSR. Erevan, 1957.

Vratzian, *Hanrapetutiun*   Simon Vratzian. *Hayastani Hanrapetutiun.* Paris, 1928.

Vratzian, *Ughinerov*   Simon Vratzian. *Kianki ughinerov: Depker, demker, aprumner.* Cairo [Vol. I] and Beirut [Vols. II–VI], 1955–1967. 6 vols.

Correction to the Notes for the Second Printing

The General Staff War Diary of the British 27th Division's Headquarters was misfiled for a time in the War Office Archives. As that diary has now been returned to its proper carton, all references to that source in the notes of this volume should be read now as WO 95/4879 rather than WO 95/4880.

The Republic of
ARMENIA

The First Year,
1918-1919

1

Toward
Independence

On the eve of World War I the historic Armenian plateau, bounded by the western branches of the Euphrates River, the Pontus and the Taurus mountain chains, and the highlands of Karabagh, was divided unevenly between the Ottoman and the Russian empires. Though in centuries past Armenian kingdoms had flourished on the plateau, no Armenian dynast had reigned there during the preceding eight hundred years. The Armenians had become a minority in the Turkish-controlled sector and formed only a slight majority in Russian Armenia, which, while not a separate legal entity, was generally acknowledged to include the provinces of Kars and Erevan, the uplands of Elisavetpol, and the southern reaches of the Tiflis *guberniia* (province).[1]

The Armenians of the Russian Empire

The discriminatory policies of the Romanov bureaucracy notwithstanding, the Armenians of the Russian Empire made impressive cultural strides during the nineteenth century. Poets and novelists rediscovered the historically Armenian character of their native land and decried the endless foreign intrusions to which it had been victim. Political societies emerged with the goals of redeeming national honor and liberating the Armenians, particularly those of the Ottoman Empire, from ever increasing oppression. Significantly, however, the Armenian intellectual and political renaissance unfolded outside the

[1] The material in this chapter is the subject of a detailed study by Richard G. Hovannisian, *Armenia on the Road to Independence, 1918* (Berkeley and Los Angeles, 1967).

1

1. TURKISH ARMENIA AND THE TRANSCAUCASUS, 1914

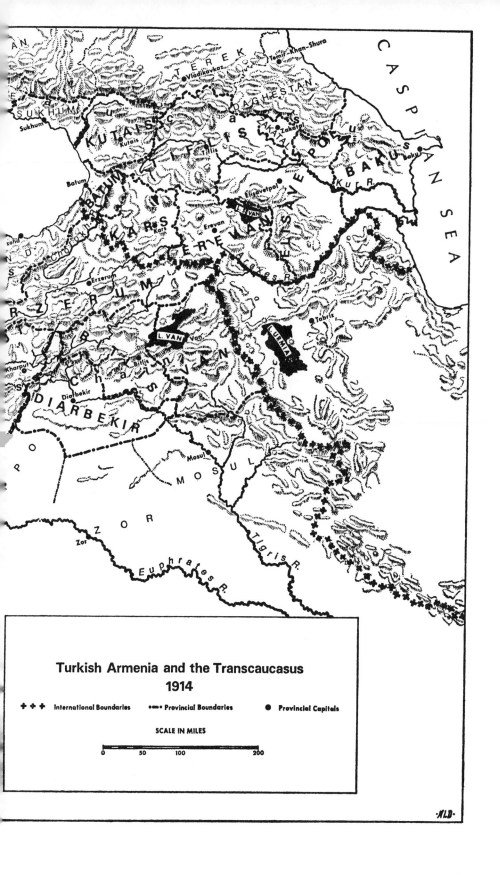

**Turkish Armenia and the Transcaucasus
1914**

✛ ✛ ✛ International Boundaries   •—•—• Provincial Boundaries   ● Provincial Capitals

SCALE IN MILES

0   50   100   200

Russian Armenian provinces. Not Erevan, but such cities as Dorpat, St. Petersburg, Moscow, Nor (New) Nakhichevan on the Don River, Baku, and Tiflis became centers of the Armenian movement.

To the Armenians of Russia this phenomenon was not at all unnatural, for Erevan was regarded as a small, relatively unimportant part of the historic homeland. Rather, attention was focused upon the eastern Ottoman provinces—Turkish Armenia—the cradle of the nation (see map 1). It was thus logical that the influential political organization, Hai Heghapokhakan Dashnaktsutiun (Armenian Revolutionary Federation), though formed in Tiflis, should dedicate itself to the emancipation of the Turkish Armenians.[2] All the while, Erevan remained in the backwaters of Armenian intellectual, economic, and political life.[3] Yet, ironically, it was in the province of Erevan that the Republic of Armenia was to emerge unheralded in 1918.

Of the two million Armenians in the Romanov Empire in 1914, approximately 1,780,000 lived interspersed with Russians, Georgians, and Muslim peoples in the several provinces of Ciscaucasia and Transcaucasia (see maps 1, 2). In Transcaucasia alone, the Armenians numbered 1,685,000 (22.2 percent), the Georgians, 1,741,000 (22.9 percent), and the Muslims, 3,089,000, of whom 1,791,000 (23.6 percent) were Tatars. By individual provinces the highest concentrations of Armenians were in Erevan, 669,000 (60 percent), Elisavetpol, 419,000 (33 percent), Tiflis, 415,000 (28 percent), and Kars, 119,000 (30 percent). In the city of Tiflis, the administrative center of the Caucasus, they represented no less than 45 percent of the population, followed by the Russians and only then by the Georgians, the historic masters of that exciting metropolis.[4]

---

[2] Documents relating to the origins and program of Dashnaktsutiun are included in the party's publications, *Divan H. H. Dashnaktsutian* (Boston, 1933–1934), 2 vols.; and *Hushapatum H. H. Dashnaktsutian, 1890–1950* (Boston, 1950). See also Mikayel Varandian, *H. H. Dashnaktsutian patmutiun* (Paris and Cairo, 1932–1950), 2 vols.

[3] By the first years of the twentieth century the population of Baku had grown to nearly 400,000, and that of Tiflis to nearly 350,000. In sharp contrast, the population of Erevan remained relatively static at less than 35,000. See M. H. Adonts, *Hayastani zhoghovrdakan tntesutiune ev hai tntesagitakan mitke XX dari skzbin* (Erevan, 1968), pp. 273–279.

[4] Abeghian, "Mer harevannere" (May, 1928), p. 139, and (June, 1928), pp. 154–155; A. Shakhatuni, *Administrativnyi peredel Zakavkazskago kraia* (Tiflis, 1918), pp. 61–73. Detailed population statistics for each of the Transcaucasian provinces, based on the official *Kavkazskii kalendar'*, are found in US Archives, RG 256, 867B.00/4/10/11/23. Figures differing from those included in the text are cited by Adonts, *op. cit.*, p. 279. See also Britain, FO 371/4381, 490/490/PID. The provinces of the Ciscaucasus, lying to the north of the main mountain range, included Daghestan, Terek, Stavropol, Kuban, and Chernomorie.

The Muslims and the Georgians of Transcaucasia

Like the Armenians, the Muslims of Transcaucasia, most of them Shiʻa Tatars (Azerbaijanis), were scattered through every province but in considerably larger numbers. The descendants of Mongol-Turkic invaders, they endured as the dominant ethnic-religious element and landholding group until the Russian absorption of the Caucasus in the nineteenth century.[5] It was only under Romanov dominion that the Armenians succeeded in regaining numerical superiority in the Erevan guberniia and the Christian peoples combined came to outbalance the adherents of Islam in Transcaucasia. By the turn of the twentieth century, rivalry between Armenians and Tatars had reached dangerous proportions, for the Armenian peasants were no longer willing to accept the status of tenant or sharecropper and the active Armenian commercial classes had begun to undermine the power and prestige of the Muslim landed aristocracy.[6] Tsarist bureaucrats, in pursuance of the policy of divide and rule, fanned the smoldering antagonism until it burst into sporadic warfare.

By the eve of World War I the Muslims had made considerable organic progress, as schools and newspapers were founded and political societies were formed. The Musavat (Equality) party, drawing membership from the intellectual circles, the emerging bourgeoisie, and the more enlightened aristocracy, was the most pervasive of these Muslim organizations. Strongly influenced by Pan-Islamic ideologies, the Musavat party set as its goals the political, economic, and social regeneration of all Muslim nations, the adoption of liberal constitutional reforms, and the establishment of firm bonds among the Muslim peoples within and beyond the Russian Empire.[7]

[5] For a general history of Azerbaijan, see Akademiia Nauk Azerbaidzhanskoi SSR, Institut Istorii, *Istoriia Azerbaidzhana*, ed. I. A. Guseinov *et al.* (Baku, 1958–1963), 3 vols. in 4 pts. For the period during and preceding the Muslim invasions, see Ziia Buniiatov, *Azerbaidzhan v VII–IX vv.* (Baku, 1965); Movses Dasxurançi (Daskhurantsi), *The History of the Caucasian Albanians*, trans. C. J. F. Dowsett (London, 1961).

[6] A useful study of the ethnic and class structure in the Caucasus at the beginning of the twentieth century is that of B. Ishkhanian, *Narodnosti Kavkaza* (Petrograd, 1916). See also D. Ananun, *Rusahayeri hasarakakan zargatsume*, Vol. III (Venice, 1926), pp. 265–281, 420–506 *passim*.

[7] Materials on the formation and program of the Musavat party are included in the following publications: M. E. Rassoul-Zadé, *L'Azerbaidjan en lutte pour l'Indépendance* (Paris, 1930); Mirza-Davud Guseinov, *Tiurkskaia Demokraticheskaia Partiia Federalistov "Musavat" v proshlom i nastoiashchem* ([Tiflis], 1927); Mir-Yacoub, *Le problème du Caucase* (Paris, 1933); Mehmet-Zade Mirza-Bala, *Milli Azerbaycan hareketi: Milli Az. "Müsavat" halk fırkası tarihi* ([Berlin], 1938); S. D. Dimanshtein, ed., *Revoliutsiia i natsional'nyi vopros*, Vol. III (Moscow, 1930), pp. 341–345.

2. THE ADMINISTRATIVE SUBDIVISIONS OF TRANSCAUCASIA

The Georgians were no more numerous than the Armenians in Trancaucasia, but they held several distinct advantages. Almost all lived in the contiguous provinces of Tiflis, Kutais, and Batum, the lands of their historic kingdoms. In contrast with the Armenians, they had never lost their self-awareness. Georgian monarchs had reigned into the nineteenth century, and the social structure remained largely intact. The Georgian countryside was more productive and fertile than Russian Armenia, and a favorable geographic position made the world beyond the Caucasus readily accessible. Moreover, Georgia had been spared many of the devastating invasions that had ravaged Armenia.[8]

Although the Armenians and Georgians were Christian peoples and shared many traditions, they had in some ways become rivals. The competition stemmed in large measure from the growing power of the Armenian bourgeoisie and its rapid infiltration into and domination of Tiflis, the natural capital of Georgia and of all Transcaucasia. The Armenian merchant classes had even begun to spread their surplus capital into the rural districts, corroding the authority and economic base of the vitiated Georgian aristocracy.[9] Many Georgian and Armenian intellectuals, having espoused the tenets of socialism, mocked this conflict. But their belief that they could unite against the parasitic aristocracy of the one people and the exploiting bourgeoisie of the other proved unfounded, for the mantle of Armenian socialism was much too thin and that of Georgian socialism much too chauvinistic.

Georgian political thought found its strongest expression in Marxist doctrines. A number of Georgian Marxists held important posts in the Russian Social Democrat Labor Party and gained prominence in the international labor movement. Nearly all, with such notable exceptions as Iosif V. Jugashvili (Stalin) and Prokopii A. Japaridze, adhered to the Menshevik faction of Social Democracy and branded the

[8] For general histories of Georgia, see Alexandre Manvelichvili, *Histoire de la Géorgie* (Paris, [1951]); W. E. D. Allen, *A History of the Georgian People* (London, 1932); David Marshall Lang, *The Last Years of the Georgian Monarchy, 1658–1832* (New York, 1957); Cyril Tumanoff, *Studies in Christian Caucasian History* ([Washington, D.C., 1963]).

[9] US Archives, RG 256, 184.01602/23, Report of American Field Mission to South Russia, Tiflis Party; M. Philips Price, *War and Revolution in Asiatic Russia* (New York, [1918]), pp. 264–265. Ishkhanian establishes that nearly 20 percent of the industry and trade of all Caucasia was controlled by Armenians as compared with less than 10 percent by Georgians. Ananun, *op. cit.*, p. 421, cites official sources to show that of the 7,929 commercial houses in Tiflis in 1901, Armenians owned 4,026; Georgians, 2,021; Russians, 1,450; Germans, 126; and others, 74. Nearly all the Armenian business establishments were situated in the fashionable neighborhoods of the city. See also Adonts, *op. cit.*, pp. 284–285.

Bolshevik program and strategy as unorthodox and opportunist.[10] In 1917 these Menshevik champions were to take an active role in the Provisional Government and the soviets of Russia, and in 1918 they were to redirect the tenor of their leadership to serve the independent Republic of Georgia.

The Armenians of the Ottoman Empire

The approximately two million Armenians of Turkey were even more widely dispersed than those of the Russian Empire. They made up a sizable element in Constantinople, the coastal cities, and in Cilicia, that fertile region along the Mediterranean Sea where an Armenian principality and kingdom had held sway from the eleventh through the fourteenth centuries. Yet, despite this broad distribution, most Turkish Armenians still inhabited their historic plateau lands, which formed the six eastern Ottoman *vilayets* (provinces) of Sivas, Erzerum, Kharput, Diarbekir, Bitlis, and Van (see map 1).[11]

During the early centuries of Ottoman domination, the Armenians did not meet insuperable obstacles in preserving their national identity, and, although some were constrained to embrace Islam and more were subjected to economic exploitation, they learned to live in peace

[10] Information on the origins of the Social Democratic movement in Georgia and biographical sketches of Menshevik leaders are included in the following publications: Grigorii Uratadze, *Vospominaniia Gruzinskogo Sotsial-Demokrata* (Stanford, 1968); N. Zhordaniia, *Moia Zhizn'* (Stanford, 1968), pp. 1–62; Paul Gentizon, *La résurrection géorgienne* (Paris, 1920), pp. 170–178; Wladimir Woytinsky, *La démocratie géorgienne* (Paris, 1921), pp. 47–70; Karl Kautsky, *Georgia: A Social-Democratic Peasant Republic*, trans. H. J. Stenning (London, [1921]), pp. 17–22. See also *Istoriia Kompartii Gruzii*, pp. 5–100; V. B. Stankevich, *Sud'by narodov Rossii* (Berlin, 1921), pp. 220–223. According to statistics prepared by the Communist Party of Georgia, there were 374 Bolsheviks in that country in 1907, 464 in 1910, and 505 in 1913. See N. B. Makharadze, *Pobeda sotsialisticheskoi revoliutsii v Gruzii* (Tbilisi, 1965), p. 361.

[11] An analysis of the population statistics relating to the Armenians of the Ottoman Empire is made by Hovannisian, *Road to Independence*, pp. 34–37. Broad discrepancies exist between figures given in Turkish sources and those cited in Armenian sources. For the Turkish contentions, see, for example, *Les Turcs et les revendications arméniennes* (Paris, 1919); [Milli Kongre], *The Turco-Armenian Question: The Turkish Point of View* (Constantinople, 1919); *Memorandum of the Sublime Porte Communicated to the American, British, French and Italian High Commissioners on the 12th February 1919* (Constantinople, 1919), pp. 4–8 and annex; Esat Uras, *Tarihte Ermeniler ve Ermeni Meselesi* (Ankara, 1950), pp. 131–147, 676–683. For the Armenian contentions, see, for example, *Réponse au mémoire de la Sublime-Porte en date du 12 février 1919* (Constantinople, 1919), pp. 13–23, 32–35, and annexes; Kévork-Mesrob, *L'Arménie au point de vue géographique, historique, statistique et cultural* (Constantinople, 1919), pp. 59–75. See also US Archives, RG 256, 867.00/3/7/8/18/31/58; Britain, FO 608/108, File 384/2/4.

with their Muslim overlords and neighbors. This situation changed radically by the nineteenth century, however, as burgeoning corruption and oppression accompanied the decline of the Ottoman Empire. Armenian villagers found it progressively more difficult to safeguard their property, goods, and families from marauding Kurds and other mounted bands.[12]

Significantly, the political and economic deterioration of the Ottoman Empire was paralleled by an Armenian cultural reawakening. Deeply permeated by the intellectual currents of Europe, the Armenian renaissance found expression in the novel, the essay, the drama, and in the field of education. Literature inspired political thought, which in turn engendered more intense dissatisfaction and unrest among this subject people. By the latter part of the nineteenth century the Armenakan party in Van had begun to advocate constitutional and economic reforms, the Hnchakian Revolutionary (subsequently Social Democrat Hnchakian) party, especially influential in Constantinople and in Cilicia, was clamoring for the creation of a separate Armenian state, and Dashnaktsutiun, having extended its network from the Caucasus into Turkish Armenia, was pressing for Armenian self-administration and far-reaching social and economic changes within the structure of the Ottoman Empire.[13]

The capricious diversions of Europe into the so-called Armenian question aggravated the plight of the Armenians of Turkey. The inconsistent and often contradictory policies of the Continental Powers

[12] Numerous documents regarding the plight of the Armenians in the Ottoman Empire have been published in Parliament's *Sessional Papers (Accounts and Papers)*, particularly under the heading of *Turkey*. This source is cited hereafter as British Parliament, *Papers*. See also Gegham Ter-Karapetian, *Hoghayin hartse hayabnak nahangneru medj* (Constantinople, 1911); A. S. Hambarian, *Agrarayin haraberutiunnere Arevmtian Hayastanum (1856–1914)* (Erevan, 1965); Haik Ghazarian, *Arevmtahayeri sotsial-tntesakan ev kaghakakan katsutiune 1800–1870 tt.* (Erevan, 1967); A. N. Nersisian, *Arevmtahayeri tntesakan u kaghakakan vijake ev nrants rusakan orientatsian 19-rd dari aradjin kesin* (Erevan, 1962); H. G. Vardanian, "Arevmtahayeri sotsialakan ev azgayin jnshman uzheghatsume Berlini Kongresits heto," *Patmabanasirakan handes*, 3 (1964), 69–78.

[13] Material on the Armenian literary and political renaissance is extensive. For representative views, see V. A. Parsamian, *Hai azatagrakan sharzhumneri patmutiunits* (Erevan, 1958); Louise Nalbandian, *The Armenian Revolutionary Movement* (Berkeley and Los Angeles, 1963); Leo [A. Babakhanian], *Tiurkahai heghapokhutian gaghaparabanutiune* (Paris, 1934–1935), 2 vols., cited hereafter as *Tiurkahai*; A. O. Sarkissian, *History of the Armenian Question to 1885* (Urbana, Ill., 1938); Mikayel Varandian, *Haikakan sharzhman nakhapatmutiun* (Geneva, 1912–1914), 2 vols.; Mesrop Djanachian, *Patmutiun ardi hai grakanutian* (Venice, 1953); Akademiia Nauk Armianskoi SSR, Institut Literatury imeni M. Abeghiana, *Hai nor grakanutian patmutiun*, Vols. I–III (Erevan, 1962–1964).

did not alleviate Armenian woes but instead deepened the sultan's suspicion of his Armenian subjects and impressed upon him the danger of continued foreign interference. Yielding to European coercion in 1895, Sultan Abdul-Hamid II promulgated an Armenian reform program, but, as had happened before, external intervention was not sustained by force.[14] In Abdul-Hamid's appalling response to European meddling, an estimated 150,000 to 300,000 Armenians were massacred.[15]

In 1908 the Armenians of the Ottoman Empire hailed the "Young Turk" (Ittihad ve Terakki) revolution, which compelled Abdul-Hamid to submit to a constitutional regime based on civil and religious liberties for all Ottoman subjects and parliamentary representation for the several nationalities of the empire. Ironically, it was these same Young Turks, the disciples of European liberal, positivist, nationalist ideologies, who were to perpetrate that which no sultan had ever contemplated—solving the Armenian problem by extirpating the entire Armenian population. A series of international crises involving the Ottoman Empire between 1908 and 1913 culminated in the triumph of Turkish chauvinism over Ottoman liberalism and in the ascendancy of the dictatorial element of Ittihad ve Terraki. From mid-1913 until the end of World War I, the empire lay in the firm grip of a small coterie led by Enver, Talaat, and Jemal pashas.[16]

[14] Documents relating to the European-sponsored Armenian reforms and the subsequent massacres of 1895–1896 are included in the following: British Parliament, House of Commons, *Papers*, Vol. XCV, 1896, c. 7923, Turkey no. 1; c. 7927, Turkey no. 2; c. 8015, Turkey no. 3; c. 8108, Turkey no. 6; and Vol. XCVI, 1896, c. 8273, Turkey no. 8; France, Ministère des Affaires Étrangères, *Documents diplomatiques: Affaires arméniennes: Projets de réformes dans l'Empire Ottoman, 1893–1897* (Paris, 1897), and *Supplément, 1895–1896* (1897); Germany, Auswärtiges Amt, *Die grosse Politik der europäischen Kabinette, 1871–1914*, Vols. IX–X (Berlin, 1924); Johannes Lepsius, *Armenia and Europe* (London, 1897); A. Schopoff, *Les réformes et la protection des Chrétiens en Turquie, 1673–1904* (Paris, 1904), pp. 472–526; William L. Langer, *The Diplomacy of Imperialism, 1890–1902* (2d ed.; New York, 1951), pp. 145–166, 195–212 *passim*. In addition hundreds of accounts were written by eyewitness Christian missionaries and by the Armenians themselves.

[15] For the failure of the reform plan and abandonment of the Armenian Question by the Continental Powers, see British Parliament, House of Commons, *Papers*, Vol. XCV, 1896, Turkey no. 2; Vol. XCVI, 1896, Turkey no. 8; and Vol. CI, 1897, c. 8305, Turkey no. 3; Germany, Auswärtiges Amt, *op. cit.*, Vols. X and XII, pt. 1 (1924); France, Ministère des Affaires Étrangères, Commission de Publication des Documents Relatifs aux Origines de la Guerre de 1914, *Documents diplomatiques français (1871–1914)*, 1ᵉ sér., Vol. XIII (Paris, 1943), cited hereafter as France, *1871–1914*; Langer, *op. cit.*, pp. 321–350.

[16] Interpretations of the Young Turk revolution and government are made by Ernest Edmondson Ramsaur, *The Young Turks* (Princeton, 1957); Feroz Ahmad, *The Young Turks* (Oxford, 1969); A. J. Toynbee, *Turkey: A Past and a Future* (New York, 1917); Victor Bérard, *Le mort de Stamboul: Considérations sur le gouverne-*

With Turkey beset by external and domestic problems, Imperial Russia, after years of calculated silence, found it expedient to protest anew the excesses to which the Turkish Armenians were subject. Foreign policy considerations, alarm over German economic penetration deep within Anatolia, and fear that a desperate Turkish Armenian population would rebel and that the consequent insurrection might then spill over into Transcaucasia, all contributed in 1913 to Russia's decision to propose a fresh scheme of Armenian reforms in the Ottoman Empire. After months of controversy the six Continental Powers, already divided into the Triple Alliance and the Triple Entente, finally arrived at a compromise measure, to which the Ottoman government yielded in February, 1914. The plan, though much less comprehensive than the original Russian draft, was the most satisfactory and workable Armenian reform program yet adopted. Granted considerable cultural and political autonomy, the six vilayets of Turkish Armenia, along with the Trebizond vilayet, were to be consolidated into two administrative regions, each having a European inspector general. The arrival of the two inspectors general in the summer of 1914 seemed to be an indication that Armenian aspirations verged on fruition.[17] But the triumph was deceptive, for by the summer of 1916 it was no longer possible to speak of Armenian self-administration in the Ottoman Empire. By that time the Armenian plateau and Cilicia had been denuded of their Armenian inhabitants. The Ittihadist dictatorship seized the opportunity provided by World War I to rid the empire of the Armenian question by ridding it of the Armenians.

World War I and the Armenians

The outbreak of war in the summer of 1914 exposed the Armenians on both sides of the Russo-Turkish border to extreme dangers. Influential Turkish Armenian spokesmen pleaded in vain with the It-

---

ment des Jeunes-Turcs (Paris, 1913); Wilhelm Feldmann, *Kriegstage in Konstantinopel* (Strassburg, 1913). See also Great Britain, Foreign Office, *British Documents on the Origins of the War, 1898–1914*, ed. G. P. Gooch and Harold Temperley, Vol. V (London, 1928), nos. 196–217, cited hereafter as Britain, *Origins.*

[17] A clear presentation of the reform proposal and final compromise is made by Roderic H. Davison, "The Armenian Crisis, 1912–1914," *American Historical Review,* LIII (April, 1948), 481–505. See also Russia, Ministerstvo Inostrannykh Del, *Sbornik diplomaticheskikh dokumentov: Reformy v Armenii* (Petrograd, 1915); Germany, Auswärtiges Amt, *op. cit.,* Vol. XXXVIII (1926); Britain, *Origins,* Vol. X, pt. 1 (1936); France, *1871–1914,* 3ᵉ sér., Vols. VII–IX (1934–1936); Vahan Papazian, *Im hushere,* Vol. II (Beirut, 1952), pp. 241–258, 543–583; Leo [A. Babakhanian], *Hayots hartsi vaveragrere* (Tiflis, 1915), pp. 301–357.

tihadist government to preserve the neutrality of the Ottoman Empire. Instead, at the end of October, the Turkish fleet bombarded Russia's Black Sea installations, and shortly thereafter the Ottoman army set out to regain the Transcaucasian provinces ceded to Russia in 1829 and 1878.[18] Enver Pasha, the Minister of War and the most dynamic of the Ittihadist rulers, was driven by an even greater vision—the creation of a Turkic empire extending from Constantinople to Central Asia. Exhilarated by this prospect, Enver personally directed the Caucasus campaign in the winter of 1914–1915, but his 100,000-man force was decimated by the bitter cold of the Armenian plateau and by the stubborn resistance of several Russian divisions assisted by three Armenian volunteer units from Transcaucasia.[19]

With the Ottoman Empire committed to war, the Turkish Armenian leaders exhorted their people to fulfill every obligation of Ottoman citizenship. Their apprehensions were eased somewhat when Enver Pasha himself praised the valor of the Turkish Armenian soldiers.[20] Such attestations, however, did not forestall implementation of the Ittihadist plan for what was to be the first genocide in modern history.

In April of 1915, using the pretext that the Armenians inhabited the war zones, offered aid and comfort to the enemy, and plotted a na-

[18] The events and activities culminating in the involvement of the Ottoman Empire in the World War are described and interpreted in the following works: Ulrich Trumpener, *Germany and the Ottoman Empire, 1914–1918* (Princeton, 1968), pp. 3–6i; Carl Mühlmann, *Das deutsch-türkische Waffenbündnis in Weltkrieg* (Leipzig, [1940]), pp. 12–27; Ernest Jackh, *The Rising Crescent: Turkey Yesterday, Today and Tomorrow* (New York and Toronto, [1944]), pp. 7–23; Bernadotte E. Schmitt, *The Coming of the War, 1914* (2 vols.; New York and London, 1930), II, 274, 431–440; E. K. Sargsian, *Ekspansionistskaia politika Osmanskoi imperii v Zakavkaz'e nakanune i v gody pervoi mirovoi voiny* (Erevan, 1962), pp. 129–172; Kurt Ziemke, *Die neue Türkei: Politische Entwicklung, 1914–1929* (Stuttgart, 1930), pp. 20–34; Luigi Albertini, *The Origins of the War of 1914*, trans. Isabella M. Massey, Vol. III (London, 1957), pp. 605–623; Harry N. Howard, *The Partition of Turkey* (Norman, Okla., 1931), pp. 83–115.

[19] Detailed accounts of the Caucasus campaign are given by N. Korsun, *Sarykamyshskaia operatsiia na Kavkazskom fronte mirovoi voiny v 1914–1915 godu* (Moscow, 1937); E. V. Maslovskii, *Mirovaia voina na Kavkazskom fronte, 1914–1917 g.* (Paris, [1937]), pp. 51–134; W. E. D. Allen and Paul Muratoff, *Caucasian Battlefields: A History of the Wars on the Turco-Caucasian Border, 1828–1921* (Cambridge, 1953), pp. 240–285; Price, *op. cit.*, pp. 49–58; Sargsian, *op. cit.*, pp. 181–198; Felix Guse, *Die Kaukasusfront im Weltkrieg bis zum Frieden von Brest* (Leipzig, [1940]), pp. 27–53; M. Larcher, *La guerre turque dans la guerre mondiale* (Paris, 1926), pp. 375–389; A. Harutiunian, "Sarighamishi jakatamarti dere Kovkase turkakan nerkhuzhman vtangits prkelu gordsum (1914 t. dektember)," *Banber Hayastani arkhivneri*, 2 (1967), 89–109.

[20] Johannes Lepsius, *Der Todesgang des Armenischen Volkes* (4th ed.; Potsdam, 1930), pp. 160–162; Leo, *Tiurkahai*, II, 118–119, 137, 139.

tional rising against the Ottoman Empire, Talaat Pasha, the Minister of Interior, supported by the entire Council of Ministers, ordered their deportation from the eastern vilayets. In carrying out the operation no distinction was made between deportation and massacre. With unusual speed and efficiency the Armenian intellectual, religious, and political notables were arrested, deported, and executed. The thousands of Armenians in the Ottoman army were segregated into unarmed labor battalions and ultimately slaughtered. Under various guises the men of hundreds of Armenian villages were marched away; in some instances they were massacred a short distance from their homes, while in others they were forced to trudge many days before meeting their doom. The men gone, the remainder of the population of one district after another was driven southward in the most pitiless manner. Thousands upon thousands of ravaged and tormented women and children fell to an infamous death. The carnage extended far beyond the eastern vilayets, as boatloads of Armenian inhabitants of the Black Sea littoral were dumped into the angry waters and the Armenians of Cilicia and western Anatolia were subjected in turn to deportation and massacre. Countless women and children were apportioned to Muslim households and compelled to embrace Islam.[21]

[21] Hundreds of volumes have been published regarding the Armenian deportations and massacres. For representative studies, documents, and interpretations, see Hovannisian, *Road to Independence*, pp. 48–55; [Turkey], *Aspirations et agissements révolutionnaires des comités arméniens avant et après la proclamation de la constitution ottoman* (Constantinople, 1917); Yusuf Hikmet Bayur, *Türk İnkılâbı ïarihi*, Vol. III, pt. 3 (Ankara, 1957), pp. 6–10, 35–49; Ahmed Emin, *Turkey and the World War* (New Haven and London, 1930), pp. 213–222; Aram Andonian, ed., *Documents officiels concernant les massacres arméniens* (Paris, 1920); Henry Morgenthau, *Ambassador Morgenthau's Story* (Garden City, N.Y., 1919), pp. 296–383 *passim*; Howard M. Sachar, *The Emergence of the Middle East: 1914–1924* (New York, 1969), pp. 87–115; *Hushamatian Meds Egherni, 1915–1965*, ed. Gersam Aharonian (Beirut, 1965); Jean Mécérian, *Le génocide du peuple arménien* (Beirut, 1965), pp. 47–76; Great Britain, Parliament, *The Treatment of the Armenians in the Ottoman Empire*, Miscellaneous No. 31 (1916). A copy of the Turkish plan for genocide, recovered by British officials after the World War, is in Britain, FO 371/4172, 31307/1270/44. The role of Germany in relation to the massacres is discussed by Lepsius, *Deutschland und Armenien*, and by Trumpener, *op cit.*, pp. 125–128, 200–247, 268–270, the latter author having recently disclosed much new material from the several German archives. During the 1960's historians in Soviet Armenia found it possible for the first time to broach the subject of the Armenian massacres. Representative of the new, partially unfettered approach are the following: *Genotsid armian v Osmanskoi imperii: Sbornik dokumentov i materialov*, ed. M. G. Nersisian (Erevan, 1966); Sargsian, *op. cit.*, pp. 231–291; A. N. Mnatsakanian, *Hai zhoghovrdi voghbergutiune* (Erevan, 1965); Dj. S. Kirakosian, *Aradjin hamashkharhayin paterazme ev arevmtahayutiune 1914–1916 t.t.* (Erevan, 1965). See also the commemorative issues of the Soviet Armenian journals *Sovetakan grakanutiun*, 4 (1965); *Teghekagir*, 4 (1965); *Patma-banasirakan handes*, 1 (1965).

A few Armenian districts defended themselves to the end, but only at Van, the province bordering Persia and the Russian Empire, did such resistance prove successful. The Armenians of Van held out until volunteer units and Russian divisions from the Caucasus rescued them. When the Russian army withdrew shortly thereafter, nearly 200,000 Armenians of the vilayet poured into Transcaucasia, overwhelming the Russian Armenians with the magnitude of the tragedy that had unfolded beyond the border. Turkish Armenia had become a wasteland.[22]

The Armenians of Russia, in contrast with those of Turkey, initially welcomed the outbreak of war. Suppressing the memory of Romanov Armenophobe policies, they now pledged fealty to Tsar Nicholas, who promised to free the Turkish Armenians and guarantee them the opportunity of unrestricted progress. Full of optimism, the Russian Armenians, in addition to contributing more than 100,000 men to the regular tsarist armies, formed seven volunteer contingents specifically to aid in the liberation of Turkish Armenia. The partisan tactics of the volunteers and their knowledge of the rugged terrain proved important assets to the Russian war effort.[23] But Armenian hopes were rudely shaken in 1916. Russian authorities abruptly ordered the demobilization of the volunteer units, proscribed Armenian civic activity, and imposed stringent press censorship. This sudden reversal left the Armenians aghast.[24]

Russian archival materials subsequently published by the Soviet government have shown that the tsarist strategy was quite logical. By mid-1916 Russia, Great Britain, and France had completed negotiations for the partition of the Ottoman Empire. These agreements reserved for France the westernmost sector of the Armenian plateau, Cilicia, and the Syrian coastline, allotted most of Mesopotamia and

[22] Onnik Mkhitarian, *Vani herosamarte* (Sofia, 1930); G. Sassuni, *Tajkahayastane rusakan tirapetutian tak (1914–1918)* (Boston, 1927), pp. 65–93; Sargsian, *op. cit.*, pp. 274–280; Allen and Muratoff, *op. cit.*, pp. 297–310; Maslovskii, *op. cit.*, 149–197 *passim*; Leo, *Tiurkahai*, II, 163–182, 192–194.

[23] The role of the Armenian volunteers is described in detail in the following sources: General G. Korganoff, *La participation des Arméniens à la guerre mondiale sur le front du Caucase, 1914–1918* (Paris, 1927); Edvard Choburian, *Meds paterazme ev hai zhoghovurde* (Constantinople, 1920); Gr. Tchalkhouchian, *Le livre rouge* (Paris, 1919), pp. 21–31; A. Khatisian, "Kaghakapeti me hishataknere," *Hairenik Amsagir*, X (Oct., 1932), 155–159; Ananun, *op. cit.*, pp. 540–561; Price, *op. cit.*, pp. 122–162. See also Rep. of Arm. Archives, File 157/56, *H. H. Pat., 1921*, "L'Arménie dans la Guerre Mondiale."

[24] Rep. of Arm. Archives, File 1/1, *Hayastani Hanrapetutiun, 1918 t.*; Ananun, *op. cit.*, pp. 552–553; Sassuni, *op. cit.*, pp. 108–109; Khatisian, *op. cit.*, pp. 159–161.

inland Syria to Great Britain, and awarded Constantinople, the shores of the Bosporus, and the bulk of Turkish Armenia to Russia. It is now evident that Russian postwar plans for Turkish Armenia did not, by any interpretation, include autonomy. On the contrary, the region was marked for annexation as an integral unit of the Romanov Empire and for possible repopulation by Russian peasants and Cossacks.[25] With Russian armies in firm control of most of the Armenian plateau by the summer of 1916, there was no longer any need to expend niceties upon the Armenians.

The March Revolution and Transcaucasia

Embittered by tsarist policies toward the subject nationalities, the Armenians, Georgians, and Muslims of Transcaucasia hailed the February/March Revolution of 1917, which drove Nicholas II from the throne and ended the three-hundred-year reign of the Romanov dynasty. The leaders of the several peoples of Transcaucasia, spurred by the emotions of the moment, united in appeals for regional solidarity and brotherhood within the great Russian federative democracy that would surely rise from the ruins of the Romanov autocracy.

Shortly after assuming power the Russian Provisional Government dispatched to Transcaucasia an interim regional administrative body known by the abbreviated title, Ozakom. Many regarded the Ozakom as a symbol of the new era and expected it to heal the wounds inflicted by the old regime, relieve the critical food shortage, dispel national antagonisms, strengthen the front, and foster just rule. Actually, the Ozakom had neither the means nor the will to undertake such a comprehensive program. Instead, in pursuance of the Provisional Government's policy to delay sweeping reforms until the All-Russian Constituent Assembly had convened to determine a course of action, the

---

[25] For discussions of the secret wartime treaties and their relation to Armenia, see Richard G. Hovannisian, "The Allies and Armenia, 1915–18," *Journal of Contemporary History*, III (Jan., 1968), 155–166; Howard, *op. cit.*, pp. 119–187; Sachar, *op. cit.*, pp. 152–181; S. M. Akopian, *Zapadnaia Armeniia v planakh imperialisticheskikh derzhav v period pervoi mirovoi voiny* (Erevan, 1967). The documents disclosed by the Soviet government are in the following publications: Ministerstvo Inostrannykh Del SSSR, *Konstantinopol' i Prolivy po sekretnym dokumentam b. ministerstva inostrannykh del*, ed. E. A. Adamov (Moscow, 1925–1926), 2 vols; *Razdel Aziatskoi Turtsii po sekretnym dokumentam b. ministerstva inostrannykh del*, ed. E. A. Adamov (Moscow, 1924); "Dnevnik Ministerstva Inostrannykh Del za 1915–1916 g.g.," *Krasnyi Arkhiv*, XXXI (1928), 3–50, and XXXII (1929), 3–87. For a study of the Russian advance over the Armenian plateau in 1916, see the Turkish account in Belen, *Türk Harbi*, III (1965), 3–107 *passim*, and IV (1966), 185–190.

Ozakom attempted to slow the pace of agrarian and political revolution.[26]

The inefficaciousness of the Ozakom aside, the Armenians were cheered by the Provisional Government's favorable pronouncements about the future status of Turkish Armenia. A decree published on April 26 (May 9), 1917, gave Turkish Armenia a civil administration and permitted Armenians to fill many posts therein. Moreover, Turkish Armenian refugees, previously forbidden by tsarist commanders from returning to their native villages, began to stream homeward. By the end of 1917 nearly 150,000 Turkish Armenians were rebuilding in the provinces of Van, Erzerum, and Bitlis.[27]

Armenian confidence was somewhat undermined by the disintegration of the Russian armies on every front. Weary of war and swept along by the slogan "peace without annexations and indemnities," Russian soldiers mutinied and deserted. Bolshevik defeatist propaganda urged the wretched troops to turn their weapons, not on the poor workers and peasants in uniform who stood against them, but on their own officers, and to transform the imperialist war into a class struggle. In view of the unstable conditions along the front, Armenian leaders in Petrograd prevailed upon the Provisional Government to transfer from the European theater to the Caucasus thousands of Armenian soldiers, who could be relied upon to preserve the hard-won Russian gains in Turkish Armenia. The reassignment of these troops had hardly begun, however, when the operation was interrupted by the Bolshevik coup.[28]

The fluid situation in 1917 prompted the interparty council of Russian Armenians to summon a national congress to determine Armenian policy and to select an executive board to act as the collective spokesman of the Armenian people. The congress, held in Tiflis in October, brought together more than two hundred delegates from many parts of the former Russian Empire.[29] Only the Armenian Bolsheviks, still

[26] The organization, prerogatives, and activities of the Ozakom (Osobyi Zakavkazskii Komitet) are presented by Hovannisian, *Road to Independence*, pp. 75–78; Kazemzadeh, *Transcaucasia*, pp. 33–35; Ananun, *op. cit.*, pp. 607–609; S. E. Sef, *Revoliutsiia 1917 goda v Zakavkaz'i (dokumenty, materialy)* ([Tiflis], 1927), pp. 78–83, 194–196, 217–235 *passim;* Robert Paul Browder and Alexander F. Kerensky, eds., *The Russian Provisional Government, 1917: Documents* (3 vols.; Stanford, 1961), I, 424–426; *Bor'ba v Gruzii*, pp. 8, 79–80. For a collection of documents relating to the nationality and minority policies of the Provisional Government, see Dimanshtein, *op. cit.*, pp. 41–78.

[27] Vratzian, *Hanrapetutiun*, pp. 22–24; Papazian, *op. cit.*, pp. 441–442; Sassuni, *op. cit.*, pp. 141–143.

[28] Rep. of Arm. Archives, File 379/1, *H. H. Vashingtoni Nerkayatsutsich ev H. Amerikian Karavarutiune, 1917–1918*, Pasdermadjian to Lansing, March 4 and May 10, 1918.

[29] A résumé of the proceedings of the Armenian National Congress is given by

but a handful of men, refused to participate, alleging that the congress could be nothing more than a bourgeois-clerical assembly that would ignore the interests of the workers and peasants and intrigue to keep the downtrodden under the yoke of capitalism and imperialism.[30]

By political affiliation the majority of the delegates were Dashnakists, followed by Populists, Social Revolutionaries, Social Democrats, and nonpartisans. The Armenian Populist Party (Hai Zhoghovrdakan Kusaktsutiun), formed in March, 1917, by Armenian members of the Russian Constitutional Democrat (Kadet) organization, advanced a program of liberal, evolutionary reforms and drew its adherents primarily from among the professional-commercial classes of Tiflis and Baku. These two cities were also the centers of the small Armenian Social Revolutionary and Social Democrat elements, which, like the Populists, found little support in the native Armenian districts. The intellectual circles of Armenian Social Revolutionaries and Social Democrats were internationally oriented and either had no separate Armenian organization or else operated as component units of the all-Russian parties. Earlier, in feuds with Dashnaktsutiun, both groups had accused the dominant Armenian party of ultranationalism, excessive involvement in Turkish Armenian affairs, and failure to participate sufficiently in the Russian revolutionary movement. In 1917, however, neither Armenian Social Revolutionaries nor Social Democrats could disregard questions related to the future of the Armenian plateau.[31]

The Armenian National Congress, upholding the Provisional Government's "defensive war" policy and paying lip service to the principle of harmony and collaboration among the peoples of Transcaucasia, also called for the long overdue administrative reorganization of the

---

Hovannisian, *Road to Independence*, pp. 86–90. See also S. Masurian, "Rusahayots Azgayin Hamagumare," in *Mayis 28*, publ. of the Paris Regional Committee of Dashnaktsutiun (Paris, 1926), pp. 4–22; Ananun, *op. cit.*, pp. 639–640, 653–658; A. Terzipashian, *Nupar* (Paris, 1939), pp. 158–170.

[30] G. B. Gharibdjanian, *Hayastani komunistakan kazmakerputiunnere Sovetakan ishkhanutian haghtanaki hamar mghvads paikarum* (Erevan, 1955), pp. 122–123; *Revoliutsion kocher*, pp. 415–417; *Bor'ba v Gruzii*, pp. 88, 93–95. Terzipashian, *op. cit.*, pp. 163–164, states that Bolshevik delegates did attend the first sessions of the National Congress and declared a boycott only after being shouted down during the presentation of their program.

[31] For material on the founding and principles of the Armenian Populist, Social Revolutionary, and Social Democrat groups, see Hovannisian, *Road to Independence*, pp. 18–19, 74, 278 n. 133; Ananun, *op. cit.*, pp. 91–106, 329–349, 604–607; Dimanshtein, *op. cit.*, pp. 401–403; Vahan Minakhorian, "Andjatakannere," *Vem*, I, 1 (1933), 110–111, and 2 (1933), 90–107. For the economic programs of the Armenian political parties, as appraised by a Soviet economic historian, see Adonts, *op. cit.*, pp. 302–429.

Caucasus.[32] It recommended that the provincial boundaries be re-drawn on the basis of ethnic and topographic unity. The Armenian lands would thereby encompass the existing Erevan guberniia and several contiguous districts in the provinces of Kars, Tiflis, and Elisa-vetpol. Although similar schemes had been proposed since 1905 at conferences sponsored by Romanov officials, it was felt that the likeli-hood of adoption was greater now that the forces of democracy had triumphed in Russia.[33] The territories marked for inclusion within the Armenian sector of Transcaucasia were nearly identical with those subsequently claimed by the Republic of Armenia.

In clear control of the National Congress, Dashnaktsutiun never-theless sought the collaboration of the minor parties in the establish-ment of a permanent executive body to be known as the Armenian National Council. The Dashnakists therefore accepted a compromise plan that allotted them only six of the fifteen places and accorded two seats each to the Populists, Social Revolutionaries, and Social Demo-crats and three seats to nonpartisans.[34] As the situation in Russia deteriorated during the following months, the responsibilities of the National Council increased; it was this executive that ultimately pro-claimed the independence of Armenia.

That Dashnaktsutiun, its compromises aside, retained the solid sup-port of the Armenian populace was demonstrated in the elections to the All-Russian Constituent Assembly in November, 1917. The Geor-gian Mensheviks, Muslim Musavatists, and Armenian Dashnakists garnered among themselves more than 75 percent of the total vote cast in Transcaucasia. This figure would have been even larger had the Russian soldiers stationed in the area not been included in the Trans-caucasian electorate, for they augmented considerably the Social Revo-

---

[32] Rep. of Arm. Archives, File 1/1; Masurian, *op. cit.*, pp. 7–8.

[33] The proposals for provincial reorganization are given in detail by Shakhatuni, *op. cit.*, pp. 61–73; Ananun, *op. cit.*, pp. 613–640; Abeghian, "Mer harevannere" (Feb., 1928), pp. 96–98. A listing of all provinces (*guberniia* and *oblast*) and counties (*uezd* and *okrug*) of Transcaucasia, together with a corresponding map, is given by Stanke-vich, *op. cit.*, pp. 209–210.

[34] Rep. of Arm. Archives, File 1/1; Vratzian, *Hanrapetutiun*, pp. 32–33. The origi-nal membership of the Armenian National Council consisted of Avetis Aharonian (chairman), Aram Manukian, Nikol Aghbalian, Ruben Ter-Minasian, Khachatur Karjikian, Artashes Babalian (Dashnakists); Samson Harutiunian, Mikayel Papa-djanian (Populists); Misha (Mikayel) Gharabekian, Ghazar Ter-Ghazarian (Social Democrats); Haik Ter-Ohanian, Anushavan Stamboltsian (Social Revolutionaries); Stepan Mamikonian, Tigran Bekzadian, Petros Zakarian (Nonpartisans). See also Dimanshtein, *op. cit.*, pp. 404–405.

lutionary and the Social Democrat Bolshevik vote. Of the fifteen slates on the ballot, the following six gained the highest totals:[35]

Social Democrat (Menshevik)	661,934
Musavat	615,816
Dashnaktsutiun	558,440
Muslim Socialist Bloc	159,770
Social Revolutionary	117,522
Social Democrat (Bolshevik)	93,581

The parties were awarded one Constituent Assembly seat for each 60,000 votes received.[36]

Some Transcaucasian delegates were still en route to Petrograd when the All-Russian Constituent Assembly, having convened for a single day on January 18, 1918, was dispersed by order of the new Bolshevik-controlled government of Russia.[37] Nearly all Transcaucasia denounced the Bolshevik tactic just as it had the October/November Revolution that, two months earlier, had overthrown the Provisional Government of Russia and brought to power the Council of People's Commissars (Sovnarkom).[38] With Baku the major exception, Transcaucasia firmly denied the Sovnarkom recognition and instead anticipated the liquidation of the Bolshevik "adventure."[39]

[35] Hovannisian, *Road to Independence*, pp. 108–109; Ananun, *op. cit.*, p. 672; Khatisian, "Kaghakapeti me hishataknere," XI (March, 1933), 146. Different totals are given by Oliver Radkey, *The Election to the Russian Constituent Assembly of 1917* (Cambridge, Mass., 1950), pp. 16–20, appendix; and by Woytinsky, *op. cit.*, p. 113.

[36] Ananun, *op. cit.*, p. 673; Vratzian, *Hanrapetutiun*, p. 30.

[37] Zhordaniia, *op. cit.*, p. 83, states that Iraklii Tsereteli was the only Georgian Menshevik to attend the Constituent Assembly and asserts that most of the Georgian leadership placed little faith in the Petrograd gathering.

[38] For representative resolutions deprecating the Bolshevik coup, see *Dokumenty i materialy*, pp. 1–3.

[39] For the stand of the Baku Soviet, see B. H. Lalabekian, *V. I. Lenine ev Sovetakan kargeri hastatumn u amrapndumn Andrkovkasum* (Erevan, 1961), pp. 21–23; Kh. S. Barseghian, *Stepan Shahumian: Kianki ev gordsuneutian vaveragrakan taregrutiun, 1878–1918* (Erevan, 1968), pp. 435–443. The Bolsheviks in Baku gained control of the local Soviet only in April of 1918 and even then had to rely on support from Social Revolutionary and Dashnakist deputies. Even though the Baku Soviet formally recognized the Russian Sovnarkom on November 13, elections then in progress for the All-Russian Constituent Assembly gave the Bolshevik slate less than 30 percent of the votes cast in Baku, 22,276 out of 71,262. The Musavat-Muslim bloc received 21,752, Dashnaktsutiun, 20,314, and the Social Revolutionary party, 18,789. With the temporary establishment of Soviet order in April, the Bolshevik–Left Social Revolutionary leadership remained dependent upon the Armenian national militia, commanded by members or sympathizers of Dashnaktsutiun. A useful Soviet account of the events from the October/November Revolution to the declaration of Soviet rule in Baku is given by A. L. Popov, "Iz istorii revoliutsii v Vostochnom Zakavkaz'e (1917–1918 g.g.)," *Proletarskaia revoliutsiia*, nos. 5–11 (May–Nov., 1924).

The Sovnarkom and Armenia

Bolshevik strategy perplexed and alarmed most Armenian leaders. Even before the coup of November, 1917, Lenin had demanded withdrawal of Russian troops from Turkish Armenia and recognition of the right of all peoples to self-determination.[40] This view, hammered forth time and again, seemed sinister to the Armenians, for a Russian evacuation would culminate in Turkish reoccupation of the eastern vilayets and would expose the Armenians of the Caucasus to the tragic fate recently suffered by the Armenians of the Ottoman Empire.

The Bolshevik maneuver was calculated to win the sympathy and support of the many thousands of war-weary soldiers and to undermine the Provisional Government. After the Bolshevik Revolution the tactic was employed to convince the Muslim world that the Sovnarkom had unconditionally renounced tsarist territorial ambitions: "We declare that the treaty on the partition of Turkey and the wresting of Armenia from her is null and void." [41] Soviet leaders reasoned that the colonial peoples, once convinced of the good intent of the new Russia, would unite in the struggle against the powerful imperialist and capitalist antagonists of the West.

The Sovnarkom's decree "About Turkish Armenia," published in January, 1918, invoked the principle of self-determination as a cover under which to recall the Russian armies. The decree advocated the return home of all Turkish Armenian deportees and refugees and the creation of a native militia force and of a popular provisional administration on the Armenian plateau.[42] Actually, this plan was rendered unrealistic, if not cynical, by the Russian abandonment of Turkish Armenia. To Russian Armenians and Turkish Armenians alike, self-determination under the prevailing circumstances was out of the question. That the Sovnarkom's maneuver was a necessary step in demonstrating the absence of imperialistic designs by the new Russian

[40] Alfred G. Meyer, *Leninism* (Cambridge, Mass., 1957), pp. 145-155; Lenin, *Sochineniia*, XXXII, 289-290, and XXXIV, 232, 379; B. A. Borian, *Armeniia, mezhdunarodnaia diplomatiia i SSSR*, Vol. II (Moscow and Leningrad, 1929), pp. 262-263, 277; H. Sahakian, *Meds Hoktembere ev azgayin hartsi ludsume Andrkovkasum* (Erevan, 1967), pp. 6-8, 12-13.

[41] *Dokumenty SSSR*, Vol. I (Moscow, 1957), p. 35. See also Iu. V. Kliuchnikov and A. Sabanin, eds., *Mezhdunarodnaia politika noveishego vremeni v dogovorakh, notakh i deklaratsiiakh*, Vol. II (Moscow, 1926), p. 94.

[42] *Dokumenty SSSR*, I, 71-75, 93-94; H. M. Elchibekian and A. M. Hakobian, *Urvagdser Sovetakan Hayastani patmutian*, pt. 1 (Erevan, 1954), pp. 19-20; M. V. Arzumanian, "Leninskii 'Dekret o Turetskoi Armenii'," *Vestnik obshchestvennykh nauk [Lraber hasarakakan gitutiunneri]*, 1 (1968), 23-28.

government has been affirmed by a noted (purged and posthumously rehabilitated) Soviet historian, who explained, "The Armenian question thus became the means and not the end." [43]

An equally severe blow was dealt the Armenians by the Sovnarkom's acquiescence in the Treaty of Brest-Litovsk, March 3, 1918. By the terms of that treaty, Soviet Russia ceded to the Central Powers more than a million square miles with nearly sixty million inhabitants. Lenin's government also acknowledged the right of the Ottoman Empire to sovereignty over all Turkish Armenia and, although having no actual jurisdiction in Transcaucasia, tacitly forfeited to Turkey the districts of Kars, Ardahan, and Batum. The treaty also stipulated that Russian armed forces were to complete their withdrawal from Turkish Armenia and the three Transcaucasian districts within eight weeks. And the Sovnarkom promised to utilize every available means to disperse and destroy the Armenian "bands" operating in Russia and in the "occupied provinces" of Turkey.[44] The Armenians, who had attempted to man the Turkish front in spite of the massive Russian desertions and the proceedings at Brest-Litovsk, now accused the Sovnarkom of a nefarious betrayal.

The Commissariat and the Seim

Prompted by the Bolshevik seizure of power in central Russia, a multinational congress of Transcaucasian leaders met in Tiflis in November, 1917, to create a provisional regional executive board, the Commissariat, for the purpose of maintaining order until the establishment of a democratic federative Russian republic.[45] The Transcaucasian Com-

---

[43] Borian, op. cit., p. 262.

[44] Dokumenty SSSR, I, 121, 199–200; United States, Department of State, Papers Relating to the Foreign Relations of the United States, 1918: Russia, Vol. I (Washington, D.C., 1931), pp. 442–476. See also Jane Degras, ed., Soviet Documents on Foreign Policy, Vol. I (London, New York and Toronto, 1951), pp. 50–55; Akdes Nimet Kurat, "Brest-Litovsk müzakereleri ve barısı (20 aralık 1917–3 mart 1918," Belleten, XXXI (July, 1967), 375–413.

[45] US Archives, RG 59, 861.00/711/719, Smith (Tiflis) to Secretary of State, Nov. 23 and 25, 1917; Hovannisian, Road to Independence, pp. 106–108; Ananun, op. cit., pp. 662–663; Dokumenty i materialy, pp. 3–10; Khatisian, Hanrapetutian zargatsume, pp. 17–18. A Bolshevik deputation composed of Filipp I. Makharadze, Mikha G. Tskhakaia, and Amaiak (Hmaiak) M. Nazaretian attended the meeting long enough to denounce the counterrevolutionary nature of the gathering and to declare that any form of government other than Soviet order would be reactionary. See G. Zhvaniia, Velikii Oktiabr' i bor'ba Bol'shevikov Zakavkaz'ia za Sovetskuiu vlast' (Tbilisi, 1967), pp. 121–123; Ia. Shafir, Grazhdanskaia voina v Rossii i men'shevistskaia Gruziia (Moscow, 1921), pp. 3–4.

missariat (which included three Georgians, three Muslims, three Armenians, and two Russians) and the Seim, the legislature organized in February, 1918, were heavily encumbered by their pretense that Transcaucasia formed an integral unit of the (nonexistent) Russian democracy, while in fact they were being driven to cope with situations that demanded independent action. The longer Transcaucasia held to the myth of union with Russia, the deeper it sank into contradiction and confusion. The Armenians persistently rejected the slightest suggestion of separation from Russia. Only under the aegis of a powerful Russian republic, they felt, could Russian Armenia and Turkish Armenia be merged into a progressive autonomous region. The Georgian Menshevik leadership also held to the principle of Russia, one and united, but most Muslim spokesmen, although initially advocating a federated Russian republic, were soon drawn toward Turkey by racial and religious bonds.

In December, 1917, the Commissariat and the (anti-Bolshevik) Russian Army Command of the Caucasus negotiated with the Ottoman Empire a truce that left most of Turkish Armenia under Transcaucasian control.[46] Because the regular Russian divisions were deserting this region en masse, the Russian Command then authorized the formation of the Armenian Army Corps, composed of three substrength divisions. The Armenian Corps, commanded by General Tovmas Nazarbekian (Foma I. Nazarbekov), took up positions along the demarcation line from Van to Erzinjan, while a smaller Georgian force filled in from Erzinjan to the Black Sea. Several thousand men now defended a 300-mile front formerly secured by a half million Russian regulars.[47]

At the beginning of 1918 the Transcaucasian executive was hurtled into chaos by a well-calculated Ottoman maneuver, a proposal to begin bilateral discussions for a permanent peace. The Commissariat, by its own definition, was an interim body empowered to deal only with local affairs. Moreover, both Georgian and Armenian leaders knew that, alone, Transcaucasia could wield little power at the bargaining table. Nevertheless, unsuccessful in efforts to strike upon a satisfactory alternative, the Commissariat finally accepted the Ottoman offer in

[46] *Dokumenty i materialy*, pp. 11–23; *Dokumenty SSSR*, I, 53–57; Aram Amirkhanian, *Rus ev turk zinadadare: Patmakan antsker, 1917–1918* (Fresno, Calif., 1921); Belen, *Türk Harbi*, IV, 204–206.

[47] Rep. of Arm. Archives, File 1/1; Korganoff, *op. cit.*, pp. 77–88; A. Poidebard, "Rôle militaire des Arméniens sur le front du Caucase après la défection de l'armée russe (décembre 1917–novembre 1918)," *Revue des études arméniennes*, I, pt. 2 (1920), 149–151; Allen and Muratoff, *op. cit.*, pp. 457–459; Sargsian, *op. cit.*, pp. 337–338.

mid-February, 1918.[48] Then on March 1 the Seim announced its "realistic" and "moderate" foundations for peace. Transcaucasia would waive its right to Turkish Armenia and would consent to the restoration of the Russo-Turkish border of 1914 on condition that certain provisions be made regarding the self-administration of Turkish Armenia within the framework of the Ottoman Empire. The Armenian deputies, a minority in the Seim, clearly understood that adoption of this program would shatter the cherished vision of a liberated Turkish Armenia, most of which still remained under the jurisdiction of the Armenian Army Corps. Yet, also equally aware that adamance would bring even greater misfortune to their people, they sullenly yielded to the plan sponsored by the Georgian and Muslim factions of the legislature.[49]

The Trebizond Conference

Just as the Transcaucasian delegation was about to depart for Trebizond to conduct pourparlers with officials of the Turkish government, a wire from Brest-Litovsk announced that Soviet Russia had recognized the right of the Ottoman Empire to reoccupy Turkish Armenia and to extend into Kars, Ardahan, and Batum.[50] The Sovnarkom's action left Transcaucasia in an untenable bargaining position yet with no choice but to begin negotiations. When the Trebizond conference commenced on March 14, 1918, it became apparent that the fears of the Transcaucasian leaders were well founded. Husein Rauf Bey, the chief Ottoman delegate, proved intractable in his demand that the Treaty of Brest-Litovsk serve as the basis for all further proceedings. He was not in the least impressed by the arguments that the Sovnarkom had no jurisdiction in Transcaucasia and that Turkey and Transcaucasia had already agreed to negotiate before the Treaty of Brest-Litovsk was concluded.[51]

The large Transcaucasian delegation, headed by Georgian Menshe-

[48] *Dokumenty i materialy*, pp. 24–40, 52–57, 60, 62–66; US Archives, RG 84, American Consulate, Tiflis, General Correspondence, 1917–1919, File 711, Consular reports and enclosures, Jan.–March, 1918.

[49] *Dokumenty i materialy*, pp. 73–84; S. T. Arkomed, *Materialy po istorii otpadeniia Zakavkaz'ia ot Rossii* (Tiflis, 1923), p. 17; Ananun, *op. cit.*, pp. 675–676; Leo, *Tiurkahai*, II, 200; Vratzian, *Hanrapetutiun*, pp. 60–61.

[50] *Dokumenty i materialy*, pp. 85–86.

[51] *Ibid.*, pp. 107–119, 132–139; Khatisian, *Hanrapetutian zargatsume*, pp. 28–33; Arkomed, *op. cit.*, pp. 27–35; Hovannisian, *Road to Independence*, pp. 131–134, 138–140; Al. Stavrovskii, *Zakavkaz'e posle Oktiabria* (Moscow and Leningrad, [1925]), pp. 116–118.

vik A. I. Chkhenkeli, was rendered helpless not only by the overbearing Turkish attitude but also by violent internal discord. The divergent views of the Georgian, Muslim, and Armenian delegates reflected the basic differences among the three peoples. The Muslims, bound by race, religion, and ideology to the rulers of Turkey, favored prompt acceptance of all Ottoman demands. They kept Rauf Bey fully informed about the activities and the closed caucuses of the Transcaucasian delegation. The Georgians recognized the inevitability of making a number of further concessions, but these, they maintained, should be focused upon Kars, an Armenian district, in order to save Batum, a vital Georgian coastal region. The Armenian delegates angrily retorted that Transcaucasia could never survive without the mighty bastion of Kars and insisted that the conditions for peace as voted by the Seim should constitute the maximum concession.[52]

Away from Trebizond, the growing disunity among the Transcaucasian peoples racked the Commissariat and the Seim and erupted into armed conflict between Muslims and Christians in nearly every province of Transcaucasia. With the land torn by civil strife the political leverage of the Turkish representatives in Trebizond was further strengthened. But Enver Pasha and his fellow military commanders did not intend to await the outcome of the diplomatic wrangling; instead they determined to take forcibly the territories that the empire had been awarded at Brest-Litovsk. Claiming that Armenian bands had perpetrated atrocities against Muslims in the occupied eastern vilayets, the Ottoman Third Army, headed by General Mehmed Vehib Pasha, violated the demarcation lines established by the recent truce and swept into Turkish Armenia. In March, 1918, the key citadel of Erzerum fell, and by early April Ottoman divisions approached the international frontier of 1914. The battle for Turkish Armenia had been quickly decided; the struggle for Russian Armenia was now at hand (see map 3).[53]

Distressed by the critical diplomatic and military setbacks sustained by Transcaucasia, delegation chairman Chkhenkeli informed Rauf Bey that the Treaty of Brest-Litovsk would henceforth be accepted as the

[52] Arkomed, op. cit., pp. 42–44; O. Minasian, "Vneshniaia politika zakavkazskoi kontrrevoliutsii v pervoi polovine 1918 goda," Istorik marksist, 6 (1938), 68.

[53] Rep. of Arm. Archives, File 1406a/26a, H. H. D. Amerikayi Kedronakan Komite, 1918; Allen and Muratoff, op. cit., pp. 459–464; Dokumenty i materialy, pp. 41–51; Kandemir, Karabekir, pp. 142–158; Korganoff, op. cit., pp. 89–121; Kadishev, Interventsiia v Zakavkaz'e, pp. 43–48; E. F. Ludshuveit, Turtsiia v gody pervoi mirovoi voiny 1914–1918 gg.: Voenno-politicheskii ocherk (Moscow, 1966), pp. 161–174; Belen, Türk Harbi, V (1967), 149–155.

basis for their negotiations. Chkhenkeli then wired his government and the leadership of the Georgian Menshevik organization, urging them to uphold his unauthorized action as the only possible means of saving Batum, the outlet to the external world and the terminus of the oil pipeline from Baku.[54] The mood prevailing in Tiflis, however, contrasted sharply with the cold realism of Akakii Chkhenkeli. Menshevik orators in the Seim exclaimed that submission to the terms of Brest-Litovsk would be tantamount to the self-destruction of the entire Caucasus. Expressing greater determination than ever before, the Georgians pledged, to the resounding applause of the Armenian deputies, a resolute defense of the front. But while Georgian sabers rattled in the Seim, Muslim spokesmen made it known that they would not take arms against a kindred people and that they were prepared to support those elements attempting to bring about a just and lasting settlement. Unaffected by this ominous declaration the now united Armeno-Georgian bloc ordered Chkhenkeli's delegation to return to Tiflis and acknowledged the existence of a state of war between Transcaucasia and Turkey.[55]

The Transcaucasian Federative Republic

The resolve of the Georgians to defend Transcaucasia was short-lived. On April 14, 1918, only a few hours after the Seim had recalled its delegation from Trebizond, Ottoman troops captured Batum, thus dampening Georgian zeal.[56] The Menshevik faction in the Seim now bowed to the Ottoman conditions for the resumption of negotiations: a declaration of Transcaucasia's total separation from Russia and the recognition of the territorial rights of Turkey. Thus, on April 22, 1918, the Mensheviks, supported by all Muslim groups in the Seim, proposed the establishment of the independent democratic Transcaucasian Federative Republic.[57] Once again the Armenians were cast upon the horns of a dilemma. Their army corps still held the fortress of Kars and, according to military experts, could stave off the Turkish offensive for at least two months. And yet, if the Armenians should reject the com-

[54] *Dokumenty i materialy*, pp. 159–160; Arkomed, *op. cit.*, pp. 51–54; Kh. H. Badalian, *Germana-turkakan okupantnere Hayastanum 1918 tvakanin* (Erevan, 1962), p. 92.

[55] Mir-Yacoub, *op. cit.*, p. 103; *Dokumenty i materialy*, pp. 163–184; Badalian, *op. cit.*, pp. 91–92; Stavrovskii, *op. cit.*, pp. 24–29; Vratzian, *Hanrapetutiun*, pp. 78–82; Zhordaniia, *op. cit.*, pp. 84–85.

[56] Rep. of Arm. Archives, File 1406a/26a; Allen and Muratoff, *op. cit.*, pp. 465–466.

[57] Arkomed, *op. cit.*, p. 66; Vahan Minakhorian, "Batumi khorhrdazhoghove," *Hairenik Amsagir*, XIV (March, 1936), 93–94.

3. THE TURKISH OFFENSIVE OF 1918

LEGEND

+++ Russo-Turkish Boundary, 1914

···· Demarcation Line, February 1, 1918

═══ Primary Roads

┼┼┼ Railroads

2-13 Date of Occupation

Scale in Miles

0   50   100

BLACK SEA

PERSIA

Lake Van

Lake Sevan

Tiflis
Kutais
Akstafa
Karakilisa
Vorontsovka 5-26
5-22
Borzhom
Bozhom
Hamamlu
Akhalkalak
Akhaltsikh
Alexandropol
5-15
Erevan
Maku
Nakhichevan
Bayazit
Manziker
Khoi
Van
4-7
Sardarabad
Sarikamish
Kars
A-25
4-18
A-5
Ardahan 3-19
Merdenek
Ozurget
Batum 4-15
4-19
Arvin
Ardahan
Hasankal
Erzerum 3-12
Alashkert
Khnus
Mush
Sassun
Bitlis
Ognot
Kighi
Mamakhatun
Rize
Gumushane
Baiburt
Erzinjan 2-13
Kemakh
Trebizond
Shabin-Karahisar
Ordu
Samsun
Sivas

bined Georgian-Muslim tactic in the Seim, they would have to continue the struggle alone. Desperately trying to avoid isolation as the specter of new massacres loomed ever nearer, the dejected Armenian deputies endorsed with bitterness the proclamation of Transcaucasian independence. It was an act dictated by external military pressure and regarded by many Armenians as a horrifying stride toward the consummation of Enver Pasha's Pan-Turkic goals.[58]

Akakii Ivanovich Chkhenkeli, the proponent of peace, was entrusted with the formation of the cabinet of the Transcaucasian Republic. While still premier-designate, however, Chkhenkeli ordered the Armenian Army Corps to surrender Kars. The command, issued without the knowledge of either the Seim or the Armenians who had agreed to serve in the cabinet, threw the populace of Kars into utter panic. Within a few hours thousands of Armenians were fleeing eastward toward the borders of the Erevan guberniia. On April 25, 1918, regiments of the Ottoman Third Army marched into the fortress and seized its enormous stockpiles of arms and matériel.[59]

The Armenian leaders in Tiflis, learning belatedly of Chkhenkeli's furtive maneuver, rescinded their decision to participate in his cabinet and indignantly demanded the overthrow of the "perfidious" Georgian. The Menshevik chiefs admitted that Chkhenkeli had acted in bad faith but would agree to topple him only if an Armenian, preferably Hovhannes Kachaznuni, took the reins of government. The Georgians were well aware that the Armenians could not accept such a proposal, for the Turks would regard its adoption as the restoration of a war cabinet. With Kars already lost the possibility of an effective Armenian defense had vanished, and with Kachaznuni as the premier of Transcaucasia a renewed Turkish offensive would bring added devastation to the Armenians. Thoroughly humiliated, the Dashnakists now withdrew their resignations and joined Chkhenkeli's cabinet, which was confirmed by the Seim on April 26, 1918.[60] There was no other way

---

[58] *Dokumenty i materialy,* pp. 200–222; Ananun, *op. cit.,* pp. 681–682; Vratzian, *Hanrapetutiun,* pp. 84–86.

[59] For documents and accounts of the surrender of Kars, see Hovannisian, *Road to Independence,* pp. 162–166; *Dokumenty i materialy,* pp. 224–255; Rep. of Arm. Archives, File 1/1; Badalian, *op. cit.,* pp. 90–156; Belen, *Türk Harbi,* V, 157–161; Korganoff, *op. cit.,* pp. 123–128, 137–156. Ludshuveit, *op. cit.,* p. 181, shows that included in the rich booty taken by the Turkish army at Kars were 11,000 rifles, nearly 2 million bullets, 67 cannons, 19 machine guns, and a year's supply of dry bread (*sukhari*).

[60] Vratzian, *Hanrapetutiun,* pp. 93–94; Khatisian, *Hanrapetutian zargatsume,* pp. 42–45; *Dokumenty i materialy,* p. 229. The cabinet of the Transcaucasian Republic included Akakii I. Chkhenkeli, Noi V. Ramishvili, Noi G. Khomeriki, Grigorii T.

to spare the remaining districts of Russian Armenia from the Turkish onslaught.

The Batum Conference

As premier and foreign minister of the Transcaucasian Federative Republic, Chkhenkeli led a new delegation to Batum to resume negotiations. His government was now prepared to accede to all provisions of the Treaty of Brest-Litovsk. During the first session on May 11, however, the Ottoman representative, Halil Bey, announced that this concession no longer sufficed. Since blood had been shed after the Trebizond conference, he explained, the original Ottoman terms could no longer be proffered. Then declaring any further discussion unnecessary, Halil presented a preformulated draft treaty and demanded its immediate acceptance. The Ottoman Empire now laid claim not only to Turkish Armenia and the districts of Kars, Ardahan, and Batum, but also to the counties (*uezds*) of Akhaltsikh (Akhaltskha) and Akhalkalak in the Tiflis guberniia and to the western half of the Erevan guberniia, including the Araxes river valley and the railway that connected Kars with Julfa on the Persian border. Moreover, the truncated Transcaucasian Republic was to be fully subservient to the Ottoman Empire. Chkhenkeli feebly protested that the Ottoman terms precluded the emergence of a friendly buffer state between Turkey and Russia.[61]

Without troubling to allow time for the Transcaucasian government to accept or reject the new terms for peace, Turkish military authorities ordered the invasion of the Erevan guberniia. After a spirited but short Armenian defense, the Ottoman army captured Alexandropol on May 15 and struck out in two directions: southward along the Erevan-Julfa railway and eastward along the Karakilisa-Tiflis-Baku line. A week later Turkish troops and Muslim irregulars had nearly surrounded Erevan on one front and were pressing on Karakilisa, the gateway to Tiflis, on the other.[62] Reinforced by these successes in the field, the

Georgadze (Georgians); Fathali Khan Khoiskii, Khudadat Bek Melik-Aslanov, Nasib Bek Usubbekov, Mahmed Hasan Hajinskii, Ibrahim Bek Haidarov (Muslims); Alexandre I. Khatisian, Hovhannes (Ruben I.) Kachaznuni, Avetik I. Sahakian, Aramayis A. Erzinkian (Armenians). The Armenian view regarding the strategy of the Georgian leaders is given by Beruni, "Vratsi varichnere, Kovkasi pashtpanutiune ev Hayere," *Hairenik* (daily), July 30–Aug. 11, 1919.
[61] *Dokumenty i materialy*, pp. 272-277, 312-316; Rep. of Arm. Archives, File 100/1, *H. H. Patvirakutiun, 1918: H. Ohandjaniani Tghtere*; Z. Avalov, *Nezavisimost' Gruzii v mezhdunarodnoi politike, 1918-1921 g.g.* (Paris, 1924), pp. 40-42, 45-47; Ludshuveit, *op. cit.*, pp. 182-185.
[62] *Dokumenty i materialy*, pp. 269-288 *passim*; Korganoff, *op. cit.*, pp. 157-160.

Ottoman delegation in Batum then presented Chkhenkeli an ultimatum that set aside another slice of the Erevan guberniia for Turkish annexation and required unconditional acceptance of the amended draft treaty within seventy-two hours.[63] The very existence of the Armenian people seemed at an end.

Germany, the senior ally of the Ottoman Empire, opposed Turkish violations of the Treaty of Brest-Litovsk and repeatedly directed Enver Pasha to shift his attention and military forces to the beleaguered fronts in Mesopotamia and Palestine. Germany had entered into bilateral negotiations with Soviet Russia on the future status of the Caucasus and was nearing a settlement which would place the Baku region in Moscow's sphere of influence while securing for Germany abundant raw materials, especially sorely needed petroleum. Because the Turkish offensive in Transcaucasia strained relations between Moscow and Berlin and threatened Germany's designs on this strategic crossroad, the Kaiser's government admonished Enver to honor the Brest-Litovsk boundaries, adding that it would make no further excuses for Turkish excesses against the native Christian population.[64]

When German political and military authorities learned that negotiations between Turkey and Transcaucasia were to resume at Batum, they dispatched an observer, General Otto von Lossow, to defend Germany's interests. During the Batum conference the German officer maneuvered to halt the Ottoman invasion by proposing mediation. When his services were spurned, von Lossow strongly urged his superiors to bend the Turkish strategists into submission through a show of force. Rudely treated by Halil Bey, who rejected every German attempt to interfere, von Lossow finally informed the Transcaucasian representatives of his helplessness and departed on the night of May 25, 1918. Only the Georgian members of Chkhenkeli's delegation knew that he was headed for the nearby port of Poti.[65]

By May of 1918 Georgian political leaders had concluded that the salvation of their people depended upon the intervention of Germany,

[63] US Archives, RG 59, 861.00/2015, Poole (Moscow) to Secretary of State, June 2, 1918; *Dokumenty i materialy*, pp. 309–310; Stavrovskii, *op. cit.*, pp. 108–110.

[64] German-Turkish discord and rivalry on policy relative to the Caucasus are discussed by Trumpener, *op. cit.*, pp. 167–199, 248–266 *passim*; Hovannisian, *Road to Independence*, pp. 176–179; Erich Ludendorff, *Meine Kriegserinnerungen, 1914–1918* (Berlin, 1919), pp. 498–500; Lepsius, *Deutschland und Armenien*, pp. xlv–l, 367–391 *passim*; Fritz Fischer, *Griff nach der Weltmacht* (3d ptg., Düsseldorf, 1964), pp. 738–757 *passim*; Britain, Cab 27/37, E.C. 2570.

[65] *Dokumenty i materialy*, pp. 307, 316; Khatisian, *Hanrapetutian zargatsume*, pp. 53–64; Stavrovskii, *op. cit.*, pp. 98, 107–108; Lepsius, *Deutschland und Armenien*, pp. 381–384.

while the German government, unable to restrain the Turks in Armenia, a land with no readily accessible raw materials, had resolved to bring at least Georgia into Berlin's sphere of influence.[66] Therefore, in secret meetings at Batum, von Lossow and Georgian officials drafted a provisional treaty whereby Germany would extend protection to Georgia in return for economic domination. The implementation of this plan required that the Georgians withdraw from the floundering Transcaucasian Republic and abandon the Armenians. By the time von Lossow set sail from Batum, all had been arranged. Georgia would declare her independence and send a delegation to Poti to seal officially the German-Georgian accord. With these decisions made, Georgian spokesmen in Batum engaged in informal talks with the Muslim members of the Transcaucasian delegation. A view pervading these discussions was that one of the three constituent peoples of the Transcaucasian Federative Republic would fall victim to Turkish aggression but that hopefully the other two, Georgians and Muslims, could maintain cordial mutual relations.[67] It was anticipated that the Armenians would figure no longer in the politics of Transcaucasia.

Independent Republics in Transcaucasia

The Transcaucasian Seim gathered for its final session on the afternoon of May 26, 1918. There, Menshevik orator Iraklii G. Tsereteli justified the calculated Georgian tactic. Condemning the disloyalty of the Transcaucasian Muslims and praising the valiant efforts of the Armenians, who, however, had now been defeated, Tsereteli announced that the Georgians must fend for themselves. Belief in a common Transcaucasian homeland, in a united delegation at Batum, in a community of interests had proved illusory. Thus, the Georgians had no choice but to proclaim independence and form a separate government.[68] Cries from the chamber that the Armenians, still battling the enemy, were

[66] For the decision of the Georgian National Council to appeal to Germany for protection, see *Bor'ba v Gruzii*, p. 264.

[67] Avalov, *op. cit.*, pp. 44–45, 54–61; Arkomed, *op. cit.*, pp. 74–76; D. Enukidze, *Krakh imperialisticheskoi interventsii v Zakavkaz'e* (Tbilisi, 1954), pp. 48–49. According to Enukidze, p. 58, Iraklii Tsereteli revealed to Muslim leaders of the Seim on May 25 the Georgian decision to declare independence, whereupon the Muslims prepared to take like action.

[68] *Dokumenty i materialy*, pp. 317–330; Irakly Tsérételli, *Séparation de la Transcaucasie de la Russie et indépendance de la Géorgie: Discours prononcés à la Diète transcaucasienne* (Paris, 1919), pp. 31–40.

being deserted went unheeded as the Seim adopted the Menshevik motion to dissolve the Transcaucasian Federative Republic.[69]

That same day the Georgian National Council ceremoniously proclaimed the independence of Georgia and named Noi V. Ramishvili to head a provisional cabinet.[70] The Premier's first official act was to hasten to Poti to confirm the treaty between the German Empire and the Republic of Georgia.[71] In Tiflis the German flag was hoisted alongside the Georgian banner; the Georgians had been saved.[72]

On May 27 the Muslim National Council, meeting in Tiflis, resolved to declare the independence of Azerbaijan, a republic that was to encompass "southern and eastern Transcaucasia." The act was officially proclaimed on the following day, and the governing body of the Transcaucasian Tatars, now Azerbaijanis, selected Ganja (Elisavetpol, Gandzak) as the Republic's temporary capital, since Baku still languished under the control of a coalition of Armenian and Bolshevik forces.[73] Ottoman military authorities had already promised to participate in the liberation of Baku, and during the summer of 1918 the Azerbaijani cabinet of Fathali Khan Khoiskii received extensive Turkish support, both in men and matériel. In September, after weeks of battle, the combined Turkish and Azerbaijani armies swept into the city. Much

---

[69] Khondkarian, "Opozitsian Hayastanum," I, 2, p. 78; Arkomed, op. cit., p. 77; Dokumenty i materialy, p. 330.

[70] The initial Georgian cabinet, a coalition, consisted of Ramishvili, Akakii Chkhenkeli, Grigorii Georgadze, Georgii Zhuruli, Georgii Laskhishvili, Noi Khomeriki, Shalva Alekseev-Meskhishvili, and Ivan Lordkipanidze. On June 24, 1918, Noi N. Zhordania succeeded Ramishvili as Minister-President of the Georgian republic. See G. I. Uratadze, Obrazovanie i konsolidatsiia Gruzinskoi Demokraticheskoi Respubliki (Munich, 1956), p. 83.

[71] Dokumenty i materialy, pp. 332–338; Avalov, op. cit., pp. 65–67; Arkomed, op. cit., pp. 77–78. Documents published in Bor'ba v Gruzii, pp. 275–279, show Chkhenkeli as having signed the provisional treaty on behalf of Georgia. Chkhenkeli and von Lossow did sign the draft while they were in Batum but the agreement was considered valid only after Ramishvili had certified it in Poti.

[72] For German-Georgian relations during the latter half of 1918, see Kazemzadeh, Transcaucasia, pp. 147–152, 157–162; Enukidze, op. cit., pp. 90–95; Fischer, op. cit., pp. 38–57 passim; Zhordaniia, op. cit., pp. 85–86, 88–89; Avalov, op. cit., pp. 77–157 passim; P. G. La Chesnais, Les peuples de la Transcaucasie pendant la guerre et devant la paix (Paris, 1921), pp. 58–64; Bor'ba v Gruzii, pp. 280–341 passim; Ludshuveit, op. cit., pp. 197–205.

[73] Rassoul-Zadé, op. cit., p. 18; [Republic of Azerbaijan], Le 28 Mai 1919 ([Baku, 1919]), pp. 2–4, 7–9; Rep. of Arm. Archives, File 70/2, H. H. Adrbedjani Divanagitakan Nerkayatsutsich ev Adrbedjani Karavarutiun, 1920 t., "Memorandum of the Republic of Azerbaijan." The Azerbaijani declaration of independence is quoted by Mirza-Bala, op. cit., pp. 135–136. He states that the Muslim members of the Seim constituted themselves as the Azerbaijani National Council, which then proclaimed the act of independence. For the composition of Khan Khoiskii's cabinet, see Hovannisian, Road to Independence, p. 305 n. 20.

of the Christian population had taken to the ships, but there was neither room nor time for all to flee. An estimated 15,000 Armenians were put to the sword. The Republic of Azerbaijan had at last acquired its natural capital.[74]

The dissolution of the Transcaucasian Federative Republic voided the final effort of the Armenians to forge a united front with their neighbors. On the night of May 26, 1918, the enraged Armenian National Council hurled accusations of treachery at the Mensheviks and denounced the Georgian tactic but failed to reach any positive policy decisions. The Social Revolutionary and nonpartisan members scorned the concept of a separate Armenian state, for without a doubt it would either be obliterated by or made subservient to the Turks. The Armenian Social Democrats, emulating their Georgian Menshevik colleagues, together with most Populists, insisted that there was no alternative but to declare independence. The Dashnakist members of the National Council were sharply split. Only after an emotion-charged emergency party conference did Dashnaktsutiun recommend that the National Council assume dictatorial powers over the Armenian provinces. On their return to Tiflis, Hovhannes Kachaznuni and Alexandre

---

[74] Material relating to the struggle for Baku during World War I is voluminous and highly controversial. For Soviet studies and interpretations, see *Bol'sheviki v bor'be za pobedu sotsialisticheskoi revoliutsii v Azerbaidzhane: Dokumenty i materialy, 1917–1918 gg.*, ed. Z. I. Ibragimov and M. S. Iskenderov (Baku, 1957); Ia. Ratgauzer, *Revoliutsiia i grazhdanskaia voina v Baku*, pt. 1 (Baku, 1927); L. M. Lifshits, *Geroicheskii podvig Bakinskikh Bol'shevikov* (Baku, 1964); M. S. Iskenderov, *Iz istorii bor'by Kommunisticheskoi partii Azerbaidzhana za pobedu Sovetskoi vlasti* (Baku, 1958), pp. 162–360; Barseghian, *op. cit.*, pp. 395–618. Ludshuveit, *op. cit.*, pp. 207–258. For accounts by British officers, see Britain, Cab 27/24, Eastern Committee Minutes, and WO 32/5671, Naval Operations; L. C. Dunsterville, *The Adventures of Dunsterforce* (London, 1920); Ranald MacDonell, ". . . And Nothing Long"* (London, [1938]); F. J. F. French, *From Whitehall to the Caspian* (London, 1920). For the non-Bolshevik Armenian point of view, see Korganoff, *op. cit.*, pp. 163–204; Sergei Melik-Yolchian, "Bakvi herosamarte," *Hairenik Amsagir*, III (May, 1925), 105–128; (June), 104–118; (July), 68–74; (Aug.), 97–113; (Sept.), 68–78; (Oct.), 125–129; A. Giulkhandanian, "Bakvi herosamarte," *Hairenik Amsagir*, XIX (July, 1941), 89–102; (Aug.), 101–115; (Sept./Oct.), 81–92. See also Allen and Muratoff, *op. cit.*, pp. 478–495; Kazemzadeh, *Transcaucasia*, pp. 128–146; Henry Barby, *Le débâcle russe* (Paris, 1919), pp. 160–230; Gotthard Jäschke, "Der Turanismus der Jungtürken," *Die Welt des Islams*, XXIII, 1–2 (1941), 38–41; Belen, *Türk Harbi*, V, 172–185; Winfried Baumgart, "Das 'Kaspi-Unternehmen'—Grössenwahn Ludendorffs oder Routineplanung des deutschen Generalstabs?" *Jahrbücher für Geschichte Osteuropas*, n.s., XVIII, 1 (March, 1970), 47–127, and 2 (June, 1970), 231–278. The number of Armenians killed in Baku during and after the Turkish occupation has been placed as low as 9,000 and as high as 30,000. See, for example, Allen and Muratoff, *op. cit.*, p. 495; Larcher, *op. cit.* p. 423; Tokarzhevskii, *op. cit.*, p. 160. The most thorough statistical data on Armenian losses is the study of B. Ishkhanian, *Velikie uzhasy v gor. Baku* (Tiflis, 1920).

Khatisian, the Armenian members of Chkhenkeli's delegation in Batum, advised like action, for only a declaration of independence and an immediate peace with Turkey might possibly save the situation so fraught with tragedy. After agonizing hours the National Council finally accepted this view and at noon on May 28, 1918, dispatched Kachaznuni, Khatisian, and Mikayel Papadjanian (Mikhail I. Papadjanov) to Batum with unlimited powers to conclude peace on behalf of the Armenian people or in the name of independent Armenia.[75] In such an inauspicious manner was born the Republic of Armenia.

This decision made, the Armenian National Council still postponed a public proclamation. Only after another extraordinary Dashnakist conference had determined that Armenia should be a republic under a provisional coalition government led by Kachaznuni did the National Council issue the following statement on May 30, 1918:

In view of the dissolution of the political unity of Transcaucasia and the new situation created by the proclamation of the independence of Georgia and Azerbaijan, the Armenian National Council declares itself to be the supreme and only administration for the Armenian provinces. Because of certain grave circumstances, the National Council, deferring until the near future the formation of an Armenian national government, temporarily assumes all governmental functions, in order to take hold of the political and administrative helm of the Armenian provinces.[76]

The declaration, intentionally vague, made no mention of independence or republic. Only after news of Armenian military successes near Erevan and the conclusion of peace at Batum had been verified did the National Council venture to use those terms publicly.

The Last Battles and Peace

As the Armenian National Council moved toward painful decisions in Tiflis, the Armenian people were making a final desperate stand in the Erevan guberniia (see map 4). Four Turkish divisions bolstered by many irregulars pressed upon Karakilisa and upon Bash-Abaran

[75] A. Babalian, *Edjer Hayastani ankakhutian patmutiunits* (Cairo, 1959), p. 6; Khondkarian, "Opozitsian Hayastanum," II, 1, pp. 88–89; Khatisian, *Hanrapetutian zargatsume,* p. 68; Vratzian, *Hanrapetutiun,* pp. 130–131.

[76] Rep. of Arm. Archives, File 8/8, *Hayastani Hanrapetutiun, 1919 t.;* Ananun, *op. cit.,* p. 683; Vratzian, *Hanrapetutiun,* pp. 131–132. For a published French translation of the declaration, see A. Poidebard, "Le Transcaucase et la République d'Arménie dans les textes diplomatiques du Traité de Brest-Litovsk au Traité de Kars, 1918–1921," *Revue des études arméniennes,* IV, 1 (1924), 37.

4. THE BATTLES OF MAY, 1918

LEGEND

Turkish forces

Armenian forces

On the defensive

5-15 Date

0 10 20 MILES

and Sardarabad, the strategic approaches to the last remaining Armenian city—Erevan. But to the wonder of all, the populace, uniting with the Armenian Army Corps, stemmed the Turkish tide. The fierce pitched battles during the final days of May, 1918, routed the Ottoman forces, which fell back toward Alexandropol. Inspired by the uplifting experience of victory, the Armenians advanced on Alexandropol convinced that they would sweep the Turks out of all Russian Armenia.[77] And yet, with the troops almost in sight of the key fortress, General Nazarbekian ordered the Armenian Corps to halt. The National Council had informed him that a cease-fire had been arranged at Batum and that negotiations for peace were in progress. Such an announcement coming a few days earlier would have been greeted with extreme relief and thanksgiving, but it now drew angry jeers from soldiers and peasants alike. The decision of the military and political leaders was dictated, however, by the knowledge that the ammunition depots were nearly empty and fresh Turkish reinforcements were nearby. Should the tide of battle once again turn in favor of the Ottomans, the Armenian catastrophe would be complete. Rejection of the cease-fire could not be risked. So it was that the tragedy-saturated hostilities between Turks and Armenians abated.[78]

When peace negotiations began at Batum, Halil Bey pressed for immediate acceptance of the boundaries set forth in his earlier ultimatum to the Transcaucasian delegation. The Armenians would be permitted to retain some 4,000 square miles, less than half the Erevan guberniia. On June 2, after news of the Armenian victories around Erevan had reached Batum, the Ottoman delegation, assenting "for the sake of friendly relations" to a minor territorial rectification, grudg-

---

[77] Accounts of the battles of May, 1918, are in Allen and Muratoff, *op. cit.*, pp. 469–476; *Miatsial ev Ankakh Hayastan*, publ. of H. H. Dashnaktsutiun (Constantinople, 1919), pp. 7–39; Rep. of Arm. Archives, File 1/1 and File 8/8. Earlier passed over in silence or belittled by Soviet Armenian writers, these battles have been acclaimed by the historians publishing in the 1960's. In May of 1968, on the fiftieth anniversary of the struggle, the government of Soviet Armenia dedicated a memorial monument and park on the field of Sardarabad. For the new approach by Soviet historians, see, for example, Sargsian, *op. cit.*, pp. 399–401; H. G. Turshian, *Sardarapati herosamarte* (Erevan, 1965); Dj. Kirakosian, "Hisun tari aradj (Sardarapati herosamarti aritov)," *Banber Erevani Hamalsarani*, 2 (1968), 36–53; Martin Martirosian, "Sardarapati jakatamarte," *Banber Hayastani arkhivneri*, 1 (1969), 151–166; "Park zohvadsnerin" (editorial), *Sovetakan grakanutiun*, 5 (1968), 102–104. Soviet military historian E. F. Ludshuveit (*op. cit.*, pp. 186–190) not only describes the resistance of the "Armenian Dashnak forces" and the populace but also emphasizes that these battles near Erevan eased considerably the pressure on Baku and slowed the Turkish advance toward that prime objective.

[78] Rep. of Arm. Archives, File 157/56, *H. H. Patvirakutiun, 1921*, and File 1406a/26a; Vratzian, *Hanrapetutiun*, pp. 121–122.

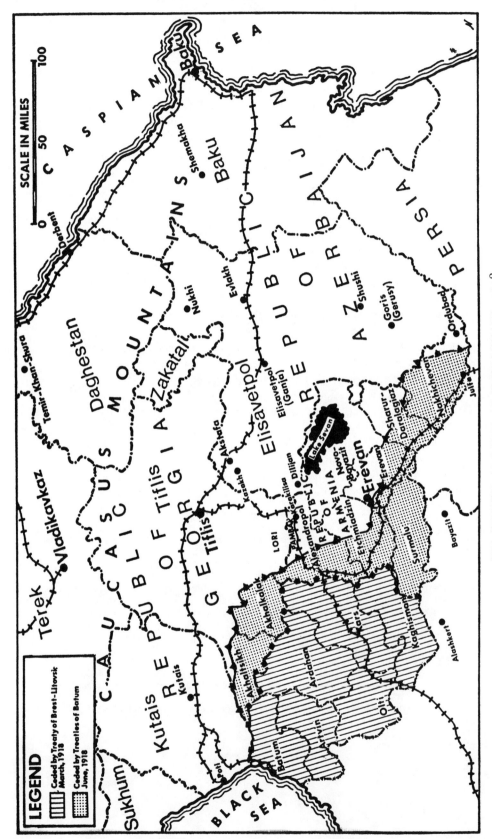

5. THE TERRITORIAL LOSSES OF TRANSCAUCASIA, 1918

ingly allotted Armenia an additional 400 square miles. That was the maximum concession.[79] The Treaty of Peace and Friendship between the Republic of Armenia and the Ottoman Empire, signed on June 4, 1918, left to Armenia the uezd of Novo-Bayazit and the eastern halves of the uezds of Alexandropol, Etchmiadzin, Erevan, and Sharur-Daralagiaz (see map 5). Other important provisions bound Armenia to grant full religious and cultural liberties to Muslim inhabitants, to reduce drastically the size of the army, to expel all representatives of nations hostile to the Central Powers, and to ensure the unhindered transit of Ottoman troops and supplies across the Republic. Should Armenia fail to honor these obligations, the Turkish army reserved the right to intervene. The exchange of ratified copies of the treaty was scheduled to take place at Constantinople within a month.[80] Georgia and Azerbaijan also concluded treaties with the Ottoman Empire that day, but the settlement imposed upon Georgia lacked several of the harsh terms of the Armenian treaty, while the Azerbaijani-Ottoman document was more in the nature of an alliance.[81]

On June 6 the Armenian peace delegation returned to Tiflis and presented the onerous Treaty of Batum to the National Council. Study of the document revealed that Transcaucasia had been sheared of more than 17,000 square miles, approximately 20 percent of its territory. Almost 75 percent of this loss had been in the provinces of Kars and Erevan. In the surrendered territories the majority of the 1,250,000 prewar inhabitants had been Armenian, with more than 400,000 in the ceded sector of the Erevan guberniia alone. During the Turkish invasion most of these people had fled northward into Georgia and beyond the Caucasus Mountains or had crowded into the eastern highlands of the Erevan guberniia.[82]

[79] Khatisian, *Hanrapetutian zargatsume*, pp. 69–71.

[80] Rep. of Arm. Archives, File 1/1; Badalian, *op. cit.*, pp. 172–199; Poidebard, "Le Transcaucase," pp. 37–50.

[81] D. Z. T., "La première République musulmane: L'Azerbaidjan," *Revue du monde musulman*, XXXVI (1918/1919), 254–255; Avalov, *op. cit.*, p. 95; *Dokumenty i materialy*, pp. 340–368; La Chesnais, *op. cit.*, pp. 106–108; Jäschke, *op. cit.*, pp. 34–36; Mirza-Bala, *op. cit.*, p. 137. For materials on Ottoman-Azerbaijani relations during the summer of 1918 and for evidence of growing friction between Khan Khoiskii's cabinet and Nuri Pasha, the chief Turkish commander in Azerbaijan, see *Bor'ba v Azerbaidzhane*, pp. 12–13, 17–18; *Istoriia gosudarstva i prava Azerbaidzhanskoi SSR: Velikaia Oktiabr'skaia sotsialisticheskaia revoliutsiia i sozdanie Sovetskoi gosudarstvennosti v Azerbaidzhane*, publ. of Akademiia Nauk Azerbaidzhanskoi SSR, Sektor Filosofii (Baku, 1964), pp. 270–275.

[82] Kadishev, *Interventsiia v Zakavkaz'e*, p. 64; D. S. Zavriev, *K noveishei istorii severo-vostochnykh vilaetov Turtsii* (Tbilisi, 1947), pp. 70–71; Rep. of Arm. Archives, File 1/1 and File 74/1, *H. H. Patvirakutiun ev Divanagitakan Nerkayatsutschutiun Tajkastanum, 1914–1918 t.t.* See also Ananun, *op. cit.*, pp. 685–686.

In mid-1918 the remnants of the Armenian people were left a mangled bit of land that, for lack of a better term, they called a republic. But as pitiful a state as was the Republic of Armenia in May, 1918, its very existence was, nevertheless, an amazing accomplishment. The inglorious birth of the Republic followed four years of devastating warfare, the decimation of the Turkish Armenian population, the illusory hopes prompted by the first Russian revolution of 1917, the disastrous policy of the Sovnarkom at Brest-Litovsk, the relentless Turkish invasion of 1918, the disintegration of Transcaucasia, and, finally, the frantic efforts of the Armenian leaders to save the nation from total annihilation. The decision for independence had been extremely difficult to reach, but the Armenians were soon to find that they faced far greater tribulations in making independence something more than a declaration. The new government turned to the problems of a barren and isolated land, abounding with rocks and mountains, orphans and refugees, heartache and misery.

2

The
First Steps

Having traveled the road to independence, Armenia was faced with the urgent need to steer somehow through the indescribable turmoil, to form a rudimentary administrative system, and to maintain the precarious peace with the ever dangerous Ottoman Empire. These problems placed upon the national leaders the obligation to move from Tiflis, with its many conveniences, to Erevan, the bleak, unimposing town designated as the capital of Armenia. There, in the midst of lawlessness and anguish, they endeavored without the benefit of preexisting ruling apparatus or traditions to create the foundations of government. The central bureaus, chancelleries, state buildings, arsenals, printing presses, and railroad garages of Transcaucasia were left behind in Tiflis and became the rich inheritance of the new Georgia. Moreover, without exception, every Armenian industrial and commercial center lay outside the narrow bounds of the rural, underdeveloped Armenian republic. During the latter half of 1918, with Ottoman armies pressing on the borders from the west and south, with Turkish-supported Azerbaijani forces threatening from the east, and with German-patronized Georgian units poised on the north, it seemed on more than one occasion that the sorely distressed Republic of Armenia would disintegrate.

The Cabinet

While still in Tiflis the Armenian National Council on June 9, 1918, called upon Hovhannes Kachaznuni to form a coalition government. Kachaznuni's party, Dashnaktsutiun, felt that a coalition was of utmost importance for, having been created as a revolutionary society to emancipate the Turkish Armenians, it was neither structured as nor intended to evolve into a legal ruling organism. Though it had gained considerable experience in leading the National Council and participating in the Transcaucasian Commissariat and Seim, Dashnaktsutiun was not prepared to shoulder alone the onerous duty of guiding an independent country during such unfavorable times. But coalition was difficult to achieve because Dashnaktsutiun had established a near monopoly on Armenian political life in the Caucasus, and the other parties, while finding limited support among the intellectual and professional classes, lacked a popular base.[1]

It soon became apparent that the obstacles to coalition could not be overcome. The Populists insisted that Dashnaktsutiun must bear the responsibility for Armenian misfortunes and thus withdraw from the political arena in favor of new elements. But even had this plan been accepted it could not have been implemented, for the Social Democrats and the Social Revolutionaries absolutely refused to participate in a cabinet dominated by the bourgeois Populists. Furthermore, in any other combination, the Social Democrats would collaborate only on the condition that they be accorded several influential ministries of their choice, a demand vociferously opposed by the Social Revolutionaries. On June 30, 1918, after three weeks of futile negotiations, the National Council finally authorized Kachaznuni to organize his cabinet on an individual basis rather than along interparty lines. Thereupon, Kachaznuni presented his brief list of ministers, all Dashnakists except for the nonpartisan Minister of Military Affairs:[2]

PREMIER (MINISTER-PRESIDENT)	Hovhannes Kachaznuni
FOREIGN AFFAIRS	Alexandre Khatisian
INTERNAL AFFAIRS	Aram Manukian
FINANCIAL AFFAIRS	Khachatur Karjikian
MILITARY AFFAIRS	Hovhannes Hakhverdian (Akhverdov)

By that time Armenia had been independent, at least nominally, for a full month, yet the only semblance of administration in the districts around Erevan remained a popular dictatorship headed by Aram Manukian, a hero of the resistance at Van in 1915 and in the Erevan

[1] Arsham Khondkarian, "Opozitsian Hayastanum," II, 1, p. 92; US Archives, RG 256, 184.01602/23.
[2] Vratzian, *Hanrapetutiun*, p. 156; Khondkarian, "Opozitsian Hayastanum," II, 1, pp. 92–97; A. Babalian, *Edjer Hayastani ankakhutian patmutiunits* (Cairo, 1959), pp. 9–10; Rep. of Arm. Archives, File 72, *H. H. Nerkayatsutschutiun Ukrayinayum, 1918–1928 t.t.*

guberniia in May, 1918, and by Dro (Drasdamat Kanayan), a renowned partisan commander. The two leaders, regarded by many of their contemporaries as the true founders of the Republic, were not relieved of their duties even after Kachaznuni's cabinet had been confirmed by the National Council, because the official government still tarried in Tiflis.[3] Spokesmen for the Populist and Social Revolutionary parties insisted that, while Kachaznuni's cabinet could serve as a regional authority at Erevan, the National Council must remain in Tiflis to safeguard the interests of all Russian Armenians. Both parties, their centers of strength being Tiflis and Baku, equated transferral of the National Council with dereliction of nearly one million Armenians living in Georgia, Azerbaijan, and the North Caucasus. The impasse prevailed until mid-July when Aram "Pasha" gave final notice that he would stay at his post no longer and Kachaznuni threatened to resign as premier. Faced with a cabinet crisis even before the government had begun to function, the opposition parties now ruefully consented to the basing in Erevan of both the cabinet and the National Council.[4]

The circumstances under which the Armenian ruling bodies left Tiflis on July 17, 1918, clearly reflected the rapid exacerbation of Armeno-Georgian antagonism. In violation of accepted protocol, there were no Georgian officials at the railway station to bid the Armenian dignitaries farewell. Instead, the departing leaders, who on the previous day had paid a courtesy visit to the Georgian government, were denied entrance to the waiting suite and constrained to stand upon the platform several hours before a locomotive and a few filth-covered coaches were made available. Ironically, it was only through the forceful protests and intervention of German and Turkish officers assigned to accompany Kachaznuni to Erevan that the National Council was permitted to take along some of its belongings, including three automobiles, and that the humiliated Armenians were spared a detailed inspection at the Georgian border. Because the Ottoman army now stood on the direct line to Erevan, the party had to follow a circuitous route passing over a few miles of Azerbaijan. The welcome given by Azerbaijani officials, complete with music, speeches, and banquets,

[3] Events in Erevan following the Russian Revolution of February/March, 1917, are given by Arshaluis Astvadsatrian, "Arame," *Vem*, II, 6 (1934), 25–35, and III, 1 (1935), 57–71; Hovakim Melikian, "Arian janaparhov," *Hairenik Amsagir*, III (Nov., 1924–July, 1925); John Elder, "Memories of the Armenian Republic," *Armenian Review*, VI (Spring, 1953), 3–12; Ambartsum (Hambardzum) Elchibekian, *Armeniia nakanune Velikogo Oktiabria (fevral'-oktiabr' 1917 goda)* (Erevan, 1963). See also Rep. of Arm. Archives, File 1/1.

[4] Khondkarian, "Opozitsian Hayastanum," I, 3, pp. 42–46; Vratzian, *Hanrapetutiun*, pp. 157–158.

contrasted sharply with the recent ordeal in Tiflis. It must have been difficult to believe in that atmosphere of cordiality that Armeno-Azerbaijani disputes were far more fundamental and complex than the issues dividing Armenians and Georgians.[5]

On July 19 the Armenian cabinet and National Council were greeted at the outskirts of Erevan by Aram, Dro, and General Nazarbekian. Together the entourage rode into the nation's capital. The scene that unfolded before the newly arrived leaders defied description. The midsummer air was heavy with the umbra of death. The diseased and starving people were cast like shadows upon a backdrop of mud hovels and mire. It was said that the Turks had begrudged the Armenians enough land for a mass cemetery, and this appraisal seemed scarcely exaggerated during the first torturous months of the Republic. The native inhabitants and refugees subsisted on a few grains of wheat and a broth of grasses and herbs; but by the onset of winter even these were gone.

Armenia's Legislature, the Khorhurd

Amidst this "formless chaos" Armenia laid her legislative foundations. Elections then being out of the question, the four political parties agreed to triple the membership of the National Council and transform it into a legislature. Thus when the Khorhurd convened on August 1, 1918, it was composed of 18 Dashnakists, 6 Social Revolutionaries, 6 Social Democrats, 6 Populists, and 2 nonpartisans. In addition, 6 Muslims, 1 Yezidi, and 1 Russian were seated as representatives of the Republic's minorities.[6] The opening session was attended by military and religious notables, members of the Muslim and Russian councils of Erevan, and the envoys of the Ottoman Empire, Persia, the Ukraine, Austria-Hungary, and Germany. Avetik Sahakian, president of the Khorhurd, reviewed the tragic events leading to independence but concluded optimistically that the concept of statehood was taking root and that brighter days lay ahead. Although the Republic was small in size, deprived of its best lands, and unable to provide for all

[5] Rep. of Arm. Archives, File 65/1, *Vrastani Divanagitakan Nerkayatsutsich ev Vrastani Karavarutiun, 1918*, "Gruziia i Armeniia: Obzor vneshnei i vnutrennei politiki za vremia s 18 iiulia do 29 sentiabria"; Djamalian, "Hai-vratsakan knjire" (Sept., 1928), pp. 120–121; Babalian, *op. cit.*, pp. 8–9; Vratzian, *Hanrapetutiun*, pp. 158–159.

[6] Rep. of Arm. Archives, File 72, Bulletin no. 17; Lepsius, *Deutschland und Armenien*, pp. 421–422. The membership of the Khorhurd and the seating arrangement of the "fractions" therein are given by Hovannisian, *Road to Independence*, p. 309 nn. 93 and 94.

its citizens, Armenia's boundaries would not remain inflexible forever: "I believe that our borders will expand with the iron force of life, with the defense of our just and indisputable rights to the [Turkish-] occupied lands. . . ." [7] Following several addresses of felicitation, the red, blue, and orange tricolor of Armenia was raised atop the Khorhurd, and the legislature turned to the business at hand.

Two days later, on August 3, Hovhannes Kachaznuni appeared before the Khorhurd to outline his cabinet's program. The state of the nation, he lamented, was one of utter disorganization. The wars, revolutions, and invasions of the preceding years had totally disrupted the economy, judicial order, administrative mechanism, and transportation-communication systems. The Premier announced that in view of this catastrophic situation he would lay aside long-range goals and idealistic phrases characteristic of inaugural addresses. The government's foremost objective would be to deliver the nation from the clutches of anarchy by striving to safeguard the life and property of all inhabitants, to restore the avenues of communication, and to succor the refugee population. In foreign affairs, it would honor all treaty obligations and would attempt to secure Turkish withdrawal from the occupied portions of the Republic as well as the return of refugees to their native districts. Every effort would be made to gain a share of the common goods and assets of the former Transcaucasian Federative Republic and to determine Armenia's boundaries with Georgia and Azerbaijan on the basis of the ethnic principle, the only acceptable criterion in democratic states.[8] These goals, which Kachaznuni termed realistic, were in fact quite illusive and unattainable in 1918.

Discussion of Kachaznuni's program dominated the agenda of the next few sessions. The parties of the left complained that entire areas of government activity had been neglected. The Social Revolutionaries were particularly aroused by the failure to consider Armeno-Russian relations, while the Social Democrats sharply rapped the omission of a plank on labor. Haik Azatian, chairman of the Social Democrat faction, likened Kachaznuni's tactic to that of the despised tsarist minister, Stolypin, who had attempted to hoodwink the masses by propounding "first peace, then reforms." The single Bolshevik of the Social Democrat faction, Arshavir Melikian, took the rostrum to extol world

[7] Rep. of Arm. Archives, File 72. Records of the proceedings of the Khorhurd have been published in part under the title "Hayastani Khorhrdi ardzanagrutiunnere," *Vem*, II (1934), nos. 4–6, III (1935), nos. 1–3, cited hereafter as "Ardzanagrutiunnere."

[8] "Ardzanagrutiunnere," II, 4, pp. 120–122; Rep. of Arm. Archives, File 72, Bulletin no. 15; Vratzian, *Hanrapetutiun*, pp. 164–166.

revolution and to belittle the concept of national independence. The parties of the right, including the Populists and the representatives of the ethnic minorities, expressed satisfaction with the cautious, essentially conservative platform of the cabinet. There had been nothing in Kachaznuni's address to indicate that Dashnaktsutiun was a socialist party and a member of the Second International. The benches of the right therefore joined with the center, Dashnaktsutiun, to give Kachaznuni a vote of confidence. Even the SR's and the SD's did not cast dissenting ballots. As long as Ottoman armies infested the Erevan guberniia, the parties of the left chose to abstain rather than to vote in opposition.[9]

Domestic Issues

Although a coalition cabinet had not materialized, Armenia was nevertheless governed along coalitional lines by virtue of the ascendancy of the legislature. Through its several standing and special committees, each composed of three Dashnakists and one representative of each of the other Armenian factions, the Khorhurd assumed numerous executive functions during the first months of the Republic.[10] The multipartisan committees of finance, administrative affairs, education, provisions, refugees, land, labor, local government, and medical-sanitary affairs strongly influenced the corresponding state ministries. Many controversial issues were settled in committee, but among those that reached the floor and occasioned bitter disputes in the Khorhurd and between the Khorhurd and the cabinet were the unbridled spread of cholera, public disarmament, educational policies, and refugee problems.

Cholera reached epidemic proportions by the end of August, 1918. The meager supply of medications and disinfectants had been exhausted and there was no hope of receiving new shipments from abroad. It was impossible to quarantine the infected, who lived among the populace in crowded, unsanitary hutches. The refugee masses, roaming the countryside in search of food, spread the disease over the breadth of the land. Dr. Hovhannes Ter-Mikayelian, chairman of the Khorhurd's medical-sanitation committee, decried the inefficacy of the

[9] Khondkarian, "Opozitsian Hayastanum," II, 4, pp. 80–83; "Ardzanagrutiunnere," II, 5, pp. 92–102; Rep. of Arm. Archives, File 72, Bulletin no. 20. For a useful analysis of the policies of each opposition party during the first months of the Republic, see Khondkarian, "Opozitsian Hayastanum," II, 3, pp. 42–60.

[10] "Ardzanagrutiunnere," II, 5, pp. 102–104, and 6, p. 87; Khondkarian, "Opozitsian Hayastanum," II, 4, pp. 73–79.

Ministry of Interior and urged that his own committee be vested with dictatorial powers to cope with the crisis. He upbraided the nation's physicians and intellectuals for shirking the responsibility to educate the public in hygienic practices and to minister to the rural sick. Aram Manukian refuted the charges leveled at his department and offered proof of significant progress in stemming the disease. Overriding Aram's objections, however, the legislature named the medical-sanitation committee the supreme authority in the crusade against cholera, a battle finally won at the end of November, 1918.[11] But as the wave of cholera ebbed, an even more avaricious killer reared its ugly head—typhus.

The proposal of the Ministry of Interior to disarm the citizenry provoked the most intense domestic controversy of 1918. Its decrees and decisions unheeded, the government was scandalized by the insolence of gangs of bandits, who robbed and killed in broad daylight. These so-called "mauserists"[12] had become so bold as to extend their activities into Erevan itself. As matters stood, Aram warned, the government could not establish law and order or wield real authority until the entire civilian population had been disarmed and taught to respect discipline. He refuted the argument that an armed populace constituted an important military asset; it was an asset only for anarchy.[13]

The parties of the left flatly rejected Aram's proposal. Social Democrat Tadeos Avdalbekian contended that the question involved a vote of confidence or no confidence in the people and that the Minister of Interior was sorely mistaken in associating anarchy with the freedom to carry arms. Citizens possessed weapons in many countries where anarchy was unknown. What was actually needed, Avdalbekian continued, was to rid the land of corrupt officials, who ignored and violated the directives of the government and brought discredit to it. The citizenry would disarm of its own accord once the central government had shown itself capable of enforcing judicial procedures and of protecting all inhabitants.[14]

[11] Rep. of Arm. Archives, File 72; "Ardzanagrutiunnere," II, 6, pp. 89–90; Khondkarian, "Opozitsian Hayastanum," III, 1, pp. 72–74.

[12] The term is derived from Mauser, the rifle carried by many of the bandits. The weapon bears the name of its German inventor, Peter Paul Mauser (1838–1914), a developer of the bolt-action rifle. The rifle was first patented in 1868 in the United States and by the turn of the century had been adopted by several armies, including that of the Ottoman Empire. It was a common firearm among the Turkish Armenian guerrillas and revolutionaries. The word "mauserist" connotes violence and lawlessness and until the 1960's was invariably used by Soviet historians to characterize the regime of independent Armenia.

[13] "Ardzanagrutiunnere," II, 6, pp. 91, 93–94.

[14] Ibid., pp. 91–92.

In a stinging denunciation Haik Azatian mocked Aram Manukian and the party Dashnaktsutiun, which for years had exhorted the Armenian people to arms but now, after having achieved this aim, sought to render that same people defenseless. Reminding his colleagues of the constant foreign threat and of the rampant brigandage, Azatian exclaimed that anarchy would be overcome, not by depriving the peasantry of its weapons, but only by the enactment of revolutionary legislation in the areas of land reform, labor, and sanitation and by the equitable distribution of goods. Dashnakist Sahak Torosian retorted that the SD's, in suddenly becoming champions of the right to bear arms, seemed to have forgotten their former condemnation of Dashnaktsutiun's efforts to that end. The present circumstances, Torosian declared, were totally unlike those that had existed when Dashnaktsutiun led the struggle against the oppression of sultans and tsars. Armenia was now independent and the welfare of the Republic required an unarmed populace.[15]

Populist spokesman Stepan Malkhasian announced that stringent arms control and a trenchant policy toward criminals were intrinsic to his party's principles. Still, because of the abnormal conditions and the probability that only peaceful elements would submit to disarmament, the Populist faction could support Aram's proposal only if the operation were to begin after complete domestic security had first been attained. Even then, the disarmament should start in the most unmanageable border districts and progress gradually inward to the capital.[16]

That many members of Dashnaktsutiun were themselves not convinced of the wisdom of the measure was revealed in the adoption of the proposal by a meager vote of fifteen to seven. Well over half the Khorhurd had abstained.[17] Furthermore, passage of legislation was quite a different matter from enforcement. Unwilling or unable to depend upon the government for protection, Armenia's inhabitants, Christian and Muslim alike, clung to their weapons.

The schools of Armenia, destroyed or closed during the Turkish invasion, had to begin operations anew. Both the government and the legislative committee on education recognized that sweeping curricular and structural changes were impractical for the time being. Moreover, the legislative committee opposed a state monopoly in education and recommended that individual patrons and civic, ethnic, and social groups be encouraged to maintain schools. In view of the govern-

[15] Ibid., pp. 94, 95.
[16] Ibid., p. 92.
[17] Vratzian, Hanrapetutiun, p. 170; "Ardzanagrutiunnere," II, 6, p. 95.

ment's dire financial straits, the primary responsibility for school support would devolve upon the local communities. Eventually a ministry of education would coordinate the school system and effect a degree of uniformity in the curriculum.

While all political parties were in general accord, the Social Revolutionaries and Social Democrats attempted to circumscribe the right of the Church of Armenia to continue its traditional role in education. There were members in both factions who favored a total ban on parochial schools. The SR's, realizing that they lacked sufficient support to enact such a measure, then demanded that parochial schools be deprived of state aid and that, should the clergy contrive to bar qualified groups from using church-owned structures as schools, these properties be confiscated forthwith. The SD's added that not a kopek would be allocated for religious instruction and that the principle of separation of church and state must be fully enforced. Offended and angered by this fusillade, the Populists rose in defense of the Church, whose service in education they deemed vital and beneficial. They also contended that the central government was obligated to provide a national network of schools, since to make funding a purely local concern would deprive numerous impoverished villages of schools and lead to wide disparity in educational opportunities.[18]

Dashnakist Sirakan Tigranian, chairman of the education committee, explained that the government's refusal to requisition church-owned properties was based on the right of educational freedom. In any case the issue was meaningless, he claimed, since the Church was cooperating in every way possible and had already welcomed the use of its buildings as community schools. Education, Tigranian continued, would be secular in nature with allowance for optional religious training, and the language of instruction would be determined by the community that supported the particular school. The Muslim and Russian inhabitants were to enjoy complete educational freedom and to be represented in the projected state council of education.[19] With these guidelines Armenia prepared for the first day of classes on October 1, 1918. The results, though modest, were significant, for by the end of the year more than 130 schools had resumed operations.[20]

[18] Rep. of Arm. Archives, File 72; "Ardzanagrutiunnere," III, 1, pp. 75–77.

[19] "Ardzanagrutiunnere," III, 1, pp. 78–82.

[20] Rep. of Arm. Archives, File 8/8. The laws and regulations enacted by the Khorhurd were published as *Hayastani Khorhrdi hastatads orenknere, 1918–1919 t.* (Erevan, 1919). Excerpts are included in the appendix of Vratzian, *Hanrapetutiun*, pp. 518–529. A report in Britain, FO 371/4950, 2738/36/58, shows that in 1918–1919 there were 135 elementary schools with 11,136 pupils and 10 secondary (middle-level) schools with 313 students.

The homeless, disease-ridden masses in the Erevan guberniia were an incessant scourge to Kachaznuni's government. Some 300,000 refugees had crowded within the suffocating bounds of the barren republic.[21] The Turkish army held the fertile Araxes river valley, and all routes to and from Armenia were sealed. By the end of September, 1918, the state granaries were nearly empty. To feed the refugees the Minister of Interior levied arbitrary food quotas upon the few districts not devastated by the war. These extralegal measures evoked a bitter response in the affected villages and in the Khorhurd. The charge of aspiring to perpetual dictatorship was hurled at Aram Manukian. Even more distressing to the critics were reports that men in military uniform were terrorizing the peasantry and seizing its goods in the name of the Armenian government. Minister of Military Affairs Hakhverdian explained that the thieves were army deserters and promised that unauthorized personnel found in uniform would be meted harsh punishment; the irregularities continued nonetheless.[22] But the crowning insult was draped upon the government by a number of provincial officials who enriched themselves by stealing from the state reserves and trading the precious foodstuffs for hard metals, gems, and other valuables.

In an attempt to strike upon a fiscal program that would provide revenue for refugee relief and to secure tighter control over the meager food supply, the government established a monopoly on the sale and distribution of grain. The venture drew the complaints of the nonsocialist factions of the Khorhurd. The Populists, respected for their business acumen, maintained that the monopoly had precipitated an artificial shortage of food. The peasantry, well aware that the prices set by the government were far below the actual retail value of the grain, had resorted to hoarding and to illegal sales. If the monopoly were abandoned in favor of a free economy, the Populists explained, a large supply of grain would reach the public and famine would be averted. The argument failed to impress Dashnaktsutiun and the other socialist factions of the legislature, which not only authorized the ex-

[21] Rep. of Arm. Archives, File 1/1. Reports published by Lepsius, *Deutschland und Armenien*, pp. 410, 418, 421, 425, establish the number of refugees as more than 500,-000. Based on documents in the Central State Historical Archives of the Armenian Soviet Socialist Republic, S. T. Alikhanian shows 650,000 Armenian refugees in territories of the former Russian Empire. Of these, 400,000 were within the present bounds of Soviet Armenia, and 150,000 were in Georgia. See his *Haikakan Gordseri Komisariati gordsuneutiune (1917–1921)* (Erevan, 1958), p. 112. See also Britain, FO 371/3658, 47290/68107/512/58.

[22] "Ardzanagrutiunnere," III, 1, pp. 75, 83–85; Khondkarian, "Opozitsian Hayastanum," II, 3, pp. 59–60.

tension of the grain monopoly but also broadened the economic controls by nationalizing the entire cotton crop, an immediate source of state income.[23]

Unable to care for all refugees, the government did nevertheless undertake several random measures for relief. The few million rubles brought from Tiflis by the cabinet were rapidly exhausted, primarily in organizing the orphan population as wards of the state and in affording employment to refugee women by reactivating a number of textile mills. By the end of 1918 the legislature had allocated, from all sources combined, more than 30 million rubles, but it is by no means certain that the treasury had sufficient funds to cover the drafts.[24] There is no doubt, however, that, regardless of how concentrated the effort, the government could not have overcome the critical food shortage. The Populist thesis associating a free market economy with the existence of an abundance of goods was invalid; the croplands were either devastated or occupied by foreign troops. Yet this terrible economic dilemma in the summer and autumn of 1918 came to be regarded as only a mild prelude to the agony awaiting the people of Armenia during the pitiless winter that approached.

The Supplicants

As the government in Erevan grappled with domestic crises, Armenian representatives in the capitals of the Central Powers, the Ukraine, and Soviet Russia strove to win recognition, diplomatic support, and economic assistance for the Republic. For five months, until the end of World War I, they toiled under trying and humiliating conditions, with petitions, statistics, and logic as their only means.

Berlin became the hub of Armenian activities, for it was believed that only Germany held the power to restrain the Turks and to force them back to the boundaries drawn in the Treaty of Brest-Litovsk. Officials in the German Foreign Ministry repeatedly assured the Armenian envoys, Hamazasp Ohandjanian (Dashnakist) and Arshak

[23] "Ardzanagrutiunnere," III, 1, pp. 82–83; Vratzian, *Hanrapetutiun*, p. 170 and appendix.
[24] Rep. of Arm. Archives, File 1/1; Vratzian, *Hanrapetutiun*, p. 171 and appendix. Allocations were also made for Armenian refugees in Georgia, particularly those who eventually returned to their devastated villages in Akhalkalak. In March, 1919, Davit Davitkhanian, a member of the former Georgian Parliament, became Armenia's Tiflis representative for refugee and welfare matters. His colleague, Tigran Avetisian, was named to coordinate Armenian refugee affairs in the North Caucasus. See *Bor'ba* (Tiflis), April 18, 1919, p. 1, and June 4, p. 2.

Zohrabian (Social Democrat), that the Turks would be made to comply.[25] The initial optimism of the Armenian supplicants faded as the weeks passed, however, for Germany could neither constrain the Turks nor even secure their permission for the repatriation of Armenian refugees. Moreover, Germany persistently denied the Republic of Armenia official recognition. Secret German-Soviet negotiations then in progress were leading toward Berlin's acceptance of Russian domination over southern and eastern Transcaucasia in return for a share of the petroleum of Baku and the inclusion of Georgia in the German sphere of influence. In a policy that verged on dualism, the German Foreign Ministry agreed to aid Armenia by enforcing the Treaty of Brest-Litovsk even as it promised Soviet Russia that the Reich would neither recognize Armenia nor intervene in the affairs of southern and eastern Transcaucasia.[26]

Upon learning of these secret parleys, the Armenian delegates denounced the proceedings as irresponsible and illogical. Ohandjanian attempted to impress Soviet diplomat Adolf A. Ioffe with the justice and validity of Armenian aspirations. While the Soviet slogan advocating self-determination and peace without annexations was admirable in principle, the violation of its intent, Ohandjanian argued, had resulted in the desolation of Turkish Armenia, the surrender of Kars, Ardahan, and Batum, and the invasion of the Erevan guberniia. In order to salvage the last few districts of Russian Armenia, a republic had been proclaimed, but voracious enemies were casting glances toward even this pitiful state. Russian support for Armenia, a natural ally, was therefore imperative. Ioffe made professions of sympathy and consented to relay Ohandjanian's appeals from Berlin to Moscow.[27]

In the Kremlin, meanwhile, Hakob Zavriev (Zavrian) and Liparit Nazariants contended that Soviet recognition of Armenia would forestall the obliteration of the infant republic by the Pan-Turkists and the transformation of the entire Caucasus into a solid Islamic stronghold. The Armenian supplicants in Moscow warned that the realiza-

[25] The handwritten reports of Ohandjanian and Zohrabian are preserved in Rep. of Arm. Archives, File 100/1, and File 353; *H. H. Berlini Nerkayatsutschutiun, 1918–1919*. Other relevant material is included in File 72, Bulletins of the Armenian Commissariat, Kiev. See also Hovannisian, *Road to Independence*, pp. 217–220, 223–224; Lepsius, *Deutschland und Armenien*, pp. 401–402, 404–408, 411–412, 417–418.

[26] These negotiations and the events leading to them are described by John W. Wheeler-Bennett, *Brest-Litovsk: The Forgotten Peace, March 1918* (London, 1938), pp. 311–348. See also Ulrich Trumpener, *Germany and the Ottoman Empire, 1914–1918* (Princeton, 1968), pp. 186–194.

[27] Rep. of Arm. Archives, File 100/1, Memorandum; Hovannisian, *Road to Independence*, pp. 218–219.

tion of Enver Pasha's goals would render inconceivable any future Transcaucasian association or confederation with Russia.[28] All such appeals went unheeded, however, as the Soviet leadership was by the summer of 1918 no longer tolerant of non-Bolshevik Armenian spokesmen.[29] And even had this not been the case, the Armenian petitions would still have been powerless to prevent the conclusion, in August, 1918, of the German-Soviet supplementary treaty, which partitioned the Caucasus into two large spheres of influence.[30]

By the beginning of September, Armenian diplomatic labors in Moscow, Berlin, and even Vienna had been frustrated. In an ironic paradox Armenia now turned to the Ottoman Empire. Grand Vizier Talaat Pasha, a principal organizer of the massacres of 1915, set out to abrogate the supplementary treaty and to advise German recognition of Armenia, for understandably the Ottoman Empire preferred a feeble and dependent state around Erevan to a bilateral division of the Caucasus between Russia and Germany.[31] Talaat's attempt to void the treaty failed, but during his stay in Berlin he did win tacit German acceptance of Turkey's decision to recognize the Transcaucasian republics and to assist in the creation of Muslim states in the North Caucasus and Turkestan. In return, Talaat gave assurances that Ottoman armies in Azerbaijan, Armenia, and North Persia would be withdrawn as soon as this proved feasible.[32] Whatever comfort the Armenians might have derived from this protocol was nullified by news that Turkish and Azerbaijani divisions had just marched into Baku and massacred thousands of Armenians. Formalistic promises and supplementary treaties aside, the Ottoman army remained firmly entrenched in Transcaucasia until the end of World War I.

The Armenian Mission in Constantinople

In June, 1918, soon after the Ottoman Empire had dictated the treaties of Batum to the three Transcaucasian republics, German officials in-

[28] Rep. of Arm. Archives, File 74/1; Gabriel Lazian, *Hayastan ev hai date (Vaveragrer)* (Cairo, 1946), pp. 214–216; Ruben [Ter-Minasian], *Hai heghapokhakani me hishataknere*, Vol. VII (Los Angeles, 1952), pp. 261–263.

[29] Armenian-Soviet relations are discussed in chapter 12 below.

[30] Part VI of the supplementary treaty dealt with the Caucasus. See *Dokumenty SSSR*, I, 443–444; Jane Degras, ed., *Soviet Documents on Foreign Policy*, Vol. I (London, New York and Toronto, 1951), pp. 96–98.

[31] Rep. of Arm. Archives, File 100/1; Joseph Pomiankowski, *Der Zusammenbruch des Ottomanischen Reiches* (Leipzig, 1928), pp. 369–370, 373.

[32] Gotthard Jäschke, "Der Turanismus der Jungtürken," *Die Welt des Islams*, XXIII, 1–2 (1941), 44–47; Carl Mühlmann, *Das deutsch-türkische Waffenbündnis im Weltkrieg* (Leipzig, [1940]), pp. 212–213; Trumpener, *op. cit.*, pp. 194–195.

formed the Armenian leadership, then still in Tiflis, that these treaties would not be countenanced by Berlin and that they would be revised in Constantinople by a conference of all Transcaucasian states and Central Powers. Heartened by the possibility that Armenia would not have to ratify the ironfisted Batum treaty, the National Council hurriedly dispatched a mission to the shores of the Bosporus.[33] There, the delegation, composed of Avetis Aharonian (chairman), Alexandre Khatisian, and Mikayel Papadjanian, waited impatiently and in vain for the conference to open. The Germans ascribed the delay to the Turks, whereas both Enver and Talaat tossed the responsibility back upon Berlin. The views of the two Central Powers had diverged so widely that neither seemed anxious to expose their rivalry to the scrutiny of an international conference.[34] As each day passed in anticipation, the Armenian mission attempted to gain at least unilateral concessions from the Ottoman government.

The most trying and delicate task of Aharonian's delegation was to cultivate a favorable disposition among the Turkish leaders. The reports of Aharonian, Khatisian, and the mission's secretary, Hakob Kocharian, described the debasing interviews with Enver and Talaat. The supplicants humbled themselves as far as to express gratitude to the Ottoman Empire for tolerating the establishment of the Armenian republic. During these discussions Talaat cast the blame for Armenian misfortunes upon the Kurds, the military authorities, and the irresponsible local officials, but he also charged the Armenians with disloyalty to the Ottoman homeland. Enver Pasha, the most candid official in these insincere sessions, received the Armenian envoys with reserve, offered no sympathy, and categorically rejected all entreaties for the limited expansion of Armenia. The Ittihadist party, he observed, had after considerable deliberation consented to allow, on former Russian territory, a small Armenian state that could never in any way affect the interests of the new Turkish empire. The borders as defined in the Treaty of Batum would remain firm. By contrast, Sultan Mehmed VI (Vahideddin) bewailed the suffering of the Armenians and, according

[33] Khatisian, *Hanrapetutian zargatsume*, pp. 77–78; Rep. of Arm. Archives, File 100/1, Khatisian to Ohandjanian. The minutes and handwritten reports of the Armenian mission to Constantinople are preserved in Rep. of Arm. Archives, File 74/1 and File 100/1. See also Kh. H. Badalian, *Germanaturkakan okupantnere Hayastanum 1918 tvakanin* (Erevan, 1962), pp. 47–48.

[34] Rep. of Arm. Archives, File 100/1, Reports of July 13, 20, 30, and August 6, 16, 1918. German-Turkish antagonism arising from conflicting interests in the Caucasus is discussed by Pomiankowski, *op. cit.*, pp. 362–369, 372–373; Lepsius, *Deutschland und Armenien*, pp. 393–431 *passim;* Mühlmann, *op. cit.*, pp. 200–211; Trumpener, *op. cit.*, pp. 167–199, 244–268.

to a delegation report, even disclosed his impatience with the Ittihadist rulers.[35]

The specific objectives of Aharonian's delegation included Ottoman evacuation of Pambak (Bambak) and southern Lori, a region not annexed but nonetheless occupied by Turkey. The Pambak district (*uchastok*) in the Alexandropol uezd of the Erevan guberniia and the contiguous Lori uchastok in the Borchalu uezd of the Tiflis guberniia were both claimed by Armenia (see map 5). Despite numerous statements by the Ottoman Ministry of War that Turkish troops would soon withdraw, the recall order was not issued until mid-October, when the defeat of the Central Powers had become imminent.[36]

The Armenian delegation also sought permission for refugees to return to the Ottoman-occupied sectors of Russian Armenia. Relieving the population burden might possibly deliver the Armenian republic from total famine. Throughout June and July, 1918, the Ittihadist masters were unrelenting, but in late August they granted a minor concession, allowing repatriation to within 20 kilometers of the Alexandropol-Julfa railway in the central sector of the Erevan guberniia. As few villages existed in that specific strip of rugged volcanic highland, Aharonian repeatedly requested that the thousands of refugees from the rich adjacent river valley be authorized to return. Enver Pasha was not moved.[37]

Boundary disputes involving the three Transcaucasian republics were placed before representatives of all the Central Powers in Constantinople. The Armenian mission submitted charts, maps, and statistical data to substantiate its claim that no viable state could exist on the little rocky land left to Armenia. Should the Republic expand to the Brest-Litovsk boundaries, however, it would then embrace some 20,000 square miles and have a chance to survive. But the issue was extremely complicated, for much of this territory—the Erevan guberniia and several districts of the Elisavetpol and Tiflis guberniias—was also claimed either by Georgia or by Azerbaijan. Even if the Ottoman Empire were to relinquish the lands east of the Brest-Litovsk boundaries, Armenia would be limited to a mere 6,000 square miles, 8 per-

[35] Rep. of Arm. Archives, File 100/1, Reports of July 3 and Sept. 6, 7, 1918. Khatisian, *Hanrapetutian zargatsume*, pp. 79–85, presents a résumé of the interviews between the Armenian mission and the representatives of the Ottoman Empire and other Central Powers. See also Badalian, *op. cit.*, pp. 48–50, 239–244; Lepsius, *Deutschland und Armenien*, pp. 413–414.

[36] Rep. of Arm. Archives, File 100/1, Reports of July 13 and 30, 1918, and File 72, Bulletin no. 18.

[37] Rep. of Arm. Archives, File 100/1, Report of Aug. 24, 1918. See also Lepsius, *Deutschland und Armenien*, pp. 401–434 *passim*.

cent of Transcaucasia, should the pretensions of Georgia and Azerbaijan be realized. The Central Powers could, however, establish equity and peace in the region by endorsing the Armenian proposal that would accord 38 percent of Transcaucasia to Azerbaijan, 33 percent to Georgia, and 29 percent to Armenia.[38] This solution did not go unchallenged by the alert Georgian delegation led by Evgenii Gegechkori and the Azerbaijani delegation led by Mehmed Emin Rasulzade and Ali Mardan Topchibashev, likewise in Constantinople to defend the interests of their respective nations.

Not until the autumn of 1918, and then for reasons other than the validity of the Armenian arguments, did Ottoman officials offer conditional support on the territorial question. In September, after Germany and Soviet Russia had ratified the supplementary treaty dividing the Caucasus into two zones of influence, Enver Pasha intimated to Aharonian and Khatisian that Turkey would uphold Armenia's bid for Lori and Pambak and might eventually condone the Republic's expansion to the Brest-Litovsk boundaries. The Ittihadists favored the inclusion of these uchastoks within Armenia rather than Georgia, a German protectorate. Then, at the end of September, Talaat Pasha announced that his government would grant Armenia concessions even greater than those sought by Aharonian's delegation in the preceding weeks.[39] These, however, were his last official words on the subject, for a few days later, in the prelude to Ottoman capitulation to the Allies, Talaat's cabinet fell.

The maneuverability of the Armenian supplicants had increased considerably by mid-October, 1918, when Ahmed Izzet Pasha, the new Grand Vizier, pressed for an accord with Aharonian to demonstrate to the Allied victors that animosity no longer existed between Turk and Armenian. He soon revealed that Turkish armies had been ordered to pull back to the Brest-Litovsk boundaries and promised that the Ottoman government would release and compensate Armenians conscripted for forced labor, would permit refugees to repatriate, and would take steps to retrieve Armenian women and children held in Muslim households.[40]

[38] Rep. of Arm. Archives, File 74/1, and File 104/3, *H. H. Patvirakutiun, 1919 t.: Hashtutian Konferens.*

[39] Rep. of Arm. Archives, File 100/1, Reports of Sept. 7, 10, 21, and Oct. 1, 5, 1918; Khatisian, *Hanrapetutian zargatsume*, p. 93.

[40] Rep. of Arm. Archives, File 74/1, Ottoman Foreign Ministry to Aharonian, Oct. 25, 1918, and File 100/1, Ottoman Ministry of War to Aharonian, Oct. 28, 1918, and Delegation reports of Oct. 22 and 24, 1918. See also Badalian, *op. cit.*, p. 245, Abdul Kerim to Djamalian, Tiflis, Nov. 2, 1918.

At the end of October, as an Ottoman delegation was about to set
sail for the isle of Lemnos to sue for peace, Husein Rauf Bey called
upon Alexandre Khatisian. The two men had sat on opposing sides
at the Trebizond conference several months earlier. Now Rauf, named
to lead the deputation to Port Mudros, had come to urge the Armenian
mission to accompany him as evidence of Armeno-Turkish cordiality.
He indicated that in return the Turkish government would relinquish
Kars and Ardahan, restore the boundaries of 1914, and possibly even
accede to an additional minor territorial rectification in favor of Armenia. What the Transcaucasian Seim had sought in March, a ranking
Ottoman official himself now offered. But the wheel had turned full
circle, and in October, 1918, it was the Armenians who found the
suggested Turkish concessions unacceptable.[41] Khatisian, Aharonian,
and Papadjanian did not sail with Husein Rauf to Port Mudros but
remained in Constantinople until the terms of the armistice were made
known. Then, appointing Ferdinand Tahtadjian to serve as Armenia's chargé d'affaires in the Ottoman capital, they departed for Erevan
as the harbingers of peace and a new day in the history of the Republic
of Armenia.[42]

The Mudros Armistice and Armenia

Armenians the world over rejoiced at news of the Mudros Armistice,
October 30, and the German surrender, November 11, 1918. With
Turkey vanquished, the Allies could now satisfy the Armenian demand
for justice and retribution.[43] Sentiment aside, however, those who
carefully read the terms of the Mudros Armistice had valid cause for
misgivings. It was quite lenient and, in reference to Armenia, imprecise.
The twenty-five articles included provisions for the release of all interned Armenians, the demobilization of Ottoman armies except for
a force sufficient to maintain order and guard the frontiers, and the
immediate evacuation of North Persia and most of Transcaucasia,

[41] Khatisian, *Hanrapetutian zargatsume,* p. 94.
[42] *Ibid.,* pp. 94–95; Rep. of Arm. Archives, File 74/1.
[43] Consult the following for materials on the armistice preliminaries, including the
preparation of the armistice terms by the British War Office and Admiralty: Britain,
Cab 23/8, War Cabinet Minutes, 480(2), 484(3), 486(2), 488(4), 492(9), and Cab 24/67,
G.T. 6068, 6069; Britain, *Naval Operations,* V, 351–354, 418–421; David Lloyd George,
War Memoirs, Vol. V (Boston, 1936), pp. 36–37, 55–62, 255–260, and Vol. VI (1937),
pp. 200–208, 240–243; Lord [Maurice] Hankey, *The Supreme Command, 1914–1918*
(2 vols.; London, [1961]), II, 841–844; *The Times History of the War,* Vol. XX (London, 1919), pp. 101–103; Frederick Maurice, *The Armistice of 1918* (London, 1943),
pp. 17–20.

with the remainder of that region to be cleared if demanded by the Allies after an investigation. The Ottoman government also consented to Allied occupation of Batum and Baku and the intervening railway system and acknowledged that the Allies reserved the right to march into any part of the six Armenian vilayets "in case of disorder." [44]

During the deliberations aboard the H.M.S. *Agamemnon* at Port Mudros, October 26–30, Vice Admiral Sir Somerset Arthur Gough-Calthorpe, the Allied negotiator and British Commander in Chief in the Mediterranean, had made several significant concessions to the Ottoman Empire. In the original draft of the armistice, as preformulated in London, the Allies required the immediate evacuation of all Transcaucasia and retained the right, in case of disorder, to occupy not only the six Armenian vilayets but also the entire region of Cilicia. The Ottoman delegation first persuaded Calthorpe to permit the Turkish armies to hold, at least temporarily, the province of Kars and a part of the province of Batum and then succeeded in disassociating the status of Cilicia from that of the eastern vilayets.[45] The Mudros Armistice, in its revised and final form, did not even reestablish the boundaries of 1914 nor did it make provision for enforcement of a rapid supervised demobilization. The primary objective of the Allies, particularly Great Britain, was to open the Straits, occupy the forts along the Dardanelles and Bosporus, and gain access to the Black Sea. On these terms, there could be no compromise.[46] Armenian lead-

[44] The rough minutes of the negotiating sessions at Mudros are in Britain, FO 371/5259, E5732/5732/44. Rear Admiral Michael Culme Seymour and three other British naval officers were also present during the negotiations, which were concluded at 9:40 p. m. (local time) on October 30. An official text of the armistice is in Great Britain, Parliament, House of Commons, *Sessional Papers (Accounts and Papers)*, 1919, Cmd. 53. See also Britain, WO 106/1433 and /1571; Maurice, *op. cit.*, pp. 85–87; H. W. V. Temperley, *A History of the Peace Conference of Paris*, Vol. I (London, 1920), pp. 495–497; Harry R. Rudin, *Armistice, 1918* (New Haven, 1944), pp. 410–411; United States, Department of State, *Papers Relating to the Foreign Relations of the United States, 1918*, Supplement 1: *The World War* (2 vols.; Washington, D.C., 1933), I, 441–443.

[45] The memoirs of the secretary of the Turkish delegation provide a valuable account of the Mudros negotiations and the changes that the Ottoman representatives were able to make in the draft terms. See Âli Türkgeldi, *Moudros ve Mudanya mütarekelerinin tarihi* (Ankara, 1948), pp. 27–73. See also G. Jäschke, "Die Südwestkaukasische Regierung von Kars," *Die Welt des Islams*, n.s., II, 1 (1952), 47; Britain, *Naval Operations*, V, 354–357; Belen, *Türk Harbi*, V, 208–214.

[46] On October 22 the British government relayed to Calthorpe twenty-four terms to be included in the armistice with Turkey, instructing, however, that the immediate implementation of the naval clauses "will so inevitably make us master of the situation that we do not wish you to jeopardise obtaining them, and obtaining them quickly, by insisting unduly on all or any of the rest, or indeed by raising any particular one of the remaining twenty if you think it might endanger success in getting

ers were alarmed that the armistice implied continued Ottoman sovereignty in Turkish Armenia, and they bitterly questioned how disorders involving Armenians might arise in those provinces, the Christian population long since having been deported, massacred, or driven into exile.[47]

Had the Armenians known of several directives circulated by the Ottoman Ministry of War, they would have expressed still greater consternation. In October, 1918, Izzet Pasha recalled the Turkish divisions to the Brest-Litovsk boundaries; yet at the same time the

---

the vital four at once." By October 30 Gough-Calthorpe and the Ottoman representatives had reached an accord on all terms except clause 16, relating to the surrender of the Turkish garrisons in Cilicia, and clause 24, relating to the right of the Allies to occupy Cilicia and the six Armenian vilayets: "The Turkish delegates agreed to most of the remaining conditions, but Raouf urged that Clauses 16 and 24 might well be modified. Admiral Calthorpe, who had rather reluctantly insisted that the negotiations should be finished that night, and was anxious that the armistice should be signed without rancour, modified these two contested clauses very considerably during the last hours of the negotiations." See Britain, *Naval Operations*, V, 356, 419–421.

A contemporary evaluation of the Mudros Armistice, in *The Times History of the War*, XX, 103–104, reads: "The armistice made the military and naval situation of the Allies perfectly secure, but they were less severe than the Turks had reason to expect. . . . The weakness of the armistice lay in that it did not bring home to the Turks in Anatolia the completeness of the defeat they had sustained and that no adequate provision was made for the security of the Armenians." For subsequent armistice modifications to Turkey's advantage, see the British War Office's classified document, *Execution of the Armistice with Turkey*, in WO 106/64.

[47] The rivalries that characterized Anglo-French postwar relations in the Near East were coming into sharp focus at this time. Premiers Lloyd George and Clemenceau engaged in heated exchanges over the British maneuver that excluded French representatives from the negotiations aboard the H.M.S. *Agamemnon*. Vice Admiral Gough-Calthorpe was technically responsible to the joint Allied commander of Mediterranean naval operations, a French admiral, and apparently also to the Senior Officer in the Aegean, French Vice Admiral Amet. Yet when Amet asked to participate in the negotiations, Calthorpe, in Lloyd George's words, "refused to share the business with him." See Lloyd George, *op. cit.*, VI, 279. The British Premier maintained that the naval forces in the Aegean were actually commanded by Admiral Gough-Calthorpe, but the official history, Britain, *Naval Operations*, V, 251–252, confirms that Admiral Amet was in fact the "Senior Officer."

At an inter-Allied conference meeting in Paris while the armistice was being negotiated, Lloyd George and Clemenceau each stated his country's right to a position of prominence in the Near East and attempted to minimize the military contributions of the other nation. In response to Clemenceau's protestations about recent British actions, Lloyd George exclaimed that there were a half million Imperial troops on Turkish soil and that these forces had suffered thousands upon thousands of casualties in that theater. "The other Governments," he continued, "had only put in a few nigger policemen to see that we did not steal the Holy Sepulchre!" When it became evident that the French could not alter the proceedings at Mudros, Clemenceau grudgingly bowed to the "fait accompli." See Lloyd George, *op. cit.*, VI, 276–280; Hankey, *op. cit.*, pp. 844–845; Maurice, *op. cit.*, pp. 22–23. The effect of Allied rivalries upon the fate of Armenia is discussed in chapter 10 below.

Ministry of War authorized army officers in Transcaucasia to enter into the service of the North Caucasus and Azerbaijani republics. In November Azerbaijani military leaders and Nuri Pasha, commander of the Caucasus-based Army of Islam, concluded a pact which permitted all Ottoman officers and enlisted men who so desired to join the army of Azerbaijan. The Republic of Azerbaijan was to pay these volunteers regularly, grant them annual furloughs, and make provision for their families in Turkey.[48] Whether or not this agreement had any bearing on the situation, hundreds of Turkish soldiers did remain in the Caucasus after their divisions had drawn back into the provinces of Van, Erzerum, Kars, and Batum. These *askers* were to take an active role in the border warfare between Armenia and Azerbaijan and in the Muslim rebellions in the Erevan guberniia.

Ottoman Withdrawal from the Caucasus

During the autumn of 1918, while Armenian diplomats labored abroad, a ray of hope filtered into Armenia. The Allied victories on distant fronts seemed to prompt the Turkish intruders to grant occasional favors. In mid-August a train was permitted to pass from Erevan to Tiflis for the first time in weeks. Mehmed Ali Pasha, the Ottoman representative in Armenia, even consented to sell Finance Minister Karjikian a few carloads of grain from the Turkish-controlled outskirts of Erevan.[49] In Tiflis, meanwhile, Ottoman envoy Abdul Kerim Pasha assured the Armenian chargé d'affaires, Arshak Djamalian, that Turkish troops would soon evacuate Pambak and southern Lori and that Armenian refugees would be allowed home. On a visit to the Armenian capital in late August, General Halil Pasha, an influential Turkish commander and the uncle of Enver Pasha, informed Kachaznuni's cabinet that refugees could return to a small part of the occupied sector of the Erevan guberniia. Then, on October 5, as the Ottoman Empire prepared to capitulate, Halil appointed several officers to arrange for the transfer of Lori and Pambak to Armenia.[50] On October 18 Armenian companies marched into the two districts and came

[48] Sabahattin Selek, *Millî mücadele: Anadolu ihtilâli*, Vol. I (Istanbul, 1963), pp. 151, 155. See also Britain, Cab 27/36, E.C. 2298, E.C. 2342, and Cab 27/37, E.C. 2418; E. F. Ludshuveit, *Turtsiia v gody pervoi mirovoi voiny 1914–1918 gg.: Voenno-politicheskii ocherk* (Moscow, 1966), pp. 263–264.

[49] Rep. of Arm. Archives, File 72; Vratzian, *Hanrapetutiun*, p. 169.

[50] Rep. of Arm. Archives, File 65/1, Report of Sept. 19 and 25, 1918; Khondkarian, "Opozitsian Hayastanum," II, 4, p. 86.

face to face with German and Georgian border patrols. The scene had been set for a military conflict between Georgia and Armenia.[51]

During the month of November the Ottoman army of occupation gradually withdrew from the Erevan guberniia. In the last phase of this operation, the Turkish forces abandoned the railway from Erevan to Alexandropol on December 5 and delivered the fortress of Alexandropol to Colonel Nesterovskii's Armenian units the following day. The Ottoman Empire thus relinquished nearly 6,000 square miles of the Erevan guberniia.[52]

As the Armenian soldiers advanced, the full significance of the saying, "the Turk has passed here," was bruisingly demonstrated. The richest districts of the Erevan guberniia had been stripped bare of crops, animals, implements, and all other movable goods. Only a shadow of the former Armenian villages remained. Clothing, furniture, utensils, pottery, even doors and windows had been carted away. Not one operable locomotive or freight car remained along the entire railway line; every depot lay in shambles. Rubble filled the streets of Alexandropol as the result of the Turkish decision to detonate the powder and ammunition before the evacuation. This devastation had taken place despite Mehmed Ali's promise of an orderly withdrawal without looting or irregularities. A share of the spoils was concentrated in the Muslim-populated southern districts of the guberniia, but most of it, thousands of tons of cotton, sugar, and grain, and several hundred thousand animals, was moved toward Kars. The little that might have been missed was picked clean by other Turkish regiments as they passed over Armenia in retreat from North Persia.[53]

Terrifying stories were told by the Armenians who had endured six months of Turkish domination. They had been beaten, robbed, and exploited. The suffering had been especially intense in the district of Pambak, where Turkish Armenian refugees had been used as targets for bayonet practice and more than 8,000 young men had been driven toward Erzerum as slave labor. The women of numerous villages had been ravished. When the Turkish armies departed they took from this small district alone more than 125,000 head of livestock,

[51] The Armeno-Georgian territorial conflict is discussed in chapters 3 and 4 below.
[52] Rep. of Arm. Archives, File 1/1. For an account of the Turkish administration in Alexandropol during the summer and autumn of 1918, see *Hairenik* (daily), Feb. 27, 1919, p. 2.
[53] US Archives, RG 256, 861K.00/5, Report of Wilbur E. Post and John O. Arrol, and RG 59, 861.00/4017. See also Rep. of Arm. Archives, File 9/9, *Hayastani Hanrapetutiun, 1919 t*; Britain, FO 371/3657, 3404/3409/16547/512/58, and Cab 27/39, E.C. 2862.

30,000 farm implements, 6,000 carts and wagons, and 18,000 tons of grain and other foodstuffs.[54] Subsequent depositions of the victims filled countless pages; but words, no matter how descriptive, failed to convey the magnitude of the horror and destruction in the lands retrieved by the Republic of Armenia.

In spite of such catastrophe, the hope and perhaps even the belief arose at the end of 1918 that the Republic could indeed survive as an independent state and that the recovery of Kars and all Turkish Armenia was no longer a mere flight of fantasy. The great Allies— France, Great Britain, and the United States of America—had repeatedly proclaimed that the Armenians would be indemnified and that never again would they be allowed to experience "the blasting tyranny of the Turk." The Armenian question, the Allies pledged, would be settled "according to the supreme laws of humanity and justice." [55]

With this outlook the Armenians welcomed the British decision to take control of strategic points in Transcaucasia, under provision of the Mudros Armistice. On October 31, 1918, the War Office instructed the Imperial Expeditionary Army in Mesopotamia to occupy Baku and the surrounding oil fields.[56] In pursuance of this directive Acting Major General William Montgomerie Thomson, the commander of the North Persia Force,[57] ordered the last Ottoman contingents out of

---

[54] E. K. Sargsian, *Ekspansionistskaia politika Osmanskoi imperii v gody pervoi mirovoi voiny* (Erevan, 1962), pp. 389–391; Vratzian, *Hanrapetutiun*, pp. 179–180; V. A. Mikayelian, *Hayastani giughatsiutiune Sovetakan ishkhanutian hamar mghvads paikari zhamanakashrdjanum (1917–1920 t.t.)* (Erevan, 1960), pp. 59–61. Numerous documents and depositions pertaining to Armenian losses during the Turkish occupation are in the Central State Historical Archives of the Armenian SSR, fund 200, work 1271.

[55] For a résumé of Allied pledges, see Richard G. Hovannisian, "The Allies and Armenia, 1915–18," *Journal of Contemporary History*, III (Jan., 1968), 145–155; André Mandelstam, *La Société des Nations et les Puissances devant le Problème Arménien* (Paris, 1926), pp. 310–313.

[56] Richard H. Ullman, *Anglo-Soviet Relations, 1917–1921*, Vol. II: *Britain and the Russian Civil War, November 1918–February 1920* (Princeton, 1968), p. 50. See also Britain, Cab 23/8, War Cabinet Minutes, 495(5). On November 13 the War Office called attention to "the great importance of insisting from the outset on the recognition of the supremacy of British interests in any undertaking in the North or South Caucasus and the Don country." See Ullman, *op. cit.*, p. 45. That same day a conference at the Foreign Office, concurring in the view that "considerations both of honour and of interest demand that we should keep Bolshevism from the regions East of the Black Sea, i.e., the Caucasus, the Don country, and Turkestan," accepted the inevitability of British military involvement in Transcaucasia. See Britain, Cab 23/8, War Cabinet Minutes, 502(Appendix), and Cab 27/24, E.C. 2392.

[57] The North Persia Force was organized to supersede Major General Lionel Charles Dunsterville's ill-fated Dunsterforce after its withdrawal from Baku in September,

Baku on November 14 and three days later arrived there from Enzeli with several companies of the 39th Infantry Brigade and representatives, official and unofficial, of the Allied nations.[58] Shortly thereafter a part of the British Salonica Army transferred to Constantinople, where General George Francis Milne established headquarters of the so-called Army of the Black Sea, with jurisdiction over an extensive area including Anatolia and the Caucasus. Milne dispatched Major General George Townshend Forestier-Walker's 27th Division to safeguard the vital centers in the western provinces of Transcaucasia.[59] In late December, Batum, the western terminus of the Transcaucasian railway system and of the oil pipeline from Baku, was occupied.[60] Much to the chagrin of the Georgian government, the port, city, and

1918. Thomson had previously commanded the 14th Division of Lieutenant General Sir William Raine Marshall's Mesopotamia Expeditionary Force. For details, see Britain, *Campaign in Mesopotamia*, IV (1927), and the war diaries in Britain, WO 95.

[58] For descriptions of this operation, see Britain, Cab 45/107, WO 95/4955, and WO 106/917. See also *The Times History of the War*, XX, 92; US Archives, RG 256, 861K.00/5; A. Raevskii, *Angliiskaia interventsiia i Musavatskoe pravitel'stvo* (Baku, 1927), pp. 32–33, 40–41; Kadishev, *Interventsiia v Zakavkaz'e*, p. 164; Britain, *Campaign in Mesopotamia*, IV, 329–330. The British garrison in Baku numbered nearly 1,500 men at the end of November, 1918, and was bolstered to just more than 2,000 by the beginning of 1919. The basic strength of what became known as Thomson's Force, Baku, was drawn from the 7th Battalion, North Staffordshire Regiment, the 7th Battalion, Gloucestershire Regiment, the 9th Battalion, Royal Warwickshire Regiment, and the 9th Battalion, Worcestershire Regiment. See the war diaries of the 39th Infantry Brigade, headquarters and individual battalions, in Britain, WO 95/4955. See also Britain, *Order of Battle*, Pt. 3A (1938), p. 41.

[59] For materials relating to the British Salonica Army and to the composition and command personnel of the 27th Division, see Britain, *Operations in Macedonia*, 2 vols.; Britain, *Order of Battle*, Pt. 1 (1935), pp. 97–103, and Pt. 4 (1945), pp. 55–62. On November 21, 1918, the Cabinet, having sanctioned the use of Imperial troops to occupy the Batum-Baku railway, requested the Director of Military Operations to instruct General Milne to prepare to ship one division to Batum. See Britain, Cab 23/8, War Cabinet Minutes, 502(Appendix) and 505(3), and Cab 27/24, E.C. 2392. The War Office informed General Milne on December 11 that "our policy in the Caucasus at present is to ensure that the terms of the Armistice are complied with in full by the Turks, to re-open the railway and pipe-line between the Black Sea and the Caspian, and to that end to occupy Baku and Batoum, and probably Tiflis, and so much as may be necessary of the railway." See Britain, WO 33/695, no. 2908 and Cab 27/38, E.C. 2709.

[60] The Georgian chargé d'affaires in Batum, Diomid A. Topuridze, reported that a British mission had come ashore on December 15. See *Bor'ba v Gruzii*, pp. 354–356. The information is probably accurate inasmuch as British war vessels, primarily the H.M.S. *Liverpool*, had anchored off Batum as early as December 5. The headquarters company and the main force of the 80th Brigade of the 27th Division sailed into harbor on December 21 and 22. Most units disembarked on the twenty-third, and headquarters went ashore the following day. The 81st Brigade arrived on December 30 and the 82d Brigade on January 8. See the headquarters and brigade war diaries in Britain, WO 95/4880 and /4890–4895.

surrounding district were constituted as a British military governorship under Acting Brigadier General W. J. N. Cooke-Collis, commander
of the 80th Infantry Brigade.[61] Then, after a series of strained, even
hostile Georgian and British diplomatic exchanges, Forestier-Walker
directed a battalion of the 80th Brigade to proceed to Tiflis.[62] Soon
British spokesmen were to carry greetings and messages of encouragement to Erevan.[63] Almost simultaneously, however, Armenia was to
be distressed and disillusioned by the modus operandi of His Majesty's
military commanders in the Caucasus.

Coalition in Government

The momentous changes on the international scene had a whole-
some effect on the political situation in Armenia. Many who previously
had used the appellations "republic" and "independence" with undisguised skepticism now began to feel that an independent republic
could be more than a mere phantasm. The Populist party in particular
modified its position and in October, 1918, indicated a readiness to
enter the cabinet. Samson Harutiunian and Minas Berberian, distinguished members of the Tiflis bourgeoisie, traveled to Erevan to lay
the groundwork for a more active Populist role in government.[64]

By this time Dashnaktsutiun, too, desired a reshuffling of the cabinet.
Throughout the preceding perilous months the party had tolerated and
even condoned the supremacy of the legislature with its dispropor-

[61] William James Norman Cooke-Collis was appointed military governor on December 25 and officially received the district from the departing Turkish vali (governor) on December 30. See Britain, WO 95/4880, 80th Brigade War Diary. See also
Dokumenty i materialy, pp. 424–427; Britain, Operations in Macedonia, II, 306–309.

[62] The 4th Battalion, Rifle Brigade, departed for Tiflis on December 30 and arrived
there on New Year's Day, after having encountered numerous Georgian delaying
tactics along the rails. General Forestier-Walker made his entry into the Georgian
capital on January 2 and, acting on General Milne's authorization, established 27th
Division headquarters there on January 19. By that time the 81st Brigade and much
of the 82d Brigade had also transferred to Tiflis. See the headquarters and brigade
war diaries in WO 95/4880 and /4890–4894.

[63] On January 1, 1919, Forestier-Walker informed the Georgian and Armenian governments of his jurisdiction and responsibilities in enforcing the terms of the armistice until the world peace conference had arranged a permanent settlement. He
invited the two governments to communicate with the Allies through his headquarters and made known that General Thomson possessed similar powers in eastern
Transcaucasia. See Rep. of Arm. Archives, File 333/3, H. H. Londoni Nerkayatsutschutiun ev Britanakan Karavarutiune, 1919; Bor'ba v Gruzii, pp. 363–364; Britain,
WO 95/4880, 27th Division War Diary.

[64] Vratzian, Hanrapetutiun, p. 173.

tionate political complexion. Nonetheless, new municipal elections in Erevan once again demonstrated that the Khorhurd's composition did not reflect public sentiment. The vote for Dashnaktsutiun was more than double that of all other slates combined.[65] Growing bolder as the Turkish threat waned, Dashnaktsutiun began to challenge the dominance of the legislature. The Khorhurd's impotence and the alleged combination in it against Dashnaktsutiun were denounced by the party press, which complained sarcastically that "the opposition groups each have six deputies but scarcely five followers." [66] Party militants even packed the gallery with spectators who interrupted the legislative sessions with raucous outbursts.

The Khorhurd's objection to a government-sponsored measure of no great import provided Hovhannes Kachaznuni the pretext to assert that he had received a no-confidence vote and to tender his resignation, thus precipitating the Republic's first cabinet crisis. The strategy was so well planned that in a single session the Khorhurd both accepted Kachaznuni's resignation and called upon him to form a new cabinet. Significantly, the Populist deputies voted with Dashnaktsutiun. While determined to enhance the authority of the cabinet, Kachaznuni and Dashnaktsutiun's central executive, the Bureau, were not averse to a coalition in government. On the contrary, they maintained that such an arrangement would raise the Republic's prestige among Allied ruling circles and Armenian communities abroad.[67]

At the end of October and the beginning of November, 1918, Kachaznuni conferred with leaders of the other parties, only to face irreconcilable demands once again. The Social Democrats would join no coalition unless granted the portfolios of Internal Affairs and Foreign Affairs, whereas the Social Revolutionaries refused to countenance either a Social Democrat in Internal Affairs or a Populist in Foreign Affairs. The intransigence of the SD's and the SR's perturbed Dashnaktsutiun but little, for the party was actually far more intent upon collaboration with the Armenian bourgeoisie, whose professional experience, commercial aptitude, and educational achievements were deemed vital to the Republic and whose liberal and constitutional principles would appeal to the democracies of the West. Dashnaktsutiun appeared quite ready to lay aside its cloak of socialism, a cloak that had been worn ever so lightly by many prominent members. Offering the parties of the left few concessions, Kachaznuni con-

[65] Khondkarian, "Opozitsian Hayastanum," II, 3, p. 50.
[66] Ibid., II, 4, pp. 87–89, 92.
[67] Ibid., pp. 89–92; Rep. of Arm. Archives, File 72.

centrated his efforts upon the Populists, to whom he promised a gradualist approach in social and agrarian reforms.[68]

On November 4, 1918, despite the acerbic remonstrances of the SR and SD factions, the Khorhurd confirmed the coalition cabinet of Dashnakists and Populists. For the first time the opposition socialist parties cast negative ballots against the government on a vital issue. This tactic was a promising sign, for it indicated that Armenia had taken a small, faltering step toward a regular parliamentary system.[69] The composition of Kachaznuni's new cabinet showed that Dashnaktsutiun, although holding fewer than half the posts, retained a dominant position by virtue of its control of the premiership and the strategic ministries of Foreign Affairs and Internal Affairs.[70]

PREMIER (MINISTER-PRESIDENT)	Hovhannes Kachaznuni	*Dashnaktsutiun*
FOREIGN AFFAIRS	Sirakan Tigranian	*Dashnaktsutiun*
INTERNAL AFFAIRS	Aram Manukian	*Dashnaktsutiun*
MILITARY AFFAIRS	Hovhannes Hakhverdian	*Nonpartisan*
FINANCIAL AFFAIRS	Artashes Enfiadjian	*Populist*
JUDICIAL AFFAIRS	Samson Harutiunian	*Populist*
ENLIGHTENMENT (PUBLIC INSTRUCTION)	Mikayel Atabekian	*Populist*
PROVISIONS	Levon Ghulian	*Populist*
WELFARE (PUBLIC ASSISTANCE)	Khachatur Karjikian	*Dashnaktsutiun*

The Republic of Armenia had traveled a precarious path during its first months but had managed to survive. The end of the World War and the withdrawal of the Turkish armies engendered new enthusiasm and hope. Yet, on the other hand, the easing of external pressures permitted the hostilities among the Transcaucasian republics to resurface. To Kachaznuni's coalition government fell the immediate taxing responsibility of seeking a satisfactory solution to the imminently explosive territorial disputes with the Republic of Georgia and with the Republic of Azerbaijan.

[68] Rep. of Arm. Archives, File 65/1, Djamalian to Armenian mission, Berlin; Khondkarian, "Opozitsian Hayastanum," II, 4, pp. 92–94; Vratzian, *Hanrapetutiun,* pp. 173–174.

[69] Rep. of Arm. Archives, File 72; Khondkarian, "Opozitsian Hayastanum," II, 4, pp. 94–95.

[70] Rep. of Arm. Archives, File 1/1; Lazian, *op. cit.,* p. 174.

3

The
Foundations of
Conflict

The emergence of independent republics in Transcaucasia created a multiplicity of new and distressingly entangled problems. Under Russian domination, Transcaucasia had been constituted as a major administrative unit of the Romanov realm, much of its food had come from beyond the Caucasus Mountains, and its economy had been integrated to a considerable degree with that of the empire as a whole. This no longer held true in 1918, however, as chaos gripped Russia and seething mutual antagonisms divided the peoples of Transcaucasia. Furthermore, each of the nascent republics promptly measured political and economic security in terms of area controlled and thus strove to gain the maximum possible land. Territorial disputes loomed as the greatest impediment to satisfactory relations among the republics of Armenia, Georgia, and Azerbaijan.

The century of Russian rule in Transcaucasia had provided a measure of homogeneity, yet national and religious particularisms persisted and intense resistance to assimilation surged time and again. In actions calculated to undermine indigenous national-religious cohesion, the tsarist government had drawn and redrawn internal boundaries, often incorporating into a single province many different peoples and contrasting topographic formations.[1] Such policies gave

[1] For documents and studies of tsarist administrative policies in the Caucasus, consult *Akty sobrannye Kavkazskoiu Arkheograficheskoiu Kommissieiu* (Tiflis, 1866–1904), 12 vols.; A. Shakhatuni, *Administrativnyi peredel Zakavkazskago kraia* (Tiflis, 1918); S. Esadze, *Istoricheskaia zapiska ob upravlenii Kavkazom* (Tiflis, 1907); *Kavkazskii kalendar'* (Tiflis, 1846–1916); Hovannisian, *Road to Independence*, pp. 7–15; T. Kh. Hakobian, *Erevani patmutiune* (Erevan, 1959–1963), 2 vols.; A. Sh. Mil'man, *Politicheskii stroi Azerbaidzhana v XIX–nachala XX vekov* (Baku, 1966).

Transcaucasia, already an ethnic polyglot, the semblance of even greater racial interspersion.[2] Official population statistics for the individual provinces in 1916 (table 1) bear out the complexity of the situation. The figures in the table point up a cause for potential rivalry between Georgia and Armenia over parts of the Tiflis guberniia and between Azerbaijan and Armenia over broad sectors of the Elisavetpol and Erevan guberniias. They also reveal that, while the Armenians and Muslims were spread throughout Transcaucasia, the Georgians were concentrated in the provinces of Tiflis, Kutais, and Batum, their historic homelands. Still, in the Tiflis guberniia, the most populous of the provinces, the Georgians failed to form a majority.

The Deterioration of Armeno-Georgian Relations

For more than two thousand years Armenians and Georgians had been neighbors, enjoying an extraordinary record of peaceful association. Christian peoples, they shared numerous traditions, including related erstwhile dynastic families. Yet in 1918, as both nations struggled for survival, their inexperienced governments were quick to take offense and to assume uncompromising attitudes. The former bonds degenerated into jealousy and distrust.

Feeling betrayed, the Armenians ascribed the collapse of the Transcaucasian Federative Republic to the Georgians, who upon securing German protection had abandoned Armenia to the Turkish hordes. The embittered and envious Armenians were stung again as control of Tiflis was wrenched from their grasp. They charged that the Georgian Mensheviks, bringing dishonor to the internationalist and humanitarian principles of the Social Democratic movement, had most brazenly unmasked their chauvinism by allying with the aristocracy to oppress the Armenian plurality of Tiflis. In conduct equally nefarious,

---

[2] According to the *Kavkazskii kalendar'* for 1917 (Tiflis, 1916), the 6,973,800 inhabitants of Transcaucasia (not including Daghestan) were divided into the following ethnic-religious groupings:

Armenian Apostolic	1,722,500	Shi'a Muslim	1,485,200
Armenian Orthodox	2,200	Sunni Muslim	817,200
Armenian, other faiths	56,900	Kurd, Muslim	97,100
Georgian Orthodox	1,641,000	Yezidi	40,400
Georgian Muslim	139,300	Gypsy	40,200
Russian Orthodox	352,600	Jew	65,900
Russian Sectarian	99,500	European	50,200
Mountaineer, Muslim	117,000	Other Christian	198,600
Mountaineer, other faiths	46,900		

TABLE 1
POPULATION OF THE TRANSCAUCASIAN PROVINCES IN 1916

Province	Total population	Shi'a Muslim (primarily Tatar)	Sunni Muslim (Turco-Tatar)	Kurd (Muslim and Yezidi)	Armenian	Georgian	Russian	Other Christian
Kars	364,000	19,000	83,000	68,000	118,000	—	19,000	18,000[a]
Batum	123,000	700	14,000	600	15,000	79,000[b]	9,000	3,000
Tiflis	1,473,000	39,000	129,000	56,000	411,000	580,000	150,000	40,000
Kutais	1,034,000	—	—	—	5,000	993,000	16,000	2,000[c]
Erevan	1,120,000	366,000	9,000	55,000	670,000	400	16,000	4,000
Elisavetpol	1,275,000	478,000	305,000	4,000[d]	419,000	1,000	37,000	18,000
Baku	1,281,000	583,000	293,000	700	120,000	10,000	177,000	12,000

[a] There were also 38,000 Gypsies in Kars. The statistics include no data on the population of Olti, the smallest of the four counties of Kars.

[b] More than 70,000 of the Georgians in Batum (Ajaria) were Muslim.

[c] There were some 18,000 Jews in the Kutais guberniia.

[d] Other sources show that there were 15,000 Kurds in the Elisavetpol guberniia.

Source: United States of America, the National Archives, Record Group 256, 867.B.00/10. See also A. Shakhatuni, Administrativnyi peredel Zakavkazskago kraia (Tiflis, 1918), pp. 61, 68, 71–72.

the Georgian government had sealed the escape routes to refugees fleeing before the Turkish armies. Nearly 80,000 Armenians from Akhalkalak alone had been denied sanctuary. Of this destitute mass, stranded
in the rugged Bakuriani highland until the end of the World War,
some 30,000 perished.[3]

The Georgians indignantly refuted every accusation, asserting that
a nation could not be blamed for saving itself and that, were the
circumstances reversed, the Armenians would have followed the same
course. Moreover, the Armenians, having found refuge in Georgia for
decades past, were now unscrupulously violating the goodwill of the
Georgian people by aspiring to dominate the country. They filled
many quarters of Tiflis, and their bourgeoisie nearly monopolized the
commerce and enjoyed ownership of the most luxurious mansions.
Tiflis had in fact been transformed into a Russo-Armenian city, but,
as it had again become the capital of free Georgia, the perpetuation
of this singularly abnormal situation could be tolerated no longer.
Furthermore, declared the Georgians, inhumanity was not one of their
national attributes; the Armenian indictment was baseless. Georgia
was actually teeming with so many thousands of refugees that her
economic welfare was in jeopardy. These people roved in lawless, looting bands, stealing, marauding, and spreading contagion. It was incumbent upon the Georgian government to protect its citizenry by
sealing the borders. Only by coincidence had the brunt of this action
fallen upon the misfortunate Armenians of Akhalkalak.[4]

Lori and Akhalkalak

A trenchant source of Armeno-Georgian antagonism sprang from
rivalry over Lori and Akhalkalak (see map 6). The uchastok (district)

---

[3] Henri Barbusse, *Voici ce qu'on a fait de la Géorgie* (Paris, 1929), pp. 28, 114. Rep.
of Arm. Archives, File 230/129, *H. H. Patvirakutiun, 1919*; Lepsius, *Deutschland und
Armenien*, pp. 405, 410, 412, 417–418; Mikayel Varandian, *Le conflit arméno-géorgien
et la guerre du Caucase* (Paris, 1919), pp. 72–73; S. T. Alikhanian, *Haikakan Gordseri
Komisariati gordsuneutiune (1917–1921)* (Erevan, 1958), pp. 116–117.

[4] Excerpts from the Georgian newspapers *Ertoba, Bor'ba, Gruziia,* and *Sakartvelos
Respublika* are included in press bulletins in Rep. of Arm. Archives, File 65/1 and
File 72. See also Djamalian, "Hai-vratsakan knjire" (Sept., 1928), pp. 121–123. D.
Ananun, *Rusahayeri hasarakakan zargatsume,* Vol. III (Venice, 1926), p. 437, shows
that in 1906 the Tiflis City Duma was composed of 53 Armenians, 14 Georgians, 10
Russians, 1 Pole, 1 German, and 1 Turk (Tatar). Between 1870 and 1916, 9 of the 11
mayors of Tiflis were Armenian. For the growing antagonism between the Georgian
aristocracy and the Armenian bourgeoisie, see the memoirs of the last Armenian
mayor, Alexandre Khatisian (A. I. Khatisov), "Kaghakapeti me hishataknere," *Hairenik Amsagir,* X (April, 1932), 86–89.

of Lori, located between Pambak and the Khram River in the northern reaches of the volcanic Armenian plateau, had been detached from the Erevan guberniia in 1862 and added to the Tiflis guberniia. Historically, under the Arsacid (Arshakuni) dynasty of the first to fifth centuries A.D., Lori constituted the county of Dashir, and, under the Bagratid (Bagratuni) dynasty, ninth through eleventh centuries, it formed the core of the Armenian subkingdom of Gugark. Then, after a period of vassalage to the Seljuk Turks, Lori was included in the realms of the Georgian branch of the Bagratids, but it eventually fell to the Mongols and to Safavid Persia. Late in the eighteenth century King Iraklii II restored Georgian sovereignty over the district for a few years until all eastern Georgia was annexed by Russia in 1801.[5] Under Romanov rule most of historic Lori was organized as the Lori uchastok, whereas the remainder was apportioned among the three other uchastoks of the Borchalu uezd.[6] The population of the Lori uchastok was basically Armenian: 42,000 in 1914, as compared with 8,500 Russians, 3,350 Greeks, 3,300 Tatars, and fewer than 100 Georgians. Another 25,000 Armenians lived in neighboring districts of the Borchalu uezd, and the Armenian element was likewise predominant in the adjacent southern sector of the Tiflis uezd.[7]

[5] Abeghian, "Mer harevannere" (Jan., 1929), pp. 126–129; Rep. of Arm. Archives, File 16/16, *Hayastani Hanrapetutiun, 1920 t.*, "Memorandum on the Controversy between the Republics of Georgia and Armenia Concerning Their Frontiers," and File 74/1; Djamalian, "Hai-vratsakan knjire" (April, 1928), pp. 83–84. For studies on the land, people, and history of Lori, consult the following: Lewond Movsesian, "Histoire des rois Kurikian de Lori," trans. Frédéric Macler, *Revue des études arméniennes*, VII, pt. 2 (1927), 209–265; Arshak Alboyajian, *Patmakan Hayastani sahmannere* (Cairo, 1950), pp. 125–127, 209–231, 259–260, 281–289, 337–344; L. H. Babayan, *Hayastani sotsial-tntesakan ev kaghakakan patmutiune XIII–XIV darerum* (Erevan, 1964), pp. 194–208; I. Gharibian, "Lori kaghake matenagrutian medj," *Banber Erevani Hamalsarani*, 1 (1968), 209–214.

[6] The Borchalu uezd was subdivided into the Trialet, Ekaterinenfeld, Lori, and Borchalu uchastoks and encompassed approximately 300 villages, nearly 70 of which fell within the Lori uchastok. An outstanding, comprehensive study of the Borchalu uezd, its geography, climate, economy, political history, folklore, and ethnography, is that of Ervand Lalayan, a pioneer Armenian sociologist and ethnographer. Lalayan founded and edited the highly reputed *Azgagrakan handes*, published in Shushi (Vol. I only) and in Tiflis. See his "Borchalui gavare," *Azgagrakan handes:* VI (1901), 271–437, VII (1902), 197–262, and VIII (1903), 112–268.

[7] US Archives, RG 256, 184.01602/90, Moore (Tiflis) to Tyler (Paris), for Westermann. See also Shakhatuni, *op. cit.*, p. 72; Abeghian, "Mer harevannere" (Feb., 1928), p. 100, and (Jan., 1929), p. 131. In all uchastoks of the Borchalu uezd combined, the Armenians formed 40 percent of the population, the Muslims, 29 percent, and the Georgians, scarcely 5 percent. A Georgian memorandum prepared in May, 1919 (now in Britain, FO 371/4940, 5325/1/58), shows the population of the Borchalu uezd to have been 65,777 Armenians, 45,493 Tatars, 26,175 Greeks, 9,525 Russians, 8,146 Georgians, and 2,986 Germans.

Lying to the west of the Borchalu uezd, Akhalkalak (Akhalkalaki), historically the Armenian Javakhk and the Georgian Javakheti, had alternated between Georgian and Armenian rule until it passed to the Georgian Bagratids in the eleventh century. At the end of the thirteenth century Akhalkalak began a long semiautonomous existence which endured into the seventeenth century, when it was absorbed by the Ottoman Empire and included in the *eyalet* (province) of Akhaltsikh. By the time Akhalkalak was annexed to the Russian Empire in 1829, the population, though primarily of Georgian stock, had been Islamicized.[8] To avoid becoming Romanov subjects, most of these Muslims forsook their native villages and relocated within the revised boundaries of the Ottoman Empire. As this movement was paralleled by an exodus of thousands of Turkish Armenians from the regions of Erzerum and old Bayazit, the abandoned hamlets of Akhalkalak were resettled by Christian immigrants. The ethnic reversal was so complete that, in 1916, 83,000 of the 107,000 inhabitants were Armenians, whereas Russians, Georgians, Tatars, Greeks, and other nationality groups made up the remaining 24,000.[9]

Between 1905 and 1916, at conferences dealing with the feasibility of introducing into Transcaucasia the limited self-governing agrarian administrative units known as *zemstvos*, Armenian spokesmen advocated the realignment of existing provincial boundaries to make them coincide with those of the several projected zemstvos. By this plan Lori and Akhalkalak of the Tiflis guberniia, the Alexandropol uezd of Erevan, and two counties of Kars would have been combined into a zemstvo-province named Shirak. These conferences brought about neither the adoption of the zemstvo system nor the adjustment of provincial boundaries, but the Armenian representatives were nonetheless heartened by the declarations of Georgian Menshevik leaders

[8] Abeghian, "Mer harevannere" (Dec., 1928), pp. 117–120; Rep. of Arm. Archives, File 16/16. For a reliable historical and sociological study of Akhalkalak, see Ervand Lalayan, "Djavakhk," *Azgagrakan handes*, I (1895), 117–380. See also Cyril Toumanoff, *Studies in Christian Caucasian History* ([Washington, D.C., 1963]), pp. 435–499 *passim*.

[9] US Archives, RG 256, 867B.00/4/10; Rep. of Arm. Archives, File 74/1. Shakhatuni, *op. cit.*, pp. 71–72, shows that of the 108,500 inhabitants of Akhalkalak 84,275 (77.6 percent) were Armenian. Abeghian, "Mer harevannere" (Feb., 1928), p. 100, and (Dec., 1928), p. 121, uses statistics of the Russian government to show that in 1914 there were 81,004 Armenians, 9,557 Muslims, 7,185 Russians, and 6,895 Georgians in the Akhalkalak uezd. The *Kavkazskii kalendar'* for 1917 classified the population of the county as follows: Russian, 7,500; Orthodox Georgian, 7,400; Muslim Georgian, 2,999; Armenian Apostolic, 69,300; Armenians of other denominations, 13,500; Kurd, 9,000; Sunni Muslim, 5,400; Jew, 200; European, 100.

1. HOVHANNES KACHAZNUNI   2. ALEXANDRE KHATISIAN   3. SIRAKAN TIGRANIAN

4. ARAM MANUKIAN   5. ARTASHES ENFIADJIAN   6. SAMSON HARUTIUNIAN

7. MIKAYEL ATABEKIAN   8. MINAS BERBERIAN   9. AVETIK SAHAKIAN

10. ARSHAM KHONDKARIAN

11. ARSHAK DJAMALIAN

12. CATHOLICOS GEVORG V

13. GENERAL TOVMAS
NAZARABEKIAN

14. DRASTAMAT
KANAYAN (DRO)

15. GENERAL
ANDRANIK OZANIAN

16. NOI ZHORDANIA

17. AKAKII CHKHENKELI

18. EVGENII GEGECHKORI

19. NOI RAMISHVILI

20. FATHALI KHAN KHOISKII

21. SULTAN MEHMED VI

22. ENVER PASHA

23. TALAAT PASHA

24. NURI PASHA

25. HALIL BEY

26. HUSEIN RAUF BEY

27. AHMED IZZET PASHA

28. YAKUB SHEVKI PASHA

29. ADMIRAL S. A. GOUGH-CALTHORPE

30. GENERAL GEORGE F. MILNE AND STAFF

upholding the ethnic principle (with allowance for geographic and economic factors) in determining the future internal boundaries of Transcaucasia.[10]

Soon after the February/March Revolution of 1917, the Russian Provisional Government revived the zemstvo question. A conference of Transcaucasian leaders meeting in Petrograd submitted recommendations to the Ministry of Interior, which then forwarded the project to Tiflis for implementation by the regional administration, the Ozakom. In its turn the Ozakom appointed a fifteen-man committee to work out the details, but basic differences between Armenian and Muslim members resulted in deadlock. During these discussions the Georgian Mensheviks again conceded that Lori and Akhalkalak should be joined to an Armenian province if the zemstvo system were introduced. This stand they took despite the vociferous opposition of the antisocialist Georgian National Democrats, who insisted that the entire Tiflis guberniia was intrinsically Georgian and must remain so.[11]

The October/November Revolution put an end to the Ozakom and its various committees, and the Turkish invasion of Transcaucasia made further discussion of the zemstvo superfluous, at least for a time. In June, 1918, the treaties of Batum awarded the Akhalkalak uezd to the Ottoman Empire, and even on the Transcaucasian side of the new boundary Turkish regiments remained in control of Pambak and the southern part of Lori. In a countermaneuver Georgian units led by German officers took possession of northern Lori and established outposts along the Kamenka (Dzoraget) River.[12] The seasoned Menshevik statesman, Noi Zhordania, hastened to reassure the Armenian National Council that this occupation would be temporary and that following a return to normalcy Georgia would once again honor the ethnic principle.[13]

[10] Abeghian, "Mer harevannere" (Dec., 1927), p. 149, (Feb., 1928), pp. 96–97, (Dec., 1928), pp. 125–126, and (Jan., 1929), p. 127; Rep. of Arm. Archives, File 65/1; Armiano-gruzinskii konflikt, pp. 1–4. For details of the Armenian proposals, see Shakhatuni, op. cit., pp. 100–117; Ananun, op. cit., pp. 417–419, 437–446, 613–653.

[11] Hovannisian, Road to Independence, pp. 92–93; Rep. of Arm. Archives, File 65/1; Djamalian, "Hai-vratsakan knjire" (April, 1928), pp. 87–89; Ananun, op. cit., pp. 652–656; Armiano-gruzinskii konflikt, pp. 7–10.

[12] The major Georgian-German outposts were in the villages and settlements of Vorontsovka, Haidarbek, Alexandrovka, Tsater, Kober, and Korinj. The Turkish line extended along the right bank of the Kamenka River through the villages of Novo-Pokrovka, Jalal-oghli, Nikolaevka, Gerger, Vartablur, Kurtan, and Dara-Kend and then eastward between the stations of Kober and Kolageran to the settlements of Marts and Lorut. See Iz arm-gruz otnoshenii, p. 13.

[13] Rep. of Arm. Archives, File 65/1, Djamalian to Ramishvili, and File 107/6,

Thereafter, on behalf of the Armenian National Council, Khachatur Karjikian, Gevorg Khatisian, and General Gabriel Korganian met with a special Georgian committee charged with defining the exact boundaries of the Republic of Georgia. During that conference the international Menshevik leader, Iraklii Tsereteli, stunned the Armenians by outlining the Georgian case for sovereignty over every uezd of the Tiflis guberniia, together with the Pambak uchastok of the Erevan guberniia. The more Armenian-populated territory included within Georgia, he argued, the safer the inhabitants would be. The Armenians would at least be spared the viciousness of the Turk, and they would reinforce the Christian element in Georgia as a bulwark against the Muslims. Vehemently protesting the new Menshevik tactic the Armenian representatives persuaded the Georgian committee to reconsider the issue and to resume the discussions in a few days. But before the two sides met again, Georgian newspapers carried the official announcement that the Tiflis guberniia was in its entirety an integral unit of the Republic of Georgia.[14]

The Menshevik reversal could logically be defended. Georgian acceptance of the ethnic principle in Lori and Akhalkalak had come at a time when all Transcaucasia had been combined into an extensive region (krai) of the Russian Empire. With the establishment of independent republics, however, circumstances had changed radically. The Republic of Georgia deemed possession of Akhalkalak and Lori essential. Historic, geographic, cultural, and economic considerations now overshadowed the ethnic principle. Georgian kingdoms had encompassed both districts, which together constituted a natural defensive boundary. These highlands also provided lush summer pastures for herdsmen of the plains to the north and, combined with those plains, formed an economic unit bound to Tiflis, not to Erevan.[15] Furthermore, the Mensheviks now flaunted a document long since uncovered by Georgian nationalists, the Russo-Georgian treaty of 1783. This compact not only had placed the realms of King Iraklii II under the protection of Empress Catherine II but also had provided that, should

H. H. Patvirakutiun, 1919 t.; Varandian, op. cit., p. 74; Paul Miliukov, "The Balkanization of Transcaucasia," New Russia, II (July 8, 1920), 303; Iz arm-gruz otnoshenii, pp. 12–13.

[14] Denikin, Ocherki smuty, III (1924), 51–52; Armiano-gruzinskii konflikt, p. 11; Iz arm-gruz otnoshenii, pp. 10–11; Rep. of Arm. Archives, File 16/16 and File 65/1; D. Enukidze, Krakh imperialisticheskoi interventsii v Zakavkaz'e (Tbilisi, 1954), pp. 119–120.

[15] Iz arm-gruz otnoshenii, p. 10; Britain, FO 371/4940, 5325/1/58; Djamalian, "Haivratsakan knjire" (April, 1928), pp. 92–93.

the remaining historic Georgian territories subsequently be liberated from Muslim overlords, they too would be added to the domains of Iraklii or his successors. The Republic of Georgia, as heir to the Georgian kingdoms, thus staked its claim to Akhalkalak and Lori.[16]

The pretensions of Armenia rested on equally logical foundations. Ethnically, Lori and Akhalkalak were indisputably Armenian. Geographically, they formed an extension of the Erevan guberniia and contrasted with the Georgian lowlands to the north. Strategically, they afforded a natural, easily defended frontier that in the hands of any other power would thrust menacingly toward the heart of Armenia. Economically, these highlands were rich in pastures, forests, and mineral resources, which were vital to Armenia, a land otherwise exceedingly limited in natural wealth.[17]

Throughout the summer and autumn of 1918, despite the seriousness of the controversy, neither Armenia nor Georgia could enforce her claims. Southern Lori and all Akhalkalak remained under Turkish domination; the two republics did not even share a common frontier. Moreover, the Armenians of northern Lori enjoyed greater security under German protection than did their compatriots south of the Kamenka, where Turkish violence and pillage were rampant. The cardinal complaint of the Lori Armenians during this time arose from attempts to induct the village youth into the Georgian army. On three separate occasions Arshak Djamalian, the Armenian chargé d'affaires in Tiflis, protested this infringement and reminded Georgian officials of their pledge that the occupation of Lori would not be permanent. He insisted that Georgia had no right to recruit men in "an integral part of the Republic of Armenia." [18]

The Armenian Maneuver in Lori

In October, 1918, Turkish regiments withdrew from Pambak and southern Lori, thus eliminating the corridor between Georgia and Armenia. General Halil Pasha apparently kept Armenian military authorities better informed of the evacuation timetable than he did Georgian officials, and on October 18 Armenian companies attached to Dro's headquarters at Dilijan rapidly occupied southern Lori from

---

[16] For the text of the treaty of 1783, see *Traité conclu en 1783 entre Catherine II, impératrice de Russie, et Irakly II, roi de Géorgie* (Geneva, 1919).

[17] Rep. of Arm. Archives, File 107/6, "La République arménienne et ses voisins"; Abeghian, "Mer harevannere" (Dec., 1928), pp. 120–122, and (Jan., 1929), pp. 129–131; Shakhatuni, *op. cit.*, pp. 16–62, 175–180 *passim*.

[18] Rep. of Arm. Archives, File 65/1, Communiqués of July 27, Aug. 23, and Sept. 28, 1918, and File 74/1, Djamalian to Aharonian, Sept. 28, 1918.

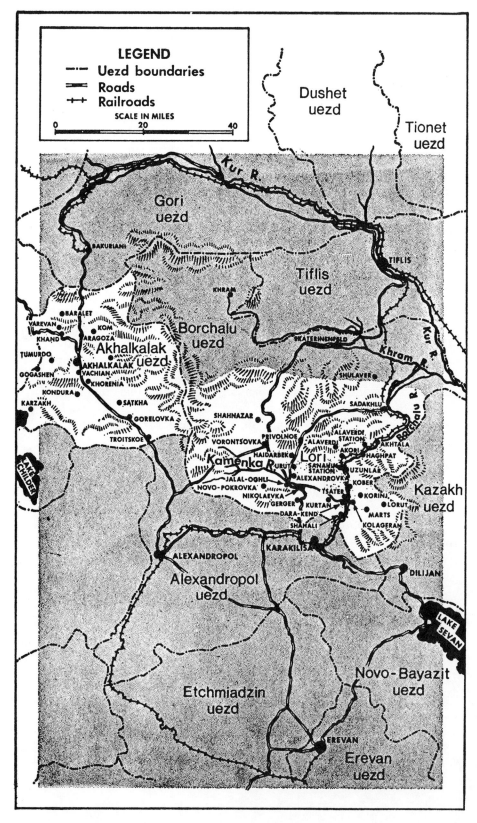

6. LORI AND AKHALKALAK

Shahali station, on the border of the Erevan guberniia, to the Kamenka River.[19] Small patrols even moved along the railway to Tsater and Kober at the edge of the Georgian-controlled sector of Lori. Evidently, the Armenian strategy was to probe and, in the absence of resistance, to advance farther to the north. But the German and Georgian detachments at the nearby station of Sanahin quickly informed Tiflis of the operation and appealed for reinforcements.[20]

Georgian Foreign Ministry officials wrote Djamalian the next day that the Republic of Georgia, while willing to settle differences peaceably, could not but view the unilateral Armenian maneuver as an unfriendly act.[21] Then on October 20 Minister of Military Affairs Grigorii Georgadze instructed the commander of the Georgian armored trains, located near Sanahin, to transmit an ultimatum to Armenian headquarters demanding immediate withdrawal of Dro's forces from the Tiflis guberniia. By this time the Armenian strategists had, it seems, laid aside plans to seize all northern Lori and therefore allowed Georgian units to retrieve Kober and Tsater. The presence of German officers on the Georgian side undoubtedly tempered Armenian spirits. This tactical retreat notwithstanding, Armenia had gained possession of southern Lori by October 21.[22]

On the twenty-second the Tiflis government, adopting a policy of caution, ordered its army to defend the positions held prior to the Turkish evacuation.[23] Still, minor incidents involving a handful of men on each side continued to occur for several days. Armenian detachments even moved back into Tsater and took the small village of Korinj (Karindj). The crisis, though serious, was almost amusing. In his communiqués the Georgian commander, General Tsulukidze, reported that Armenians had wounded one of his men and were behaving in a rude and insolent manner. They had even attempted to take captive several Georgian officers but had withdrawn to their own lines when the Georgians had scolded them. Tsulukidze also expressed

---

[19] Vratzian, *Hanrapetutiun*, pp. 171–172. As early as September, 1918, Halil Pasha gave assurances that Armenia would receive Pambak and Lori. See Rep. of Arm. Archives, File 74/1, Report of Sept. 21, 1918; also Lepsius, *Deutschland und Armenien*, p. 432.

[20] *Iz arm-gruz otnoshenii*, pp. 14–15.

[21] Rep. of Arm. Archives, File 65/1, Asst. Minister of Foreign Affairs Gvardjaladze to Diplomatic Representative of Armenia, Oct. 19, 1918; Khatisian, *Hanrapetutian zargatsume*, pp. 101–102.

[22] *Iz arm-gruz otnoshenii*, pp. 17–20, 26; Rep. of Arm. Archives, File 65/1, Commander of Armored Trains (Goguadze) to Armenian Commander (Dro) at Dilijan; *Armiano-gruzinskii konflikt*, p. 13; Vratzian, *Hanrapetutiun*, p. 183.

[23] *Armiano-gruzinskii konflikt*, p. 14; *Iz arm-gruz otnoshenii*, pp. 24–25.

concern over the disappearance of young men from the Armenian villages under his jurisdiction. And indeed they soon reappeared, descending the hillsides to capture a cannon and the six Georgian soldiers who accompanied it. The odyssey ended on October 26 when the Armenian invaders were ordered by their superiors to abandon Korinj and Tsater and a Georgian counteroffensive army, some fifty soldiers and four officers, succeeded in recapturing the two outposts.[24]

Meanwhile, tempers flared in Tiflis and Erevan. The Georgian ultimatum to clear the Tiflis guberniia arrived in Erevan on the evening of the twenty-first, shortly before the expiration hour. Premier Kachaznuni described the situation to the Khorhurd the next day, pointing to the repeated assurances by the Central Powers and by General Halil Pasha himself that both Pambak and Lori would be restored to Armenia. In Kachaznuni's estimation, the Georgian ultimatum was superfluous and offensive. The legislature responded by lauding the cabinet's "conciliatory attitude" yet demanding that Dro counter any Georgian show of force.[25]

Kachaznuni relayed to Tiflis the decision to reject the already expired ultimatum and added an appeal for peace. In a separate message to Premier Noi Zhordania, he gave notice that the Armenian army was under strict orders to hold the district between Shahali and the Kamenka River. He expressed "confidence" that the Menshevik chief of state had not forgotten his solemn pledge that Georgia harbored no lasting pretensions to Lori.[26] Then on October 26, making light of the Armenian foray into Korinj, Tsater, and Kober as having been either a misunderstanding or a necessary defensive measure, Kachaznuni announced that Armenian troops would not advance beyond the territory cleared by the Turkish army. He pressed for an Armeno-Georgian conference to resolve all existing differences.[27]

In a more detailed explanation on October 31, 1918, Chargé d'affaires Djamalian assured Acting Foreign Minister Noi Ramishvili that Armenia's action was not prompted by aggressive intentions. The brief occupation of Kober had resulted from the absence of a Georgian garrison there. The Armenians, not knowing on which side of the former

---

[24] *Iz arm-gruz otnoshenii*, pp. 26–37 *passim*.

[25] Rep. of Arm. Archives, File 65/1; Vratzian, *Hanrapetutiun*, pp. 184–185.

[26] *Iz arm-gruz otnoshenii*, pp. 23–24; *Armiano-gruzinskii konflikt*, pp. 17–18; Rep. of Arm. Archives, File 65/1, Kachaznuni to Djamalian, Oct. 23, 1918.

[27] Rep. of Arm. Archives, File 65/1, Kachaznuni to Dro, and Dro to Lt. Col. Korolkov, Oct. 26, 1918; *Iz arm-gruz otnoshenii*, p. 36. Apparently Khatisian, *Hanrapetutian zargatsume*, p. 103, and *Dokumenty i materialy*, pp. 448–449, are in error in dating the communiqué October 27, 1918.

demarcation line the station lay, had "respectfully withdrawn" when a German officer furnished the information. Asserting that all of Lori was indisputably and inalienably Armenian, Djamalian added that his government nonetheless desired to gain recognition of its just rights through diplomatic, nonmilitary means.[28] And finally, on November 1, the Georgian Parliament received from the Armenian Khorhurd an appeal for an amicable solution "in the name of the centuries-long brotherly relations of the two peoples." [29]

The Georgians, on their part, were not ones to spare words. Ramishvili announced to Djamalian on October 23 that Georgia had decided "for the love of peace" not to press beyond the positions originally held, but he warned that if the Armenian units remained in Korinj and Tsater or if they contrived to seize any more of the Tiflis guberniia the Republic of Georgia would be left no alternative but to regard this as an act of war.[30] The commander of the German military expedition in Georgia also brought pressure to bear by advising Djamalian that Erevan's maneuver was ill-timed and that Germany was obligated to support her protectorate. Georgian authorities declared martial law in Lori on October 24 and appointed General Tsulukidze to serve as the military governor. He was instructed to deal harshly with armed bands operating behind the Georgian lines but to refrain from a direct assault upon the Armenian positions at Korinj and Tsater.[31]

The Georgian Parliament gathered in extraordinary session on the twenty-sixth, the very day the Armenian units retreated from the two settlements. The deputies were stirred as Ramishvili exclaimed that the entire Tiflis guberniia was and would remain Georgian and Georgadze sternly promised that the army would crush disorder and anarchy in the Republic. In a resolution markedly similar to its Armenian counterpart, the Georgian Parliament commended the government for its devotion to the cause of peace and, at the same

[28] Rep. of Arm. Archives, File 65/1, Djamalian to Foreign Minister of Georgia. *Iz arm-gruz otnoshenii*, pp. 40–42, dates the document October 30.

[29] Like the Armenian National Council, the Georgian National Council was reorganized and, on October 18, 1918, formed into a legislature, with twenty-four places assigned to the Republic's minorities. The ten Armenian deputies were seated on November 1. See G. I. Uratadze, *Obrazovanie i konsolidatsiia Gruzinskoi Demokraticheskoi Respubliki* (Munich, 1956), p. 83.

[30] *Dokumenty i materialy*, p. 449; Rep. of Arm. Archives, File 353, Greenfield to Ohandjanian, and File 65/1, Ramishvili and Lordkipanidze to Djamalian, Oct. 23, 1918.

[31] *Iz arm-gruz otnoshenii*, pp. 32, 35; *Armiano-gruzinskii konflikt*, p. 15; Vratzian, *Hanrapetutiun*, p. 184.

time, admonished it "to prevent the intrusion of foreign arms within the boundaries of Georgia." [32]

The first round of the Armeno-Georgian conflict had ended favorably for Armenia. She had retained control of southern Lori even though probes farther north had shown that Georgia would react and that German influence was still to be considered. From the Georgian point of view, the Armenian maneuver had come with alarming suddenness. Unable to enforce its ultimatum to Erevan, the Menshevik government had acted with moderation and had initiated no retaliatory moves. The episode revealed that the Armenians were not so powerless as had been generally thought. The Georgian army began to mass additional troops and supplies along the now common frontier and placed the Armenian villages of northern Lori under strict surveillance in order to forestall a guerrilla outburst that might provide Armenia with a new pretext to intervene.

Muslim-Armenian Dissonance

Hostility between Armenians and Muslims was deep-seated and much more fundamental than the friction between Armenians and Georgians. Beginning in the eleventh century the Azerbaijanis had swept into southern and eastern Transcaucasia as Turco-Islamic conquerors and had eventually driven the indigenous Christian population from the fertile river valleys and plains. Thus as lowlands gave way to hills and mountains, the Armenian element became increasingly evident. Yet there were many exceptions to this general pattern; Muslim hamlets lay nestled in the Armenian highlands, while many Armenian villages had persevered down through the centuries in the Araxes river valley.

Economic factors also contributed to the mutual antagonism. As a sedentary people the Armenians were at odds with the nomadic or seminomadic Muslim tribesmen who drove their flocks to highland summer pastures. The age-old struggle between farmer and herdsman was clearly enunciated in Transcaucasia. Moreover, of the Muslim military-feudal nobility, many had acquired extensive landed domains that included Armenian villages. But during the eighteenth and especially the nineteenth centuries, thousands of Armenians succeeded in freeing themselves of obligations to these beks, aghas, and khans,

---

[32] *Iz arm-gruz otnoshenii*, pp. 25, 42. The chambers of the Georgian Parliament were in the palace of the former Romanov Viceroy for the Caucasus. See US Archives, RG 256, 861K.00/119.

and the emerging Armenian bourgeoisie learned to compete favorably with the old Tatar elite. Under Russian rule the Armenian commercial and industrial magnates began to strike roots even in Baku, whose cosmopolitan population soon relegated the indigenous Tatars to the status of a minority. And throughout the Caucasus the relative numerical strength of the Armenians grew at the expense of the dominant Muslim elements.

The racial, religious, and economic antipathies had burst into open warfare in 1905. Beginning in Baku and spreading to every other province of Transcaucasia, the battles took a heavy toll in life and caused material damage totaling millions of rubles. Tsarist officials were accused of fanning the hatred in order to divert the attention of the Caucasus from the mainstream of the Russian revolution of 1905. Not until that revolution had run its course in 1907 did the "Armeno-Tatar war" abate.[33] In 1918 hostilities again erupted as the Armenians clung to a strong Russian orientation while the Azerbaijani Tatars looked to Turkey to reestablish Muslim hegemony in Transcaucasia.

The Elisavetpol Guberniia

Any possibility of satisfactory Azerbaijani-Armenian relations was precluded by the bitter struggle over parts of the Elisavetpol guberniia (see map 7). The province, created in 1868 by combining the eastern highlands of the Tiflis and Erevan guberniias with the western steppes of the Baku guberniia, was an artificial entity in terms of ethnic and geographic homogeneity. Russian statistics for 1916 show that Muslims outnumbered Armenians two to one in the guberniia but that Armenians constituted nearly 70 percent of the population in the mountainous districts. Still, since the uezds of the guberniia were so structured as to extend from the mountains to the plains, only in the Shushi (Shusha) uezd were the Armenians an absolute majority.[34]

In its quest for the possession of the Elisavetpol highland region,

[33] Consult the following for descriptions and analyses of the Armeno-Tatar hostilities of 1905–1907: Aramayis, *Mi kani glukh hai-trkakan endharumnerits* (Tiflis, 1907), 2 pts.; Filipp Makharadze, *Ocherki revoliutsionnogo dvizheniia v Zakavkaz'e* (Tiflis, 1927), pp. 238–247, 298–308; Ananun, *op. cit.*, pp. 165–264; A. Giulkhandanian, *Hai-tatarakan endharumnere* (Tiflis, 1907), and his *Hai-trkakan endharumnere* (Paris, 1933); Mikayel Hovhannisian, *Kovkasian Vandean* (Tiflis, 1907); Armen Garo [G. Pasdermadjian], *Aprvads orer* (Boston, 1948), pp. 163–179; Luigi Villari, *Fire and Sword in the Caucasus* (London, [1906]), pp. 144–208 *passim*, 217–221, 265–291, 331–338.

[34] US Archives, RG 256, 867B.00/10. Detailed population statistics for the Elisavet-

commonly known as Mountainous Karabagh, the Republic of Armenia compiled an array of justifications. Erevan and Karabagh shared a common language, religion, and culture. Karabagh formed the eastern-most component of the Armenian plateau and, rising several thousand feet above sea level, contrasted sharply with the Azerbaijani steppeland far below. This mountain fastness, rich in mineral deposits, forests, and alpine pastures and renowned for its honey, beeswax, silk, and leather products, provided Armenia a natural frontier and guarded the routes of descent to the Araxes valley and the plain of Ararat. With-out Karabagh the physical unity of Armenia would be destroyed and, equally important, the major barrier between the Muslims of Azer-baijan and the Turkic peoples of the Ottoman Empire would be eliminated.[35]

The land of Karabagh, a part of the Armenian erstwhile provinces of Utik, Artsakh, and Siunik, had through the ages nurtured a steady procession of writers, artists, builders, teachers, religious patriarchs, and soldiers. Even after the extinction of the last Armenian kingdom on the plateau in the eleventh century, the separate principality of Siunik had endured, its mountains long a beacon to the Armenians submerged in the Muslim deluge below.[36] In later centuries thousands of Christians found refuge in Karabagh under the patronage of native lords, *meliks*, who, in return for acknowledging the nominal suzerainty of transitory Turkoman states and the Safavid Persian empire, enjoyed autonomy in the five principalities of Gulistan, Jraberd, Khachen,

---

pol guberniia, subdivided into the uezds of Elisavetpol, Nukha (Nukhi) Aresh, Kazakh, Jevanshir, Shusha (Shushi), Jebrail, and Zangezur are included in RG 256, 867B.00/4/10 and 184.01602/62, and in RG 84, Tiflis Consulate, 1919, pt. 4, File 711. See also [Delegation of the Republic of Armenia], *Données statistiques des popula-tions de la Transcaucasie* (Paris, 1920); and *Revendications de la Délégation de Paix de la République de l'Azerbaidjan du Caucase présentées à la Conférence de la Paix à Paris, 1919* ([Paris, 1919]).

[35] US Archives, RG 59, 867.00/1100, and RG 256, 184.01602/23; Britain, FO 608/82, 342/5/4/10328; Shakhatuni, *op. cit.*, pp. 16–17, 22–25, 35–56; Abeghian, "Mer hare-vannere" (Oct., 1928), pp. 136–137; Rep. of Arm. Archives, File 16/16 and File 70/2. For a valuable socioeconomic and ethnographic study of this district, see Ervand Lalayan, "Varanda," *Azgagrakan handes*, II (1897), 4–244.

[36] Rep. of Arm. Archives, File 1/1 and File 107/6. For a history of this region and the subkingdom of Siunik, see T. Kh. Hakobian, *Urvagdser Hayastani patmakan ashkharhagrutian* (Erevan, 1960), pp. 252–255, 275, 302, 309–311, and his *Siuniki tagavorutiune* (Erevan, 1966); Alboyajian, *op. cit.*, pp. 139–146, 263–265, 274–277; M. S. Soghomonian, "Artsakh-Gharabaghi patmutiunits," *Banber Hayastani arkhiv-neri*, 1 (1969), 127–139; T. M. Sahakian, "Siuniats tagavorutian himnume ev nra kaghakakan dere XI darum," *Patma-banasirakan handes*, 3 (1966), 220–228; B. Haru-tiunian "Siuniats tagavorutian himnadrman taretive," *Banber Erevani Hamalsarani*, 1 (1969), 145–153. See also US Archives, RG 256, 184.021/23.

Varanda, and Dizak.[37] During the seventeenth century Karabagh gave rise to the pioneers of the Armenian emancipatory struggle, adventurers who attempted to entice the monarchs of Russia and other European powers to embark on a crusade to liberate the great plateau. The first Russian military contingents appeared in the eighteenth century, and finally at the beginning of the nineteenth century, after a series of devastating Muslim incursions, Karabagh was annexed to the Romanov Empire. By then only one of the melikdoms remained and the region had become severely depopulated.[38]

The introduction of Russian rule did not fulfill Armenian aspirations, for Karabagh, instead of regaining autonomy, was absorbed into a succession of larger administrative units and ultimately into the Elisavetpol guberniia. Beginning in 1905, at the conferences dealing with the zemstvo system, the Armenians had attempted to disassociate the mountains from the plains of Elisavetpol by proposing the creation of a separate zemstvo-province for the highlands alone. Of the 529,000 inhabitants in the projected province, 365,000 would have been Armenian, 134,000 Muslim, and 28,000 of other nationalities. The scheme, although endorsed by the Russian viceroy and with certain reservations by a special committee of the Provisional Government in 1917, was, for stated reasons, never adopted.[39]

The Azerbaijani case for Karabagh was not unimpressive. The Armenian arguments needed only to be reversed. Though the Armenians had enjoyed a degree of autonomy in the past, the region had nonetheless been included in the Muslim khanates of Ganja and Karabagh. During the several centuries before the Russian conquest, the Muslims had prevailed throughout Transcaucasia and, in spite of Russian favoritism to the Christians, still outnumbered each of the Christian peoples taken separately. In the Elisavetpol guberniia Muslims constituted the majority in seven of the eight uezds and, even in the heart of Mountainous Karabagh, Tatars and Kurds formed a significant minority. The Armenians, the Republic of Azerbaijan

[37] For studies of the five (khamsa) melikdoms of Karabagh, see Alboyajian, op. cit., pp. 393-401; Leo [A. Babakhanian], Hayots patmutiun, Vol. III (Erevan, 1946), pp. 744-877 passim.

[38] The emancipatory struggle of the Armenians of Karabagh and their attempts to gain Russian protection are described in the following works: G. A. Ezov, ed., Snosheniia Petra Velikago s armianskim narodom: Dokumenty (St. Petersburg, 1898); Leo, op. cit., pp. 491-924 passim; Ashot Hovhannisian, Drvagner hai azatagrakan mtki patmutian (Erevan, 1957-1959), 2 vols.; A. Khachatrian, Armianskie voiski v XVIII veke: Iz istorii armiano-russkogo voennogo sodruzhestva (Erevan, 1968).

[39] Shakhatuni, op. cit., pp. 63-71, 93, 141; Abeghian, "Mer harevannere" (Feb., 1928), p. 97; Rep. of Arm. Archives, File 70/2.

charged, strove to carve out of Elisavetpol only those districts that were suitable to their political ends, but in so doing they threatened the geographic, economic, and political unity of the region. The addition of pockets of Christian concentration to Armenia in this manner would be unjust, illogical, and deleterious to the welfare of all concerned.[40]

For Azerbaijan, the steppes and mountains of Elisavetpol were not contrasting entities; on the contrary, they were the complementary components of a single unit, fitting perfectly into the Muslim pastoral economy. If hills and steppes were separated, countless Muslim herdsmen, deprived of summer pastures, would face certain ruin. Armenian suggestions, such as an irrigation project on the steppes, the diversion to new pastures in northern Azerbaijan, or an Armeno-Azerbaijani treaty for Muslim pasturage privileges in "Armenian" Karabagh, were neither convincing nor acceptable solutions to the Azerbaijanis.

Azerbaijan believed that Karabagh was strategically as vital to her as it was to Armenia. It was a towering natural frontier which, under the control of another power, would leave Azerbaijan perpetually vulnerable. That the Elisavetpol guberniia was bound to Azerbaijan was clearly demonstrated by the fact that nearly every primary road led eastward toward Baku, not westward to Erevan. The Armenians of Karabagh depended on Baku for a large share of their supplies, and thousands of them were either seasonal laborers or permanent employees in the oil fields and offices of that rapidly expanding metropolis on the Caspian Sea.[41]

The disputed mountainous region of the Elisavetpol guberniia had come to be divided into three distinct sectors by mid-1918. The smallest of these, the southwestern half of the Kazakh uezd with Dilijan as its major town, had been incorporated into the Armenian republic from the outset. The second district, Mountainous Karabagh proper, encompassed most of the Shushi uezd and parts of the Elisavetpol (Gulistan), Jevanshir, and Jebrail (Kariagin) uezds and was populated by approximately 165,000 Armenians, 59,000 Muslims (20,000 of whom lived in or near the town of Shushi), and 7,000 Russians.[42] Separated from Mountainous Karabagh by a solid buffer of Kurdish-Tatar settlements,

[40] US Archives, RG 256, 184.021/23; Rep. of Arm. Archives, File 1/1 and File 16/16. The khanates of Ganja and Karabagh are discussed in Alboyajian, op. cit., pp. 379–385.

[41] US Archives, RG 59, 867.00/1100; Rep. of Arm. Archives, Files 5/5, Hayastani Hanrapetutiun, 1919 t., and File 107/6.

[42] Rep. of Arm. Archives, File 70/2 and File 105/4, H. H. Patvirakutiun, 1919: Hushagrer. Statistics in File 3/3 show 137,000 Armenians and 47,000 Tatars in Moun-

the third sector, Zangezur, dominated the strategic southern passageway to the Araxes river valley and Erevan guberniia.[43]

Mountainous Karabagh in 1918

During the first half of 1918, even as interracial warfare was consuming Baku, Ganja, and Erevan, the Armenians and Muslims of Mountainous Karabagh lived in relative peace. Although acknowledging the nominal authority of the Transcaucasian Commissariat and Seim in Tiflis, Mountainous Karabagh was actually autonomous, governed by a biracial, interparty council. A tenuous balance prevailed until the Turkish invasion of Transcaucasia, the disintegration of the Federative Republic, and the creation of the three independent states. The Republic of Azerbaijan then selected nearby Elisavetpol (Ganja) as its provisional capital and appealed for Turkish assistance in order to establish sovereignty over the Baku guberniia and the remainder of the Elisavetpol guberniia—Karabagh and Zangezur.[44]

Nuri, the half brother of Enver Pasha, answered the summons, based his Army of Islam at Ganja, and led the campaign against Baku. As long as Turkish divisions stood in Transcaucasia, the feeble Republic of Armenia could scarcely whisper its claim to the highlands of Elisavetpol. Yet the rugged Armenian mountaineers rejected Nuri's demands to accept the suzerainty of Azerbaijan and to allow the entry of Turkish troops into Shushi. The so-called People's Government of Karabagh, elected by the First Assembly of Karabagh Armenians at the beginning of August, 1918, returned Nuri's envoys empty-handed.[45]

Following the Ottoman conquest of Baku the Muslim hero again commanded the Armenians to submit, but in reply the Second Assembly of Karabagh, September 20–24, insisted that the status quo be preserved until the announced conference between the Transcaucasian

tainous Karabagh, while figures in US Archives, RG 84, Tiflis Consulate, 1919, pt. 4, File 711, show 150,000 Armenians and 58,000 Muslims.

[43] For detailed material on the land, people, and history of Zangezur, see Ervand Lalayan's studies in *Azgagrakan handes:* "Sisian," III, 1 (1898), 102–272; "Zangezur," III, 2 (1898), 7–116; "Zangezuri gavar," IX (1905), 175–202. See also the recent useful study by Stepan Lisitsian, *Zangezuri hayere* (Erevan, 1969).

[44] For events in Karabagh prior to the Turkish invasion, see US Archives, RG 84, Tiflis Consulate, 1919, pt. 4, File 801, *Dokladnaia zapiska,* March 13, 1919; Rep. of Arm. Archives, File 1649, *H. H. D.: Gharabagh;* E. Ishkhanian, "Depkere Gharabaghum: jshdumner ev ditoghutiunner," *Hairenik Amsagir,* XI (Sept., 1933), 85.

[45] Rep. of Arm. Archives, File 1649; Ishkhanian, *op. cit.,* p. 86. Dates in the text are given in accordance with the Gregorian calendar, currently in use, even though most sources consulted date the events in Karabagh according to the Julian calendar, which was used throughout the Russian Empire until 1918.

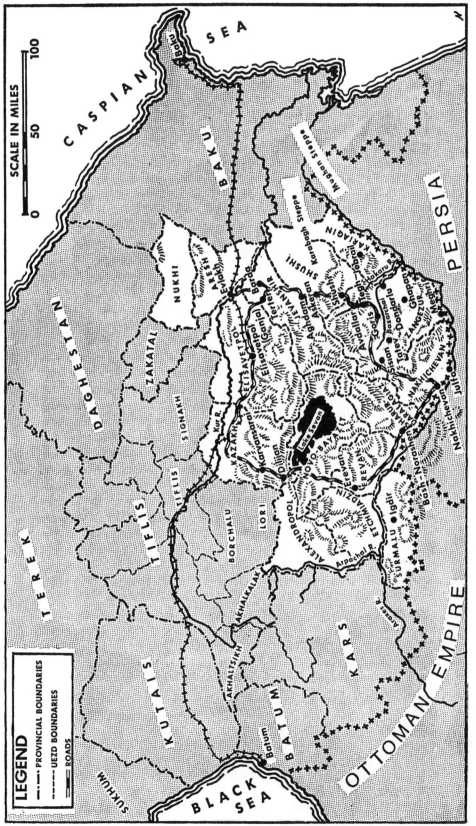

7. THE EREVAN AND ELISAVETPOL GUBERNIIAS

states and the Central Powers had met in Constantinople and arranged a settlement. The momentous Muslim victory in Baku having freed more Turkish troops for action against Karabagh, Nuri ordered Colonel Jemil Javid Bey to advance his regiments upon Shushi.[46] Already the Azerbaijani army and Muslim irregulars had overcome the two-week resistance of the large Armenian village of Gharaghshlagh, thus severing Karabagh from Armenian Zangezur. With Gharaghshlagh in ashes, Nuri Pasha renewed his ultimatum.[47]

When the tragic fate of the Armenians of Baku became known in Karabagh, many leaders despaired. The mayor of Shushi, Gerasim Melik-Shahnazarian, and influential spokesmen of the commercial classes now urged the Third Assembly of Karabagh Armenians, October 1–5, to yield in order to avert the otherwise inevitable massacre. At long last, as nearly 5,000 Turkish troops ascended through the pass of Askeran, the Third Assembly complied with the ultimatum and opened the way to the heartland of Karabagh. On October 8 (September 25), 1918, Jemil Javid Bey and Azerbaijan's representative, Ismail Khan Ziatkhanov,[48] led the Turkish units into Shushi. The Ottoman military authorities promised peace and justice to the Armenian inhabitants, but they had been in Shushi less than a week when they arrested some sixty civic leaders and intellectuals, erected gallows in the central square, and, despite pledges to the contrary, disarmed the townsfolk.[49]

Shushi had submitted. Yet the outlying districts continued to resist and to deny recognition to either Ottomans or Azerbaijanis. With a

---

[46] Jemil Javid, the former commander of the 11th Caucasus Division, is identified in several sources as Jemal Jahid, Jevad Jamil, or Jamil Jevad. A Soviet military historian shows that his command had been reorganized to include several regular and irregular Azerbaijani units, whereupon it was identified as the Caucasus Muslim Division or the 1st Azerbaijani Division, with Colonel Jemil Javid being elevated to the rank of major general in the Azerbaijani army and granted the title of pasha. See E. F. Ludshuveit, *Turtsiia v gody pervoi mirovoi voiny 1914–1918 gg.: Voenno-politicheskii ocherk* (Moscow, 1966), p. 259. The Azerbaijani army was integrated into Nuri Pasha's Army of Islam, a component of the Army Group of the East, which combined under General Halil Pasha's command nearly all Ottoman forces operating along the Caucasus–North Persian front. See Belen, *Türk Harbi*, V, 166–171 and table 14.

[47] G. A. Hovhannisian, "Msmnayi jakatamarte," *Banber Erevani Hamalsarani*, 3 (1968), 150–151; Rep. of Arm. Archives, File 1649; Ishkhanian, *op. cit.*, pp. 86–89.

[48] Ludshuveit, *op. cit.*, p. 259, identifies Ziatkhanov as Adil Khan Ziatkhanov, the Azerbaijani Minister of Military Affairs.

[49] Rep. of Arm. Archives, File 69a/1a, *H. H. Adrbedjani Divanagitakan Nerkayatsutsich ev Adrbedjani Karavarutiun, 1919 t.*; G. A. Hovhannisian, *op. cit.*, pp. 151–152; Ishkhanian, *op. cit.*, pp. 90–91; E. K. Sargsian, *Ekspansionistskaia politika Osmanskoi imperii v Zakavkaz'e nakanune i v gody pervoi mirovoi voiny* (Erevan, 1962), pp. 410–411.

partisan commander in each of Karabagh's four historic central districts, Khachen, Jraberd, Varanda, and Dizak, the Armenians defied the Turks, whose forays into the countryside resulted in ambush and disaster.[50] As World War I drew to a close, the Armenians of Mountainous Karabagh looked expectantly toward the peaks of Zangezur, where throughout the summer months a native militia and bands of Turkish Armenians led by Major General Andranik Ozanian had been battling one Muslim village cluster after another.

Zangezur

The uezd of Zangezur, an area of 2,744 square miles subdivided into the districts of Sisian, Goris, Ghapan (Kafan), and Meghri, formed the strategic passageway between eastern Transcaucasia and the Erevan guberniia. Zangezur, like Karabagh, was inhabited by a mixed population, made up in 1916 of 101,000 Armenians and 120,000 Muslims, Sunni and Shi'a combined. Yet, because only Muslims inhabited the peripheral southeastern slopes, the Armenians held a numerical superiority in the central subdistricts.[51] In 1917, after the February/March Revolution in Russia, an interparty executive of Muslims and Armenians ruled over Zangezur from the town of Goris (Gerusy), but the progressive deterioration of relations between the two peoples culminated late that year in the Muslim decision to establish a separate administration based at the village of Dondarlu. Famine during the winter of 1917–1918, a by-product of the upheavals in Russia and Transcaucasia, aggravated racial tensions so that by spring the Armenians had resolved to bar the yearly trek of thousands of Muslim herdsmen toward the alpine pastures. Mounted detachments of Turkish Armenians from Khnus, Sassun, and Van prepared to enforce the decision.[52]

By June of 1918 interracial warfare had enveloped Zangezur. Armenian couriers dispatched to Erevan pleaded for officers and matériel, but, with Turkish armies poised just a few miles from the capital, the

---

[50] Hovak Stepanian, "Andranike Siuniats erkrum," *Vem*, IV, 4 (1936), 51–52; Ishkhanian, *op. cit.*, pp. 91–93; G. A. Hovhannisian, *op. cit.*, pp. 152–153. The partisan commanders of Karabagh in 1918 were Bagrat Ghazanjian in Khachen; Aleksan Dayi (Dey) Balasian, Jraberd; Sokrat Bek Melik-Shahnazarian, Varanda; Artem Lalayan, Dizak.

[51] US Archives, RG 59, 867.00/1100. See also RG 256, 184.021/23 and 867B.00/10. In the Armenian project for provincial reorganization in Transcaucasia, the peripheral Muslim districts of Zangezur were to have been detached, thus creating a unit with 88,000 Armenians, 2,000 other Christians, and 46,000 Muslims.

[52] Vratzian, *Hanrapetutiun*, pp. 296–298; Rep. of Arm. Archives, File 1649.

Republic could give little more than moral support. At that critical moment General Andranik arrived in Zangezur with an irregular division estimated to have from three to five thousand men, followed by many thousands of refugees from Turkish Armenia and the occupied provinces of Russian Armenia.[53] Andranik had refused to acknowledge the Republic of Armenia as anything but a pawn in the grip of Turkey, and he labeled the humiliating Treaty of Batum the work of traitors. Determined to disassociate himself from the Republic, Andranik initially attempted to unite with the British expeditionary force operating in North Persia, but he had to backtrack to Nakhichevan when his columns were intercepted by Turkish divisions near Khoi. In July the stranded multitude of soldiers and refugees left the Araxes river valley and moved up into the mountains of Zangezur.[54]

Although the presence of some 30,000 refugees in Zangezur intensified famine conditions, the local Armenian leaders welcomed Andranik, for they knew that the Turkish army had made its way into the Erevan guberniia below and was threatening Zangezur from the direction of Ganja and Mountainous Karabagh. It seemed as if Zangezur was destined to become the last center of Armenian resistance. Throughout the months of September and October, Andranik's men and the local populace feverishly prepared for the anticipated Turkish invasion. Andranik struck at the defiant fortified Muslim villages that controlled the major routes connecting the four subdistricts of Zangezur. The process of transforming Zangezur into a solidly Armenian land had begun.[55]

The destruction wrought by Andranik drew sharp protests in Erevan from General Halil Pasha, who threatened the Armenian government with retaliation. In reply Premier Kachaznuni claimed to possess no

[53] *General Andranik*, pp. 75–81. See also Vratzian, *Hanrapetutiun*, pp. 298–299; G. Sassuni, *Tajkahayastane rusakan tirapetutian tak (1914–1918)* (Boston, 1927), p. 183. A report in US Archives, RG 59, 867.00/1100, asserts that Andranik arrived in Zangezur with 12,000 men and 40,000 refugee followers, whereas a communiqué by Andranik himself in RG 256, 861K.00/5, states that he reached Zangezur with 2,000 armed men and organized another 6,000 while in the highland.

[54] For accounts of Andranik's activities and campaign in North Persia and Nakhichevan before his "Special Striking Division" ascended to Zangezur, see *General Andranik*, pp. 41–75; Stepanian, "Andranike Siuniats erkrum," IV, 3 (1936), 70–74; M. Avetian, *Hai azatagrakan azgayin hisnamia (1870–1920) hushamatian ev Zor. Andranik* (Paris, 1954), pp. 195–208; US Archives, RG 256, 184.021/6.

[55] These operations are described in *General Andranik*, pp. 82–118; Stepanian, "Andranike Siuniats erkrum," IV, 4 (1936), 59–71; US Archives, RG 256, 861K.00/5; Rep. of Arm. Archives, File 8/8. Several of the Turkish Armenian units parted company with Andranik during the summer of 1918 and descended over Daralagiaz to Erevan where they entered the service of the Armenian republic.

jurisdiction over the partisans. He reminded Halil that Nuri Pasha, having declared the entire Elisavetpol guberniia Azerbaijani territory, had banned regular Armenian units from Zangezur. Certainly, therefore, Armenia should not be held responsible for the prevailing state of affairs in that region. Kachaznuni's sincerity might well have been doubted, but his arguments were reasonable.[56]

Karabagh's Appeal to Zangezur

Meanwhile, the Armenian militia commanders of Karabagh appealed for assistance from Zangezur. By the end of October, 1918, Andranik had concentrated his troops at Korindzor, Tegh, and Khndzoresk, the border villages of Zangezur. Optimism and impatience grew in the Armenian ranks as news circulated that the Turks would soon abandon Karabagh. Now was the time to establish firm Armenian rule there. But Andranik did not act with the decisiveness and daring of his earlier campaigns. Instead he postponed the offensive until he had received written guarantees of support from the leaders of both Zangezur and Karabagh. These he had in hand by mid-November, but just as he prepared to move out on the eighteenth, he received word from the mayor of Shushi, Gerasim Melik-Shahnazarian, and one of the partisan chiefs of Karabagh, Sokrat Bek Melik-Shahnazarian, to postpone action for another ten days. During that interval they hoped to persuade the native Muslim leaders not to resist the advance of the Armenian force from Zangezur. If any such negotiations took place, they were fruitless and only delayed Andranik's foremarch until the end of November. The time lost proved crucial.[57]

The road from Zangezur to Shushi passed through some twenty Muslim villages in the narrow Zabukh and Hakaru (Akera) river valleys and the intervening heights of Markiz and Haji-Samlu. Led by Sultan Bek Sultanov the Kurds and Tatars of this mountain stronghold were experienced fighters. Hence as Andranik's men struck out toward Karabagh at dawn on November 29, 1918, they were met by a hail of bullets and pinned down by the entrenched Muslim defenders. The battle raged for three days before Andranik's columns, suffering heavy casualties, finally overran the Muslim positions, seized the commanding

---

[56] Rep. of Arm. Archives, File 65/1, Djamalian to Armenian mission, Constantinople, Sept. 23 and 26, 1918; Lepsius, *Deutschland und Armenien*, p. 435.

[57] *General Andranik*, pp. 121–146; Rep. of Arm. Archives, File 8/8; Sarur [Asur], "Gharabaghi ktsume Adrbedjani," *Hairenik Amsagir*, VII (June, 1929), 128, 130; Ishkhanian, "Depkere Gharabaghum," XI (Oct., 1933), 111–115; Stepanian, "Andranike Siuniats erkrum," IV, 5 (1936), 52–57.

heights, and drove into several Muslim villages, including Avdallar (Abdalar), the major barrier to Shushi. The way to the heartland of Karabagh now lay unobstructed. In a day's rapid march Andranik could reach Shushi, only 26.5 miles (40 versts) away.[58]

But the Armenians had waited too long. Hardly had they moved into Avdallar when an automobile flying a white flag and bearing English Captain G. F. Squire and French Captain Nicolas Gasfield approached from the direction of Shushi.[59] The officers delivered to Andranik an urgent message from Major General W. M. Thomson, who had recently come ashore at Baku as commander of the Allied forces in eastern Transcaucasia. Thomson informed Andranik that, since the World War was over, any further Armenian military activity would adversely affect the solution of the Armenian question, soon to be taken under consideration by the peace conference in Europe. Reiterating this admonition, the Allied envoys persuaded Andranik to halt the offensive and to return to Goris, retaining jurisdiction over Zangezur until General Thomson forwarded further instructions. Andranik, sharing his people's faith in the Allies, could not but accede.[60] When the Armenians withdrew to Goris on December 4, Muslim bands promptly razed the three remaining Christian villages between Karabagh and Zangezur, further separating the two mountain districts.[61]

In Karabagh, meanwhile, a self-appointed Armenian administration took charge following the Ottoman evacuation in November, 1918.[62] Acting as an interim government until a regional assembly could meet to select an official body, the five-man Armenian council, composed of the mayor of Shushi and one representative each from Varanda, Khachen, Jraberd, and Dizak, gained the informal recognition of British officers who arrived in December. Soon, however, the British military

[58] General Andranik, pp. 146–152; Arsen Mikayelian, "Gharabaghi verdjin depkere," Hairenik Amsagir, I (May, 1923), 162–163; Sarur, op. cit., p. 129; Stepanian, "Andranike Siuniats erkrum," IV, 5 (1936), 57–62. A report in US Archives, RG 84, Tiflis Consulate, 1919, pt. 4, File 710, states that Andranik was within 35 versts (23.2 miles) of Shushi.

[59] Squire was a company commander of the 7th Battalion, Gloucestershire Regiment, 39th Brigade, and Gasfield belonged to the 6ᵐᵉ Régiment des Hussards and was attached to the French military mission in the Caucasus.

[60] US Archives, RG 84, Tiflis Consulate, 1919, pt. 4, File 801, and RG 256, 861K.00/5; Rep. of Arm. Archives, File 8/8; General Andranik, pp. 152–159. See also Britain, Cab 27/36, E.C. 2368, 27/37, E.C. 2429, and 27/38, E.C. 2717.

[61] Vratzian, Hanrapetutiun, p. 282; Rep. of Arm. Archives, File 9/9. The devastated villages were Harar, Spitakashen, and Petrosashen.

[62] G. A. Hovhannisian, op. cit., p. 153, states that the Turkish troops left Karabagh on October 31 (November 13), 1918. British sources show that several Turkish contingents lingered on in Karabagh at least until the end of December. See Britain, Cab 27/38, E.C. 2707, and Cab 27/39, E.C. 2818 and E.C. 2998.

mission in Shushi was insisting that the Armenian council act only in local, nonpolitical matters, such as economic rehabilitation and refugee relief. General Thomson, it was explained, would relay directives concerning the provisional political organization of Karabagh.[63] When Thomson finally forwarded those directives in January of 1919, the Armenians of Karabagh and Kachaznuni's coalition government in Erevan were thoroughly shaken. A new phase in the struggle for Mountainous Karabagh had begun.[64]

The Erevan Guberniia

Until the end of 1918 the Armeno-Azerbaijani controversy in the Erevan guberniia was of necessity restricted to districts not occupied by the Ottoman army. Azerbaijan attempted to deny to Armenia what was left of the uezds of Nakhichevan and Sharur-Daralagiaz and the eastern half of Novo-Bayazit (see map 5). Immediately upon Turkish withdrawal from the guberniia in December, however, Azerbaijan extended her claims to include the entire uezds of Nakhichevan, Sharur-Daralagiaz, and Surmalu, and generous strips of the Etchmiadzin and Erevan uezds, including the very outskirts of the Armenian capital.[65]

Azerbaijan substantiated these pretensions by underscoring the fact that historically the territories in question had lain within the Muslim khanates of Nakhichevan and Erevan. Even after the two khanates had been annexed to Russia in the nineteenth century, then combined and reorganized as the Erevan guberniia, and eventually populated by thousands of Armenian immigrants, the southern districts remained basically Muslim. Indeed, according to Russian statistics for 1916, the Muslim peoples—Shi'a Tatars and Sunni Turks and Kurds—formed a majority in three of the seven uezds of the Erevan guberniia:[66]

---

[63] Rep. of Arm. Archives, File 9/9, and File 1649, "Mikayeliani zekuitse Gharabaghi verdjin depkeri masin." The small British mission, with officers at Shushi and Goris, was headed by Major W. D. Gibbon, commander of the 9th Battalion, Worcestershire Regiment. He was relieved of the post in February, 1919, by Major G. N. G. Monck-Mason.

[64] See chapter 6 below.

[65] Rep. of Arm. Archives, Files 74/1, 105/4, and 107/6. See also US Archives, RG 256, 861K.00/106 F.W.; [Delegation of the Republic of Azerbaijan], Carte de la République de l'Azerbaïdjan.

[66] US Archives, RG 256, 867B.00/10; Rep. of Arm. Archives, File 118/17, H. H. Patvirakutiun, 1920: Hashtutian Konferens. Other sources show that as late as 1914 the Muslims held a slight numerical superiority in the Erevan uezd as well. See Abeghian, "Mer harevannere" (Feb., 1928), p. 99.

Uezd	Muslim	Armenian
Nakhichevan	81,000	54,000
Surmalu	73,000	33,000
Sharur-Daralagiaz	51,000	29,000
Erevan	88,000	107,000
Novo-Bayazit	51,000	129,000
Etchmiadzin	42,000	115,000
Alexandropol	9,000	202,000

Most of the Muslims were Tatars, bound by language, religious sect, custom, and ancestry to the people of the Republic of Azerbaijan. The ethnic principle, contended the Baku government, required that the disputed lands be joined to the Azerbaijani Muslim state.

Armenia argued that the Araxes valley, around which the controversy raged, rose 2,500 to 4,000 feet above sea level and was not at all linked topographically with eastern Transcaucasia, where the steppes and plains seldom attained a height of 1,000 feet. The valley of the Araxes, situated like a Swiss mountain valley, was clearly a part of the Armenian plateau. Although Muslims did predominate in certain village clusters, the region as a whole contained an Armenian majority. Manipulation of the principle of self-determination as a pretext to cut into the heart of the Armenian republic could not be tolerated. As evidence of its historic Armenian character, the Araxes valley, a part of the ancient province of Vaspurakan, cradled the ruins of Armavir, Artashat, Vagharshapat, and Dvin, the capital cities of successive Armenian kingdoms. In view of the waves of Muslim invasion, massacre, enslavement, and deportation, it was not surprising that the Christian Armenian majority had been dissipated in several districts.[67]

Economically, the richest farmland of Russian Armenia lay in the Araxes valley, which alone was suited to subtropical agriculture and could yield profitable surplus for export. Its 40,000 dessiatines (108,000 acres) of irrigated land were vital to Armenia, yet they were small indeed when compared with Azerbaijan's 700,000 dessiatines (1,890,000 acres). The valley linked Armenia and Persia; through it ran the railway from the border at Julfa northward to Erevan and Alexandropol, whence it extended westward to Kars and Sarikamish and northeastward to Karakilisa and Tiflis, the main junction on the Batum-Baku line. As a strategic corridor, the Araxes valley dominated the most accessible southwestern approach to Zangezur and Karabagh. Armenia had little chance of gaining those two mountainous districts without

[67] Rep. of Arm. Archives, File 5/5 and File 118/17; Abeghian, "Mer harevannere" (Sept., 1928), pp. 128-130, 136; Britain, FO 608/82, 342/5/4/10328.

first securing Sharur-Daralagiaz and Nakhichevan. And finally, control over the southern half of the Erevan guberniia was essential to deter the menace of Pan-Islam and Pan-Turan. Armenia could not allow Azerbaijan and Turkey to share a common frontier.[68]

Not all territorial disputes in Transcaucasia involved Armenia. The Republic of Georgia and the Volunteer Army of Russia vied for control of the Black Sea littoral from Sochi to Sukhum (Sukhumi, Sukhumkale) and the mountainous land extending to the southeast, while the native Abkhazians and Ossetians strove to escape both Georgian and Russian rule. Azerbaijan, Georgia, and the Mountaineer Confederation of the North Caucasus tangled over the self-contained *okrug* (county) of Zakatal, which, though overwhelmingly Muslim in population but historically at times associated with Georgia, was held inalienable by each.[69] Azerbaijan also challenged Georgia's right to much of the Tiflis guberniia, claiming either in part or in their entirety the uezds of Signakh, Tiflis, Borchalu, Akhaltsikh, and Akhalkalak. And since Armenia, too, demanded Akhalkalak and the southern half of Borchalu, all three Transcaucasian republics were embroiled in these contests. Azerbaijan's territorial aims, far more extensive than those of the other states, included nearly two-thirds of the Transcaucasus and, if realized, would confine Armenia to some 5,000 square miles, little more than the rugged land originally salvaged by the Republic in June of 1918.[70] But even this was not the full scope of the land hunger in Transcaucasia. When the Ottoman armies withdrew from Kars and Batum in the winter of 1918–1919, the conflicting claims of Georgia, Azerbaijan, and Armenia immediately spilled over into these western provinces as well.

The opposing aspirations of the Transcaucasian republics had become sharply defined by the end of 1918. Each of the newly independent states, finding its borders elastic, attempted to stretch outward at the expense of the others. And while each could logically justify its position, in the end it was political strength and force of arms that counted.

[68] Rep. of Arm. Archives, File 16/16.

[69] Haidar Bammate, "The Caucasus during the War," *Current History*, X (April, 1919), 123; US Archives, RG 256, 867K.00/6/7/51; Kadishev, *Interventsiia v Zakavkaz'e*, p. 171. According to Russian statistics for 1916 (867B.00/10), the population of Zakatal (Zakataly) was 92,600, of whom 2,500 were Armenian, 4,600 Georgian, 41,800 Mountaineer, and 42,800 Sunni Muslim. The Shi'a sect, the major element in Azerbaijan, had only 600 adherents in Zakatal.

[70] Rep. of Arm. Archives, File 104/3, "Les frontières de la République de l'Azerbaïdjan," and Files 105/4 and 107/6; US Archives, RG 256, 861.00/106 F.W.; *Dokumenty i materialy*, pp. 436–438.

4

The
Armeno-Georgian
Entanglement

To their lasting embarrassment, Armenia and Georgia, beset by extreme crisis conditions and, above all, thoroughly convinced that vital national interests were at stake, plunged into warfare in December, 1918. The conflict exposed the two republics to the ridicule of political enemies and of skeptics who questioned the feasibility of independent states in the Caucasus. Indeed, the inglorious two-week war rudely shook the faith of foreign supporters and sympathetic officials.

A Stillborn Transcaucasian Conference

As the border crisis in Lori eased in late October, 1918, and Armenia and Georgia appealed simultaneously for a peaceful solution to their disputes, the Republic of Georgia, in a conciliatory gesture, sent Simeon (Semën) Gurgenovich Mdivani, a member of Parliament, to Erevan for negotiations.[1] Yet at the same time the Georgian government initiated a diplomatic episode that gave affront to Armenia and evoked Armenian charges that Georgia was aspiring to hegemony over all Transcaucasia. Georgia's inadequate attention to protocol and to the wording of communiqués was in part responsible for triggering

---

[1] *Iz arm-gruz otnoshenii*, p. 44; Vratzian, *Hanrapetutiun*, p. 191. Mdivani was a member of the Social Federalist organization, a minor Georgian party whose program included a number of principles also advocated by Dashnaktsutiun, the dominant party in Armenia.

the Armenian accusations and for negating what might otherwise have been a most constructive act.

In a message dated October 27, 1918, Acting Foreign Minister Noi V. Ramishvili advised the governments of Armenia, Azerbaijan, and the Mountaineer Republic of the North Caucasus and Daghestan that, with conclusion of the World War imminent, the future of the peoples of the former Russian Empire would soon be determined. Motivated by the conviction that the nations of Transcaucasia could attain their respective goals only if they stood united, Georgia, he continued, now summoned the sister republics to a conference in Tiflis, to begin at midday on November 3, 1918. Each state should empower two delegates to work toward a solution to the following questions "which the government of the Georgian republic has decided to place before the conference":

1. The mutual recognition of the independence of the nations whose governments are invited to the conference.

2. The settlement of all controversies, not excluding boundary disputes, by agreement of the interested governments or, in the absence of such agreement, through arbitration.

3. The reciprocal obligation not to conclude pacts of any kind with other governments to the detriment of any one of the peoples participating in the conference.

4. The establishment of a solid front and mutual support at the world peace congress for the purpose of securing recognition of the republics' independence and of defending their common interests.[2]

This invitation was not intended, the interpretation of several authors aside, to give offense; yet so it did. Without preliminary consultation Georgia had dictated the time, place, participants, and agenda of the conference even though representatives of the other governments were then in Tiflis. A prominent non-Menshevik Georgian statesman has likened the invitation to "a circular of the Ministry of Internal Affairs" rather than an international communication.[3] With the recent trouble in Lori fresh in mind, the Armenians found it most difficult to regard the Georgian maneuver as a gesture of goodwill. Chargé d'affaires Djamalian informed Ramishvili on October 31 that the Georgian proposal had been relayed to Erevan and that Ar-

[2] Rep. of Arm. Archives, File 65/1, Georgian Ministry of Foreign Affairs to Diplomatic Representative of Armenia, Oct. 27, 1918; Dokumenty i materialy, pp. 428–429.

[3] Z. Avalov, Nezavisimost' Gruzii v mezhdunarodnoi politike, 1918–1921 g.g. (Paris, 1924), p. 167.

menia would undoubtedly be favorably disposed. Still, he could not but regret that the Tiflis government had not thought it wise to conduct preparatory discussions regarding the organization of the conference.[4] As it was, even if Armenia had actually been willing, she could not have selected and dispatched a delegation by November 3. In fact, because of communication and transportation difficulties, only on November 7, four days after the conference was to have opened, did a copy of the Georgian note reach Erevan.[5]

An evaluation of Armenian policy indicates that the agenda proposed by Georgia created misgivings more fundamental than the overbearing tone of the summons. Territorial disputes, Armenia believed, should be settled by the states directly involved rather than through arbitration of a four-nation panel. This procedure would obviate the threat of power blocs at a general conference, where the Mountaineers could be expected to support Azerbaijan's claims to the disputed sectors of the Elisavetpol and Erevan guberniias, and both Muslim states could gain Georgia's vote in return for upholding Georgian claims to the Armenian-populated southern districts of the Tiflis guberniia. The memory of Muslim-Georgian coalitions in the Transcaucasian Commissariat and Seim was painfully vivid for the Armenians. Nor did Armenia desire to recognize the anomalous confederative republic of Mountaineers, where Nuri Pasha and other Turkish officers still held sway. The lands of the Terek and Daghestan were not integral to Transcaucasia proper, yet the inclusion of the Mountaineer representatives at the proposed conference would serve to augment Muslim power throughout the region.[6]

The last item on the proposed agenda also disturbed Erevan. Armenia had no intention of joining in a united front at the peace conference in Europe, for in late 1918 she appeared to hold a tremendous advantage on the international scene. Of all the Transcaucasian states, Armenia alone had elicited widespread sympathy in Europe and America. Armenophiles the world over were demanding that justice be done. The unification of Russian Armenia and Turkish Armenia seemed a very real prospect. Governments supporting the reestablishment of a single, indivisible Russia were inclined to view Armenia as an exception and permit the disassociation of Russian Armenia

[4] Rep. of Arm. Archives, File 65/1, Djamalian to Georgian Ministry of Foreign Affairs, Oct. 31, 1918; Dokumenty i materialy, p. 429.

[5] Iz arm-gruz otnoshenii, p. 53.

[6] Rep. of Arm. Archives, File 3/3, Report of May 10, 1919; Khatisian, Hanrapetutian zargatsume, pp. 100–101; Vratzian, Hanrapetutiun, pp. 187–188; Mikayel Varandian, Le conflit arméno-géorgien et la guerre du Caucase (Paris, 1919), pp. 89–91.

from Russia, but they were not willing to make similar concessions in the case of Azerbaijan and especially not in that of the Mountaineer Confederation, which was totally unknown to most Europeans.[7] Armenia expected to attend the peace conference in a very special capacity. She was the "Little Ally," had struggled heroically, though desperately, against the Turkish invasion, and remained free of the shadows cast upon Georgia, Azerbaijan, and the Mountaineers by their wartime associations with the Central Powers. Armenian efforts for a united Transcaucasian front against Turkey had failed. Now the concept of a united front at Paris seemed ludicrous indeed.

On November 8, the day after Ramishvili's communiqué was received in Erevan, the Khorhurd of Armenia denounced the tactless Georgian proposal. Especially vociferous were the Social Democrat legislators, who hitherto had staunchly defended their Georgian comrades. Menshevik Abraham Malkhasian now vilified the "dictatorial aspirations" of Zhordania's cabinet and termed its action "a violation of the principle of equality and evidence that one government is attempting to impose its will upon another." After the expression of similar sentiment by all other factions, the Khorhurd unanimously resolved to abstain from the Tiflis conference, but in so doing it called upon the cabinet to arrange a new gathering, according due regard to all parties, the time, place, and agenda to be determined by preliminary mutual consent. It insisted, however, that the agenda not include boundary disputes, for these should be settled bilaterally.[8]

Two days later, on November 10, delegates of the other three republics met for the first time in Tiflis. Georgia was represented by

[7] The Mountaineer peoples of the North Caucasus and Daghestan declared independence from Russia in May of 1918. They welcomed the Ottoman armies and sent representatives to Constantinople to establish formal bonds. During the autumn of 1918 the Turkish 15th Infantry Division occupied much of Daghestan, and the division leader, Iusuf Izzet Pasha, was given the title of military commander of the "Republic of the Caucasus." See E. F. Ludshuveit, *Turtsiia v gody pervoi mirovoi voiny 1914–1918 gg.: Voenno-politicheskii ocherk* (Moscow, 1966), pp. 260–262; Belen, *Türk Harbi*, V, 185–200. Many Ottoman officers and troops remained among the North Caucasus tribesmen after the Turkish surrender. For material relating to this republic, see the work of one of its founders, Haidar Bammate, *Le Caucase et la révolution russe* (Paris, 1929), and his memoranda in US Archives, RG 256, 861G.00/3; Britain, FO 371/3661–3662, 61656/85034/1015/58, and FO 371/4381, File 490/PID. See also RG 256, 184.01602/23 and 861K.00/6/7/8/51; "Traité de Paix et d'Amitié entre le Gouvernement Impérial Ottoman et le Gouvernement de l'Union des Montagnards du Caucase," *Die Welt des Islams*, n.s., V, 3–4 (1958), 259–262; "Gorskaia kontrrevoliutsiia i interventy," comp. by A. Ivanov, *Krasnyi Arkhiv*, LXVIII (1935), 125–153; S. D. Dimanshtein, ed., *Revoliutsiia i natsional'nyi vopros*, Vol. III (Moscow, 1930), pp. 369–379.

[8] Rep. of Arm. Archives, File 65/1; Vratzian, *Hanrapetutiun*, p. 148.

Minister of Interior Noi V. Ramishvili and by Evgenii P. Gegechkori, who had just taken charge of the Ministry of Foreign Affairs; Azerbaijan by her plenipotentiary to Georgia, Mohammed Iusuf Jafarov, and by Dr. Mustafa Bek Vekilov; and the Mountaineers by Minister of Interior Pshemakho Kotsev and by Minister of Finance Vassan-Ghirai Jabagi. The session opened with a welcoming address by Premier Zhordania. Then, since the Armenians were absent, the delegates deferred the conference for another three days. Notified of this action, Simeon Mdivani, the Georgian envoy in Erevan, advised his government not to proceed with the meeting until he and the Armenian leaders had settled certain basic issues. Foreign Minister Sirakan F. Tigranian had already made it quite clear that Armenia would not participate in any conference that dealt with territorial questions.[9]

When the delegates of the three republics assembled again on November 14, the Armenians were still absent. Incensed by the behavior of the Erevan government, Jafarov urged the conference to turn to its agenda. Ramishvili recommended that discussions remain informal pending the arrival of the Armenian spokesmen and that decisions made during the unofficial sessions be adopted as binding if the Armenians did not appear by a specified date. Jafarov rejected this suggestion and proposed that the republics having representatives present consider this conference as totally new, thus eliminating the need for unofficial commissions or further delays. The delegates arrived at no clear solution but consented to request once again that Armenia send a pair of negotiators empowered to enter into treaty arrangements. They then recessed until November 20.[10] Foreign Minister Gegechkori instructed Mdivani to inform Kachaznuni's government that the conference would open officially at the next session, with or without Armenian collaboration.[11]

Mdivani earnestly endeavored to allay the apprehensions in Erevan. He explained that, in view of the momentous changes on the world scene and the absence of regular channels of communication, preliminary negotiations would have consumed much valuable time. Georgia, he continued, had acted in good faith and in the belief that once the delegations had gathered in Tiflis they could alter or add to the agenda.[12] By November 17 he had met with some little success, for

[9] Dokumenty i materialy, p. 430; Iz arm-gruz otnoshenii, pp. 48–49, 53–54.
[10] Dokumenty i materialy, pp. 432–434.
[11] Rep. of Arm. Archives, File 65/1, Georgian Foreign Minister to Diplomatic Representative in Armenia, Nov. 20, 1918; Dokumenty i materialy, pp. 434–435.
[12] Rep. of Arm. Archives, File 65/1, Résumé of conversation.

Foreign Minister Tigranian had assented, with certain reservations, to Armenian participation in a Transcaucasian conference. Mdivani cautioned his government, however, that a delegation could not reach Tiflis before the next scheduled session, and he urged a further postponement until at least the twenty-seventh.[13]

Five days later, on November 22, Gegechkori wired that the meeting had been set back, for the very last time, until the thirtieth.[14] But then followed a sullen message divulging news that the entire conference had fallen apart. Gegechkori was offended by Armenia's capriciousness, and he felt that the very concept of a general Transcaucasian meeting might be compromised for a long time to come.[15] In his reply of December 5 Mdivani reiterated the reasons for Armenia's absence, adding optimistically that, in view of his recent understanding with the Erevan government, a delegation would arrive in Tiflis shortly.[16]

The Transcaucasian conference dispersed, however, without having officially convened. The responsibility for the fiasco lay to a considerable degree with the Armenians. It was unfortunate that the new republics had failed to come together at this relatively early date, for the slight possibility existed that, had they conferred, subsequent events would not have taken their ultimate deleterious course. On December 8 Mdivani departed for Tiflis taking a promise from Tigranian that he would follow immediately after welcoming a French envoy then en route to Erevan[17] and after attending to matters related to the Turkish evacuation of the Erevan guberniia. Tigranian, who had agreed to enter into bilateral negotiations with the Georgian cabinet, was certain the delay would last no longer than two weeks.[18]

---

[13] *Dokumenty i materialy*, p. 436; *Iz arm-gruz otnoshenii*, p. 57.

[14] *Dokumenty i materialy*, p. 436; Rep. of Arm. Archives, File 65/1, Gegechkori to Mdivani, Nov. 22, 1918.

[15] *Dokumenty i materialy*, p. 435, dates the communiqué December 2, 1919, whereas *Iz arm-gruz otnoshenii*, p. 58, dates it December 3. According to the copy in Rep. of Arm. Archives, File 65/1, December 3 is correct.

[16] *Iz arm-gruz otnoshenii*, p. 59.

[17] The French representative Antoine Poidebard, an Armenian-speaking army officer, landed at Baku with General Thomson on November 17 and, by his account, arrived in Armenia on December 6 and in Erevan on December 13, 1918. See his "Rôle militaire des Arméniens sur le front du Caucase après la défection de l'armée russe," *Revue des études arméniennes*, I, pt. 2 (1920), 161, and his *Voyages au carrefour des routes de Perse* (Paris, 1923), p. 126. In a report to the Georgian government, however, Mdivani claimed to have wired Poidebard in Alexandropol on December 13 and to have received Poidebard's reply from that city on December 14, 1918. See *Iz arm-gruz otnoshenii*, pp. 114–116.

[18] *Iz arm-gruz otnoshenii*, pp. 60–61, 99.

Before that fortnight had passed, however, Armenia and Georgia were at war.

Diplomatic Sparring

While Mdivani acted as intermediary regarding the Transcaucasian conference, he also engaged the Erevan government on the conflicting claims to Lori and Akhalkalak. When on November 12 Foreign Minister Tigranian cited Menshevik declarations acknowledging the Armenian character of these lands, the Georgian representative rejoined that the recent extraordinary political changes in the Caucasus had rendered such statements invalid. Every foot of the Tiflis guberniia was now needed by the Republic of Georgia to implement plans for social and agrarian reforms. The ethnic principle must be laid aside. Georgia, Mdivani continued, could for strategic reasons even claim the northern sector of Armenia, but since the Turkish threat had finally passed, his country would forego pretensions to Pambak and Kazakh. Georgia could not, however, relinquish Akhalkalak and Lori. During this and subsequent interviews Tigranian and Premier Kachaznuni indicated a willingness to make certain concessions should Georgia support Armenia's claim to Mountainous Karabagh. Georgia, they reasoned, could be of little assistance in Erevan's bid for Turkish Armenia but could, with regard to Karabagh, bring pressure to bear on Azerbaijan. Mdivani demurred, for he felt that Georgia, through her contacts in European countries and especially among socialist circles, could further Armenia's westward expansion, whereas the problem with Azerbaijan was fraught with bewildering complexities.[19]

In the midst of these verbal exchanges, Foreign Minister Gegechkori instructed Mdivani on November 19 to stand firm on Akhalkalak, but, if necessary, to entertain possible amendments in Lori, a district already occupied in part by Armenia. The communiqué was two-pronged, however, for it also required that in no event "should a single interest of Georgia be compromised." [20] Ten days later Mdivani announced to Armenian foreign ministry officials his authorization to conclude a preliminary boundary agreement, which would then be submitted to Tiflis for confirmation. He suggested that the existing border between the Tiflis and Erevan guberniias become the permanent international boundary and inquired if there were "any objec-

[19] Ibid., pp. 63–67.
[20] Ibid., p. 62. This document is dated November 18, 1918, in *Velikaia Oktiabr'skaia revoliutsiia*, pp. 241–242.

tions" to such an arrangement.[21] There were, of course, objections, as Mdivani well knew. On December 1 Tigranian reiterated Armenia's adherence to the ethnic principle, which during 1917 and a part of 1918 had also been honored, with allowance for certain geographic considerations, by the leadership of the "Georgian democracy." By this arrangement Armenia was to encompass both Akhalkalak and Lori but not the adjoining uchastoks closer to Tiflis, even though Armenian pluralities existed in those districts. If, however, Georgia intended to reverse her position on Akhalkalak and Lori, Armenia would feel quite justified in bringing the other zones into contention once again. Mdivani reminded Tigranian that the question now at hand was the determination of the boundary between two sovereign nations and not, as it was earlier, between provinces or zemstvos of the same empire. Although characterizing the disputed lands as organically Georgian, Mdivani was sufficiently conciliatory in attitude to gain Tigranian's promise to continue the discussions in Tiflis.[22]

The Georgian Occupation of Akhalkalak

Throughout the summer and autumn of 1918 the uezds of Akhalkalak and Akhaltsikh in the southwestern sector of the Tiflis guberniia lay under Turkish domination. Meanwhile, the Armenian population of Akhalkalak, having fled to the barren Bakuriani highlands, succumbed en masse. Chargé d'affaires Djamalian repeatedly protested Georgia's refusal to grant these people asylum in the Armenian communities of the Borchalu uezd, particularly since most of that uezd was "rightfully Armenian." He branded the Georgian stand as not only inhumane but also a transgression into the internal affairs of Armenia.[23] Foreign Minister Tigranian appealed through Mdivani on November 13 to permit the refugees passage to the Armenian villages "under Georgian occupation," and Mdivani urged his government to act favorably upon the petition, but the Georgian cabinet remained steadfast in its decision to keep the borders sealed.[24]

In compliance with the provision of the Mudros Armistice that the

[21] Rep. of Arm. Archives, File 65/1, Mdivani to Foreign Minister of the Armenian republic, Nov. 29, 1918; *Armiano-gruzinskii konflikt*, pp. 26–27.

[22] Rep. of Arm. Archives, File 65/1, Minister of Foreign Affairs to Diplomatic Representative of Georgia, Dec. 1, 1918; *Armiano-gruzinskii konflikt*, pp. 27–29; *Iz arm-gruz otnoshenii*, pp. 71–74.

[23] Djamalian, "Hai-vratsakan knjire" (Sept., 1928), p. 124. See also *Iz arm-gruz otnoshenii*, p. 62.

[24] *Iz arm-gruz otnoshenii*, pp. 84–85.

Ottoman Empire withdraw its forces from Transcaucasia, the Ottoman representative in Tiflis, Abdul Kerim Pasha, released to the Georgian government in November, 1918, the schedule of evacuation from Akhalkalak and Akhaltsikh. But the matter was complicated by rumors that the envoy to Erevan, Mehmed Ali Pasha, had divulged similar information to the Armenians.[25] On November 30 Mdivani wired Gegechkori disquieting news that Turkish officials had supposedly offered Akhalkalak to Armenia, and he inquired whether Georgian troops had succeeded in occupying the district. Gegechkori, too, believed that some undefined form of collusion existed and that Georgia would consequently find it more difficult to deal with the Armenians.[26]

The Menshevik leaders, however, had already taken the initiative in securing the contested land. In a circular addressed to the inhabitants of Akhalkalak and Akhaltsikh, the Tiflis government explained that because of the Turkish occupation the Republic had been unable to manifest its deep concern for their welfare but that fortunately Georgia could soon recover the two districts, which temporarily would be combined under a military governorship. In a separate statement Major General K. Makaev, the officer named to serve as governor, guaranteed the proper conduct of his men but also threatened to take stern measures against any disorder or antigovernment activity.[27]

Armenian officials scoffed at the claim that the residents of Akhalkalak were Georgian subjects. Were this the case, why had Georgia sealed the borders to her own people and permitted thousands of them to perish? Only when the opportunity had come to annex Akhalkalak did Georgia suddenly discover that these unfortunate victims were actually Georgian citizens! On December 2 Tigranian protested the appointment of a military governor, and three days later he urged that Georgian troops be kept out of Akhalkalak until a peaceful solution had been reached.[28] Georgia could not have taken Tigranian's unrealistic appeal seriously. Indeed, her troops marched into Akhalkalak that very day.

As General Makaev directed the successful maneuver, a small Ar-

[25] Rep. of Arm. Archives, File 108/7, *H. H. Patvirakutiun, 1919;* A. Babalian, *Edjer Hayastani ankakhutian patmutiunits* (Cairo, 1959), pp. 26–27; P. G. La Chesnais, *Les peuples de la Transcaucasie pendant la guerre et devant la paix* (Paris, 1921), p. 152. See also Denikin, *Ocherki smuty,* IV (1925), 153; London *Times,* Jan. 24, 1919, p. 7.

[26] *Iz arm-gruz otnoshenii,* p. 79. Foreign Minister Tigranian denied the existence of any agreement with the Turks.

[27] *Bor'ba* (Tiflis), Nov. 9 and 10, 1918; *Iz arm-gruz otnoshenii,* pp. 80–82.

[28] Rep. of Arm. Archives, File 65/1, Tigranian to Mdivani, Dec. 2 and 5, 1918.

menian detachment advanced into the southeastern tip of the Akhalkalak uezd and occupied the Russian sectarian villages of Troitskoe, Efremovka, Gorelovka, and Bogdanovka (see map 8). On December 8, however, the detachment was confronted by a squadron of Georgian cavalry and a battery of artillery and ordered to withdraw. More Georgian forces arrived the next day, and on December 10 Makaev's men pressed into that sector.[29] With matters apparently under control General Makaev appointed a garrison commander and a uezd commissar for Akhalkalak and moved on to Akhaltsikh, where unrest among the Muslim inhabitants was anticipated.[30] The Armeno-Georgian confrontation had been brief and one-sided. Georgia answered Armenia's protests with two curt explanations: Akhalkalak was Georgian and the occupation was necessitated by the obligation to safeguard the populace.[31] Had the Turks cleared the Erevan guberniia earlier and had Armenian troops entered Alexandropol, on the main route to Akhalkalak, before December 6, the Armenian tactic might have been quite different. As it was, Georgian units seized the strategic points almost without a challenge.

During this crisis Georgia applied economic pressure to make the Erevan government more malleable. The routes between Georgia and Armenia were frequently closed on the pretext that the two countries had not concluded a transit agreement. One such incident involved the shipment to Erevan of forty cisterns of oil and nine cisterns of gasoline purchased in Baku. Georgia demanded 20 percent of the petroleum products in return for transit privileges but then refused to allow any trains except those of the homeward-bound Turkish army to pass to the south, assertedly because the district of Lori, through which the railway ran, was under martial law.[32] These same circumstances deprived Armenia of the little grain her representatives had managed to secure abroad.[33] The reaction of a starving people is not difficult to

[29] *Armiano-gruzinskii konflikt*, pp. 32–33; Kadishev, *Interventsiia v Zakavkaz'e*, p. 172; *Iz arm-gruz otnoshenii*, p. 127; Rep. of Arm. Archives, File 65/1, Report of Dro to Erevan Division headquarters. A vivid description of this corner of Akhalkalak has been given by H. F. B. Lynch, *Armenia: Travels and Studies* (2 vols.; London, 1901), I, 96–117.

[30] *Iz arm-gruz otnoshenii*, p. 128. Makaev's appointees were Captain Machavariani as uezd commandant and Rotmaster Abashidze as uezd commissar.

[31] *Dokumenty i materialy*, pp. 451–452; Khatisian, *Hanrapetutian zargatsume*, p. 103.

[32] Rep. of Arm. Archives, File 65/1, Djamalian to Foreign Minister of Armenia; Vratzian, *Hanrapetutiun*, p. 198.

[33] During the latter half of 1918 Armenian representatives, in particular G. S. Dsamoev (Grigor Dsamoyan) and Simon Vratzian, had persuaded the Ukrainian government in Kiev and the Volunteer Army Command in South Russia to make

imagine. Tempers on both sides had reached their limit when Armenian guerrilla activity in northern Lori plunged the two republics into
war. For Georgia it was a question of quelling an internal disturbance;
for Armenia it was an obligation to defend citizens who had fallen
under foreign domination.

Lori—Rebellion or Self-Defense?

Following the occupation of southern Lori by Dro's contingents in
October of 1918, the Georgian army reinforced its garrisons to the
north, where animosity between inhabitants and soldiers mounted
steadily. The Armenian villages were required to quarter and provision companies of Georgian troops, whose contemptuous manner and
untoward gestures to the women elicited numerous protests. The World
War now at an end, the peasantry of Lori could see no advantage in
continued Georgian rule and began to clamor for unification with Armenia. In appeals to Erevan they bitterly decried the inordinate requisition and search operations to which they were repeatedly subjected.[34]
When the large community of Uzunlar resisted on one such occasion,
the village commissar was beaten and another official killed by the
Georgian troops. Upon investigation, Georgian Lieutenant Colonel
Ramazov reported that the soldiers had been the instigators but that
in view of the organized nature of the resistance at Uzunlar the strategic
village should be searched and neutralized. He also recommended the
recall of the two offending units, which had become incompetent and
troublesome.[35]

Despite several such obvious warning signals, the situation deteriorated, and by the beginning of December northern Lori was in a state
of imminent rebellion. When emissaries from Uzunlar appeared at
Georgian headquarters near Sanahin station to protest the arbitrary
acts of violence, the district commander, General Tsulukidze, had them
arrested and then dispatched a force to deal with the unrest in the
village and round up the agents provocateurs.[36] On December 9 other
spokesmen from Uzunlar appealed to Kachaznuni's government for

available for Armenia several hundred tons of grain and sugar. Materials relating to
these transactions are in Rep. of Arm. Archives, File 72. In a report of October 12,
1918, File 65/1, Dsamoev stated that the Ukrainian government had pledged fifty carloads of grain and ten of sugar and that the Cossack leaders of the Kuban would
provide a hundred carloads of grain.

[34] Numerous like protests are preserved in Rep. of Arm. Archives, File 65/1.

[35] *Armiano-gruzinskii konflikt*, pp. 20–21; D. Enukidze, *Krakh imperialisticheskoi
interventsii v Zakavkaz'e* (Tbilisi, 1954), p. 124; Varandian, *op. cit.*, pp. 82–84.

[36] *Armiano-gruzinskii konflikt*, p. 21; Vratzian, *Hanrapetutiun*, p. 190.

measures "to save from ruin our village of a thousand houses." Their claim that Uzunlar had been under ceaseless Georgian bombardment for two days was countered, however, by the Georgian charge that the villagers had opened fire and had rolled huge boulders down upon government troops.[37] In subsequent accounts both Armenia and Georgia attempted to prove the guilt of the other. The Georgian thesis held that the inhabitants of Lori would not have rebelled had they not been incited and assisted by the regular military forces of Armenia, whereas the Armenian sources maintained that no regular units were involved until mid-December, when oppression had become so intolerable that the very physical security of the people was in question. There was doubtless some validity to both claims.

From his headquarters at Sanahin, for example, General Tsulukidze reported on December 9 that, under the guise of bandits, soldiers of Armenia's 4th Infantry Regiment were fomenting insurrection. They had disarmed the forty-five men of a Georgian cavalry troop, imprisoned the garrison at Uzunlar, and greeted a relief force with a barrage of fire. Rebellion was spreading over Lori, warned Tsulukidze, and Sanahin itself was endangered.[38] On the following day he added that no fewer than three hundred and fifty Armenians had attacked two Georgian units and that several of his men had been crushed under boulders rolled down the mountainside by Armenian partisans. The Georgian commander was certain that many of the Armenians were regulars, for their orders were given in Russian, the language still used by the Armenian military command. His dispatch that afternoon revealed the loss of two officers and several more enlisted men during an Armenian attack on Tsater. Tsulukidze admitted that the cunning Armenians, aware that an open breach would mean sure war, did not molest the border guards but instead cut behind the frontier posts and roused sedition in Georgia. He now demanded the military means to squelch the lawlessness.[39]

Control of the situation was slipping away from the Georgian authorities. General Goguadze, commander of the armored trains, informed Tiflis that the rails had been torn between Sanahin and Alaverdi stations, and Tsulukidze announced that a passenger train had been set aflame and that regulars of the Armenian 4th Infantry Regiment had pinned down his troops near the town of Alaverdi. Mean-

---

[37] Rep. of Arm. Archives, File 65/1, from Shahali station to Ministry of Military Affairs, Erevan, Dec. 9, 1918; *Armiano-gruzinskii konflikt*, pp. 22–23.

[38] *Dokumenty i materialy*, p. 452; *Iz arm-gruz otnoshenii*, p. 88.

[39] *Iz arm-gruz otnoshenii*, pp. 89–90.

while in the Vorontsovka district General Tsitsianov reported that Armenian scouts were being sheltered by friendly villages, that partisans at Agarak had captured a Georgian detachment, and that other villages, particularly Ovnagar, were joining the insurgents. Without reinforcements, declared Tsitsianov, no action could be taken, for in Agarak alone there were more than a hundred enemy troops. He was certain that regulars had sifted across the border from Jalal-oghli in southern Lori.[40]

News of the burgeoning conflagration swirled around the Armenians of Tiflis, who found themselves trapped in dangerous straits. The National Council of Armenians in Georgia obtained permission from Zhordania's cabinet to commission a delegation to help reestablish order in the troubled region. The party left Tiflis in the company of Georgia's Assistant Minister of Internal Affairs, Gerasim F. Makharadze, and Assistant Minister of Military Affairs, Major General A. K. Gedevanov (Gedevanishvili). In a message to his government soon after the group's arrival in Alaverdi on December 12, Makharadze confirmed that several Armenian villages were in open revolt and that Sanahin was besieged. He nonetheless characterized the uprising as local, with the possible implication of individual Armenian soldiers. The delegation of Tiflis Armenians, including Zhordania's Menshevik colleague Aramayis Erzinkian, emphasized the isolated nature of the disturbance and pledged to use every means available to restore harmony.[41] The reports of Makharadze and the Armenian delegation obviously did not substantiate those of Tsulukidze and Tsitsianov, who spoke of the definite intervention of regular Armenian units commanded by Russian-speaking officers.

The Last Words

The rebellion in Lori severed rail and telegraph service between Tiflis and Erevan and left Simeon Mdivani stranded in Karakilisa along with a number of Armenian officials, including Avetis Aharonian and Mikayel Papadjanian, who were en route to the Paris Peace Conference, Minister of Provisions Levon Ghulian, and Minister of Enlightenment Mikayel Atabekian. All passengers by chance on the same train to Tiflis, they first learned of the open hostilities when they reached Alexandropol on December 10. Dro Kanayan, commander of the

---

[40] *Ibid.*, pp. 91–93, 95–96; *Armiano-gruzinskii konflikt*, p. 22.
[41] Rep. of Arm. Archives, File 65/1, Telegram folder; *Iz arm-gruz otnoshenii*, pp. 93–94.

Karakilisa-Lori detachments, met with Mdivani to pledge that if the Georgian envoy could induce General Tsulukidze and the Georgian government to act with restraint he would call upon the people of Lori to remain calm. As it happened, however, Mdivani found on December 11 that the train could advance no farther than Kober, a border outpost already abandoned by the Georgians. From Kober he did make telephone contact with Tsulukidze in Sanahin and urged that no punitive action be taken against the Armenians, at least until he had been able to communicate with officials in Tiflis. Mdivani nonetheless complained that Aharonian and other influential Dashnakists were not attempting to persuade the armed villagers to let the train through to Sanahin and Tiflis; only Populist leaders Papadjanian and Atabekian had cooperated, but to no avail. Mdivani added that, as it would serve no purpose for him to remain at Kober, he was returning to Karakilisa in order to be in closer contact with the military and political strategists of Armenia.[42]

In Karakilisa Mdivani conferred once again with Dro. The Armenian commander now contended that the conflict would abate if Georgia recalled General Tsulukidze and removed the garrison at Sanahin, for Armenia would tacitly assent to the retention of a Georgian civil administration in northern Lori pending a final settlement. Distressed by Dro's stand, which he could not but regard as intrusion into the affairs of Georgia, Mdivani spoke by direct wire with Foreign Minister Tigranian. He warned that the accomplishments of the preceding weeks in Erevan would be nullified if Dro's conditions were also those of the government. Mdivani suggested that mixed Georgian-Armenian commissions be sent to pacify the villages of Lori and requested that Armenia declare publicly her opposition to the anarchy. All who had violated the laws of the land would be punished, he promised, and, while it was possible to adopt a lenient attitude toward the populace, the offending Georgian officials would be held fully accountable. Armenia, came Tigranian's reply, could not be expected to exhort "her citizens" to submit to a foreign power that had forcibly occupied their land. Application of the principle of self-determination and withdrawal of the Georgian army from Lori could alone rectify the situation.[43]

Meanwhile the Tiflis–Erevan correspondence became ever more strident. Because of disruptions in communication, some messages

---

[42] *Iz arm-gruz otnoshcnii,* pp. 92, 93, 99–103.

[43] Rep. of Arm. Archives, File 65/1, Stenograph, Dec. 11, 1918; *Dokumenty i materialy,* pp. 453–456.

never did reach their destination, whereas others arrived only after long delays. On occasion the identical text was relayed simultaneously via radio, wireless, and military channels along the frontier in the hope that one would get through. In communiqués of December 9 and 11, 1918, Tigranian decried the tyranny in Lori and admonished Georgia to cease the requisitions and oppression or else be prepared to accept the responsibility for the consequences.[44] On the latter date the Georgian Parliament heard Gegechkori's description of the crisis and adopted a resolution expressing confidence that "the government will take whatever measures necessary to defend the state from enemies, whose sole aim it is to bring forth a bloody conflict between the two neighboring peoples, spread anarchy in our land, and thus prepare grounds for the destruction of our independence and democratic republic." [45] Then on the twelfth Premier Hovhannes Kachaznuni addressed the following ominous message to Premier Zhordania:

The conduct of Georgian troops in Borchalu, in that part of Armenia occupied forcibly by Georgia, has created an intolerable situation. Only the immediate withdrawal of Georgian troops from that region can prevent new bloodshed and lead to the restoration of friendly, lasting relations between Georgia and Armenia. With this view the government of Armenia has the honor to propose to the government of Georgia that it remove its troops, without further delay, from that part of Armenia which lies within the Borchalu uezd. In the event of refusal or evasion on your part, the Armenian government will be obliged to take the necessary measures to protect the citizens of Armenia from the violence and lawlessness of the Georgian troops.[46]

The next day, even before this warning was received in Tiflis, Foreign Minister Gegechkori answered one of Tigranian's previous protests by reiterating Georgia's desire for peace but also underscoring the determination not to tolerate any meddling in the "internal affairs" of the country. He denied reports of Georgian attacks upon the Armenians in Lori and contended that the armed forces had returned fire for the first time at noon that very day, December 13.[47] In a separate wire to Mdivani, Gegechkori stated that information from Lori im-

---

[44] Rep. of Arm. Archives, File 65/1, Foreign Minister of Armenia to Foreign Minister of Georgia, Dec. 9 and 11, 1918.

[45] Khatisian, *Hanrapetutian zargatsume*, p. 107.

[46] *Armiano-gruzinskii konflikt*, pp. 33–34; Varandian, *op. cit.*, p. 86; Rep. of Arm. Archives, File 65/1, Kachaznuni to Zhordania, Dec. 12, 1918.

[47] Rep. of Arm. Archives, File 65/1, Gegechkori to Minister of Foreign Affairs of Armenia, Dec. 13, 1918; *Iz arm-gruz otnoshenii*, p. 118.

plicated the Armenian military in the hostilities at Sanahin, yet the Georgian government preferred not to believe that this violation of the borders had occurred with the knowledge of the Armenian command. Mdivani (who had departed from Erevan five days earlier) was instructed to prevail upon the Armenian government to halt the activities "of the irresponsible troops." [48]

Armenia had by this time decided on overt intervention. In his subsequent official report to the Georgian Foreign Ministry, Mdivani asserted that on December 13 Dro presented him with an ultimatum intended for the Georgian government. The message, signed by Premier Kachaznuni and relayed to Karakilisa by General Movses Silikian at midnight of December 12, was evidently the same note Kachaznuni had addressed directly to Zhordania. Mdivani had claimed to have no means to relay the ultimatum and protested that during the preceding three days his every effort to reach Sanahin with Dro's help in order to communicate with Tiflis had been ignored and frustrated.[49]

Also on the thirteenth, according to Mdivani, Dro revealed he had received orders to occupy all the Borchalu uezd south of the Khram River; preliminary activities were scheduled to begin in a few hours. It seems odd, at the very least, that Dro would have disclosed such top-secret information, but there were so many unusual facets to the episode that the account cannot be dismissed. In frantic last-minute appeals to Foreign Minister Tigranian, Minister of Welfare Alexandre Khatisian, Khorhurd members Avetik Sahakian and Stepan Malkhasian, and to the only Allied official in Armenia, French Captain Antoine Poidebard, Mdivani emphasized that the interruption in communications had probably left the Georgian government unaware of Armenia's position. Should Dro's forces advance, Armenia would be guilty not only of transgression into Georgian affairs but also of violating the accepted international practice to allow time for a reply to an ultimatum before beginning military action. The result would, in

---

[48] *Dokumenty i materialy*, p. 460. Allowing for the delay in communications between Armenia and Georgia, it is nevertheless highly improbable that Gegechkori was unaware that Mdivani had left Erevan on December 8. The Georgian publication, *Iz arm-gruz otnoshenii*, includes a report from General Tsulukidze on December 11 stating that he had talked by telephone with Mdivani, who was at Kober station in Lori. Moreover, on December 12 the Armenian deputation that had gone to Alaverdi with Makharadze reported to Tiflis on Mdivani's presence in Kober. See *Iz arm-gruz otnoshenii*, pp. 92, 94. If Gegechkori did not know of these reports, it would seem that Georgia had suffered a massive breakdown in internal communication. Such was not the case, however, for on December 14 Gegechkori himself announced in the Georgian Parliament that Mdivani had been forced to return to Karakilisa from Lori. See *Dokumenty i materialy*, p. 466.

[49] *Iz arm-gruz otnoshenii*, pp. 110–111.

any case, be war between the two republics. The futility of his labors was soon evident, and on December 14 Mdivani departed for Tiflis along the same roundabout route that the Armenian cabinet had been compelled to follow when it transferred from Tiflis to Erevan in the summer of 1918.[50]

Indignation in Georgia

Even as Armenian units started to advance on December 14, Sirakan Tigranian again appealed for a "peaceful settlement," and in Tiflis Evgenii Gegechkori informed an agitated Parliament of the government's efforts to avert war. The Georgian Foreign Minister deplored the fact that instead of a Transcaucasian conference—repeatedly postponed because of the Armenians—there was now a military confrontation. Its patience expended, the Parliament instructed the cabinet "to take all steps required to destroy the enemy attempting to spread inimical relations between the two neighboring peoples, to suppress the anarchy, and to defend the democracy of Georgia." [51]

Three days later when the "Armenian invasion" was well under way, Premier Noi Zhordania also addressed Parliament. He began in stirring words: "There has taken place that which should not have taken place." Regretfully, Armenia had incited rebellion and then had brought up her regular army. "The present Armenian government, in instigating this shameful conflict, has precipitated that which has never before occurred—war between Georgia and Armenia." Who had ever heard of war over a few incidents in a village or two? The real explanation could be found in the character of Kachaznuni's government which, "like the wolf, eats the calf because such is its nature." That government could not live in peace and was obsessed with battling one or another of its neighbors, for, like the wolf, it had to devour everything. Should not the Armenians have realized that, in view of their hostile relations with the Muslims, they must at least cling to the friendship of Georgia? But instead they had now burned this bridge as well. In Armenia, continued Zhordania, there were two political currents, one composed of men of moderation seeking a reconciliation and the other made up of militarists. Obviously the latter extremists had finally gained ascendancy, but Georgia would rise to battle this pack of "mau-

---

[50] *Ibid.*, pp. 112–116; Rep. of Arm. Archives, File 65/1, Telegram folder.

[51] *Armiano-gruzinskii konflikt*, pp. 34–35; *Dokumenty i materialy*, pp. 464–467. The latter source dates Tigranian's communiqué December 15, possibly the day the radiogram was received in the Georgian Foreign Ministry.

serists." [52] Aroused by the rhetorical eloquence, the Parliament adopted legislation to defend the Georgian republic, taking pains to emphasize that the measures were not directed against the Armenian people but against "those circles striving to break the bonds of centuries between the two neighboring nations." [53]

British officers then in Tiflis to arrange for the arrival of General Forestier-Walker's division, en route from Salonica over the Black Sea, witnessed the strange spectacle of an Armeno-Georgian war. Zhordania's cabinet, voicing strong opposition to the landing of British forces in Georgia without its permission, nevertheless did not hesitate to carry the dispute to the Allied military officials. Foreign Minister Gegechkori, in his communiqué of December 15, reviewed the crisis from the Georgian point of view and declared that the Republic "now protests before the entire world the treachery of the Armenian government." [54]

In Karakilisa, meanwhile, Captain E. Green, a British transportation officer traveling from Baku, offered his services as mediator. Armenia readily agreed and appointed a delegation to meet with Green and Georgian representatives. The group included Martiros Harutiunian (chairman) and Smbat Khachatrian (Dashnakists), Stepan Mamikonian (nonpartisan), Arsham Khondkarian (Social Revolutionary), and Grigor Ter-Khachatrian (Populist), all members of the Khorhurd.[55] Tigranian apprised the Tiflis government by wireless of the delegation's departure for Karakilisa and asked that Georgian officials also be dispatched to confer with Green. He took the opportunity to add that Georgia's regrettable "imperialistic policy" had compelled Armenia to defend her citizenry, and he reaffirmed his belief that a bilateral conference could stabilize relations between the two peoples "bound by so many historic traditions and permeated by common cultural ideals." [56] In Karakilisa Captain Green and the Armenian delegation waited in vain for Georgian envoys. And under the circumstances, with a zone of war separating the two sides, it would have been most surprising had any

[52] *Dokumenty i materialy*, pp. 473–476. See also Wladimir Woytinsky, *La démocratie géorgienne* (Paris, 1921), pp. 180–183.

[53] *Iz arm-gruz otnoshenii*, p. 138.

[54] *Dokumenty i materialy*, pp. 469–470. See also Britain, Cab 27/39, E.C. 2980.

[55] Vratzian, *Hanrapetutiun*, p. 193. Green was a staff officer of the 9th Battalion, Worcestershire Regiment. The battalion diary shows that Green had been dispatched to Alexandropol on December 6 to obtain information on the railway rolling stock. See Britain, WO 95/4955.

[56] Rep. of Arm. Archives, File 65/1, Foreign Minister of Armenia to Foreign Minister of Georgia, Dec. 18, 1918; *Armiano-gruzinskii konflikt*, pp. 36–37. This appeal has been omitted from both official Georgian publications, *Dokumenty i materialy* and *Iz arm-gruz otnoshenii*.

Georgian appeared. Apparently bewildered by the whole affair, Green departed for Baku in order to report to Major General Thomson and then to return with further instructions. That was the last heard or seen of Captain Green.[57]

The Battles

Diplomacy failed to stave off the conflict, and the military had its day upon the field. Captured Armenian documents subsequently published by the Georgian government indicate that Erevan had made detailed plans for seizure of the land up to the Khram River, and Armenian military activity would seem to verify the authenticity of those documents. At dawn on December 14, in the bitter cold of winter, components of Armenia's 4th, 5th, and 6th Regiments advanced in three columns under Colonels Ter-Nikoghosian, Nesterovskii, and Korolkov, their initial objective being the line of villages, Vorontsovka-Privolnoe-Opret-Hairum. The full strength of Dro's army, including those units held in reserve, consisted of twenty-eight companies of infantry and four squadrons of cavalry, equipped with a total of twenty-six machine guns and seven mountain cannons. The Armenians had fewer men, provisions, and ammunition than the Georgians, but they held the decisive advantage of striking into friendly territory.[58]

On the afternoon of December 14 General Tsulukidze reported that the Armenians had forced him to evacuate the Georgian headquarters at Sanahin and had surrounded Haghpat, where the inhabitants were assisting the invaders. The following day he added that the Georgian defenders were about to be encircled and that their dead and wounded had fallen into enemy hands.[59] By December 15 the Armenian regulars had taken Vorontsovka, Privolnoe, Sanahin, Mikhailovka, Alaverdi, and the heights between Haghpat and Akhova. In this initial rapid

[57] Vratzian, *Hanrapetutiun*, pp. 193–194. Denikin, *Ocherki smuty*, IV, 153–154, claims that the meeting was held at Sanahin but that Georgia did not send a delegation. Green arrived back in Baku on December 25 according to the 9th Worcestershire Battalion War Diary. Neither the battalion nor the 39th Brigade headquarters war diary makes any mention of Green's activities in Karakilisa. On January 4, 1919, Captain Green was appointed Railway Transportation Officer of the Baku district. See Britain, WO 95/4955. See also Cab 27/39, E.C. 2980.

[58] Vratzian, *Hanrapetutiun*, p. 195. Armenian orders to move forward and the assignments of the various companies and commanders, dated December 13, 1918, were taken from an Armenian prisoner, according to the Georgian government, and published in *Dokumenty i materialy*, pp. 462–464.

[59] *Iz arm-gruz otnoshenii*, pp. 121–122. On December 14 Foreign Minister Gegechkori reported to the Georgian representative in Batum that the fighting had placed the country in dire straits. See Enukidze, *op. cit.*, p. 125.

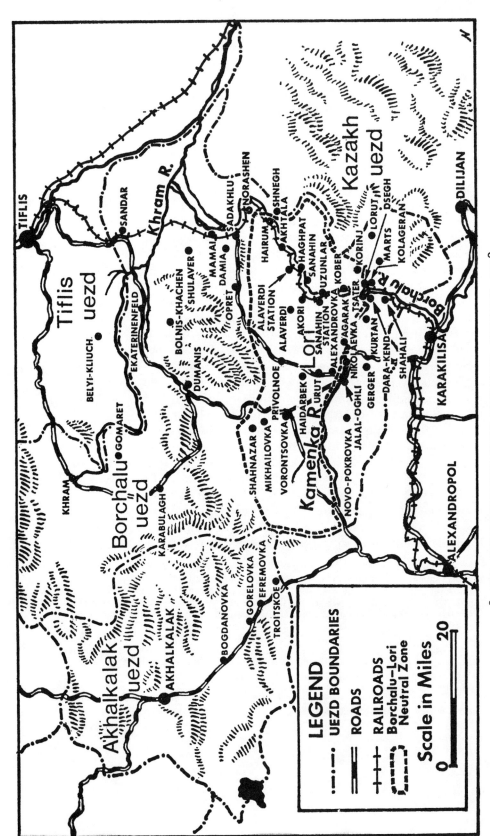

8. THE ARMENO-GEORGIAN FIELD OF BATTLE, DECEMBER, 1918

march, they captured nearly a hundred Georgian soldiers, many cavalry mounts, a locomotive and some fifty freight cars, and several machine guns and mountain cannons.[60]

At daybreak on the sixteenth the Armenian left flank, commanded by Ter-Nikoghosian, struck toward Bolnis-Khachen and Ekaterinenfeld, while Korolkov's right flank captured the station of Hairum (Airum) in a surprise attack that cost the Georgians another five hundred men, killed, wounded, or taken prisoner. The next day the Georgian 5th and 6th Infantry Regiments were caught in an Armenian pincer movement and managed to escape only after suffering sixty new casualties and abandoning two field pieces and twenty-five machine guns. During the same general operation the Armenians seized two fully equipped Georgian armored trains near the station of Akhtala. Unable to cope with the situation General Tsulukidze fled to Sadakhlu in such haste that he had to leave behind his plush personal rail coach. By December 18 the Georgians were in serious trouble. They had been driven all the way to Sadakhlu and, on their western flank, had lost Bolnis-Khachen to Ter-Nikoghosian's column. Tiflis was in an uproar; the People's Guard was mobilized and a state of emergency proclaimed.[61]

Minister of Military Affairs Grigorii T. Georgadze personally led a thousand fresh Georgian infantrymen, a cavalry squadron, and the last of the armored trains into Sadakhlu on December 18. This maneuver, however, did not deter Dro from pursuing his plan to crush General Tsulukidze. The Armenian right flank, skirting the main Georgian force at Sadakhlu, captured the friendly village of Shulaver on December 20 and approached the Khram River. Other units raided Sadakhlu, but, as they came within range of the armored train, the Armenian troops for the first time sustained heavy losses. The Georgians labored to consolidate their position even though the rails to their rear had been cut and they risked encirclement. On the twenty-second the Armenians struck again and captured Sadakhlu station and the outskirts of the village but were then hurled back once more by the Georgian troops and armored train. The next day Dro ordered twelve companies to a full-scale offensive. After hours of fierce pitched combat the Armenians gained the strategic village, taking rich bounty consisting of three locomotives, more than a hundred freight cars laden with food and ammunition, and some 130 prisoners of war. A humili-

---

[60] Kadishev, *Interventsiia v Zakavkaz'e*, p. 173; Vratzian, *Hanrapetutiun*, pp. 195–196; *Iz arm-gruz otnoshenii*, pp. 123–124.

[61] Vratzian, *Hanrapetutiun*, pp. 196–197.

ated and disgraced Tsulukidze was relieved of his command and replaced by one of Georgia's most respected military leaders, Major General Georgii I. Mazniev (Mazniashvili).[62]

Having attained Shulaver and the town of Belyi-Kliuch, the latter located in the Tiflis uezd, the Armenian forces had come within 45 versts (30 miles) of the Georgian capital. In the sporadic encounters that ensued on December 24, Mazniev's units continued to fall back, but on the next day a thousand additional troops reached the front, and, for the first time, Georgian airplanes bombed the Armenian positions near Shulaver. The startling Armenian offensive had reached its climax on December 25, the date on which Allied representatives in Tiflis demanded a halt to the senseless war.[63]

The Truce

In the midst of this crisis an Allied military commission led by British and French Lieutenant Colonels R. P. Jordan and P. A. Chardigny arrived in Tiflis from Baku. Although the mission's assignment was to hasten the withdrawal of Turkish regiments strung out along the railway from Baku to Tiflis and Alexandropol and to make arrangements for the installation and quartering of Forestier-Walker's 27th Division, soon to come ashore, Colonel Jordan readily acted upon Gegechkori's urgent appeal and protest of December 15.[64] The Armenian and Georgian forces, posited Jordan, should clear all disputed territory, Akhalkalak included, and be replaced by British troops. Inasmuch as nearly all the contested region had fallen under Turkish occupation, it seemed quite reasonable to Jordan that the British should police these lands until the peace conference had determined their future status.[65]

Georgia rejected the proposal as being a concession to Armenia and an appeasement of the aggressor. On December 21 Premier Zhordania informed his cabinet of the discussions with the Allied officers and then outlined his position:

---

[62] *Ibid.*, pp. 197–199; Rep. of Arm. Archives, File 65/1

[63] Vratzian, *Hanrapetutiun*, p. 199. The Armenian army had no airplanes in 1918.

[64] Richard Price Jordan commanded the 7th Battalion, Gloucestershire Regiment. In January, 1919, he took charge of the entire 39th Brigade at Baku. For his reports and activities pertaining to the Turkish withdrawal, see Britain, Cab 27/38, E.C. 2655, 2690, 2721, 2726, and 2770, and Cab 27/39, E.C. 2820. Pierre-Auguste Chardigny had headed the French military mission in the Caucasus during the World War and returned to Baku with the forward party of Thomson's force in November, 1918. See Britain, WO 95/4955, 39th Brigade War Diary.

[65] Enukidze, *op. cit.*, pp. 125–126; Rep. of Arm. Archives, File 65/1.

1. The Georgian government would welcome the initiative of the Allies in arranging a halt to the bloodshed.

2. The telegram to be sent to Armenia demanding an end to military activity should be relayed by the Georgian commander, not by the Allied representatives.

3. The cessation of hostilities must immediately be followed by an Armenian withdrawal to the line held before the war.

4. The duties of a proposed mixed commission should include a determination of the aggressor nation, which should then be required to make reparations.[66]

Foreign Minister Gegechkori told Jordan on the twenty-second that Georgia would agree to end the fighting only on the basis of the status quo ante bellum. Evidently the differences between the Georgian leaders and the Allied officers were not quickly resolved, for two days later Gegechkori reiterated his government's stand: "The guarantee that similar aggression not occur in the future and that all disputed questions be settled by mutual agreement or arbitration dictates the implementation of the status quo ante bellum." The Republic of Georgia would accept no alternative.[67]

As it happened, Major General Sir William Henry Rycroft, Deputy Quartermaster of the British Salonica Army, preceded the 27th Division to Transcaucasia to conduct an inspection tour. Once in Tiflis, however, he apparently discovered himself to be the ranking Allied officer and promptly decided to take charge of the negotiations.[68] More amenable to the Georgian demands than Colonel Jordan had been, Rycroft soon consented to several modifications in the original British proposal, particularly in relation to Akhalkalak. Only then did Premier Zhordania accept the British plan, which, as revised, now provided for the retention of Georgian troops in Akhalkalak and northern Borchalu and of Armenian troops in southern Borchalu, with an intervening "neutral zone" under British supervision. Armenia would thus be constrained to relinquish all territory gained during the war. Zhordania once again insisted that an international commission identify the aggressor and impose reparations.[69]

It is curious that Armenian representatives in Tiflis had not been included in these preliminary proceedings. Only on December 25, when Rycroft and Colonel Chardigny drafted a message to Premier Kachaz-

[66] *Dokumenty i materialy*, pp. 477–478.
[67] *Iz arm-gruz otnoshenii*, pp. 128–130; *Dokumenty i materialy*, pp. 478–479.
[68] Britain, *Operations in Macedonia*, II, 307.
[69] *Iz arm-gruz otnoshenii*, p. 130.

nuni, was Chargé d'affaires Arshak Djamalian summoned to sign the text. Djamalian objected to this unfair treatment and refused to place his signature to any document without instructions from his government.[70] Nonetheless, the following communiqué was wired to Erevan on the twenty-fifth, by which time all Lori together with neighboring districts in the Borchalu uezd had been occupied by Dro's army:

Major General Rycroft, now in Tiflis, Chardigny of the French Mission, in company with Zhordania and in the presence of Djamalian, have decided that military activities should cease and, over the protest of Djamalian, have resolved to create a mixed commission of English, French, Armenian, and Georgian representatives to go to the front to effect this decision. The commission is to determine the number of Georgian garrisons which are to remain in the northern sector of the Borchalu uezd and the number of Armenian garrisons in the southern sector. It will also rule on the number of garrisons the Georgians will retain in Akhalkalak, with the understanding that these should be at a minimum. The Georgians are to hold their present line, while the Armenians must withdraw to the Dsegh–Jalal-oghli perimeter. The British will take positions between the Georgian and Armenian troops and will create a mixed administration in that district, whereas the Georgian administration in Akhalkalak will be supervised by the Allies, with the guarantee that Armenian and Muslim representatives shall be included in the administration. Soon Georgian and Armenian envoys will depart for Europe, where the final boundaries will be determined by the Great Powers.[71]

The dispatch was signed by Rycroft, Chardigny, and Zhordania, who then appealed to the Armenian and Georgian commanders in the field to cease military activities. The trio announced that an Anglo-French commission, accompanied by Georgian attachés, would arrive at the front to explain the details and to implement the cease-fire.[72] Obviously the Allied officers had decided to impose their plan with or without the cooperation and approval of the Armenian government.[73]

[70] Rep. of Arm. Archives, File 66a/3, H. H. Vrastani Divanagitakan Nerkayatsutschutiun ev Vrastani Karavarutiun, 1919–1920: Teghekatu, 1919; Khatisian, Hanrapetutian zargatsume, p. 109.

[71] Rep. of Arm. Archives, File 65/1; Dokumenty i materialy, pp. 480–481.

[72] Dokumenty i materialy, p. 480. See also Britain, WO 33/965, nos. 3043 and 3050, and FO 371/3661, 2034/1015/58. Noi Zhordania later asserted that British officers, in their extreme hostility to Georgia, organized the Armenian advance over Lori but that when the Georgian army began to take the initiative the British, "having miscalculated," intervened to halt the warfare. See his Moia Zhizn' (Stanford, 1968), pp. 89–90. The communiqués signed by the Allied officers and Zhordania do not, however, lend credence to this interpretation.

[73] A Soviet historian, citing a document in the Georgian SSR Central State Archives

The mixed commission, composed of British Captain Douglas-With-ers[74] (chairman), French Captain Gasfield,[75] and Georgian Colonel Japaridze, arrived in Karakilisa on December 28 to confer with division commander General Silikian and the Armenian delegation which earlier had met with Captain Green. Delegation chairman Martiros Harutiunian attempted to alter several of the terms brought from Tiflis but finally, on instructions from Erevan, yielded to strong British pressure. Armenia agreed to acquiesce in the truce on condition that her delegation be allowed to proceed to Tiflis to clarify certain moot points in the draft settlement.[76] On December 30 Captain Douglas-Withers informed his superiors in Tiflis and Baku that Armenia had consented to the plan. Hostilities were to cease at midnight, December 31, 1918, and the Armenians would withdraw at a date to be determined in consultations at Tiflis. Douglas-Withers concurred that certain existing ambiguities in the Allied terms required clarification, and he expressed gratification at Armenia's "nobility and sincere desire for peace." [77]

---

of the October Revolution, charges that British agents had incited the war in order to secure a firm hold in Transcaucasia. A British officer, identified only as Webster, purportedly urged Georgian officials to expel all Armenians from Georgia inasmuch as their bourgeoisie were scheming to seize full control of the country's economy. The Armenians, Webster was alleged to have said, were the Jews of the Caucasus and planned to leave no Georgians in Tiflis. Thus, Georgia should turn away from dependence on Armenian capital and instead utilize British capital. The same historian claims that other British agents in Erevan were encouraging the Armenians to strike against Georgia to provide the appropriate pretext for Imperial forces to march in and create a neutral zone which the British could exploit. See V. I. Adamiia, *Iz istorii angliiskoi interventsii v Gruzii (1918–1921 gg.)* (Sukhumi, 1961), pp. 73–74. From all available historical evidence, the accusation is grossly exaggerated, if not totally unfounded. It is quite possible that individual British officers—there was a Webster—might have expressed themselves as described by Adamiia, but Armeno-Georgian hostilities in the disputed zone predated the arrival of the first British soldier at Batum, and, furthermore, not a single British representative, military or civil, was in Erevan during the entire course of the conflict.

[74] Herbert Henry Douglas-Withers, Brigade Major of the 39th Infantry Brigade, Baku, was then on a special mission in Tiflis to arrange for the transportation and billeting of British troops.

[75] Nicolas Gasfield was one of the Allied officers who earlier in December had gone to Karabagh to inform Andranik of General Thomson's directive to withdraw to Zangezur.

[76] Vratzian, *Hanrapetutiun*, p. 200; Ds. Aghayan, *Hoktemberian revoliutsian ev hai zhoghovrdi azatagrume* (Erevan, 1957), p. 205; V. L. Avagian, *Edjer Andrkovkasum otarerkria interventsiayi patmutiunits (1918 t)* (Erevan, 1957), p. 127.

[77] *Dokumenty i materialy*, pp. 483, 488–489; Khatisian, *Hanrapetutian zargatsume*, pp. 110–111. See also Britain, Cab 27/39, E.C. 2977 and E.C. 2995, and WO 33/965, no. 3073.

The Final Encounters

As talks proceeded in Tiflis and Karakilisa, the military fought to gain an advantageous field position. The momentum of the Armenian drive had slowed considerably by December 25. The troops had maintained the offensive for ten days without rest, and typhus had broken out in the ranks. No reinforcements could be anticipated, since much of the army was engaged in the unsecured southern districts of the Republic. Moreover, once the front had moved beyond the Armenian villages of Lori into the adjacent plain to the north, partisan bands no longer advanced alongside the regulars. Instead, the Armenian insurgents of Lori returned to their native villages, content with their victory and convinced that their land would be annexed to Armenia. Strategically, the Georgians now held a favorable though exceedingly precarious line. With the front approaching the Khram River and so near to Tiflis, army regulars and the People's Guard were able to join the battle quickly and logistics were simplified.[78]

From December 25 to 27 the military action entailed a series of skirmishes. The Georgians became more daring but failed to make any significant gains. On the twenty-eighth, however, General Mazniev ordered a 3,500-man battle group to a full-scale attack and by nightfall had retrieved Shulaver and several smaller villages and had inflicted nearly two hundred casualties upon the Armenians. At long last Georgia tasted victory. For the next two days there ensued a brisk contest for control of Sadakhlu. The village changed hands several times until at last the Armenians entrenched themselves at the station and the Georgians in the town.[79]

Both armies understood on the morning of December 31 that this was to be the last opportunity to secure a commanding position before the cease-fire at midnight. The battles raged all day, the Armenian columns at the center and the right making significant strategic gains but the typhus-riddled column to the left being driven back. By late afternoon Armenian companies had taken the heights east of Sadakhlu and, again outflanking the Georgians, had cut the rails at Mamai in the direction of Shulaver. When the last shot was fired, the two armies

[78] Djamalian, "Hai-vratsakan knjire" (April, 1929), p. 145; Vratzian, *Hanrapetutiun*, pp. 200–201. A prominent Dashnakist, Babalian, *op. cit.*, p. 26, has roundly criticized Kachaznuni for the Premier's excessive caution and his determination to keep the hostilities localized. Babalian claims that, although the Armenian objective was the Khram River, the Armenian military establishment, had it been unfettered by Kachaznuni, could have marched right into Tiflis and shown the Georgians where matters stood.

[79] Vratzian, *Hanrapetutiun*, pp. 201–202.

stood along a very irregular line: the Armenians dominated sites east, north, and south of Sadakhlu, whereas the Georgians had successfully penetrated to a considerable distance southwest of the village.[80]

Who won the war? The Georgians claimed major victories and insisted that the enemy would have been driven back into the Erevan guberniia had there not been a cease-fire. This the Armenians denied, contending that, had it not been for the truce imposed by the Allies, Dro's army would have completed the encirclement of the Georgian forces at Sadakhlu. Beyond the battlefield little was known of the true military situation. Several European newspapers as far away as London carried brief accounts of the conflict and, depending upon the source of their information, reported either an Armenian victory or a successful Georgian defense against an Armenian invasion.[81] Perhaps the Armeno-Georgian war might best be described as inconclusive. The Armenian columns had advanced over northern Lori and had nearly attained their goal, the Khram River, when the Allies demanded an end to the hostilities. On the other hand, after steadily retreating for the first ten days, the Georgians had shown greater courage and initiative during the last week of December. Could they have driven the Armenians out of the Borchalu uezd if the Allies had not intervened? The question remains disputed although the fact that all battles had taken place in lands formerly held by the Georgian army is not. Statistically, the Armenians had suffered fewer casualties than the Georgians and had given less than a hundred prisoners, while they had captured two armored trains, twenty-eight cannons, nearly seventy-five machine guns, two hundred loaded freight cars, and as many as a thousand Georgian soldiers.[82] But even these figures, though appearing to disprove the Georgian boast of a smashing triumph, do not in themselves prove a decisive Armenian victory.[83]

[80] *Ibid.*, pp. 203–205; Rep. of Arm. Archives, File 66a/3.

[81] Documents in the British Archives show that both the War Office and the Foreign Office were poorly informed about the happenings in the Caucasus. The British military commanders on the scene, having had little time to adjust to local conditions, even reported the Armenian army as being just one mile south of Tiflis. For the sketchy information reaching London from Constantinople, Batum, Tiflis, and Baku, see Britain, FO 371/3667, File 2897/58, and WO 33/965. Armenian representatives in Europe were extremely concerned about the war, especially over early reports of a Georgian victory. See Rep. of Arm. Archives, File 101/2, *H. H. Patvirakutiun, 1919: H. Ohandjaniani Tghtere*, Isahakian to Ohandjanian, Jan. 14, 1919, Ohandjanian to Isahakian, Jan. 11, 1919, and Ohandjanian to Varandian, Jan. 22, 1919.

[82] Denikin, *Ocherki smuty*, IV, 154; Djamalian, "Hai-vratsakan knjire" (April, 1929), p. 140; Rep. of Arm. Archives, File 66a/3; Hamo, "Hayastani Hanrapetutian erkamia kiankn u gordsuneutiune," *Hairenik: Batsarik tiv* (Boston, 1920), p. 38.

[83] An English correspondent and author, stating that he had gone to the Caucasus

The Neutral Zone in Lori

On January 1, 1919, the Allied commission led by Captain Douglas-Withers arrived back in Tiflis with General Gabriel Korganian and the Armenian delegation that had come to work out the details of the peace plan. Martiros Harutiunian and the other Armenian spokesmen asserted that the message relayed to Erevan by Rycroft, Chardigny, and Zhordania on December 25 had clearly stated that the Georgian army was to retain its "present line," that is, the positions held on that date. As such an interpretation would deprive Georgia of her gains of the final campaign and leave Shulaver and Sadakhlu under British supervision, Foreign Minister Gegechkori threatened to break off the talks if the Armenians proved adamant. The crisis passed, however, when news reached Tiflis that a British peace-keeping mission had arrived at Sadakhlu on January 2 and that on the following day the Armenian army had begun to withdraw.[84]

In Parliament Gegechkori proclaimed that the "Erevan adventure" had been liquidated. Georgia, he asserted, had proved that she had not shed first blood and had demonstrated that her neighbors could not impose their will upon the Republic. He accused Armenia of dishonorable conduct by striking precisely when other foreign armed forces were moving into Georgia. But the calculations of the Armenian government, Gegechkori announced with gratification, had miscarried. Thereupon the Parliament adopted a resolution declaring the Armenian plot to destroy Georgia's territorial integrity foiled and expressing satisfaction that the enemy had been obliged to draw back. In view of this turn of events, the resolution concluded, Georgia would be favorably inclined to begin discussions for peace.[85] The Menshevik-dominated Soviet of Workers' Deputies shared the professed exuberance of the cabinet and Parliament and extolled the People's Red Guard for shattering the coordinated scheme of Dashnaktsutiun and

---

"with the common European prejudice against the Armenians," and thus half inclined to credit the cynical view that "the Armenians were probably destined by Divine providence to be massacred," insisted that the British military authorities had saved the situation for Georgia: "The two people came to blows in December, 1918, and, to the astonishment of those who supposed the Armenians to be a race of degraded moneymakers, these routed the Georgians, and would, perhaps, have captured Tiflis, the Georgian capital, had not the Allies intervened." See C. E. Bechofer-[Roberts], *In Denikin's Russia and the Caucasus, 1919–1920* (London, [1921]), pp. 14, 257.

[84] *Dokumenty i materialy*, p. 489; US Archives, RG 59, 861.00/6583.

[85] *Dokumenty i materialy*, pp. 483–491; Denikin, *Ocherki smuty*, IV, 154.

the Armenian bourgeoisie to overthrow the Republic of Georgia.[86]

Despite these overbearing pronouncements, some of which might have been intended to cloud the real circumstances at the front, Georgian, Armenian, and Allied officials met from January 9 to 17, 1919, to finalize the provisional settlement. The conference, chaired by British Lieutenant Colonel Robert Neil Stewart, commander of the 2d Battalion, Cameron Highlanders, and attended by Gegechkori, Ramishvili, Assistant Foreign Minister Konstantin Sabakhtarashvili, and General A. K. Gedevanov for Georgia and by General Gabriel Korganian and Harutiunian's five-man delegation of legislators for Armenia, laid the bases for the resumption of diplomatic relations, for a transit agreement, and for the exchange of prisoners (which took place on January 23).[87] With extreme reluctance Armenia further assented to Georgia's temporary retention of two companies of infantry in Akhalkalak, but only on condition that the district be placed under Allied supervision and that Armenian participation in the administration be guaranteed. Lieutenant Colonel Alan Ritchie would serve as the British military representative.[88] The conference also adopted the British-sponsored plan to create a neutral zone in the Borchalu uezd, from the outskirts of Sadakhlu to the positions held by Armenia before the outbreak of the two-week war (see map 8). The commissioner general of the zone was to be an Allied officer, who, although having an Armenian and a Georgian assistant, would possess the ultimate authority in matters pertaining to the borders of the zone, the number and composition of the troops stationed in it, the administrative apparatus, and the local militia. The neutral zone, which included the productive copper mines of Alaverdi, forty-three villages, predominantly Armenian, and approximately 30 miles of railway with six stations, was divided into the districts of Uzunlar, Vorontsovka, and

[86] *Dokumenty i materialy*, p. 492
[87] *Hairenik* (daily), April 15, 1919, p. 2.
[88] Alan MacDougall Ritchie, 1st Battalion, Royal Scots (Lothian Regiment), 81st Brigade, was appointed military representative on January 26 and departed for Akhalkalak on the twenty-eighth with 4 officers and 122 enlisted men of the 2d Battalion, Duke of Cornwall's Light Infantry Regiment, 82d Brigade. For a copy of Ritchie's orders, setting forth his powers and duties in Akhalkalak, see Britain, WO 95/4880, General Staff War Diary, January, 1919, Appendix IV. Ritchie's company did not reach Akhalkalak until the end of February because of road conditions and a Muslim uprising in that district and in neighboring Akhaltsikh. Until the spring of 1919, when the Georgian army finally regained control in these troubled regions, Ritchie attempted to mediate between the opposing sides and to win the cooperation of the local Muslim councils that held sway in the interim. His criticisms of the Georgian administration and garrison in Akhalkalak are frequently recorded in the battalion and divisional war diaries. See Britain, WO 95/4891–4895.

Alaverdi. The three districts, as well as the thirteen village clusters into which they were subdivided, were each to have a native resident commissar.[89] It had already been decided that Captain A. S. G. Douglas of the 4th Battalion, Rifle Brigade, would serve as the Allied commissioner general.[90]

The Armenians of Georgia

The brunt of the war fell not upon the combatants or even the villages of Lori but upon the Armenians of Tiflis and the surrounding communities. Although Zhordania's government repeatedly underscored the distinction between the Armenian people and what it described as a clique of Armenian militarists, it nonetheless took stringent measures against the entire population. On December 24, 1918, the Parliament passed legislation making treason punishable by death and confiscation of properties, and two days later the governor of the Tiflis guberniia declared all Armenians technically prisoners of war. Those Armenians in Tiflis who were natives of the districts under enemy occupation, that is, the southern half of the Borchalu uezd, were required to register within twenty-four hours or face prosecution under the law of treason. This announcement was followed by numerous arrests and the expropriation of many Armenian-owned mansions and business establishments. Militiamen received exorbitant sums of money as ransom from wealthy Armenians, who were threatened with death or else incarceration in the dread prison of Metekh.[91]

The Armenian and Russian organizations in Tiflis protested in vain.

[89] S. Kh. Karapetian, *Zinvads apstambutiune Lorum 1921 tvakanin* (Erevan, 1955), pp. 12–14; Avagian, *op. cit.*, pp. 127–128. A copy of the settlement is in the Central State Historical Archives of the Armenian SSR, Fund 111. See also US Archives, RG 59, 861.00/6583, and RG 84, Tiflis Consulate, 1920, Press Reports.

[90] Archibald Sholto George Douglas had been in charge of a peace-keeping mission in the disputed zone since the cessation of hostilities. He was formally appointed commissioner general with the rank of Acting Major on January 27. Having one company of 4th Brigade Rifles as support, Douglas established British headquarters at Alaverdi. Like Ritchie's communiqués, the reports by Douglas were very critical of Georgian officials, particularly those in the Armenian villages lying just inside the neutral zone. See Britain, WO 95/4890, 4th Battalion, Rifle Brigade, War Diary. Colonel Stewart, who assumed temporary command of the 81st Brigade while the Armeno-Georgian conference was in progress, received instructions from 27th Division headquarters to coordinate the activities of the British military representatives in Akhalkalak and the Lori neutral zone. See Britain, WO 95/4891, 81st Brigade, War Diary.

[91] Djamalian, "Hai-vratsakan knjire" (March, 1929), pp. 121–122; Denikin, *Ocherki smuty*, IV, 154; F. Makharadze, *Diktatura men'shevistskoi partii v Gruzii* (Moscow, 1921), p. 74.

The doors of the National Council of Armenians in Georgia were sealed and members of the council were placed under house arrest. Several newspapers, including the Dashnakist *Ashkhatavor* ("Laborer") and *Nor Horizon* ("New Horizon"), the Social Revolutionary *Trudovoe znamia* ("The Labor Banner"), and the Constitutional Democrat *Kavkazskoe slovo* ("Word of the Caucasus"), were suspended. Dashnakist deputies in the Tiflis City Duma were arrested, and Armenian representatives in Parliament faced the shouts and taunts of the Georgian nationalist factions and the stony silence of the Social Democrat majority.[92]

It was with extreme relief that the Armenians of Georgia greeted the news of the cease-fire, but many new tribulations lay ahead. During January of 1919 hundreds of these people were arrested and deported to Kutais, where they were paraded through the streets as prisoners of war. This tactic, according to the Erevan government, was intended to bemuddle the fact that Georgia had actually taken few prisoners upon the field of battle and to deceive the public into believing the official propaganda boasts of a stunning Georgian victory. When the Armenian Council of Georgia was subsequently permitted to resume its activities, it denounced with acerbic indignation the unjust, cruel treatment inflicted by the Georgian government. Its protest read in part: "The explanation of the Minister of Interior that this national persecution must be ascribed to the unauthorized acts of individual officials can only leave the most onerous impression upon the Armenian public, especially since the explanation follows that which has become a most common word of late—a word about the supposed respect for the Armenian people, a word that can now only wound the sensitivity of a people living under the most debasing and oppressive of conditions." [93]

During the course of the retaliatory measures against the Armenian civilian population, the governor of the Tiflis guberniia issued to a few prominent Armenians papers that gave them the right to come and go freely and exempted them from being arrested simply because they happened to be Armenian. Highly incensed by this discrimination and hypocrisy, the widely respected Menshevik-Internationalist, Arshak G. Zohrabian (Zurabov), returned one such document to the Georgian government with the taunt that he wished to share the fate of the

[92] Kadishev, *Interventsiia v Zakavkaz'e*, p. 173; Vratzian, *Hanrapetutiun*, p. 206; Varandian, *op. cit.*, p. 92; Djamalian, "Hai-vratsakan knjire" (March, 1929), pp. 121–122, 124; *Hairenik* (daily), March 20, 1919, p. 2, from *Jakatamart* (Constantinople).
[93] Rep. of Arm. Archives, File 65/1; Djamalian, "Hai-vratsakan knjire" (March, 1929), pp. 122–125; Vratzian, *Hanrapetutiun*, pp. 205–209.

Armenian people, however bitter that fate might be. He condemned the chauvinism of his Georgian colleagues and exclaimed to Premier Zhordania that the outrageous and shameful acts being committed on the streets of the city they both loved so dearly were worse than at any time during the abhorrent days of the tsars.[94]

In the countryside, meanwhile, lawless bands and organized units of the People's (Red) Guard plundered Armenian villages and spread terror to gain retribution and to punish the "disloyal and treacherous" inhabitants. The Armenians of Shulaver and Bolnis-Khachen, for example, were driven from their homes, the town of Belyi-Kliuch was sacked, and the girls of its Armenian orphanage ravished by guardsmen.[95]

The Georgians further exploited the crisis to take control of the city administration of Tiflis by dismissing scores of Armenian civic officials, police, and workmen, and calling new municipal elections, giving notice that those eligible to vote must be registered as Georgian citizens. The Armenian plurality of Tiflis, from anger, fear, and humiliation, stayed away from the polls, as did thousands of Russians, who would not condescend to accept the status of Georgian subjects.[96] Tiflis thus finally became a Georgian city ruled by Georgians. Armenians who previously could not have imagined residing anywhere but in the magnificent capital of the Caucasus now began to look toward Erevan. If Armenia endured and expanded, the trickle of Georgian Armenians emigrating to the south would undoubtedly become a surging current.

The negative aspects of the war between Georgia and Armenia were clearly apparent and reached far deeper than the misfortunes that befell the Georgian Armenians. For more than one reason the two republics needed each other, yet they had pulled in opposite directions.

[94] Varandian, op. cit., pp. 92–94; Djamalian, "Hai-vratsakan knjire" (April, 1929), pp. 138–139; Vratzian, Hanrapetutiun, pp. 209–210.

[95] Djamalian, "Hai-vratsakan knjire" (March, 1929), p. 118, and (April, 1929), pp. 136–137; Rep. of Arm. Archives, File 66a/3. At the end of December, 1918, the Georgian Chief of Field Staff, Major General Imnadze, announced that the People's Guard was being sent against the Belyi-Kliuch region, where the Armenian villagers were reported to have joined Dro's regulars and to be causing disturbances to the rear of the Georgian lines. See Iz arm-gruz otnoshenii, pp. 125–126. The commander of the People's Guard, Valiko Jugheli, later describing the Georgian operations in the Ekaterinenfeld district, expressed anguish over the destruction of such proud and prosperous historic Armenian villages as Bolnis-Khachen. See Bor'ba, May 12, 1920, pp. 2–3.

[96] US Archives, RG 256, 861K.00/49; La Chesnais, op. cit., pp. 154–155; Djamalian, "Hai-vratsakan knjire" (April, 1929), pp. 145–147; Varandian, op. cit., p. 97.

The wounds inflicted would be long in healing. The Allied Powers, upon which the fate of Transcaucasia was so dependent, had been treated to a regrettable display of inexperience and impulsive action. They had cause to question whether anything could be made of independence in Transcaucasia or whether independence would become another word for anarchy.[97] The conflict seriously taxed the physical and material energies of the two new states at a time when their resources were insufficient to cope with domestic problems alone. While Armenian units advanced over Lori, the population of Erevan was starving and without shelter, and as the Georgian army dispatched men and supplies to the front, the Tiflis government grappled with a financial crisis and widespread internal unrest.

Still, both Armenia and Georgia could find solace in the events of December, 1918. Even though the Armenian army had been required to withdraw to its original positions, northern Lori had been taken from Georgia and made into a neutral zone under Allied supervision. Furthermore, the overconfident Georgians, their public declarations aside, knew that henceforth they must reckon with the Armenians as military equals—the battles had raged dangerously close to Tiflis. And if, as Armenia persistently charged, Georgia aspired to dominate the affairs of Transcaucasia, this goal had been dealt a severe setback.

The Georgians, too, could list positive results. Their army had been tested and had stood firm at the crucial moment. Georgia had succeeded in retaining Akhalkalak, whereas Armenia had been forced to relinquish all territory seized during the war. Moreover, as Tiflis had become the headquarters of the British command in western Transcaucasia and was more closely linked to Europe than any other capital in the Caucasus, Georgia had been able both to present her case and to negotiate directly with Allied representatives, thus gaining a decided advantage over Armenia. Zhordania's government hoped that the Armenian monopoly on European sympathy had begun to crumble and that the rights of the Georgian republic would be given proper consideration by the world peace conference, which was beginning to assemble in Paris.

[97] The general opposition of the French government to the dismemberment of the Russian Empire was fortified by the reports by Colonel Chardigny. On January 4 he wrote, "This war is new proof that the organization of the Caucasus into independent States is impossible." See Britain, WO 33/965, no. 3181.

5

The
First Winter

The first winter in the Republic of Armenia brought unbearable suffering to the people and insurmountable difficulties to the coalition government of Hovhannes Kachaznuni. Even with the evacuation of the Ottoman armies, Armenia remained landlocked and confined to the Erevan guberniia and its margins to the north in Lori and Kazakh. And within the Erevan guberniia itself, the Muslim-populated districts defied the Armenian government, while lawless bands terrorized the inhabitants and frustrated efforts to bring order to the land.

Refugees, Famine, and Pestilence

The chaotic situation in Armenia was intensified by the presence of approximately 500,000 refugees, nearly 350,000 of whom were crammed into the Erevan guberniia. These wretched people were, at the end of 1918, concentrated as follows:[1]

[1] Ds. Aghayan, *Hoktemberian revoliutsian ev hai zhoghovrdi azatagrume* (Erevan, 1957), p. 195. Statistics in the Central State Historical Archives of the Armenian SSR, Fund 68/200, work 213, show that there were 310,835 refugees and 271,041 native destitute. See S. T. Alikhanian, *Sovetakan Rusastani dere hai zhoghovrdi azatagrman gordsum (1917–1921 t.t.)* (Erevan, 1966), p. 89. A detailed statistical breakdown by the Armenian government showed the presence of 393,700 refugees in the Republic in 1919. See Rep. of Arm. Archives, File 7/7, *Hayastani Hanrapetutiun, 1919 t.* Numerous reports of American and British officials and relief workers in the Caucasus confirmed that there were at least a half million Armenian refugees, more than 300,000 of whom were crammed into the Armenian republic. See, for example, James L. Barton. *Story of Near East Relief (1915–1930)* (New York, 1930), pp. 121–124; [Herbert Hoover], *The Memoirs of Herbert Hoover*, Vol. I (New York, 1952), p. 387; US Archives, RG 84, Tiflis Consulate, 1919, pt. 3, File 360, and RG 256, 867B.4016/8 and 867B.50/1; Britain, FO 371/3658, 47290/68107/512/58, and FO 608/79, File 342/1/9.

District	Number of refugees	District	Number of refugees
Erevan	75,000	Daralagiaz	36,000
Ashtarak	30,000	Bash-Abaran	35,000
Akhta–Elenovka	22,000	Etchmiadzin	70,000
Bash-Garni	15,000	Karakilisa	16,000
Novo-Bayazit	38,000	Dilijan	13,000

These figures do not include the additional thousands who had found temporary sanctuary in Zangezur and Karabagh, Georgia, the North Caucasus, and the steppelands of Russia.

The winter of 1918–1919 was one of the longest and most severe in the annals of Erevan. The homeless masses, lacking food, clothing, and medicine, passed hellish months in blizzard conditions. The starving people sometimes demonstrated or rioted for food, but these sporadic outbursts were to no avail. The state granaries were empty. Allied officials who came to Erevan brought hope that before too long provisions would begin to arrive from abroad. Until that time the nation must persevere. But soon even this hope faded. An American eyewitness, overwhelmed by the misery, wrote:

A terrible population! Unspeakably filthy and tatterdemalion throngs; shelterless, deathstricken throngs milling from place to place; children crying aloud; women sobbing in broken inarticulate lamentation; men utterly hopeless and reduced to staggering weakness, heedless of the tears rolling down their dirt-streaked faces. As a picture of the Armenians most in evidence in Armenia I can think of nothing better than this, unless I turn to other kinds of mobs: Large numbers here and there, wide-eyed, eager, hands outstretched in wolfish supplication; teeth bared in a ghastly grin that had long since ceased to be a smile—an emaciated, skin-stretched grin, fixed and uncontrollable.[2]

The pitiful multitude lay in the snow, in partially destroyed buildings, on doorsteps of churches, eventually too weak to protest or even to beg any longer. They lived in the "land of stalking death," waiting with sunken face and swollen belly for the touch of that angel. And death came, delivering from anguish thousands upon thousands of refugees and native inhabitants alike.

Many who withstood the exposure and famine succumbed to the ravaging diseases that infested the derelict masses. Typhus was the major

[2] Eleanor Franklin Egan, "This To Be Said for the Turk," Saturday Evening Post, CXCII (Dec. 20, 1919), 14. See also Barton, op. cit., p. 121. For reports of other Americans in the Caucasus, see US Archives, RG 59, 861.00/4017 and 867.48/1118/1138/1216, and RG 256, 867B.00/74 and 867B.48/10/22.

killer, striking in every district and at every age group, taking its largest toll among the children. The phenomenon of death came to be both
expected and accepted. The insensible bodies were gathered from the
streets by the hundreds each week and covered in mass graves, often
without mourners or final rites. In January, 1919, a government report
showed that there was scarcely a household in all Erevan which had
escaped the typhus epidemic. That year in the capital alone some
19,000 people contracted the disease and nearly 10,000 died from the
three-headed monster—exposure, famine, pestilence.[3] One of hundreds
of newspaper descriptions read: "The populace is feeding upon the
bodies of dead cats and dogs. There have even been cases when a starving
mother has eaten the kidney or the liver from the corpse of her own
child. . . . The skeleton-like women and children rummage in the
refuse heaps for moldered shoes and, after cooking them for three days,
eat them." [4] The famine became so acute in Erevan that by the spring
of 1919 the daily ration of bread was reduced to 4 ounces, and this only
for those who were fortunate enough to qualify.[5]

Conditions in the outlying regions were even worse. The inhabitants
of entire villages perished. A report from Sardarabad in February, 1919,
stated: "Sixty-five percent of the population of the district has died,
and the remaining small percent has scarcely a few days of life left.
They have become skeletons in the true sense of the word; they cannot
move or even talk. . . . The dead are left in their homes for weeks,
torn to pieces by dogs. The death of whole families often passes un-
noticed." [6] Forty percent of the inhabitants of eight villages near Etchmiadzin and 25 percent of the sixteen villages in neighboring Ashtarak
had succumbed by April. During the winter of 1918–1919 the population of Talin, a district midway between Etchmiadzin and Alexandropol, was cut in half and nearly 60 percent of the Armenians in the
Surmalu uezd starved to death.[7] The following account was not at all
unusual: "On the road from Igdir to Blur a horse had died more than
a month ago, its carcass eaten by dogs, only dry bones remaining.
There, boys of eight and ten years of age, two brothers, were crushing

[3] Aghayan, *op. cit.*, p. 202; V. A. Mikayelian, *Hayastani giughatsiutiune Sovetakan ishkhanutian hamar mghvads paikari zhamanakashrdjanum (1917–1920 t.t.)* (Erevan, 1960), pp. 103–104, 180; S. H. Tovmasian, *Sovetakan Hayastane Hoktemberi dsnundn e* (Erevan, 1957), p. 56.
[4] Mikayelian, *op. cit.*, p. 108.
[5] Vratzian, *Hanrapetutiun*, p. 216.
[6] Aghayan, *op. cit.*, p. 201; Mikayelian, *op. cit.*, p. 104.
[7] H. M. Elchibekian and A. M. Hakobian, *Urvagdser Sovetakan Hayastani patmutian*, pt. 1 (Erevan, 1954), p. 35; Mikayelian, *op. cit.*, pp. 104–108; Aghayan, *op. cit.*, p. 201.

the stinking bones with rocks, taking the marrow and eating it. This example is not one, not ten, not a thousand." [8]

In the north of Armenia a similar situation prevailed. From Bash-Abaran word came that "the population has fallen upon the fields; it is grazing, swelling, and dying." From near Lake Sevan it was reported, "The native and refugee Armenians in the district of Akhta are starving. . . . Unless aid and seed-grain arrive it will be too late." But aid did not come and the following message announced, "The people have been annihilated by starvation. Hundreds are dying; the district is slipping from our hands." [9] From Karakilisa, a government official wrote: "If I say that in the fields and forests there no longer remain any greens, whether edible or inedible, believe me. On the one hand the refugees and on the other the natives are strewn upon the mountains from dawn to dusk; weak, languid, and colorless, they are quietly picking grass, making a salad, and eating it. In this way people deceive themselves in order to live a few hours, a few days more." [10] The grasses bloated, poisoned, and killed. And all the while the winter storms raged.

Nor did accounts from the east and south of Erevan bring any com-

[8] Mikayelian, *op. cit.*, p. 107. Igdir was one of Armenia's most devastated and famine-stricken districts. An American correspondent described the situation there in the spring of 1919, that is, after the freezing weather had already passed:

We found the children, such as they were, inhabiting an orphanage wherein one sickened at putridity's horrible odor, and were informed that there were neither medicines nor disinfectants wherewith to allay the conditions of the many little sick-beds. Sick? Say, rather the bed-ridden—a word which more justly describes those tiny, withered up, crone-like creatures, upon whose faces the skin seemed stretched to a drumhead's tightness; whose peering eyes shot terror and anguish, as if Death's presence were already perceptible to them, and who lay there at Famine's climax of physical exhaustion. In those young, yet grotesquely aged faces, we seemed to see a long lifetime of tragedy packed into eight or ten childish years. . . . The mud huts which we visited presented an invariable picture—a barren, cave-like interior, lacking one stick of furniture or household utensil, and with a few bleached bones scattered here and there. The occupants, stretched out on the clay floor, would half lift themselves to regard us with dazed and questioning eyes. Those gaunt faces, those attenuated bodies clad in a shagginess of filthy rags, seemed centuries removed from civilization. You felt that you had stumbled into prehistoric man's den during some great famine year. [Melville Chater, "The Land of Stalking Death," *National Geographic Magazine*, XXXVI (Nov., 1919), 417–418.]

[9] Vratzian, *Hanrapetutiun*, p. 215.

[10] Aghayan, *op. cit.*, pp. 201–202. Egan, *op. cit.*, p. 74, wrote: "Everywhere in the fields there were people down on their knees searching for grasses to eat, though I do not know why I should use the word 'fields'. . . . I did not believe there were people anywhere down on their knees eating grass. I thought it very likely that starving persons might go out and gather grasses and greens of various sorts to be prepared for food, but that men, women and children should gather like cattle in herds to graze, this I did not believe—not until I saw it."

fort; they were all alike. In the uezd of Novo-Bayazit more than 25,000 people slowly starved to death. "The women and children are like phantoms. For the love of God, spare us from death, give us bread!" [11] Into Daralagiaz fled natives of Nakhichevan, presenting a terrifying sight:

Naked, barefoot, or covering a part of their grotesque bodies with assorted rags, and bent under the burden of their little ones, the refugee population wanders from village to village begging for bread, but bread is not to be found. There are among the refugees, nourished by grass instead of bread, many cases of poisoning. Or else, as if crazed, they roam the streets uttering incoherent and disconnected phrases. Many of the refugees in this district still live under open skies and pass their days in the snow, rain, and mud. . . . Joining forces, famine and misery are harvesting this pitiful population of 17,000.[12]

For the Armenians, the winter of 1918–1919 completed the decimation that had begun with the deportations and massacres of 1915.

By the spring of 1919 the typhus epidemic had run its vicious course, the weather had improved, and the snows had begun to thaw. Conditions for survival improved slightly, although thousands more were to die before the crisis had passed. The statistics were horrifying. Approximately 200,000 people, almost 20 percent of the Republic's population, had perished by midyear. In 1919, for each 1,000 persons in Armenia there were 8.7 births and 204.2 deaths, a net loss of 195.5.[13] It was verily a land of death.

A Country of Ruin

The burden of several hundred thousand unsheltered and unemployed refugees was enough in itself to cause an economic maelstrom. Even during normal times the land under the actual jurisdiction of the Armenian government could not have supported so needy a population. The fertile soil of the Araxes valley and the once-cultivated fields of Turkish Armenia now lay under Muslim domination. As the sowing season approached in 1919, almost no seed grain was left, for the hun-

---

[11] Vratzian, *Hanrapetutiun*, p. 215.

[12] *Ibid.*

[13] A. M. Elchibekian, *Velikaia Oktiabr'skaia sotsialisticheskaia revoliutsiia i pobeda Sovetskoi vlasti v Armenii* (Erevan, 1957), p. 106; M. A. Melikian, *K voprosu o formirovanii armianskoi natsii i ee sotsialisticheskogo preobrazovaniia* (Erevan, 1957), p. 101. From among non-Soviet sources, Khatisian, *Hanrapetutian zargatsume*, p. 98, estimates that no fewer than 150,000 persons died of starvation and disease, while Vratzian, *Hanrapetutiun*, p. 169, places the figure at 180,000.

ger-crazed masses had seized every available particle. It seemed impossible to protect from the ravenous mobs even the little that was planted.

Industry had not been encouraged in Russian Armenia during the century of Romanov rule. The Erevan guberniia still retained its agrarian character, with the Shustov cognac and wine works the only significant source of industrial income. Home manufacture of furniture, textiles, implements, and handicrafts accounted for nearly all other nonagricultural revenue, but in 1919 this was extremely limited by the scarcity of raw materials. In neighboring Zangezur and Lori the copper industry had been developed by foreign firms, yet these, too, were useless to Armenia, as the mines were either flooded or else beyond the jurisdiction of Erevan. The general decline in production was further aggravated by the widespread destruction of railways, bridges, auto and rail garages and repair shops. Industrial income had never been high, but in 1919 it totaled less than 2 rubles per capita, scarcely 8 percent of the prewar level in Russian Armenia.[14]

The drastic decrease in agricultural production, which had begun during the war years, contributed heavily to the Armenian tragedy. A poor harvest in 1914 was followed by the conscription of farmhands by the thousands, the revolutionary upheavals and civil strife throughout the Russian Empire, the Turkish invasion of Transcaucasia, and the influx of nearly a half million refugees. The outcome of these bewildering events was that, of the 276,957 dessiatines (747,784 acres) of land cultivated before the World War, only one-fourth, 75,714 dessiatines (204,428 acres), was sown in 1919. Fields planted in grain, Armenia's basic agricultural product, dwindled from a total of 247,766 dessiatines (668,968 acres) to 71,778 dessiatines (193,801 acres), with the yield per dessiatine considerably less in 1919. If allowance is made for the seed grain kept in reserve, the harvest of 1919 provided some 55 pounds of breadstuff per capita. Had the crop been divided equally

---

[14] Melikian, op. cit., p. 114; Tovmasian, op. cit., pp. 69–70; G. Galoyan, Bor'ba za Sovetskuiu vlast' v Armenii (Moscow, 1957), p. 113; P. I. Engoyan, Hayastani Kompartiayi paikare respublikayi industriatsman hamar (Erevan, 1965), pp. 8–17. These and the figures following in this section pertain only to the territory now included within Soviet Armenia, that is, minus the province of Kars and the districts of Sharur, Nakhichevan, and Surmalu. For surveys of the industrial development in Armenia before 1918, see T. Kh. Hakobian, Erevani patmutiune, Vol. II (Erevan, 1963), pp. 40–100, 501–505; P. T. Voskerchian, Sovetakan Hayastani ardiunaberutiune 1920–1940 (Erevan, 1966), pp. 3–15; M. H. Adonts, Hayastani zhoghovrdakan tntesutiune ev hai tntesagitakan mitke XX dari skzbin (Erevan, 1968), pp. 187–226; Kh. G. Gulanian, Urvagdser hai tntesagitakan mtki patmutian (Erevan, 1959), pp. 73–89. See also Grigor Agababian, "The Economic Situation of the Armenian Republic," Asiatic Review, XVI (April, 1920), 310–312.

among the citizenry, each person would have received a daily ration of less than 3 ounces.[15]

Tremendous losses were also registered in the lesser cultures, as shown in the following table with the land measurements converted into acres:

Culture	Acreage in 1913	Acreage in 1919	Decrease (in percent)
Vineyard	22,733	14,602	45
Orchard	10,872	3,706	66
Potato and greens	30,393	6,178	80
Cotton	37,806	1,483	96

The overall decline in agriculture exceeded 80 percent.[16]

An appalling destruction in livestock and farm implements paralleled the ruin in industry and agriculture. Thousands of animals had been slaughtered for food by the invading Turkish armies in 1918 and thousands more were driven toward Kars when those same armies withdrew at the end of the year. Most of the remaining animals were eaten by the refugees or else succumbed to the same diseases that decimated the population during the winter of 1918–1919. The decline in animal husbandry by more than 65 percent since 1914 directly affected the agricultural yield. Thousands of farmers were left not a single draft animal and were further handicapped by the loss of their basic implement, the plough. The toll in livestock and farm equipment in Armenia, exclusive of the southern Muslim districts, was as follows (to the nearest hundred):[17]

[15] Engoyan, *op. cit.*, p. 16; Aghayan, *op. cit.*, p. 200; Mikayelian, *op. cit.*, pp. 99–100; V. N. Nerkararian, *Hayastani Kompartian zhoghovrdakan tntesutian verakangnman zhamanakashrdjanum (1921–1925 tt.)* (Erevan, 1956), p. 9.

[16] Mikayelian, *op. cit.*, p. 100. For further statistics, some varying from those cited by Mikayelian, see Akademiia Nauk Armianskoi SSR, Institut Ekonomiki, *Sovetakan Hayastani tntesakan zargatsume, 1920–1960* (Erevan, 1960), pp. 290, 292, 298–299, 313, cited hereafter as *Tntesakan zargatsume*; Aghayan, *op. cit.*, p. 200; H. S. Karapetian, *Mayisian apstambutiune Hayastanum, 1920* (Erevan, 1961), p. 46. The figures in the text do not include losses in the Armenian-populated districts controlled by Georgia or Azerbaijan. In Akhalkalak, for example, the agricultural decline was in excess of 90 percent, the population had dwindled from nearly 110,000 to 60,000, and more than seventy villages had been totally razed by the Turkish army in 1918. See N. B. Makharadze, *Pobeda sotsialisticheskoi revoliutsii v Gruzii* (Tbilisi, 1965), p. 194.

[17] These figures have been compiled from statistics cited in *Tntesakan zargatsume*, pp. 234–235; Aghayan, *op. cit.*, p. 200; Elchibekian, *op. cit.*, p. 99; and Mikayelian, *op. cit.*, pp. 101–120. According to A. S. Ambarian [Hambarian], *Razvitie kapitalisticheskikh otnoshenii v armianskoi derevne (1860–1920)* (Erevan, 1959), p. 251, the following losses in animals were registered between 1913 and 1919: large horned, from 464,000 to 294,000; small horned, from 812,000 to 470,000; horses, from 42,000 to 19,000.

Animals and implements	1914	1919	Decrease (in percent)
Total Livestock	2,364,700	747,600	68
Large-horned animals (cattle, oxen, water buffalo)	688,600	229,500	67
Horses	51,500	19,900	63
Sheep	1,378,600	405,700	71
Goats	186,000	65,200	65
Pigs	23,600	5,600	76
Implements			
Wooden ploughs	99,900	22,300	78
Metal ploughs	17,600	5,300	70

A soaring inflation resulted from these heavy losses. The assorted paper specie became nearly worthless as the price of food and essential items doubled and multiplied time and again.[18] Shrewd manipulators and speculators hoarded the remaining meager stocks, relinquishing small amounts of food to desperate people who paid with their last possessions and deeds of title. The government was faced with a catastrophe that it had not created but for which it was held accountable. It had little means to cope with the problem, as neither legislation nor decree could deliver the starving masses. At that critical moment in the history of the Armenian people, the United States of America came to the rescue, giving life, awakening fresh hopes, and opening new horizons.

American Committee for Relief in the Near East

It was private American charity that reached the Armenians first. As early as 1915, in response to Ambassador Henry Morgenthau's urgent message from Constantinople that "the destruction of the Armenian race in Turkey is rapidly progressing," an influential group of missionaries, philanthropists, industrialists, and educators founded the Armenian Relief Committee. The organization promptly collected 100,000 dollars for supplies to be distributed by American officials in Constantinople and Syria.[19] As the magnitude of the Armenian tragedy was revealed, the Committee expanded its operations, uniting late in 1915 with relief groups for Syria and Persia into the Armenian

[18] Statistics in *Tntesakan zargatsume*, p. 235, show that in comparison with 1916 the price of wheat in 1919–1920 was 5,000 percent higher, soap and oil 2,000 percent, and salt, 8,000 percent. For information on the inflationary trend that began during the World War, see Adonts, *op. cit.*, pp. 453–454.

[19] Barton, *op. cit.*, pp. 4–9, 17, 408

and Syrian Relief. During the next two years a steady flow of money and supplies was used to succor Christian refugees in the Near East, particularly destitute Armenians who had been deported to the arid plains of the Arab provinces. At the same time American missionaries and educators in Anatolia struggled to snatch an occasional Armenian from certain death. Even after Turkey severed diplomatic relations with the United States in 1917, many of these men and women remained at their posts.[20]

In contrast with the situation in the Ottoman Empire, few American educational, cultural, and religious organizations existed in the Caucasus, the region in which most of the Armenian survivors from the provinces of Van, Bitlis, Erzerum, and Trebizond took refuge. Nonetheless, in 1916 Consul F. Willoughby Smith and several other Americans in Tiflis did join with British officials of the Lord Mayor's Fund in caring for a small number of orphan children and in arranging employment, primarily spinning and weaving, for refugee women.[21] But in 1918, as the Ottoman army swept into Transcaucasia, Allied officials were recalled or compelled to leave. The consulate in Tiflis closed and nearly all Americans hurried northward beyond the Caucasus, virtually suspending relief activities. Three or four did, however, stay behind in Erevan. Throughout the latter half of 1918, despite the risks involved, they worked closely with Kachaznuni's cabinet and supervised the distribution of what little remained of their supplies.[22]

The defeat of the Central Powers enabled the American public to renew and intensify relief operations. As the channels of communication became unclogged, numerous reports from Turkey, Syria, and the Caucasus portrayed the utter wretchedness of the refugee population. In response, the Armenian and Syrian Relief, now operating as the American Committee for Relief in the Near East (ACRNE), launched a 30 million dollar campaign and in an unprecedented display of private charity succeeded in raising nearly 20 million by the end of 1919.[23]

In January, 1919, ACRNE dispatched its first cargoes and a num-

[20] *Ibid.*, pp. 13–17, 51–69.

[21] John Elder, "Memories of the Armenian Republic," *Armenian Review*, VI (Spring, 1963), 4–5; Barton, *op cit.*, pp. 18, 82–85. See also US Archives, RG 59, 867.48/691/713/891/917/930, and RG 256, 184.021/95.

[22] Elder, *op. cit.*, pp. 8–13; Barton, *op. cit.*, pp. 86–87; Rep. of Arm. Archives, File 380/2, *H. H. Vashingtoni Nerkayatsutsich ev H. Amerikayi Karavarutiune, 1917–1918;* US Archives, RG 256, 861K.00/5.

[23] Barton, *op. cit.*, p. 209.

ber of administrators and medical workers to the Near East and the Caucasus. James Levi Barton, the president of ACRNE, then led a special commission to study firsthand the basic needs of those regions. Arriving in Constantinople in February, the commission supervised the distribution of more than 10,000 metric tons of food and clothing to the poverty-stricken inhabitants there and in western Anatolia. These supplies, valued at almost 3.5 million dollars, were augmented by ACRNE's purchase of nearly 2,000 metric tons of wheat flour and milk from the American Relief Administration, a government agency.[24]

Several members of Barton's commission led field parties into Syria, Palestine, Persia, the interior of Turkey, and the Caucasus. The team traveling into the interior reported that there were no refugees to care for in Van, Bitlis, and Erzerum. Turkish Armenia was devoid of Armenians. The operations of ACRNE within the Ottoman Empire were therefore concentrated in Constantinople, Syria, Palestine, and in Anatolia as far east as Sivas-Kharput-Diarbekir-Mardin.[25]

Dr. John H. T. Main, President of Grinnell College in Iowa, headed the Caucasus field party, which sailed from Constantinople together with some thirty relief workers. In March one of the messages of the party was given wide publicity in the United States:

No bread anywhere. Government has not a pound. Forty-five thousand in Erivan without bread. Orphanages and troops all through Erivan in terrible condition. Not a dog, cat, horse, camel or any living thing in all Igdir region. Saw women stripping flesh from dead horses with their bare hands today. . . . Another week will score ten thousand lives lost. For heaven's sake hurry! [26]

After his inspection of the refugee centers, Dr. Main relayed dispatches depicting scenes that surpassed even the worst apprehensions of ACRNE. He warned that of the half million refugees in the Caucasus at least 200,000 were on the verge of starvation:

[24] Frank M. Surface and Raymond L. Bland, *American Food in the World War and Reconstruction Period* (Stanford, 1931), p. 149 and table 202, pp. 410–411; United States, Department of State, *Papers Relating to the Foreign Relations of the United States, 1919* (2 vols.; Washington, D.C., 1934), II, 819–820; Barton, *op. cit.*, pp. 109–112, 120. See also Suda Lorena Bane and Ralph Haswell Lutz, *Organization of American Relief in Europe 1918–1919* (Stanford, 1934), pp. 220, 283–284.

[25] Barton, *op. cit.*, pp. 112–116; US Archives, RG 256, 867.48/10. See also 867B.00/54/134/146; *Hairenik* (daily), March 23, 1919, p. 2; Britain, FO 371/3657, 12359/28092/512/58, and FO 608/79, 341/1/9/14786.

[26] US Archives, RG 59, 867.48/1216. See also Surface and Bland, *op. cit.*, p. 149; *American Relief Administration Bulletin*, no. 1 (March 17, 1919), pp. 29–30, cited hereafter as *ARA Bulletin*.

At Etchmiadzin I looked for a time at a refugee burial. Seven bodies were thrown indiscriminately into a square pit as carrion, and covered with earth without any suggestion of care or pity. As I looked at the workmen I saw a hand protruding from the loose earth. It was a woman's hand and seemed to be stretched out in mute appeal to me. This hand reaching upward from the horrible pit symbolized starving Armenia.[27]

Main reported that in Alexandropol alone there were more than 68,000 refugees, one-seventh of whom, nearly 10,000, died each month. The survivors did not dare return to their homes where the Muslims were now firmly entrenched. According to Main, "The Turk and his racial confederates are carrying forward with growing efficiency the policy of extermination developed during the war." This they did by confining the Armenians to the Erevan guberniia where famine and disease completed the work. If the peasants did not soon regain their fields, he warned, Armenia would be faced with another year of famine. The American educator cried out, "At this last moment, can Christian civilization do something to restore and heal!" [28]

Meanwhile, a trace of American philanthropy had begun to reach Erevan. In March, 1919, medical teams were dispatched to Armenia, and, by agreement with the cabinet, ACRNE took charge of eleven hospitals and ninety orphanages with more than 13,000 emaciated children. Unable even to feed the orphans, the government gratefully transferred their physical care to the American organization but did retain the right to supervise their education.[29] Many others from among the 30,000 waifs scattered over the land were eventually to be taken in by ACRNE, whose president declared: "The hope of the future of the Armenian nation is wrapped up in a large measure with the orphan and women problem which we are attempting to solve. The children who survived the terrible ordeal of the past five years have matured prematurely and reveal unexpected recuperative capacity.

[27] US Archives, RG 256, 867B.4016/8. See also Barton, *op. cit.*, pp. 120–122; *ARA Bulletin*, no. 9 (May 13, 1919), p. 22; *Hairenik* (daily), April 22 and 25, 1919.
[28] US Archives, RG 59, 867.48/1244, and RG 256, 867B.00/113.
[29] Rep. of Arm. Archives, File 3/3, *Hayastani Hanrapetutiun, 1919 t.;* Elder, *op. cit.*, p. 21; Barton, *op. cit.*, pp. 120, 123–124. The plight of the Armenian orphans and the helplessness of the government is discussed by T. A. Balasanian, "Mankatnere Hayastanum 1917–1920 tt.," *Banber Erevani Hamalsarani*, 2 (1968), 217–220. According to the archival sources used by Balasanian, the agreement between ACRNE and the government was entered into in March, formalized in April, and effected in May, 1919. During the period May 1 to July 1, 1919, the Armenian orphanages in Georgia were also placed under the administration of ACRNE. See *Bor'ba*, May 3, 1919, p. 4, and June 27, p. 2.

Thousands of the weaker children have perished; we deal with the survivors." [30]

By summer's end ACRNE, incorporated in August, 1919, by act of Congress as the Near East Relief (NER),[31] had sent to the Near East–Caucasus area more than 30,000 metric tons of food and clothing valued in excess of 9 million dollars. Though the records of the organization indicate that these goods were delivered to Armenia, they should in fact have shown that the recipients were the Armenian people, since at least half the supplies were distributed to the destitute in Constantinople and in the western provinces of Anatolia.[32] But even if all private American charity in the Near East and the Caucasus had been directed to the Republic of Armenia, it could not have met the basic needs of an utterly dependent population. Like nearly every country of Europe in 1919, Armenia stretched out an empty, open hand to the government of the United States. In a year when much of the world lay in ruins and was caught in the clutches of famine, the United States responded with more than a billion dollars in relief. In this enormous American crusade the trickle of supplies that reached Armenia was to shore up the Republic for its second, hopefully brighter, year of existence.

The American Relief Administration

Immediately after the armistice with Germany in 1918, the United States Food Administration shipped cargo after cargo to European shores, and Herbert Hoover sailed for France to direct the postwar relief operations of the American agencies.[33] Moreover, to overcome legal technicalities preventing the extension of aid to the "liberated" states of the Baltic, Eastern Europe, and Transcaucasia, legislation for a special appropriation of 100 million dollars was introduced in Congress. On January 6, 1919, in support of this measure, Hoover out-

---

[30] Barton, *op. cit.*, p. 119.

[31] *Ibid.*, pp. 431–437, for the Act of Incorporation.

[32] Surface and Bland, *op. cit.*, pp. 56, 150, and tables 123, 200, pp. 307, 408–409. A share of the goods dispensed in the Ottoman Empire was made available to non-Armenian needy as well. The American relief organization was not free of scandals and profiteering. See Hoover, *op. cit.*, p. 386; US Archives, RG 256, 184.021/25/29, Green to Hoover.

[33] Bane and Lutz, *op. cit.*, pp. 2–3, 10, 36–37; Surface and Bland, *op. cit.*, pp. 24–25. For the organization of the American postwar relief operations in Europe, see Bane and Lutz, pp. 1–129; Seth P. Tillman, *Anglo-American Relations at the Paris Peace Conference of 1919* (Princeton, 1961), pp. 260–267; *Paris Peace Conference*, II (1942), 625–725.

lined the needs of the several states affected, warning that starvation had already gripped Armenia. In another cable, ten days later, he added: "Food is not the only problem in Armenia and Syria. Hundreds of thousands driven out cruelly by the Turks must be reinstalled in their homes and afforded an opportunity to become self-supporting. These problems require the largest measure of support from charitable public." [34]

The "Hundred Million Dollar Appropriation" was passed into law on February 24, 1919, with the stipulation that the funds be used to assist "non-enemy countries" as well as the "Armenians, Syrians, Greeks, and other Christian and Jewish populations of Asia Minor, now or formerly subjects of Turkey." [35] The American Relief Administration (ARA), established by the legislation to direct the project, was to complete operations by the last day of June, requiring reimbursement "as far as possible" from the recipient governments or peoples. President Woodrow Wilson appointed Hoover, by executive decree, to head the ARA, and the Allied and Associated Powers named him Director General of Relief in Europe.[36] The latter decision provided an aura of international collaboration and spared the pride of the European governments, but relief activities, especially in Armenia, remained almost exclusively an American undertaking.

Even before the passage of the Hundred Million Dollar Appropriation, Hoover dispatched food administrator Howard Heinz to Constantinople to take charge of relief matters in the Balkans and Turkey. In Constantinople, Heinz cooperated with the American Committee for Relief in the Near East and transferred to its account flour and condensed milk valued at more than a half million dollars.[37] With the creation of the ARA, Hoover and Heinz sent a number of army officers to the Caucasus to make accurate and impartial assessments of the

[34] Bane and Lutz, *op. cit.*, pp. 12–13, 139–140, 148–149, 176–177; *New York Times*, Jan. 8, 1919, p. 18.

[35] Bane and Lutz, *op. cit.*, pp. 291–292. Surface and Bland, *op. cit.*, p. 34, state that the legislation was enacted on February 25, 1919. They quote the act on page 39. See also *ARA Bulletin*, no. 1 (March 17, 1919), p. 16. Congressman Edward C. Little was instrumental in the specific inclusion of the Armenians. See *Congressional Record*, 65th Cong., 3d Sess., Vol. LVII, pt. 2 (Jan. 13, 1919), p. 1372.

[36] Surface and Bland, *op. cit.*, p. 40; Bane and Lutz, *op. cit.*, p. 292. Hoover was appointed Director General of Relief in Europe on January 11, 1919, and the Supreme Economic Council was established in Paris on February 7, 1919. See Bane and Lutz, *op. cit.*, p. 176; Hoover, *op. cit.*, p. 297. Tillman, *op. cit.*, p. 263, states that Wilson appointed Hoover as Director General on January 4, 1919. For the records of the Supreme Economic Council, see *Paris Peace Conference*, Vol. X (1947).

[37] Bane and Lutz, *op. cit.*, pp. 214–216, 392; Surface and Bland, *op. cit.*, pp. 56, 149, 150, and tables 120, 140, 202, pp. 305, 322–323, 410.

situation there. The reports of these officers confirmed all that had been said before. Captain Abraham Tulin wrote: "The condition of these people is horrible beyond belief. . . . It was stated to me by British officers, and also by Americans on the ground, that cannibalism had in some places been resorted to, and that human dead were being disinterred from fresh graves and eaten. I saw some of the horrible evidences of the latter at Igdir." Armenia's remoteness, Captain Tulin continued, created major obstacles to relief operations, and Georgia, while not in need of relief, nonetheless demanded a share of any goods passing over her land in order to profiteer and deprive the Armenians. Major Edward R. Stoever added that "in the districts where refugees have congregated, no description can give any adequate idea of conditions." Armenia was in need of 8,000 tons of flour per month as well as 13,000 tons of seed grain. The Tatars, he said, had abundant grain but were unwilling to sell to the Armenians, who were further handicapped by the disruption of their irrigation canals and the lack of equipment. Stoever expressed admiration for the courage of the Armenians and for their eagerness to seize the slightest opportunity for work.[38]

At Hoover's behest, Heinz himself conducted an inspection tour of the Caucasus at the end of April, 1919. His account of Armenian agony then followed:

I found a most distressing situation throughout this country, where starvation and misery actually beggar description. It is true that the people are literally dying from lack of food and from diseases caused by malnutrition. There are 500,000 refugees who are in need of food and of these the estimate that from 200,000 to 250,000 are at the starvation point is a reasonable one. . . . The people are clad in vermin-infested rags, with no possible change or chance for improvement, because there is no clothing of any kind or textile material available at any price even if the people had the money with which to buy it.[39]

Heinz had earlier thought the reports of Captain Tulin and other ARA officials somewhat exaggerated, but now convinced, he exclaimed, "Merciful God! It's all true! Nobody has ever told the whole truth! Nobody could!" [40]

[38] US Archives, RG 256, 867B.48/15; *ARA Bulletin*, no. 12 (June 6, 1919), pp. 18–20. See also Britain, FO 608/78, File 341/1/1.

[39] Barton, *op. cit.*, pp. 122–124; *ARA Bulletin*, no. 10 (May 20, 1919), pp. 12–14. See also US Archives, RG 84, Tiflis Consulate, 1919, pt. 3, File 360.

[40] Egan, *op. cit.*, p. 15; Barton, *op. cit.*, p. 123.

Published reports of the ARA indicate that considerable aid was extended Armenia before May, 1919, yet the statistics are imprecise and somewhat contradictory. Hoover's staff planned that Armenia should receive at least 5,000 metric tons of food each month from February through July, 1919, but the operation was slow in starting.[41] The Director General of Relief subsequently informed the Supreme Economic Council in Paris that 5,252 metric tons of breadstuffs and condensed milk had been delivered to Armenia in March and another 1,457 tons in April.[42] Records of the American Relief Administration give no indication, however, that any vessel carrying either ARA or ACRNE goods made deliveries during those two months at Constantinople or at Batum, the only ports from which food would have been relayed to Armenia.[43] Even this evidence is not conclusive, however, for at the end of February, 1919, Heinz informed Hoover that an ARA cargo had been transferred to the account of ACRNE for shipment to Batum. Other figures show that as of April 30 only one ship carrying 4,521 metric tons of supplies had arrived at Batum.[44] Armenian sources reveal that British authorities brought six carloads of grain from Kars in January, 1919, that a trainload of food arrived from Batum in February, and that, as of March 29, 1919, thirty carloads of flour had entered Armenia. This apparently was the total external assistance until the arrival of the first shipment of American flour in April.[45] That several deliveries intended for Armenia did not reach their destination might account in part for these discrepancies. Transportation difficulties, to which Herbert Hoover repeatedly made reference, may have been a factor. Furthermore, American authorities

[41] Surface and Bland, op. cit., table 13, pp. 32–33. See also ARA Bulletin, no. 2 (March 24, 1919), p. 5.

[42] Bane and Lutz, op. cit., pp. 395, 494; ARA Bulletin, no. 5 (April 15, 1919), p. 6, and no. 8 (May 6, 1919), p. 32. See also Paris Peace Conference, X, 169, 171, 277.

[43] Surface and Bland, op. cit., table 111, pp. 282–289.

[44] Bane and Lutz, op. cit., p. 283; ARA Bulletin, no. 4 (April 8, 1919), p. 30, and no. 13 (May 31, 1919), p. 24. A later report showed that a ship carrying 5,021 tons of ACRNE supplies arrived in Batum on March 1, 1919. See ARA Bulletin, no. 18 (July 18, 1919), p. 21. This shipment has not been cited, however, in studies of ACRNE and ARA.

[45] Rep. of Arm. Archives, File 3/3; Khatisian, Hanrapetutian zargatsume, p. 111; Vratzian, Hanrapetutiun, p. 216. Acting Premier Khatisian reported that as of March 13, 1919, a total of 22 carloads of bread, 14 of flour, 10 of rice, and 18 cisterns of kerosene, 2 of gasoline, and 3 of oil had been received in Armenia. See Hairenik (daily), May 20, 1919, p. 2. A communiqué of the Armenian Foreign Minister on April 15, 1919, stated that the arrival in Erevan of American missionaries with flour was having a leveling effect on the runaway inflation. Vratzian maintains that the first American flour was brought into Armenia on April 28.

in the Caucasus had to divert a share of the foodstuffs to Georgia and Azerbaijan as payment for transit privileges and as evidence of good-will.[46] Finally, Armenia, as understood by Hoover and other relief officials, obviously included a much broader expanse than the terri-tory under the control of the Erevan government.

It was at the end of May, 1919, that the first substantial ARA assist-ance reached Armenia. Two American steamers cast anchor at Batum and discharged 9,946 metric tons of wheat flour and 619 metric tons of beans and peas. British authorities cleared the Batum-Tiflis-Alex-andropol-Erevan rail lines, and during the next four days the cargo, valued at more than 2 million dollars, rolled into Armenia. Three more shipments in June added another 11,000 metric tons of food. American flour had at last arrived. The Armenians would live.[47]

Captain, subsequently Major, Joseph C. Green was detailed to the Caucasus to supervise the ARA operations and the activities of some two hundred and fifty relief workers scattered throughout the region.[48] Green reported excellent cooperation from the Armenian government, which, however, required considerable direction in its attempts to assist the population. His feelings for the Georgians were clearly hos-tile. He had been in Tiflis only a short time when he was robbed and manhandled, assertedly by members of the Georgian Red (People's) Guard, who then proceeded to drive off in his automobile. Green and other Allied officials also complained of willful interference and ob-structionism by the Georgian government, which demanded relief sup-plies in return for transit privileges to Erevan and applied economic blackmail to ply Armenia toward concessions on the boundary dispute. These messages of anger and outrage wired to Paris eventually prompted Herbert Hoover to take the matter to the Peace Conference

[46] Bane and Lutz, op. cit., pp. 392, 496, 498; US Archives, RG 84, Tiflis Consulate, 1919, pt. 3, File 360, and RG 256, 867B.48/8, Hoover to Secretary of State, April 29, 1919; Britain, WO 33/974, no. 4553. Dr. Main reported that of the 3,500 tons of flour reaching the Caucasus in March and April, 1919, 2,500 tons had been sold to the British authorities and 400 tons to the Georgians. See US Archives, RG 256, 867B.48/5. A subsequent report showed that of the 7,646 tons of ACRNE food and supplies de-livered in the Caucasus between February and June, 1919, only 3,314 tons actually entered Armenia. See ARA Bulletin, no. 18 (July 18, 1919), pp. 21–22.

[47] Surface and Bland, op. cit., table 111, pp. 290–295; Bane and Lutz, op. cit., p. 650; Vratzian, Hanrapetutiun, p. 217. Bane and Lutz show (p. 651) that by June 30, 1919, the ARA had delivered and charged to Armenia 31,062 metric tons from a total 3,219,896 metric tons handled by the organization. For a breakdown of the commodi-ties sent to Armenia during the first half of 1919, see Paris Peace Conference, X, 169, 171, 277, 426–427, 428, 429, 500, 501.

[48] ARA Bulletin, no. 9 (May 13, 1919), p. 22; US Archives, RG 256, 867B.48/21.

with the recommendation that Zhordania's government be censured and threatened with political countermeasures.[49]

No further deliveries were made to Armenia until the end of August, 1919, when four more vessels discharged the last remaining supplies financed by the Hundred Million Dollar Appropriation. The August deliveries, 28,000 metric tons, constituted more than half the total food earmarked for Armenia by the ARA. Included in these final shipments were 8,000 metric tons of vitally needed seed grain, which the ARA, in collaboration with the United States Liquidation Commission and ACRNE, had acquired in the Kuban region of Russia by bartering 915.5 metric tons of hardware, implements, and miscellaneous supplies.[50] Besides its regular activities, the ARA also shipped 754 metric tons of clothing donated to Armenia by the American Red Cross. The transportation charge of 47,688 dollars was written off as a gift from the government of the United States to the government of Armenia. This clothing, together with several thousand metric tons sent by ACRNE, was to replace many tattered rags before the onset of winter.[51]

Up to the last quarter of 1919, government-sponsored and private American relief operations provided the Armenian people food and supplies valued in excess of 20 million dollars. More than half this sum, especially the share given directly to the Armenian republic, was financed through the American Relief Administration. Both ARA and ACRNE assistance was coordinated by Herbert Hoover as Director General of Relief.[52] For each ARA shipment, the Armenian government issued promissory notes to be deposited in the United States Treasury, whereas the ACRNE contributions were the direct gifts of the American people to the Armenian people.[53] The ARA deliveries

[49] US Archives, RG 84, Tiflis Consulate, 1919, pt. 3, File 360, and RG 256, 180.03502/4, 184.021/29, 184.611/582, 867B.48/32, 867B.5018/7, 861G.00/82/84. See also Rep. of Arm. Archives, File 66a/3, Press clippings; *ARA Bulletin*, no. 13 (June 13, 1919), p. 22; no. 18 (July 18, 1919), p. 19; no. 19 (July 25, 1919), pp. 36–37. Of the American officials in Tiflis, apparently only Consul Smith favored the sale of foodstuffs to the Georgians. See US Archives, RG 256, 184.021/369, Green to Hoover, June 17, 1919.

[50] Bane and Lutz, *op. cit.*, p. 287; Surface and Bland, *op. cit.*, p. 150, and tables 111, 142, 201, pp. 298–299, 326–327, 408–409; *ARA Bulletin*, no. 14 (June 20, 1919), p. 30, and no. 16 (July 4 1919), pp. 26–28.

[51] Surface and Bland, *op. cit.*, pp. 59, 135, 150–151, and tables 126, 127, 143A, pp. 308–309, 327.

[52] Bane and Lutz, *op. cit.*, p. 147; Surface and Bland, *op. cit.*, tables 75, 110, 112, 200, 201, pp. 151, 282–283, 298–299, 408–409.

[53] US Archives, RG 256, 184.021/9; Bane and Lutz, *op. cit.*, pp. 329–330; Surface and Bland, *op. cit.*, p. 150.

charged to Armenia as compared with the ARA worldwide deliveries, and the total deliveries administered through the Director General of Relief (primarily the ARA and the ACRNE shipments combined) are shown in table 2.

TABLE 2

RELIEF DELIVERIES THROUGH AUGUST, 1919 (IN METRIC TONS)

Commodity	ARA deliveries to Armenia	ARA worldwide deliveries	Director General deliveries to Armenia	Director General worldwide deliveries
Flour	34,167.1	266,706.6	43,430.5	1,253,568
Grain	8,000	155,657.4	8,000	983,979.6
Rice	1,022.3	9,472.8	1,022.3	99,039.1
Beans, peas	2,661.8	12,498.8	2,661.8	104,833.6
Pork products	49	26,748.4	49	266,979.6
Milk	3,119.8	7,039.5	4,715.7	50,653.7
Cocoa	186.9	234.5	186.9	511.5
Sugar	812.8	869.4	812.8	43,276.7
Miscellaneous food	—	14.1	6,585	873,062.2
Soap	431.5	431.5	431.5	1,110.5
Clothing and miscellaneous items	107.7	5,885.1	16,068.8	497,055.7
Total metric tonnage	50,588.9	485,558.1	83,964.3	4,178,477.7
Estimated total value	$10,630,872	$107,132,277	$20,231,455[a]	$1,101,486,783.34[b]

[a] Of this total, the sum of $71,400 in freight charges was contributed by the British government.

[b] Of the grand total, 2 percent of the tonnage and 1.8 percent of the estimated value had been assigned Armenia. Germany was the largest recipient, with 28.7 percent of the tonnage and 25.4 percent of the value of the total goods delivered.

SOURCE: Frank M. Surface and Raymond L. Bland, *American Food in the World War and Reconstruction Period* (Stanford, 1931), charts IV and V, pp. 37–38, tables 41, 108, 133, 186, 207, pp. 63, 280–281, 314–315, 394–395, 408–409.

With the expiration of the ARA in the summer of 1919, the burden of Armenian relief shifted to private agencies once again. Some degree of official involvement was maintained with the appointment of Colonel William N. Haskell as joint relief administrator in Armenia for the United States and the Allied Powers. The ARA properties and equipment located in the Near East and the Caucasus were transferred to the Near East Relief, the successor organization of ACRNE, and those ARA officials who wished to continue service in the region were placed on the NER payroll.[54] The American Relief Administration, having spared the people of Armenia absolute annihilation, passed into history.

Achievements of the Coalition Government

Such were the circumstances under which Hovhannes Kachaznuni's coalition government began to function. During the winter of 1918–1919 most of Armenia's lands lay beyond the established control of the government and contributed nothing to the state revenue, whereas the inhabitants of the remaining regions did their utmost to evade the onerous obligations imposed upon them. On occasion government officials were ejected from a village and the army had to be summoned to restrain the peasants, who were waging a desperate struggle to eke out a mere existence. Moreover, the villagers, reluctant to leave their families in the face of rampant insecurity, attempted to escape military service.[55] A government did exist in Erevan, but it was hardly the embodiment of the self-administration so long coveted by politically aware Armenians. It ruled over a land bleak with ruin, a vast graveyard that could not even enfold its dead. The troubles of the government were exacerbated by the many thousands of Turkish Armenian refugees who sought safety in the Republic but who did not consider it their country. Their only desire was to return home. The Erevan republic, bearing the strong imprint of Russia, was alien to the Turkish Armenians, whose national consciousness had been stirred far beyond that of the Russian Armenian masses.

These fundamental, vexing issues notwithstanding, Premier Kachaznuni's cabinet labored assiduously to bring order out of chaos. The Populist ministers, having been given the opportunity to put their ideals into practice, were especially enthusiastic. Trained and experienced in their respective fields, they had come to believe that Armenia could develop into a true republic. Samson Harutiunian, an outstanding attorney and civic leader, undertook to reorganize Armenia's judicial system to include branches for civil, criminal, and administrative law, appellate courts, a supreme court, and the jury system. Finance Minister Artashes Enfiadjian laid plans for the introduction of a national currency, a sound budgetary system, and a progressive income tax.

[54] Bane and Lutz, op. cit., pp. 600–601; Surface and Bland, op. cit., pp. 151–152.
[55] Elchibekian and Hakobian, op. cit., p. 39; Mikayelian, op. cit., pp. 131–134; Karapetian, op. cit., pp. 60–62, 70–74; Aghayan, op. cit., pp. 197–198.

Mikayel Atabekian, the Minister of Enlightenment, initiated studies for the eventual adoption of a general curriculum based on universal, secular, compulsory elementary education, with emphasis on technical training and the trades. He hoped to transfer the Gevorgian Academy (Jemaran) of Etchmiadzin to the capital as the first step toward founding a state university. Atabekian also envisioned the establishment of a theater and a museum in Erevan. State Controller Minas Berberian worked out procedures to guarantee the system of checks and balances in administration. The idealistic fervor of the Populist ministers eschewed reality, but it inspired hope at a time when pessimism was the prevailing sentiment among many circles in Armenia.[56]

Through the winter months the coalition government did make several modest but practical strides. The Shustov wine and cognac complex, one of the few immediate sources of state revenue, was nationalized. Several textile mills were renovated, providing employment for a few hundred refugee women. Hospitals were opened even though basic equipment and medications were lacking, and thousands of orphans were made wards of the state until the American Committee for Relief in the Near East assumed their charge in the spring of 1919.[57] In February teams of civil and mining engineers and technicians from other parts of the Caucasus and from southern Russia were employed to study the soil, survey mineral deposits, assess the industrial potential, and formulate plans for the reconstruction of Armenia. This important project was financed through a grant of 2 million rubles from the Mailov brothers, oil magnates who had amassed a fortune in Baku before the World War.[58] The government also took concrete steps to improve transportation and communication routes. When the winter snows thawed, crews of laborers repaired the railways and the depots that had been badly damaged during the Turkish evacuation and restored and expanded the telegraph network. And finally, Armenia's first naval vessel, a gunboat christened *Ashot Erkat*, was launched in the waters of Lake Sevan.[59] Then, with

[56] Vratzian, *Hanrapetutiun*, pp. 174-175.

[57] Rep. of Arm. Archives, File 66a/3; *Hairenik* (daily), June 25, 1919, pp. 1-2. See note 29 above.

[58] Rep. of Arm. Archives, File 421/1, *H. H. Hai Teghekagir Biuro Parizum, 1919 t.*, no. 59; File 66a/3, Bulletin no. 34; File 132/31, *H. H. Patvirakutiun, 1920*. See also US Archives, RG 256, 184.021/304/364.

[59] Rep. of Arm. Archives, File 13/13, *Hayastani Hanrapetutiun, 1920 t.*; and File 22/22, *Hayastani Hanrapetutiun, 1920 t.* See also Vratzian, *Hanrapetutiun*, p. 226; *Miatsial ev Ankakh Hayastan*, publ. of H. H. Dashnaktsutiun (Constantinople, 1919), p. 58. Ashot Erkat or Ashot II (914-928) was one of the more ironfisted dynasts of the Bagratid kingdom (885-1045). His campaigns restored to Armenia several provinces that had been seized by powerful Muslim emirs.

the approach of spring, the Republic turned to the vital matter of extending its boundaries to Kars and Nakhichevan.[60]

The ruling to substitute the Armenian language for Russian in the performance of all official functions was perhaps the most difficult administrative measure to implement. To discard a system of government developed during a hundred years of Romanov domination was no easy task. At the very beginning it would require the invention of hundreds of Armenian technical terms, the chaos-wrought conversion from a Cyrillic to an Armenian filing system, and such assorted particulars as the importation from Europe of typewriters in the Armenian alphabet. The major dilemma, however, lay in the fact that few of the more experienced administrators could read or write Armenian. They had passed through Russian schools, had entered the Romanov civil or military hierarchy in far-flung parts of the empire, and had become efficient within the framework of the old bureaucratic system. The Armenian government could conceivably dismiss those who were not literate in Armenian or else it could teach them to read, to write, and in many cases to speak Armenian. Either alternative held in store a host of troubles. Still, it was believed that, if the Republic was to rise as an independent nation and if it was to gain the loyalty of all Armenians, the agonizing process of transition must begin. By April of 1919, with the decision made, a few ministries had initiated the cumbersome move toward Armenianization.[61]

Crisis in Government

The accomplishments of the coalition government were outweighed by a succession of setbacks. First among these was the death of several key members of the cabinet. In November, 1918, Welfare Minister Khachatur Karjikian was assassinated by a political comrade. Karjikian, an ardent proponent of moderation and of interparty and interracial collaboration, had served in Tiflis as a member of the Transcaucasian Commissariat and as the chairman of the Dashnakist faction in the Seim. During the Turkish invasion he spearheaded the Armenian effort to win the cooperation of both Georgians and Tatars in defending the common homeland. Karjikian had even consented to

[60] The Armenian republic's expansion into Kars and Nakhichevan is discussed in chapters 7 and 8 below.

[61] This gradual transition is evidenced in the documents deposited in the Rep. of Arm. Archives. The Foreign Ministry was among the first departments to employ Armenian, whereas the Ministry of Military Affairs and the General Staff persisted in the use of Russian until the final months of the Republic.

enter the cabinet of Akakii Chkhenkeli after the Georgian leader, using his position as premier-elect of Transcaucasia, had ordered the surrender of Kars in April, 1918. The assassin, demented by the suffering of the Armenian people, blamed Karjikian for the fall of Kars and for much of the subsequent disaster. The shots he fired deprived the newly formed coalition of a staunch supporter and badly undermined the prestige of the government.[62] During the Armeno-Georgian war, Georgian Premier Zhordania characterized the murder of Karjikian as a victory for the Armenian militants, who had plotted the invasion of Lori.[63] The mission that had been sent to Constantinople to plead Armenia's case in the summer of 1918 returned to Erevan just as Karjikian's grim funeral was taking place.[64] Alexandre Khatisian, a member of that mission and the foreign minister in Kachaznuni's initial cabinet, filled the empty post as acting minister of welfare. In the spring of 1919 Sahak Torosian was appointed to head the ministry.[65]

During the first winter the typhus epidemic took a heavy toll of public officials, and in January, 1919, it claimed two other members of the cabinet. First to succumb was State Controller Minas Berberian, a wealthy patriot who had been instrumental in bringing about Populist participation in the coalition government and who had abandoned his position and life of ease in Tiflis to serve Armenia. The heaviest blow fell on January 26, when Aram Manukian lost his battle against the ravaging disease. Aram Pasha, as he was known to friend and foe alike, had been a veritable founder of the Armenian republic. While the Commissariat and Seim harangued in Tiflis in 1918, Aram established a dictatorship in Erevan and took an active role in the successful defense against the Turkish onslaught in May of that year. Following the proclamation of Armenian independence, Aram and Dro, as the de facto administration in Armenia, continued in power until Kachaznuni's cabinet finally transferred to Erevan in

[62] Khatisian, *Hanrapetutian zargatsume*, p. 97; Vratzian, *Ughinerov*, V (1966), 49. For information on Karjikian's participation in the Armenian National Council and in the Transcaucasian Commissariat and Seim, see Hovannisian, *Road to Independence*, pp. 90, 108, 141–176 *passim*, 205, 206.

[63] *Dokumenty i materialy*, pp. 475–476. See also Wladimir Woytinsky, *La démocratie géorgienne* (Paris, 1921), pp. 180–181.

[64] Karjikian's funeral is described in *Hairenik* (daily), Feb. 15, 1919, p. 1. His assassin, Egor Ter-Minasian, was sentenced to ten years at hard labor on April 17, 1919. See *Bor'ba*, April 26, 1919, p. 3.

[65] Khatisian, *Hanrapetutian zargatsume*, p. 96. For the composition of the Armenian cabinet in January, 1919, see US Archives, RG 59, 861.00/4017, and RG 256, 867B.001/1.

July. And even after the cabinet had begun to function in the capital, there were many who believed that Aram Manukian, the Minister of Interior, operated as a virtual dictator. The controversial and extralegal activities of his department provoked the ire of parties both to the right and to the left of Dashnaktsutiun. Aram's impatience with the fetters of parliamentary government was evident, and, under the conditions then existing in Armenia, it was not difficult to find ample justification for strong centralized control or even a dictatorial regime. Aram's death deepened the gloom in Erevan; the invincible leader had been vanquished.[66] The Ministry of Interior, too, devolved upon Alexandre Khatisian, but never again was it to be the strong, pervasive, effective, or contentious department that it had been under Aram Manukian.[67]

The initial enthusiasm of the Populist ministers soon faded into distress and disillusion. The filth, famine, and disease in Erevan made life unbearable; indeed existence was in constant jeopardy. The Armenian bourgeoisie, accustomed as it was to the comforts and luxuries of Tiflis, found it especially difficult to adjust to the situation. But the magnetism of Tiflis and the misery of Erevan were not all that disenchanted the Populists. As members of a liberal constitutional party, they were bitterly disappointed when they came to realize that there was little possibility for the early establishment of true parliamentary democracy. They felt intimidated by the brashness of Dashnaktsutiun and frustrated at their helplessness in face of the anarchic conditions that still prevailed.

More than one Populist minister found occasion to depart for Tiflis on pressing personal or "official" business. Their absence from Erevan was sometimes prolonged and for two ministers it was permanent. Mikayel Atabekian was the first to go. Involved in internal party strife, he opted to relinquish the Ministry of Enlightenment and return to his private concerns in Tiflis. His post was filled by another Populist, Gevorg Melik-Karageozian, who had been serving as assistant

[66] Vratzian, *Ughinerov*, V, 50–55; Arshaluis Astvadsatrian, "Arame," *Vem*, III, 1 (1935), 67–71. The records of the Armenian legislature reveal the intensity of the controversies aroused by Aram Manukian's modus operandi. See "Hayastani Khorhrdi ardzanagrutiunnere," *Vem*, II, 4–6 (1934), and III, 1–3 (1935).

[67] News of the deaths of Berberian and Manukian did not reach the United States until April of 1919. Both Premier Kachaznuni and Foreign Minister Tigranian contracted typhus but survived. See *Hairenik* (daily), April 5 and 6, 1919. A collection of articles devoted to Aram's political and governmental activities during three decades was published on the fiftieth anniversary of his death. Each of the contributors was a contemporary of Aram and an active participant in the period of the Armenian republic. See *Arame*, publ. of H. H. Dashnaktsutiun ([Beirut], 1969).

foreign minister under Sirakan Tigranian. Shortly thereafter Levon Ghulian set out for Tiflis on important business. In Ghulian's absence, Samson Harutiunian was called upon to assume the functions of the Ministry of Provisions. But he quickly followed Atabekian and Ghulian, leaving Melik-Karageozian temporarily in charge of that ministry as well. It was tragically ironic that in Armenia "there were three ministers of provisions but absolutely no provisions." Critical of his political associates and especially piqued by the directives that both Ghulian and Harutiunian continued to relay from Tiflis, Melik-Karageozian demanded an end to the parody. In mid-February, 1919, the cabinet granted him full jurisdiction in the Ministry of Provisions pending the arrival, on March 1, of the newly designated Populist minister, Kristapor Vermishian (K. A. Vermishev).[68]

The structure of the military establishment posed another formidable obstacle to efficient government. The army command, adept in the tsarist school of traditional warfare, found it extremely difficult to adjust to the needs of an unstable emerging state. The cadre knew little Armenian, used Russian both in administrative work and in the training program, and even included a considerable number of Russian officers. As in the old Russian system a large concentration of personnel was required at headquarters level. This structure decreased the combat potential of the army and placed a heavy burden on the manpower and resources of the state. The lack of weapons, ammunition, and spare parts aggravated the unwholesome situation in the military. Moreover, the men under arms were continuously involved with the Muslim insurgents and never enjoyed a span of peace adequate for advanced training or more effective organization. Desertion was widespread. Many villages tried to shelter their young men and to defy orders for new levies.[69]

In an attempt to cope with this dilemma, the government reshuffled the military hierarchy in March, 1919, and, elevating Colonel Kristapor Araratian to the rank of Major General, named him Minister of Military Affairs. Dro, the experienced partisan leader, was brought into the government as the assistant military minister. It was hoped

[68] Vratzian, Hanrapetutiun, pp. 175–176, 226; A. Babalian, Edjer Hayastani anka-khutian patmutiunits (Cairo, 1959), p. 21.

[69] Ruben [Ter-Minasian], Hai heghapokhakani me hishataknere, Vol. VII (Los Angeles, 1952), pp. 329–339; Khatisian, Hanrapetutian zargatsume, pp. 113–114; Hovh. Sahakian, "Erku tari haikakan banakin medj," in Edjer mer azatagrakan patmutenen (Paris, 1937), pp. 20–21. For unfavorable comments regarding the Armenian army, particularly its personnel, see G. Chalkhushian, Inch er ev inch piti lini mer ughin? ([Vienna], 1923), pp. 16–22.

that the pair would be able to create a tight, disciplined, yet flexible command and to prepare the army for the localized, irregular warfare in which it was engaged. This positive move notwithstanding, both time and technical-material assistance of an advanced, friendly power would be needed to forge the small but efficient army so essential to the Republic of Armenia.[70]

When the various ministerial vacancies were filled and the realignments completed in the spring of 1919, the political balance of the coalition government was unchanged. Dashnaktsutiun, in control of the strategic ministries, remained content with less than half the posts:[71]

PREMIER (MINISTER-PRESIDENT)	Hovhannes Kachaznuni	*Dashnakist*
FOREIGN AFFAIRS	Sirakan Tigranian	*Dashnakist*
INTERNAL AFFAIRS	Alexandre Khatisian	*Dashnakist*
WELFARE	Sahak Torosian	*Dashnakist*
JUSTICE	Samson Harutiunian	*Populist*
FINANCE	Artashes Enfiadjian	*Populist*
ENLIGHTENMENT	Gevorg Melik-Karageozian	*Populist*
PROVISIONS	Kristapor Vermishian	*Populist*
MILITARY AFFAIRS	Kristapor Araratian	*Nonpartisan*

Crisis in Party

Inseparable from the governmental morass was the turbulence within Dashnaktsutiun. Rivalry often flared between Hovhannes Kachaznuni and the Bureau, the supreme organ of the party. Now that Armenia was independent, Kachaznuni and several other Dashnakists who held official positions believed that a clear distinction between party and government must be established. They apparently felt that, with the formation of the Republic, the primary goal of Dashnaktsutiun had been accomplished and that the party machinery, particularly the Bureau, should fade into the background.

Differences also arose concerning the chain of command. Should the Dashnakist members of the cabinet, following normal political procedure, be responsible to the Dashnakist faction of the legislature, or should they be bound directly to the Bureau? Kachaznuni and like-minded leaders urged that the Dashnakist bloc in the legislature become the indirect link between the cabinet and the Bureau, with the

[70] Rep. of Arm. Archives, File 381/3, *H. H. Vashingtoni Nerkayatsutsich ev H. Amerikian Karavarutiune, 1919;* Vratzian, *Hanrapetutiun,* p. 226.

[71] Rep. of Arm. Archives, File 8/8; *Miatsial ev Ankakh Hayastan,* p. 50.

cabinet responsible to the legislature, and the Dashnakist bloc answerable to the Bureau.[72]

Party activists both in and out of government refuted this logic. They stressed the need for what they termed "revolutionary" action and order and insisted that all members serving in government be subservient to the Bureau's dictates. Voicing impatience with the conservatism of some Dashnakists in state positions, they complained that the cabinet leaders, particularly Premier Kachaznuni, had abandoned their revolutionary heritage and had compromised both themselves and their party by excessive flirtation with the Armenian bourgeoisie. The crisis in party rarely broke into the open, however. While the Dashnakist ministers were subjected to scathing criticism within party circles and behind the closed doors of the caucuses of the Dashnakist faction in the legislature, they invariably received a unanimous vote of confidence on the floor of the Khorhurd—as the Bureau instructed.[73]

The dissension between what might be called the revolutionary and the conservative elements in Dashnaktsutiun subsided to some extent with Kachaznuni's departure for Europe. On January 22, 1919, the Premier announced that a delegation must be sent abroad to obtain assistance in time to prevent total starvation. To impress upon the foreign nations the urgency of the situation, he proposed that the chief of state head the mission, being empowered to conclude agreements with private and government agencies for the importation of vital goods and to determine the conditions under which Armenia might float loans and conduct the sale of bonds abroad. On January 27 the cabinet gave its approval, and on February 4 the legislature voted "to authorize the Premier to travel to Europe and America in order to approach the Entente Powers and the Government of the United States of North America on behalf of Armenia's Khorhurd, with an appeal for their assistance in the importation of provisions and other essential goods lacking in Armenia." [74] Alexandre Khatisian

[72] Ruben, *op. cit.*, pp. 228–232, 271–276. For criticisms of Dashnaktsutiun's role in government, see Chalkhushian, *op. cit.*, pp. 26–36; H. Kachaznuni, *Dashnaktsutiune anelik chuni ailevs* (Vienna, 1923), pp. 31–32, 38. These analyses, written by officials of the Armenian republic after its Sovietization, were confuted by several other former members of government. See, for example, V. Navasardian, *Inch cher ev inch piti chlini mer ughin* (Cairo, 1923); S. Vratzian, *Kharkhapumner* (Boston, 1924).

[73] Rep. of Arm. Archives, File 3/3, Foreign Ministry report of April 15, 1919; Ruben, *op. cit.*, pp. 233–236, 340–341.

[74] Rep. of Arm. Archives, File 381/3, Credentials; Vratzian, *Hanrapetutiun*, p. 261. A copy of Kachaznuni's credentials, dated February 15, 1919, is in US Archives, RG 59, 860J.48/21.

was named to serve as acting premier in Kachaznuni's absence.

Kachaznuni departed for Tiflis on February 15, 1919, but British officials in the Georgian capital delayed issuing the required travel documents. It was soon revealed that the complication was attributable to suspicion of Simon Vratzian, a member of Kachaznuni's mission and of the party Bureau. Vratzian, it seems, was marked as an undesirable Dashnakist of leftist persuasions. Unwilling to sail without Vratzian, Kachaznuni returned to Erevan on April 2. Within a few days, however, the aging premier was prevailed upon to make the important journey with a new delegation. On the sixteenth Kachaznuni again entrusted the government to Khatisian and proceeded to Tiflis, where he now found the British extremely cooperative in furnishing the necessary papers for himself and his companions, Artashes Enfiadjian, the Minister of Finance, Artem (Harutiun) Piralian, an economic adviser, and Suren Melikian, a dashing, young army captain.[75]

From mid-February, 1919, Khatisian was the actual chief of state in Armenia. As mayor of multinational Tiflis for a decade, he curiously had been persona grata both to the Romanov hierarchy and to nearly the entire spectrum of revolutionary societies. He had become a master in the art of politics. Thus, under his cautious direction, tensions between party and government began to ease in Armenia. Khatisian nonetheless shared many of Kachaznuni's views about government and carefully maneuvered to enhance the position of the cabinet.[76]

Crisis in Legislature

The prestige of the Khorhurd corroded steadily during the first winter. Although a parliamentary republic had been declared and the organs for such a system had been established, Armenia lacked the experience and popular base requisite to the effective exercise of this form of government. In 1919 the aspiration to but actual absence of parliamentary rule created a strange paradox. The Khorhurd frequently adopted legislation borrowed from and apropos of more advanced states, reasoning that such laws had been tested successfully in the

[75] Rep. of Arm. Archives, File 230/129, and File 231/130, *H. H. Patvirakutiun, 1919;* Vratzian, *Ughinerov,* V, 66-67, and *Hanrapetutiun,* pp. 216-217. See also Britain, FO 371/3657, 38733/39139/512/58.

[76] Ruben, *op. cit.,* pp. 232-233, 276-278, 340-343.

countries Armenia wished to emulate. The Khorhurd, perhaps only partially conscious of its motivation, believed that upholding progressive, albeit premature, legislation might hasten Armenia's evolvement into a true parliamentary republic. Such action would also demonstrate to the Allied Powers that Armenia was worthy of their unreserved diplomatic support and economic-military assistance.

On the other hand, a number of political leaders were convinced that the existing circumstances in Armenia demanded decisive action through revolutionary decree, as opposed to the slower, more desirable, yet sometimes disastrous parliamentary process. The divergent points of view crystallized around the perplexing Muslim question. The activists emphasized that Armenia was the object of a coordinated Turco-Azerbaijani campaign to explode the Republic and that the Muslims of Armenia, as a party to the intrigue, would never submit willingly to the authority of the central government. Consequently, a policy of conciliation and gradual transition, even the granting of internal autonomy, would not ensure the loyalty of the Muslim population but would instead encourage more sedition. The proponents of this view included not only many seasoned partisan commanders but also a considerable number of state employees and legislators. The preservation of the Republic, they insisted, depended on force, the only persuasion the Muslim elements understood and respected. Those who gainsaid this argument contended that Armenia would never be secure until the sincere loyalty of all inhabitants, Christian and Muslim alike, had been won, and that this could only be attained through a policy of caution, flexibility, and compromise. The Muslim population must therefore be placated and appeased.[77]

On this issue the legislature locked in vehement debate, which became blustering as the army prepared to move into several of the Muslim-held districts of the Erevan guberniia. When the government placed the strategically located Surmalu uezd under martial law and reports of irregularities against the Muslims in that district reached the Khorhurd, impassioned denunciations sounded from the floor. The Social Revolutionary and Social Democrat deputies led the attack in an attempt to discomfit the Dashnakist-Populist majority bloc and the coalition government. The rhetoric of Social Revolutionaries Arsham Khondkarian and Vahan Minakhorian was especially eloquent in the cause of interracial harmony. The critics were unable, however, to strengthen their position with support from Muslim leaders. Indeed,

[77] *Ibid.*, pp. 213, 327–329; Babalian, *op. cit.*, pp. 44–45.

nearly all Muslim inhabitants of the Erevan guberniia utterly rejected Armenian rule, be it "revolutionary" or "parliamentary." [78]

The embarrassing tirades in the legislature aroused the activists, who jeered from the galleries and even disrupted the proceedings.[79] By March, 1919, the Khorhurd was hopelessly racked by dissension; emotions ran high and views became polarized. The legislature had deteriorated into a platform for oratory and declamation. The impasse was eventually broken on April 27 when the Khorhurd adopted a Dashnakist-sponsored motion to recess for a month and vest all its prerogatives in the cabinet during the interval.[80] The maneuver undoubtedly pleased those who favored vigorous, centralized rule in Armenia; in fact, it brought to an end the activities of the Khorhurd. Preparations for the Republic's first general elections had already been undertaken, and Dashnaktsutiun anticipated a popular mandate that would guarantee the party unchallenged ascendancy in the new parliament.[81]

The domestic crises of the Republic of Armenia during the first winter weighed heavily upon populace and leaders alike. Nowhere in the world was there greater misery than in Armenia during those terrible months. Many thousands perished without having recognized either the value or the benefits of an independent state. The unparalleled suffering was the inevitable result of the events of preceding years, but this explanation could make no difference to the ravaged masses whose appeals for salvation went unanswered. It is not sur-

[78] Vratzian, *Hanrapetutiun*, p. 227; Babalian, *op. cit.*, pp. 47–48. For the "activist" view on the Muslim question, see the appendix of Ruben's memoirs, *op. cit.*, pp. 407–409.

[79] Under the heading "Scandal in the Armenian Parliament," the semiofficial organ of the Georgian government, *Bor'ba*, March 12, 1919, p. 3, described the outlandish scene created in the Armenian legislature on February 27 when "mauserist" and "bashibazouk" elements, shouting pernicious threats, prevented the highest governing body of the country from turning to its agenda. It was reported in the issue of March 27 that, according to Armenian sources, Dashnaktsutiun's central committee in Georgia had called for the trial of Dr. Artashes Babalian as a principal organizer of the shameful demonstration.

[80] Rep. of Arm. Archives, File 6/6, *Hayastani Hanrapetutiun, 1919 t.*; Vratzian, *Hanrapetutiun*, p. 227.

[81] The Social Revolutionary organ *Znamia sotsializma* reported that only after ten days of intense negotiations had the Dashnakists succeeded in persuading the Populist deputies to support the recess motion on April 27. According to the Social Revolutionary interpretation, the Dashnakist maneuver was intended to replace *demokratiia* (democracy) with *khmbapetakratiia* (rule of the partisan chiefs), at least until the end of the forthcoming electoral campaign. See *Bor'ba*, May 6, 1919, p. 3. The electoral campaign and its results are discussed in chapter 14 below.

prising, therefore, that the crises in government, in party, and in legislature all had a common source. It was the tragedy of the Armenian people.

Yet there was hope. By the spring of 1919 Armenia had weathered the worst. The death toll dropped, and American grain reached the landlocked country. Moreover, as demonstrated in the following chapters, the Republic began to fill out into the unsecured regions of Russian Armenia. These were no small gains for a country born under the oppressive shadow of the Ottoman armies and immediately subjected to the pitiless blows of exposure, famine, and pestilence.

6

The Struggle for
Karabagh and Zangezur

It was inevitable that relations between the republics of Armenia and Azerbaijan would continue strained and hostile as long as the permanent status of Karabagh and Zangezur remained in dispute. Yet on this vital issue neither government found it possible to yield or even to compromise. Azerbaijan held advantages in material strength and physical access to the highlands, but these were attenuated by the determination of the majority of the population to unite with Armenia. In central Zangezur at the end of 1918, Andranik's partisans held sway in cooperation with a regional Armenian administration and militia, while in Karabagh, Javid Bey's Turkish division having withdrawn, a provisional executive body restored a semblance of Armenian rule. The Karabagh executive, which included the mayor of Shushi and a military representative from each of the four subdistricts, Varanda, Khachen, Jraberd, and Dizak, functioned under the shadow of the British military mission sent from Baku by Major General William M. Thomson.[1]

Toward a British Policy

The Armenian response to the occupation of strategic points in Transcaucasia by British military forces was initially enthusiastic. Shortly after his arrival in Baku General Thomson announced that the world peace conference would bring a just settlement in Karabagh and Zan-

[1] E. Ishkhanian, "Depkere Gharabaghum: jshdumner ev ditoghutiunner," *Hairenik Amsagir*, XI (Oct., 1933), 117–119; Vratzian, *Hanrapetutiun*, p. 282. The British military mission arrived in Shushi on December 8, 1918.

gezur, and he sent Major William Duff Gibbon to assist the Armenian refugees in the two centers and to arrange for the return of many of them to their native Nakhichevan. Gratified by these gestures, the Armenians were nevertheless mistaken in regarding them as manifestations of British political support. After a brief period of indecision General Thomson and especially his successor, Colonel Digby Inglis Shuttleworth, took a stand in favor of Azerbaijan's claims to Karabagh and Zangezur and demanded that the inhabitants accept the provisional jurisdiction of Fathali Khan Khoiskii's government.

There were, of course, factors other than the legitimacy of Azerbaijan's arguments which affected the formulation of British policy.[2] As rulers of an extensive colonial empire that included millions of Muslim subjects, the British stood to gain widespread goodwill for supporting the first Muslim republic in modern history. Moreover, the British strategists maintained that a politically and economically viable structure would render Azerbaijan less susceptible to Pan-Islamic or Pan-Turanic agitation and to the pervasive influences of the Ottoman Empire. At the end of 1918, they also believed that Armenia would be awarded the Ottoman eastern vilayets. It seemed reasonable, therefore, to regard Karabagh and Zangezur as compensation to Azerbaijan, whose aspirations to lands farther west would be disallowed. Several critics have singled out economic exploitation as the prime determinant in British policy. The reserve of oil at Baku was apparently inexhaustible, and access to this wealth would naturally be facilitated through the cooperation of an appreciative, indebted local government. While officials in London demonstrated that the occupation of Transcaucasia was imposing great financial strains, Great Britain nonetheless succeeded in tapping thousands of tons of petroleum products valued in the millions of pounds sterling. Whether or not "oil imperialism" dictated British policy in the Caucasus, economic factors could not have been ignored.[3]

[2] For differing evaluations of British policy in Transcaucasia, see the following: V. A. Gurko-Kriazhin, "Angliiskaia interventsiia 1918-1919 gg. v Zakaspii i Zakavkaz'e," Istorik marksist, 2 (1926), 115-120; US Archives, RG 256, Files 861G, 861K, and 867B passim; Khatisian, Hanrapetutian zargatsume, pp. 137-138, 143, 151-152, 155-156; E. A. Brayley Hodgetts, "The Strategic Position of Armenia," Asiatic Review, XVI (July, 1920), 385-394; Akademiia Nauk Azerbaidzhanskoi SSR, Institut Istorii, Istoriia Azerbaidzhana, ed. I. A. Guseinov et al., Vol. III, pt. 1 (Baku, 1963), pp. 164-169, cited hereafter as Istoriia Azerbaidzhana. The British Cabinet Office, War Office, and Foreign Office records for this period are now open and contain much fresh material for a scholarly appraisal of British policy—or lack of policy—toward the Caucasus.

[3] Many documents on Britain's interest in Baku oil are in Britain, FO 371/3668,

It was not until General Thomson had become well established in Baku, however, that he displayed partiality toward the government of Khan Khoiskii. In fact, his initial decrees were clearly heedless of Azerbaijani sovereignty. Unequivocal in his ultimatum that all Turkish and Azerbaijani military forces quit Baku before the Allied armada anchored in port,[4] he declared martial law in the city, placed British officers in charge of the police, forbade public assemblies, ordered the populace disarmed, and brought under his supervision many aspects of economic life. Among Thomson's first official pronouncements was the claim that the British expedition had come ashore with the full knowledge and consent of the "New Russian Government," having reference presumably to the anti-Bolshevik administration created at Ufa in September, 1918.[5] Revealing by his choice of words that he

---

File 1015/58, especially no. 47637. Soviet historians, using statistics of the former Azerbaijani republic, show that Great Britain exported enormous quantities of petroleum during the British occupation of Baku, November, 1918–August, 1919. F. Sh. Shabanov, *Razvitie Sovetskoi gosudarstvennosti v Azerbaidzhane* (Moscow, 1959), p. 42, states that the British took some 2.5 million pouds (40,952 metric tons) of kerosene in four months. *Istoriia Azerbaidzhana*, pp. 167–168, shows that by August, 1919, the British had exported 30 million pouds (491,425 metric tons) of petroleum valued at 113.5 million rubles. A. Raevskii, *Angliiskaia interventsiia i Musavatskoe pravitel'stvo* (Baku, 1927), pp. 20–22, 68, asserts that, during the first half of 1919 alone, the British exported via the Baku-Batum pipeline 5,793,000 pouds (94,894 metric tons) of oil, nearly 30 percent of the annual production, and that, during the latter half of the year, they acquired 14,884,000 pouds (243,812 metric tons). See also E. A. Tokarzhevskii, *Iz istorii inostrannoi interventsii i grazhdanskoi voiny v Azerbaidzhane* (Baku, 1957), pp. 173–175; D. Enukidze, *Krakh imperialisticheskoi interventsii v Zakavkaz'e* (Tbilisi, 1954), p. 173. Statistics compiled by the British Foreign Office and War Office show that for the period ending on March 31, 1919, the total cost for maintaining the British troops in the Caucasus was 810,000 pounds, 550,000 for the armed forces and 260,000 for transportation charges. During the period from April 1 to December 31, 1919, the sum increased to 3,340,000 pounds, 2,600,000 for the armed forces and 740,000 for transportation charges. See Britain, FO 371/3690, 117079/91/38. According to a British military source in US Archives, RG 256, 184.021/371, the cost of maintaining the Imperial contingents in Baku alone was 160 million Russian rubles up to March, 1919, with another 85 million earmarked for immediate expenditure.

[4] The Azerbaijani Ministry of Military Affairs and the General Staff transferred to Ganja, where they remained until the spring of 1919. See Mehmet-Zade Mirza-Bala, *Milli Azerbaycan hareketi: Milli Az. "Müsavat" halk firkası tarihi* ([Berlin], 1938), pp. 169–170; Britain, WO 106/917, and Cab 27/37, E.C. 2437.

[5] Britain, FO 371/3669, 19373/512/58, and Cab 27/37, E.C. 2457; US Archives, RG 256, 184.021/86; Raevskii, *op. cit.*, pp. 33–34; Kadishev, *Interventsiia v Zakavkaz'e*, pp. 164, 167; Enukidze, *op. cit.*, pp. 136–137; George A. Brinkley, *The Volunteer Army and Allied Intervention in South Russia, 1917–1921* (Notre Dame, 1966), pp. 91–93, 94–95; *Bor'ba v Azerbaidzhane*, pp. 27–30, 32–33, 64. According to Gaioz Devdariani, ed., *Dni gospodstva men'shevikov v Gruzii (dokumenty, materialy)* ([Tiflis], 1931), p. 39, General Thomson made specific reference to the bond between the Allies and the Ufa regime and stressed that the Allied Powers, like the legal govern-

regarded Baku as an inseparable part of Russia, Thomson continued:

In the hour of victory we are not unmindful of the great services in the Allied cause rendered by the Russian peoples in the earlier part of the War. The Allies cannot return to their homes without restoring order in Russia, and placing her in a position again to take her proper place among the nations of the world. . . .

There is no question of the Allies retaining possession of one foot of Russia. They have given their word to the Russian peoples on this point.

The internal Government of any portion of Russia is a question for the Russian peoples in which the Allies in no way interfere. We come simply to restore order by removing the Turkish and German centres of unrest which remain to prevent the establishment of peace and prosperity. All races and religions will receive the same treatment at our hands. Local and Municipal Administrations will be appointed provisionally by me and will have our support, and we shall confine our attention to the restoration of law and order. . . .

I look forward, with the assistance of all moderate and thinking men in Baku, to the easy and early accomplishment of the duty which lies before me and the troops under my command, and that we may return at an early date to our country, having helped Russia to take her share in the victory which has been achieved over our common enemies.[6]

This apparent rejection of Azerbaijan's bid for independence jeopardized the future of Khan Khoiskii's cabinet, which had, after all, been installed in Baku on the strength of Turkish bayonets.[7] But his

---

ment of Russia, could not recognize any independent entities that had been formed on Russian territory.

[6] Britain, FO 371/3667, 11067/11067/58. See also US Archives, RG 256, 861K.00/5; Brinkley, *op. cit.*, pp. 93–94.

[7] On December 6 General Thomson urged his superiors to formulate a comprehensive, clear-cut policy regarding the Caucasus. He stressed that the local population hated Russia and would look favorably on a British or French protectorate as a guarantee against oppression. Thomson advised that the British army take control of the transportation, post and telegraph, customs and excise, state banks, and police in the Caucasus and also prepare to occupy the region in three stages:

a. The occupation of TIFLIS and the advance Northwards up the Georgian [Military] Road towards VLADIKAVKAZ of a sufficient force to hearten the many anti-Bolshevik elements into a united move which would clear Vladikavkaz and the Railway [of the Bolsheviks].

b. The occupation of the other Republican "capitals" of ERIVAN and PETROVSK [Daghestan], where the Officer in Command gives [would give] direct orders to the local Government and insists on their execution.

c. Occupation of KARS and JULFA (also TABRIZ if found necessary). The disbandment of all troops in the Caucasus other than British and those actually fighting the Bolsheviks is an essential preliminary to the restoration of order.

Secret societies, agitators and the gutter press must be firmly dealt with.

public statements aside, Thomson actually sought the most expeditious means to supplant the Ottoman-oriented government with a local administration in which all major ethnic and religious groups would be represented. He deemed this the most judicious way of controlling the region until Great Britain and the Peace Conference had shaped the destiny of the Transcaucasian lands. Spokesmen for the Armenian population, then in the process of returning to Baku from Enzeli and other temporary havens, responded favorably to a proposal to implement the scheme, but negotiations between Azerbaijani and Russian representatives proved futile. The Russians tended to consider some future all-Russian constituent assembly as the sole body empowered to determine the fate of territories previously included within the Romanov Empire, whereas the Azerbaijanis insisted that their country had formally separated from Russia and that the purpose of the current talks was simply to facilitate Armenian and Russian participation in the government of the Azerbaijani republic.[8]

Khan Khoiskii maneuvered skillfully to make it appear that the Russian National Council of Baku was unreasonable and inflexible, and a fruitless personal attempt to intercede with the Russian leaders convinced Thomson of the validity of the charge. By December Azerbaijani statesmen had succeeded in gaining the sympathy of the British commander. To provide evidence of Azerbaijan's dedication to demo-

---

Whatever the decision of the Peace Conference our occupation must be prolonged.

See Britain, FO 371/3667, 5890/5890/58. See also Cab 27/37, E.C. 2458 and E.C. 2527, and Cab 27/38, E.C. 2780.

Thomson's straightforward, if somewhat imperialist-tinged, proposal was not endorsed by the policy makers in London who suggested that "it might be advisable to caution General Thomson to exercise greater reserve in these matters" and "to instruct the War Office to telegraph at once to say that the military commanders both at Batum and Baku should be informed that it was no part of His Majesty's Government's policy to embark on any operations at any distance from the Baku-Batum line, as our troops in that area were intended for the purpose of protecting the railway and maintaining through communications from the Black Sea to the Caspian." See Britain, Cab 27/24, Eastern Committee, 48th Minutes. Undersecretary of State for Foreign Affairs Lord Curzon quipped that the fulfillment of Thomson's program would take "two years, if not five, or possibly ten." He complained that since the War Office had taken over the direction of affairs in the Caucasus, the Foreign Office had been left poorly informed about the military and political events there, even though the Foreign Office would be held responsible for any resulting complications. See Britain, FO 371/3667, 19030/5890/58. See also Richard H. Ullman, *Anglo-Soviet Relations, 1917–1921,* Vol. II: *Britain and the Russian Civil War, November 1918–February 1920* (Princeton, 1968), pp. 82–84.

[8] Britain, FO 371/3667, 19030/5890/58; B. Baikov, "Vospominaniia o revoliutsii v Zakavkaz'i (1917–1920 g.g.)," *Arkhiv russkoi revoliutsii,* IX (1923), 149–151; Brinkley, *op. cit.,* pp. 93–94; US Archives, RG 256, 184.021/86.

cratic principles, they established a national parliament.[9] Although the Muslim groups combined held firm control therein, the popular Musavat party laid claim to only a third of the seats, and several places were held in reserve for representatives of the ethnic minorities.[10] Thereafter, Khan Khoiskii reorganized his cabinet on a broader political base in order to absolve Azerbaijan from the stigma of her Ottoman birth and to satisfy Thomson's demand for a local administrative coalition.[11] Finally on December 28, 1918, General Thomson acknowledged Khan Khoiskii's government as the only legal local authority pending the ultimate settlement by the Peace Conference.[12] The proponents of a free and independent Azerbaijan had won an impressive, if not momentous, victory.

[9] British consent to the creation of the Parliament was given by General Thomson on December 3, 1918, according to a document cited in *Istoriia gosudarstva i prava Azerbaidzhanskoi SSR: Velikaia Oktiabr'skaia sotsialisticheskaia revoliutsiia i sozdanie Sovetskoi gosudarstvennosti v Azerbaidzhane*, publ. of Akademiia Nauk Azerbaidzhanskoi SSR, Sektor Filosofii (Baku, 1964), p. 277.

[10] The legislature convened on December 7, 1918, and elected Ali Mardan Topchibashev as its chairman. For the political, social, and ethnic structure of the Azerbaijani Parliament, see *Istoriia Azerbaidzhana*, pp. 169–170; Kazemzadeh, *Transcaucasia*, pp. 166–167; Richard Pipes, *The Formation of the Soviet Union* (rev. ed.; Cambridge, Mass., 1964), p. 206; US Archives, RG 256, 861K.00/5. The Musavat-Nonpartisan bloc controlled 38 of the 96 seats. Pipes shows that 11 of the deputies were Armenian, whereas a report of the Tiflis party of the American Field Mission to South Russia, May 1, 1919, states that 5 Dashnakists and 4 Populists had entered the Parliament in deference to British insistence. See RG 256, 184.021/14. A press release in Rep. of Arm. Archives, File 69a/1a, announced the participation of 7 Dashnakists, 5 from Baku and 2 from Elisavetpol, in the Azerbaijani legislature. Mirza-Bala, *op. cit.*, pp. 154–155, states that the Parliament was to have had 120 members but that in fact there were never more than 95 deputies, of whom 75 were Muslim, 10 Armenian, 5 Russian, and 5 of other minorities. He shows the Musavat bloc as having 39 seats. No other party had more than 11 representatives in the legislature. Statistics in *Istoriia gosudarstva i prava Azerbaidzhanskoi SSR*, p. 278, show that 43 of the 96 members of Parliament were feudal landlords (khans and beks); 15 petroleum industrialists; 12 commercial magnates; and at least 8 religious notables.

[11] For the composition of Khan Khoiskii's coalition cabinet, see Adil Khan Ziatkhan, *Aperçu sur l'histoire, la littérature et la politique de l'Azerbeidjan* (Baku, 1919), pp. 79–80; [Republic of Azerbaijan], *Le 28 Mai 1919* ([Baku], 1919]), pp. 14–15. See also *Istoriia Azerbaidzhana*, p. 170.

[12] M. E. Rassoul-Zadé, *L'Azerbaidjan en lutte pour l'Indépendance* (Paris, 1930), p. 19; Ziatkhan, *op. cit.*, p. 74; Raevskii, *op. cit.*, pp. 46–47; Mirza-Bala, *op. cit.*, pp. 164–165; *Le 28 Mai 1919*, p. 15. See also Denikin, *Ocherki smuty*, IV, 164–166. The provisional policy guidelines of Great Britain at the end of 1918 supported the formation of Caucasian states independent of Russia. See Britain, Cab 23/8, War Cabinet Minutes, 511(Appendix), Cab 27/36, E.C. 2392, Cab 27/38, E.C. 2715A, WO 33/965, nos. 2908, 3274, and FO 371/3661, 41025/1015/58.

Governor-General Khosrov Bek Sultanov

Once having secured British recognition, although partial and unofficial, Premier Fathali Khan Khoiskii impressed General Thomson with the urgency of restoring law and order in the unmanageable districts of the Elisavetpol guberniia. As this goal was in no way contradictory to British policy, Thomson sanctioned Khan Khoiskii's appointment on January 15, 1919, of Dr. Khosrov Bek Sultanov as provisional governor-general of a region encompassing both Mountainous Karabagh and Zangezur.[13] Functioning under the jurisdiction of the Ministry of Interior, Sultanov's primary assignment was "to establish the rule of government in that region, where anarchy has become especially widespread and where the maintenance of order by ordinary means has been found to be extremely difficult."[14] The Armenians were shocked into disbelief, not only by this overt British patronage of Azerbaijan, but also by the choice of governor-general. The Armenian militia still dominated the situation in Zangezur, and, had General Thomson not intervened to stay Andranik's advance in December of 1918, Armenia would have established control over Karabagh as well.

Dr. Sultanov, an influential Musavatist and a wealthy landlord in Karabagh, bore a notorious reputation. During the summer of 1918, as a powerful aide of Nuri Pasha, he had incited the Muslim inhabitants of Karabagh against their Armenian neighbors and had taken an active role in the conquest of Baku. His Pan-Turanic views and his intimacy with the Turkish Ittihadist commanders were common knowledge. General Thomson could not have been ignorant of these facts when he condoned the appointment of Sultanov, a man feared and hated by the Armenians of Karabagh.[15]

On January 26, 1919, even before news of the appointment had been confirmed in Erevan, the Armenian government denounced Azerbaijan's intention to establish a governor-generalship within the limits of the Jevanshir, Jebrail, Shushi, and Zangezur uezds as a "violation of the territorial rights of Armenia."[16] In reply, Azerbaijan asserted "in-

[13] US Archives, RG 256, 861K.00/5; P. G. La Chesnais, *Les peuples de la Transcaucasie pendant la guerre et devant la paix* (Paris, 1921), p. 158; Ziatkhan, *op. cit.*, pp. 65–66.

[14] *Istoriia gosudarstva i prava Azerbaidzhanskoi SSR*, p. 285.

[15] US Archives, RG 256, 184.01602/23; Rep. of Arm. Archives, File 9/9. American representatives in the Caucasus protested Sultanov's appointment on the same grounds as the Armenians. See US Archives, RG 84, Tiflis Consulate, 1919, pt. 4, File 710; RG 256, 867.00/158, and 867B.00/151/156.

[16] Rep. of Arm. Archives, File 8/8, Armenian Foreign Ministry to Foreign Minister of Azerbaijan.

disputable and irrevocable" title to the region and labeled the Armenian protest as "a violation of our sovereignty and an attempt to interfere in our internal affairs." [17]

With the controversy still budding, Major General George Townshend Forestier-Walker, commander of the Tiflis-based 27th Division, apprised the Armenian government on February 19 of a principle assertedly adopted by the Allied peacemakers: "The possession of disputed territory gained by force will seriously prejudice the claims of the aggressor. All must await the decision of the Peace Conference." [18] Five days later, on February 24, temporary Brigadier General Verney Asser, representing Forestier-Walker in Erevan, handed Foreign Minister Tigranian a communiqué, relayed via Tiflis, from General Thomson: "Dr. Sultanov is leaving for Shusha in the capacity of governor-general in the districts of Zangezur, Shusha, and Karabagh [sic]. He is taking this action without imposing any conditions regarding Azerbaijan's future jurisdiction there. He is going only to preserve law and order." [19]

Tigranian gave Forestier-Walker immediate notice that "the Armenian government cannot consider the transmission of the wire from General Thomson as an expression of even indirect recognition of Azerbaijan's right, albeit temporary, to subject to the administration of Dr. Sultanov the contested sectors of the said counties." The only tolerable arrangement, he insisted, would be the maintenance of the status quo until the Paris Peace Conference had given its decision on the boundaries. In the same message Tigranian inquired whether the directive regarding "the possession of disputed territory gained by force" had been communicated to the Baku government as well.[20]

Appealing directly to General Thomson on March 11, Tigranian again contended that the instructions of the Peace Conference would be violated should Azerbaijan initiate unilateral action. He reminded Thomson that during the war Karabagh had defended its freedom

[17] Rep. of Arm. Archives, File 66a/3, Khan Khoiskii to Foreign Minister of Armenia.
[18] Rep. of Arm. Archives, File 7/7, Commander of British Forces to President of the Armenian Government.
[19] Khatisian, Hanrapetutian zargatsume, p. 153; Rep. of Arm. Archives, File 9/9, Brig. Gen. V. Asser to Foreign Minister of Armenia. General Asser, commander of the 27th Division Artillery, was assigned to Erevan on February 1. He served there as the British military representative until the beginning of March, when he was appointed military governor of Kars. See Britain, WO 95/4880, 27th Division Headquarters, General Staff, War Diary.
[20] US Archives, RG 84, Tiflis Consulate, 1919, pt. 4, File 710; Khatisian, Hanrapetutian zargatsume, p. 154; Rep. of Arm. Archives, File 3/3, Foreign Minister to British Commander, Feb. 25, 1919.

tenaciously and now regarded itself as part of the Republic of Armenia. Any forcible attempt by Azerbaijan to impose her will would unquestionably give rise to grievous consequences. Therefore, the office of the "so-called governor-general" should be suspended, at least in Armenian Karabagh, so that recourse to constructive negotiations might follow. Thomson found the Armenian suggestion unacceptable.[21]

The British Mission in Shushi

Alarmed by the adroit strategy of Azerbaijan, the provisional Armenian administration in Shushi summoned the Fourth Assembly of Karabagh to deal with the crisis and to demonstrate that the rejection of Sultanov was unqualified and unanimous. The Fourth Assembly, February 10–21, 1919, spurned an invitation to send deputies to the Parliament in Baku and protested vociferously Khan Khoiskii's charge that the concern shown for Karabagh by Armenia was tantamount to involvement in the domestic affairs of Azerbaijan: "Mountainous Karabagh, as a component of the Republic of Armenia, denies Azerbaijani authority in any form whatsoever." In messages relayed to General Thomson, Kachaznuni's cabinet, and the Armenian delegation in Paris, the sixty-six–member Assembly appealed for an effective defense of the "fundamental rights" of Mountainous Karabagh. Before adjourning, the conference elected a permanent executive, the Council of Karabagh, and charged it with the primary responsibility of ensuring Mountainous Karabagh's inclusion within the Republic of Armenia.[22]

The Fourth Assembly was still in session when Dr. Khosrov Bek Sultanov arrived in Shushi with two members of the Baku Armenian Council and a company of Imperial troops led by Major G. N. G. Monck-Mason of the 84th Punjabi Regiment, Indian Army.[23] Taking

[21] Rep. of Arm. Archives, File 66/2, *Vrastani Divanagitakan Nerkayatsutsich ev Vrastani Karavarutiun, 1919,* Foreign Minister to General Thomson.

[22] Rep. of Arm. Archives, File 69a/1a and File 1649; US Archives, RG 84, Tiflis Consulate, 1919, pt. 4, File 710. See also Britain, FO 608/82, 342/5/4/7743.

[23] A press bulletin of February 24, 1919, in Rep. of Arm. Archives, File 69a/1a, states that 200 sepoys had arrived in Shushi where they were welcomed by the Armenian population but received with hostility by the Muslim inhabitants. The war diary of the 84th Punjabis shows that the regiment, commanded by Godfrey Noel Grey Monck-Mason and formerly a part of the 17th Infantry (Indian) Division in Mesopotamia, was among the first units of the 27th Division to go ashore at Batum on December 22. Ordered to Baku on January 23, 1919, the regiment was attached to the 39th Brigade of the Thomson's Force. On February 5 Monck-Mason and D Company were instructed to assume charge of the British mission at Shushi. Three days later the company entrained for Evlakh, whence it marched overland to

charge of the local British military mission, Monck-Mason informed the newly elected Council of Karabagh that Sultanov's appointment had been explicitly authorized by General Thomson. The Governor-General would have an Armenian assistant for civil affairs and would be guided by a mixed advisory board composed of three Armenians, three Muslims, and a member of the British mission.[24] Then, in a formal message, Monck-Mason reassured the Armenian representatives that the provisional arrangement would have no bearing on the future permanent status of Karabagh, but he also warned: "The British mission declares by means of this communiqué that all orders of the Governor-General or his aides must be executed to the word by the population. The most stringent measures will be taken to deal with those who refuse to comply." [25]

Major Monck-Mason's coaxing notwithstanding, the Karabagh Council remained adamant, replying that the native inhabitants "express their vexation at these coercions and make it known to the world that they will not submit to the authority of the government of Azerbaijan." For the sake of peace, however, they would be willing to accept, as an alternative to complete self-government, the creation of an interim administration headed by an English officer.[26]

Rejecting this "concession," the British mission then addressed itself to the Karabagh militia commanders, all four of whom were then in Shushi, ordering them to acknowledge Dr. Sultanov as governor-general or else to sign the following protocol:

We, the undersigned, have examined the project in the official communication which the chief of the British Mission proposes to publish. We are not disposed to recognize the authority of the officials of the government of Azerbaijan under any form whatsoever, either in the limits of Karabagh or of Zangezur.
We refuse likewise to figure among the members of the council being formed for the administration of the region.
We consider ourselves informed by the chief of the Mission that any

---

Shushi. The garrison at Shushi was strengthened a month later by the arrival of B Company. Several light armored vehicles and sections of the field ambulance corps and other auxiliary services were attached to the British mission. The effective strength of the mission at the end of April, 1919, was 4 British officers, 16 British, other ranks, and 204 Indian, other ranks. The remaining two companies of 84th Punjabis and the regiment headquarters company, temporarily under Major Reginald Tyrer, were dispatched for service at Petrovsk. See Britain, WO 95/4955.

[24] US Archives, RG 84, Tiflis Consulate, 1919, pt. 4, File 711; Rep. of Arm. Archives, File 9/9, Project.

[25] Rep. of Arm. Archives, File 1649, Monck-Mason to Karabagh Armenian Council.

[26] US Archives, RG 84. Tiflis Consulate, 1919, pt. 4, File 801; Rep. of Arm. Archives, File 9/9.

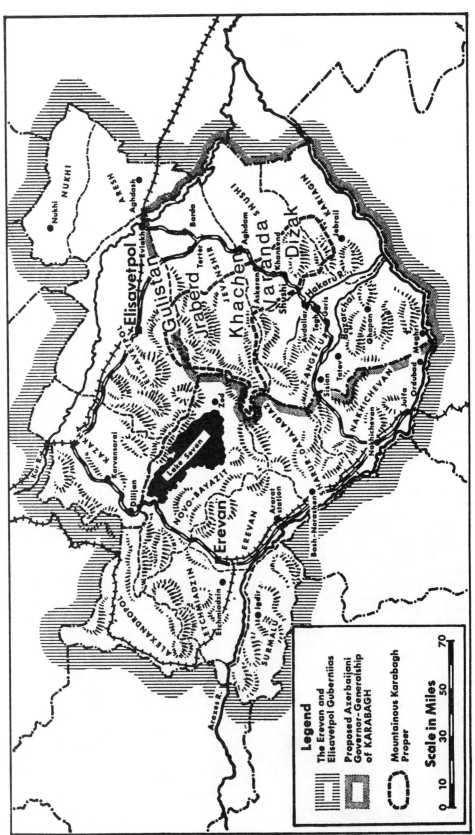

9. KARABAGH AND ZANGEZUR

Legend

The Erevan and
Elisavetpol Guberniias

Proposed Azerbaijani
Governor-Generalship
of KARABAGH

Mountainous Karabagh
Proper

Scale in Miles
0   10   30   50   70

belligerent action against the government of Azerbaijan will be regarded as if it were directed against the government of Great Britain.

We cannot guarantee how the districts which we head may be affected by the publication of this appeal.[27]

The four leaders, stating their allegiance to the Karabagh Council and disclaiming jurisdiction in political matters, returned the ultimatum unsigned. The British mission responded with a sharp rebuke and the demand that, inasmuch as the stand taken by the Karabagh Council was totally inadmissible, the commanders endorse the British plan without reservation or else place their signatures upon the self-incriminating document. They did neither, reiterating only that as mere soldiers charged with the defense of Varanda, Khachen, Dizak, and Jraberd they possessed no authority in political matters.[28]

Still hoping to find some way to bring about the peaceful acquiescence of the Karabagh Armenians, Monck-Mason solicited the intercession of the two Baku Armenian Council members who had accompanied him to Shushi. Gerasim Balayan and Levon Zarafian had given their word to General Thomson that they would strive to pacify their agitated compatriots in Karabagh. Once they had arrived in the highland and had seen the situation firsthand, however, both joined the critics of the British project. Angered by what he considered a breach of faith, Monck-Mason had the pair placed in an armored car and exiled. Word of this "abusive treatment" circulated rapidly. The shops and central market of Shushi closed and soon an angry crowd gathered outside Monck-Mason's headquarters. The tension eased only after the British mission consented to return Balayan and Zarafian. The pledge, however, was not honored.[29]

Alternative Proposals

With the belief that the senior British officers in Transcaucasia would be more accommodating if the Armenian case were presented directly, the Karabagh Council dispatched Bishop Vahan and one of its members, Hrand Bagaturian, to Tiflis on February 24, 1919. The appeal

[27] US Archives, RG 84, Tiflis Consulate, 1919, pt. 4, File 801, *Dokladnaia zapiska*, March 13, 1919; Rep. of Arm. Archives, File 69a/1a, Report of Feb. 27, 1919; Britain, FO 608/82, 342/5/4/7743.

[28] US Archives, RG 84, Tiflis Consulate, 1919, pt. 4, File 710; Rep. of Arm. Archives, File 1649.

[29] Ishkhanian, *op. cit.*, pp. 120–121; Sarur [Asur], "Gharabaghi ktsume Adrbedjani," *Hairenik Amsagir*, VII (June, 1929), 134–135; Rep. of Arm. Archives, File 1649, Report of Arsen Mikayelian.

they submitted to General Forestier-Walker repeated that which had been said so often: The Karabagh Armenians had defended their liberty against all enemies and had laid aside their arms only in deference to General Thomson, whom they regarded as the spokesman for Great Britain. But Azerbaijan had taken advantage of this show of good faith by concentrating troops at such strategic places as Askeran, Khankend, and Kariagin. The native inhabitants trusted, nonetheless, that the Paris Peace Conference would respect their determination to become citizens of the Republic of Armenia. The scheme to clamp an Azerbaijani governorship on the counties of Zangezur, Shushi, Jebrail, and Jevanshir was totally unacceptable, and any move to enforce it would lead to regrettable strife. Consequently, the British should compel all Azerbaijani officials and soldiers to withdraw from Karabagh and should take direct control of the situation until the Peace Conference had rendered its decision.[30]

Through Bishop Vahan and Bagaturian, the Karabagh Council also submitted a draft proposal for an interim administration. It provided that Mountainous Karabagh proper be governed by a mixed council of seven Armenians, three Muslims, and, with the mutual consent of Armenia and Azerbaijan, one representative from each republic. The chief of the British mission in Shushi would serve as the ex-officio head of government and would possess the power to regulate council proceedings and to veto any decision. The British command would place observers at all strategic sites and would regulate troop movements. Zangezur was to be excluded from consideration because it already had its own autonomous administration and the situation there was quite dissimilar from that prevailing in Karabagh. Hrand Bagaturian and Bishop Vahan requested that the appeal and the project of the Karabagh Council be forwarded to His Majesty's Government and supreme military command.[31]

Armenian envoys carried copies of these same documents to British headquarters in Baku and petitioned General Thomson to prohibit the installation of Azerbaijani officials in Mountainous Karabagh. The project of the Karabagh Council or any one of the following alternatives would, they said, be acceptable to the Armenians as a temporary

[30] US Archives, RG 84, Tiflis Consulate, 1919, pt. 4, File 710, Appeal to Commander of Allied Forces in Transcaucasia, Feb. 24, 1919; Rep. of Arm. Archives, File 9/9 and File 69a/1a. A copy of the appeal in Britain, FO 608/82, 342/5/4/7743, shows one of the signatories to be Karabagh Council member Anushavan Ter-Mikayelian rather than Bishop Vahan.

[31] US Archives, RG 84, Tiflis Consulate, 1919, pt. 4, File 710 and File 801, Project, Feb. 20, 1919; Rep. of Arm. Archives, File 9/9. See also Bor'ba March 22, 1919, p. 2.

settlement: (1) inclusion of Mountainous Karabagh into the Republic of Armenia; (2) restoration of the administrative structure as it had existed in Karabagh before the Turkish offensive in 1918; (3) establishment of a British governor-generalship for Mountainous Karabagh proper, that is Armenian-populated Karabagh; (4) creation of a British governor-generalship for all Karabagh, partitioned, however, into distinct zones of Armenian and Muslim self-rule. General Thomson, now appearing a bit more flexible, no longer rejected unequivocally the Armenian appeals but did maintain that only the original British-supported solution could ensure the return of peace.[32]

Early in March, 1919, at General Thomson's request, the Armenians of Karabagh selected a new delegation to negotiate for a modus vivendi. Yet Major Monck-Mason disallowed the six-man delegation, insisting that the chairman and two vice-chairmen of the Karabagh Council be included. The Armenians were apprehensive of Monck-Mason's motives, for they realized that the Council would be severely handicapped if its officers were forcibly detained in Baku. Nonetheless, after several conferences at the British mission, Council Chairman Aslan Melik-Shahnazarian agreed to lead the deputation. But as the party prepared to depart Monck-Mason angrily charged that armed men known to the Karabagh Council had harassed two of Sultanov's appointees, and he warned that all such violations would be regarded as expressions of hostility toward Great Britain. Since the Armenians had obstinately rejected the opportunity to participate in the administration, they had no right to interfere in the conduct of official duties and must submit to Governor-General Sultanov's directives. The chief of the British mission concluded, "I ask from you not opposition but cooperation." Aslan Melik-Shahnazarian feigned amazement at the inference of bad faith and told Monck-Mason that the Council was prepared to resign so that the British, if they desired, could summon another Karabagh assembly to elect a new executive body. Knowing that the outcome of such a move would not decrease Armenian intransigence but might easily embarrass the British, Monck-Mason chose to ignore Melik-Shahnazarian's "suggestion," and the delegation proceeded to Baku.[33]

When the Armenian leaders arrived in the Azerbaijani capital, they discovered that General Thomson had just departed post haste for

---

[32] Rep. of Arm. Archives, File 3/3 and File 69a/1a.

[33] US Archives, RG 84, Tiflis Consulate, 1919, pt. 4, File 801; Rep. of Arm. Archives, File 9/9, British Mission, Shushi, to Armenian National Council, and National Council to Chief of British Mission.

Tiflis to replace the ailing Forestier-Walker as senior British commander in Transcaucasia. Colonel D. I. Shuttleworth, one of Thomson's staff officers, was left in charge of the Imperial forces in Baku.[34] He displayed quick impatience with the Armenians and straightforward sympathy for the Azerbaijanis. On April 3, 1919, after several unproductive sessions with the Armenian delegation, he publicized the following circular:

The English Command declares to the entire population of the counties of Shusha, Zangezur, Jebrail, and Jevanshir that:
1. the government of Azerbaijan, by its decision of January 15, 1919, has appointed Dr. Sultanov as governor-general, and he enjoys the cooperation of the English Command;
2. in conformity with existing laws, a six-man council of capable Armenians and Muslims is to be formed in the governor-generalship to minister to the needs of the entire population;
3. an officer of the English Mission may join the council as the representative of the English Command;
4. the Azerbaijani treasury will be responsible for the salaries of officials and for all other expenses in the governor-generalship;
5. the final solution to all disputed questions will emanate from the [Paris] Peace Conference;
6. the English Mission will be informed in advance about all military movements within the bounds of the governor-generalship;
7. with this communiqué the English Command wishes to emphasize that in order for the Governor-General to fulfill the obligations placed upon him, including preservation of law and order in the governor-generalship, all regulations and directives issued by the Governor-General and his bureaus must be enacted without opposition, and the English Command lends its full support to all legally adopted measures.[35]

[34] Forestier-Walker was discovered to have severe diabetes mellitus, requiring immediate hospitalization. Thomson departed for Tiflis on March 9 and began his duties at 27th Division headquarters the following day. Lieutenant Colonel R. P. Jordan, who since January, 1919, had served as acting commander of the 39th Brigade in Baku, also departed on March 9 for leave in the United Kingdom. The distinction between the 39th Brigade and the somewhat more encompassing Thomson's Force ended on March 11, when all Imperial contingents in the Caspian region were attached to the 39th Brigade, and Shuttleworth transferred 39th Brigade headquarters to those of the former Thomson's Force. Thus, Shuttleworth led all British troops in Azerbaijan and at Petrovsk and Krasnovodsk. In January, 1919, the 39th Brigade had come under the jurisdiction of General Milne's Army of the Black Sea, and on March 16 it was attached to the 27th Division, headquartered in Tiflis, with Major General Thomson commanding. For the structure and interrelationships of the Army of the Black Sea, the 27th Division, the Thomson's Force, and the 39th Brigade, see Britain, WO 95/4880, /4950, and /4955. See also Britain, *Order of Battle*, Pt. 3A, pp. 36–42.

[35] Rep. of Arm. Archives, File 9/9, Commander of British Military Mission at Baku,

The declaration drew violent protests from the people of Karabagh and the government of Armenia. On April 16 Foreign Minister Tigranian characterized the directive to submit to Sultanov "without opposition" as intolerable, and he again appealed for temporary British rule in Karabagh as an alternative to the strife that Azerbaijani domination would inevitably produce.[36] Meanwhile, in Karabagh itself, the militia chiefs led their men back into Varanda, Khachen, Dizak, and Jraberd. The partisan units, stationed in Shushi since December of 1918, had lost much of their cohesiveness and militant spirit. In the countryside, their basic source of strength, they hopefully could be redisciplined to withstand the threats and coercion of Azerbaijanis and British alike.[37]

The Fifth Assembly of Karabagh

Determined to settle the deepening crisis, Shuttleworth, who was promoted to Brigadier General on April 19, 1919,[38] instructed the Karabagh Council to summon the Fifth Assembly of Karabagh and then traveled to Shushi to expound his views in person. During the opening session of the Fifth Assembly, April 23–29, both General Shuttleworth and Dr. Sultanov made lengthy appeals for what they termed a rational solution. They promised that the rights and security of the Armenian inhabitants would remain inviolate. Shuttleworth also laid strong emphasis on economic factors, asserting that Mountainous Karabagh would starve were it separated from the plains to the east and the vital railway link at Evlakh on the Batum-Tiflis-Baku line.[39]

The Assembly's reply on April 25 was heavy with emotion. The Armenians of Karabagh did uphold the right of their Tatar neighbors to self-determination, but they demanded the same freedom for themselves. The refusal of the Baku government to acknowledge that right

D. I. Shuttleworth. See also File 3/3, Tigranian to Aharonian, May 6, 1919, and File 115/14, *H. H. Patvirakutiun, 1920*, British Commander, Tiflis, to Foreign Minister of Armenia, April 16, 1919.

[36] US Archives, RG 84, Tiflis Consulate, 1919, pt. 4, File 710, Foreign Minister to Commander of British Forces in Transcaucasia; Britain, FO 371/3659, 84448/512/58, and FO 608/82, 342/5/2/11654; Rep. of Arm. Archives, File 9/9.

[37] Ishkhanian, *op. cit.*, p. 123; Rep. of Arm. Archives, File 1649; Sarur, *op. cit.*, p. 135.

[38] Britain, *Order of Battle*, Pt. 3A, p. 36. The 39th Brigade War Diary indicates that Shuttleworth's promotion was retroactive to March 23, 1919. See Britain, WO 95/4955.

[39] Rep. of Arm. Archives, File 1649, Mikayelian report; Vratzian, *Hanrapetutiun*, p. 285; Sarur, *op. cit.*, p. 136. See also Denikin, *Ocherki smuty*, IV, 170.

had precipitated the crisis. The Assembly felt compelled to declare that "Azerbaijan has been and remains an accomplice and ally of the Turks in all measures taken against the Armenians in general and against the Armenians of Karabagh in particular." Azerbaijan had welcomed the Turkish invasion of Transcaucasia, had committed treason and sabotage, and now, having not abandoned the hope that the Turk would one day return, was subjecting the Armenian population to an economic boycott and systematic persecution. The violent acts of brigandage and plunder multiplied "even as the representatives of the power of England are at our side to protect us." The Azerbaijanis, true to their Turkic forebears, the reply continued, labored fervidly to extirpate the Armenians, who were the only civilized element, the only channel to Europe, and the only champions of liberty. In answer to the economic arguments raised by Shuttleworth, the Assembly maintained that the safe and unhindered flow of goods was essential to the welfare of all Transcaucasia and that the issue should not be exploited to justify the tyrannical rule of Azerbaijan. Muslim herdsmen would not be denied summer pasturage in Karabagh unless the Armenians were driven to defend their hard-won freedom. Finally, the Armenians of Karabagh set forth their refusal to believe that Great Britain would attempt to reimpose the yoke of servitude and suggested that the British commander need only conduct a referendum to test the popular and representative nature of this official reply: "The decision of the Fifth Assembly never to submit is dictated by the unyielding will of the entire Armenian population of Karabagh, a will which the delegates to this congress may not disobey, because they cannot accept the responsibility for the bloody eventualities that will result from the forcible imposition of Azerbaijani rule upon Mountainous Karabagh." [40]

General Shuttleworth felt that he had done his utmost, within the limits of British policy guidelines, to resolve the dispute. His personal mission to Karabagh having failed, he now made it known that no longer could he oppose Azerbaijan's decision to take action.[41] Already,

[40] Rep. of Arm. Archives, File 9/9, Fifth Karabagh Congress to General Shuttleworth, and "Rapport Officiel" of July 14, 1919. See also File 231/130, Aharonian to Balfour, June 20, 1919; and US Archives, RG 84, Tiflis Consulate, 1919, pt. 4, File 801.

[41] Shuttleworth returned to Baku on April 26 and three days later gave the Azerbaijani government authorization to make political arrests and to regulate the freedom of speech and public assembly. See Britain, WO 95/4880 and /4955. American officials reported that Shuttleworth condoned the Azerbaijani economic boycott of Karabagh and gave permission to starve the Armenians into submission. See US Archives, RG 59, 867.00/893, and RG 256, 184.021/23.

the Azebaijani army had dispatched fresh troops to Karabagh and the government had given public notice of its intentions. On March 28, 1919, Premier Khan Khoiskii informed the Georgian republic and the Allied representatives in Baku and Tiflis that the small Azerbaijani detachments at Khankend, Askeran, and elsewhere in Karabagh had been viciously attacked by Armenian bands and that, in view of this sedition, the government had adopted preventive measures to enforce law and order in the region.[42]

Consultations in Erevan

While Shuttleworth coaxed and threatened in Baku and in Shushi, Major General Thomson attempted to reason with the Armenian government. On March 27, two weeks after taking charge of British headquarters in Tiflis, Thomson paid an official visit to Erevan. During a five-hour conference with Acting Premier Alexandre Khatisian and Foreign Minister Sirakan Tigranian, he reiterated the argument that Karabagh could not subsist without food imported by way of Evlakh on the Batum-Baku railway. As there was no direct passage or suitable road between Erevan and Karabagh, only the provisional jurisdiction of Azerbaijan could guarantee that the single available supply route would remain open. General Thomson made no excuses for Sultanov's disreputable past, but he believed that, as a leading Musavatist and a highly capable person, Sultanov could be very useful. In what he termed a concession to Armenia, Thomson gave his word that Azerbaijani troops would not be allowed beyond Khankend, meaning that they would not be quartered in Shushi and that the governor-generalship would not actually include Zangezur. Moreover, Dr. Sultanov would be subject to the directives of Major Monck-Mason and could take action of a substantive nature only with the express consent of the British mission in Shushi. The Erevan government would even be permitted to assign a liaison officer to the British mission. To Khatisian's appeal that Karabagh be cleared of Azerbaijani troops and placed temporarily under English administration, Thomson snapped that Sultanov, even if hated by all, was indispensable in British efforts to assist the people. Given an official position and made aware that he was responsible for the welfare of the district, Khosrov

---

[42] *Gruziia* (Tiflis), March 31, 1919. See also Rep. of Arm. Archives, File 9/9. The British mission in Shushi reported in mid-April that Governor-General Sultanov was disregarding instructions to inform the mission of Azerbaijani troop movements in Karabagh. See Britain, WO 95/4880, 27th Division War Diary.

Bek Sultanov would undoubtedly facilitate the movement and distribution of supplies. In conclusion Thomson stated once again that the establishment of a governor-generalship in Karabagh did not infer permanent Azerbaijani sovereignty there.[43]

General Sir George F. Milne, commander of the British Army of the Black Sea, with jurisdiction over the broad expanse from Constantinople to Transcaspia, expressed the same views a month later, on April 30, during his first official tour of Armenia. He agreed to study Khatisian's request for British supervision in Karabagh, but when the Armenian leaders became so bold as to inquire about news that a number of Armenians had been exiled from Karabagh as provocateurs, Milne refused to discuss the matter further, directing that all local questions be taken up with General Thomson, the senior officer in charge of Transcaucasian affairs.[44]

With the knowledge and consent of General Thomson, Mikayel (Misha) Arzumanian, an unofficial representative of Armenia, set out to investigate the situation in Karabagh and report his findings to the Erevan government.[45] It happened that his arrival in Shushi coincided with General Shuttleworth's appearance before the Fifth Assembly of Karabagh. On April 29, chafing under the rebuff just delivered by the Assembly, Shuttleworth urged Arzumanian to talk sense into his adamant countrymen. He also insisted that the difficulties would quickly dissolve if the Armenian government would acknowledge Azerbaijan's jurisdiction over Karabagh. It soon became clear, however, that Arzumanian was as intransigent as the Fifth Assembly. He was exiled forthwith.[46]

Armenia then appointed an official envoy, Prince Hovsep Arghutian (Kniaz' Dolgorukii-Argutinskii), one of the few advocates of compromise in Karabagh. In Shushi for several days, he conferred with the British mission, the Karabagh Council, and local notables, seeking means to loosen the tightly knotted controversy. General Shuttleworth, who had come once more to the troubled region on May 10, pressed

[43] Rep. of Arm. Archives, File 8/8, Report of Foreign Minister, March 28, 1919. See also File 66a/3. For a partial published account of the interview, see Bor'ba, April 10, 1919, p. 4.

[44] Rep. of Arm. Archives, File 3/3, Stenographic record of interview.

[45] It was announced in Bor'ba, April 9, 1919, p. 4, that Arzumanian was an official representative of the Armenian government and that accompanying him to Karabagh as his secretary would be Haik Ter-Ohanian.

[46] Vratzian, Hanrapetutiun, p. 285; Ishkhanian, op. cit., p. 123; Sarur, op. cit., pp. 135-136. The entry for May 5 in the 27th Division War Diary reads simply, "Armenian liaison officer has not been behaving himself satisfactorily and is being sent back to Baku." See Britain, WO 95/4880.

Arghutian to make a public declaration that the Armenian government had assented to provisional Azerbaijani rule in Karabagh. A simple announcement to that end would, he contended, usher in the peace that was yearned for by all. Arghutian could make no such statement, but he willingly called upon the Armenians of Karabagh and Zangezur to cooperate with the British authorities and to permit the annual migration of Muslim herdsmen to the highland pastures. Shuttleworth, dissatisfied by what he regarded as an evasive Armenian maneuver, then took Arghutian along to Zangezur with the demand that the envoy direct his compatriots to submit to Sultanov. The reception Shuttleworth encountered in Goris (Gerusy) was so hostile, however, that he returned exasperated to Baku on May 19.[47] And Arghutian, educated to the polarizations in Karabagh and Zangezur, arrived back in Erevan on the twenty-third, his belief in the feasibility of compromise badly undermined though not yet abandoned.[48]

Bloodshed in Karabagh

The crisis in Karabagh was whipped into carnage in June of 1919. Arghutian's intermediation had borne no positive results, and the Azerbaijani army brought in more troops after General Shuttleworth had gone blustering for the second time to Baku. On June 2 the Armenian leaders of Karabagh were called before Major Monck-Mason, who handed them a writ from Shuttleworth requiring a pledge to desist from any further political activity. No one was allowed to exit from the British mission until all had affixed their signatures beneath the radiogram. On the following day Dr. Sultanov had the nearby Azerbaijani garrison ring the Armenian sector of Shushi and then ordered the Karabagh Council to surrender the fortress held by Ar-

[47] The 27th Division War Diary for May, 1919, contains many interesting observations and details of these events. On Shuttleworth's advice General Thomson attempted to pressure the Armenian government by ordering the refugee repatriation in districts south of Erevan suspended until the cabinet publicly disavowed all agitators in Karabagh and Zangezur. The punitive measure was revoked upon receipt of Acting Premier Khatisian's diplomatically worded response, together with the remonstrances of General K. M. Davie, the British military representative in Erevan. See pp. 243–244 below.

[48] Ishkhanian, op. cit., p. 125. The Armenian coalition government, particularly while under Kachaznuni's leadership, has been blamed for not having taken decisive action in Karabagh at a time when Turkey had just been defeated and Azerbaijan was thoroughly demoralized by the occupation of Baku. Kachaznuni's vacillation assertedly precluded the adoption of a clearly defined policy, either to cede Karabagh or to defend it. See A. Babalian, Edjer Hayastani ankakhutian patmutiunits (Cairo, 1959), pp. 30–33.

menian militiamen. The Council's noncompliance prompted a menacing show of Azerbaijani arms on June 4. Soon the shops were shuttered, the marketplace deserted, and the anticipated sound of gunfire echoed over the city. The Armenian barricades and even the British mission came under heavy Azerbaijani fire, but the Governor-General failed to dislodge the Armenian defenders.[49]

Jarred by the sudden outburst, Major Monck-Mason appealed to both sides to cease fire and permit the posting of British pickets between them. Sultanov refused to halt the military activity unless the Karabagh Council was arrested and delivered to him. Monck-Mason hoped that the stipulation could be met simply by coercing the Armenian executive to retire from Karabagh. He therefore summoned the Karabagh Council, assertedly to be apprised of new instructions from General Shuttleworth. Alerted to the possibility of a deception, the Council sent only three members to the British mission, where Monck-Mason told them that Shuttleworth had ordered the entire Karabagh Council to quit the district. The trio, claiming to have no knowledge of the whereabouts of the other members, submitted to exile. Plans of the local Dashnakist committee to rescue them by ambushing the British armored car as it passed through the countryside met with no success. As that fateful day wore on, Monck-Mason demanded in the name of His Majesty's Government that all combatants relinquish their positions to Imperial troops. At dusk the hard-pressed Armenians yielded, but the Azerbaijanis, still having been denied victory, remained defiant. An uneasy calm settled over the city.[50]

The unexpected difficulties encountered by the Azerbaijani units in Shushi led the Governor-General to call forth his brother, Sultan Bek Sultanov, the chief of nearly 2,000 mounted Tatar-Kurdish irregulars. On the morning of June 5, this large band attacked Khaibalikend, a strategic Armenian village just 2 miles from Shushi. The armed villagers successfully repulsed the assault throughout most of the day, but then regular Azerbaijani companies controlling the outskirts of Shushi joined the fray. By nightfall Khaibalikend had been looted and burned and many of the inhabitants killed. Thereafter the Muslim raiders fell upon the nearby smaller villages of Krkejan, Pahliul, and Jamillu, as well as several remote hamlets. When the gunfire and flames

[49] Ishkhanian, op. cit., pp. 124–125; Vratzian, Hanrapetutiun, p. 286; Rep. of Arm. Archives, File 66a/3, Report of June 10, 1919; Sarur, op. cit., pp. 136–137.

[50] US Archives, RG 256, 867B.4016/4/6, and 184.021/23, Jenkins to Ammission, June 16, 1919; Vratzian, Hanrapetutiun, p. 286. One sepoy attached to the British mission was killed and another wounded by Azerbaijani fire. See Britain, WO 95/4880, 27th Division War Diary; US Archives, RG 59, 861.00/6583.

abated a few days later, an estimated six hundred Armenians were dead and the affected villages lay in ruin.[51] The British mission and the Armenians of Shushi had been unable to lend support to the settlements under attack, and the Armenian militia in the countryside had revealed its inability to counterbalance the forces of the Governor-General. Doctor Sultanov, while disclaiming the involvement of regular army units, had made it painfully clear to the Armenians that the alternative to submission was bloodshed. Azerbaijani troops now marched triumphantly through the streets of Shushi.[52]

The Protests

News of massacre in Karabagh brewed a storm of protest in Armenian government circles, the national Church of Armenia, and scores of Armenian communities throughout the Caucasus. Major General George Norton Cory, since May, 1919, General Thomson's replacement as British commander in Transcaucasia,[53] was beset by pleas and demands to safeguard the Armenians of Karabagh and to punish the principal offender, Khosrov Bek Sultanov. In Erevan thousands joined

[51] US Archives, RG 59, 867.00/893/1100, and RG 256, 184.021/23/60, 867B.00/139/151, and 867B.4016/4/5/6. See also Vratzian, Hanrapetutiun, pp. 286–287; Rep. of Arm. Archives, File 66a/3, Bulletin no. 87. A British officer on the scene reported that of Khaibalikend's 700 inhabitants only 11 men and 87 women survivors had been found. The massacre, he stated, had been fully visible from Sultanov's residence in Shushi. In another sector an English officer had persuaded 200 Kurds to cease their attack by claiming that the order had emanated from Sultanov. The villages of Pahliul and Krkejan were in the vicinity of Khankend, the headquarters of the Azerbaijani forces in Karabagh. See Britain, WO 95/4880, Report of June 11, 1919.

[52] Sultanov asserted that the Azerbaijani units in Karabagh had been bolstered in order to guarantee the passage of Muslim nomads to their summer pastures without incident. The Armenians had nonetheless fired upon the nomads, who thus were constrained to burn the Armenian villages. See Gruziia, June 18, 1919; Rep. of Arm. Archives, File 9/9. Azerbaijani soldiers, escorted by officers of the British mission, occupied the Armenian barracks of Shushi on June 7. See Britain, WO 95/4880.

[53] On May 10, 1919, General Thomson informed the governments of the Transcaucasian republics that an Italian force would soon be relieving the British troops, that he was going to England on furlough, and that Major General Cory was taking command of the 27th Division. See Rep. of Arm. Archives, File 8/8; Bor'ba, May 13, 1919, p. 1; Bor'ba v Gruzii, p. 415. Cory, the Chief General Staff Officer of General Milne's Salonica Army, had gone to Constantinople shortly after the Mudros Armistice to arrange for the arrival of the Allied fleet. He then served on the headquarters staff of Milne's Army of the Black Sea until being assigned to relieve General Thomson. See Britain, Operations in Macedonia, II, 267–271, 311; Britain, Order of Battle, Pt. 1, p. 97, and Pt. 4, p. 55. Cory arrived in Tiflis on May 10 and Thomson departed on the evening of May 12. See the 27th Division War Diary, Britain, WO 95/4880. Thomson's appraisal of events in the Caucasus, written en route back to England, is in Britain, Cab 45/107.

in angry demonstration and all political parties united in condemning the repressions. Social Democrat Davit Ananun, Social Revolutionary Arsham Khondkarian, and Dashnakists Vahan Khoreni and Dro delivered impassioned orations at a mass meeting, which shouted its approval of a resolution declaring:

The extent to which the Armenian people have been massacred in Turkey, in Karabagh, in Azerbaijan has exceeded all that has gone before. It is enough! We can tolerate no longer the slaughter of our women and children under the very eyes of the representatives of the great peoples of Europe. . . . We protest emphatically and express our boundless admiration for our brothers of Karabagh, who are struggling heroically against the tyranny of Sultanov, in the name of civilization and the self-determination of peoples.[54]

In Tiflis other thousands surged through the streets during a rally sponsored by more than forty Armenian societies and presided over by poet laureate Hovhannes Tumanian. The resolutions of this and countless similar gatherings wherever a sizable Armenian community existed called for the intercession of the Allies, the removal of Sultanov, the indictment of the guilty, and the union of Karabagh with Armenia.[55]

American officials in the Caucasus echoed the Armenian protests. In messages to the Department of State and the American peace delegation in Paris, they deprecated the essentially pro-Muslim policy of the British. Consul F. Willoughby Smith, returning to his post in Tiflis after the war, had opposed Sultanov's appointment from the very outset and repeatedly vilified the Musavatist leader as if he were an old personal foe. In March, Smith predicted that unless the British recalled Sultanov with absolute haste and took charge themselves disaster in Karabagh would soon follow. He gave credence to the Armenian arguments against Sultanov and labeled the Governor-General's appointment as tantamount to a declaration of Muslim imperium in Karabagh. The Consul berated the Allied military leadership, claiming it should have been responsible enough to exclude from office such infamous Turkish agents as Sultanov.[56]

---

[54] Vratzian, *Hanrapetutiun*, pp. 287–288; Rep. of Arm. Archives, File 66a/3, Release of the Armenian Press Bureau, Tiflis.

[55] US Archives, RG 84, Tiflis Consulate, 1919, pt. 4, File 801 and File 840.1, and RG 256, 867B.4016/5. See also Vratzian, *Hanrapetutiun*, pp. 287 288; Britain, FO 608/82, 342/1/2/13339/15316.

[56] US Archives, RG 84, Tiflis Consulate, 1919, pt. 4, File 710, Memorandum, March 28, 1919.

Shortly before the clash in Karabagh, Smith retired from the United States consulate at Tiflis. His departure after several years of service in the Caucasus deprived Armenia of a staunch, outspoken supporter.[57] The end of Smith's colorful diplomatic career had no basic effect, however, upon the attitudes and recommendations of the American officials in Tiflis. Consul W. L. Jenkins,[58] Vice-Consul H. A. Doolittle,[59] Major Joseph C. Green of the American Relief Administration,[60] and B. B. Moore[61] of the Tiflis party of Lieutenant Colonel E. Francis Riggs' American Field Mission to South Russia were one in their continuance

[57] Felix Willoughby Smith, born in 1872 of American parents in Russia, left his New York law offices to enter the diplomatic corps in 1909. He was appointed Consul at Batum in April, 1914. The consulate was transferred to Tiflis in 1916 because of the military operations on the Turkish-Caucasus front and then temporarily closed in May, 1918, as the result of the Ottoman invasion of Transcaucasia. Smith made his way to the United States via Moscow, Stockholm, and London, and then in January, 1919, sailed back to Tiflis to resume his consular duties. He relinquished his post in May, 1919, to Consul John Quinby Wood pending the arrival of his assigned replacement. The extraordinary diplomat died in Battle Creek, Michigan, on January 11, 1920, six months after his return home. For papers relating to his diplomatic service, see US Archives, RG 59, *United States Consular Officers by Post, 1789–1939*, Consular Posts, Batum and Tiflis; and *Personal Records of Commissioned Diplomatic and Foreign Service Officers*, F. W. Smith, Book 120, 123/Sm 52.

[58] William Lancaster Jenkins, Consul at Trebizond from July, 1916, to January, 1918, had fled the Caucasus, together with Smith and other American officials, in late May, 1918. He was dispatched to open the Odessa consulate in January, 1919, but was forced to abandon that office hastily in April because of the occupation of the Crimea and surrounding territory by the Red Army. Jenkins was then detailed to the Tiflis consulate, taking charge in mid-May and remaining at that post until the beginning of July, when he was transferred on his own request to the Funchal consulate on the Portuguese island of Madeira. See US Archives, RG 59, *United States Consular Officers by Post, 1789–1939*, Consular Posts, Tiflis and Trebizond; and *Personal Records of Commissioned Diplomatic and Foreign Service Officers*, W. L. Jenkins, Book 103, 123/J 41.

[59] Hooker Austin Doolittle had served as vice-consul at Tiflis from the beginning of 1917 until the consulate's closure in 1918. After the World War, in January, 1919, he was initially assigned, with Jenkins, to the Odessa consulate but was soon instructed to proceed to Tiflis. Resuming his duties in Tiflis on March 6, 1919, he was put in charge of the consulate on July 1, when Jenkins departed for Funchal. Doolittle remained the senior American official in Tiflis until Consul Charles Kroth Moser arrived in January, 1920. See US Archives, RG 59, *United States Consular Officers by Post, 1789–1939*, Consular Posts, Tiflis and Odessa; and *Personal Records of Commissioned Diplomatic and Foreign Service Officers*, H. A. Doolittle, Book 91, 123/D 721, and C. K. Moser, Book 111, 123/M 85.

[60] See pp. 141–142 above.

[61] Benjamin Burgess Moore, a civilian member of the Riggs Mission, arrived in Tiflis on March 17, 1919. His reports to the American Commission to Negotiate Peace were unusually thorough and reveal a clear understanding of the complicated problems of the Caucasus. The Tiflis party of the Riggs Mission was authorized to continue in the field even after Riggs himself and the sections in Russia had been recalled. Moore's detailed reports are included in US Archives, RG 256, Files 184.016, 184.01602, and 184.021.

of Smith's critical view of British policy, his warnings against the Muslim and Pan-Turanic threats to Armenia, and his pleas for more active assistance to the Armenian republic.

When reports of the bloodshed in Karabagh reached Tiflis, Jenkins angrily reviled British strategy, especially the sanctioning of an Azerbaijani economic blockade to compel the Armenians to submit.[62] Benjamin Moore, who in April had forecast massacres in Karabagh unless Sultanov was removed, led a team of American investigators to Shushi less than a week after the carnage. He then cabled his military superiors in Paris: "The British solution of placing Karabagh and Zangezur under Azerbaijan has proved a disastrous failure which has lowered Allied prestige throughout the Caucasus. Peace cannot be established in the Caucasus until Armenia's legitimate claims in this district receive some form of satisfaction." [63] American relief workers in Tiflis and Shushi urged the United States peace delegation to persuade the British to expel all Turco-Tatar agents and warriors from Russian Armenia, including Karabagh and Zangezur. Vice-Consul Doolittle voiced the opinion of nearly every American in the Caucasus: "Under present conditions relief without military support practically amounts to fattening the victim for the slaughtering." Great Britain, Doolittle added, had been unwilling to defend the Armenians. He was especially perturbed by news that Dr. Sultanov, who had been recalled to Baku shortly after the massacre, was being reinstated as governor-general.[64]

Sultanov's departure from Shushi gave rise to conflicting accounts. The Azerbaijani government alleged that he had simply been summoned to Baku for consultations, whereas the British command in Tiflis announced that, at its insistence, the Governor-General had been suspended from office and ordered to face formal charges. The most prevalent report, repeated several times in American dispatches, confirmed the arrest and imprisonment of Sultanov.[65] General Cory

[62] US Archives, RG 256, 867B.4016/4.

[63] US Archives, RG 256, 184.021/23 and 184.01602/97.

[64] US Archives, RG 84, Tiflis Consulate, 1919, pt. 4, File 800, Telegram, and RG 256, 867B.00/192.

[65] See, for example, US Archives, RG 59, 861.00/4759; RG 84, Tiflis Consulate, 1919, pt. 4, File 800; RG 256, 184.021/26, 867B.4016/8, and 861G.00/70. British officials in Tiflis assured Acting Premier Khatisian in June, 1919, that Sultanov would be brought to account. See Rep. of Arm. Archives, File 66/2, Report of June 23, 1919. According to F. J. F. French, *From Whitehall to the Caspian* (London, 1920), p. 166, the British military authorities condemned Sultanov's actions and demanded his recall, but as Sultanov was back at his post shortly after the massacre the British command decided to yield to the fait accompli.

himself assured the Armenian cabinet that Sultanov and other offenders had been recalled. The head of the 27th Division nevertheless rejected the Armenian petition to place Karabagh under British rule, adding that the Erevan government had exceeded its prerogatives in even making such a request. Armenia, Cory continued, should be thankful that the British authorities no longer required the inclusion of Zangezur within the bounds of the governor-generalship. He regretted that the Armenian leaders, instead of showing gratitude for this concession, had secretly stoked the smoldering embers in Karabagh.[66]

A British team sent to the highland to investigate the causes of the violence verified the common knowledge that Sultanov had stationed irregulars around Shushi and had then utilized them as agents of massacre. Chief investigating officer Lieutenant Colonel C. H. Clutterbuck reported that, had Sultanov so willed, blood need not have been shed and that the Governor-General should therefore be held accountable.[67] Similar findings were presented in the Azerbaijani Parliament by Armenian deputies who had just returned from Shushi, but the Muslim majority in the legislature ruled that "there is no evidence to indicate any illegality in the actions of the Governor-General." [68]

Whether Sultanov was summoned to Baku merely for consultation, was suspended, or was actually arrested, the fact remains that he was neither permanently removed nor punished in any way. Apparently the strength of Shuttleworth's patronage outweighed the incriminating evidence. Sultanov returned to Shushi before the end of June and, his awesomeness enhanced, resumed the difficult assignment of bending the Armenians to submission.[69] The American officials were appalled

[66] Rep. of Arm. Archives, File 3/3 and File 9/9, Cory to Council of Ministers of Armenia, June 18, 1919.

[67] Britain, WO 95/4880; US Archives, RG 256, 867B.00/156; Rep. of Arm. Archives, File 25/25, *Zinvorakan Nakhararutian Hramanner, 1920 t.*, and File 66a/3, Bulletin no. 71. Cecil Hulton Clutterbuck had earlier been the British liaison officer with Colonel Lazar F. Bicherakhov's Cossack force in North Persia and Baku. See Britain, *Campaign in Mesopotamia*, IV, 172, 202–203, 236–238.

[68] Vratzian, *Hanrapetutiun*, p. 289; *Gruziia*, July 18 and 22, 1919; Rep. of Arm. Archives, File 66a/3, Bulletin nos. 87 and 92.

[69] The 27th Division War Diary for June, 1919, includes many entries relating to the "Shusha Affair." On the seventh it was recorded that the President (Premier) of Azerbaijan had consented to remove Sultanov. The entry on the eleventh noted that action was being taken with the Azerbaijani cabinet to dismiss Sultanov and to punish those responsible for the recent massacre. That same day General Cory instructed Shuttleworth in Baku to press for Sultanov's early replacement. On the eighteenth a report from Monck-Mason revealed that just before Sultanov had departed from Shushi to Baku, the Governor-General made a conciliatory speech to the Armenians, during which he placed the blame for the recent outrages on the British. On the same day, Cory wired Shuttleworth that on no account was Sultanov to be

by what they termed irresponsible and disgraceful British policy, complaining that the Imperial command had first requested American support in putting Sultanov on the gallows, only to turn about and lead the villain back to Shushi.[70] Almost without exception, however, the Americans expressed grave apprehensions when it became known that preparations were under way to close the British mission in Karabagh. On July 19 Vice-Consul Doolittle cabled his superiors in Washington and Paris, "Tartars have become so arrogant owing to reports that British will move." The Armenians were to be deprived of whatever restraining influence the British mission might still have possessed. The incomprehensible course of British actions and the intolerable conditions in Karabagh, exclaimed Doolittle, constituted "a gratuitous self-inflicted blow to [the] good will and prestige of the Allied Nations." [71]

---

permitted to return to Karabagh, whether in an official or in a private capacity. Shuttleworth was also told to demand an explanation as to how Sultanov came "to betray the trust reposed in him." On June 20, 39th Brigade headquarters in Baku reported that the Azerbaijani government, acting in bad faith, had allowed Sultanov to slip away. A week later, when the tenacity and evasiveness of Sultanov and the Azerbaijani cabinet seemed to be leading them toward favorable results, Cory, in response to an inquiry from General Headquarters in Constantinople, advised General Milne that no action against the Azerbaijani government was being suggested for the time being. He nonetheless assured Milne that Sultanov would be barred from Karabagh. In fact, however, Sultanov was already on his way back to Shushi. See Britain, WO 95/4880.

[70] US Archives, RG 59, 861.00/6583. See also RG 84, Tiflis Consulate, 1919, pt. 4, File 710, and RG 256, 867B.00/192.

[71] US Archives, RG 256, 867B.00/173. A news release in Rep. of Arm. Archives, File 66a/3, Bulletin no. 122, shows the last British troops as having departed from Shushi on August 13, 1919. An announcement that the British mission in Karabagh had been closed appeared in Bor'ba on September 1, p. 3. The most reliable source, the British war diaries, reveal that shortly after the bloodshed in Shushi the 9th Battalion, Royal Warwickshire Regiment, was instructed to proceed from Baku to Karabagh but that the orders were countervened before the battalion had reached its destination. Then on June 10 Major Reginald Tyrer, acting commander of the 84th Punjabi Regiment, left for Shushi to take charge of the British mission, as Major Monck-Mason was being recalled to India. It was at that juncture that General Headquarters of the Army of the Black Sea directed the 27th Division to prepare for withdrawal from the Caucasus. In the preliminary phases the outlying units were to be recalled to their respective brigade headquarters. By the end of June all but one platoon of the 84th Punjabis had returned to Baku. Major Tyrer apparently closed the mission at Shushi on August 16. Two days later his single detachment boarded a military train at Evlakh and proceeded to Batum with the main body of the Punjabi regiment. This sequence of events has been reconstructed on the basis of entries in the war diaries of the 27th Division Headquarters, 39th Brigade Headquarters, 84th Punjabi Regiment, 13th Light Armored Motor Battery, 39th Brigade Trench Mortar, and 9th Battalion, Royal Warwickshire Regiment. See Britain, WO 95/4880 and /4955. Just before the full withdrawal was announced, British medical officers had selected Shushi as the site for a convalescent camp and summer recreation area, some 5,000

Division and Vacillation in Karabagh

The return of Sultanov to Shushi demonstrated that the Armenians of Karabagh had given their allegiance to a government that could do little more than lodge loud protests. The pessimism resulting from this realization, together with the strain of months of severe hardship, divided the exhausted Armenian leadership. The mayor, the commercial and professional classes, and the local branch of the Populist party came to regard further resistance as an invitation to irreparable disaster. Mountainous Karabagh must therefore come to terms with Azerbaijan. On the other hand, most Dashnakist leaders, the Karabagh Council (which had fled to the countryside), the partisan commanders, and the rural population still denied the advisability of surrender. But even among the latter groups, the resolve to resist was attenuated by the growing fear that there was no deliverance.[72]

Heartened by the course of events turning in his favor, Governor-General Sultanov prevailed upon Bishop Vahan and several other prominent citizens to persuade the Karabagh Council to summon a new assembly. The Council assented even though it had recently denounced Sultanov to Allied representatives and had emphasized that, despite the Azerbaijani military occupation of Shushi, Karabagh would never submit.[73] On June 29 the Sixth Assembly of Karabagh convened in the village of Shosh (Shushikend), a short distance from Shushi. Musavatist spokesman Shafi Bek Rustambekov attended and promised the delegates that the Baku government would deal benevolently with Karabagh. For the first time the Armenians revealed a willingness to listen. But a sense of impending doom shrouded the Sixth Assembly, for the British War Office had already announced plans to withdraw the Imperial forces not only from Shushi but from the entire Caucasus. Moreover, Dr. Sultanov, at whose request the delegates had gathered, made no conciliatory gesture. Instead he now chose to ignore the Assembly and abruptly departed for additional consultations in Baku. Placed in this awkward situation, which rendered further discussions superfluous, the Armenian representatives adopted basic guidelines for a settlement, appointed a committee of three to negotiate in Baku, and then adjourned.[74]

In those guidelines the Armenians of Karabagh showed themselves

feet above the hot and humid Azerbaijani steppeland. See the 40th Field Ambulance War Diary, WO 95/4955.

[72] Sarur, op. cit., pp. 139–140; Rep. of Arm. Archives, File 1649.

[73] Rep. of Arm. Archives, File 1649, Mikayelian report; Sarur, op. cit., p. 140.

[74] Vratzian, Hanrapetutiun, pp. 289–290; Sarur, op. cit., p. 140.

ready to compromise, although they insisted that the government of Azerbaijan acknowledge them as an equal party during the forthcoming discussions. Karabagh would yield to the provisional jurisdiction of Azerbaijan in return for complete administrative and cultural autonomy. Azerbaijan must agree not to appoint Muslim officials in Karabagh, claim permanent suzerainty over the district, direct troops toward Zangezur, or attempt to disarm the Armenian population.[75]

These terms were carried to Baku by Aramayis Ter-Danielian and Gerasim Khachatrian (Dashnakists) and Ruben Shahnazarian (Populist). Muslim bandits killed Khachatrian en route, but the other two reached the Azerbaijani capital, where, after preliminary talks with the Baku Armenian Council and Karabagh Compatriotic Union, they entered into direct negotiations with Sultanov and members of the cabinet.[76] A modified version of the Armenian proposal was approved by the government of Premier Nasib Bek Usubbekov,[77] who had succeeded Fathali Khan Khoiskii in April, but the Armenian envoys withheld their signatures pending a vote of confirmation by the Seventh Assembly of Karabagh. The Azerbaijani leaders took advantage of the opportunity to alter the terms even more and then sent the revised project to Shushi with Dr. Sultanov and Ruben Shahnazarian, branded a collaborator by many of his Armenian contemporaries. Learning of these unacceptable changes, the Karabagh Council dispatched one of its members, Nerses Nasibian, to Baku with instructions to press for adoption of the original plan and to seek the advice of Armenia's diplomatic representative, Tigran A. Bekzadian.[78]

The Submission of Mountainous Karabagh

As the Seventh Assembly of Karabagh gathered in the village of Shosh on August 12, a bellicose mood blazed briefly once again. The Assembly's first official act was the adoption of a resolution denounc-

[75] Rep. of Arm. Archives, File 1649; Sarur, op. cit., p. 141.

[76] Vratzian, Hanrapetutiun, p. 290; Sarur, op. cit., pp. 140–141. Rep. of Arm. Archives, File 1649.

[77] For the composition of Usubbekov's cabinet, see Le 28 Mai 1919, p. 19; Bulletin d'Informations de l'Azerbaïdjan (Paris), no. 1 (Sept. 1, 1919), p. 1. See also US Archives, RG 256, 184.021/14 and 184.01602/23. Usubbekov's inaugural address on the state of the nation, upheld in the Azerbaijani Parliament by a vote of 46 to 21, was published in Bor'ba, April 27, 1919. It was at about this time that the British authorities permitted the Azerbaijani army to return to Baku. See Ziatkhan, op. cit., p. 81. According to Mirza-Bala, op. cit., p. 170, the General Staff transferred from Ganja to the capital in June of 1919.

[78] Rep. of Arm. Archives, File 66a/3, Bulletin no. 101, and File 1649, Mikayelian report; Sarur, op. cit., pp. 141–142.

ing the murders of Gerasim Khachatrian and two delegates en route to Shosh from Jraberd. The Assembly was unanimous in its rejection of an appeal from a deputation led by Bishop Vahan to transfer the sessions to the city of Shushi and to espouse a policy of conciliation. On the fourteenth Dr. Sultanov responded to the failure of the emissaries, whom he himself had sent out, with an ultimatum to the Seventh Assembly to accept the project of the Azerbaijani government within forty-eight hours or else be subjected by force of arms.[79]

At that crucial moment Nerses Nasibian returned from Baku bringing word that there existed no possibility of outside aid. Tigran Bekzadian had intimated that Karabagh must fend for itself. The Assembly then selected a six-man committee to determine what defense measures the Karabagh Council and the partisan groups might take should the Armenians decide to continue their resistance. This committee, too, returned a discouraging report: the Karabagh Council, with almost no funds remaining, had reached the limit of its resourcefulness, and the militia had nearly exhausted its supply of ammunition.[80] Finally, on August 15, 1919, the disheartened Assembly, having found no alternative, empowered fifteen of its members to conclude a settlement with Sultanov. But placing little faith in the promises and guarantees of the Azerbaijani government, the Assembly instructed the Karabagh Council to form a committee of self-defense to prepare a course of action in the event the forthcoming agreement was violated.[81]

On August 22, 1919, after nearly a week of final negotiations in Shushi, the Armenian delegation attended a public ceremony at which Dr. Sultanov, Bishop Vahan, and other Muslim and Armenian notables spoke of interracial brotherhood and of the vital need to end the mutually calamitous strife. Having thus paid the required lip service, the Armenian representatives affixed their signatures to the document confirming the submission of Karabagh. Because of its importance in the subsequent history of Armenian-Azerbaijani relations, the agreement is here given in its entirety:[82]

[79] Vratzian, *Hanrapetutiun*, pp. 290–291; Sarur, *op. cit.*, p. 142; Rep. of Arm. Archives, File 66a/3, Bulletin no. 122.

[80] Sarur, *op. cit.*, p. 142; Rep. of Arm. Archives, File 1649, Mikayelian report.

[81] Rep. of Arm. Archives, File 9/9, Memorandum, and File 1649. An account in File 66a/3, Bulletin no. 122, states that twenty delegates were sent to negotiate with Sultanov.

[82] *Azerbaidzhan* (Baku), August 28, 1919; Rep. of Arm. Archives, File 9/9 and File 66a/3, Bulletin no. 123. See also "Provisional Accord between the Armenians of Karabagh and the Government of Azerbaijan," *Eastern Europe*, I (Oct. 16, 1919), 158–160; *Bor'ba*, Aug. 31, 1919, p. 3; *Hairenik* (daily), Oct. 25, 1919, p. 4.

Whereas the fate of Mountainous Karabagh shall be determined by the Peace Conference, whereas every hostile encounter is disastrous to the nationalities inhabiting Karabagh, and whereas in whatever way the question of Karabagh may be settled, the Armenians and Muslims will continue to live together, the Seventh Assembly of Karabagh Armenians, in its fourth morning session of August 15, 1919, resolved to uphold the following points constituting the temporary agreement with the government of the Republic of Azerbaijan:

1. The contracting parties accept this provisional agreement until the Peace Conference renders a decision, which both sides shall accept as an equally binding solution.

2. The Armenian-populated mountainous sector of Karabagh (Dizak, Varanda, Khachen, Jraberd), in the uezds of Shushi, Jevanshir, Jebrail, regards itself to be provisionally within the boundaries of the Azerbaijani republic.

3. The Shushi, Jevanshir, and Jebrail uezds remain as a distinct administrative unit within the governor-generalship of Karabagh, and the internal structure of that unit shall be such that the administration of the mountainous Armenian sector is composed of Armenians, with the rights of minorities guaranteed.

4. In the mountainous portion of Karabagh (Dizak, Khachen, Varanda, and Jraberd), administrative officials shall be named on the recommendation of the Armenian members of the council [see point 5].

5. A six-member council of three Armenians and three Muslims shall be created in the governor-generalship of Karabagh.

6. The council's Armenian members are to be chosen by the assembly of the Armenian population of Mountainous Karabagh. The assembly has the right to reelection.

7. All fundamental questions of an interracial nature cannot be acted upon until they have first been considered by the council.

8. The council has the right of initiative in matters relating to the arrangements and the administration of the governor-generalship.

9. The council has the right to oversee and counterbalance the administration of the governor-generalship but without the right to interfere in the operations of the administration.

10. The post of governor-general's assistant in civil affairs shall be established, and an Armenian must be appointed to that post.

11. The Armenian assembly shall present to the government of Azerbaijan two candidates for the position of assistant in civil affairs, one of whom will be confirmed.

12. The Armenians of Karabagh shall enjoy the right of cultural autonomy.

13. The right of cultural autonomy is to be vested in the National Council of Karabagh Armenians, which will be elected by the periodically convened assemblies of Karabagh Armenians. The assembly is summoned by the National Council.

14. The government of the Azerbaijani republic shall regulate the

activities of the Armenian National Council through Armenian intermediaries.

15. The [Azerbaijani] garrisons shall be stationed at Khankend and Shushi in peacetime strength.

16. Any and all movements of armed forces in the mountainous Armenian-inhabited sectors of the Shushi, Jevanshir, and Jebrail uezds of Karabagh shall require the consent of two-thirds of the council.

17. No person may be subjected to persecution, either by judicial or executive procedures, for his political convictions.

18. All Armenians who have been constrained to leave for political reasons shall have the right to return to their homes.

19. The disarming of the Armenian and Muslim population shall be suspended in Karabagh until the question of Karabagh is resolved by the Peace Conference.

Note: In view of the fact that a general disarmament has been declared for all Azerbaijan, there can only be talk of suspension.

20. The government of the Azerbaijani republic is to give material and moral assistance to the population of Karabagh for the rapid restoration of the devastated Muslim and Armenian villages.

21. For the purpose of improving interracial relations, the council shall periodically sponsor general and local Armenian-Muslim congresses.

22. There will be absolute freedom of assembly, speech, and press. But because a state of martial law exists throughout Azerbaijan, meetings shall be authorized by the administration.

23. All crimes of private and official persons shall be prosecuted according to judicial procedure, except for the felonies and criminal acts excluded from the normal judicial order by the binding decision of June 11, 1919, of the Committee for State Defense of the Azerbaijani republic.[83]

24. No one shall be persecuted for having taken part in interracial clashes up to the present time.

25. This agreement comes into effect from the moment of its acceptance by the Seventh Assembly of Karabagh Armenians.

26. This agreement shall remain in effect in all circumstances—besiegement, warfare, and so forth.

The delegates appointed by the Seventh Assembly of Karabagh are authorized to conclude with the Azerbaijani government the final provisional agreement, which has been approved by all members of the Assembly, to select the two candidates for the post of civil assistant to the provisional governor-general and the three members of the council formed alongside the governor-general, and to settle all technical questions relating to the administration of Karabagh on the basis of the provisional agreement that has been accepted.

---

[83] The Azerbaijani Committee for State Defense is discussed on p. 380 below.

In a published résumé of the settlement, Dr. Sultanov declared, "Henceforth a new era has begun in the life of the population of Karabagh." [84] Indeed, an Armenian assistant in civil affairs, Giga Kalantarian, was soon named and three other Armenians were selected to serve on the council established by the agreement. The crisis had apparently passed. Roads were opened and the economic boycott lifted. Sultanov skillfully circumvented the article forbidding the disarming of Armenians by putting on the payroll Armenian collaborators who would buy rifles and ammunition at a high price. The money received by an Armenian villager for a single rifle was often enough to sustain a family for several weeks. The local self-defense committees organized by the Karabagh Council found it increasingly difficult to take effective countermeasures against this devitalizing maneuver. [85]

The settlement of August 22, 1919, was a personal triumph for Khosrov Bek Sultanov and a national victory for Azerbaijan. After months of withering defiance, Karabagh had finally bowed to the provisional rule of Azerbaijan. And provisional rule was an imposing stride toward permanent control. Whatever tactic it might adopt in the future, the Republic of Armenia was never to succeed in dislodging Azerbaijan from this Armenian-populated highland. Besides her own tenacity, Azerbaijan had benefited from the patronage of the British commanders, from the failure of the Paris Peace Conference to take action on the controversy, and from the general helplessness of the Armenian government. All that remained to the Armenians was the promise of autonomy for Karabagh and the compensation that Zangezur had not as yet been included within the governor-generalship.

Karabagh had been Azerbaijan's greatest obstacle to success in Zangezur. Now, however, there was reason to believe that ere long both Zangezur and Nakhichevan could be drawn into the Muslim republic. Less than a week after the Armenian capitulation in Karabagh, Mehmed Emin Rasulzade, a founder and publicist of the Musavat party, wrote in the official Baku daily, *Azerbaidzhan*:[86]

Karabagh, that beautiful spot of our fatherland, has been freed from the clutches of our stubborn neighbors, who were disrupting our eco-

---

[84] Vratzian, *Hanrapetutiun*, pp. 293–294.

[85] Sarur, *op. cit.*, pp. 143–144; Arsen Mikayelian, "Gharabaghi verdjin depkere," *Hairenik Amsagir*, I (May, 1923), 166; Rep. of Arm. Archives, File 1649, Report of Khachik Melkumian. According to information in File 66a/3, Bulletin no. 122, it was Arsen Hovhannisian who was appointed assistant for civil affairs, while Kalantarian is listed as one of the members of the council.

[86] *Azerbaidzhan*, Aug. 28, 1919. See also Vratzian, *Hanrapetutiun*, p. 294.

nomic life, and, by controlling the upper currents of our waters, were attempting to place us in a terrible dilemma. Rejecting a course of further needless bloodshed, the Armenian people have elected to seek a peaceful settlement and have accepted the sovereignty of Azerbaijan.

Nakhichevan is an indivisible part of Azerbaijan and, because of the heroic and dedicated patriotism of its children, has exercised the right to rebel in order to unite with the fatherland, from which it had been treacherously wrenched. Nakhichevan has expelled Armenia's imperious army of occupation.

As for Zangezur, which has become an agony for us and which looms in the middle as a threat to our aims, we have reason to hope that in the near future it too will be rendered harmless and that an unobstructed road will open out from the Astara River and the bridge at Samur [Daghestan] all the way to the Araxes River and the bridge at Julfa [Persia]. With this success an important part of the territorial aspirations of Azerbaijan will have been satisfied.

The Republic of Azerbaijan soon made preparations to transform Rasulzade's prediction into reality. In direct violation of points 15 and 16 of the temporary agreement of August 22, the Azerbaijani army ordered its men to march across Karabagh and concentrate along the border with Zangezur.

Andranik's Departure from Zangezur

During the winter of 1918–1919 Zangezur was isolated from the Armenian centers of Karabagh and Erevan by snowbound roads and intervening Muslim-populated strongholds. The burden of approximately 30,000 refugees intensified the famine and epidemic conditions and gave wings to boundless inflation. Friction between newcomers and natives mounted steadily.

On his withdrawal from Karabagh to Goris in December of 1918, General Andranik met with British officers, who suggested that the Armenian companies prepare to dig in for the winter in Zangezur. Andranik was quick to state his apprehensions, for he knew that a prolonged stay in the snow-covered highland would invite added disaster. A group of Armenian military and refugee leaders who met in conference on December 23 also concluded that Zangezur could not support the multitude until spring, that the soldiers would be forced into the undesirable role of policemen if they did remain, and that most of them were impatient to set out in search of members of their families who might have survived the massacres and havoc of the war years. The gathering agreed that the first logical step in relieving the strain in Zangezur would be the repatriation of the more than

15,000 refugees whose homes were in Nakhichevan, the adjoining district that had just been evacuated by the Ottoman armies. Both Andranik and the extraordinary conference called upon the British command to provide for the refugees in the interim. Major W. D. Gibbon, General Thomson's liaison officer, arrived with limited supplies and a million rubles contributed by the Armenians of Baku. This aid, however, was not enough to sustain the refugees for long. Gibbon then traveled to Nakhichevan to arrange for the proposed repatriation, but he encountered unbridled Muslim hostility and recommended, on his return to Zangezur, that the refugees stand fast for the time being. He could not guarantee the safety of the Armenians should they descend to the Araxes river valley.[87]

By the end of February, 1919, Andranik, tormented by anxiety and impatience, protested to the British mission that no longer could he sit idly in Zangezur. On General Thomson's instructions, Gibbon suggested that the Armenian partisan groups ride unarmed through Karabagh to the Baku-Tiflis railway at Evlakh, whence they would be transported to Tiflis and beyond. Andranik found the plan unacceptable, for it would deprive his men of their arms and lead them far astray. Moreover, it would require them to sell their horses before entraining at Evlakh. The farmers of Armenia had dire need of livestock, particularly horses, and Andranik was reluctant to let his mounts fall into Azerbaijani hands.[88] After protracted deliberations Andranik finally resolved to descend into the Erevan guberniia and the plain of Ararat by the hazardous passage over Daralagiaz. The throngs of refugees, who had followed Andranik for months, were panic-stricken by news of the General's impending departure, and it was with the utmost difficulty that they were finally persuaded to wait in Zangezur until the snows had thawed and the promised American supplies had arrived. With the primary routes over Nakhichevan sealed, a mass movement any earlier would have brought certain death.[89]

On March 22, 1919, Andranik bade farewell to Goris and led his "Special Striking Division" across Sisian through deep snowdrifts to Daralagiaz. After a tortuous march of three weeks the frostbitten company of men and horses reached the railway station of Ararat. Dro, Armenia's Assistant Minister of Military Affairs, and Sargis Manasian,

---

[87] *General Andranik*, pp. 160–167, 178–179; Hovak Stepanian, "Andranike Siuniats erkrum," *Vem*, IV, 5 (1936), 65–66. See also US Archives, RG 84, Tiflis Consulate, 1919, pt. 4, File 710, Andranik to General Thomson, and RG 256, 861K.00/5.

[88] Stepanian, *op. cit.*, pp. 66–67; *General Andranik*, pp. 183–185. See also Britain, WO 95/4955, 39th Brigade War Diary.

[89] Stepanian, *op. cit.*, pp. 67–69; *General Andranik*, pp. 185–189.

Assistant Minister of Internal Affairs, were among the officials who welcomed Andranik and offered to transport his exhausted partisans by rail to Erevan. But the Turkish Armenian leader rejected the invitation to be accorded a hero's reception in the capital, for he still believed that the "traitors" in Erevan shared the responsibility for the devastation of his beloved homeland and the annihilation of his people. Andranik bypassed Erevan and halted at Etchmiadzin, which, as the seat of the Church of Armenia, seemed somehow to lie beyond the jurisdiction of Kachaznuni's government, scarcely 10 miles away.[90]

General Andranik was optimistic that the British allies would authorize him to lead the thousands of Turkish Armenian refugees homeward. To his bitter disappointment, however, the British command not only forbade such a movement but also rejected his proposal to attach the "Special Striking Division" to the Imperial forces in Transcaucasia. With visions dashed and spirits dampened, Andranik ordered the demobilization of his veteran contingents.[91] Many of the Turkish Armenian partisans enlisted in the army of the Armenian republic and became its most trustworthy elements, but Andranik and a number of aides set out for foreign shores.[92] In France, Great Britain, and finally the United States, the legendary general aroused Armenophiles to demand loudly and incessantly the liberation of Turkish Armenia. He lived in the hope that he would one day return to direct the occupation of his native land, but like so many other Armenian expectations this, too, proved illusionary.[93]

[90] Vratzian, *Hanrapetutiun*, p. 299; *General Andranik*, pp. 189–210. The British authorities observed Andranik's movements closely. After General Davie failed in an attempt to reconcile Andranik's differences with the Armenian government, he advised 27th Division headquarters to get Andranik out of the country as soon as possible. See the war diaries of the 27th Division and the 82d Brigade in Britain, WO 95/4880 and /4894.

[91] Vardges Aharonian, *Andranik, marde ev razmike* (Boston, 1957), pp. 165–166; *General Andranik*, pp. 210–217. The ranks of the "Special Striking Division" had dwindled to 1,350 men by this time. See also Britain, FO 371/3658, 43519/45517/80231/512/58.

[92] Accompanied by Major Gibbon, Andranik and 250 of his men departed for Tiflis on April 27, 1919. While in the Georgian capital Andranik had several interviews with staff officers and the commander of the 27th Division. General Thomson, acting on authorization from General Milne, provided Andranik and his followers transportation to Constantinople in mid-May. See Britain, WO 95/4880, 27th Division War Diary, and WO 33/974, no. 4470.

[93] Andranik journeyed from Batum to Paris and London where he attempted in vain to persuade the Allied governments to undertake the military occupation of Turkish Armenia. He then sailed to the United States to participate in a campaign to raise funds for the Armenian army. Andranik eventually established residence in Fresno, California, where he died in 1928. His body was shipped abroad for interment in Armenia, but the Moscow government refused to grant the necessary author-

Armenian Supremacy in Zangezur

With Andranik's exodus from Zangezur the district became more vulnerable to Azerbaijani designs. But even before the departure of the "Special Striking Division," the Central National Council of Zangezur, the Armenian governing body, had recognized the gravity of the situation and requested provisions and weapons from Erevan. The urgency of the appeals increased when it became clear that Azerbaijan, supported by General Thomson, had named Dr. Sultanov as governor-general of both Karabagh and Zangezur. The Central National Council implored Kachaznuni's coalition government to appoint an Armenian provincial governor and regular officials for Zangezur. Reluctant at that early stage to defy or even antagonize the British commanders in Transcaucasia, the Armenian government responded cautiously by dispatching only Lieutenant Colonel Arsen Shahmazian as provincial commissar. Although Shahmazian had instructions to coordinate the campaign to bring Zangezur into the Republic, his appointment was never confirmed by Premier Kachaznuni or Acting Premier Khatisian, thus allowing them to disclaim the active involvement of their cabinet in the struggle of the Zangezur Armenians.[94]

Colonel Shahmazian arrived in Goris on March 6, 1919, and three weeks later participated in an expanded meeting of district leaders. The conference reorganized the local governing body and renamed it the Regional Council of Zangezur and Karabagh. The Regional Council, having as its primary objective the absorption of the two districts into the Armenian republic, brought together an unusual combination of Dashnakists, Bolsheviks, and nonpartisans—seven natives of Zangezur and five exiled leaders of Karabagh. The activities and jurisdiction of the body, its title aside, were in reality limited to Zangezur alone. Within the uezd the Regional Council worked effectively, establishing a general staff and an extraordinary committee for military affairs and designating chiefs for the detachments assigned to the five subdistricts: Sisian, Tatev, Tegh-Khndzoresk, Ghapan, and Meghri.

---

ization. The Armenian hero was therefore laid to rest in Paris. During recent years in Soviet Armenia there has emerged a strong current of popular sentiment insisting on Andranik's reinterment in Erevan. The issue has been complicated, however, by the objections of Soviet Azerbaijan, which continues to brand Andranik as a reactionary oppressor of Muslim villagers. The difficulties notwithstanding, Soviet Armenian scholars have prepared extensive materials on Andranik for publication when conditions permit. And among the general public, stories and songs about Andranik's feats, his photographs in military dress, and memorial items abound.

[94] Vratzian, *Hanrapetutiun*, pp. 300–301; Aharonian, *op. cit.*, p. 166.

Nikolai Hovsepian presided over the civil administration, while Arsen Shahmazian continued as provincial commissar and as liaison officer with Erevan. The Armenians of Zangezur prepared to defy Azerbaijan and, if necessary, the representatives of Great Britain as well.[95]

During the first months of 1919 the British commanders pressed Zangezur to accept peaceably the temporary rule of Azerbaijan. In late April, the power of persuasion having failed, General Shuttleworth himself traveled to Goris to demand recognition of Khosrov Bek Sultanov as governor-general of Zangezur. But confronted with undiminished intractibility, he retired to Baku, only to return two weeks later with a section of the 13th Light Armored Motor Battery and authorization from General Thomson to arrest all Armenian agitators.[96] Again accorded an icy reception, Shuttleworth responded with threats of force, even aerial bombardment, but these words spoken in anger, instead of intimidating the Armenians, incited them to a boisterous armed demonstration. The 39th Brigade commander, himself now intimidated, retreated hastily to Shushi.[97] He accused the Armenian government of "playing a double game" by disclaiming, on the one hand, the least involvement in Zangezur and even publicly disavowing Shahmazian, while, on the other hand, secretly financing Shahmazian, Arzumanian, and other agents who fomented the Armenian opposition in Karabagh and Zangezur. Shuttleworth left the highland region for the last time on May 19, thoroughly convinced of the incorrigible nature of the Armenians.[98]

The efforts of Major Monck-Mason were no more successful. During his meetings in Goris with the Armenian Regional Council, he promised that, in return for the right to maintain order in Zangezur, Azerbaijan would safeguard the communication and transportation routes and would supply food and other desperately needed goods. In a lengthy session on May 2 the chief of the British mission insisted in particular that the Armenians not attempt to obstruct the seasonal ascent of Muslim herdsmen to alpine pasture. That Monck-Mason had failed to make even a little progress was clearly evidenced in the Regional Council's formal reply the following day:

[95] Vratzian, Hanrapetutiun, pp. 301–302.

[96] Britain, FO 95/4880 and /4955. See also US Archives, RG 256, 184.021/23 and 184.01602/60.

[97] Khatisian, Hanrapetutian zargatsume, p. 155; A. G. Soghomonian, Kaghakatsiakan krivnere Zangezurum (Erevan, 1968), p. 22. The small British mission and escort in Zangezur withdrew on May 18, although Shuttleworth had originally intended to retain them in Gerusy (Goris) until Azerbaijani troops had arrived there. See Britain, WO 95/4880, 27th Division War Diary.

[98] Britain, WO 95/4880, Report of May 18, 1919.

1. All acts of aggression against Zangezur, an integral part of the Republic of Armenia, would be met with ironfisted contravention.

2. Herdsmen living beyond the boundaries of the Republic of Armenia would, under no circumstances, be permitted in the mountains of Zangezur.

3. Law and order had been preserved in Zangezur even while the rest of the Caucasus and all Russia had been engulfed by anarchy. There was absolutely no need for Azerbaijan to establish law and order in a region where these already existed.

4. The world peace conference had dictated that the status quo be maintained in disputed regions until a settlement was announced. Zangezur should not be excepted from that ruling.

5. Throughout the Turkish-Azerbaijani "adventure" during the World War, Zangezur had succeeded in preserving its freedom and separate administrative structure. Allied officers who first arrived in Zangezur could confirm this incontrovertible fact.

The Armenian declaration ended in a defiant tone: "Each and every transgression against our self-government, regardless on whose part, will violate the status quo and shall thus be countered by unremitting resistance from us." [99]

And already the "resistance" had begun. From the middle of April, 1919, the armed encounters between the Armenians on the one side and the native Muslim inhabitants and the incoming herdsmen on the other grew in frequency and ferocity. The Armenian military organization proved effective as the Muslims of central Zangezur were driven into the peripheries of the uezd, down to the steppes in the east, or across the Araxes River into Persia. The bloodshed in Zangezur stirred Azerbaijan to shower Armenia with protests, but the Armenian government denied any wrongdoing. On June 21 the Baku newspaper *Azerbaidzhan* carried a dispatch from Khosrov Bek Sultanov stating that Armenian bands in Zangezur had sealed the passes and stranded 10,000 Muslim nomads with 150,000 head of livestock. Claiming that the annihilation of both nomads and livestock was certain unless the impasse was broken forthwith, Sultanov urged his government to act with determination and to give him free reign in discharging "the ponderous responsibilities that I have for tens of thousands of human beings." [100]

The Armenians of Zangezur, disregarding the threats of the Azerbaijani government and the British officers, stubbornly held their

[99] Vratzian, *Hanrapetutiun*, pp. 302–303; Rep. of Arm. Archives, File 1649.
[100] Quoted in *Bulletin d'Informations de l'Azerbaïdjan*, no. 1 (Sept. 1, 1919), p. 5.

ground. Faced with a fait accompli and indomitable defiance, the British strategists eventually modified their policy by tacitly admitting to the status quo in Zangezur, but only on condition that Mountainous Karabagh submit to Azerbaijan. On May 29 General Cory, the new commander of the 27th Division, instructed Shuttleworth, "You should inform the Azerbaijan Govt that any attempt on their part to enforce their administration in the Zangezur district will be looked upon by me as an offensive military action on their part." [101] Three days later he wrote Acting Premier Khatisian that Azerbaijan had been told to resign herself to the local Armenian rule in Zangezur.[102] In a subsequent note on June 18, Cory termed the arrangement a major concession to the Armenians, who nonetheless had done little to show their appreciation.[103]

By the time the Armenians of Karabagh had yielded to Azerbaijani jurisdiction, it was clear that Zangezur would remain, at least temporarily, beyond Sultanov's control. The cabinet of Nasib Bek Usubbekov had acknowledged this fact during negotiations with the representatives of Karabagh, and it was confirmed by the provisional accord of August 22, 1919, whereby the uezds of Shushi, Jevanshir, and Jebrail, but not Zangezur, were placed within the Azerbaijani governor-generalship of Karabagh.

A round in the struggle for Karabagh and Zangezur had drawn to a close, but neither Armenia nor Azerbaijan considered the battle at an end. The Armenian General Staff urged the cabinet to gird for a decisive campaign in Zangezur and emphasized that gaining possession of Karabagh was imperative, as it was the only effective means of thwarting the Turkish and Azerbaijani goal to unite.[104] The Azerbaijani General Staff, on the other hand, cautioned Governor-General Sultanov that "the Armenians will not accept the permanent loss of Karabagh." They would utilize every suitable opportunity to seize the district and would undoubtedly strike at a time when Azerbaijan was engaged against General Denikin, whose Volunteer Army had already manifested its hostility to the Republic. So that the strength of the Azerbaijani army would not be dissipated in a possible war on two

[101] Britain, WO 95/4880, 27th Division War Diary.

[102] Rep. of Arm. Archives, File 8/8, No. 13-12. Cory met directly with Khan Khoiskii's government on June 4 and insisted that until the situation eased Azerbaijan should not try to assert her authority in Zangezur. See Britain, WO 95/4880, 27th Division War Diary.

[103] Rep. of Arm. Archives, File 3/3.

[104] *Ibid.*, File 7/7, "Rapport du Chef de l'Etat-Major Général," June 17, 1919, no. P 0176.

fronts, the General Staff deemed indispensable the formation of Kurdish auxiliary units. These mounted squadrons would police Karabagh and relieve, if necessary, several regular army contingents for service elsewhere: "Azerbaijan must be prepared for a conflict with the Volunteer Army and its natural and permanent ally, Armenia." [105]

By autumn of 1919, after months of strife and irregular warfare, Armenia and Azerbaijan had come to dominate the territories on opposite sides of the demarcation line inadvertently drawn in December, 1918, by General Thomson's directive that Andranik pull back to Zangezur. The subsequent efforts of Thomson, Shuttleworth, and Monck-Mason and of the Armenian and Azerbaijani governments to erase that line had failed. Such was the state of affairs when the 27th Division began its withdrawal from Transcaucasia, thus removing from the embattled region whatever capacity for restraint the British forces might have been able to exercise. The republics of Armenia and Azerbaijan entered their second year of independence, glaring at each other from atop the mountains of Karabagh and Zangezur.

[105] Rep. of Arm. Archives, File 8/8, no. 4007, Sept. 7, 1919, Baku, Chief of Staff to Governor-General of Karabagh. Brinkley, op. cit., p. 358 n. 80, cites what appears to be the same message by General Sulkevich, now included in the D. P. Dratsenko Documents at the Hoover Institution.

7

The
Annexation
of Kars

During the spring of 1919 the Republic of Armenia expanded into Kars and the southern half of the Erevan guberniia, where few Armenians remained after the Ottoman invasion of 1918. The coalition government, despite its extreme disappointment in British policy regarding Karabagh, depended heavily upon Allied support in penetrating to the Russo-Turkish and Russo-Persian boundaries of 1914. The Republic's annexation of Turkish Armenia when sanctioned by the Paris Peace Conference could not be seriously anticipated until control had first been established over the western and southern districts of Russian Armenia.

The Kars Oblast

The Kars oblast, formerly the Ottoman *sanjaks* (districts) of Kars and Ardahan, had been added to the Romanov Empire in 1878 as the result of the Russo-Turkish War (see map 10). The oblast, 7,200 square miles in area, was then populated predominantly by Muslims, but by the first years of the twentieth century the Armenians had regained a plurality and the Christians a majority in two of the four okrugs (counties):[1]

[1] B. Ishkhanian, *Narodnosti Kavkaza* (Petrograd, 1916), p. 36; A. Shakhatuni, *Administrativnyi peredel Zakavkazskago kraia* (Tiflis, 1918), pp. 72–73; Abeghian, "Mer harevannere" (Feb., 1928), p. 100. See also US Archives, RG 256, Inquiry Document no. 11. For accounts of the Kars oblast under Russian domination, see A. M. Poghosian, *Sotsial-tntesakan haraberutiunnere Karsi marzum, 1878–1920* (Erevan, 1961); D. S. Zavriev, *K noveishei istorii severo-vostochnykh vilaetov Turtsii* (Tbilisi, 1947).

10. THE KARS OBLAST

Okrug	Total population	Armenian	Turco-Tatar	Kurd	Other (primarily Christian)
Kars	192,000	81,000	54,000	11,000	46,000
Kaghisman	83,000	35,000	6,000	27,000	15,000
Ardahan	89,000	5,000	50,000	25,000	9,000
Olti	40,000	5,000	27,000 (with Kurds)		8,000

From 1905 onward Armenian political leaders advocated the inclusion of Kars, Kaghisman, and a small sector of Ardahan within an Armenian zemstvo-province, but World War I and the Turkish assault eliminated all possibility of implementing the proposal. In April of 1918 more than 100,000 panic-stricken Armenians from the Kars oblast fled to the Erevan and Tiflis guberniias, where until the end of the year they shared the misery of the Turkish Armenian refugees.[2] When the Ottoman divisions evacuated the Erevan guberniia in December, most of these people crowded into Alexandropol, the gateway to Kars, in expectation of news that the Allies had compelled the Turkish army to clear the oblast. Yet the Allies did not act decisively, and the pitiful throng, having to pass the long, severe winter of 1918–1919 under open skies, was decimated by freezing cold, disease, and starvation. Those who ventured to cross the Arpachai River into the oblast were not seen again. The Ottoman Ninth Army of General Yakub Shevki Pasha still stood at Kars

The Mudros Armistice and Kars

Clause 11 of the Mudros Armistice required the immediate withdrawal of Ottoman armies from all Transcaucasia except the Kars oblast and a portion of the Batum oblast, with the stipulation that these districts too would be evacuated should the Allies, "after they have studied the situation there," so demand. During the final weeks of 1918 nearly 50,000 soldiers from Ottoman divisions operating in the North Caucasus, Azerbaijan, Georgia, Armenia, and North Persia streamed into Kars and Batum.[3] The slight chance that the Ottoman Empire might

[2] US Archives, RG 256, 861K.00/5 and 867B.50/1; Khatisian, *Hanrapetutian zargatsume*, p. 131. For discussions of the Armenian zemstvo plan as it pertained to Kars, see Abeghian, "Mer harevannere" (Feb., 1928), p. 97; Shakhatuni, *op. cit.*, pp. 73–76, 124–127, 132–133; G. M. Tumanov, *K vvedeniiu na Kavkaz zemskago samoupravleniia* (Tiflis, 1905), pp. 59–68.

[3] The composition of the Ottoman army on the Caucasus front and the geographic distribution of its divisions at the end of World War I are given by Belen, *Türk*

be allowed to retain the two oblasts vanished, however, on November 11 when Grand Vizier Ahmed Izzet Pasha received the following communiqué from the British Commander in Chief in the Mediterranean, Vice Admiral Gough-Calthorpe:

Supplementary Clause 11 of Terms of Armistice.
I am directed by the British Government to request Your Excellency to order the complete evacuation of all Turkish troops and Turkish elements situated behind [beyond] the pre-war frontier between Turkey and Russia. The retention of any such troops or elements in Azerbaijan cannot be countenanced on any grounds whatever. This evacuation to be complete must include Halil Pasha, Nuri Pasha, and Ahmet the father of Enver as well as all Turkish officers and men who have been despatched for service in any capacity in the Army of Islam. The British Government directs me to emphasize that they will only consider this clause of the Armistice to have been carried out when it is definitely established that the foregoing has been done. I request that Your Excellency will inform me when orders have been given and again when the evacuation is completed.[4]

Rather than defy the command outright, the Ottoman government adopted delaying tactics and sought permission for the Ninth Army to winter at Kars. A mass movement of troops across the snow-covered plateau would wreak extreme hardships on the Ottoman army. Chief of Staff Jevad Pasha took precautions nevertheless and ordered General Yakub Shevki to prepare both men and supplies for an immediate evacuation should it prove necessary. The Ottoman position was further undermined on November 24 when the General Staff received news that the decision to require the Turkish withdrawal from Kars, Ardahan, and Batum had been made by the Supreme Allied War Council.[5] Informed of these developments the following day, Shevki

---

Harbi, V, 205–206; Sabahattin Selek, *Milli mücadele: Anadolu ihtilali*, Vol. I (Istanbul, 1963), p. 151. See also M. Larcher, *La guerre turque dans la guerre mondiale* (Paris, 1926), pp. 591–595.

[4] Tevfik Bıyıklıoğlu, "Mondros mütarekenamesinde Elviyei Selâse ile ilgili yeni vesikalar," *Belletin*, XXI (Oct., 1957), 573–574. Numerous misspellings in English in Bıyıklıoğlu's text have been corrected for inclusion of the message here. The British Admiralty had relayed the conditions of the supplementary clause to Calthorpe on November 8. See Britain, WO 106/64, "Execution of the Armistice with Turkey."

[5] On November 14 Jevad Pasha had requested that, because the Turkish divisions could not subsist behind the 1914 frontier, the 12th Division and the 3d, 9th, 11th, and 36th Caucasus Divisions be retained in the Ardahan-Kars-Alexandropol-Julfa-Tabriz area of Transcaucasia and North Persia. But General W. R. Marshall, chief of Great Britain's Mesopotamia Expeditionary Force, advised the War Office on November 20 that the Turks had already concentrated enormous stores of foodstuffs behind the border and that their request was "an impudent bluff." The War Office then in-

Pasha protested that, inasmuch as an on-the-spot Allied investigation had not taken place at Kars, the British directives were in violation of the Mudros Armistice. He counseled his government to forestall the evacuation, at least until the Allies had conducted the prescribed investigation. Yakub Shevki also stated his concern over the identity of the military force that would supplant his army at Kars. He insisted that, while he could raise no stringent objection to the return of Russian armies, neither the Georgians nor the Armenians had the right to assume control. Abandoning the province to either one of these anarchic elements would result in the annihilation of countless thousands of innocent people. In view of this grim prospect, General Shevki concluded, the Muslims of Kars, Ardahan, Batum, and lands beyond had resolved never to submit.[6]

Yakub Shevki Pasha had not relayed exaggerated information. The Muslim leaders of Kars, advised and aided by the Ninth Army commander and his staff, prepared for a defense of the region. As early as November 5, 1918, they had begun their organizational work by forming the Kars Muslim Council (Kars İslâm Şûrası), led by Hilmi [Uran] Bey and Fahreddin [Erdoğan] Bey. This provisional body was superseded in December by the Muslim National Council (Millî İslâm Şûrası), a twelve-man board headed by Fahreddin Bey and Jihangirzade (Cihangiroğlu) Ibrahim, a regiment commander in the Turkish army and a local leader of the Ittihadist party.[7] With weapons, ammunition, and instructors provided by Yakub Shevki Pasha, the Muslim *shura* (council) placed nearly 8,000 men in the field and claimed jurisdiction over the entire province. Even if the Ninth Army were forced to evacuate, the partisan legion was ready to defy both Armenians and Georgians.[8]

---

structed General Milne to inform Jevad that "his ingenuous excuse" could not be accepted and that the Turkish divisions would have to be disposed of wherever they could be maintained to the west of the prewar frontier. When Ottoman officials pled "climatic and transport" difficulties, Admiral Calthorpe, who had been named British High Commissioner in Constantinople, was instructed on November 24 to reply that "we were not in the least influenced by their alleged difficulties and that we insist that the terms of the Armistice should be executed in the fullest sense of the word." See Britain, WO 106/64, "Execution of the Armistice with Turkey," and Cab, 27/37, E.C. 2415.

[6] Bıyıklıoğlu, *op. cit.*, pp. 575-576.

[7] Gotthard Jäschke, "Beiträge zur Geschichte des Kampfes der Türkei um ihre Unabhängigkeit," *Die Welt des Islams*, n.s., V, 1-2 (1957), 23, cited hereafter as "Beiträge"; Fahrettin Çelik, "Kars eli tarihi," in *Kars*, ed. Kemal Çilingiroğlu et al. (Istanbul, 1943), pp. 40-42. See also Dankwart A. Rustow, "The Army and the Founding of the Turkish Republic," *World Politics*, XI (July, 1959), 524.

[8] Tarik Z. Tunaya, *Türkiyede siyasî partiler, 1859-1952* (Istanbul, 1952), pp. 486-

Forestier-Walker's Initial Arrangements

To Major General G. T. Forestier-Walker, the ranking Allied officer in western Transcaucasia until March, 1919, fell the responsibility of supervising the Ottoman withdrawal from Kars. Meeting in Alexandropol with Armenian Foreign Minister Tigranian on January 6, Forestier-Walker revealed plans to place the oblast under British military jurisdiction. Although rejecting an appeal to sanction Armenia's expansion to the prewar Ottoman frontier, he did authorize the Armenian government to appoint the civil officials for the British military governorship of Kars. This was an important concession to Armenia, he said, especially in view of the fact that Georgia had gained no such privilege when Brigadier General W. J. N. Cooke-Collis was installed as military governor of Batum.[9]

Forestier-Walker crossed the Arpachai into the Kars oblast the next day, January 7, and there, in an interview aboard his train, imparted to Yakub Shevki Pasha the following directives, recorded subsequently as a memorandum:

1. Forestier-Walker gave official notice of his intent to direct both the civil and the military administration of the Kars oblast. His representative, a military governor, would arrive on or about January 12 with a company of two hundred soldiers and the necessary civil officials provided by the Armenian government.

2. Shevki Pasha must raise no obstacles to the free movement of trains and people and must guarantee the proper conduct of his troops. In order to avoid conflicts with the native populace, he must confine his men to their camps and depots and to the principal evacuation routes to Erzerum. The Allies would hold him directly responsible for all encounters beyond these sites.

3. Beginning on January 15 Armenian officials acting under the English military governor would manage the railway and telegraph from Alexandropol to Kars, while Turkish officials responsible to the military governor would continue to oversee the railway from Kars to the Turkish frontier for the duration of the evacuation.

4. The Turkish withdrawal should be completed, except in the event of heavy snowfalls, by January 25. Should the evacuation not proceed with "reasonable rapidity," the British commanding officer at Constan-

---

487; Selek, *op. cit.*, pp. 152, 154; Jäschke, "Beiträge," pp. 23–24, and his "Die Südwestkaukasische Regierung von Kars," *Die Welt des Islams*, n.s., II, 1 (1952), 48–49, cited hereafter as "Kars."

[9] US Archives, RG 256, 184.021/1; Rep. of Arm. Archives, File 333/3.

tinople (General Milne) would be advised that Yakub Shevki had resorted to obstructionism.

5. The goods and properties of private citizens and the former (Russian) government were inviolable. Shevki's army could remove only what had been brought to Kars from Turkey.

6. Since the native population was faced with severe famine, the Turkish army could keep only enough grain to provide each soldier with one kilogram (2.2046 pounds) of grain per day for one month. The English military governor would watch over all other food supplies, and Forestier-Walker would consider releasing additional grain to the Turkish army if the allocated amount proved insufficient.

7. The Turkish army would be required to pay for the grain it was to draw, but a decision whether the Ottoman Empire must make reimbursements for goods previously carried away or requisitioned was left to the Allied Powers.

8. The military governor would, on his arrival in Kars, take control of the wireless and the telegraph lines. All instruments needed to operate the radio station, even if the legitimate property of the Ottoman government, were to be left intact.[10]

These instructions having been communicated to Yakub Shevki Pasha, General Forestier-Walker returned to Alexandropol and there concluded an arrangement with Tigranian regarding the Armenian administrative role in the military governorship of Kars. Dated January 8, 1919, the memorandum provided that, pending action by the Paris Peace Conference, all civil officials were to be appointed by the Armenian government. They were to be responsible to the Ministry of Interior yet also subject to the decisions of the English military governor in matters requiring his intercession. Should serious disagreement arise from this duality in authority, the British commander in Transcaucasia would, after consultation with the Armenian government, render a final judgment. The Armenian officials, the memorandum went on, should be ready to depart on January 12. They would take charge of the railway and telegraph lines as far as the city of Kars on January 15 and, following the completion of the Ottoman evacuation, the railway from Kars to Sarikamish and the Turkish frontier. For the time being the central administration of Kars would be entrusted exclusively to Armenian civil officials, while the Muslims would participate in the various municipal councils in proportion to their numbers prior to the Turkish occupation. Moreover, the British command reserved the right

[10] Britain, FO 608/78, 342/1/6/3681; US Archives, RG 256, 184.021/2; Rep. of Arm. Archives, File 8/8 and File 333/3.

to exclude from the jurisdiction of the central provincial government certain districts inhabited almost entirely by Muslim peoples.

The document also noted that, to maintain law and order in Kars, the Armenian army would form a gendarmerie, which would be strictly limited in size and would advance gradually as the Turkish forces withdrew. Above all, the militia must respect the rights of the indigenous population, for "the Muslim inhabitants of Kars are extremely apprehensive about the introduction of an Armenian administration, even under an English governor." All officials must exhibit great tact in order to dispel this fear and "to demonstrate that the Armenians are capable of laying aside racial prejudices when they assume power." Precautions should be taken to guard against excesses by the gendarmerie, with all offenders meted swift, harsh punishment: "Such action will constitute a significant vindication of Armenian authority, and, if tranquillity is preserved while the Peace Conference is determining the future of Transcaucasia, the [Armenian] government shall be worthy of commendation by the Allied Powers." The willingness of Armenia to collaborate with the English military governor, the memorandum concluded, did not in any way compromise the Republic's pretensions to Kars or restrict its endeavors to gain a favorable ruling from the Paris Peace Conference.[11]

Soon after negotiating this provisional accord, General Forestier-Walker assigned Captain Clive Errington Temperley, the adjutant of the 4th Battalion, Rifle Brigade, to serve as military governor with the rank of local Lieutenant Colonel, and Hovhannes Kachaznuni's cabinet named Stepan Korganian, an experienced administrator, to act as civil governor.[12] In sum, Forestier-Walker's directives to Yakub Shevki Pasha and his agreement with Sirakan Tigranian were a triumph for the Republic of Armenia and a logical step toward Armenian sovereignty over the province of Kars. Some 100,000 refugees would, it seemed, be able to reclaim their homes before winter's end. Starving Armenia would be slightly relieved of her refugee burden and would also find it possible to dip into the great stores of foodstuffs concentrated at Kars.

[11] Rep. of Arm. Archives, Files 7/7, 10/10, and 333/3; Britain, FO 371/3669, 25355/25355/58; Central State Historical Archives of the Armenian SSR, Fund 200, work 109.

[12] Rep. of Arm. Archives, File 7/7, Report of Jan. 13, 1919. Britain, WO 95/4890, 4th Battalion, Rifle Brigade, War Diary, and 95/4880, 27th Division, Headquarters, General Staff, War Diary.

The South-West Caucasus Republic

While Armenia selected officials to administer the Kars oblast, the Muslim population of that province girded for self-defense. On January 17–18, 1919, more than a hundred delegates from far-flung districts met in Kars to chart a course of united resistance. The Ittihadist-oriented conference chaired by Dr. Esad Oktay of Childer resolved to reject both Armenian and Georgian authority and to establish an autonomous state, the South-West Caucasus Republic. Its ruling organ, the South-West Caucasus Provisional Government (Cenub-u-Garbî Kafkas Hükû-meti Muvakkatai Milliyesi), would operate in accordance with the interests of Turkey and tolerate no malfeasance toward the Turkish nation. The new republic would encompass an uninterrupted expanse from Adjaria on the Black Sea to Nakhichevan on the Persian border, use Turkish as its official language and the Ottoman flag as its standard, respect the rights of non-Muslim minorities, and honor the sectarian divisions within the faith of Islam. A legislature (mejlis), to be elected by democratic procedures, would be empowered to select a permanent government. The delegates warned that, although the friendship of all neighboring peoples was welcome, any attempt by the European victors to sever the eastern vilayets of the Ottoman Empire and award them to another people would provoke the South-West Caucasus Republic to rise in defense of its right to remain a part of the Turkish nation. The provisional administration led by Jihangirzade Ibrahim Bey prepared to coordinate the activities of Muslim shuras from Batum to Ordubad. An official envoy, Zenel Agha-oghli (Zeinalov) was dispatched to Tiflis to plead the Muslim case before the representatives of the Allied Powers and Transcaucasian states. And other emissaries, including Fahred-din Bey, the foreign minister of the South-West Caucasus Provisional Government, crossed into Turkey to establish direct contact and to collaborate with the founders of the nascent Nationalist movement.[13]

Through an appeal relayed on the eve of the Muslim conference, the Kars shura hoped to make itself known to President Wilson, King George, President Poincaré, the Paris Peace Conference, the Allied Mediterranean Commander, and the American, British, and French

[13] Jäschke, "Beiträge," p. 24, and "Kars," pp. 49–51; Çelik, op. cit., pp. 42–43. According to the memoirs of Ibrahim Cihangiroğlu, included in the latter source, these principles were set down at the end of 1918. The South-West Caucasus Provisional Government, commonly known simply as the Kars shura, represented itself as the government of all the people by co-opting individuals from among the local Greek and Russian population. See also Tunaya, op. cit., pp. 488–489; Cevat Dursunoğlu, Milli mücadelede Erzurum (Ankara, 1946), pp. 45–46; Britain, FO 371/3658, 80231/512/58.

Commissioners in the Ottoman capital. The communiqué stated that in the "southern Caucasus" there were no Armenians and that the machinations of Great Britain to thrust Armenian officials upon the Muslim population were inspiring deep resentment and vigorous opposition. British authorities in Batum, it was charged, had promised that only Imperial troops would enter Kars while, instead, an attempt had just been made to install Gazganoff (Korganoff) as governor and a certain Palyanos as vice-governor. The British were plotting to slap Armenian rule on a land where "there is not one single Armenian." It could not be forgotten, the message continued, that "the Armenians have burnt more than 1,000 Mohammedan villages, and massacred about 100,000 Mohammedan women and innocent children." If, prior to the general peace, any further efforts were made to impose Armenian dominion, the Muslims would take arms and, invoking Wilsonian principles, defend themselves to the last man. "We have sworn not to allow these blood-thirsty brutes to live among us. Unless 3,000,000 Mohammedans are first killed, the Armenians will never occupy and rule our country." The cable was signed by Ibrahim Bey on behalf of all Muslims of Kars, Ardahan, Olti, Kaghisman, Batum, Iyindir (Igdir?), Khamarlu, Nakhichevan, and Ordubad.[14]

Although American and British officials gave little heed to the message, the challenge of the Muslim leaders deserved not to have been taken lightly.[15] This fact had already been substantiated when Lieutenant Colonel Temperley and a number of Armenian officials led by Stepan Korganian had, under escort of a single company of the 4th Battalion, Rifle Brigade, set out for Kars. Hundreds of armed Muslims intercepted the party and, rifles aimed, threatened to open fire unless the Armenians returned whence they had come. Swayed by this show of force, Colonel Temperley ordered the Armenian officials to quit the Kars oblast, and, much to the dismay and chagrin of the Armenian government, granted informal recognition to the Muslim shura.[16] Under

[14] Britain, FO 371/3658, 42884/512/58; US Archives, RG 256, 861K.00/9. See also Britain, FO 371/3669, 22072/22072/58, and FO 608/84, File 347/1/1; US Archives, RG 256, 861K.00/11 and 867.00/51 F.W., and RG 59, 861.01/40.

[15] A memorandum in the files of the American delegation advised in regard to the situation in Kars that "the whole matter may be considered as part of the program of Turkish agitation to maintain the supremacy of the Turkish and Mohammedan element in the Caucasus." See US Archives, RG 256, 867B.00/77. The British Director of Military Intelligence reported that the Muslim communiqué was clearly exaggerated in an attempt to keep the Armenians from returning, and General Milne wired from Constantinople that there were "no grounds for Moslem fear of annihilation." See Britain, FO 371/3658, 50074/58109/512/58.

[16] Rep. of Arms. Archives, File 3/3, Foreign Minister to Aharonian, March 6, 1919;

these circumstances the South-West Caucasus Provisional Government was willing to endure Temperley's presence in Kars.[17]

The military and political situation having balanced in favor of the local shura, General Yakub Shevki Pasha complied with Forestier-Walker's orders and gradually withdrew the Ottoman Ninth Army. He took care, however, to conceal large caches of arms and ammunition throughout the Kars oblast and to leave behind individual officers to direct and assist the Turco-Muslim population. Shevki departed for Erzerum at the end of January, 1919, and by mid-February, 42,000 of the approximately 47,000 Turkish soldiers who were in the Caucasus when the war ended had drawn behind the Russo-Turkish frontier of 1914.[18] Of these veteran troops, many thousands remained with their mobilized regiments in the vilayets of Van, Bitlis, Erzerum, and Trebizond and became the core of the Turkish Nationalist armies of General Kiazim Karabekir and Mustafa Kemal Pasha.[19]

US Archives, RG 256, 184.01602/23; Vratzian, *Hanrapetutiun*, p. 219; Zavriev, *op. cit.*, p. 75.

[17] In a wire of January 19 General Forestier-Walker approved Temperley's handling of the problem and instructed him to continue working in cooperation with the local shura. The British military governor of Kars was reinforced on January 23 with the remainder of the 4th Battalion, Rifle Brigade, minus the company under Captain Douglas in the Borchalu neutral zone and one platoon that had been sent on temporary duty to Nakhichevan. As the 4th Rifles advanced along the Alexandropol-Kars railway, detachments were detailed to stand guard over several military storehouses once belonging to the Russian army. One platoon went on to Sarikamish near the Russo-Turkish prewar boundary. Between five and six hundred British troops thus occupied the Alexandropol-Kars-Sarikamish line by the end of January, 1919. A single troop of Lothian and Border Horse provided mounted support. See the brigade and division war diaries in Britain, WO 95/4880 and /4890.

[18] US Archives, RG 59, 861.00/6583. The slow-paced Ottoman evacuation had evoked repeated protests from General Milne. He maintained that the Ottoman orders to withdraw were so worded as to encourage noncompliance and that Turkey's real reason for procrastinating was to gain time to convoy grain and massive loot from Kars to Erzerum. He urged that Great Britain threaten the Sublime Porte with severe retaliatory measures. In Kars, meanwhile, Shevki Pasha assured Colonel Temperley that the Ninth Army would be gone by the end of January. On instructions from General Forestier-Walker, Temperley did not attempt to hold Shevki to the grain quotas dictated by Forestier-Walker on January 7. Even after the main Ottoman force had withdrawn, a number of Turkish soldiers were employed by Temperley to guard the remaining stockpiles in Kars. They were relieved at the end of February by a Russian gendarmerie, which had been recruited in Tiflis. The last Ottoman contingent was reported to have cleared the city of Kars on March 6 and the province on March 15, 1919. See Britain, WO 33/965, nos. 3180, 3243, and 3616, and WO 95/4880 and /4890, War Diaries.

[19] The distribution of Shevki's divisions after their withdrawal from Transcaucasia is given by Selek, *op. cit.*, pp. 88–89; Britain, WO 106/64 and /1475; Belen, *Türk Harbi*, V, 232–237.

The Armenian Reaction

The expulsion of governor-elect Korganian and his staff elicited bitter remonstrances from Foreign Minister Tigranian. The British, he protested to Forestier-Walker, had failed to enforce their decisions and had been humiliated by an outrageous act that had reassured the Turks that the slightest expression of discontent would guarantee them the power to dictate. After the inexcusable fiasco just enacted at Kars, who could doubt that the Turks would be more arrogant and adamant than ever![20]

In a lengthy report to Armenian envoys in Europe, Tigranian characterized British policy as cataclysmic. It was true that the Imperial forces in the Caucasus were inadequate to subdue all opposition, but there were other equally grim factors. The British commanders, imbued with England's almost traditional Russophobia, distrusted the Armenians for their Russophile tendencies. This apprehension had recently been exposed once again in Forestier-Walker's insistence that the Russian Volunteer Army's representative in Erevan (Lesley) return to Ekaterinodar. The reappearance of Russia, whether tsarist, republican, or communist, in Transcaucasia was most distasteful to the English military establishment. Herein, Tigranian pointed, lay the determining factor in the British refusal to permit Armenia to consolidate her lands. Convinced that the Turks afforded a powerful bulwark against Russia and that the Muslims of Kars constituted a dependable anti-Russian element, the British authorities had promptly discarded the agreement to establish an Armenian civil administration in the province. Clearly, the British preferred not to rely on the Armenians, whom they regarded as "more Russian than the Russians themselves." The stigma of Russophilia, whether actual or imagined, was continuing to compromise the interests of Armenia. Somehow, concluded the Foreign Minister, the European Powers must be brought to the realization that the forces of Turkism were strangling Armenia and promoting the Ittihadist conspiracy to sweep the Armenian people from the face of the earth.[21]

The rebuff handed the Armenians by the South-West Caucasus Republic proved particularly tragic to the refugees from Kars, some 60,000 of whom had congregated in Alexandropol awaiting permission to return home.[22] They had prepared to move across the Arpachai River,

[20] Rep. of Arm. Archives, File 3/3, Foreign Minister to Allied Commander, Jan. 21, 1919.

[21] Vratzian, *Hanrapetutiun*, pp. 219–221.

[22] US Archives, RG 256, 867B.00/113 and 867B.4016/8; Kadishev, *Interventsiia v Zakavkaz'e*, p. 166.

only to be told to spend the remainder of the winter in Alexandropol, without food and shelter. On January 25, 1919, Premier Hovhannes Kachaznuni pleaded with General Forestier-Walker to rescind the latest directive prohibiting the repatriation and instead to honor his original pledge to supervise the immediate resettlement of the refugees. The British reversal, Kachaznuni complained, had placed his government and his people in an untenable position, for it confined them to an area that had been totally looted and denuded by the Ottoman armies. Pending more constructive action, the British should at least release a share of the wheat stored at Kars, the rightful possession of the Republic of Armenia.[23] At the end of the month Kachaznuni informed the British authorities that the last reserves of food had been exhausted and hospitals and orphanages had received no bread for two days. Unless the grain at Kars was made available soon, the nation would face extinction.[24] Several days later on February 7 the Premier added: "The Armenians were fully convinced that, with the victory of the Allies and their arrival in the Caucasus, the situation would improve. But I am compelled to state that a sense of indignation, apprehension, and disillusionment has started to creep into their minds. They are beginning to think that it makes no difference to the Allies whether they live or die." [25]

Despite the urgency of these appeals, the British military strategists followed a solicitous policy, striving to avoid conflict with the Muslim partisans of Kars. Colonel Temperley, having reached a working arrangement with the shura, officially the South-West Caucasus Provisional Government, opposed any further attempt to install Armenian administrators and even made harsh demands on Armenian officials at Alexandropol, the major railway junction linking Kars and Tiflis.

[23] Rep. of Arm. Archives, File 3/3, Minister-President to Allied Commander; *Velikaia Oktiabr'skaia revoliutsiia*, pp. 254–255. See also US Archives, RG 256, 184.021/1.

[24] Rep. of Arm. Archives, File 8/8; A. M. Elchibekian, *Velikaia Oktiabr'skaia sotsialisticheskaia revoliutsiia i pobeda Sovetskoi vlasti v Armenii* (Erevan, 1957), pp. 105–108; *Velikaia Oktiabr'skaia revoliutsiia*, p. 255.

[25] D. Enukidze, *Krakh imperialisticheskoi interventsii v Zakavkaz'e* (Tbilisi, 1954), pp. 188–189. An American observer traveling with relief officials in Armenia wrote: "Alexandropol is a blasted town (the handiwork of the Turk upon retreating), with streets like the Slough of Despond; low, flat houses; long lines of sackclothed people, sitting, lying, dozing, and dying. . . . Utter silence brooded over Alexandropol—a silence profound and sinister, as if the whole town were muffled out of respect for continuous burial. We found no violence, no disorder. The people showed the gentle somnolence of lotus-eaters, as they sat there in the long sunbathed streets, feeding on hope." See Melville Chater, "The Land of Stalking Death," *National Geographic Magazine*, XXXVI, 5 (Nov., 1919), 407.

Kachaznuni's cabinet was quite helpless to act upon the complaints lodged against the "haughty and insolent Englishman." [26]

In Tiflis, meanwhile, Aramayis Erzinkian (Social Democrat) and Hovsep Arghutian (Dashnakist) sought the intercession of Brigadier General William Henry Beach, Director of Military Intelligence in the Caucasus. They predicted another year of famine unless the natives of Kars could return in time to sow their fields. Beach commiserated but offered little hope, contending that there was no way to protect the repatriates. He promised the Armenian spokesmen his moral support but stated that their nation must endure patiently until the Paris Peace Conference had taken action.[27]

In F. Willoughby Smith, the Armenians had an indefatigable ally, but only with exhortative messages to the American Mission to Negotiate Peace and to an unresponsive Department of State could the American Consul at Tiflis serve the people whom he esteemed so highly. In these communiqués before his retirement in May, 1919, Smith criticized the British authorities for the unnecessary and calamitous barriers they had thrown up before the refugees. The British, he reported, had come to believe that the Russian Armenian refugees should not repatriate until that right had also been given the Turkish Armenian refugees. But, because the problem of Turkish Armenia had become an international issue requiring definitive measures by the Peace Conference, a considerable delay could be anticipated in repatriating the prewar inhabitants of the Ottoman eastern vilayets. There were no logical grounds, however, to detain the refugees from Kars, which was a part of Russian Armenia. Smith questioned the sincerity of the British explanation that a ten-regiment division would be needed to supervise the return of the Russian Armenian refugees, and he called upon the Allied Powers to oust Turkish agitators and officers from the Kars oblast.[28]

Opposing Interests in Kars

Throughout February and March of 1919, the South-West Caucasus Provisional Government waxed powerful. For a time it even extended its loose network into the Tiflis guberniia, where Muslim insurgents ex-

[26] Rep. of Arm. Archives, File 9/9; *Velikaia Oktiabr'skaia revoliutsiia*, pp. 256–258. See also Denikin, *Ocherki smuty*, IV, 147.

[27] Rep. of Arm. Archives, File 66a/3.

[28] US Archives, RG 59, 867.4016/404; RG 84, Tiflis Consulate, 1919, pt. 4, File 800; RG 256, 867.00/139 and 867B.00/74. Benjamin B. Moore shared many of Smith's sentiments. See especially RG 256, 184.01602/23.

pelled the Georgian garrisons from Akhalkalak and Akhaltsikh.[29] The
Republic of Georgia consequently joined Armenia in unbridled opposition to the new rival state in Transcaucasia. Premier Noi Zhordania
excoriated British policy for having contributed to the rebellions on
Georgian territory and thus having obliged the Georgian army to
restore order by force. Moreover, Zhordania exclaimed, Forestier-
Walker's tolerance of the Muslim shura at Kars, a province rightfully
and intrinsically Armenian, was scandalous.[30] The Georgian press,
too, sided with Armenia and expressed satisfaction that Erevan had
wisely turned the center of its attention from north to west—to Kars
and Turkish Armenia—the historically correct and natural direction.
Still, the Tiflis publicists, while upholding Armenia's pretensions to
the city, fortress, and most of the province of Kars, nonetheless asserted
Georgia's right to the northern districts, particularly the Ardahan
okrug.[31]

The Republic of Azerbaijan displayed an equally keen interest in
matters affecting the western provinces of Transcaucasia. Most inhabitants in the lands claimed by the South-West Caucasus Republic were
Muslim and related in many ways to the Azerbaijanis. Of the Transcaucasian republics, only Azerbaijan granted recognition and extended
moral support to the Kars shura. Premier Khan Khoiskii even declared
that hostility from any quarter to that government would be regarded
as enmity toward Azerbaijan.[32] His cabinet urged General Thomson
to respect the right of self-determination and to shield the South-West
Caucasus Republic from Georgian and Armenian aggression. The only
acceptable alternative to the permanent existence of the new state
would be Azerbaijani annexation of all its territory—from Batum to
Kars and from Akhaltsikh to Ordubad. Initially, British authorities in
Baku assured Khan Khoiskii that the status quo would be preserved in

[29] In his frequent reports to 27th Division headquarters, Lieutenant Colonel
Ritchie, the British military representative in Akhalkalak and Akhaltsikh, drew at-
tention to the provocative influence that the Kars shura was having upon the Muslim
inhabitants of the two districts. See Britain, WO 95/4880, 27th Division War Diary.
[30] " 'Demokraticheskoe' pravitel'stvo i angliiskoe komandovanie," comp. by Semen
Sef, Krasnyi Arkhiv, XXI (1927), 130, and XXV (1927), 98–104, cited hereafter as
"Gruziia i angliiskoe komandovanie." See also Enukidze, op. cit., pp. 162–164; Bor'ba,
March 30, 1919, p. 2, and April 11, p. 2. Forestier-Walker had instructed the British
military governor at Kars to impress upon the local Muslim administration that the
extension of its activities beyond the provincial boundaries would not be tolerated.
See Britain, WO 95/4880, 27th Division War Diary.
[31] Rep. of Arm. Archives, File 66a/3, Press clippings. See also G. I. Uratadze,
Obrazovanie i konsolidatsiia Gruzinskoi Demokraticheskoi Respubliki (Munich, 1956),
pp. 86–87.
[32] Rep. of Arm. Archives, File 66a/3, Press clippings.

Kars, but General Thomson did not honor this pledge after he transferred to Tiflis in March to become the ranking Allied officer in Transcaucasia.[33]

The Muslim leadership of Kars had by that time grown so brash as to ignore and even defy the directives of Colonel Temperley and his replacement, Brigadier General Verney Asser.[34] Bound ever more closely to the Ottoman Empire and the still-mobilized Turkish divisions just beyond the border, the South-West Caucasus Provisional Government pursued a fixed purpose to rid itself of all external supervision, including that of the British commanders.[35]

Reports of the military governor of Kars revealed that Muslim bands had attacked and stripped members of his staff, had broken into the storehouses and stolen weapons, and were mobilizing the youth of the province.[36] In one incident, mounted irregulars surrounded a rail convoy transporting grain to Alexandropol. The British escort returned fire during the ensuing skirmish, killing three of the besiegers. Unable to halt the train the Muslims then vented their rage upon several Russian gendarmes attached to the British mission.[37] On March 10 General Asser wired division headquarters that the shura had doggedly flouted instructions to drop the title South-West Caucasus Republic and to restrict its activities to the province of Kars.[38] A staff officer arriving in Tiflis five days later added that "the shura is completely out of hand and cannot be compelled to obey British orders unless the British garrison in Kars is much increased."[39]

These reports helped to convince General Thomson that the Armenian and Georgian armies should be authorized to occupy the province

[33] Kadishev, Interventsiia v Zakavkaz'e, p. 166; Kazemzadeh, Transcaucasia, pp. 199–200.

[34] Asser took over as British military governor on March 2, 1919, while Temperley transferred to Erevan in the capacity of military representative. While serving in Erevan, Temperley underwent a progressive change of attitude. In reports to 27th Division headquarters, he expressed concern over the difficulties faced by the Armenian government. He frequently tried to pacify outlying Muslim settlements that rejected Erevan's jurisdiction. Temperley returned to division headquarters at Tiflis (in company with General Andranik and Major Gibbon) on April 28 and assumed temporary command of the 4th Battalion, Rifle Brigade, on May 1. See the division and brigade war diaries in Britain, WO 95/4880 and /4890.

[35] See pertinent reports and evaluations in US Archives, RG 59, 861.00/6583; Rep. of Arm. Archives, File 3/3; Denikin, Ocherki smuty, IV, 147; Uratadze, op. cit., p. 87; Kadishev, Interventsiia v Zakavkaz'e, p. 171.

[36] Britain, WO 95/4890, 27th Division War Diary.

[37] Bor'ba, April 5, 1919, p. 4; Britain, WO 95/4880, 27th Division War Diary, March, 1919, Appendix III.

[38] Britain, WO 95/4880, 27th Division War Diary.

[39] Ibid.

with support from the 27th Division. Informing General Headquarters
in Constantinople that the shura was radiating dangerous propaganda,
he asked permission to reinforce the British garrison at Kars.[40] The
next day, March 14, Thomson summoned Georgian and Armenian
officials to acquaint them with his sentiments and to urge the two countries to resolve their differences. By the comprehensive arrangement he
proposed, Armenia would administer the Kaghisman and Kars okrugs,
Georgia the northern half of Ardahan, and the British military governor of Batum the Olti okrug and the remainder of Ardahan. In the disputed districts beyond the Kars oblast, Armenia was to accede to Georgian rule in Akhalkalak and the northern sector of Lori, including the
village and mines of Alaverdi, while Georgia was to acknowledge Armenian jurisdiction over the rest of Lori, including the village and station
of Sanahin. Thomson recommended that men under arms be held to a
minimum in these latter districts and that local problems be settled by
native councils composed of representatives of the various political
parties, nationalities, and faiths. The Armenian spokesmen, baited
with the offer of the Kars and Kaghisman okrugs, raised no objection
to Georgian rule in northern Ardahan, but they tactfully circumvented
Thomson's unacceptable solution to the controversy over Akhalkalak
and Lori.[41]

General Milne's outlook paralleled that of his chief deputy in the
Caucasus, but he hesitated to grant the request to strengthen the Kars
garrison. The General Officer Commanding, Army of the Black Sea,
was bound by a Cabinet decision, relayed in a War Office directive of
February 15, that the British forces at Kars and other locations away
from the Batum-Tiflis-Baku railway and the port of Petrovsk should
be called in as soon as the Turkish army had completed its evacuation
of the Caucasus. The communiqué continued: "It is realised that there
will be considerable risk of internal disorder and even open hostilities
breaking out between rival States and factions in withdrawing outlying
detachments from such places as Kars and leaving the provinces to their
own devices. It is not intended that armed intervention by British
troops should be resorted to to quell such disturbances, but you should
endeavour to do what is possible by means of British Missions to the
various seats of local Governments to compose such differences." [42]

[40] Ibid.
[41] Rep. of Arm. Archives, File 3/3, Report of conversation; Velikaia Oktiabr'skaia
revoliutsiia, pp. 260–262. See also Britain, FO 371/3658, 80231/512/58, and FO 608/82,
342/5/2/11688.
[42] Britain, FO 371/3661, 31192/1015/58.

Evidently advised by Milne to alter his proposals to conform with these instructions, General Thomson prepared a revised scheme which in effect constituted a volte-face. The British military governorship at Kars was to be terminated and the 4th Battalion, Rifle Brigade, and attached units were to be withdrawn. Lieutenant Colonel G. A. Preston[43] would relieve General Asser, using only the title of military representative, and the Muslim shura would be given increasing latitude in administering the province.[44] Putting the plan into action Thomson accompanied Preston to his new post on March 24 and in secret guidelines issued two days later directed the colonel (1) to allow the functions of the military governorship to lapse; (2) to augment steadily the rights and prerogatives of the shura; (3) to remain aloof from internal affairs so long as human life was not in danger or British troops had not been the victim of violence by the inhabitants; (4) to pull the men under his command into Kars and to desist from deploying units to outlying positions without specific authorization from division headquarters; (5) to regard as his area of jurisdiction that region over which the shura asserted control; (6) to avoid the use of force in attempting any reparations but to exercise whatever influence possible to get people (Armenian refugees) back to their homes to resume normal lives; (7) to return the 4th Rifles to division headquarters as soon as two companies of Preston's own Gurkha battalion had arrived in Kars.[45]

This order, which represented a final effort to minimize British obligations in Kars by sanctioning the continued and enhanced predominance of the South-West Caucasus Provisional Government, was soon rescinded. The flow of reports about the shura's seditious activities and Ittihadist bent, coupled with the spread of unrest and defiance throughout Turkey, finally induced General Milne to give precedence to his own judgment. Lieutenant Colonel Alfred Rawlinson had scouted the eastern Ottoman vilayets and the Kars oblast, only to confirm that numerous Muslim bands, armed with Turkish rifles and machine guns and led by Turkish officers, were operating freely throughout the lands claimed by the South-West Caucasus Republic. Although the Ottoman Ninth Army had formally relinquished the province, the

[43] George Allen Preston commanded the 2d Battalion, 6th Gurkha Rifle Regiment, formerly a component of the 42d Infantry Brigade, 15th (Indian) Division, on the Mesopotamian front. On their transfer to the 27th Division, the 2/6 Gurkhas were first attached to the 80th Brigade at Batum and then, after proceeding to Tiflis in March, 1919, to the 82d Brigade.

[44] Britain, WO 95/4880, 27th Division War Diary.

[45] *Ibid.*, G.S. 212/9. General Asser arrived back in Tiflis on March 29 and resumed active command of the divisional artillery.

drawing power of the Ottoman Empire still prevailed there.[46] Thus by the end of March, Milne had laid aside the War Office directive and determined to overthrow the Kars shura. He traveled to Batum for long conferences with Thomson on April 2 and 3. When he turned back to Constantinople and Thomson to Tiflis, the operation had been planned in full. Colonel Preston was instructed by wireless to disregard the operational guidelines issued him the previous week, to revive the title of British military governor, and to work under General Davie, who would arrive shortly with fresh troops and further particulars.[47]

Occupation of the Kars Oblast

In keeping with the dramatic shift in policy, General Thomson, while still at Batum on April 2, cabled Tiflis to alert General Keith Maitland Davie, commander of the 82d Infantry Brigade and, since January 19, of all troops in the Tiflis sector, to make immediate preparations to depart as the British military representative at Erevan.[48] Then, in an order dated April 4, 1919, Davie was named General Officer Commanding of the 27th Division's Southern Command, a new subsector that was to include Erevan, the neutral zone in the Borchalu uezd, the Nakhichevan district, and the province of Kars.[49] Placed in charge of the Imperial forces in those regions, Davie was enjoined to implement the following policy:

KARS Province and NAKHICHEVAN Area will be handed over to the Armenian Government for administration pending the settlement by the Peace Conference.

The Military Governorship of BORCHALOU will be done away with, and this area will be taken over for administration by either Georgia or Armenia or divided between them; this question has yet to be settled.

Repatriation up to the old Russian Frontier will be commenced,

[46] A. Rawlinson, *Adventures in the Near East, 1918–1922* (London and New York, 1923), pp. 155–162.

[47] Britain, WO 95/4880, 27th Division War Diary.

[48] *Ibid.*, WO 95/4994, 82d Brigade War Diary. Davie relinquished command of the Tiflis garrison to Brigadier General Francis Stewart Montague-Bates, who arrived from Constantinople on April 3 to assume command of the 81st Brigade. Since mid-January the 81st Brigade had been under the acting leadership of Lieutenant Colonel R. N. Stewart, the 2/Cameron Highlander who had presided at the Armeno-Georgian peace conference and was then named to coordinate the activities of the British missions at Akhalkalak and the Borchalu (Lori) neutral zone.

[49] In a collateral order General Thomson created four subcommands in Transcaucasia: Baku (Shuttleworth), Tiflis (Montague-Bates), Erevan (Davie), Batum (Cooke-Collis).

and the Armenians gradually re-instated, the whole to be completed by 30th April 1919.

The KARS SHURA will be dispersed as soon as possible and its leaders deported.

The Turks of whom you have the least suspicion will be arrested and sent to Tiflis.

The above arrangements will be completed by April 30th and the British troops withdrawn leaving only a Mission with the Armenian Govt.

As for the specific course of action in Kars, the head of the Southern Command was directed:

1) to transfer there at once to arrange for the dispersal of the shura and for the deportation of its leaders, this to be accomplished before either the introduction of an Armenian administration or the repatriation of the refugees;

2) to report as soon as possible whether he could carry out the arrests with the 4th Battalion Rifles and the 2d Battalion Gurkhas alone or whether it would be necessary to await further reinforcements;

3) to apprehend, in addition to the shura leaders, any other persons deemed prudent and to deport both groups immediatly to Tiflis;

4) to draw in all British detachments before the beginning of the operation or, if this could not be done for strategic reasons, to strengthen those outlying units to ensure that no British personnel would be taken hostage by the Tatars;

5) to instruct Lieutenant Colonel Preston, the military governor, to manage provincial affairs through whatever kind of local council considered advisable or procurable until such time as the Armenian administration was introduced and the whole province eventually governed and garrisoned by the Armenian republic;

6) to distribute proclamations that were to be sent out from Tiflis regarding the dispersal of the shura, utilizing airplanes (two landed at Kars on April 13) for this work;

7) to begin as quickly as feasible the repatriation of Armenian refugees up to the prewar Russo-Turkish frontier, it being made clear that no protection could be given refugees passing beyond this line and that any who so ventured would be proceeding at their own risk;

8) to accomplish all the above measures in time to allow the withdrawal of British troops from the province by April 30, 1919.[50]

General Davie arrived in Kars on April 6 with the 82d Brigade headquarters company and two sections (four armored cars) of the 13th

---

[50] Britain, WO 95/4894, 82d Brigade War Diary, G.S. 273.

Light Armored Motor Battery. Two trains brought in the 2d Battalion, 6th Gurkha Rifles, the next day, followed on April 9 by the 1st Battalion, 23d Sikh Pioneers.[51] The Indian battalions, together with auxiliary medical, signal, engineering, and artillery contingents, increased the British garrison at Kars to some 2,500 men.[52] Moreover, a detachment of the 82d Machine Gun Battery manned the Armenian armored train at Alexandropol and the Armenian army concentrated 2,000 troops in that city to lead the repatriation of the refugees, who stirred with excitement all along the border.[53]

Only after these preparations had been completed did General Milne inform London that he had sent the Gurkha and Sikh battalions to Kars and had ordered the arrest of the shura and all Turkish officers in the province. This action had been necessitated, he explained to the War Office, by the brazen anti-Entente attitude of the shura, its collaboration with the Ottoman Ninth Army headquartered nearby at Erzerum, and its open fraternization with Turkish officers working in disguise all about Kars. There was the further danger that the enormous military stockpiles, which had been impossible to remove because of snowdrifts, might fall into enemy hands; the British occupation would now allow for the transferal or destruction of these goods. Milne enunciated his confidence that quick, firm action would avert bloodshed. As soon as Armenian control had been established at Kars and the refugees repatriated in time to sow their fields, the men of the 27th Division

[51] The 1/23 Sikh Pioneer Regiment, led by Lieutenant Colonel Hugh Frederic Archie Pearson, was one of the Indian battalions General Milne had dispatched to Transcaucasia to replace English and Scottish battalions scheduled for rotation and demobilization. The 1/23 Sikhs disembarked at Batum on March 9, were ordered to Tiflis on April 4, and, to the surprise of their commander, were sent straight on to Kars on April 7. The battalion diary for April 9, 1919, reads: "Arrive ALEXANDROPOL at 0300 hours and leave 1000 hours. Whole place utterly wrecked. Thousands of Armenian refugees awaiting repatriation. Finally arrive KARS. KARS absolutely wrecked and burnt down except for a few houses and barracks now occupied by Tartars." See Britain, WO 95/4885 and /4886.

[52] The effective strength of each of the Indian battalions was approximately 800 men. On April 11 they took over guard duties from the 4/Rifle Brigade, the ranks of which had dwindled through partial demobilization. Colonel Pearson was named by Military Governor Preston to take acting command of all Imperial contingents at Kars. See Britain, WO 95/4880, /4885, /4890, and /4894.

[53] Khatisian, Hanrapetutian zargatsume, p. 132, states that, during a conference held at Alexandropol in March and attended by him, Dro, and Generals Davie, Beach, Hovsepian, and Pirumian, a plan was devised according to which 1,500 Imperial and 1,200 Armenian troops were to begin a joint advance along the railway and main road to Kars. The Armenian strength was to be progressively increased to 3,000 men. Armenian sources err in showing that Colonel Temperley was supposed to remain in Kars as the military governor. Preston was then the British governor, whereas Temperley was serving as the military representative at Erevan.

would be recalled, thereby fulfilling the War Office directive of February 15.[54]

Shortly before the operation was to commence, General Thomson summoned Acting Premier Khatisian to Tiflis to inform him that, as a result of General Milne's recent decisions, many of Armenia's requests could now be treated favorably. The refugee masses would be repatriated westward to Kars and southward to Nakhichevan. It was only reasonable, Thomson insisted, that Armenia should reciprocate by making concessions in other troubled areas. Her claims to Mountainous Karabagh, Akhalkalak, and a part of the Borchalu neutral zone should be dropped. As before, however, the British officer could elicit nothing more than a noncommittal reply.[55] In his tactics to resolve the cardinal territorial conflicts prior to the British withdrawal from the Caucasus, Major General Thomson was roundly criticized by American officials. Benjamin B. Moore, chief of the Tiflis party of the American Field Mission to South Russia, termed the British plan unjust and illogical, especially as it would have left the Alaverdi copper mines to Georgia. Thomson had consulted neither the French nor the American representatives in Tiflis before thrusting this scheme upon Khatisian and, in Moore's view, had violated the dictum that only the Paris Peace Conference possessed the authority to rule on the fate of disputed territory.[56]

General Thomson, taking little note of this isolated American opinion and amazed by the intransigence of the Transcaucasian statesmen, nonetheless focused upon the basic feature of the new British strategy and printed a proclamation, dated April 10, 1919, announcing the dissolution of the South-West Caucasus Provisional Government. He specifically emphasized, Moore's accusation aside, that the Peace

[54] Britain, WO 33/965, no. 4095, and FO 608/78, 342/1/6/7050.

[55] Rep. of Arm. Archives, File 8/8. The 27th Division War Diary shows that while Khatisian was in Tiflis, April 6–9, he and Thomson were joined in conference by Georgian Foreign Minister E. P. Gegechkori. The Georgian government was blunt in its rejection of the proposal to divide the neutral zone with Armenia, thus angering Thomson, who deprecated the "extravagant claims" of Zhordania's cabinet and demanded that the Georgian armed forces at Akhalkalak be reduced to two companies, the limit established by the Armeno-Georgian peace settlement in January but recently exceeded because of Muslim disturbances inspired by the Kars shura. Upon receipt of a more judiciously stated Georgian note, Thomson permitted matters to stand in Akhalkalak. See Britain, WO 95/4880.

[56] US Archives, RG 256, 184.01602/28. For other criticisms of British policy, see 184.01602/60; John Elder, "Memories of the Armenian Republic," *Armenian Review*, VI (Spring, 1963), 20–21.

Conference would determine the ultimate status of Kars and all other contested districts.[57]

At Kars, meanwhile, General Davie and Colonel Preston deployed platoons of Gurkhas to bolster the outlying British posts and finalized their master stroke against the shura. They were not overly perturbed by intelligence reports that the shura had called the provincial chieftains to arms in order to block any attempt to bring back the Armenians. Davie casually interviewed several members of the local government and learned that the legislative assembly, the mejlis, met three afternoons weekly. Two of his staff officers attended the session of April 10 to acquaint themselves with the layout.[58] Colonel Preston then wrote the shura that he would be present at the assembly meeting on Saturday the twelfth in order to impart some vital information.

Shortly after Preston had entered the assembly on the appointed day, a company of Gurkhas surrounded the building and disarmed the sentinels. The British military governor then proceeded to read Thomson's proclamation dissolving the shura. Faced with Gurkha rifles, the deputies offered no resistance and watched helplessly as ten of their leaders were transferred under escort of an armored car to a waiting train. At the depot they were joined by four other "undesirables" who had been taken in the city after brief skirmishes that had resulted in the wounding of a 4th Battalion rifleman and the death of three Muslim defenders.[59] At six-thirty that evening, following the arrival of the Armenian armored train from Alexandropol, the captive notables, among whom were shura chairman Ibrahim Bey and the ministers of interior, war, provisions, and post and telegraph, were sped to Tiflis and, in compliance with instructions from General Milne, deported to Constantinople and ultimately to the isle of Malta.[60]

[57] Kazemzadeh, Transcaucasia, p. 200. See also Dursunoğlu, op. cit., p. 46. Evidently, it was intended that Davie should move against the Kars government on April 10, as his orders of the fourth stated that proclamations on the dispersal of the shura would be forwarded from Tiflis. Davie himself noted that the operation had been delayed slightly to provide time to strengthen the British units stationed outside Kars. See the war diaries of the 27th Division and 82d Brigade, WO 95/4880 and /4894.

[58] The British authorities made no distinction between the ministerial council (shura) and the assembly (mejlis) of Kars, referring to them collectively as the shura. On the day that the British staff officers scouted the mejlis, organized in January with a proposed membership of 120, it was attended by 52 deputies.

[59] Britain, WO 95/4994, 82d Brigade War Diary, April, 1919, Appendix F, 82G/27, and /4880, 27th Division War Diary. See also US Archives, RG 256, 184.01602/35 and 867B.48/16.

[60] The names and positions of the prisoners are listed in Britain, WO 95/4994,

After an existence of three months the South-West Caucasus Republic had collapsed. On the night of the overthrow, town criers passed through the streets reading the decree of dissolution, and Imperial forces patrolled the city until dawn. On April 13 Davie declared the province under martial law, and Preston summoned several members of the former government to organize a provisional administrative council. By decision of the British commanders the new shura, which formally convened on April 15, was composed of 4 Tatars, 2 Greeks, 1 Kurd, 1 Russian, and 1 Molokan (Russian sectarian) and was chaired by Esad Oktay, the president of the dispersed mejlis.[61] For several days after the near bloodless coup, the 2/6 Gurkhas and 1/23 Sikhs conducted a house-to-house search for weapons and, on orders from Milne and Thomson, emptied many of the forts, loading arms and matériel on trains bound for Tiflis and beyond. Large quantities of military equipment that General Davie assessed as obsolete were burned.[62]

The swift British blow at Kars drew contrasting responses from Armenia's neighbors. Azerbaijan denounced the liquidation of the South-West Caucasus Republic and charged Great Britain with a shameful breach of faith.[63] The Sultan's government in Constantinople stated its distress to Admiral Calthorpe, the British High Commissioner, as it relayed a wire from Kars protesting the arrest of the Muslim leaders.[64] Georgia, on the other hand, applauded the demise of the shura, which for a time had wrested control of Akhalkalak and Akhaltsikh from Tiflis. Also welcome was General Thomson's authorization for a small Georgian force to advance from Akhaltsikh into the northern part of

April, 1919, Appendix F/1, and in FO 371/3658, 80231/512/58. Two of the men were released after questioning in Tiflis and allowed to return to Kars. The others were sent to Batum on the evening of April 13 and three days later placed aboard a ship bound for Constantinople. A wire from General Milne to detain the arrested leaders in Batum pending further instructions did not arrive in time, and General Thomson strongly urged his commanding officer not to send the twelve back to the Caucasus. See WO 95/4880, and WO 33/965, no. 4204.

[61] For a primary account of this procedure and the composition of the new shura, see Britain, WO 95/4894, April, 1919, Appendix H, 82/G/32. Davie termed the selection of Esad Bey as not sound, since "he is a man who is imbued with the previous traditions of the so-called S.W. Caucasus Republic, of which he was President." The appointment had been advised by Colonel Preston, who felt that the respected Muslim leader could be useful. Davie left Preston with instructions to send Esad Bey under arrest to Tiflis if his attitude "is not all that is desired."

[62] See the brigade and battalion war diaries in Britain, WO 95/4885, /4890, and /4894.

[63] US Archives, RG 256, 861K.00/93; Rep. of Arm. Archives, File 66a/3, Press clippings.

[64] Britain, FO 371/3658, 75875/512/58, and FO 608/78, 342/1/6/10793.

the Ardahan okrug.[65] But the enthusiasm of Zhordania's cabinet was not lasting. Negative reports by British military observers on the behavior of the Georgian troops in Ardahan, the opposition of Military Governor Cooke-Collis to any Georgian expansion in the direction of Batum, where Georgian irredentist propaganda was rampant, and the strong dislike of General Milne for the Menshevik leadership in Tiflis culminated in orders, sustained by threats, for the Georgian army to recall its men from that peripheral district of the Kars oblast.[66]

The Transfer of Authority

With the situation in Kars apparently well in hand, Brigadier General Davie traveled the 50 miles to Alexandropol on April 17 to discuss the forthcoming repatriation with Acting Premier Khatisian. The plan the two adopted provided that the refugee convoys proceed from Alexandropol to Kars and from Kulp (Goghb) to Kaghisman. The main body of refugees, who were massed at Alexandropol, would advance by rail and by road starting on April 21. The repatriates whose villages lay between Alexandropol and Kars would follow the Armenian army on foot, parting company as they approached their homes. A British troop of fifty mounted men under an officer of the 1/23 Sikhs was to move out with the soldiers and peasantry. The city inhabitants would be trained to Kars, as would natives of towns and settlements extending to the Turkish frontier. From Kars the latter group would fan out gradually, occupying the villages nearest the city and then pressing forward until

[65] For contemporary Georgian accounts of this operation, see *Bor'ba*, April 27, 1919, p. 2, and April 29, p. 2.

[66] Milne refused to receive any Georgian officials during his stay in Tiflis on May 1 and 2. The British war diaries reveal the lack of a well-defined policy regarding the Georgian maneuver in Ardahan. Commands were given and rescinded depending on the disposition prevailing at British headquarters. An interesting game of evasion was implemented by Georgia. Soon after receiving a British directive in late April to withdraw the Georgian force, the Minister of Military Affairs reported full compliance, whereas a British officer at Merdenek, some 20 miles southwest of Ardahan, wired that Georgian troops had advanced to the vicinity of the town. On May 15 General Milne modified his decision once again by authorizing the retention of a fifty-man Georgian garrison in northern Ardahan, but this arrangement, too, was revoked on receipt of several reports about the "shameless" actions of the soldiers. Throughout the summer of 1919 Zhordania and his ministers insisted that no contingents remained in Ardahan, while British intelligence proved the contrary and one officer even warned that the Georgians were "half way to Kars." Matters were further aggravated by persistent reports of Georgian incursions into the province of Batum. For a fascinating day-to-day sketch of these events, see Britain, WO 95/4880, /4890, and /4894. See also "Gruziia i angliiskoe komandovanie," XXI, 156–157, 161; Noi Zhordaniia, *Moia Zhizn'* (Stanford, 1968), pp. 101–102.

the remoter hamlets had been attained. British detachments at Kaghisman, Sarikamish, and Merdenek would assist in the operation.[67]

Khatisian agreed to Davie's suggestion that the infusion of an Armenian administration should be measured and cautious. The governor-designate, Stepan Korganian, and various assistants representing the ministries in Erevan would begin their duties on April 19. Initially, they would merge with the provisional shura under Colonel Preston, who would stay on temporarily as the British military governor. In due time an Armenian preponderance in government would be achieved, commissioners dispatched to oversee matters in the countryside, and full Armenian jurisdiction established throughout the province.[68]

Implementation of the plan was precise. On Saturday, April 19, Colonel Preston welcomed Korganian back to Kars and commenced the transfer of power.[69] Two days later the 2,000-man armed column under General Harutiun Hovsepian (Ossipov) struck out from Alexandropol, followed by streams of refugees, more than 50,000 of whom were repatriated the first month.[70] Hovsepian's troops made their entry into Kars on April 24, having earned high praise from the attached British officer whose reports regarding their exemplary behavior were relayed to the headquarters of the 27th Division in Tiflis and of the Army of the Black Sea in Constantinople. On April 28, 1919, the Armenian 2d Infantry Regiment relieved the Gurkha Rifles and the Sikh Pioneers standing guard over the forts and the city. Kars had been united to the Republic of Armenia.[71]

The assumption of responsibility by the Armenian army was witnessed by George F. Milne and William M. Thomson, who were conducting a final inspection of their men at Kars and Sarikamish. Satisfied

[67] Britain, WO 4894, 82d Brigade War Diary, April, 1919, Appendix G, 82/G/25, and Appendix K, 82/G/43.

[68] Ibid., Appendix L, 82/G/44. Khatisian had been assured by both Davie and Thomson that Armenia would not be required to retain the provisional Kars shura.

[69] The arrival of the Armenian administrators on April 19 has apparently led several authors to conclude that the South-West Caucasus Provisional Government was overthrown on that day instead of the actual date one week earlier, April 12. See, for example, Tunaya, op. cit., p. 488; Dursunoğlu, op. cit., pp. 46–47; Çelik, op. cit., p. 44; W. E. D. Allen and Paul Muratoff, Caucasian Battlefields (Cambridge, 1953), p. 498.

[70] Rep. of Arm. Archives, File 3/3, Foreign Minister to Aharonian, May 6, 1919; Bor'ba, May 21, 1919, p. 2; US Archives, RG 256, 184.01602/28 and 867B.4016/16. For a graphic description of the hardships suffered by the refugees after their return, see Eleanor Franklin Egan, "This To Be Said for the Turk," Saturday Evening Post, CXCII (Dec. 20, 1919), 74, 77.

[71] Britain, WO 95/4894, 82d Brigade War Diary, April, 1919, Appendix S, 82/G/56.

that the steps outlined in the orders issued to General Davie on April 4 had been effectively executed, they entrained for Erevan on the evening of the twenty-eighth for conferences with Khatisian's cabinet.[72] The Armenian government, while highly gratified by the extension of its authority to Kars, was nonetheless disquieted by the impending British withdrawal.[73] During consultations on April 30, Alexandre Khatisian urged that the battalions be kept in Kars for a few months, but Milne, stern in his refusal, revealed that they would depart around the middle of May.[74] The intervening two weeks, he calculated, would give ample time for Korganian's administration to take root. The Armenian refugees, Milne continued, must not under any circumstance advance beyond the prewar boundary into Turkish Armenia, for mobilized Ottoman divisions stood along the border, contrary to British orders, and a critical situation could easily be provoked. Adding a word of encouragement, or perhaps exhortation, the commander of the Army of the Black Sea expressed confidence that the Armenians would prove themselves capable administrators. This belief, he stated, had prompted him to sanction Armenia's expansion to include the entire Kars oblast excepting northern Ardahan and western Olti. Still, the Armenians might be wise to follow the tested British practice of replacing tired, outspent officials. Stepan Korganian, a sincere old gentleman, should step aside in favor of a younger and more alert governor.[75] Milne had put tactfully that which General Davie had reported in blunt terms to division headquarters and to Khatisian himself. In receipt of news that Korganian, while en route to Kars, had been pretentious and arrogant in dealing with the mayor of a strategically located Muslim town, Davie warned that such ineptitude should not be tolerated, particularly under the delicate circumstances prevailing in the province just awarded Armenia.[76]

During the lengthy meeting of April 30, Khatisian voiced strong ob-

[72] Ibid., WO 95/4880.

[73] Completion of the withdrawal was originally scheduled for April 30. Khatisian traveled to Tiflis twice to plead for an extension, and General Davie cautioned his superiors that abandoning Armenia before she had been given sufficient time to establish her jurisdiction in Kars and Nakhichevan would lead to certain bloodshed. On April 18 General Thomson informed Khatisian that the troops would remain pending the forthcoming visit of Commander in Chief Milne, who would make the ultimate decision.

[74] The 4th Battalion, Rifle Brigade, was already en route to Batum, whence all but cadres embarked on the homeward voyage at the end of May.

[75] Rep. of Arm. Archives, File 8/8. Stenographic notes. See also Britain, WO 95/4880.

[76] Davie's appraisals of Korganian are in Britain, WO 95/4894, 82d Brigade War Diary, April, 1919, Appendix Q, 82/G/50, and Appendix U, 82/G/60.

jections to the requisitioning of military stockpiles at Kars by the British army and the conveyance of these goods to eastern Transcaucasia. Armenia, in her struggle for survival, had urgent need of all this matériel. Milne replied that the military warehouses in Kars were brimming and that the British were only drawing weapons and ammunition to be sent to General Denikin. It seemed odd, he continued, that Khatisian should complain, since the Volunteer Army would turn these arms against the Russian Bolshevik regime, which everyone knew was also an adversary of the Armenian republic.[77] Milne's explanation did not correspond with one given the Georgian government a short time later by Thomson's successor, Major General Cory, who asserted that the materiel from Kars was intended, not for the Volunteer Army, an avowed enemy of the Georgian republic, but for the Transcaspian Turkoman forces struggling against the Bolsheviks.[78]

Before the discussion of April 30 had turned from military questions, Khatisian drew attention to the fact that only two million of the five million rounds of ammunition promised Armenia had been delivered from Kars. General Milne, seconded by Thomson, now insisted that two million rounds were quite sufficient for Armenia's defense. He felt obliged to point out once again that the war was over and that the Allies had not fought the past four years to encourage the growth of regional armies. Khatisian could not but take issue, emphasizing that a strong army was requisite to the preservation of peace. He wondered if the British commanders were really that misinformed about the threats to the Republic, both from within and without.[79]

The wholesale removal of supplies and weapons from Kars continued for many days after Milne and Thomson had returned to Tiflis. Armenian military leaders, exasperated by this alarming drain, floundered helplessly in search of effective countermeasures. A futile attempt by General Movses Silikian to intercept a loaded train passing through Alexandropol en route to Baku elicited a sharp reprimand and warning

[77] Rep. of Arm. Archives, File 8/8. See also US Archives, RG 256, 184.021/8.

[78] "Gruziia i angliiskoe komandovanie," XXI, 157–161. See also Bor'ba v Gruzii, pp. 435–436.

[79] Rep. of Arm. Archives, File 3/3 and File 8/8. The actual reason for Milne's admonition is discerned in a report that General Davie relayed from Kars on April 16: "I can find no trace of anything like 5,000,000 rounds Russian S.S.A. [small arms ammunition] here. All I have been able to discover is being sent to ALEXANDROPOL. 861,-600 rounds were sent on the 14th inst[ant]. 997,800 was loaded yesterday and will be despatched today. In addition about 400,000 remain to be sent. This is all the Russian stuff which can be found. There is about 2,500,000 to 3,000,000 rounds of British ammunition." See Britain, WO 95/4894, 82d Brigade War Diary, April, 1919, Appendix I, 82/G/39.

from British headquarters. Some one hundred cannons and field guns, many carloads of artillery shells and assorted spare parts, and tons of raw cotton were taken from the forts and storage depots of Kars. Director of Military Intelligence General Beach tried to calm the frantic Armenian officials by repeating Milne's rationalization that the Volunteer Army would use this matériel against a common enemy. But even were this so, the very fact that some of the heavily laden trains were headed for Baku, the capital of Azerbaijan, was in itself sufficient to sustain the apprehensions in Erevan.[80]

The Armenian Administration in Kars

By mid-May, 1919, nearly all the Imperial forces at Kars had been withdrawn, and the initially hesitant Armenian government assumed both civil and military responsibility for the province.[81] The Armenian railway administration extended its network to include the Alexandropol-Kars-Sarikamish line, and Armenian troops advanced southward into Kaghisman, southwestward into Sarikamish, northwestward into Merdenek, and northward to the environs of Ardahan. This seemingly favorable turn of fortune was crowned on May 10 when Acting Premier Khatisian and General Davie rode through the city of Kars in a military parade. On Sunday, the eleventh, they attended thanksgiving services in the historic Church of the Apostles, where Khatisian ex-

[80] Rep. of Arm. Archives, File 8/8, Report of Commander in Chief Nazarabekov. See also Poghosian, *op. cit.,* pp. 311–312.

[81] On May 1, the day after Milne and Thomson had met with Khatisian, disturbances in Baku and Petrovsk were reported. Thomson immediately ordered his General Officer Commanding, Southern Command, to hasten two companies of 1/23 Pioneers and of 2/6 Gurkhas to Tiflis. The Pioneers and Section A of the 99th Field Artillery Battery departed on May 4 and were followed three days later by the half brigade of Gurkhas. The crisis in the Caspian sector apparently having passed, these companies did not go on to Baku. During the next two weeks the evacuation proceeded rapidly. The Sikh Pioneer War Diary for May 12 reads: "Receive preliminary warning of leaving KARS. Repatriation of Armenians in KARS district practically completed. Remarkable change in the appearance of KARS and surrounding country now Armenians have returned." The Pioneer battalion headquarters and last two companies having entrained two days later, the final entry written at Kars added: "No one sorry to leave such a desolate spot." The Gurkha detachments at Sarikamish, Merdenek, and Kaghisman were concentrated at Kars on May 16 and with their battalion headquarters departed for Tiflis the next day. The infantry was gone. By that time, too, the single troop of Lothian and Border Horse had transferred to Alaverdi in the Borchalu neutral zone, and the detachment of the 82d Machine Gun Battery had reentrusted the armored train to an Armenian crew. On May 20 the two British airplanes evacuated Kars, and a week later the wireless section left. And finally on June 8 the four vehicles of the 13th Light Armored Motor Battery crossed the Arpachai, leaving only a British military mission at Kars.

claimed optimistically that the Armenian army would soon be in the plain of Alashkert, just beyond the old frontier.[82] Davie appointed Captain H. R. Prosser to remain at Kars in charge of a small British military mission and then with Khatisian departed for Erevan to coordinate the repatriation in the direction of Nakhichevan.[83]

The Kars oblast had been restored to Armenia, but Armenia was not yet its master. Kurdish chieftains, Tatar beks, and Turkish *askers* remained in control of many outlying districts. Armenian garrisons stood at Sarikamish, Kaghisman, Merdenek, and several other towns, but these could be likened to frontier outposts in hostile territory. In Olti powerful Kurdish chief Jafar Bey barred the Armenians from most of the okrug; in Kaghisman, Ayyub Pasha regarded much of the country as his private domain and reserved for himself the right to determine who might pass through it; in the village cluster of Aghbaba, not far from Alexandropol, some 40,000 Muslims resolved to forbid the entry of any Armenian officials, civil or military. Turkish agents roved freely between Olti and Sarikamish, maintaining liaison with the nearby Ottoman divisions. The Armenian government faced, at best, a long, painful process of transforming its theoretical suzerainty into effective actual control.[84] In a few districts Muslim collaborators facilitated this endeavor. Kurdish chieftain Kadimov, commissioned a colonel in the Armenian army, led southern Ardahan into allegiance to Erevan. Muslim notables elsewhere accepted official posts and were inscribed on the government payrolls. Yet resentment against Armenian rule ran deep among most Muslim inhabitants of the Kars oblast.[85]

[82] For descriptions of these happenings, see Rep. of Arm. Archives, File 8/8 and File 22/22; Vratzian, *Hanrapetutiun*, p. 222. According to Khatisian, *Hanrapetutian zargatsume*, p. 134, the occupation of Kars provided Armenia with a vital supply of grain, a few automobiles, and abundant mechanical parts and instruments which were used to reopen several motor and railway garages. Moreover, with the dense alpine forest around Sarikamish now within the borders, Armenia had gained a valuable source of lumber.

[83] Colonel Preston, the former British military governor of Kars and commander of the 2/6 Gurkhas, was killed in a fall from his horse on May 6. With much less authority than a military governor, Captain Prosser, a member of the Gloucestershire Regiment and an 82d Brigade intelligence officer, used the title British Military Representative, Kars.

[84] Rawlinson, *op. cit.*, pp. 197–219; Rep. of Arm. Archives, File 7/7, Report of the General Staff, and File 8/8a, *Hayastani Hanrapetutiun, 1919 t.*, Intelligence report of Schneur.

[85] Khatisian, *Hanrapetutian zargatsume*, p. 134; Rep. of Arm. Archives, File 3/3, Foreign Ministry to Aharonian, May 6, 1919. Kadimov subsequently came under suspicion of having been bribed to serve as a secret agent of Azerbaijan and Turkey. See Ruben [Ter-Minasian], *Hai heghapokhakani me hishataknere*, Vol. VII (Los Angeles, 1952), pp. 209–210.

The problems confronting the government of Armenia were further complicated by rivalry between the civil and military authorities in Kars. Governor Stepan Korganian, contrary to General Davie's evaluation of him, persistently advocated a cautious policy of peaceful penetration, propounding that the inclusion in the administration of all ethnic and religious groups was the means to success. This view was not shared by General Daniel Bek Pirumian, named commandant of Kars fortress, or by General Harutiun Hovsepian, commander of the newly arrived 2d Infantry Regiment.[86] The military men regarded conciliation and pacification as an admission of weakness. The slightest resistance, they maintained, should be crushed, for only through a display of power could Armenia gain the passivity and cooperation of the Muslim population. This dichotomy between the civil and military establishments permeated even the lowest echelons of the provincial administration and precluded the implementation of an efficient, unified program. Moreover, while Hovsepian and Pirumian joined in opposition to Stepan Korganian, each maneuvered to eclipse the other in authority.[87]

Many native Muslim leaders, bewildered for a time by the arrest and deportation of the South-West Caucasus Provisional Government and by the sudden introduction of Armenian rule, were soon to renew their defiance of Erevan. Nevertheless, not long after Armenia's annexation of Kars, Premier Khatisian felt secure enough to tour the province. At every stop along his circular route from Alexandropol to Kars, Kaghisman, Sarikamish, and Ardahan, he was welcomed by deputations of Kurds, Tatars, Greeks, and Russians, who swore allegiance to the Armenian government and pledged to strive toward interracial and interfaith harmony. Alexandre Khatisian was impressed and encouraged, but the true feelings of most non-Armenians were undoubtedly suppressed in these manifestations of goodwill. The fact that an armed escort, two generals, and several Allied officials accompanied the Armenian chief of state might well have conditioned the warm reception accorded him.[88]

[86] US Archives, RG 256, 184.021/26.

[87] Khatisian, *Hanrapetutian zargatsume*, pp. 133–134; T. Baghdasarian, "Hayastani Hanrapetutian verdjaluisin," in *Edjer mer azatagrakan patmutenen* (Paris, 1937), p. 235.

[88] Khatisian, *Hanrapetutian zargatsume*, pp. 135–137; *Hairenik* (daily), Dec. 28, 1919, p. 3.

8

Expansion
to Nakhichevan

The Republic of Armenia was never free of the specter of enemy encirclement. Several million Muslims populated the neighboring provinces of Turkey and Azerbaijan, and, between those two countries, in the southern heartland of Armenia, another 300,000 dominated the Araxes river valley. Although the number of Armenians was twice that of Muslims in the Erevan guberniia as a whole, the Tatars held sway over most of the countryside and along the primary communication and transportation routes, and they formed a majority in the southern uezds of Surmalu, Sharur-Daralagiaz, and Nakhichevan (see maps 9, 11).[1] Even on the outskirts of Erevan, the more than twenty Muslim villages of the Zangibasar district bristled in opposition to the Armenian government. Moreover, Azerbaijan's claims to the entire region were substantial and, as demonstrated in the preceding chapters, the seriousness of her intent was not to be taken lightly. At times agents sent from Baku and Turkish officers who had remained after the Ottoman withdrawal vied for positions of leadership, yet both groups were one in their determination to withstand an Armenian southward thrust.[2]

In spite of these obstacles, the Armenian government realized that it must gain control of the rich lands extending to the Persian frontier

[1] Abeghian, "Mer harevannere" (Feb., 1928), p. 99, and (Sept., 1928), pp. 130, 134. See also US Archives, RG 59, 867.00/1100; Rep. of Arm. Archives, File 6/6.

[2] Numerous intelligence reports on the activities of the Turkish officers who spearheaded the Muslim resistance in Armenia are included in Rep. of Arm. Archives. Additional information on this subject, supplied by American and British officials in the Caucasus, is in US Archives, Record Groups 59, 84, 256 passim, and in the British Foreign Office, War Office, and Empire Delegation archives for 1919.

to steady the Republic. The probes to the south began almost simultaneously with the end of the World War. Emboldened by the Allied
victories, armed bands of Turkish Armenians, natives of Sassun and
Mush, expelled the inhabitants of several Muslim villages in Daralagiaz during November and December, 1918, and in their stead settled 15,000 refugees. For Armenia the maneuver was highly significant,
as it secured the treacherous mountain route from Erevan to Zangezur
at a time when the main road leading over Sharur and Nakhichevan
was tightly sealed by the Tatars.[3]

Nearly 100,000 Armenian inhabitants of the southern uezds had
fled during the Turkish invasion of 1918. Following the Mudros
Armistice those who had taken refuge near Erevan clamored for the
military protection necessary for them to return home. In December
small army units led the first refugee caravans across the Araxes River
into Igdir, the administrative center of the Surmalu uezd, where
Mount Ararat rises to a towering height above the plain. Strategically
situated, the Surmalu uezd bordered upon the Kars oblast, the Bayazit
sanjak of the Erzerum vilayet, and the khanate of Maku in northern
Persia. Over it lay the passageway between the Muslim centers of
Kars and the so-called Arasdayan republic, the autonomous Muslim
district around Sharur-Nakhichevan in the Araxes river valley. The
thousand-man Armenian 8th Infantry Regiment could do little more
in Surmalu than establish garrisons at critical points from Kulp
(Goghb) near the southern margin of the Kars oblast to the Persian
frontier. Minister of Military Affairs Hakhverdian could not spare
additional troops to secure the uezd.[4]

In the county of Erevan, meanwhile, other detachments and refugee
convoys moved unhindered as far as Khamarlu, 15 miles to the south
of the Armenian capital. A combined force of army regulars and
Turkish Armenian partisans then proceeded along the Erevan-Julfa
railway to relieve the isolated Armenian town of Davalu, thus by-
passing Vedibasar, a populous Muslim district centering on the
large village of Baouk (Büyük) Vedi. By mid-December, 1918, the
Armenian units had attained the southern administrative boundary
of the Erevan uezd and were preparing to march through the defile
known as Wolves Gates (Volch'i Vorota) into Sharur.[5] Just at that time,

[3] Ruben [Ter-Minasian], *Hai heghapokhakani me hishataknere*, Vol. VII (Los Angeles, 1952), pp. 207–208; G. Sassuni, *Tajkahayastane rusakan tirapetutian tak (1914–
1918)* (Boston, 1927), pp. 185–186.

[4] T. Baghdasarian, "Hayastani Hanrapetutian verdjaluisin," in *Edjer mer azatagrakan patmutenen* (Paris, 1937), pp. 202–203.

[5] Rep. of Arm. Archives, File 3/3, Foreign Minister to Aharonian; John Elder,

however, the Armeno-Georgian war erupted in Lori. Unwilling to risk simultaneous encounters with the Muslims of Sharur-Nakhichevan, the Armenian command ordered a temporary halt on the southern sector and recalled the forward contingents to Davalu.[6]

The British Military Governorship

In January, 1919, Allied officials in Tiflis having intervened to bring an end to the two-week war between Armenia and Georgia, General Hakhverdian readied his force at Davalu to resume the move toward Sharur. On the eve of the operation, however, Muslim spokesmen from Sharur and Nakhichevan arrived, offering to negotiate for terms that would obviate the impending bloodshed. In the ensuing parleys Kachaznuni's cabinet consented to stay the march for up to ten days, during which time the Tatar envoys would attempt to pacify their people and convey to them the pledge that the advancing army and administration would respect in full the fundamental rights of all inhabitants, Muslim and Christian.[7]

On January 18, before the expiration of the ten days, Captain F. E. Laughton passed through the Armenian lines en route to Nakhichevan as the British military representative.[8] Once in that center of the Arasdayan republic, Laughton conferred with the ruling council (shura), which protested against the imminent Armenian occupation and left no doubt that Sharur and Nakhichevan were prepared for self-defense. Laughton drafted a provisional armistice satisfactory to the shura and, returning to Armenian field headquarters on January 21, demanded in the name of His Majesty's Government the cessation of all military action. Pending further directives from Tiflis, he would oversee matters in Sharur-Nakhichevan.[9] Unwilling at that stage to flout British injunctions and, probably more instrinsically, lacking the necessary military power to subject a region reportedly held by an irregular Muslim soldiery of up to ten thousand well-armed men, the

"Memories of the Armenian Republic," *Armenian Review*, VI (Spring, 1963), 14–15. See also Veysel Ünüvar, *İstiklâl harbinde Bolşeviklerle sekiz ay 1920–1921* (Istanbul, 1948), pp. 15–16.

[6] Vratzian, *Hanrapetutiun*, p. 219; Rep. of Arm. Archives, File 3/3.

[7] *Ibid.*

[8] Frederick Eastfield Laughton, who also acted as the temporary second in command of the 2d Battalion, Cameron Highlander Regiment, 81st Brigade, was escorted to Nakhichevan by one platoon of A Company, 4th Battalion, Rifle Brigade, under Lieutenant F. L. Schwind.

[9] Britain, WO 95/4880, 27th Division, General Staff, War Diary; Rep. of Arm. Archives, File 3/3.

Armenian government yielded to the temporary arrangement dictated by Captain Laughton.[10]

Having achieved this respite, Laughton submitted an urgent report to 27th Division headquarters, recommending the creation of a military governorship at Nakhichevan and the issuance of orders for Armenia to remove her armed forces from the southern part of Erevan county. On January 26 General George T. Forestier-Walker placed the communiqué before a staff conference attended by Director of Military Intelligence William H. Beach, Chief of Staff Charles C. Grattan-Bellew, 81st Brigade Commander Robert N. Stewart, and assistants. At the end of the deliberations he announced that Laughton would be installed as military governor with the local rank of Lieutenant Colonel and that one company from the 82d Brigade would be dispatched immediately as Laughton's escort.[11]

The formal instructions to the military governor, dated January 26, 1919, were relayed to him with the company of Duke of Cornwall's Light Infantry, which entrained for Nakhichevan three days later.[12] Colonel Laughton was to discharge his functions in collaboration with the existing shura or any other body he might select, and he was to make it known that the governorship had been established solely to preserve law and order until the Paris Peace Conference had ruled on the future of the district. The boundaries of the governorship were well defined in the west and the south by the Araxes River, Laughton could determine a suitable line in the east, and the administrative division between the Erevan and Sharur uezds would mark the northern limit. As regards the second major suggestion Laughton had made, the instructions continued: "If you consider that the necessity for maintaining order requires you to extend your Northern boundary so as to include tracts of preponderatingly Moslem character, you will inform the Armenian Government of the fact, and unless the Armenian Government objects, you will so extend it. If the Armenian Govt objects, the question will be referred to D H Q [Division Headquarters]." [13]

[10] Rep. of Arm. Archives, File 9/9; Ruben, *op. cit.*, p. 212.

[11] Britain, WO 95/4880, 27th Division War Diary, January, 1919, Appendix 1.

[12] At the same time as the 132 men of B Company, 2d Battalion, Duke of Cornwall's Light Infantry Regiment, departed for Nakhichevan, C Company set out as escort to Colonel Ritchie, the newly appointed British Military Representative, Akhalkalak. See above, p. 121, n. 88. Colonel Laughton's initial escort of 4th Brigade Rifles rejoined the main body of the battalion, which was then at Kars in support of British Military Governor C. E. Temperley.

[13] Britain, WO 95/4880, 27th Division War Diary, January, 1919, Appendix 2.

The Armenian government did, of course, object when Laughton arrived in the capital to announce that only civil officials could be left in the southern sector of Erevan county and that these must be enjoined to follow his directives. In response to the protests arising from this fiat and from the recent British decision to abandon the introduction of an Armenian administration in Kars,[14] Forestier-Walker sent Brigadier General Verney Asser to Erevan on February 1 with the assignment to explain the reasons for this policy and to deliver an official letter giving assurances that the interim arrangements would in no way prejudice the ultimate disposition of the territories in question. He then traveled in person to Sharur, picking up Asser in Erevan and arriving on February 6 in the town of Bash-Norashen where Colonel Laughton awaited him. In conference aboard the divisional train, the commanding officer of the Imperial forces in western Transcaucasia approved the proposal to expand the governorship of Nakhichevan to include the southern part of the Erevan uezd, from the county line near Wolves Gates and the village of Sadarak northward to the Vedichai (Uvachai) tributary of the Araxes. This district would form a separate zone within the governorship and be managed by Armenian officials but without any armed support. Instead, the 82d Brigade would detail a second company to serve as a peacekeeping body. In the larger region of Sharur-Nakhichevan the Muslim shura would remain in charge.[15]

The plan adopted, Forestier-Walker proceeded to Erevan with the directive that, except for a fifty-man garrison at Davalu, the Armenian army was to be drawn north of the Vedichai by February 8. The remonstrances of Kachaznuni's cabinet were unavailing, and on the tenth the armed column fell back across the stream to Khamarlu.[16] That same day a company of Gloucesters left Tiflis en route to Mount Ararat station to patrol the strip of the Erevan uezd just added to the British military governorship of Nakhichevan.[17]

[14] See above, pp. 206–209.

[15] Britain, WO 95/4880, 27th Division War Diary, February, 1919, Appendix 1.

[16] Rep. of Arm. Archives, File 3/3; Britain, WO 95/4880, 27th Division War Diary, Report of Laughton, Feb. 10, 1919. See also US Archives, RG 256, 184.021/7.

[17] Lieutenant H. B. Boughton led the 112 men of D Company, 2d Battalion, Gloucestershire Regiment, and small auxiliary detachments to Mount Ararat station, arriving there tardily on February 14 because of a blizzard. The station was adjacent to Davalu, presently the town of Ararat on the southwestern administrative boundary of the Armenian SSR. The Gloucestershire War Diary (WO 95/4895) contains vivid descriptions of the district and the plight of the Armenian population there.

In another decree issued in February, Forestier-Walker forbade the Armenian army from consolidating its positions in Surmalu, across the river from the county of Erevan and the northern edge of Sharur. Minister of Military Affairs Hakhverdian complained that these unreasonable fetters had endangered the very existence of the Republic, as they rendered the small contingents at Igdir, Molla-Kamar, and Kulp defenseless. Restricted to these posts the 8th Infantry Regiment could not prevent the Muslims of Kars and Sharur-Nakhichevan from joining forces, and if the key village of Aralikh, linking Sharur and Surmalu, took arms, the Armenian soldiers would be encircled and annihilated. It was therefore imperative that the army be permitted to occupy Aralikh, where, according to intelligence reports, preparations for insurrection were far advanced. The urgency of the plea failed to impress the 27th Division commander, who withheld authorization for any further Armenian military ventures in the south.[18]

Having bowed to Forestier-Walker's regulations, the coalition cabinet of Hovhannes Kachaznuni desperately sought some way to repatriate refugees to the southern districts. In petitions to the British officers in Erevan and Tiflis, the government submitted that, since the Armenian army had not been allowed to assume the responsibility, the British should themselves lead the wretched masses homeward. Such appeals were overshadowed, however, by Colonel Laughton's caveats against a premature repatriation that might easily signal the resumption of interracial warfare.[19] Major William D. Gibbon, who since January, 1919, had been assisting the refugees stranded in Zangezur, did attempt to arrange for the return of at least several thousand originally from the Nakhichevan area, but he met with utter failure. Nor was the intercession of the few American missionaries and relief workers any more fruitful. With Erevan in the clutches of famine they traveled to the Araxes valley to purchase grain but were accorded such a hostile reception that they considered themselves fortunate to have escaped alive.[20]

An air of despondency hovered over government circles in the midst of winter. There seemed to be no end to Armenia's myriad misfortunes. Racked by an unsheltered, hunger-crazed, and disease-ridden population, the Republic had now suffered two major political setbacks: Kars and most of the Araxes valley had slipped beyond its grasp.

[18] US Archives, RG 256, 184.021/7; Rep. of Arm. Archives, File 8/8.
[19] Rep. of Arm. Archives, File 3/3; Britain WO 95/4880, 27th Division War Diary, Reports of Laughton, Feb. 20 and 26, 1919.
[20] Elder, op. cit., pp. 16–18; Rep. of Arm. Archives, File 3/3.

11. THE SOUTHERN UEZDS OF THE EREVAN GUBERNIIA

Foreign Minister Tigranian's report to the Armenian delegation in Paris throbbed with frustration:

Thus, Sharur and Nakhichevan have also been taken from us (even if temporarily) and transformed into a British military governorship (Kars style); we were even constrained to keep troops out of a district (Vedibasar) lying on our side of that boundary.

The Turks are making concerted preparations to play the same game in Surmalu.

Karabagh is being attached to an Azerbaijani governor-generalship under British patronage.

Akhaltsikh, Akhalkalak, Batum have all fallen under the domination of the Turanians of Kars, who have expelled the Georgian garrisons.

And so, in the era of British commanders, the Turkism [Turkic element] of Transcaucasia enjoys conditions even more favorable than it did during the victorious German-Ottoman occupation.

These are facts and realities that cause us grave apprehensions and extreme distress.

The primary reason for this is, of course, the relative weakness of the English armed forces here. Just as Germany yielded to the demands and whims of the Turkish commanders last summer and autumn, so too do the English generals now retreat before the aggressive designs and activities put in motion by Ottoman officers. The facts here recorded not only bespeak the impotence of Armenia but even more they mark the downfall of England—for the British military governorships are nothing but veils, delicate and sheer, under which the real Turkish authority and power are clearly defined.[21]

The British Reversal

Not until the British commanders had become disquieted by the apparent recrudescence of Pan-Turanianism did they reconsider the wisdom of utilizing the existing local power structures as the most commodious means of keeping some sort of order in the entangled and complicated Caucasus. The turnabout in policy vis-à-vis Sharur-Nakhichevan occurred, as in the case of Kars, during the two months that William M. Thomson served as the senior Imperial officer in Transcaucasia.

By the time Thomson transferred from Baku to division headquarters at Tiflis on March 10, the tenor of the reports from British military representatives and governors at Kars, Erevan, Akhalkalak, Nakhichevan, and other outposts had changed drastically, and the office of intelligence had come to believe that a fine Ottoman thread bound

[21] Vratzian, *Hanrapetutiun*, pp. 219–220; Rep. of Arm. Archives, File 3/3.

these districts together and drew the Muslim inhabitants into tighter opposition to the Allied victors. From Nakhichevan, Colonel Laughton began to characterize the shura as "truculent"; the authority he had presumed to possess was slipping away. The single company of Gloucesters headquartered at Ararat station, for example, was much too small a force to prevent the frequent looting and killing of Armenians in the Vedichai-Sadarak zone. Laughton's attempt to impose a penalty on the native villages of the offenders led to a defiant show of weapons and the foreboding departure of the womenfolk. The labors of Colonel Temperley, then acting as the military representative in Erevan, to mollify the aroused chieftains and khans were of no success. This unrest, he concluded, was not an isolated incident, for the mobilization in the Sadarak district was linked with that in Aralikh, Kaghisman, and Kars. Turkish propaganda was spilling across the Araxes from Maku and Aralikh, agitating the Muslim population from Baouk Vedi to Nakhichevan.[22]

Tigranian's assessment that the British military governorships were ephemeral was overstated, but there were few who would dispute the fact that in Nakhichevan the Tatar nobility led by Rahim Khan, Abbas Quli Khan, and Kalb Ali Khan directed affairs. Moreover, Azerbaijani agents such as Samed Bey and Turkish officers such as Captain Halil Bey arrived to assist in the campaign against Armenian incursions and to forge a bridge between the Ottoman Empire and Azerbaijan and ultimately between Nationalist Turkey and Soviet Russia.[23] With a growing sense of insecurity Colonel Laughton requested reinforcements, especially as the effective strength of the two companies under his command had dwindled through the departure of many men scheduled for demobilization. On March 16 General Thomson dispatched Indian replacements, two full companies of the 1st Battalion, 2d Rajput Light Infantry Regiment, for the reduced British units at Ararat-Davalu and Nakhichevan.[24] The commanding officer of the Rajputs, Lieutenant Colonel J. C. Simpson, followed a

[22] See, in particular, the war diaries for March, 1919, in Britain, WO 95/4880.

[23] US Archives, RG 84, Tiflis Consulate, 1919, pt. 4, File 800, and RG 59, 867.00/1100; Khatisian, *Hanrapetutian zargatsume*, p. 137. See also Karabekir, *Istikldl Harbimiz*, p. 65.

[24] The Rajput Battalion, formerly a component of the 51st Brigade, 17th (Indian) Division, on the Mesopotamian front, arrived at Batum on February 21, 1919, transferred to Tiflis, March 9–11, and was attached to the 81st Brigade. C Company under Captain Percy Tidswell Adams went to Nakhichevan, and B Company under Captain Thomas Paige Cook, to Ararat, whereas the other two companies of the battalion were dispersed along the Transcaucasian railway system as guards for British military trains.

week later under orders to relieve Laughton as military governor, a transition completed at the beginning of April.[25]

As General Thomson inclined toward coming to grips with the Muslim ferment that spanned much of western Transcaucasia, he empowered his military representative at Erevan to revise southward the Vedichai-Sadarak zone and, if judged necessary, to permit the Armenian army to occupy the northern part of that district.[26] In his conversations with Acting Premier Khatisian, Thomson now conceded that the Erevan-Julfa railway was indispensable to Armenia and that the relocation of Muslims living directly south of Erevan along that line might be justified. Should displacement become unavoidable, he added, the affected inhabitants must be fully compensated and given the means to resettle in Sharur and Nakhichevan.[27] The increased accomodativeness was further evidenced in the recommendations that Brigadier General Beach prepared for submission to the British Empire Delegation at the Peace Conference. In the maps Beach drew and forwarded to Paris, Karabagh was included in Azerbaijan, but Kars, Surmalu, Sharur, Nakhichevan, and Zangezur fell within the proposed boundaries of Armenia.[28]

It was not until the decisive strategy conference held at Batum on April 2 and 3, however, that the Commander in Chief, Army of the Black Sea, and the leader of his forces in the Caucasus gave definite form to the British reversal. In the sequential orders appointing Keith Maitland Davie the General Officer Commanding, Southern Command, 27th Division, the instructions pertaining to the Erevan region read:

The Military Governorship of NAKHICHEVAN will be abolished and the district handed over to the Armenian Govt. so as to allow the withdrawal of British troops by 30th of April 1919.

This should be done in consultation with the Armenian Government and be subsequent to the arrest of the KARS SHURA.[29]

[25] The British war diaries do not reveal the exact date that John Chalmers Simpson replaced Laughton, although a report based on British military sources, now in US Archives, RG 59, 867.00/1100, shows it to be April 3, 1919. The war diaries do note that Laughton returned to Tiflis on April 12 and that the two companies he had commanded as military governor preceded him on March 27 and 28. Laughton's own Cameron battalion as well as the Cornwall and Gloucester battalions transferred to Batum at the end of May to await demobilization and the homeward journey to the United Kingdom.

[26] Britain, WO 95/4880, 27th Division War Diary.

[27] Rep. of Arm. Archives, File 8/8.

[28] Khatisian, *Hanrapetutian zargatsume*, pp. 132, 137-138; Rep. of Arm. Archives, File 231/130.

[29] Britain, WO 95/4894, 82d Brigade War Diary, April, 1919, Appendix A, G.S. 273.

In the flurry of directives that sent the 2/6 Gurkhas and the 1/23 Sikhs to Kars to overthrow the South-West Caucasus Republic, a detachment of the 81st Machine Gun Battery was detailed to install modern weapons on and to man Armenia's second armored train, assigned to the Erevan sector, and the two remaining companies of 1/2 Rajputs were taken off railway guard duty and directed to join Colonel Simpson and battalion headquarters at Nakhichevan.[30]

Elated by the rapid turn of events the Armenian government planned to bring Sharur-Nakhichevan into the Republic as a separate province, subdivided into the districts of Goghtan (Ordubad), Nakhichevan, and Sharur with the respective administrative centers in the towns of Akulis, Nakhichevan, and Bash-Norashen. Gevorg Varshamian was named to serve as the first governor. A special committee composed of Varshamian, Khatisian, Dro, and General Hakhverdian finalized the details of the annexation even though unanimity of opinion on procedure was lacking. Dro, supported by the militant leaders outside the committee, insisted that a full-scale sweep to Nakhichevan was the only means by which Erevan could be freed from the perpetual threat of insurrection and isolation and by which the Muslim population could be bent to make its peace with the government. The other committee members and the cabinet demurred, albeit for differing reasons. One group, convinced that conciliation and accommodation pointed the way to ascendancy, upheld the policy espoused by Stepan Korganian in Kars and advocated a cautious, peaceful approach to gaining Muslim obedience and loyalty. The second group, probably the majority, believed that Armenia must take swift advantage of the favorable British disposition while it lasted; valuable time must not be lost in a thorough, progressive military occupation. Instead, an Armenian civil administration should be installed in Nakhichevan at the earliest possible moment. This meant, of course, that scores of hostile Muslim villages would dominate the expanse between Erevan and Nakhichevan, but, with the Armenian army in control of the railway and the important towns along its route, the outlying areas would eventually submit. It was this policy that prevailed, in part on the strength of British suasion.[31]

The well-executed seizure of power at Kars reassured the British strategists that the procedure at Nakhichevan could be as smooth,

---

[30] Lieutenant H. J. Trueman took command of the armored train. The two Rajput companies, leaving Akstafa, Elisavetpol, Kvirili, Alexandropol, and other railroad junctions, concentrated at Nakhichevan between April 19 and 30.

[31] Vratzian, *Hanrapetutiun*, p. 222; Khatisian, *Hanrapetutian zargatsume*, p. 138.

thus permitting the withdrawal of the Imperial troops within the time limit set by Commander in Chief Milne. General Davie first discussed this phase of his assignment with Khatisian at Alexandropol on April 17 and then proceeded to Erevan to appraise the military scheme worked out by Dro. Armenia's foremost warrior called for a high-powered march to incorporate the southern counties in three stages: Davalu and the rest of the Vedichai-Sadarak zone, May 1–5, Bash-Norashen to Nakhichevan, May 5–10, Nakhichevan to Ordubad and Akulis, May 10–15. He requested that the 1/2 Rajputs move into Sadarak and stand guard along the railway from that pivotal village to Nakhichevan, a distance of some 40 miles. British observers, Dro suggested, should be sent into the settlements that were to be occupied to witness that he was treating all nationalities equally, since he intended to disarm the entire population regardless of race.[32]

Davie and Colonel Simpson, the new military governor of Nakhichevan, evaluated Dro's plan during a rendezvous at Ararat station on April 19. Simpson favored the proposals except for the manner in which his battalion was to be utilized. He advised that it would not be feasible for the Rajputs to patrol the railway inasmuch as "the line crosses numerous culverts, which could be easily destroyed by anyone, and to hold the line effectively would require posts about 20 yards apart." A sounder course, he suggested, would be to have the armored train pick up two select Armenian companies at Khamarlu on the eve of the general advance and speed them to Wolves Gates. They would secure that defile, which was the key to the region beyond, and await the arrival of the main force after it had neutralized Sadarak. The single company of Rajputs at Ararat station would cut the telegraph wires so that the towns from Davalu southward might not be alerted. Inasmuch as the military governor would be nearly isolated at Nakhichevan on commencement of the offensive, Simpson insisted that the three remaining Rajput companies should stand firm at battalion headquarters.[33]

Davie concurred in these amendments and forwarded the plan to Tiflis for confirmation.[34] But General Thomson rejected the strategy of both Dro and Simpson. On April 23 he dictated his own instructions and admonitions, which Davie personally imparted to Dro the

[32] Britain, WO 95/4894, 82d Brigade War Diary, May, 1919, Appendix P, 82/G/47, Enclosure A.
[33] *Ibid.*, Enclosure B.
[34] *Ibid.*, Appendix N.

next day and put before the Armenian government in a letter which read in part:

> The force is unnecessarily strong. It is likely to cause trouble being provocative. The proposal to disarm the inhabitants is not practicable and is not to be attempted.
> The task is the repatriation of refugees of all nationalities. It is intended that the NAKHICHEVAN area will be handed over to the Armenian Government and the Military Governorship of NAKHICHEVAN will be abolished; it is not intended that the plan decided upon should be an Armenian military invasion. . . .
> I consider that a force of 2000 Infantry, 2 Field Guns and a Squadron of Cavalry should suffice for the purposes required with the assistance of the British troops in that area. . . .
> Further, for the carrying out of repatriation of refugees, Col. Simpson will occupy with 100 men each the following villages, namely—DAVALU, SADARAK, YAIDJI and DJAGRI. The remainder of the British force will be at NAKHICHEVAN. . . .
> Every effort must be made to avoid conflict and it must be understood that a purely military occupation of the area will not lead to the best results.
> The Armenian Government should please arrange to have a civilian administration of carefully selected capable men ready to take up the government of the NAKHICHEVAN area. To this council or temporary administration it is advisable for harmonious working that representatives of the local element should be appointed.[35]

Agreeing to abide by these regulations Dro requested the deployment of four field guns instead of two and stated that in order to make adequate preparations to feed the troops and refugees the operation should be held up until May 3. Davie consented to the use of the additional artillery and guaranteed that by the designated date Rajput detachments would be at the villages specified in Thomson's instructions.[36]

Generals Milne and Thomson arrived in Erevan following their final inspection tour of Kars and during their lengthy conference with Alexandre Khatisian on April 30 reviewed details of the maneuvers that were to conclude the British military commitment in the sector placed in the 27th Division's Southern Command. Thomson again cautioned against an armed invasion, as this would violate the principle of peaceful penetration. He also stipulated that, prior to the foremarch, circulars be distributed to the Muslim inhabitants vouch-

[35] Ibid., Appendix T, Enclosure, 82/G/53.
[36] Ibid., Appendix R, 82/G/57.

safing the inviolability of their lives and property on condition that they make no attempt to impede the operation. The advance of Armenian troops and refugees, Thomson added, must proceed only under General Davie's supervision, and the right of repatriation was to apply to all displaced persons. Muslims who had fled the environs of Erevan and Daralagiaz must be allowed to reclaim their homes.[37]

The Dispatches of Khan Tekinskii

While these arrangements were being made, Azerbaijan's envoy to Erevan, Khan Tekinskii, labored ceaselessly to prevent Armenia from absorbing Sharur and Nakhichevan. Beginning with the day of his arrival in March, 1919, Tekinskii kept the Azerbaijani government posted, through coded messages, on conditions in the southern districts. He appealed for large sums of money to bolster the Muslim resistance and urged a show of force on Armenia's northeastern frontier to relieve the pressure on Sharur-Nakhichevan. The Armenian intelligence corps soon learned to decipher the dispatches and provided the cabinet and the chief of staff with the revealing texts.[38]

Khan Tekinskii's initial wires supplied general information on the composition of the Armenian army and on the prevailing internal situation in the Republic. Then on April 16, 1919, he relayed the startling unofficial news that the British command, in addition to condoning Armenia's expansion into Kars, had sanctioned her annexation of Sharur and Nakhichevan. Should this prove true, he continued, Azerbaijan must exhort the Muslims of India, Turkestan, Afghanistan, and the entire Caucasus to unite against an intrigue that would subject millions of Muslims to "a half million Armenians." In his message of April 29 Tekinskii accurately reported to Foreign Minister Mohammed Iusuf Jafarov, who was then in Tiflis to attend a conference, that Armenia would announce the annexation of Nakhichevan on

[37] Rep. of Arm. Archives, File 8/8, Stenographic notes of conversation; Khatisian, *Hanrapetutian zargatsume*, pp. 138–139.

[38] The communiqués are included in Rep. of Arm. Archives, File 132/31. Not until mid-1920 did the Armenian government disclose the fact that it had been able to decipher the messages. Since Azerbaijan had been Sovietized by that time and the code was no longer in use, the Armenian Ministry of Foreign Affairs published the wires of Khan Tekinskii and other Azerbaijani officials under the title, *Gaghtni pastatghtere: Adrbedjani davadrakan gordsuneutiunits mi edj* (Erevan, 1920), cited hereafter as *Adrbedjani pastatghtere*. British intelligence officers in the Caucasus verified the authenticity of the dispatches, some of which are also included in Britain, WO 33/965, and FO 371/3659, 131563/512/58.

May 3. Then divulging the ominous news that the British authorities had ordered the expulsion of all Azerbaijani officials from Nakhichevan, Khan Tekinskii inquired whether his government would make troops available, if only under the guise of volunteers, should the Muslim population take arms.[39]

The diplomat's channels apparently reached far up into the Armenian administration, for he had considerable knowledge of the private consultations between Khatisian, Milne, and Thomson on April 30. In order not to alert the Erevan government to his tapping of guarded state secrets, Tekinskii deemed it imprudent that he personally protest the British decision regarding Nakhichevan before it had been made public. Consequently, he urged the Azerbaijani Foreign Minister to enter into direct conversations with the two English generals, who were then en route back to Tiflis. When, as he had forewarned, an Armenian column began the advance on May 3, Khan Tekinskii implored his government to concentrate troops on the borders of Armenia. He gave assurances that the people of Nakhichevan were prepared to resist but, out of fear of the British, were waiting for Azerbaijan to beckon.[40]

It was undoubtedly with extreme distress that Tekinskii read Acting Foreign Minister Adil Khan Ziatkhanov's wire from Baku, dated May 5, 1919, stating that the Azerbaijani army could not intervene for the present but that the government had taken the question under advisement and would issue vigorous protests against the scheme to wrench Nakhichevan from its fatherland, the Republic of Azerbaijan. Four days later, on May 9, Tekinskii reported that Armenian troops had concentrated at Davalu in the southern reaches of the Erevan uezd but had not as yet penetrated into Sharur, where Muslim irregulars armed with machine guns stood in readiness. He was concerned that no news had come from the Azerbaijani military attaché operating in those districts. On the fourteenth, in words of desperation, Khan Tekinskii exclaimed that the Armenian seizure of all Nakhichevan was imminent. With undisguised sarcasm he asked whether Azerbaijan was at all interested in the fate of the region. Ziatkhanov's reply on May 18 disclosed that "certain existing circumstances" prevented the government from providing direct military assistance but Azerbaijan would be deeply gratified were the native inhabitants to stand tenaciously against the Armenian aggressors.[41]

[39] *Adrbedjani pastatghtere*, pp. 17–20, Tekinskii's nos. 6, 10, 60, 71, 72.
[40] *Ibid.*, pp. 21–22, Tekinskii's nos. 74, 82, 83.
[41] *Ibid.*, pp. 22–24, Ziatkhanov's nos. 36, 38, and Tekinskii's nos. 92, 98.

The Armenian Occupation of Sharur-Nakhichevan

As Tekinskii exchanged communiqués with Jafarov and Ziatkhanov and as the Azerbaijani government addressed protests to British headquarters and to the Paris Peace Conference, Dro gave the order for his men to move out from Khamarlu. The arrangement to extend Armenia's jurisdiction over Nakhichevan was made public on May 3 in a declaration signed by Dro and witnessed by General Davie. "The War is finished," it began; "sufferings and torture of the people must come to an end." By decision of the Allies and the Armenian government, components of the Erevan detachment, headed by Dro, were to proceed to Nakhichevan to secure peaceful conditions for all inhabitants. Dro demanded unwavering discipline from his men: "I address you, troops under my command. You are representatives of the Government. You must protect life and property of all citizens of the Republic without distinction of nationality." Field courts martial, he warned, would deal harshly with brigands, unit commanders would be held personally responsible for any breach of order, and every officer, soldier, or militiaman who attempted to incite one segment of the population against the other would be shot forthwith. "Remember that our State is called the Republic of Armenia, that is, republic of all the people inhabiting Armenia." Then directing his words to the civilian population, Dro continued: "I address you as well, inhabitants of Nakhichevan. I have come with my troops to Nakhichevan by order of my Government and of the Allies to bring back to their homes both Armenian and Mohammedan refugees. All land illegally seized on the territory of our republic must be returned to their original owners. All citizens, be they Armenians or Tartars, who dare to resist this legal desire of the working people will be punished summarily. Villages which resist will be declared beyond the law and subjected to fire and iron." [42]

This formality completed, Dro coordinated the advance of General Shelkovnikov's regulars and the Turkish Armenian partisans led by Mushegh Avetisian's mounted Sassun squadron. Passing through the Muslim villages south of Khamarlu, the offensive column was greeted by the Armenian enclave at Davalu with bread and salt, the traditional symbol of welcome. [43] But there the operation faltered. General Thom-

[42] This English translation is taken from US Archives, RG 256, 184.021/15. For the more precise text in Armenian and in Russian, see Rep. of Arm. Archives, File 66a/3; and *Kavkazskoe slovo* (Tiflis), May 3, 1919. See also *Bor'ba*, May 4, 1919, p. 2.

[43] Vratzian, *Hanrapetutiun*, pp. 222-223.

son, clearly irritated by what he could regard only as a severe breach of faith, wired Davie to halt the repatriation, using armed force if necessary. Digby I. Shuttleworth, the General Officer Commanding, Baku Command, had just sent word of renewed Armenian defiance in Zangezur, incited by Shahmazian and other agents secretly linked with Erevan. Not until that collusion had been abandoned was the Nakhichevan repatriation to resume.[44]

Thomson's pointed directive jeopardized the carefully laid plan to extend the Republic's boundaries southward. Khatisian angrily protested to General Davie that he had no control over the actions of the Regional Council in Zangezur. It was unreasonable to expect that the Armenian government could reverse by writ the determination of all Zangezur to withstand the alien rule of Azerbaijan. Davie, who had labored assiduously to ensure the success of the Nakhichevan project, required little persuasion and, in relaying Khatisian's explanation to Thomson on May 7, made clear his own view: "As regards the question of suspending the movement into the NAKHICHEVAN area, I most strongly represent that this will be fatal to our prestige and will have a disastrous effect on the situation amongst the TARTAR population not only in the NAKHICHEVAN but also in the KARS area. I beg that the repatriation and advance may be allowed to continue as arranged. If this be suspended it will affect, in addition to what I have said above, the refugees, the army and the very existence of the Armenian Govt. itself. I cannot urge this too strongly." [45]

The next day Davie and Khatisian hastened to Tiflis to plead their case. The Armenian leader assured General Thomson that his cabinet was not responsible for the state of affairs in Zangezur but would do all in its power to pacify the mountainous district. He would willingly assign an official to accompany Shuttleworth on that officer's next trip to Zangezur and would appeal for a local arrangement granting Tatar herdsmen the right to continue their annual migrations to summer pasture.[46] Sufficiently mollified by the afternoon of the ninth, Thomson rescinded the punitive decree, which if sustained might also have upset the timetable for the British withdrawal. Permission to resume the advance was wired to Dro.[47]

Khatisian and Davie returned to Erevan on May 12, having first de-

---

[44] Britain, WO 95/4880, 27th Division War Diary, and 95/4894, 82d Brigade War Diary, May, 1919, Appendix A, G 866.

[45] *Ibid.*, Appendix B, B.M. 153.

[46] It was during this interval that Prince Hovsep Arghutian was sent to Karabagh and Zangezur. See above, pp. 174-175.

[47] Britain, WO 95/4880.

toured from Alexandropol to Kars to assess the progress of the Armenian administration and of the British evacuation. On the following
day the two took governor-designate Gevorg Varshamian and his staff
aboard train, passed through General Shelkovnikov's column as it
now pressed into Sharur, and sped ahead to Nakhichevan.[48] The party
was met at the railway station by Colonel Simpson and a Rajput honor
guard and by Kalb Ali Khan Nakhichevanskii, the Arasdayan republic's war minister, a colonel formerly in the service of Russia and of
Great Britain, and the descendant and heir of the khans of Nakhichevan. When Davie announced that, by decision of the Great Powers,
Sharur and Nakhichevan were to be united temporarily to the Armenian republic, Kalb Ali Khan decried the injustice.[49] But soon the
tension slackened, as Nakhichevanskii assumed the role of host and,
feting the British and Armenian officials in his home, led the entourage to the county seat of government to confer with the local notables.

During the ensuing confrontation the Muslim spokesmen presented
their terms for a provisional settlement: there could be no Armenian
officials in Nakhichevan except for the civil governor, and the former
Armenian inhabitants could not return. Khatisian countered these
unacceptable demands with the explanation that there would be a
mixed administration and a Muslim assistant governor, that the Armenian military units would be strictly disciplined and employed
only to preserve order, and that the Muslims must recognize the right
of the Armenian refugees to repatriate and reclaim their properties.
The Acting Premier concluded with an appeal for "a new era of
friendly relations between the two neighboring peoples." There was,
in fact, a rather close resemblance between what Khatisian required
of the Muslims of Nakhichevan and what Dr. Sultanov was even then
demanding of the Armenians of Karabagh. The Muslim leaders were
incensed, but, subjected to Davie's frequent citation of "His Majesty's
Government," yielded to the seemingly inevitable.[50]

From Nakhichevan, Khatisian and Davie traveled southward all the
way to the frontier with Persia. This vital route to the outside world

[48] *Ibid.,* 95/4894, May, 1919, Appendix D, 82/G/95. Vratzian, *Hanrapetutiun,* p. 223,
states that Dro, too, accompanied Davie and Khatisian to Nakhichevan.

[49] When the declaration placing Nakhichevan under Armenian jurisdiction was first
published, Khan Nakhichevanskii petitioned Great Britain, through Davie, to
permit the district's reunification with Persia. See the 82d Brigade War Diary for
May, 1919.

[50] Khatisian, *Hanrapetutian zargatsume,* pp. 139-141. Khatisian has misdated this
episode May 18.

finally stood open to Armenia. At Julfa, Khatisian wired salutations to Persian Prime Minister Vosuq ed-Dowleh, who replied by extolling the traditional bonds between Armenia and Persia and welcoming the Republic of Armenia as a neighbor.[51] Khatisian returned to Erevan on May 16, leaving Governor Gevorg Varshamian to begin his prodigious duties. Four days later the first company of Armenian soldiers entered Nakhichevan.[52]

Thus, Davie had carried out his orders of April 4, 1919. The General Officer Commanding, Southern Command, made a final inspection of Nakhichevan on May 22 in company with General G. N. Cory, who, as the new chief of the British forces in Transcaucasia, instructed Colonel Simpson to prepare his battalion for withdrawal commencing on May 30. Cory broke his return journey at Erevan to inform Khatisian that only a military mission under Lieutenant (local Captain) F. L. Schwind would be retained at Nakhichevan.[53] Thereafter, the evacuation proceeded rapidly. Colonel Simpson and battalion headquarters departed from Nakhichevan on June 1. The rear guard left three days later and was joined en route at Bash-Norashen and Ararat station by the Rajput detachments that had kept the peace in several Muslim villages during the Armenian advance.[54]

All districts included in the Southern Command had been cleared of organized Imperial units by June 7, the day division headquarters informed General Davie that Lieutenant Colonel J. C. Plowden was arriving to replace him, but only in the capacity of British Military Representative, Erevan.[55] On the twelfth Davie officially introduced Plowden to Khatisian and paid a farewell visit to the Armenian government, which expressed deep-felt gratitude to the prime executor of the coups at Kars and at Sharur-Nakhichevan. Two days later, after Davie had arrived in Tiflis, General Cory ruled that the duties of the

---

[51] *Ibid.*, p. 141. Shortly thereafter, Persia and Armenia exchanged economic missions. See Rep. of Arm. Archives, File 66a/3.

[52] Vratzian, *Hanrapetutiun*, p. 223. In a report to division headquarters, General Davie made the following appraisal of Varshamian: "The man appears to me well suited for the appointment. He is 45 years of age, a man of the world and sympathetic to the Tartars. From what I could gather at NAKHICHEVAN I think that things will settle down quite quietly there in a short space of time."

[53] Schwind had headed Colonel Laughton's initial escort and had then proceeded with the platoon to Kars, where he took command of D Company, 4th Battalion Rifles. Schwind was officially notified of his appointment as British Military Representative, Nakhichevan, on May 15, 1919.

[54] Britain, WO 95/4891; US Archives, RG 59, 861.00/6583 and 867.00/1100.

[55] John Chichele Plowden had previously served as commander of the 2d Battalion, King's Shropshire Light Infantry Regiment, which was based at Batum and attached to the 80th Brigade.

General Officer Commanding, Southern Command, 27th Division, had been fulfilled and that the post was therefore terminated.[56] Headquarters would keep abreast of subsequent events in that area through the small missions placed at Nakhichevan, Erevan, Alaverdi, Kars, and Ardahan.[57]

The Repatriation

During the summer of 1919 thousands of refugees from Kars, Nakhichevan, Sharur, Surmalu, and the southern part of the Erevan uezd streamed back to their native villages. The painful task of beginning anew was welcomed by the refugees, most of whom disregarded government efforts to regulate the repatriation. Unable to stem this uncontrollable, sometimes disastrous movement, the government did provide what assistance it could. The Minister of Interior allocated a million rubles to stock food and supplies at stations along the routes of return, and a special committee of the legislature adopted the following interim measures: (1) the appointment of administrative commissars for each reoccupied village, district, and county; (2) the organization of a mounted militia of 100 to 200 men for each county; (3) the selection of officials to precede or accompany the refugees and arrange for their resettlement; (4) the establishment of roadside rest, food, and medical stations, not only to assist the refugees but also to keep them on the main roads in order to avoid any distasteful incidents; (5) the authorization for only native inhabitants to return initially and then, after it had been determined what vacant lands remained, the extension of this privilege to other refugees as well; (6) the appointment of individual parliamentary commissars, legislators native to each of the affected districts, to act as the highest authority during the repatriative operations.[58]

[56] Britain, WO 95/4894.

[57] The British Military Representative, Ardahan, began his duties on May 24 under the direct jurisdiction of Batum Military Governor Brigadier General W. J. N. Cooke-Collis. The company of 4th Brigade Rifles serving with Captain A. S. G. Douglas in the neutral zone between Armenia and Georgia was recalled on April 22, leaving Douglas at Alaverdi to continue his duties with a small escort. At Akhalkalak, which lay just beyond the area included in Davie's Southern Command, the company of Duke of Cornwall's Light Infantry withdrew at the beginning of May. On the seventeenth of that month Major R. Letters, who had been the acting commander of the 2d Battalion, Cameron Highlanders, from January 15 to April 3, departed from Tiflis to relieve Colonel Ritchie as British Military Representative, Akhalkalak. He was left with a small sepoy escort led by Lieutenant J. W. Dippie of the 1st Battalion, 67th Punjabi Regiment.

[58] Vratzian, *Hanrapetutiun*, pp. 223–224.

As exhilarating as the turn of events may have seemed to the Armenian government and people, the Republic still rested on precarious foundations. It would take years, perhaps decades, to restore the livestock, implements, fields, and villages to even their prewar level. And striking new roots in a land that had become a Muslim domain would be no easy task. The partial establishment of Armenian rule had been facilitated by the confusion that had beset the Muslim population, at times divided into rival groups of Turks, Tatars, and Kurds. Almost all were united, however, in irreconcilability to the alien Armenian government. Moreover, the return of Muslim refugees to the highlands of Erevan and Daralagiaz again rendered Armenia's southern flank ever so vulnerable. This repatriation, to which Khatisian and Dro had reluctantly assented in negotiations with Thomson and Davie, removed the Damoclean sword Armenia had held over Vedibasar, the Muslim stronghold below. With the sentry-like positions once more in friendly hands, the leaders of Vedibasar could venture to launch a sweeping rebellion in the lowland corridor between Erevan and Nakhichevan.[59]

As viewed in Baku the events of April and May, 1919, imperiled the fate of the Muslims of the Kars oblast and the Erevan guberniia and touched upon the vital interests of Azerbaijan. Nasib Bek Usubbekov's government was outraged by the revised state of affairs and sought effective countermeasures.[60] The departure of the small but awe-inspiring British contingents from both Kars and Nakhichevan gave reason to believe that the good fortune of Armenia would not endure for long. On June 4, 1919, Khan Tekinskii, informing his superiors of the British withdrawal from Nakhichevan, urged that all oil consignments to Armenia be suspended and that funds be provided for the now-united Muslim shuras of Sharur, Nakhichevan, and Ordubad. In reply Foreign Minister Jafarov promised the requested financial aid and commended the Azerbaijani envoy for his valiant dedicated

[59] Rep. of Arm. Archives, File 8/8; Ruben, op. cit., pp. 207–208. During the Armenian advance into Nakhichevan, the British command had rejected Dro's plan to occupy the Aralikh district in Surmalu. Shortly after Colonel Plowden arrived in Erevan, he recommended that the ban be lifted in view of the seditious activity in Surmalu, but General Cory reiterated Davie's contention that the Armenians already had their hands full and that the status quo should be preserved in that border area pending action by the Paris Peace Conference. See Britain, WO 95/4894, June, 1919, Appendix E, B.M.E. 2, and 95/4880, June 16, 1919.

[60] Examples of Azerbaijani protests against the Armenian annexations are in Bulletin d'Informations de l'Azerbaïdjan, no. 2 (Sept. 8, 1919), pp. 2–4, and no. 3 (Oct. 13, 1919), pp. 1–6.

service.[61] Throughout the following weeks Tekinskii continued to exhort the Baku government to strike at Armenia. On June 20 he relayed the disquieting news that Dro's troops had occupied many strategic points in Sharur and Nakhichevan. The shura of Nakhichevan, he reported, had petitioned the Allied Powers regarding Armenian brutality and had protested that, despite the solemn pledges of Khatisian and General Davie, many peaceful inhabitants were being disarmed and arrested. Khan Tekinskii expressed fear that Muslim resistance might crumble, for according to recent information only a force of three hundred partisans remained in the field. Armenia, he emphasized in his wire of June 22, was the sole veritable enemy of Azerbaijan. The honor and future of the nation summoned the Republic of Azerbaijan to rise to the challenge.[62]

By the end of its first year the Republic of Armenia had established nominal jurisdiction over the Kars oblast and the southern uezds of the Erevan guberniia. Largely as the result of the abrupt reversal in British policy, it seemed that the borders of the still-evolving state would encompass most of the geographic region that had become known as Russian Armenia. Technically, the southwestern and western limits of the Republic had now reached the Russo-Turkish frontier of 1914. Turkish Armenian refugees were already pressing into Surmalu and Kars, coming one step closer to the fulfillment of their obsessing fixation—to plough once again the soil of Van, Bitlis, Erzerum, and lands beyond. Whether the barriers between Russian Armenia and Turkish Armenia would be lifted was incumbent upon the decisions of the Paris Peace Conference and the actions of the Allied Powers.

[61] *Adrbedjani pastatghtere*, pp. 26–28, Tekinskii's nos. 129, 130, and Jafarov's no. 1599.
[62] *Ibid.*, pp. 28–31, Tekinskii's nos. 150, 151, 153, 184, 202.

9

Armenia at
the Peace Conference

Throughout the oppressive months of 1919, Armenian leaders anxiously awaited news that the Paris Peace Conference had at last resolved the destiny of their people. While often critical of the actions of the Allied commanders in the Caucasus, the Erevan government nonetheless believed that the victorious powers were committed to the creation of a free and united Armenian state. The question was not whether the nation would exist as an independent entity but rather how soon its definitive boundaries would be drawn and how extensive they would be. The Armenian world was delirious with visions of a resurrected fatherland.

Although the Republic of Armenia was isolated and ridden with tragedy at the end of the World War, a succession of messages from abroad augured a promising future. One such wire, relayed via Baku, read in part:

> The war is over. The Allies have triumphed. There is revolution in Germany. The peoples of Austria have declared independence. Belgium, France, Alsace, the Rhineland, Serbia, Rumania are evacuated. The British have taken Constantinople, Samson, Trebizond, Batum, Poti, Odessa. The Turks are to clear the Caucasus, which will then be occupied by the Allies, who will recognize the local governments. . . . The separation of Constantinople and Armenia from Turkey has already been decided. It is probable that your region [Russian Armenia] will be united with Turkish Armenia. The Armenians are recognized as belligerents and have been given a place at the Peace Conference. . . .[1]

[1] Vratzian, *Ughinerov*, V, 35–36.

Desideratum and Delegation

In receipt of several like communiqués and much new information imported by the Armenian mission which returned from Constantinople in late November, 1918, the legislature devoted several sessions to the selection of a delegation to the world peace conference and to the formulation of what it considered a realistic and equitable settlement. Among the deputies there were those who, uplifted by the Allied successes, looked forward to a redeemed homeland that would include the provinces of Erevan and Kars, the disputed districts of the Elisavetpol and Tiflis guberniias, and, from beyond the prewar boundary, the six vilayets of Turkish Armenia, the Trebizond vilayet along the Black Sea, and the region of Cilicia on the Mediterranean—Armenia from Sea to Sea.[2]

Somewhat less exuberant, the legislative majority resolved to seek only the unification of Russian Armenia and Turkish Armenia, with an outlet on the Black Sea and the protective guidance of a great power, preferably the United States of America. The question of Mediterranean ports, Cilicia, and the Trebizond vilayet was passed over in silence. A few officials, foremost of whom were Premier Kachaznuni and Ruben Ter-Minasian, a member of the Bureau of Dashnaktsutiun, considered even this goal to be illusive. Armenia, they contended, should be satisfied with the Russian and Turkish Armenian provinces and, instead of a coastline of her own, transit privileges to one or more ports on the Black Sea.[3]

On December 3, 1918, the Khorhurd named Avetis Aharonian to head Armenia's delegation to Paris. The eminent author, regarded as the melancholy and wrathful voice of national woes and retribution, had long been active in civic life. He had served as the chairman of the Armenian National Council when that body declared the independence of Armenia, and he had accepted the humiliating and delicate task of negotiating with the Ittihadist leaders in Constantinople.[4] With his experience, albeit limited, in international diplomacy and a knowledge of the French language, Aharonian seemed the logical person to

[2] Khatisian, *Hanrapetutian zargatsume*, p. 98; Vratzian, *Hanrapetutiun*, pp. 176–177.

[3] Khatisian, *Hanrapetutian zargatsume*, p. 97; Vratzian, *Ughinerov*, V, 44–45. Kachaznuni asserted that the Republic could be made viable with the inclusion of the historic Armenian provinces of Vaspurakan (Van), Taron (Mush), and Bardzr Haik (Erzerum), that is, only the eastern half of Turkish Armenia.

[4] For materials relating to Aharonian's activities in 1917–1918, see Rep. of Arm. Archives, File 74 and File 101/1; Hovannisian, *Road to Independence*, pp. 90, 217, 230–238.

represent the Republic in Paris. Though his candidacy was opposed by several of his own Dashnakist comrades, especially the younger radicals who considered him a romantic of mediocre ability, Aharonian received the overwhelming mandate of the Khorhurd. Designated second delegate, in order to reflect the coalitional nature of Armenia's government, was wealthy Populist leader Mikayel Papadjanian, a past member of the Russian State Duma, the Ozakom, the Armenain National Council, and the mission to Constantinople.[5] To complete the delegation, the legislature chose Hamazasp (Hamo) Ohandjanian, a minister in the former Transcaucasian Commissariat and a ranking Dashnakist, who was then in Switzerland establishing contact with Allied officials.[6] Tigran Mirzoyants, also a Dashnakist, joined the delegation as first secretary. The team was enlarged in the spring of 1919 when General Gabriel Korganian (Korganov), appointed military adviser, and Artem Piralian (Piralov), a Populist picked as an expert in statistics and economics, reached Paris. In addition, Aharonian coopted several technical assistants and secretaries from among his compatriots in Europe.[7]

Aharonian's official credentials, signed by Premier Hovhannes Kachaznuni and Foreign Minister Sirakan Tigranian on December 7, 1918, read in part: "The delegation is commissioned to represent the government of the Republic and to participate in all conferences and conventions taking place in Europe and America. It is empowered to sign treaties, conventions, and other official acts pertaining to all matters for which the present mandate is conferred." Because there existed no channels of direct communication between Erevan and Paris and because dispatches entrusted to couriers would be long in reaching their destination, Aharonian was granted broad prerogatives. Without further recourse to the cabinet or legislature, he could vest part or all of his authority in other members of the delegation, and he could create commissions for specific assignments away from Paris.[8]

From the day of his return from Constantinople to Erevan, Aharonian had emphasized the immediate need for official representation in Paris, yet the Republic's delegation was repeatedly delayed en route. It departed promptly on December 8, 1918, but was unable to proceed beyond Karakilisa because of the crisis in Lori, which was turning

[5] Khatisian, *Hanrapetutian zargatsume*, p. 98; Vratzian, *Ughinerov*, V, 44, 46.

[6] Documents and reports relating to Ohandjanian's activities in Germany, Austria, and Switzerland are included in Rep. of Arm. Archives, File 100/1 and File 101/2.

[7] Papers relating to these appointments are in Rep. of Arm. Archives, File 230/129.

[8] Rep. of Arm. Archives, File 11/11, *Hayastani Hanrapetutiun, 1920 t.*, Credentials.

into the Armeno-Georgian war. Forced to detour via Dilijan and Ak-stafa, the party ultimately arrived in Tiflis on December 18, having expended ten days to complete the first leg of the journey, a distance of scarcely 200 miles. It was then detained by the Georgian government, which actually arrested Mirzoyants and refused transit privileges to any Armenian group at a time when Dro's troops were marching toward the Khram River. Aharonian appealed to Major General William H. Rycroft, but the British officer sustained Georgia's position, reiterating that as long as the war continued the Armenian spokesmen would be held hostage in Tiflis. When the Allied-imposed truce ended the two-week war, Aharonian was still denied the necessary passage documents until Brigadier General W. J. N. Cooke-Collis, the military governor of Batum, apparently interceded in his behalf.[9] Finally, on January 9, 1919, after three weeks in the Georgian capital, the delegation entrained for Batum, whence Aharonian, Mirzoyants, and Mesdames Aharonian and Ohandjanian embarked for Constantinople.[10] To the ire of officials in Erevan, Papadjanian stayed behind in order to attend to family business in Tiflis and Baku. He was then kept waiting until May by the unexplained reluctance of the British authorities to issue travel papers.[11]

The delegation reached Constantinople on January 13, 1919, and remained there a week before it was able to secure passage to Marseilles. The enthusiastic reception accorded Aharonian by the survivors of the Turkish Armenian holocaust deeply touched the distinguished envoy. A few months earlier, when he had come to Constantinople as a supplicant, these people had been afraid to reveal themselves. But now, with Allied warships anchored in the Bosporus, Aharonian could meet freely with the remnants of what had once been the impressive center of the Western Armenian cultural renaissance.[12]

[9] A. Aharonian, "Mi kani jshdumner," *Hairenik Amsagir*, I (Oct., 1923), 80–81; Rep. of Arm. Archives, File 333/3.

[10] Several years later Aharonian was accused of having lost valuable time by waiting in Tiflis to secure a visa for his wife. See A. Babalian, *Edjer Hayastani ankakhutian patmutiunits* (Cairo, 1959), pp. 34–35. (Reprinted from a series in *Hairenik Amsagir,* Vol. I.) For the refutation of this and other charges leveled at him, see Aharonian, *op. cit.*, pp. 79–81.

[11] Correspondence regarding this delay is in Rep. of Arm. Archives, File 230/129, nos. 108, 144, 145; File 319/1, *H. H. Patvirakutiun ev Fransiakan Karavarutiune, 1919,* Communiqué of April 4, 1919, and File 333/3, Communiqué of April 16, 1919; Britain, FO 371/3658, 60618/81546/512/58, and FO 608/94, 361/1/2/3910/4570/6533/11531. According to *Bor'ba*, May 3, 1919, p. 4, Papadjanian departed for Europe on April 30.

[12] *Jakatamart* (Constantinople), Jan. 14, 1919. For an account of Aharonian's reception and activities in Constantinople, see Vahram H. Torgomian, "Hushatetres," *Vem,* VI, 1 (1938), 57–59.

In his official capacity Aharonian conferred with Ferdinand Tahta-djian, Armenia's minister plenipotentiary, Lewis Heck, the recently appointed United States Commissioner in Constantinople,[13] Thomas B. Hohler, the British minister plenipotentiary and Vice Admiral Gough-Calthorpe, the British High Commissioner.[14] Aharonian described the catastrophic conditions prevailing in Armenia and explained that wheat was selling for more than 4 rubles a pound in Erevan as compared with a half ruble in the North Caucasus and South Russia. He implored the British, who had both men and vessels available, to expedite the purchase of the low-priced grain in the north and undertake its shipment to starving Armenia. The Allied representatives could do no more than relay the appeal to Washington and to London.[15]

Aharonian sailed through the Dardanelles on January 20 and, after

[13] Lewis Heck, formerly Deputy Consul General at Constantinople, received instructions on November 30, 1918, to return to the Ottoman capital as United States Commissioner. This was not a move by the United States to resume diplomatic relations with Turkey, however, as Heck was specifically told that all diplomatic matters should remain with the Swedish legation, which had represented American interests since the rupture of Turkish-American relations in April of 1917. Following his arrival on December 27, 1918, Heck frequently relayed to Paris and Washington the cables and reports of American officials in the Caucasus and the interior vilayets of the Ottoman Empire. In April of 1919 he returned home on sick leave and was then assigned to the Near Eastern Division of the Department of State. In Constantinople, Gabriel Bie Ravndal, former United States Consul General there, reopened his offices in March and also assumed Heck's vacant post in May, 1919. See US Archives, RG 59, *United States Consular Officers by Post, 1789–1939*, Consular Post, Constantinople. See also Henry P. Beers, *U.S. Naval Detachment in Turkish Waters, 1919–1924* (Washington, D.C., 1943), pp. 2, 5–6.

[14] On November 9, 1918, the Foreign Office instructed Calthorpe to serve as High Commissioner, with the immediate goal of ensuring the execution of the Mudros Armistice. In the capacity of High Commissioner, Calthorpe was to be responsible to the Foreign Office, but this assignment, he was told, should not interfere with his regular obligations to the Admiralty. Rear Admiral Richard Webb was appointed Assistant High Commissioner to represent Calthorpe during his absences on duty or on leave from Constantinople. See Britain, Cab 27/37, E.C. 2416. On November 11 the Foreign Office cabled Calthorpe:

You will see from instructions which will reach you by Admiral Webb that we have no wish whatever to minimize the defeat and capitulation of the Turks. On the contrary in the interests of the future of the Near East we are determined that Turkish domination over subject races shall irrevocably be ended. It is best that the Turks should realize from the outset that these are the terms we intend to impose. . . .

You will see from the above that we wish you to observe the strictest reserve in your relations with the Turkish Government and to refuse to be drawn into any discussion as to the eventual peace settlement.

See Cab 27/36, E.C. 2333. Calthorpe sailed into Constantinople with the Allied armada on November 13, 1918.

[15] Rep. of Arm. Archives, File 230/129, nos. 33–34. See also US Archives, RG 256, 867B.48/1; Britain, FO 371/3659, 9745/12425/512/58.

a rough eleven-day voyage over the Mediterranean, went ashore to a festive welcome by the Armenian colony of Marseilles. On February 4, 1919, at long last, he detrained in Paris, a full two months after having been designated President of the Delegation of the Republic of Armenia.[16]

Exclusion from the Peace Conference

During the weeks that Aharonian was journeying from Erevan to Paris, the Allied governments made final arrangements for the Peace Conference, and newspapers carried feature articles on the delegations and personalities who were to attend. To the indignation of countless Armenophiles, the Republic of Armenia was not included on the list of delegations. The question of membership had posed a troublesome problem to the major powers and had been the subject of numerous dispatches between Paris, London, and Washington. In a memorandum prepared in November, 1918, American technical adviser David Hunter Miller counseled that until the situation in Russia improved "it would seem impracticable to admit formally to the Peace Congress any representative, either of Russia as a whole or of any of its nationalities which may have attempted to set up national governments." He expressed the opinion that "national groups not forming states, such as the Armenians, the Jews of Palestine, and the Arabs, would doubtless be received and heard through their representatives by Committees of the Congress, but could not be admitted to the Congress as member powers." [17] This same view was repeated by Miller and his colleague, James B. Scott, as part of a skeleton draft treaty that they submitted to Secretary of State Robert F. Lansing on December 30, 1918. In it they conceded that Finland and Poland, former Romanov domains, could be admitted, yet even though "the separate kingdom of Hedjaz has to some extent been recognized by Great Britain, and independence is claimed for Armenia," there was no need to include either as member nations.[18]

The ultimate decision on membership was made by the ranking Allied heads of government, who met in January, 1919, and determined

[16] Rep. of Arm. Archives, File 230/129, no. 40. Aharonian's reception and speeches in Marseilles are described in *Hairenik* (daily), Feb. 27, 1919, p. 1, and March 2, p. 1.

[17] *Paris Peace Conference*, I (1942), 362–363, and, for material on the question of membership, 223–281. A slightly different wording of the memorandum is given by Miller, *Documents*, II (1924), 56: "Some national groups without state governments, such as Armenians, Jews in Palestine, and Arabs, may be heard by committees of the Congress, but cannot be admitted as member powers."

[18] *Paris Peace Conference*, I, 312.

that only the victorious belligerents and those states that had broken relations with the Central Powers would be seated, while neutral countries would be heard in a limited capacity. The inclusion of the Imperial Dominions and India assured Great Britain a bloc of votes, just as the membership of a number of Central and South American states ("theoretical belligerents") guaranteed the United States a pervasive influence. Czecho-Slovakia, Poland, and the Hejaz, none independent at the beginning of World War I, were also seated, as was the new entity of Yugo-Slavia.[19] The admission of the Hejaz was founded upon strong British support. No power interceded on behalf of Armenia.

Still, the question of Armenia's status remained muddled even as the Peace Conference opened. The French newspaper *Matin* reported that the Allies had placed the Armenians in the same category as Poles and Czechs, peoples granted official representation. Mikayel Varandian, a Dashnakist intellectual prominent in European socialist circles, wrote Hamo Ohandjanian on January 22 that French President Raymond Poincaré had given assurances that the Armenians, Poles, and Czechs would be seated; furthermore, several British journals had recently listed Armenia on the roster of delegations.[20] Such fictive hopes notwithstanding, Armenia was excluded from the Peace Conference when the first plenary session convened on January 18, 1919.[21] The Allied position was perhaps best expressed by President Woodrow Wilson, stating that "on every hand among the delegates to the Peace Conference, I find the most sincere and outspoken sympathy with the Armenians," but that, regretfully, it was "technically very difficult to assign representatives to political units which have not yet been received into the family of nations." Armenia's cause, Wilson was quick

---

[19] For material on the organization and preliminaries of the Peace Conference, see Ray Stannard Baker, *Woodrow Wilson and the World Settlement* (3 vols.; Garden City, N.Y., 1923), I, 97–209; Seth P. Tillman, *Anglo-American Relations at the Peace Conference of 1919* (Princeton, 1961), pp. 69–85; Miller, *Documents*, Vols. I–II; *Paris Peace Conference*, I, 119 ff., and III (1943), 1–90. The composition and personnel of the individual bodies of the Peace Conference, as they existed in April, 1919, is given by Miller, I (1924), 377–499.

[20] Rep. of Arm. Archives, File 101/2, Varandian to Ohandjanian, Jan. 14 and 22, 1919. Negotiations among the major powers on the question of membership and the number of places to be given the various delegations continued until the eve of the opening of the Peace Conference. See Charles T. Thompson, *The Peace Conference Day by Day* (New York, 1920), pp. 112–113, 115–117.

[21] That the proceedings of the Peace Conference were dominated by the leaders of the great powers alone is reflected in the fact that only seven plenary sessions were held, and these were either ceremonial in nature or summoned to ratify the decisions and acts of the inner, select circle.

to add, would be advanced with such dedication that it would be tantamount to having Armenian delegates actually seated in the chambers.[22] Such arguments were rejected by Armenophile societies as well as by thousands of aroused private citizens and public officials who failed to understand the grounds on which Czechs, Poles, and Arabs could be seated while a people that had sacrificed half its numbers was being denied a place at the Peace Conference.[23]

Two Armenian Delegations

The arrival of Aharonian's delegation in Paris complicated the Armenian scene, for another deputation, the Armenian National Delegation, was already at work there under the leadership of Boghos Nubar Pasha, son of a finance and foreign minister of Egypt and himself once the director of the Egyptian State Railways. Nubar was a polished Levantine gentleman, fluent in French, wealthy and conservative, and well known to the European diplomatic corps.[24] In 1912, at the close of the First Balkan War, he had been appointed by the Supreme Patriarch, Catholicos Gevorg V, as a special envoy to the European Powers in hopes of persuading them to coerce the Ottoman government to promulgate effective reforms in the Turkish Armenian vilayets. In London and Paris, Nubar was joined by several prominent Turkish Armenian intellectuals and clergymen in what became known as the National Delegation. At the beginning of 1914 those representatives and all politically aware Armenians were gratified by the eventual compromise reform measure that pointed the way to the solution of many Turkish Armenian grievances. When World War I swept away the reform together with most Turkish Armenians, the National Delegation redirected its energies, laboring to win an Allied commitment to

[22] *New Armenia*, XI (April, 1919), 63. See also *Hairenik* (daily), March 27, 1919, p. 2.

[23] Numerous appeals and petitions urging Armenia's admission to the Peace Conference are deposited in US Archives, RG 256, File 867B and File 183.9 *Armenia;* and Britain, FO 371, File 512/58. See also Camille Mauclair, ed., *Pour l'Arménie libre* (Paris, 1919); *Hairenik* (daily), Jan.–March, 1919; London *Times*, Jan. 30, 1919, p. 6; *Christian Science Monitor*, Jan. 23, 1919, p. 2, and Jan. 30, p. 1.

[24] For information on the Nubarian family, particularly Boghos Nubar and his father Nubar, see Vahan G. Zardarian, comp., *Hishatakaran, 1512–1912*, Vol. II (Constantinople, 1911), pp. 277–296, and *Hishatakaran, 1512–1933*, n.s., Vol. III (Cairo, 1934), pp. 47–81; *Encyclopaedia of Islam*, Vol. III (Leiden, 1936), pp. 946–948; Ervand Otian, *Poghos Pasha Nupar* (Constantinople, 1913); A. Terzipashian, *Nupar* (Paris, 1939), pp. 245 ff.

free the Armenian provinces from Ottoman bondage.[25] It was largely on Boghos Nubar's initiative that the Légion d'Orient, an Armenian volunteer corps, was organized to serve under the French colors. The Legion participated in several major campaigns in Palestine and Syria and, at the end of the war, occupied strategic sites in Cilicia.[26] Nubar also lent support from afar to Catholicos Gevorg's personal envoy to the United States, Garegin Pasdermadjian (Armen Garo), in the latter's attempts to obtain American aid for the Armenian forces holding the Caucasus front in 1918.[27] Both spokesmen petitioned that, once the war was over, the United States of America take their people under its protection.[28]

During the latter part of 1918 Boghos Nubar redoubled efforts to secure the status of belligerent for the Armenians so that they would be assured a place in the forthcoming peace conference. On October 25 he made formal application to that end;[29] and on November 30 he declared, in the name of the Armenian people, the unification of all historic Armenian territories.[30] In addition, to give his delegation a broader popular mandate and to facilitate deliberations on certain issues affecting the future of the nation, Nubar summoned an all-Armenian congress, which, as it happened, assembled in Paris shortly after Aharonian's arrival.[31]

[25] For material on the formation and activities of the National Delegation, see Rep. of Arm. Archives, File 241/140, *H. H. Patvirakutiun: Azgayin Patvirakutiun*, and File 295/2, *H. H. P.—Azgayin Patvirakutiun, 1918*; Leo [A. Babakhanian], *Tiurkahai heghapokhutian gaghaparabanutiune*, Vol. II (Paris, 1935), pp. 88–89, 197–198, 204, 207–208; D. Ananun, *Rusahayeri hasarakakan zargatsume*, Vol. III (Venice, 1926), pp. 523–525.

[26] Documents and materials relating to the Légion d'Orient are included in Rep. of Arm. Archives, File 1/1, File 241/140, and File 504, *Azgayin Miutiun Kilikio ev Siurio, 1919–1924;* Britain, FO 608/271, Eastern Mission, File 5. For accounts of the postwar activities of the Legion in Cilicia, see R. de Gontaut-Biron, *Comment la France s'est installée en Syrie (1918–1919)* (Paris, 1922), pp. 53–57, 97–99, 213–221; Tigran Boyajian, *Haikakan Legeone* (Boston, 1965); E. Brémond, *La Cilicie en 1919–1920* (Paris, 1921); Britain, FO 608/83, File 342/8/2.

[27] US Archives, RG 59, 867.22/24; Rep. of Arm. Archives, File 379/1.

[28] United States, Department of State, *Papers Relating to the Foreign Relations of the United States, 1917*, Supplement 2: *The World War* (2 vols.; Washington, D.C., 1932), I, 791–795; Rep. of Arm. Archives, File 380/2.

[29] United States, Department of State, *Papers Relating to the Foreign Relations of the United States, 1918*, Supplement 1: *The World War* (2 vols.; Washington, D.C., 1933), I, 894–895, cited hereafter as *US Papers, 1918*. See also US Archives, RG 256, 867B.00/302; Rep. of Arm. Archives, File 379/1.

[30] Britain, FO 406/41, no. 198498. The full text of Nubar's declaration is given by André N. Mandelstam, *La Société des Nations et les Puissances devant le Problème Arménien* (Paris, 1926), pp. 58–59. See also *New York Times*, Jan. 2, 1919, p. 2.

[31] *Hairenik* (daily), Feb. 4, 1919, p. 1. The National Congress is discussed in chapter 14 below.

Boghos Nubar, like so many others in the Armenian dispersion, lacked confidence in the Republic of Armenia. That small state had, after all, emerged in the eastern extremities of the Armenian plateau, on lands only partially re-Armenianized during the preceding several decades. The traditional Armenia, the focus of nineteenth-century reform and revolutionary movements, lay to the west in Turkish Armenia. Moreover, the Republic of Armenia was located entirely within former Romanov domains and could not possibly extricate itself from issues pertaining to all Russia. To bind the future of Armenia to the solution of the acutely complicated Russian question would obviously not benefit the Armenian people. Ideological and personality factors also influenced Nubar's attitude. The dominant party in the Erevan government was Dashnaktsutiun, revolutionary and socialist. Nubar had use for neither revolution nor socialism, while the chairman of the Republic's mission, Avetis Aharonian, seemed to epitomize both. There was no need for a second delegation in Paris, a delegation led by a highly independent, sometimes disdainful, author.

The presence of two Armenian delegations did indeed portend division and dissension, especially as their goals were not identical. Aharonian had instructions to advance the Republic's claims to the six eastern vilayets with a corridor to the Black Sea, whereas Boghos Nubar, together with most Armenians in the diaspora, sought much more. Nubar could not but regard the limited objectives of the Erevan government as treacherous folly. He insisted that the "Araratian republic" dissolve itself and merge into an Armenia extending from Caucasia to Cilicia. Nubar's chagrin over the Republic's failure to demand Cilicia and the Mediterranean seaports for Armenia was shared by many other leaders. Archbishop Eghishe Turian, scholar and for a time Patriarch of Constantinople, aptly expressed the sentiment of nearly all surviving Turkish Armenians in declaring that without Cilicia there could never be a viable Armenian state. Possession of Cilicia, a land bountiful in natural resources and agriculture, an Armenian population and cultural center, the locus of a medieval Armenian kingdom, would enable the new Armenian nation to face westward. And it was upon the West that the realization of so many national aspirations rested.[32]

In professing to represent all Turkish Armenians, regardless of religious denomination and political inclination, Boghos Nubar was in large part justified, at least during the months immediately following

[32] Rep. of Arm. Archives, File 241/140.

the war. Though opposed to Dashnaktsutiun, he had intimate acquaintances and associates within that party, including such noted figures as Mikayel Varandian, Garegin Pasdermadjian, and Hamo Ohandjanian. Dashnakist leaders throughout the dispersion found themselves in a quandary, for while loyal to the Republic of Armenia they held goals no different from those of Boghos Nubar. Turkish Armenians of Dashnakist persuasion did not disguise their support for the basic program of Nubar Pasha and the National Delegation.

Responsible men on both sides, recognizing that a conflict between the two delegations would be fraught with potential disaster, probed for a modus vivendi. Turkish Armenian Dashnakists in Paris urged Aharonian not to omit a valid claim to thousands of square miles of "historic Armenian territory." Such arguments were forceful, for there was convincing evidence that both the United States and Great Britain favored the formation of an Armenian state having a Mediterranean coastline. Avetis Aharonian succumbed to the euphoria that had settled over the Armenophile world. Unable to communicate expeditiously with Erevan, he stretched the prerogatives vested in him and altered the Khorhurd's guidelines of December to make them conform with the general aims of the National Delegation. He and Boghos Nubar also agreed that henceforth the two delegations, while preserving their individual identities, would unite on all fundamental issues as the "Delegation of Integral Armenia," with Nubar representing the Turkish Armenians primarily and Aharonian the Russian Armenians and the Republic of Armenia.[33] In this manner the two leaders, dissimilar in character and never on close personal terms, reached a working arrangement. But it was Aharonian who had yielded. Still relatively inexperienced in European politics, he had submitted to the direction of a man who moved with confidence in continental diplomatic circles, who was acknowledged as a reputable Armenian spokesman by Allied officials, and who presumably was best qualified to judge the disposition of the victorious powers.

[33] This arrangement has not been clearly understood by one recent historian who has accepted a misleading account that Boghos Nubar was the President of the "All-Armenian Delegation." For an appraisal of the Armenian delegates by William L. Westermann, the American adviser on the Near East, see Peter Faradjian, "A Scholar Examines Our Paris Delegates," *Armenian Review*, IX (Spring, 1956), 79–84. Various other views are included in US Archives, RG 256, 867B.oo/81/84/85; E. J. Dillon, *The Inside Story of the Peace Conference* (New York and London, [1920]), p. 86; *Le Petit Parisien* as reprinted by *Hairenik* (daily), April 1, 1919, p. 2; Abraham Mitrie Rihbany, *Wise Men from the East and from the West* (Boston and New York, [1922]), pp. 204–205.

Armenia in the Postwar Policy
of the United States

A study of the Allied proposals for peace would reveal that Boghos Nubar Pasha had good cause to admonish the Republic of Armenia to revise its objectives. Armenophiles on every continent, both in and out of government, were clamoring for a swift application of justice. None were more vocal than the Americans. The American Committee for the Independence of Armenia (ACIA), organized in 1918 and led by former ambassador to Germany James Watson Gerard, was not to be taken lightly, for among its ranks were Congressional leaders of both parties, more than twenty state governors, and a host of noted clergymen, industrialists, and philanthropists. The organization's members literally filled many pages of *Who's Who*.[34] In December, 1918, Henry Cabot Lodge, an official of ACIA, sponsored a Senate resolution advocating the establishment of an independent Armenian republic encompassing Russian Armenia, the six vilayets of Turkish Armenia, and even a district in North Persia claimed neither by the Armenian republic nor by the Armenian National Delegation.[35] President Wilson made no attempt to conceal his support for nearly every plank of the American Committee and endorsed unequivocally the concept of Armenian independence. The flow of Armenophile sentiment was synthesized by Senator William H. King: "Armenia must be freed from Turkish rule and receive the sympathetic support and protection of the Allied Powers until she has clothed herself with the habiliments of national authority and sovereign power. The Armenian people must be given their own lands, devastated and depopulated though they may be. Material as well as sympathetic aid must be extended in order that they may establish a strong virile and liberal republic." [36]

[34] The organization published a résumé of its labors under the title, *A Report of the Activities: The American Committee for the Independence of Armenia, 1918–1922* (New York, 1922), cited hereafter as *ACIA Activities*. Although, by intent, no Armenian American was invited to membership in the ACIA, Gerard and other prominent members of the organization were strongly influenced by Vahan Cardashian, a Yale graduate in law and Director of the Armenian Press Bureau, New York. Cardashian apparently penned many communiqués issued under the signatures of ACIA officers.

[35] *Congressional Record*, 65th Cong., 3d Sess., Vol. LVII, pt. 1 (Dec. 10, 1918), p. 237. The Persian district in question, lying between the Araxes River and Lake Urmia, had once been a part of the historic Armenian province of Vaspurakan.

[36] *New Armenia*, XI (Feb., 1919), 30–31. On February 13, 1919, King introduced Senate Resolution 454, which read:

Whereas the Armenian nation has for many centuries occupied certain regions

Aside from these public declarations and resolutions, the official guidelines of the United States demonstrated that Nubar's territorial aspirations, highly unrealistic by present-day standards, conformed closely with the then prevailing American policy. Far from a delirious mirage, an Armenia from sea to sea seemed a very real possibility. The United States Inquiry,[37] the corps of experts brought together at the President's behest to prepare recommendations for the postwar settlement, advised as early as December, 1917: "It is necessary to free the subject races of the Turkish Empire from oppression and misrule. This implies at the very least autonomy for Armenia and the protection of Palestine, Syria, Mesopotamia and Arabia by the civilized nations." [38] Shortly thereafter, in January, 1918, President Wilson delivered his celebrated Fourteen Points, the Twelfth of which called for "an absolutely unmolested opportunity of autonomous development" for the subject nationalities of the Ottoman Empire. He had intended to mention Armenia specifically but was dissuaded from being so precise by his trusted aide and confidant, Colonel Edward Mandell House.[39] Yet, in issuing an interpretive statement relative to the Fourteen Points, Inquiry Secretary Walter Lippmann and New York *World* editor Frank I. Cobb emphasized that Armenia should be assigned a "protecting power" and given a Mediterranean seaport.[40] This inter-

---

in Asia Minor, extending from Ararat to the Gulf of Alexandretta, including the southern littoral of the Black Sea, in the region of Trebizond; and

Whereas the Armenians are capable of self-government, and their common interests and aspirations make proper the erection of a national Armenian Government in said region: Now, therefore, be it

Resolved, That it is the sense of the Senate that Armenia be constituted a free and independent country, and that the Armenian people be permitted to erect therein a free national republic for the maintenance of their national rights and the perpetuation of their native language, culture, and traditions.

See *Journal of the Senate of the United States of America*, 65th Cong., 3d Sess. (Feb. 13, 1919), p. 148.

[37] For materials on the organization and activities of the Inquiry, see *Paris Peace Conference*, I, 9–200; Lawrence E. Gelfand, *The Inquiry: American Preparations for Peace, 1917–1919* (New Haven and London, 1963).

[38] *Paris Peace Conference*, I, 52. This memorandum is cited as Inquiry Document no. 887 by Lawrence Evans, *United States Policy and the Partition of Turkey, 1914–1924* (Baltimore, [1965]), p. 74.

[39] Evans, *op. cit.*, pp. 75–76.

[40] Charles Seymour, ed., *The Intimate Papers of Colonel House*, Vol. IV (Boston and New York [1928]), p. 129; *US Papers, 1918*, p. 412; Miller, *Documents*, II, 79. The pertinent paragraphs of the interpretive statement read as follows:

It is clear that the Straits and Constantinople, while they may remain nominally Turkish, should be under international control. This control may be collective or be in the hands of one Power as mandatory of the league.

Anatolia should be reserved for the Turks. The coast lands, where Greeks pre-

pretation indicated that Cilicia was to be included in the projected Armenian state, whether autonomous or fully independent.

In September, 1918, during the final phase of the war, the Department of State issued preliminary guidelines for use by the American Commission to Negotiate Peace. Two salient points read:

The Ottoman Empire to be reduced to Anatolia and have no possessions in Europe. (This requires consideration.)

Armenia and Syria to be erected into protectorates of such Government or Governments as seems expedient from domestic as well as an international point of view; the guaranty being that both countries be given self-government as soon as possible and that an "Open-Door" policy as to commerce and industrial development will be rigidly observed.[41]

William Linn Westermann, adviser on Western Asian affairs, subsequently elaborated on these points in his "Report on the Just and Practical Boundaries of the Turkish Empire." Self-determination was disallowed as the sole criterion for delineating boundaries in these lands; religious, economic, topographic, strategic, and linguistic factors were to be considered as well. Armenia, Westermann observed, probably should be a separate entity, and, were Armenia so established, Constantinople and the Straits should be internationalized. Inasmuch as the Armenians would form scarcely 35 percent of the population in their rather extensive state, strong external supervision would be essential.[42]

The Inquiry, having been reorganized in Paris as the Division of Territorial, Economic and Political Intelligence of the American Commission to Negotiate Peace, submitted comprehensive recommen-

dominate, should be under special international control, perhaps with Greece as mandatory.

Armenia must be given a port on the Mediterranean and a protecting power established. France may claim it, but the Armenians would prefer Great Britain.

[41] Robert Lansing, *The Peace Negotiations: A Personal Narrative* (Boston and New York, [1921]), pp. 195–196. Evans, *op. cit.*, p. 90, identifies this document as a private memorandum of Lansing entitled "The Essentials of Peace." The five American Commissioners subsequently named to attend the Paris Peace Conference were Woodrow Wilson, Robert F. Lansing, Colonel Edward M. House, General Tasker H. Bliss, the former Chief of Staff, and Henry White, a career diplomat who happened to be a Republican. Many historians have concluded that Wilson's difficulties with the Republican opposition in the Senate might have been considerably mitigated had he been willing to include in the delegation a prominent Republican leader such as Elihu Root or William Howard Taft, men who supported the basic outlines of the President's program for peace.

[42] Gelfand, *op. cit.*, pp. 248–249.

dations to President Wilson and the United States delegation on January 21, 1919. Points relative to Armenia were included under several headings. Under "Russia" the Intelligence advised that "encouragement be given" to the reunification of the border regions within a democratic federative Russian state but that "there be excepted from the general application of the principle above mentioned Finland, Poland, the Armenians of Transcaucasia, and probably Lithuania." These exceptions represented "nationalities whose severance from the Russian Empire would not destroy the Russian economic fabric, and would at the same time liberate peoples, who, because of historic oppressions and geographical position, would probably develop a stronger political and economic life if permitted to separate from the rest of the former Russian Empire." [43]

Under the heading "Transcaucasia" the American Intelligence recommended that "the Armenians of Transcaucasia be given permanent independence as a part of the new Armenian state." Within the Romanov Empire, they had constituted a peripheral group: "No local differences set them apart from their kinsmen in Turkey, and they should be reunited with the rest of the Armenian population in that region in order (1) to give the new state every reasonable element of strength; (2) to follow the principle of grouping in a common domain people of like religion, political sympathies and speech." By contrast, Georgia and Azerbaijan could conceivably receive "provisional" independence pending a clarification of the Russian problem and of their relationship to the permanently independent Armenian state.[44]

Constantinople and the Straits, the proposals continued, should be organized as an international zone, and an Anatolian Turkish state should be created away from the strategic waterways but extending no farther east than the Anti-Taurus Mountains. In these specific lands there lived "a solid block of Turkish Moslems," who as a sound Anatolian peasantry had a chance of "independent development." They would clearly benefit from being relieved of "the burden of governing alien peoples of different faith, whose oppression by the Turk has reacted upon him morally and politically, with well-known evil effects." [45]

And finally under the heading "Armenia" it was recommended that a separate country of that name be established and placed under the

[43] Miller, *Documents*, IV (1924), 219–220. See also US Archives, RG 256, 185.112/1 and 861.00/145.

[44] Miller, *Documents*, IV, 229–230.

[45] *Ibid.*, pp. 254–258.

guidance of a mandatory power serving on behalf of the League of Nations. The boundaries of the new state were clearly "fixed by nature," the Anti-Taurus Mountains in the west and the Taurus Mountains in the south being "topographical features of the first rank." Armenia would thus gather in the Cilician region with Adana and a Mediterranean outlet, Trebizond with its Black Sea harbors, and the six Turkish Armenian vilayets except for districts south of the Taurus and west of the Anti-Taurus. To these lands would be added the Russian Armenian provinces of Kars and Erevan and the counties of Akhaltsikh (not officially claimed by the Armenian republic) and Akhalkalak (see map 12). The Armenian problem, it was admitted, was "singularly difficult" since within the borders as delineated the Armenians were nearly everywhere a minority, constituting not more than 30 or 35 percent of the population. Consequently, a liberal interpretation of self-determination was required:

The principle of majorities should not apply in this case, because of the conditions under which the Armenian people have lived in the past. They have suffered from every handicap of nature and man; they have been massacred and deported by hundreds of thousands; they have been subject of international political intrigue; and at this moment, helpless and weak as they are, they are being pressed for the unfavorable settlement of their affairs by big Powers seeking to define spheres of future political and commercial interests. It would be a departure from the principle of fair dealing if at this time their every claim were not heard with patience, and their new state established under conditions that would in some manner right historic wrongs.[46]

The settlement outlined by the American experts and advisers differed little from the desideratum of Boghos Nubar Pasha and the most optimistic of Armenians.

Armenia in the Policy of Great Britain

The British guidelines for peace varied only in detail from the American plan. On more than one occasion Prime Minister David Lloyd George exclaimed that Armenia would never be restored "to the blast-

[46] *Ibid.*, pp. 259–260. The Western Asian Division of the American Commission to Negotiate Peace recommended that Karabagh and Alexandretta also be included in Armenia. It estimated that the population of the Armenian state would be, according to prewar statistics, 40 percent Armenian, 23 percent Turco-Tatar, and 20 percent Kurdish. See US Archives, RG 256, 867.00/31. See also 867B.00/8.

ing tyranny of the Turk." [47] Similar statements were made by Foreign Secretary Arthur James Balfour and by Assistant Foreign Secretary Lord E. A. Robert Cecil, who declared before Parliament "that we must not allow the misdeeds of the Turks to diminish the patrimony of the Armenians . . . that there ought to be no division of Armenia and that it ought to be treated as a single whole. . . ." [48] In January of 1917 the Allied governments defined one of their war aims as "the setting free of the populations subject to the tyranny of the Turks; and the turning out of Europe of the Ottoman Empire as decidedly foreign to Western civilisation." [49] A year later Lloyd George recited publicly that "Arabia, Armenia, Mesopotamia, Syria and Palestine are in our judgment entitled to a recognition of their separate national condition." [50] The Middle East objectives pronounced jointly by Great Britain and France on November 8, 1918, shortly after the capitulation of the Ottoman Empire, included "the complete and final emancipation of all those peoples so long oppressed by the Turks," and the establishment of "national governments and administrations which shall derive their authority from the initiative and free will of the peoples themselves." [51] This document merely affirmed what had been stated more effusively and eloquently in the halls of Parliament and in the Chamber of Deputies. The British viewpoint was summarized by Premier Lloyd George: "From the moment war was declared, there was not a British statesman of any party who did not have it in mind that if we succeeded in defeating this inhuman Empire, one essential condition of the peace we should impose was the redemption of the Armenian valleys forever from the bloody misrule with which they had been stained by the infamies of the Turk." [52]

During the closing weeks of 1918 the Foreign Office drafted tentative but definite suggestions for the Turkish settlement. In a memorandum circulated on November 21 the following observation was made:

[47] See, for example, Great Britain, Parliament, House of Commons, *Parliamentary Debates*, 5th ser., Vol. C (1917), col. 2220; David Lloyd George, *War Memoirs*, Vol. III (Boston, 1934), p. 64.

[48] House of Commons, *Parliamentary Debates*, 5th ser., Vol. CXC (1918), col. 3268. For similar pronouncements by Cecil, see *Current History*, IX, pt. 1 (Dec., 1918), 401, 402; *New Armenia*, X (Nov., 1918), 175.

[49] David Lloyd George, *Memoirs of the Peace Conference* (2 vols.; New Haven, 1939), II, 496, cited hereafter as *Conference Memoirs*.

[50] Carnegie Endowment for International Peace, *Official Statements of War Aims and Peace Proposals, December 1916 to November 1918* (Washington, D.C., 1921), p. 231.

[51] *Paris Peace Conference*, II, 274–275. Several sources and authors give either November 7 or November 9 as the date of this document.

[52] Lloyd George, *Conference Memoirs*, II, 811–812.

It would be expedient to extend the area of Armenia as widely as possible, so as to include all territories north of the boundary in which there is a mixed population of Turks, Armenians, and Kurds. . . . The principle of equality for all elements in the population is not disputed. On the other hand, in settling the proportional claims of these various elements to a voice in the government of the country, it should be laid down in Armenia that the dead and exiles should be taken into account, and Armenian immigrants from other parts of the world into Armenia should be given the same facilities as Jewish immigrants into Palestine for settling down in their ancestral home." [53]

The frontiers of Armenia as traced on an attached map extended from the Cilician shores northward along the Anti-Taurus Mountains to the Black Sea at a point just west of Ordu and from the Gulf of Alexandretta eastward along the Taurus Mountains, thus encompassing the six Armenian vilayets. The Karabagh district was circled and an accompanying explanation given: "There is a large Armenian population in the mountains, which preserved its liberty against Persia in the pre-Russian period, and has held out against the Turkish invader during the last few months. On historical grounds it should go to Armenia, but there is also a strong Azerbaijani element in the population, and the best permanent settlement might be to bring about a segregation of the Armenians and Azerbaijanis into separate areas by persuading the Karabagh Armenians to emigrate to the Erivan district and the Erivan Azerbaijanis to Karabagh." Along the line marking the proposed northeastern boundary of Armenia, the counties of Akhalkalak and Akhaltsikh fell on the Georgian side, even though, it was stated, they were populated primarily by the Armenian descendants of refugees from Turkey: "On the grounds of nationality, therefore, these districts ought to belong to Armenia, but they command the heart of Georgia strategically, and on the whole it would seem equitable to assign them to Georgia, and give their Armenian inhabitants the option of emigration into the wide territories assigned to the Armenians towards the south-west." [54]

These preliminary recommendations were put before the Eastern Committee of the British War Cabinet on December 2.[55] Earl (George

[53] Britain, Cab 27/37, E.C. 2525.

[54] *Ibid.*, Map 2 and notes. See also Cab 27/36, E.C. 2359. The district around Urfa was shown as being in question between the future Armenian and Arab states.

[55] In 1918 and at the beginning of 1919, the shaping of British policy regarding Armenia and the Caucasus devolved primarily upon three bodies: The War Cabinet, its Eastern Committee, and the Imperial War Cabinet. The War Cabinet, a compact group of from five to seven members, had been formed by Lloyd George in December, 1916, to respond more expeditiously to the numerous wartime issues. In March of 1918

Nathaniel) Curzon of Kedleston, the committee chairman, briefly reviewed the Armenian question as it had developed since 1878 and the contributory role of Great Britain in enabling the Ottoman government to circumvent its promises to enact effective Armenian reforms: "Those pledges on the part of the Turks, it is unnecessary to say, were never fulfilled; and those of us who have been in politics during the last quarter of a century remember well the Parliamentary troubles that arose out of the series of massacres of Armenians by the Turks that disfigured the years 1895 to 1897, that were repeated in the year 1909, and that culminated in, perhaps, the most atrocious crime of all, the practical extermination of the Armenians in many parts of the country in the second year of the war, 1915." During all that period, Curzon continued, the European Powers had done little more than address futile protests to the Sublime Porte. After the beginning of the World War, however, responsible British spokesmen had listed the liberation of the Armenians as one of the fixed aims of His Majesty's Government.[56]

Lord Curzon then outlined the ways in which the reconstitution of Armenia could serve the interests of the British Empire:

Now as to our general policy with regard to Armenia, I imagine that there can be little doubt, whether we look at it from the point of view of our pledges or of our political interest. We have to have an independent Armenia, an Armenia which, if not now, at some time in the future, and whether its boundaries are narrow or wide, shall be a self-

---

the War Cabinet organized the Eastern Committee to deal with questions relative to lands extending from the eastern shores of the Mediterranean to the borders of India. Lord Curzon chaired the Eastern Committee, among the membership of which were Foreign Secretary Balfour, Assistant Foreign Secretary Cecil, Lieutenant General Jan Christiaan Smuts of South Africa, Secretary of State for India Edwin Samuel Montagu, and Chief of the Imperial General Staff Sir Henry Hughes Wilson. The deliberations of the War Cabinet and the Eastern Committee spilled over into sessions of the Imperial War Cabinet, composed of the War Cabinet and representatives, usually the premiers, of the British Dominions and of India. The Imperial Cabinet sat frequently at the end of 1918 to plan British strategy for the Paris Peace Conference. Most of its membership then transferred to Paris as the British Empire Delegation. Since the Dominions and India had contributed heavily to the British war effort and since their army divisions would be required to serve in the occupation of any additional areas such as the Caucasus, the Imperial War Cabinet rightfully participated in formulating Great Britain's Eastern guidelines. See Richard H. Ullman, *Anglo-Soviet Relations, 1917–1921*, Vol. II: *Britain and the Russian Civil War, November 1918–February 1920* (Princeton, 1968), pp. 64–67. The minutes and papers of the Eastern Committee are included in Britain, Cab 27/24–39. The Committee was dissolved on January 10, 1919, after which Eastern policy became the purview of the periodically summoned Interdepartmental Conference on Middle Eastern Affairs, likewise chaired by Lord Curzon.

[56] Britain, Cab 27/24, Eastern Committee, 40th Minutes (Annex).

governing community. Our reasons for desiring that object are, it seems to me, three in number. In the first place, adopting the terminology which has become popular with regard to Palestine, we desire to provide a national home for the scattered peoples of the Armenian race. As long as they are diffused in helpless and hopeless minorities, in areas inhabited for the most part by the Kurds and Turks, every man's hand is raised against them, and any chance of settled life or autonomous existence cannot be said to exist. Secondly, we want to set up an Armenian State as a palisade, if I may use the metaphor, against the Pan-Turanian ambitions of the Turks, which may overflow the Caucasian regions and carry great peril to the countries of the Middle East and East. Thirdly, we want to constitute something like an effective barrier against the aggression—if not now, at any rate in the future—of any foreign Powers, impelled, by ambition or by other motives, to press forward in that direction. That, I think, is a fair statement of the reasons for which probably all of us here desire the erection of an independent Armenian State.[57]

The exhaustive discussion initiated by Curzon's lengthy remarks revealed that the several departments of government represented in the Eastern Committee concurred by and large in the desirability of an independent Armenia and in the absolute necessity to afford that country the guidance and protection of one of the Powers, conceivably France or the United States of America.[58]

Although some differences among the Cabinet Office, Foreign Office, War Office, and India Office remained to be worked out, Great Britain's basic postwar posture was officially set forth in a memorandum dated February 7, 1919. His Majesty's Government advocated the following eleven steps affecting the Turkish settlement:[59]

1. To detach the non-Turkish portions of the Ottoman Empire.

2. To sever, in addition, those lands where experience had shown that the security and autonomous development of the minorities could not be guaranteed under continued Turkish rule. This point applied to Armenia, where Turks and Kurds taken together formed a majority.

3. To qualify the principle of self-determination, in that Armenians

[57] *Ibid.*

[58] Sir Henry Wilson subsequently submitted a memorandum cautioning against the possibility of excessive French influence in the Middle East, particularly if all Armenia were to be placed under her direction. He therefore suggested that Russian Armenia and Turkish Armenia be treated as separate entities and that they not be allowed to unite. The Eastern Committee recognized that, by virtue of the Sykes-Picot Agreement of 1916, France had a rightful claim to prominence in much of Turkish Armenia. See Cab 27/24, Eastern Committee, 42d Minutes, and Cab 27/38, E.C. 2632.

[59] US Archives, RG 256, 185.513/14 and F.W. 867.00/480B. See also Harry N. Howard, *The King-Crane Commission* (Beirut, 1963), pp. 12–20. For a similar memorandum, dated February 18, 1919, see Britain, FO 608/83, 342/8/4/7442.

and Jews had "for historical reasons" claims to consideration out of proportion to their numbers.

4. To provide the detached regions the guidance of a mandatory power.

5. To maintain Anatolia as a Turkish state with its eastern borders fixed along a line where the solid Turkish element gave way to mixed Kurdish, Turkish, Greek, and Armenian populations. Thus, the north-south Samsun-Kaisaria-Selefke line would be included in Anatolian Turkey, whereas the Kerasund(Gerisun)-Sivas-Mersina line would not.

6. To organize a separate state beyond the Kerasund-Sivas-Mersina line, in the lands where the Ottoman government had been unwilling and unable to fulfill its obligations. The new country, roughly Cilicia and the six eastern vilayets, should be given its historic name, "Armenia."

7. To lay Armenia's boundaries in the south from Alexandretta on the Mediterranean Sea to Diarbekir and along the Tigris River to the Persian frontier; in the east, along the Persian border; and in the north, along the Black Sea to a point between Trebizond and Surmene. If the Armenian provinces of the Caucasus should be integrated into the new state, then the boundary would be fixed to encompass the districts of Olti, Kars, Alexandropol, Erevan, and Julfa (including Nakhichevan).

8. To place upon the Peace Conference the obligation to ensure tranquillity in Armenia and to assist in the nation's development. This stipulation was essential because, even before the massacres that had begun in 1895, the Armenians had been a minority in these lands taken as a whole and could therefore not organize as a homogeneous national unit.

9. To grant the Armenians, who were the only existing articulate element, the right to select the mandatory power most suitable to them. The mandatory should aid in Armenia's reconstruction, secure justice for all nationalities, and prepare the Armenians for the time when they would take full control of the administration. Because the Armenians were a prolific people and thousands of exiles would soon repatriate, it was anticipated that they would eventually establish a numerical superiority in their country.

10. To urge the Peace Conference to accord provisional recognition to the Armenian republic in Transcaucasia as well as to any other state established in the region without, however, prejudicing the will of the people if they should favor reunion or federation with Russia. In order to settle the discord between Armenia and Azerbaijan, the Armenian

population of Karabagh should be exchanged for the Muslim population of the Erevan guberniia.[60]

[60] During December, 1918 the Eastern Committee had held several long and charged sessions regarding a Caucasus policy, with Curzon and Montagu representing strongly opposed points of view. Curzon and other senior members of the Foreign Office considered the Caucasus as being pivotal to British interests in the East, whereas Secretary of State for India Montagu maintained that concern for the nebulous states between the Black and Caspian seas would be an extravagant waste. In a resolution the Eastern Committee adopted on December 16, Curzon made some attempt to reconcile the two positions but was frequently challenged by Montagu who had his dissent recorded on points that seemed to open the way to increased British involvement in the Caucasus. The thirteen-point resolution read:

1) We desire to see strong independent States—offshoots of the former Russian Empire—in the Caucasus.

2) Of these States Georgia is the most advanced and has the strongest claims to early recognition.

3) Recognition of the remaining States, viz., Daghestan, Azerbaijan, and Russian Armenia, must depend on the march of events and their successful assertion of an autonomous existence.

4) Whether Russian Armenia shall have a separate existence (as distinct from Turkish Armenia) will be determined in the main by the attitude of the people themselves.

5) Whether the independent States of the Caucasus combine hereafter in a Federation, or prefer to remain separate is a matter for their own determination.

6) Similarly their relations to the present or future Government or Governments of Russia is a matter that in the main concerns themselves.

7) If it is decided at the Peace Conference, either as a result of a request from the States, or at the instance of the League of Nations (should such be set up), that the services of a Great Power are required for a period to protect international interests in the areas concerned, the selection of America would be preferable to that of France, but is not in itself desirable. The selection of France would on broad grounds of policy and strategy be undesirable. Only in the last resort, and reluctantly if pressed to do so, might Great Britain provisionally accept this task.

8) In any case we have no intention of annexing any of these territories, or converting them into a British Protectorate, or of accepting any commitments which will involve the permanent maintenance of large British forces in the Caucasus.

9) It is important for the time being to maintain British naval control of the Caspian.

10) The ultimate settlement should provide if possible for the declaration as free ports of Batum, Poti, Trebizond, and Baku, and for free transit on the railway from Batum to Baku.

11) Special steps may require to be taken for the safeguarding of international interests in the city and oil fields of Baku.

12) In the reconstitution of Georgia, it will be desirable to include within its boundaries the Moslem Georgians of Batum and Lazistan.

13) If an independent Armenian State be constituted out of either the six Armenian vilayets or a smaller area, and if a Great Power be called upon either by the League of Nations, or by the people themselves, to act as protector to the new State, Great Britain should refrain from advancing claims, and should support the case either of America or France, preferably, in the interests of a revision of the Sykes-Picot Agreement of 1916, of France. See Cab 27/24, Eastern Committee, 43d Minutes; Cab 27/37, E.C. 2715A; and Cab 24/72, G.T. 6512. Montagu's dissenting memorandum is in Cab 24/72, G.T. 6329. See also Ullman, *op. cit.*, pp. 76–81.

11. To establish Batum and Poti as free ports and to guarantee free dom of transit to all points within Transcaucasia (see map 12).

The British memorandum demonstrated that London and Washington stood in general agreement regarding the future status and scope of Armenia. Already on January 29, 1919, soon after the Peace Conference had convened, the British Empire Delegation submitted a draft resolution recommending the total disengagement of Armenia from the Turkish Empire. The proposal was adopted the following day by the Supreme Allied Council, known also as the Council of Ten, the actual decision-making body composed of the heads of state and foreign ministers of the United States, Great Britain, France, and Italy and the former premier and foreign minister of Japan.[61]

Italy, Greece, and France

The Italians and even more emphatically the Greeks added their voices in support of Armenian aspirations. During the last months of the war a group of high-ranking Italian officials, including the mayor of Rome and former Premier Luigi Luzzatti, founded the Italian Committee for Armenian Independence.[62] In October, 1918, Foreign Minister Baron G. Sidney Sonnino wrote Boghos Nubar Pasha, "I assure your Excellency that the Royal Government will act with the utmost solicitude in safeguarding the interests of Armenia, whose sufferings have made a profound impression on us."[63] Then in a message to James Gerard of the American Committee for the Independence of Armenia, Sonnino confirmed "the sentiments of heartfelt sympathy with which the Royal Government follows the constant and noble efforts of Armenia for her independence and unity."[64] As World War I came to an end the Italian Chamber of Deputies adopted a resolution favoring Armenian independence, and on November 18, 1918, Premier Vittorio Emanuele Orlando exclaimed, "Say to the Armenians that I make their cause my cause."[65]

[61] *Paris Peace Conference*, III, 795, 805–808, 816. See also *Christian Science Monitor*, Jan. 16, Feb. 16, 24, 25, and May 3, 1919. The Council of Ten was composed of Georges Clemenceau, Stephen Pichon, David Lloyd George, Arthur Balfour, Vittorio Orlando, Sidney Sonnino, Woodrow Wilson, Robert Lansing, Marquis Kimmochi Saionji, and Baron Nobuaki Makino.

[62] London *Morning Post* as reprinted in *New Armenia*, X (Sept., 1918), 144.

[63] *Il Giornale d'Italia*, Oct. 4, 1918, as reprinted in *New Armenia*, X (Nov., 1918), 175.

[64] James W. Gerard, *England and France in Armenia* ([New York, 1920]), p. 2.

[65] Rep. of Arm. Archives, File 344/1, *H. H. Hromi Nerkayatsutschutiun ev Italakan Karavarutiune, 1918; New Armenia*, X (Dec., 1918), 191.

In Athens, the Parliament declared its admiration for the struggle "to restore the Armenian race" and expressed the conviction that the Greek government, "in its démarches at the congress of peace, will demand the definitive recognition and consecration of the just aspiration of the Armenian people." [66] During his presentation of the Greek case before the Paris Peace Conference on February 3 and 4, 1919, Premier Eleutherios K. Venizelos reaffirmed his solidarity with the Armenians. The Turkish settlement, he said, must allow for a "broad and generous interpretation" of Wilsonian principles, for it would otherwise be impossible to solve the Armenian question and "so put a stop to the sufferings of those people, who had lost through massacres over one million people during the course of the war." Armenia, Venizelos asserted, should include Cilicia, the six Armenian vilayets, Russian Armenia, and even the vilayet of Trebizond, although the latter was ethnically Greek and an indigenous movement to create a small self-governing Pontic state had begun there.[67] Venizelos's proposals, too, paralleled the American and British recommendations. A further expression of Armeno-Hellenic unity was evidenced in the joint appeal of the Armenian and Greek patriarchs of Constantinople, beseeching Venizelos never to allow the return of Turkish dominion over historic Armenian and Greek lands.[68]

It was significant that, in the postwar Allied peace formulations regarding Armenia, the loudest note of discord sounded from the French, despite the fact that Premier Georges Clemenceau had assured Boghos Nubar in July of 1918 that the Republic of France "has not ceased to place the Armenian nation among the peoples whose fate the Allies intend to settle according to the supreme laws of Humanity and Justice." [69] The secret Entente agreements of 1915–1916 had reserved for France all Cilicia and much of Sivas, Kharput, and Diarbekir, territories now claimed on behalf of Armenia. Even though tsarist Russia had been overthrown and the Bolshevik government had exposed and repudiated the pacts, France still held them to be generally valid, espe-

---

[66] *Le Temps*, Jan. 6, 1919, p. 2. Recognition of the Armenian republic by Greece was reported in the *Christian Science Monitor* on Jan. 10, 1919, p. 1.

[67] US Archives, RG 256, 180.03101/29; *Paris Peace Conference*, III, 868, 873.

[68] *Memorandum of the Oecumenical Patriarchate and of the Armenian Patriarchate of Constantinople for the Peace Conference, February 25, 1919* ([Paris, 1919]).

[69] Rep. of Arm. Archives, File 65/1; *Armenia's Charter* (London, 1918), pp. 14–15. Aristide Briand, the predecessor of Clemenceau, declared in November, 1916: "When the hour for legitimate reparation shall have struck, France will not forget the terrible trials of the Armenians, and in accord with her Allies, she will take the necessary measures to ensure for Armenia a life of peace and progress." See *Le Temps*, Nov. 7, 1918.

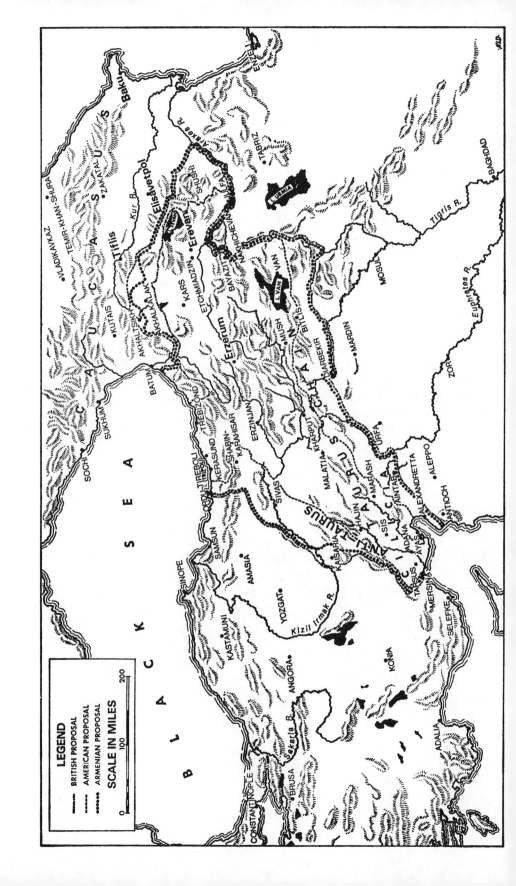

LEGEND

BRITISH PROPOSAL
AMERICAN PROPOSAL
ARMENIAN PROPOSAL

SCALE IN MILES

0   100   200

cially since Great Britain had based much of her postwar Middle East policy and strategy on them.[70] On December 27, 1918, former Premier Aristide Briand announced in the Chamber of Deputies that the wartime agreements would be honored if sanctioned by the French legislature and the Peace Conference.[71] Two days later Foreign Minister Stephen Pichon declared that the incontrovertible rights and interests of France in Cilicia and other Western Asian lands were based on "historic conventions and more recent contracts." [72]

In an apparent move to gain sure possession of Cilicia, France insisted that the region be joined to Syria, a land definitely marked for French rule even though British military contingents still stood there. From the Quai d'Orsay, the Foreign Ministry lent active support to a Syrian congress, which, meeting in Marseilles, demanded Cilicia for Syria.[73] When reports of new Muslim excesses against the Armenians of Adana and Aleppo filtered into Paris, Armenophiles charged the government of Georges Clemenceau with complicity, and the American Committee for the Independence of Armenia threatened to expose the nefarious collusion. The accusation could not be substantiated, of course, and, even if French intrigue did exist, world opinion seemed formidable enough to guarantee Armenia's expansion to the Mediterranean Sea. Among Frenchmen themselves, there was a large and impressive rank advocating for Armenia a settlement no less favorable than that recommended in the American and British guidelines.[74] But it was unfortunate for Armenia that Allied rivalries were to multiply as each week of 1919 passed. Great Britain, France, and Italy played for high stakes in the Mediterranean and the Near East, while the United States proved incapable of acting with clear resolve. And whereas the resultant delays in concluding peace would ultimately

[70] A résumé of these agreements as they related to Armenia is given by Richard G. Hovannisian, "The Allies and Armenia, 1915–18," Journal of Contemporary History, III (Jan., 1968), 155–165.

[71] Howard, op. cit., p. 9.

[72] New York Times, Jan. 2, 1919, p. 2. See also Evans, op. cit., p. 115; H. W. V. Temperley, ed., A History of the Peace Conference of Paris, Vol. VI (London, 1926), p. 143.

[73] A number of French officials, including Henri Franklin-Bouillon, President of the Foreign Affairs Commission of the Chamber of Deputies, participated in the Syrian Congress. See Christian Science Monitor, Feb. 25, 1919, p. 8. The official statement of the Francophile Syrian Central Committee is in Paris Peace Conference, III, 1024–1038; and in Miller, Documents, XIV (1925), 399–416, and XVII (1926), 154–156. See also Rep. of Arm. Archives, File 101/2, Varandian to Ohandjanian, Jan. 10, 1919.

[74] French journalist Gustave Hervé synthesized this viewpoint with the following expression: "France entertains too deep a sympathy for the Armenian people and a too strong sense of right not to renounce, in the interests of Armenia, what the treaties of 1916 allotted her." See New Armenia, XI (April, 1919), 63.

frustrate many designs of the Allied Powers, they would literally destroy Armenia.

Aharonian's Bid for Admission

When Aharonian reached Paris at the beginning of February, 1919, the Peace Conference had already convened without having reserved a place for Armenia. Still, it was thought in some quarters that, with the presence of an official delegation from the Republic of Armenia, a more forceful case for admission could be made. Upon his arrival in the French capital, Aharonian managed to secure interviews with several Allied delegates. During one such meeting with Stephen Pichon on February 10, he complained that Armenia, despite tremendous sacrifices, had been excluded from the council in which her destiny was to be determined. The French Foreign Minister commiserated but repeated the Allied policy that only organized states could participate. Alert to the opportunity Aharonian emphasized that the Armenian republic had been organized months earlier and possessed at least as much right to representation as had been granted the Yugo-Slav, Czech, and Arab states. Pichon then touched upon a more tenable justification—the Russian problem. The Allies in general and France in particular were pledged to the restoration of "democratic Russia" and would therefore find it difficult to treat with Armenia before considering the entire Russian question. It was impossible, Pichon declared, to seat Armenia while Russia was barred from the Peace Conference. Aharonian noted that, as Finland and Poland had gained their independence and Bessarabia had been annexed by Rumania, the principle of an indivisible Russian empire was no longer valid. Like Bessarabia, Armenia had been abandoned by Russia and forced to fight alone. Independence had been won on the field of battle. Pichon conceded that there was a valid analogy and suggested that, if Aharonian were to submit to the Peace Conference a memorandum to that effect, he would do his best to uphold the Armenian position.[75]

The French Foreign Minister thus conveniently terminated an interview filled with arguments much too cogent. But there was, in fact, no course available to Armenia other than that advised by Pichon. Aharonian sent a memorandum to the Peace Conference and to nearly every delegation in Paris on February 12, reviewing the salient events in the Caucasus from the Russian retreat to the establishment of Armenian independence and insisting that, because Armenia had been

[75] Avetis Aharonian, *Sardarapatits Sevr*, pp. 7-8.

forsaken by Russia in the negotiations at Brest-Litovsk, had continued the battle in the name of the Allies, and had finally achieved independence through the blood of her people, she deserved recognition and a place at the world conference of peace.[76] Three days later Aharonian again urged that Armenia be accorded the same international rights as had been granted the former Romanov territories of Poland and Finland.[77]

Thereafter, on every occasion, both appropriate and not so appropriate, Aharonian and Boghos Nubar pressed the issue; but as each week passed, the likelihood of admission became more remote. The Allied Powers, enmeshed in the German settlement and beset by the entreaties of countless ethnic and religious groups, rejected the Armenian petitions. The American delegation eventually came to favor the seating of the Armenians but at a time when France and other Allies had long since committed men and matériel in the name of a reunified, democratic Russia. The United States could not assert the point too strongly, for such insistence would place upon her a moral obligation much heavier than she was ready to shoulder.[78]

Presentation of the Armenian Case

In a joint memorandum dated February 12, 1919, Boghos Nubar and Avetis Aharonian submitted the Armenian claims to the Peace Conference.[79] The lengthy document reviewed six centuries of Ottoman domination—a story of violence, pillage, torture, rape, forced conversion, deportation, starvation, and massacre. "After such deeds the case is settled; the Allies have already, by the solemn declarations of their Statesmen, undertaken to definitely liberate Armenia from a tyranny unparalleled in History. The War of Peoples, followed by the Peace of Peoples, must needs give Armenia her complete Independence." The Armenians had shed "torrents of blood" for that independence and had upheld the Allied cause on the Caucasus front, in Palestine

[76] Rep. of Arm. Archives, File 104/3 and File 230/129, no. 39. See also US Archives, RG 256, 867B.00/49; Christian Science Monitor, May 29, 1919, p. 2.

[77] Rep. of Arm. Archives, File 104/3, note verbale, and File 230/129, nos. 41–44; US Archives, RG 256, F.W. 867B.00/49.

[78] Rep. of Arm. Archives, RG 256, F.W. 867B.00/131, Westermann memo.

[79] The memorandum in its French original and its English translation is in Rep. of Arm. Archives, File 104a/3a, H. H. Patvirakutiun, 1919 t.: Hashtutian Konferens, and File 107/6. The loosely translated and somewhat ungrammatical English version has been published as The Armenian Question before the Peace Congress, cited hereafter as Armenian Question. For the Armenian translation, see Haikakan Hartse Khaghaghutian Zhoghovin Ardjev ([Boston, 1919]).

and Syria, and in France itself. They were true belligerents, having lost nearly a quarter of their total world population. No other belligerent nation, whether victor or vanquished, had suffered such a heavy toll.

Independent Armenia, contended Nubar and Aharonian, must include the following lands:

1. The vilayets of Van, Bitlis, Diarbekir, Kharput, Sivas, Erzerum, and Trebizond, excluding districts south of the Tigris tributaries and west of the Ordu-Sivas line.

2. The four Cilician sanjaks of Marash, Khozan (Sis), Jebel-Bereket, and Adana, with the port of Alexandretta.

3. The Armenian republic in the Caucasus, inclusive of the province of Erevan, the southern portion of the Tiflis guberniia (Lori and Akhalkalak), the southwestern sector of the Elisavetpol guberniia (Mountainous Karabagh and Zangezur), and the province of Kars except for northern Ardahan (see map 12).

The Armenians, they asserted, had formed an absolute majority in the Ottoman eastern vilayets fifty years earlier, when the concentrated waves of persecution, the destruction of numerous villages, the massacre of countless Armenians, and the flight of additional thousands had begun. Moreover, despite this unbearable oppression, the Armenians had persevered as the largest single ethnic group in their historic homeland. On the eve of World War I, there had been in the six eastern vilayets, Trebizond, and Cilicia, 1,403,000 Armenians as compared with 943,000 Turks and 482,000 Kurds. In Cilicia alone, the nearly 200,000 Armenians had made up a plurality of the 500,000 inhabitants.[80] True, thousands had perished during the war years, but "THE VOICE OF ALL ARMENIANS LIVING AND DEAD MUST BE HEARD." The indigenous Muslim population, too, had been decimated by the military campaigns and the resulting epidemics and famine, so that with the return of the Armenian deportees and expatriates and especially with the incorporation of the Russian Armenian provinces the newly independent nation would come to possess a relative Armenian majority.[81]

The Armenian spokesmen maintained that a fundamental aspect of Ottoman administrative policies had been the attachment of peripheral Muslim districts to the Armenian vilayets as a means of dissipating the Armenian preponderance and creating an artificial Muslim majority. They recommended, therefore, that the Peace Conference establish a

[80] For a presentation of differing sets of population statistics, see Hovannisian, *Road to Independence*, pp. 34–37. See also US Archives, RG 256, 867.00/3/8/18/31/58, and 867B.00/3/8; Britain, FO 608/108, File 384/2/4.

[81] *Armenian Question*, pp. 1–8.

mixed commission to revise these unnatural frontiers. Armenia would raise no objection to the detachment of lands west of Ordu-Sivas and south of Diarbekir-Van, in so-called Kurdistan. As for Trebizond, Aharonian and Nubar admitted that Greeks heavily outnumbered Armenians, but they explained that the port and its environs provided the only major outlet for all northern Armenia. Premier Venizelos had already declared that Greece would not claim the province and that it should be included in Armenia. Equal justice and the right of autonomous development would, of course, be guaranteed the Pontic Greek population.[82]

The memorandum termed the Syrian demand for Cilicia preposterous. Before the war no more than 20,000 Arabs had lived in that region, the natural boundary of which, contrary to the contentions of the French-supported Syrian Committee, was the Amanus range near Alexandretta and not the Taurus Mountains. "The Armenian people, deprived of Cilicia, separated from the natural ports of Mersina and Yourmourtalik (Ayas), would be condemned to languish in the mountains, without intercourse with the Mediterranean world, without the power to breathe, and, to use the expression oft used, Armenia would thus be deprived of her lungs. Her life and future are on the Mediterranean." This disagreement notwithstanding, the bonds of Armeno-Syrian friendship and solidarity were "cemented by centuries of equal sufferings," and none "more than we can wish the constitution of a free and strong Syria as neighbour of the Armenian State." [83] Indeed, a leading, if not the foremost, Arab spokesman Emir Feisal had laid no claims to Cilicia, either in his memorandum presented to the Peace Conference on January 29 or during his personal appearance on February 6. Feisal had instead defined the upper boundary of the Arab lands as a line south of Alexandretta-Diarbekir. When questioned on the number of Arabs living in areas such as Anatolia and Cilicia, "Emir Feisal replied that there were a few in the Adana district; a few in the

[82] A deputation led by the Greek Metropolitan of Trebizond, Archbishop Chrysanthos, petitioned the Paris Peace Conference to recognize the right of Pontus to independence. For centuries a Graeco-Hellenic center, Trebizond (Trapezus) had been the capital of the extensive empire of Mithridates Eupator, second and first centuries B.C., and of the sometimes autonomous, sometimes independent Byzantine "Empire of Trebizond," A.D. 1204–1461. Thus, even though Premier Venizelos advised that the Pontic shores should be included within the Armenian republic, there was considerable local sentiment favoring the creation of a separate state, the Republic of the Euxine Pontus. See Britain, FO 371/3659, 110915/512/58, and FO 608/82, File 342/8/1; US Archives, RG 256, 867B.00/42; *New York Times*, April 13, 1919, Pt. IV, p. 13; London *Times*, Feb. 28, 1919, p. 9.
[83] *Armenian Question*, pp. 6–7.

Tarsus and Mersina area; but none in Anatolia. In all these regions they were a small minority and the Arabs were not claiming minority rights anywhere." [84]

The joint memorandum of Nubar and Aharonian also held forth the subject of future responsibilities by proposing that Armenia be placed for at least twenty years under the collective general protection of the Allies or the League of Nations and under the direct guidance of a specific mandatory power. Among its immediate duties, the mandatory nation would be expected to disarm the civilian population, expel Turkish officials from Armenian territory, punish those who had perpetrated or participated in the massacres, oust nomadic tribes that were fomenting unrest, relocate the Muslim immigrants who had recently settled in the region, and retrieve Christian women and children kept in Muslim households. Moreover, the Peace Conference should require the Ottoman government to pay an indemnity, "making good the damages of all kinds suffered by the Armenian Nation through massacres, deportations, spoliations, and devastations of the Country." On her part, Armenia would be willing to assume a share of the prewar Ottoman public debt.[85] The concluding sentence of the memorandum cautioned: "The Armenian question is not solely a local and national one; it concerns the Peace of Europe, and upon its solution depends the pacification, the progress and the prosperity of the Near East." [86]

Attached to the joint memorandum were complementary notes, statistical data, and maps—all intended to fortify the Armenian stand. The Armenian plateau and Cilicia were shown to be a single organic entity, geographically, economically, and historically. Population figures were given in detail to expose the obvious falsifications in the statistics submitted by Ottoman officials and to prove, by citing European sources and the archives of the Armenian Patriarchate of Constantinople, that Armenians had represented and would still represent at least a plurality in the proposed Armenian state. The third and final appendix to the memorandum described the Republic of Arme-

[84] *Paris Peace Conference*, III, 889–890, 894; Miller, *Documents*, IV, 300, and XIV, 227–234. See also *Current History*, X, pt. 1 (April, 1919), 72–73. Sherif Husein, the leader of the wartime Arab rebellion against the Ottoman Empire and the father of Emir Feisal, had waived any possible claims to the Adana-Mersina area in 1915. See Lloyd George, *Conference Memoirs*, II, 660–661.

[85] A separate memorandum on reparations and indemnities was submitted to the Peace Conference and considered by one of its subsectors. That memorandum is discussed in relation to the activities of the Armenian National Congress in chapter 14 below.

[86] *Armenian Question*, p. 8.

nia in the Caucasus, with its significant historic sites and centers of
Armenian concentration. The constituent lands of the Republic, the
Peace Conference was reminded, had been artificially severed from
their natural extensions to the west; now the time had come to right
this historic wrong:

> Consequently it would be a negation of justice to separate the ancient
> territories of Turkish Armenia from those of Russian Armenia under
> any pretext or for any cause whatsoever; it would, so to speak, be to
> pull to pieces a living body; and it would also create a new and per-
> manent cause for fresh persecutions, fresh oppressions and fresh blood-
> shed.
> In the name of justice, in the name of our rights of centuries, in the
> name of the irresistible aspirations of the two Armenian communities
> of Russia and Turkey, in the name of the inevitable historical necessity
> which sooner or later must triumph, we claim the absolute and final
> union of the two fragments of the same nation.[87]

The Armenians had stated their case, boldly and explicitly.

Boghos Nubar Pasha and Avetis Aharonian appeared in person before the Council of Ten on the afternoon of February 26, 1919. While
the pair waited in the anteroom of the Council's chamber at the Quai
d'Orsay, Aharonian, according to his political diary, offered to speak
first. The proposal was accepted immediately by Nubar, who remarked
in what had become his native language, "Les petits rôles passent le
premier." [88] Ushered before the Council of Ten, the Armenian leaders communicated orally their memorandum of February 12, Aharonian emphasizing the wartime military contributions of the Armenian
people and the urgency of Armenia's unification and Nubar smoothly
providing additional details about Cilicia and analyzing population
statistics in answer to critics who asked how there could be an Armenia when there were not enough Armenians to populate it.[89]

Two days later, on February 28, the Parisian newspaper *Le Temps*
captioned its résumé of the Armenian claims, "L'Empire Arménien." [90]
Despite the sarcasm of certain French journalists and the amazement
of some statesmen, the Armenian representatives intently pursued the
goal of a united Armenia. During the weeks following their historic
moment before the Council of Ten, they submitted scores of memoranda, charts, maps, and graphs in defense of Armenia's "patrimony."

---

[87] *Ibid.*, pp. 11–25, schedules 1–5, maps 1–3.
[88] Aharonian, *Sardarapatits Sevr*, p. 12.
[89] *Paris Peace Conference*, IV (1943), 147–156; Miller, *Documents*, XV (1925), 86–100.
[90] *Le Temps*, Feb. 28, 1919, p. 1.

The delegations of the major nations accepted the bulk of literature, some listened to the arguments, but none would make a binding commitment. Direct contact with the United States Commission to Negotiate Peace was usually arranged through the good offices of William L. Westermann, the American adviser on Western Asian affairs and a moderate Armenophile. He was instrumental in convincing such officials as Ray Stannard Baker, director of the American press bureau in Paris, Isaiah Bowman, Chief of Territorial Questions, and, on a few occasions, Woodrow Wilson himself to receive the Armenian spokesmen. During one of these interviews on April 17, 1919, President Wilson assured Aharonian and Nubar that he would do his utmost to secure for Armenia all territories outlined in the memorandum of February 12, but he cautioned that the problem was extremely delicate since other powers coveted the very same lands.[91] Three weeks later correspondent Edward J. Dillon told Aharonian that, according to a highly placed, trustworthy (but spurious) source, the formation of an Armenian state from the Mediterranean to the Caucasus had definitely been settled upon by the peacemakers.[92]

The staff members of the British Empire Delegation most accessible to Aharonian were Sir V. A. Louis Mallet, Assistant Undersecretary of State for Foreign Affairs and chief Near Eastern adviser, and his deputy, Arnold J. Toynbee, the formulator of several of the British postwar position papers. Both were courteous and sympathetic but firmly rejected Armenia's pretensions to Mountainous Karabagh, recommending instead implementation of the proposal to exchange the Armenian population of Karabagh for the Muslim population of the Erevan guberniia. Pointing to a large wall map of Western Asia, Mallet and Toynbee indicated the expanse between Erevan and the Mediterranean, territory presumably reserved for Armenia. Under these circumstances and in view of Azerbaijan's need for "living space," they found Armenia's intransigence regarding Karabagh unreasonable.[93]

Although Boghos Nubar had collaborated closely with the French government during the war, it was the French who were now least receptive to the Armenian spokesmen. Opposing interests in Cilicia chilled official French sentiment for Armenia. For example, in reply to Aharonian's request for assistance, Jean Gout, the chief of the

[91] Aharonian, *Sardarapatits Sevr*, pp. 18–19.

[92] *Ibid.*, p. 85.

[93] Rep. of Arm. Archives, File 230/129, and File 333/3; Aharonian, *Sardarapatits Sevr*, pp. 20–21.

Asiatic Section of the Quai d'Orsay, quipped that, since there was so much external pressure for the inclusion of Cilicia within Armenia, supplications should be made to the future mandatory of Armenia, certainly not to France.[94] Few French officials were so curt; some even revealed genuine sympathy. Aharonian was highly impressed by the perspicacity of Léon Bourgeois, a former premier and foreign minister then serving on the League of Nations Commission of the Peace Conference. Expressing reservations about his government's Near East policies, Bourgeois promised to work for Armenia's admission to the conference and to advance her interests as best he could.[95] Bourgeois, however, was not among the inner circle that then determined the strategy of France.

Conflicting Claims in Paris

Armenian objectives came into conflict not only with those of the French and the Syrians in regard to Cilicia but, on a greater scale, also with those of the Persians, Georgians, and Azerbaijanis. Persia, technically neutral during the World War, had nonetheless been fair game for German agents and for Russian, British, and Turkish armies of occupation. Foreign Minister Ali Quli Khan Moshaver ul-Mamalek now appeared in Paris to seek compensation for the havoc wrought by the Germans, Russians, and Turks and the end of special privileges wrangled from Persia by certain coercive foreign powers.[96] The Persian territorial claims, submitted to the Peace Conference in memorandum form in March, 1919, were aimed at recreating "L'Empire-Persan." The new Persia, it was posited, should be permitted to retrieve broad expanses of Central Asia, stretching from the Amu Darya (Oxus) River to the Caspian Sea, and the Transcaucasian khanates lost to tsarist Russia in the nineteenth century, that is, nearly all the territories of the republics of Armenia and Azerbaijan and a part of the North Caucasus. Nor was this the full extent of the Persian irredenta, for claims were also laid to Kurdistan, a land assertedly populated by "Iranian" elements and encompassing, according to a map attached to the memorandum, northern Mesopotamia and roughly the Turkish

[94] Toynbee cautioned the British delegation that the communiqués received from Gout were "a particularly poisonous attempt to embroil Armenians, Arabs and British with one another." See Britain, FO 608/83, 342/8/2/4238.

[95] Aharonian, *Sardarapatits Sevr*, pp. 16–17, 19–20.

[96] Anglophile Prime Minister Vosuq ed-Dowleh apparently sent his "troublesome" foreign minister to Paris in order to be rid of him during the months that negotiations leading to the Anglo-Iranian treaty of August, 1919, were in progress.

Armenian provinces of Van, Bitlis, Diarbekir, and Kharput.[97] The fanciful pretensions recited by Ali Quli Khan were held in derision by the Allied peacemakers, who, at British insistence, granted the Persian delegation neither its requested seat in the conference proceedings nor even the courtesy of an official audience.[98]

Several leading American and European journals commented unkindly on the Persian memorandum, while in Erevan, the semiofficial daily *Haradj* ("Forward") refuted Persia's title to any part of Russian or Turkish Armenia. There the matter rested. Ali Quli Khan Moshaver ul-Mamalek was soon appointed envoy to Constantinople, and he subsequently traveled to Moscow to engage in negotiations leading to the celebrated Soviet-Iranian treaty of 1921.[99] The Persian government privately disavowed the memorandum of March, 1919, and the document had no perceptible adverse effect upon Armeno-Persian relations.[100] The claims were not even mentioned in the official exchanges between Erevan and Teheran. Throughout 1919 the Republic of Armenia regarded Persia as its sole friendly neighbor.[101]

[97] *Claims of Persia before the Conference of the Preliminaries of Peace at Paris, March, 1919* ([Paris, 1919]). See also *Christian Science Monitor*, April 19, 1919, p. 1; Miller, *Documents*, XVII, 452–453.

[98] Records of the Foreign Office and the Empire Delegation show that London was resolved to deny Persia a place at the Peace Conference and to do whatever possible to neutralize Moshaver ul-Mamalek. The United States delegation initially favored the seating of Persia, and the issue was raised by several other delegations during the course of the Peace Conference but with no positive results. For primary papers on Great Britain's Persian policy, see Britain, FO 371, File 150/34 for 1919, FO 608, Files 375/1/7 and 375/3/5, and Cab 27/38, no. 2772. See also *Paris Peace Conference*, I, 245–263, 310, and V (1946), 153, 498; Miller, *Documents*, XVII, 40–42; Dillon, *op. cit.*, pp. 444–445.

[99] The Persian patriot was assigned to Constantinople as a dodge to prevent his return to Iran where he would likely become an annoyance to the Anglophile element. See *British Documents*, Vol. IV (1952), p. 1234; Britain, FO 608/98, 375/1/7/ 14200. The British strategy, as revealed in correspondence between Lord Curzon and Foreign Secretary Balfour, was to hold the Persian question in abeyance at Paris until the completion of the Anglo-Iranian treaty, after which Moshaver ul-Mamalek and all others would be confronted with a fait accompli. On news of the Persian minister's transfer to Constantinople, Balfour quipped, "the sooner he goes the better." See File 375/1/7, especially nos. 8172 and 14243.

[100] Premier Vosuq ed-Dowleh deprecated the "independent actions" of Ali Quli Khan and explained to British officials that the views expounded by the Persian delegation in Paris did not reflect the position of the Teheran government. See Britain, FO 608/101, File 375/3/5, especially no. 12175.

[101] After British interests in Persia had been protected by the Anglo-Iranian treaty, the new Foreign Minister, Prince Firuz Mirza Nusrat ed-Dowleh, was invited to London for further consultations. In the Foreign Office and particularly during his conversations with Lord Curzon, Nusrat ed-Dowleh did revive the Persian case for parts of Central Asia, Transcaucasia, and Kurdistan. In a memorandum relating to this tactic, Lord Curzon explained: "I should add that Nosret ed-Dowleh justified his

Georgia, Azerbaijan, and the Confederation of the North Caucasus, all having been discredited by wartime associations with the defeated Central Powers, encountered numerous difficulties in sending delegations to Paris. They eventually persuaded the British authorities in Tiflis to issue travel documents to Constantinople, but once in the Ottoman capital their representatives were denied permission to proceed farther because of the hostility of the French government.[102] Meanwhile, Georgian statesmen who were already in England, Switzerland, and Italy passed several anxious weeks before they were finally allowed to cross the French border as private citizens.[103] At the beginning of 1919 European endorsement of Georgian and Azerbaijani independence was by no means a foregone conclusion, and the prospect for the recognition of the Mountaineer Confederation of the North Caucasus and Daghestan was even dimmer. A bloc of states headed by France considered these regions as integral to Russia but tended to regard Armenia, whose historic lands had but partially fallen within the Romanov Empire, as a separate entity.[104] Despite these

general attitude, not on the ground of the feasibility of the particular proposals, but on the pleas that the present opportunity should not be lost of stating claims which, unless formulated, might be treated as abandoned, and some of which, in the general Asiatic welter, there might be a chance of realizing. Why should not the Persians be given as good a chance of recovering territories that had once belonged to them, as Afghans, or Russians, or anybody else?" For documents and materials on this issue, including Persian proposals for a plebiscite in Nakhichevan and the British refusal to support that suggestion or many other Persian territorial pretensions, see Britain, FO 371, File 150/34 for 1919; *British Documents*, IV, 1225–1274.

[102] The British Foreign Office assured the French ambassador in London that Great Britain would honor a specific request of the Quai d'Orsay not to recognize Georgia or the other self-styled states in the Caucasus. The opposition of France to these republics, especially to Georgia, was buttressed by the reports of Colonel P. A. Chardigny, head of the French military mission in Tiflis, characterizing Zhordania's government as extremist and incapable of conducting the affairs of state honestly. See Britain, FO 371/3661, 1015/1015/58, and WO 33/965, no. 3737.

[103] A Georgian chamber of commerce in London and information office in Berne attempted to counteract the misinformation caused by "irresponsible news bureaux, whose agents are either unconsciously ignorant of the facts or in the pay of the Imperial [Russian] or Bolshevist interests." See *Current History* X, pt. 1 (April, 1919), 39–40.

[104] The British Foreign Office was inclined to favor the organization of Caucasian buffer states, as evidenced in the Eastern Committee's deliberations of December, 1918. Lord Curzon had then described Georgia as "the most highly developed, progressive, and cultured of these states" and "the most entitled to independence." He was much less affirmative in his views of the North Caucasus Confederation and of Azerbaijan, and, in general, British policy toward the Caucasus remained malleable pending the march of events. Moreover, the Georgian cause in London was undermined by the British military commanders in the field, who asserted that Zhordania's government was radical, antagonistic, and untrustworthy. General Milne, in particular, was convinced that Georgia was led by the "worst kind of Bolshevik elements"

formidable handicaps the envoys from Tiflis, Baku, and Temir-Khan-Shura, the Mountaineer capital, labored diligently to publicize their respective causes.

As early as December of 1918 unofficial Georgian spokesmen in London circulated documents outlining the events that had led to the rebirth of national independence and defining the territories of the Republic of Georgia, including those districts not yet under the jurisdiction of Zhordania's government—Lori, Olti, Ardahan, the Batum oblast, and, from beyond the Russo-Turkish frontier, the region known as Lazistan in the eastern half of the Trebizond vilayet. They challenged Armenia's right to any part of the Tiflis guberniia or the northern half of the Kars oblast and insisted that the Armenian quest for a Black Sea port be directed away from Batum and its adjacent coastline in the Trebizond vilayet.[105] In response to the petitions of these representatives, the Foreign Office stated on December 30, 1918, that it would look with sympathy upon the concept of Georgian independence yet carefully worded the communiqué so that it might not be interpreted as a willingness to recognize the Republic of Georgia, even in an informal capacity.[106]

Having persevered through many distressing situations in Constantinople, the official Georgian delegates, Nikolai Semenovich Chkheidze and Iraklii Georgievich Tsereteli, managed to reach Paris by March, 1919, whereas most of their aides and advisers were compelled to return to Tiflis.[107] The reputations of the two distinguished Menshevik

---

and that the Georgian army was a red-flag–waving rabble. When the Georgian delegation arrived in Constantinople, Admiral Calthorpe added his disapproval by advising the War Office that "some most undesirable individuals" were among the group. See Britain, FO 608/83, 342/8/4/4453, and FO 371/3661, 13524/29843/1015/58.

[105] US Archives, RG 256, 861G.00/22; Paris Peace Conference, II, 283. Zurab Avalov (Avalashvili) and David Gambashidze acted as the Georgian representatives. They were joined in late December, 1918, by Konstantin Gvardjaladze, previously Assistant Foreign Minister of the Georgian republic. For other memoranda submitted by this group, see Britain, FO 371/3661, 1015/3293/4907/1015/58.

[106] Z. Avalov, Nezavisimost' Gruzii v mezhdunarodnoi politike, 1918–1921 g.g. (Paris, 1924), pp. 161–164; Britain, FO 371/3661, 1015/1015/58. Foreign Office officials Professor James Young Simpson and George Jardine Kidston, revealing a better understanding of Caucasian politics than that demonstrated by their War Office colleagues, emphasized that "by modern standards" the Georgian government was moderate and most certainly anti-Bolshevik." Still, the Foreign Office informed the British High Commissioner in Constantinople that the Georgian delegation should not assume that it could proceed to Paris on the strength of sympathetic expressions. See FO 371/3661, 13524/16316/29691/1015/58.

[107] W. S. Woytinsky, Stormy Passage (New York, [1961]) pp. 426–427. For the composition and description of the original Georgian delegation, as reported by Vice Admiral S. A. Calthorpe, see Britain, FO 371/3661, 13524/16228/29843/1015/58, and FO 608/87, 352/2/1/3097.

leaders were well established among European diplomatic and especially socialist circles. Chkheidze had chaired the Petrograd Soviet in 1917 and Tsereteli had served both in the Soviet and in the Russian Provisional Government. Following the Bolshevik coup they had fled, together with other Menshevik chiefs, to their native Caucasus where they helped to guide Georgia toward independence. Perhaps it was their uncompromising anti-Bolshevik attitude that persuaded the Quai d'Orsay to suffer their presence in Paris. In any case they now appeared, not as Marxist internationalists, but as Georgian patriots.[108]

The Georgian delegation, submitting its initial memorandum to the Peace Conference on March 14, 1919, attempted to rationalize the circumstances that had constrained the Republic to turn to Germany during the World War. Chkheidze and Tsereteli summarily absolved their country from any complicity against the Allies and then enumerated the constituent territories of the Republic of Georgia: the provinces of Tiflis, Kutais, and Batum, the districts of Sukhum, Zakatal, Olti, and Ardahan, and a large sector of the Trebizond vilayet (see map 13). These were not Georgia's maximal pretensions, they declared, considering that the Republic had acknowledged the importance of certain "historic Georgian territory" to its neighbor states and had therefore moderated its proposals.[109]

Of the petitions addressed to the Peace Conference by the Caucasian governments, only those of the Mountaineer Confederation of the North Caucasus and Daghestan did not overlap the claims of Armenia. This unusual and fortunate phenomenon had been determined by geography, as interposed between those two regions were the Georgian and Azerbaijani republics. The official Mountaineer delegation, led by Abdul Medjid Chermoev, was likewise halted in Constantinople for a long while.[110] In the meantime the Confederation's envoy in Berne, Haidar Bammat (Bammatov), relayed to Paris numerous memoranda asserting his country's right to the mountains and valleys of

[108] Georgian Premier Noi Zhordania later explained that Chkheidze and Tsereteli were sent abroad because they were known in Europe and could serve to enhance the international stature of Georgia, whereas they would be ineffectual in attempting to address themselves to domestic matters, which required the attention of the Zhordania-type "worker" element. See his *Moia Zhizn'* (Stanford, 1968), pp. 91–92.

[109] US Archives, RG 256, 861G.00/5; Britain, FO 608/88, 356/2/2/4366; Délégation Géorgienne à la Conférence de la Paix, *Memoire présenté à la Conférence de la Paix* (Paris, 1919). Subsequent Georgian memoranda are in US Archives, RG 256, 861G.00/74/105; Britain, FO 608/88, 356/2/2/5214/5741.

[110] For correspondence regarding the North Caucasus delegation while it was in Constantinople, see Britain, FO 371/3661, 16228/17907/28311/29691/30358/32362/47183/53346/1015/58.

the Caucasus range.[111] But much of this territory was also coveted by the Volunteer Army, Soviet Russia, the Kuban Cossacks, Georgia, and Azerbaijan, and these forces, as if to add to the complication, maneuvered against one another to extend their own spheres in the highlands that had preserved the identities of the Kabardians, Avars, Chechens, Ossetians, Ingush, and many other mountain peoples. By the time Bammat and Chermoev succeeded in transferring to Paris in the spring of 1919, the Volunteer Army had overrun most of Ciscaucasia.[112]

The Republic of Azerbaijan, in contrast with Armenia and Georgia, advanced no claims to Ottoman territory but enunciated from the outset that it was deserving of the greater part of Transcaucasia. Azerbaijani envoys in Constantinople at the end of the World War were quick to redirect their attention to the Allied officials who disembarked a few days after the Mudros Armistice. Ali Mardan Topchibashev and Mehmed Emin Rasulzade, eminent Muslim intellectuals and political modernists, identified the territory of Azerbaijan as the Baku and Elisavetpol guberniias, the southern districts of the Tiflis and Erevan guberniias, and the county of Zakatal.[113] In subsequent months, following the Turkish withdrawal from Transcaucasia, the cabinet of Fathali Khan Khoiskii revised this description to include most of Daghestan and a much enlarged area of the Erevan guberniia. In addition, tangential claims were made to the Batum and the Kars oblasts by insisting that, if these provinces were not organized as an autonomous Muslim region, they then be incorporated into Azerbaijan.[114] The implementation of either alternative would have created a broad corridor between Russian Armenia and Turkish Armenia, and Azerbaijan alone or in league with the proposed new Muslim state would have completely encircled the Erevan republic.

The Azerbaijani delegation to the Paris Peace Conference was stranded in Constantinople for many weeks.[115] When in April of 1919

---

[111] Bammat described himself as the Foreign Minister of the Mountaineer Confederation. Memoranda submitted by him and other representatives of the North Caucasus are in US Archives, RG 256, 861G.00/3, 861K.00/6/7/8/51; Britain, FO 371/3661, 61656/85034/1015/58, and FO 608/195, File 602/1/3; Miller, *Documents*, XVII, 489-491. For papers dealing with Great Britain's policy toward and relations with the Confederation of the North Caucasus, see FO 371/4381, File 490/PID.

[112] See pp. 365-373 below.

[113] US Archives, RG 256, 867.00/86; Britain, FO 608/84, 342/12/1/643. See also FO 371/3667, 9514/1015/58.

[114] Rep. of Arm. Archives, File 69a/1a; US Archives, File 256, 861K.00/93.

[115] The full membership of the delegation, which was reconstituted at the beginning of 1919, is given in Britain, FO 371/3661, 16228/17907/1015/58. See also

Ali Mardan Topchibashev was at last given permission to proceed to Paris, it was largely through the good offices of Woodrow Wilson, supported by the British Foreign Office. The President, as a matter of principle, could find no just grounds on which to exclude Azerbaijani representatives when a host of other unrecognized emissaries had been allowed to invade the French capital.[116] Upon arriving in Paris, Topchibashev followed the path cut by Aharonian, Nubar, and a parade of other supplicants by soliciting interviews with Allied officials of whatever stature or capacity. On May 23 he inquired of Sir Louis Mallet if Great Britain would act as the mandatory power for Azerbaijan and uphold the Republic's bid for recognition. The chief Near Eastern adviser made certain that nothing encouraging could be construed from his reply: A British mandate over Azerbaijan was totally out of the question and the matter of recognition was within the purview of the Peace Conference as a whole.[117]

Topchibashev submitted the Azerbaijani case to the Peace Conference in a memorandum of even greater length than its verbose Georgian and Armenian counterparts and replete with detailed information on the history, culture, geography, economy, and population of the state.[118] The pains taken to prepare the extensive document were rewarded by the prolonged silence of the peacemakers. Nor would the sacrosanctum in Paris grant Topchibashev's petition to present the

---

Kazemzadeh, *Transcaucasia*, p. 265; A. Raevskii, *Angliiskaia interventsiia i Musavatskoe pravitel'stvo* (Baku, 1927), pp. 50–51. One member, Ahmed Aghaev (Agha oghlu Ahmed), was taken into custody for his Ittihadist activity and alleged bonds with the former ruling clique of Turkey.

[116] *Paris Peace Conference*, V, 407. When, in a sudden volte-face, the French government allowed Chkheidze and Tsereteli to advance to Paris in late February, Topchibashev protested this preferential treatment. Both the British High Commissioner and the General Officer Commanding, Army of the Black Sea, put aside their personal contempt for the Caucasian governments to sustain the complaint and to advise London that the French maneuver could bring no good to the touchy situation in the East. The Foreign Office therefore recommended to the Quai d'Orsay that the Azerbaijani and Mountaineer delegations be authorized to enter France, but for several weeks more Foreign Minister Pichon remained intransigent. Only in April did he finally give notice that a pair of delegates from each of the Muslim republics would be tolerated in Paris. The rest of the delegates and staff members either returned home or eventually sifted into France to rejoin their colleagues. See Britain, WO 33/965, no. 3599, and FO 371/3661, 27212/28311/29691/30358/32362/47183/53346/1015/58.

[117] *British Documents*, Vol. III (1949), 325–326; Britain, FO 406/42, no. 24, and FO 608/84, 342/12/1/10979.

[118] US Archives, RG 256, 861K.00/103 F.W./106; *La République de l'Azerbaïdjan du Caucase* (Paris, 1919); *Claims of the Peace Delegation of the Republic of Caucasian Azerbaijan Presented to the Peace Conference in Paris* (Paris, 1919).

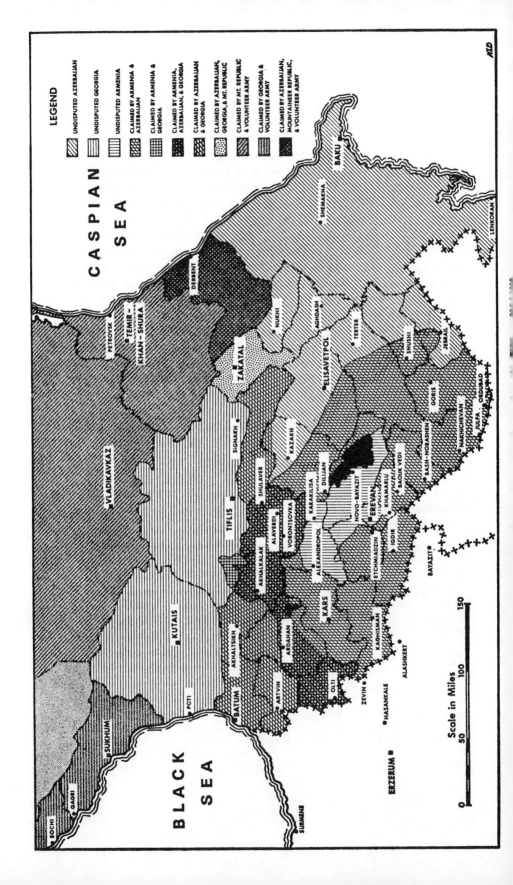

Azerbaijani views in person.[119] Finding the French and British completely unresponsive, Topchibashev addressed President Wilson directly, requesting that the United States recognize Azerbaijan, support her application for admission to the Peace Conference and the League of Nations, accord her military assistance, and consent to the exchange of diplomatic missions. Making a show of fair play, Wilson begrudged the Azerbaijani delegation an interview, but with cold formality he proceeded to advise Topchibashev that the fragmentation of the world was not a goal of the statesmen gathered in Paris. The Azerbaijanis might attract a wider audience, he suggested, if they would put forward a platform based on a confederation of the several Transcaucasian peoples. In any case, the President concluded, the status of Azerbaijan could not be resolved until the perplexing Russian question had been settled.[120]

Discouraged by Wilson's demeanor but still hoping to alter the attitude of the Peace Conference, Topchibashev then turned to Avetis Aharonian, asking that Armenia publicly espouse the principle of a Caucasian confederation. Aharonian may have gained some little comfort in reminding Topchibashev that only one year earlier there had been just such a union, which, however, had been abandoned by certain of its constituent peoples. Still, rather than issue an unqualified rebuke, Aharonian went on to explain that before all else the fate of Turkish Armenia had to be determined. Not until the two sectors of the Armenian nation had once again been united could confederation or any new combination in Transcaucasia be considered. And then it would be necessary to take into account the will and political direction of the Turkish Armenians. Never again would Caucasian Armenia act of or for herself alone.[121]

[119] Topchibashev officially protested the uncivil treatment his delegation had received from the Peace Conference. See Britain, FO 608/84, 342/12/1/18271.

[120] Raevskii, *op. cit.*, p. 53. See also Kazemzadeh, *Transcaucasia*, p. 266.

[121] Aharonian, *Sardarapatits Sevr*, pp. 23–24.

10

The
Allied Response

The first phase of the Paris Peace Conference ended on June 28, 1919, when the Treaty of Versailles was imposed on the shattered German Empire. Although European matters and the establishment of the League of Nations dominated the attention of the peacemakers during that initial period, the Eastern question smoldered just beneath the surface and occasionally erupted, with all its convolutions, into the proceedings. Avetis Aharonian and Boghos Nubar Pasha, in fundamental opposition to the Allied dictum to defer the Turkish settlement until the European treaties had been concluded, importuned the world leaders (1) to recognize the Republic of Armenia, (2) to repatriate Armenian refugees and expel Muslim settlers from Turkish Armenia, (3) to undertake the military occupation of Turkish Armenia, and (4) to select forthwith a mandatory nation for Armenia. In each case, the response in Paris was either negative or indecisive. The United States and the Allies all eventually concurred in the desirability of an Armenia from sea to sea but none was willing to provide the means necessary to transform that sentiment into reality.

Recognition and Assistance

Recognition of the Armenian republic had been urged by Armenophiles since 1918. Avetis Aharonian merely made the request official. In petitions to the Peace Conference, heads of state, and various delegations, he cited as qualifications for recognition Armenia's sacrifices and heroism. The republic that had emerged in Russian Armenia should, he maintained, serve as the core of the future expanded independent country of Armenia.[1] As the weeks multiplied into months, the plea grew in urgency. Reluctance of the world powers to grant recognition, protested Aharonian, was depriving Armenia of the possibility to float desperately needed loans and was emboldening the many forces conspiring to destroy the fledgling republic.[2] In communiqués that soon became hopelessly repetitious Aharonian complained to Lloyd George, Clemenceau, Wilson, Balfour, Pichon, Lansing, and other prominent delegates that each passing day saw another 2,000 victims added to the death toll and that Armenia had become a horrendous cemetery even though a simple declaration from the Peace Conference would have enabled her to negotiate for life-giving food, clothing, and medicines.[3]

Armenophile societies in Great Britain, France, Italy, Switzerland, Denmark, and especially the United States supported Armenia's bid. The American Committee for the Independence of Armenia submitted petitions bearing the names of thousands who advocated recognition of the de facto government in Erevan. Even as the Peace Conference began its activities, twenty-five governors made public their hope for a reconstructed Armenia "within her historic boundaries," a view reiterated in separate petitions by hundreds of American clergymen.[4] By April of 1919 several advisers to the American delegation in Paris had come to favor recognition in order to provide Armenia sufficient international stature to float a 20 million dollar loan. This same reasoning was advanced by ACIA executive members James W. Gerard, Cleveland H. Dodge, and William Jennings Bryan in a cable to President Wilson. The trio further urged that the United States assist Armenia in securing arms and ammunition for defense.[5] At the beginning of June President Wilson, whose personal sentiments were clearly in consonance with such views, was undoubtedly stirred by an appeal from thirty state governors who asked recognition for the de facto Armenian government so that the representatives of "that courageous Christian Armenian nation can participate in the Peace Conference at a time their question will be taken under consideration." Distressed by the unfortunate incumbent complications, Wilson was constrained to reply that

[1] See, for example, US Archives, RG 256, 867B.00/49/65/66; Rep. of Arm. Archives, File 3/3 and File 230/129. See also *Christian Science Monitor*, Jan. 30, 1919, p. 1, and April 22, p. 4.
[2] Rep. of Arm. Archives, File 230/129, nos. 87, 182–184.
[3] *Ibid.*, Files 230/129, 319/1, and 333/3.
[4] US Archives, RG 256, 867B.00/62; *Hairenik* (daily), Feb. 20, 1919, p. 3; *A Report of the Activities: The American Committee for the Independence of Armenia, 1918–1922* (New York, 1922), p. 8, cited hereafter as *ACIA Activities*.
[5] US Archives, RG 256, 867B.00/113.

Armenia's case was not unique and that it was most difficult to treat these like situations with disparity. He nonetheless promised to do everything possible for the "welfare of Armenia." [6]

That the Armenian republic had risen on territory once included in the Russian Empire proved a major obstacle to recognition. In a delegation paper of June 7, regional adviser William L. Westermann stated that, inasmuch as formal recognition, which he had long endorsed, was plainly contrary to the policies of the European Allies, he felt bound to counsel Secretary of State Lansing to explain to Aharonian that the whole issue must be deferred at least until after the Turkish settlement. Such a procedure would avoid antagonizing the Russian "democratic elements," which were enjoying the moral, material, and physical support of the Allies. His personal sympathies undisguised, Westermann recommended that, pending recognition, Armenia be afforded increased humanitarian aid.[7] The matter had apparently already been closed on June 5 as President Wilson instructed Lansing to impart to the Armenian delegation his deep regret that existing circumstances precluded recognition for the time being.[8] No power was willing in 1919 to assume even the moral implications inherent in official acknowledgment of the Republic of Armenia.

As Westermann had hoped, American charitable assistance to Armenia did continue throughout the year. In April, 1919, Aharonian and Nubar entered into contract arrangement with relief officials Herbert C. Hoover and Robert A. Taft, whereby Armenia was granted 5,000 metric tons of wheat, with subsequent additional allotments to be made if possible.[9] The American Relief Administration, as previously noted, delivered more than 50,000 metric tons of food to the Armenians by the end of summer. Aharonian also attempted to secure sundry supplies and equipment from the surplus depots of the American Expeditionary Force in Europe, but, lacking international recognition and foreign credit, Armenia failed to qualify.[10] American philanthropy tempered the misery of Armenia, but the source of that misery could not be sealed

---

[6] *Hairenik* (daily), June 8, 1919, p. 1, and June 13, p. 1. The governors of the following states signed the wire to the President: Arizona, Connecticut, Delaware, Florida, Georgia, Idaho, Iowa, Louisiana, Maryland, Minnesota, Nevada, New Hampshire, New Mexico, New York, North Carolina, North Dakota, Ohio, Oklahoma, Oregon, Pennsylvania, Rhode Island, South Carolina, South Dakota, Tennessee, Texas, Washington, West Virginia, Wisconsin, Wyoming, and the territory of Puerto Rico.

[7] US Archives, RG 256, 867B.00/131, Westermann to Kirk.

[8] *Ibid.*, Wilson to Lansing.

[9] Rep. of Arm. Archives, File 111/10, *H. H. Patvirakutiun, 1919*; US Archives, RG 256, 184.021/9.

[10] Rep. of Arm. Archives, File 144/43, *H. H. Patvirakutiun: Tntesakan Hartser.*

until the refugee population had been repatriated. To that problem Aharonian's delegation addressed itself unceasingly during the first phase of the Paris Peace Conference.

Armenian Refugees and Muslim Settlers

The concentration of half a million refugees in Transcaucasia rendered ineffectual nearly all Armenian plans for reconstruction. Allied and American representatives in the Caucasus reported that as long as the refugee crisis existed both the Turkish Armenians and the indigenous Russian Armenians would be condemned to unremitting torment.[11]

Meanwhile in a series of communiqués beginning on February 15, 1919, Avetis Aharonian underscored the time element and warned the Paris Peace Conference that the masses of refugees would perish were they denied access to their land much longer. It was essential, he insisted, to rekindle the hearths of 200,000 homes before the sowing season had passed.[12] In March, Aharonian wrote Peace Conference President Clemenceau and foreign ministers Pichon, Balfour, Sonnino, and Lansing, deprecating the fact that the trepidation generated in Turkey by the Allied victory had been painfully short-lived. Even though the Ottoman Empire had long since capitulated, Turkish Armenia still languished under the hand of the butcher, the refugee throngs, denied the right to reclaim their villages, died of starvation and disease all along the border, and countless Christian women and children remained prisoners of the harem. The Young Turks (Ittihadists) and their followers had been heartened by this apparent Allied abandonment of Armenia. With the admonition that the destruction of Armenia would expose the victorious powers themselves to grave danger, Aharonian demanded swift action to apprehend and expel the Turkish rabble-rousers in the Caucasus, to sanction the occupation of Turkish Armenia, and to make possible the safe repatriation of all Armenian refugees.[13]

Reports relayed to Paris by Allied and Armenian officials in Constantinople gave credence to the charges made by Aharonian. As early as January, 1919, there came news that Armenian refugees attempting

[11] See, for example, US Archives, RG 59, 861.00/4017; RG 84, American Consulate, Tiflis, 1917–1919, File 711; and RG 256, 184/10602.23 and 867B.48/8.

[12] Rep. of Arm. Archives, File 6/6 and File 230/129, nos. 64, 66, 87; US Archives, RG 256, 867B.00/49/66.

[13] Rep. of Arm. Archives, File 230/129, nos. 99–103. See also US Archives, RG 256, 867B.00/71/72.

to reclaim their homes in the nearer regions of Asia Minor were being driven back or massacred; Armenian women in Muslim households feared to reveal themselves to Allied investigators; and adherents of Ittihad ve Terakki, waxing strong in Anatolia, were threatening to continue the massacres of the Armenians so that "not one will be alive to protest." [14] American Commissioner Lewis Heck warned that in the interior provinces "conditions are steadily growing worse in every way, that some officials guilty of worst atrocities and deportations still retain their posts, that Moslem population is as arrogant as ever, not realizing defeat, because of lack of show of force by Allies, that many political prisoners have not been released in spite of general amnesty, . . . that with weakness of Government and public order further local outrages are possible." [15] Weeks later the Assistant British High Commissioner in Constantinople, Rear Admiral Richard Webb, reported no improvement. "Insecurity and disorder in the internal provinces of Turkey are rife," he emphasized; bands of brigands dominating the countryside were perpetrating fresh atrocities. [16] In view of this anarchic situation, the Allied authorities in the Near East attempted to stay the "premature" repatriation of the surviving Armenian deportees in Asia Minor, but all such efforts were in vain, for, as characterized by one British correspondent, "the homing sense of the Armenian is ineradicable." [17] On April 1, 1919, the heads of the Apostolic, Protestant, and Roman Catholic Armenian communities of the Ottoman Empire jointly protested the murder of refugees en route to their native villages and, inasmuch as the Ottoman government had made no effort to restore order, implored the Allied countries to intervene. [18]

Aharonian again took the grievance to the Peace Conference on May

---

[14] See, for example, Britain, FO 371/3657, 12425/12919/12920/23450/31312/512/58; Current History, IX, pt. 2 (March, 1919), 419–420; Hairenik (daily), March 5, 1919, p. 1, March 8, p. 4, and April 22, p. 3; Laurence Evans, United States Policy and the Partition of Turkey, 1914–1924 (Baltimore, [1965]), p. 171; Christian Science Monitor, April 18, 1919, p. 1.

[15] Miller, Documents, IV, 180.

[16] London Times, April 19, 1919, p. 10; Hairenik (daily), April 19, 1919, p. 5. For other reports on the difficulties of the surviving Armenians in the Ottoman Empire, see US Archives, RG 256, 867B.00/15/26/28/31/102/149/165/178; Britain, FO 371/4172, File 1270/44, FO 371/3658, 55143/512/58, and FO 608/78, File 342/1/5.

[17] London Times, Jan. 22, 1919, p. 7. See also Britain, WO 106/1435 passim.

[18] US Archives, RG 59, 867.4016/410, and RG 256 F.W. 867.00/159; Rep. of Arm. Archives, File 231/130. For a generally reliable account of conditions and activities of the Armenians remaining in the interior Ottoman provinces after the Mudros Armistice, see Les Mémoires de Mgr. Jean Naslian Evêque de Trebizonde sur les événements politico-religieux en Proche-Orient de 1914 à 1928. Vol. II (Vienna, [1957]). See also Britain, FO 608/78, File 342/1/5.

9. In a tone heavy with disillusionment, he lamented that, "while one side of the civilized world is rejoicing at the approach of peace," the Armenian nation was being allowed to die: "After four years of heroic sacrifice and unheard of suffering, the Armenian people had the right to hope that the end of the war would bring them relief. Six months have passed and our sufferings continue with the same intensity. Armenian homes are still occupied by the Turks, hundreds of thousands of our refugees are still massed on the frontier of Turkish Armenia dying from famine, from epidemics, and from privations without end." The Armenian people, concluded Aharonian, now addressed the world leaders once more "to offer a cry of distress" and to exclaim that they "do not understand this unjust treatment." [19]

In June, having received detailed information from his government, Aharonian protested that while General Milne, the commanding officer of the British Army of the Black Sea, continued to forbid the repatriation of the Turkish Armenians, a sinister scheme set in motion by Turkish officials progressed unimpeded.[20] The Ottoman government, he charged, had taken advantage of the vacillation and disunity in Paris to hasten the implementation of a project to populate the ravaged Turkish Armenian lands with Muslim colonists, the muhajirs. A number of Kurdish tribes, their names, sizes, and chieftains listed in the memorandum, were already moving in from North Persia; and the massive influx of Muslim refugees from the Balkan states and European Turkey was even more menacing. Unofficial sources revealed that the Ottoman government had appropriated 3 million gold pounds to establish these emigrant groups in the eastern vilayets. Some 200,000 muhajirs from Rumelia alone were reported to be in the vicinity of Angora (Ankara) and Konia, en route to usurp the historic Armenian lands and thereby to bring about a fait accompli that no future Allied decision could reverse. It was especially incomprehensible and intolerable, the Armenian delegation complained, that these violations had been initiated and financed by a Turkish cabinet ostensibly under the control of the Allied Powers. The victorious nations should, at the very least, intervene to oust the muhajirs and prevent all other plots to defraud Armenia of her legacy.[21] No government dared respond positively to the

[19] Miller, Documents, XVIII (1926), 256–257; Rep. of Arm. Archives, File 230/129 and File 333/1. Earlier similar appeals are included in Miller, XVII, 366–368, 390–392.

[20] Rep. of Arm. Archives, File 3/3 and File 116/15, H. H. Patvirakutiun, 1920.

[21] For materials on the muhajirs and the movement of Kurdish tribes into Turkish Armenia, see Britain, FO 371/3658, 68052/77798/77890/512/58, and 371/3659, 86068/86314/88849/89595/98469/512/58; Rep. of Arm. Archives, Files 230/129, 231/130, 333/3, and 421/1.

Armenian appeal, for to have done so would also have required a military commitment. Reports reaching Paris throughout 1919 indicated that the Muslim settlers, abetted by Ottoman officials, continued to stream into the abandoned Armenian villages.

The outcry of Armenophile societies embarrassed the peacemakers but did not remove their paralysis in the Armenian case. There were, moreover, voices that supported neither the contentions nor the appeals of Avetis Aharonian and Boghos Nubar Pasha. To such influential military authorities as Sir Henry H. Wilson, British Chief of the Imperial General Staff,[22] and Rear Admiral Mark L. Bristol, Senior American Naval Officer at Constantinople,[23] the Armenian claims were

[22] Field Marshal Sir Henry Hughes Wilson had served as the British Permanent Representative on the Supreme War Council from its establishment at Versailles in late 1917 until February, 1918, when he was elevated to Chief of the Imperial Staff. He has been credited with a significant role in the Allied victory, particularly by his crucial revamping of the enervated British armies on the Western front. A native of Ireland but a Protestant and staunch Unionist, Wilson ultimately condemned Lloyd George's postwar policies, especially those pertaining to the Irish question and the Sinn Fein. The Field Marshal retired from the General Staff in February, 1922, extremely embittered by the course of world events and the actions of Lloyd George. In June of that year he was assassinated by Irish nationalists. For highly sympathetic biographies of this controversial, conservative leader, see C. E. Callwell, *Field-Marshal Sir Henry Wilson* (London, [1927]), 2 vols.; and Basil Collier, *Brasshat: A Biography of Field-Marshal Sir Henry Wilson* (London, [1961]). A recent reevaluation has been made by Bernard Ash, *The Lost Dictator: A Biography of Field-Marshal Sir Henry Wilson* (London, [1968]).

[23] Mark Lambert Bristol had held several command positions during the World War and was appointed temporary Rear Admiral in July, 1918. On January 8, 1919, the Navy Department instructed Bristol to proceed to Constantinople as chief of the United States Naval Forces in the Eastern Mediterranean (also identified as the United States Naval Detachment in Turkish Waters). On January 28, Bristol raised his flag on the USS *Scorpion*, a station ship that had been interned by the Ottoman government since the disruption of Turco-American relations in April, 1917. In May of 1919 the American Commission to Negotiate Peace designated Bristol as "Chief Political Officer of the United States at Constantinople temporarily," thus making him senior to Consul General G. Bie Ravndal, who apparently disapproved of Bristol's administrative policies. On August 12, 1919, Bristol received appointment as United States High Commissioner at Constantinople, a post he retained until June 25, 1927. See US Archives, RG 256, 867.00/174; *Christian Science Monitor*, Feb. 4, 1919, p. 9; Henry P. Beers, *U.S. Naval Detachment in Turkish Waters, 1914–1924* (Washington, D.C., 1943), pp. 1–6. Bristol was an outspoken critic of Armenian aspirations and of American involvement in an Armenian mandate. Through his cables and personal letters to ranking members of the Department of State and of Congress, he, more than any other American official in the Middle East, influenced the decisions that proved disastrous to Armenian interests. Bristol was also instrumental in bringing about the resumption and normalization of Turkish-American diplomatic and economic relations. Several streets, squares, schools, and other establishments bear his name in Turkey today. The voluminous papers of Admiral Bristol, arranged in 161 boxes, are now deposited in the Manuscript Division of the Library of Congress. They constitute valuable source material for American-Turkish and American-Armenian relations in the post–World War I period.

outrageous. In his reports to the American Commission to Negotiate Peace, Bristol fulminated against Armenian pretensions and insisted that there was no such thing as "Armenia" in the sense of a national entity. Emphasizing that Armenian leaders by their own admission were attempting to use the refugee issue for political ends, he denounced all plans to repatriate the Turkish Armenians without the consent of the proper Ottoman authorities. The only possible alternative to Turkish control and supervision of the operation, he insisted, would be total Allied military occupation of the affected region, a most improbable eventuality.[24]

While initiating no firm action on behalf of the Armenian refugees, the United States government was sufficiently discomfited to put the question, albeit rather belatedly, to the Peace Conference. On July 5, 1919, William H. Buckler, adviser on Russian affairs, first recommended to the American delegation that the Peace Conference take under consideration the feasibility of repatriating "a certain number" of Armenian refugees prior to September 1. The return of even a few thousand farmers would reduce the food shortages anticipated the following year. British officers in the Caucasus, he suggested, could direct the entire operation.[25] As this recommendation was made after President Wilson had departed permanently for the United States, it was Secretary of State Lansing who proposed to the Peace Conference on July 7 that action be taken "to bring exiled Armenian agriculturalists back to the country, and to dispossess the Turkish usurpers of their land." He asked that General Milne be consulted on means to implement the plan

[24] US Archives, RG 256, 867B.00/155 and 867B.48/23. Bristol frequently criticized the "theorists and sentimentalists" who gave undue attention to the Armenians, a people having "no past history to show that they are capable of governing themselves or governing anybody else." His assessment that the Armenian pleas for immediate repatriation were nothing more than a base political maneuver is enunciated in the following representative dispatch:
At a long conference with the acting President of the Armenian Republic [Khatisian], several facts were brought out. One of these is that the Russian Armenians desire to have the Turkish Armenians who are now refugees in their country repatriated to Turkey and the principal reason is that if they are not repatriated, the Armenians will lose control of so-called Turkish Armenia. Also it is evident that the President of the Armenian republic thinks principally, if not exclusively, of the political situation rather than the suffering and starvation of the people, not only of the Russian Armenians but the Turkish Armenian refugees in the country. In reply to a question he practically stated that if trouble were caused by the forcible repatriation of the Turkish Armenians, this was of less interest than the political aspirations of the Armenians.
See Bristol Papers, Box 16, War Diaries, Reports of April 29, May 25, and June 12, 1919; Box 36, Correspondence of June 25, 1919.
[25] Paris Peace Conference, VII (1946), 40–41. See also US Archives, RG 256, 180.03801/92, 180.0501/27, and 867B.5018/8.

under the provisional supervision of British forces operating in the region. Foreign Secretary Balfour rejected forthwith any implication that the protection of the repatriates should devolve upon Great Britain. Somewhat lamely, Robert Lansing rejoined that all he desired was a report from Milne; who could object to a report? This understood, the motion to seek the advice of the General Officer Commanding, Army of the Black Sea, was smoothly adopted and the issue just as smoothly shelved.[26]

The Proposed Occupation of Turkish Armenia

The Mudros Armistice required a sweeping demobilization of the Ottoman army, yet the Allies took no effective measures to ensure compliance in the interior Asiatic provinces. A noted American historian has concluded: "In the Armistice with Turkey the Allies were concerned with the strategic access to Russia rather than with internal order. In addition to assuring their access to the Black Sea they secured the right to occupy the forts of the Dardanelles and Bosphorus." [27] Turkish Armenia did not lie along the waterways leading to Russia. This fundamental weakness in the Mudros Armistice was promptly recognized by supporters of Armenia. Members of Parliament shouted for immediate and total Ottoman demobilization in Turkish Armenia and even the military occupation of the region were it necessary to attain this goal.[28] On October 31, 1918, the day the armistice came into force, Cleveland H. Dodge and two officers of the American Board of Missions, William W. Peet and James L. Barton, petitioned the Department of State to do everything within its power to compel the Ottoman army to evacuate Turkish Armenia and Trebizond.[29] That same day Armenian envoy Garegin Pasdermadjian, together with Mihran Sevasly of the Armenian National Union of America,[30] submitted a similar appeal

[26] *Paris Peace Conference*, VII, 40–41; US Archives, RG 256, 180.03501/1 and 867B.48/27.

[27] Arno J. Mayer, *Politics and Diplomacy of Peacemaking* (New York, 1967), p. 95. See also Henry H. Cumming, *Franco-British Rivalry in the Post-War Near East* (London, 1938), p. 56.

[28] See, for example, Great Britain, Parliament, House of Commons, *Parliamentary Debates*, 5th ser., Vol. CX (1918), cols. 3239-3267; and House of Lords, *Parliamentary Debates*, 5th ser., Vol. XXXII (1919), cols. 34–41. See also *Christian Science Monitor*, Jan. 15, 1919, p. 3; *The Times History of the War*, Vol. XX (London, 1919), p. 104.

[29] US Archives, RG 59, 867.48/1075.

[30] For a résumé of the activities of the Armenian National Union, see *Teghekagir Hai Azgayin Miutian Amerikayi, 1917–1921* (Boston, 1922). See also Manuk G. Jizmejian, *Patmutiun Amerikahai kaghakakan kusaktsutiants, 1890–1925* (Fresno, Calif., 1930), pp. 360–376.

to Secretary of State Lansing with the further request that a temporary inter-Allied administration be established in Turkish Armenia.[31] It was unfortunate for the Armenians, however, that the peoples of the Allied countries were demanding, not more involvement, but a drastic reduction or even renunciation of commitments abroad.

As reports of Turkish armistice violations inundated Paris, Aharonian and Nubar, working in unison as the Delegation of Integral Armenia, implored the Allies to occupy Turkish Armenia or at least furnish aid and guidance so that the Armenian army could do so.[32] Of the victorious powers, only Great Britain had sizable forces in the Near East and the Caucasus, but the War Office viewed these as being dangerously overextended and sparse. Chief of the Imperial General Staff Sir Henry Wilson hoped even to extricate General Milne from "the very scattered situation" around the Black Sea. According to his biographer, or perhaps more accurately his hagiographer, "Sir Henry was most appreciative of the admirable work that was being done by our troops in this out of the way part of the world, but he realized that we did not possess the military forces requisite for undertaking police work in territories in which the Empire was not vitally interested." Although General Wilson was contemptuous of the "frocks" (frock-coated civilians) who determined British and Allied policy and who "fumbled" around the Paris Peace Conference, he found that his desire to divest Great Britain of her military liability in Constantinople, Syria, and Transcaucasia was shared in large measure by both Premier Lloyd George and Foreign Secretary Balfour.[33]

[31] US Archives, RG 59, 763.72/12246.

[32] Rep. of Arm. Archives, File 9/9 and File 230/129. See also US Archives, RG 84, Tiflis Consulate, 1917–1919, File 711, and RG 256, 867B.00/55/60/71/108/120/131; Britain, Cab 27/39, E.C. 3001, and FO 608/79, File 342/1/9, and 608/82, File 342/7/1.

[33] Callwell, *op. cit.*, II, 163–164, 167–168. During its deliberations of December, 1918, the War Cabinet's Eastern Committee attempted to define a policy regarding the maintenance of Imperial troops in the Caucasus. Lord Curzon urged that Britain "exercise some measure of political control over Transcaucasia," that Batum and Baku be internationalized and the railway connecting these western and eastern extremities of the Caucasus be placed under British supervision, and that the emergent republics be bolstered in order to block the return of Russian rule in the Caucasus. Curzon's contentions were challenged by his colleagues of the Eastern Committee, particularly by Secretary of State for India Montagu and by Foreign Secretary Balfour. Montagu held that the dissipation of Imperial power in so nonvital a region as the Caucasus would be foolhardy, while Balfour, piqued that he had not been consulted about the dispatch of the 27th Division to Batum, added that if Russia was in a position to crush the Caucasus, "why not." In another session, during a discussion of whether to retain or withdraw the British brigades in the Caucasus, Curzon exclaimed, "You cannot take them away and have everybody cutting everybody else's throat," in rejoinder to which Montagu was now the one to query "why not?" Arthur Balfour shared this view: "I feel much disposed to say with Mr. Montagu . . . if

Lloyd George announced in the Council of Ten (Supreme Allied Council) on January 30 that Great Britain could not be expected to continue shouldering the military responsibility in the Near East, "especially as she had not the slightest intention of being the mandatory in many of the territories she now occupied, such as Syria and parts of Armenia [Cilicia]." The same, he said, was true in the case of the Caucasus. The only action taken by the Council of Ten that day was to instruct the Military Representatives of the Supreme War Council to investigate and report on "the most equitable and economical distribution among these Powers of the burden of supplying military forces for the purposes of maintaining order in the Turkish Empire and Transcaucasia. . . ." [34]

they want to cut their own throats why do we not let them do it . . . as I understand we do let the tribes of the North West Frontier, outside our own [Indian] frontier, cut each other's throats in moderation." When the matter was brought before the Imperial War Cabinet, composed of the British War Cabinet and representatives of the Dominions and India, a somewhat vague, interim decision was made "that the British forces should not be withdrawn from the Caucasus until after the Turkish and German forces had been withdrawn; that a second British division should not be sent to the Caucasus without Cabinet authority; and that British forces should not be maintained there longer than could be avoided." For a presentation of these candid discussions, see Richard H. Ullman, *Anglo-Soviet Relations, 1917–1921*, Vol. II: *Britain and the Russian Civil War, November 1918–February 1920* (Princeton, 1968), pp. 64–81. Papers relating to this general question are deposited in Britain, Cab 27/24 and 27/37–39.

[34] US Archives, RG 256, 180.03101/25; Britain, Cab 25/118, 1A–1B, 4C; *Paris Peace Conference*, III, 805–808, 816–817, gives only the preliminary minutes of this session, whereas Miller, *Documents*, XIV, 104–111, includes both preliminary and revised minutes. The words "and Transcaucasia" in the text were added on January 31 and inserted in the revised minutes, issued on February 1, 1919. Earlier, on January 28, Lloyd George had made the following statement, as paraphrased in the minutes of the session: "Great Britain now occupied territories where they had no intention of remaining even if the League of Nations asked them to stay. For instance British troops occupied Russian Armenia and Serbia. They did not wish to be there, but someone had got to be there. Was Great Britain to be compelled to keep its troops there until the League of Nations was a going concern? . . . It appeared that they were now maintaining large forces—over 170,000 British troops alone in Syria, Caucasus, East Africa, and other out-of-the-way places. Those troops must sooner or later be withdrawn, but they could not do that without knowing who would take their place. They could not withdraw and leave the people to massacre each other." See Miller, XIV, 51.

Most minutes printed in the United States *Paris Peace Conference* series were circulated by the British secretary, Sir Maurice P. A. Hankey. The originals or mimeographed copies of the minutes are in Britain, Cabinet Record Group 28, *Allied (War) Conferences*, and in Cabinet Record Group 29, *International Conferences*. The minutes of the Council of Ten are in Cab 28/6–9; the peace conference memoranda for 1919 are in Cab 29/1–27; the minutes of the British Empire Delegation meetings are in Cab 29/28; and the minutes of the Council of Four (see below p. 318) are in Cab 29/37–40. Only the published form of these minutes, as printed in the *Paris Peace Conference* series, are cited in this study.

The Military Representatives were apparently not adept at interpreting the procedures of the politicians and consequently aroused the ire of the Council of Ten by posing a number of questions on which they themselves should have been the experts.[35] When at last on February 10 the Military Representatives did report, they not only recommended a considerable reduction of Allied troops in the Ottoman Empire and the Caucasus but also enumerated which countries should be assigned the specified zones of occupation: Italy was named to supersede Great Britain in the Caucasus and to hold Konia in Asia Minor; France, to assume control in Syria and in Cilicia; and Britain, to occupy Palestine and Mesopotomia, including Mosul.[36] The Council of Ten, now annoyed that its prerogatives had been infringed upon by the Military Representatives, ruled that the recommendations were essentially political and therefore solely within the purview of the Peace Conference.[37] Although the matter was tabled for consideration the following day, this was in fact the last time for nearly three months that it was discussed in formal session. The topic, apparently by British request, was erased from the agenda for February 11.[38]

Meanwhile on February 8, President Wilson, in response to Allied pressure to have America assume a share in "garrisoning" the Near East, cabled Secretary of War Newton D. Baker, asking him to weigh the legality of sending troops to Turkey in view of the fact that the United States had not declared war on the Ottoman Empire. Wilson had been instrumental in preventing that declaration, but he now hoped it might be possible to employ troops in Constantinople and Armenia because of "American interest in those areas." Three days later Baker firmly cautioned against the deployment of troops, for although such action might be technically permissible, the clangorous public demands to bring the boys home were growing ever more intense.[39]

In their futile efforts to have the Turkish armies ousted from the eastern vilayets, Aharonian and Nubar scurried back and forth between the Hôtel de Crillon, housing the American Commission to Negotiate Peace, and the Hôtel Astoria, headquarters of the British

[35] Britain, Cab 25/118, nos. 2B and 3A; Paris Peace Conference, III, 837–838; Miller, Documents, XIV, 157–158.

[36] Ray Stannard Baker, Woodrow Wilson and the World Settlement (3 vols.; Garden City, N.Y., 1923), III, 6; Evans, op. cit., p. 104; Britain, Cab 25/118, nos. 5C, 6A–9A, 12A, and Cab 25/126 S.W.C. 365A.

[37] Paris Peace Conference, III, 955–956; Miller, Documents, XIV, 313–315.

[38] French Foreign Minister Pichon subsequently revealed that the topic had been set aside at the request of British Colonial Secretary Lord Alfred Milner. See Baker, op. cit., p. 6.

[39] Evans, op. cit., p. 105, citing the Wilson Papers.

Empire Delegation. The United States and Great Britain heartily endorsed each other for the military undertaking. Representative of this mutual commendation was an episode on March 3 when Sir William G. E. Wiseman, chief British adviser on American affairs, called upon Colonel Stephen Bonsal, a distinguished foreign correspondent serving as secretary to Wilson, to ferret out what the President might be contemplating in regard to Armenia. Bonsal guilefully responded that perhaps the chief executive was contemplating nothing at all. With obvious satisfaction Bonsal recorded in his political diary that when Wiseman, as anticipated, expressed amazement at the reply, "I then showed him a copy of the Prime Minister's speech made at Guild Hall in 1916, which with malicious purpose I had held on my desk for some weeks. As he seemed to shy away, I read it aloud. 'Britain is resolved to liberate the Armenians from the Turkish yoke to restore them to the religious and political freedom they deserve and of which they have been so long deprived.' " Bonsal continued the taunt, "It seems to have been your job, and you accepted it at least a year before we entered the war. Why should the President barge in. *Après vous, messieurs les Anglais.*" [40]

William Westermann, too, believed that the British could, without encountering serious difficulties, penetrate Turkish Armenia to a depth of at least 100 to 150 miles. He expressed this conviction to his colleagues, Ray S. Baker and Isaiah Bowman, in an informal meeting attended by Aharonian on March 26.[41] At first unreceptive to the plan, Bowman, who was Chief Territorial Specialist of the American Commission to Negotiate Peace, gradually became captivated by Westermann's enthusiasm, yet he cautioned that the competition among the European Powers had to be taken into account. The Armenians had become the unfortunate victims of these intrigues. Still, he thought the British could and should undertake the occupation, as they alone had the manpower available and the United States army possessed no authorization to serve in the Near East. Agreeing to take the matter once again to the Secretary of State and the President, Bowman and Westermann advised Aharonian to confer with the proper British officials, who could be given every assurance that a decision to send the

[40] Stephen Bonsal, *Suitors and Suppliants: The Little Nations at Versailles* (New York, 1946), p. 191.

[41] Baker, *op. cit.*, II, 24, later wrote of the Armenian representatives: "Scarcely a day passed that mournful Armenians, bearded and black-clad, did not besiege the American delegation or, less frequently, the President, setting forth the really terrible conditions of their own ravished land."

Imperial forces into Turkish Armenia would win the warm endorsement of the United States.[42]

At the Astoria the following day Aharonian and Boghos Nubar obtained an interview with Sir Louis Mallet and Arnold Toynbee. Mallet minced no words in revealing that British military authorities had definitely ruled out all possibility of occupation and had even scheduled the 27th Division's withdrawal from the Caucasus. He was at a loss to explain the attitude of the Americans, for while they showed a keen interest in the mandate for Armenia they nonetheless expected the British to police the country. Great Britain had no troops to spare, concluded Mallet; Aharonian and Nubar should turn back to the Crillon. Refusing to be dismissed so abruptly, Aharonian then pleaded for the resources the Armenian army would need in order to attempt the occupation alone. Mallet retorted that such imprudent action would doubtless lead to interracial warfare; the Armenians must simply be patient.[43]

When the American advisers at the Crillon were informed of these proceedings, they promised to apprise Lansing and, if necessary, to place the Armenian representatives in direct communication with President Wilson.[44] This pledge was not, however, in keeping with official American policy. Robert Lansing, a vehement opponent of United States involvement in Armenia and a strategist whose annoyance with those who expressed contrary views was intense, noted, "Westermann's attitude shows [the] folly of having inexperienced men attempting to outline policies of govt." [45] With the austere Lansing in charge of the Department of State, there was a dolefully sagacious quality to Stephen Bonsal's diary entry, "Poor Nubar! Poor Aharonian! Unfortunate Armenians! Our promises are out the window and the reconstituted Armenian state has not a Chinaman's chance." [46]

Great Britain, meanwhile, made preparations to abandon the Cau-

---

[42] Aharonian, *Sardarapatits Sevr*, pp. 13–14.

[43] *Ibid.*, pp. 14–15. Descriptions of a previous interview on March 9, 1919, are in Britain, FO 371/3657, 39367/512/58, and in US Archives, RG 256, 867B.00/60. Mallet's advice differed somewhat from that of Major General William Thwaites, Director of Military Intelligence, who wrote the Foreign Office on March 19 that the Armenian forces, totalling some 12,500 men, "should be sufficient to police the area mentioned, if the Armenian Army really intends to do so." He was, however, in agreement with Mallet that the "maintenance" of the Armenians should be left to the Power that assumed the Armenian mandate. See FO 371/3658, 44511/512/58.

[44] Aharonian, *Sardarapatits Sevr*, pp. 15–16.

[45] Harry N. Howard, *The King-Crane Commission* (Beirut, 1963), p. 45 n. 2.

[46] Bonsal, *op. cit.*, p. 196.

casus. In late February the War Office advised "handing over Transcaucasia to Italy," and several days later the Cabinet conceded that the
continued occupation of the region was not feasible. Crossing over to
Paris at the end of March, Sir Henry Wilson met with Italian Chief of
Staff General Armando Diaz to arrange for the Italian army to replace
Milne's forces "in and about Transcaucasia." Lloyd George, under
strong pressure to bring the troops home, endorsed this action although he admitted that it would not sit well with the indigenous population, the Russian Volunteer Army, and the President of the United
States.[47] In April the Italian government dispatched a sizable military
mission under Colonel Melchiorre Gabba to reconnoiter the Caucasus,
but at the same time it complicated matters by disclosing imperialistic
designs on the eastern Adriatic and Asia Minor.[48] Premier Orlando was
determined that despite the solid opposition of the other powers Italy
would assert her "just rights," which he insisted had been guaranteed
by the secret wartime agreements of the Allies.[49]

[47] Callwell, op. cit., II, 171–172, 176. General Jan C. Smuts of South Africa, a member of the British War Cabinet's Eastern Committee, had suggested as early as December 9, 1918, that Italy be permitted to take control in the Caucasus, particularly if
this arrangement would effectively exclude France from that region. See Ullman, op.
cit., p. 75.

[48] The War Office informed General Headquarters in Constantinople that the
Italian mission was departing from the port of Taranto on April 25 and that Gabba
(identified as N. R. Gabba) would be accompanied by Colonel Claude Bayfield Stokes,
a British officer who had served in the Caucasus. News of the mission's arrival at
Batum was entered in the 27th Division War Diary on May 10, 1919. See Britain,
WO 33/365, no. 4248, and WO 95/4880. See also A. Raevskii, Angliiskaia interventsiia
i Musavatskoe pravitel'stvo (Baku, 1927), p. 57; US Archives, RG 84, Tiflis Consulate,
1919, pt. 4, File 801. Throughout much of the spring and summer of 1919, the quasi-
official Georgian newspaper, Bor'ba, reported on the mission's activities, particularly
those demonstrating that the Italians were busily assessing the economic potentials
of Transcaucasia. In London, Lord Curzon, who as Acting Undersecretary of State
was in charge of the Foreign Office while Balfour and Cecil participated in the Paris
Peace Conference, decried the decision to permit the Italians to move into the Caucasus. The Italians could only inspire anarchy, he warned, and their appearance between the Black and Caspian seas would be followed by internecine war and before
long the victory of Bolshevism. See Britain, FO 608/83, 342/8/4/7919. See also the objections of the Foreign Office's Russian experts in FO 406/42, no. 16.

[49] The Italian claims in Asia Minor were based on the Treaty of London, April,
1915. In return for Italy's pledge to join the Allied side, the Entente governments
had acknowledged that "Italy is interested in the maintenance of the balance of
power in the Mediterranean and that, in the event of the total or partial partition
of Turkey in Asia, she ought to obtain a just share of the Mediterranean region
adjacent to the province of Adalia. . . ." In another section of the same article, the
Triple Entente conceded that "if France, Great Britain and Russia occupy any territories in Turkey in Asia during the course of the war, the Mediterranean region
bordering on the Province of Adalia within the limits indicated above shall be reserved to Italy, who shall be entitled to occupy it." The Italian case in detail is pre-

It was the crisis precipitated by the landing of Italian troops along the Mediterranean coastline of Turkey and by reports that several Italian warships lay off the coast of Smyrna (Izmir), which prompted the Peace Conference to turn once more to the suspended question of occupying portions of the Ottoman Empire. On May 5, during the indignant Italian boycott of the sessions, Lloyd George emphasized that the assignment of definite zones of occupation would serve to forestall Italy's plan to engulf the whole of Anatolia. He proposed that the United States furnish troops for Constantinople and Armenia, the British withdraw from the Caucasus to have men available to counteract possible Italian moves in Asia Minor and Bulgaria, the French garrison Syria, and the Greeks be authorized to occupy Smyrna, "since their compatriots were actually being massacred at the present time and there was no one to help them." Lloyd George suggested that a decision be taken quickly before the return of the Italian delegation, but President Wilson was reluctant to press the issue since "he did not know where he was to find the American troops." He felt that the Allied Supreme Commander, General Ferdinand Foch, would be uneasy should American units be transferred from the occupied zone in Germany and that furthermore, in view of the nature of the projected operation, "the British troops were the only ones accustomed to this kind of business." [50] Neither President Wilson nor Clemenceau was pleased with General Henry Wilson's announcement that the Italians were, by previous agreement, to supplant the British in the Caucasus, or with Lloyd George's reminder that, while the Italian takeover would create "Hell" in the region, no other government had volunteered to assume the obligation. The United States, he said, was the logical power to protect Armenia, since the people there would gratefully welcome such a move. Sir Henry Wilson observed that his "Cousin," Woodrow Wilson, was "terrified" when told that one large division for the Constantinople zone and "anything up to five for Armenia" would be required.[51] His position most discomfiting, the President interjected that the question was much too crucial to determine in a hurry. He would confer with his military advisers and requested that General Wilson also consult

---

sented by René Albrecht-Carrié, *Italy at the Paris Peace Conference* (New York, 1938). See especially pp. 200–209 and document no. 3 (Treaty of London) and document no. 6 (Treaty of St. Jean de Maurienne).

[50] US Archives, RG 256, 180.03401/144; *Paris Peace Conference*, V, 466–468, 472. See also Paul Mantoux, *Les délibérations du Conseil des Quatre (24 mars–28 juin 1919)* (2 vols.; Paris, 1955), I, 486–487.

[51] Callwell, *op. cit.*, II, 187–188.

with General Tasker H. Bliss and Admiral William S. Benson of the American delegation.[52]

After meeting with Bliss and Benson, General Wilson recorded that the two men had agreed "Congress would not look at the idea of America going to Constantinople and Armenia, and [they] said my Cousin would be crushed out over such a proposal." [53] Indeed, during the session of May 6, President Wilson "regretted to have to say that his legal advisers informed him that he had no authority to send troops to Turkey." He had done his utmost, but the law was explicit in regulating the use of troops outside the United States. He would willingly sponsor legislation to grant that authority when he submitted the German peace treaty to Congress for ratification.[54] The Covenant of the League of Nations would be included in the treaty, and it was the President's sincere desire that, under the auspices of the League, the United States might assist the Near East in general and Armenia in particular.

The diplomatic game played in Paris by Lloyd George, Wilson, and Clemenceau failed to bring about the occupation of Turkish Armenia, but it did lead to a decision that had far-reaching consequences for Armenia. The three world leaders agreed that British, French, and American battleships should be dispatched to the waters around Smyrna where an Italian naval squadron had been espied and that a Greek military expedition be put ashore at Smyrna to defend the Christian population purportedly exposed to renewed Turkish atrocities.[55] The disembarkation of Greek troops on the night of May 14–15 was to infuse the shattered Turks with a hitherto unknown degree of nationalism, to reverse the entire postwar situation in the Near East, and, indirectly, to draw Armenia into the maelstrom of destruction.

These eventualities could hardly have been presaged at that time, yet the Armenian spokesmen clearly recognized the jeopardy to their cause and begged for at least token Allied intervention to thwart the "secret idea" of the Turks to block the restoration of Armenia as a prerequisite to the ultimate creation of a Pan-Turanian empire. "A contingent, no matter how limited, would be sufficient," Nubar exclaimed, "for the

---

[52] *Ibid.*, p. 188. See also *Paris Peace Conference*, V, 468.

[53] Callwell, *op. cit.*, II, 188.

[54] US Archives, RG 256, 180.03401/145; *Paris Peace Conference*, V, 482. See also Mantoux, *op. cit.*, I, 488.

[55] The deliberations culminating in the decision to sanction the Greek military occupation of Smyrna are included in Britain, FO 608, Files 381/1/1 and 383/1/6; Baker, *op. cit.*, II, 189–194; *Paris Peace Conference*, V, 412–413, 422, 483–484, 501–505, 553–558, 570–571, 577, 578; Mantoux, *op. cit.*, I, 510, II, 32–34, 39–44, 51–52; James B. Gidney, *A Mandate for Armenia* (Kent, Ohio [1967]), pp. 105–122.

appearance of the Allied flags in these sparsely populated regions would at the present time, we are convinced, prevent further misfortunes from which your Government would desire to spare us." [56] By mid-1919 it came to be almost expected that such petitions, submitted with sad regularity, would meet with no encouraging response. On June 2, as the doors closed before the Armenian delegation, Avetis Aharonian appealed once again to President Wilson, seeking at least "the means to equip and train the Armenian army." Touched with sorrow, the President instructed Lansing to inform the Armenian envoys that for the nonce it was quite impossible to grant the request.[57]

The Armenophiles

For Woodrow Wilson, bound by the laws and the mood of his recoiling country and an increasingly alienated Congress, it must have been distressing to receive the many hundreds of cables and letters calling for active American support of Armenia. As early as January, 1919, some seventy-five Congregational ministers besecched Wilson to champion Armenia's right to a free and independent national existence and to uphold his own stated principle that "the interest of the weakest is as sacred as the interest of the strongest!" [58] Widely published in American and British newspapers was the appeal of more than ninety American bishops to the Archbishop of Canterbury and the Archbishop of York: "With utmost horror we hear sinister rumor of the possibility of a continuance of Turkish suzerainty over unhappy Armenia. Through your lordships we ask that the Anglican churches do their utmost to prevent the repetition of so hideous a crime. The honor of our churches and the allied democracies demands that Armenia be unconditionally liberated from Turkish rule and restored to her own people." [59] In March outspoken Congressman Edward C. Little advocated American military intervention, maintaining that no more than five or six thousand marines would be required to police Armenia and assist in the building of her armed forces.[60]

On the initiative of the American Committee for the Independence of Armenia, a cardinal, 85 bishops, 20,000 clergymen, 40 state governors, and 250 college and university presidents petitioned Wilson to

[56] Miller, *Documents*, XVIII, 211–212.
[57] Rep. of Arm. Archives, File 230/129; US Archives, RG 256, 867B.00/131.
[58] *New York Times*, Jan. 27, 1919, p. 8. See also Gidney, *op. cit.*, p. 79.
[59] *Christian Science Monitor*, Jan. 1, 1919, p. 7.
[60] *Hairenik* (daily), March 13, 1919, p. 3.

aid in the establishment of an independent Armenia bordering the Black and the Mediterranean seas, to recognize the de facto Erevan government, and to bolster Armenia in every way possible.[61] Addressing the graduating class of 1919, Grinnell College President John H. T. Main, recently returned from his agonizing inspection tour of Armenian refugee centers, declared: "There are many difficult things that we ought to do, that we must do, whether we want to do them or not. But the Armenians are worth any cost of time and labor or money that may be involved. The Armenians are the one stabilizing influence in the group of nations that dwell in the region between the Caucasus Mountains and Constantinople." [62] On June 22 a group of prominent Americans synthesized the basic message conveyed in the numerous appeals—Charles Evans Hughes, James W. Gerard, Elihu Root, Henry Cabot Lodge, John Sharp Williams, Alfred E. Smith, Frederic Courtland Penfield, Charles W. Eliot, and Cleveland H. Dodge called on Woodrow Wilson to restore to Armenia her independence, unity, and integral lands and to give her people means for self-defense by furnishing supplies to equip an army of 50,000.[63] It was not without significance that Wilson's powerful political opponents were among the signatories.

European phil-Armenian organizations, too, stirred with activity. All invoked the exalted principles propounded by the President of the United States. In Paris on February 28 a mass rally chaired by the erudite philologist, Antoine Meillet, and addressed by Albert Thomas, Herbert Adams Gibbons, and Premier Eleutherios K. Venizelos, acclaimed a resolution reflecting the spirit of those publicized by the American supporters of Armenia.[64] Other such meetings took place in Geneva, Lausanne, Brussels, and Rome. In June British Armenophiles gathered in Westminster where General Andranik sat as guest of honor and Viscount Herbert John Gladstone, son of the late renowned champion of Armenia, presided. The younger Gladstone declared: "Armenia for generations has been spoken of, written of, sympathized with; there have been floods of sympathy. But until the time of the war little

[61] US Archives, RG 59, 763.72119/4142, and RG 256, 867B.00/62; *ACIA Activities*, p. 24; *Hairenik* (daily), April 26, 1919, p. 4, and May 22, p. 3. See also *Christian Science Monitor*, June 6, 1919, p. 4; *Congressional Record*, 66th Cong., 1st Sess., Vol. LVIII, pt. 1 (May 23, 1919), p. 156. Wilson replied on May 4 that he fully agreed the United States should accept responsibility in Armenia.

[62] *New Armenia*, XI (Oct., 1919), 157.

[63] US Archives, RG 59, 860J.01/12; *ACIA Activities*, p. 25. See also Gidney, *op. cit.*, p. 169, citing the House Papers.

[64] *L'Eclair* (Paris) as reprinted in *Hairenik* (daily), April 1, 1919, p. 3.

else. The time for action on her behalf has now arrived." Members of Parliament Viscount James Bryce, Lord Henry Cavendish-Bentinck, Thomas Power O'Connor, and Aneurin Williams and scholars Noel Buxton and G. P. Gooch each demanded the recognition of the Armenian republic and the restoration of Armenia within her historic boundaries. They chastised the leniency and hypocrisy so glaringly revealed in the Mudros Armistice and held the Allies honor bound to return this land to its ageless and veritable masters. O'Connor exclaimed, "I am proud, my old Gladstonian friends, that forty-five years ago we were fighting for the cause of Armenia, that we were as right then as we are right now, though we had to confront in those days a mad, stupid and villainous movement in favor of the Turks." Before adjourning, the British crusaders resolved: "That this Meeting expresses its satisfaction at the prospect that Turkish rule, which has desolated Armenia during centuries, will be now forever extinguished there, and trusts that the new Armenian State, which is to be set up with the friendly aid of the League of Nations, will embrace all the Armenians who dwell within the limits of the ancient Armenian Kingdom, including those who inhabit Cilicia on the south and Trans-Caucasia on the north, where an Armenian independent Republic already exists." [65]

The moving, often sentimental outbursts of one segment of American and European public opinion notwithstanding, there was in June, 1919, little in the way of concrete encouragement which Aharonian could relay to Erevan. As the first phase of the Peace Conference drew to a close, the solution to the Eastern question and, consequently, to Armenia's future was not in sight. Having accorded primacy to European issues, the Allied Powers, despite the misgivings and warnings of certain officials in their foreign ministries and peace delegations and in the field, found no compelling reason to believe that a humbled Ottoman Empire might transform into a defiant Turkey. Then too, in deferring the Turkish settlement, the peacemakers provided themselves with a certain escape hatch: a European nation forced to compromise on continental issues might be compensated with territories or zones of influence in the Near East. Recourse to such a solution was attempted repeatedly but with unhappy results. The fruitless and monotonous Armenian pleas and warnings that since the armistice "four months have passed," "five months have passed," "six months have passed," and "seven months have passed," failed to bring the Turkish peace treaty

[65] Rep. of Arm. Archives, File 333/3; *Christian Science Monitor*, June 23, 1919, p. 1; *Hairenik* (daily), April 25, 1919, p. 2, and July 20, pp. 1–2. Details of the rally are given in *New Armenia*, XI (Oct. 1919), 148–150.

any closer. Instead, Anglo-French rivalry flared ever more brilliantly in Western Asia and, to the chagrin of all except themselves, the Italians determined to transform the Mediterranean once again into Mare Nostrum. Meanwhile, the roots of Turkish resistance took hold from Constantinople to the Caucasus. Emboldened by Allied dissension and humiliated by British, French, Greek, Italian, Arab, and Armenian pretensions to their lands, the shabby but still mobilized Turkish divisions in the interior provinces resolved to test the confused and contradictory strategies of the victors in war.[66]

The Mandate Question

Though the Turkish settlement was assigned a secondary priority on the crowded agenda of the Peace Conference, delegations from the East were heard, special committees were created to conduct investigations and submit recommendations, and guidelines were adopted regarding the eventual disposition of the conquered lands. After considerable discussion and compromise it was generally agreed that the non-Turkish portions of the Ottoman Empire would be established as mandates or trust territories of the advanced powers. Thus, contrary to the secret wartime pacts of the Allies, France and Great Britain would not annex outright any part of Western Asia, but they would nonetheless be guaranteed an indefinite period of control in those lands.[67]

Lloyd George regarded the implementation of the mandate principle a feasible solution to the Armenian question:

It was obvious that we could not agree to any settlement which would leave the remnant of the persecuted population of Armenia to the cruel mercies of the race which had massacred, outraged and pillaged it for a generation and continued it through and right up to the end of the War. But Armenia, with its depopulated and dispirited remnants, could not stand alone against the Turks on the one hand, and the Bolsheviks on the other. It was therefore essential that we should find a mandatory Power which would undertake as a humane duty the protection of this harried Christian community in the mountains of Armenia. . . .
Russia would have been the most fitting choice for a mandatory in Armenia and the Straits. Up to the Revolution her religious sympa-

[66] The emergence of the Turkish resistance movement is discussed in chapter 13 below.

[67] The deliberations on the issue of whether victorious states should annex the colonies of the Central Powers or else transform them into mandates are in *Paris Peace Conference*, III, 718–728, 736–771 *passim;* Miller, *Documents,* XIV, 10–12, 22–34, 36–52. See also Evans, *op. cit.,* pp. 94–100; Seth P. Tillman, *Anglo-American Relations at the Peace Conference of 1919* (Princeton, 1961), pp. 85–98.

thies were engaged in a crusade for the protection of the Christian communities of Turkey. It was her military intervention that had emancipated the Christians of the Balkans and a portion of the Christians in the Armenian valleys. Had it not been for our [British] sinister intervention, the great majority of the Armenians would have been placed, by the Treaty of San Stefano in 1878, under the protection of the Russian flag.[68]

But all this had now passed. Because Russia was no longer in a position to annex Turkish Armenia and Constantinople, areas previously reserved for her, some new arrangement was required. None of the remaining Allied Powers was inclined to serve as the mandatory for Armenia, a desolate land rich only in problems. France, of course, coveted Cilicia and the economically promising mineral deposits extending toward Sivas and Diarbekir, but the colonialist elements in Paris no longer regarded these districts as integral to Armenia. Thus, if the United States could be led to accept the Armenian mandate, the European Allies would consider the void neatly filled. The unanimity of European sentiment on this issue has been corroborated by Lloyd George:

Neither Britain nor Italy was prepared to step into the abandoned shoes of Russia, and although France was ready and even eager at that time to secure dominion over the Southern part of Armenia, she was by no means prepared to extend her control to the Northern part of the province. French, British and Italians alike were driven to the conclusion that America alone was capable of discharging adequately the responsibilities of a mandatory. When the delegates of the Great Powers assembled at the Conference examined the difficulties, it became clear that America was the only mandatory who would have been acceptable to all alike.[69]

In January, 1919, even while arrangements for the Peace Conference were yet incomplete, British officials made known their hope that the United States would take charge in Constantinople and Armenia, and Lloyd George raised the subject during his very first postwar business meeting with President Wilson.[70] The British enthusiasm to thrust the Armenian mandate upon America was quite understandable to David Hunter Miller: "Doubtless the United States will get such of those as

[68] David Lloyd George, *Memoirs of the Peace Conference* (2 vols.; New Haven, 1939), II, 810–811.

[69] *Ibid.*, p. 813.

[70] Miller, *Documents*, I, 74; Lloyd George, *op. cit.*, I, 117–118. See also the minutes of the meetings of the British Empire Delegation in Britain, Cab 29/28.

Great Britain thinks too difficult for herself, and those will lie in the hands of the United States as a bulwark of the British Empire; such as Armenia." [71] A later analyst remarked that "the tribulations sure to arise in these two areas [Constantinople and Armenia] were certain to exceed the profits to be taken from them—there were no rich oil fields there—so it was assumed that rich Uncle Sam would play the role of the Good Samaritan." [72] These assessments aside, the United States was the unanimous choice of not only the Allies but of the Armenian people themselves.[73]

By January 30, 1919, the authoritative Council of Ten of the Paris Peace Conference had achieved sufficient compromise on the mandate system to adopt a statement of principles. It was decided that, because Germany had misgoverned her colonies and might continue to use them as menacing submarine bases, they would not be restored to her. The section relating to the Ottoman Empire read: "For similar reasons, and more particularly because of the historical misgovernment of the Turks of subject peoples and the terrible massacres of Armenians and others in recent years, the Allied and Associated Powers are agreed that Armenia, Syria, Mesopotamia, Palestine and Arabia must be completely severed from the Turkish Empire. This is without prejudice to the settlement of other parts of the Turkish Empire." The erstwhile German and Turkish possessions inhabited by peoples not yet prepared for self-government were to be made the "sacred trust of civilization," as embodied in the League of Nations. But for several of the non-Turkish Ottoman peoples there was to be a somewhat different arrangement: "Certain communities formerly belonging to the Turkish Empire have reached a stage of development where their existence as independent nations can be provisionally recognized subject to the rendering of administrative advice and assistance by a mandatory power until such time as they are able to stand alone. The wishes of these communities must be a principal consideration in the selection of the mandatory power." [74]

That same day, during the afternoon session of the Council of Ten, Woodrow Wilson busily engaged in evading commitments. He rejected a proposal to assign temporary mandates at once, arguing that it would

[71] David Hunter Miller, *The Drafting of the Covenant* (2 vols.; New York, 1928), I, 47.

[72] Thomas A. Bailey, *Woodrow Wilson and the Lost Peace* (New York, 1947), p. 170.

[73] Representative Armenian petitions for American protection are in US Archives, RG 256, 183.9 *Armenia/3/13½*; Rep. of Arm. Archives, File 230/129.

[74] *Paris Peace Conference*, III, 785–786, 795–796; Miller, *Documents*, XIV, 111, 130–131; Charles Seymour, ed., *The Intimate Papers of Colonel House*, Vol. IV (Boston and New York, [1928]), pp. 319–320.

be far more expedient simply to provide for military control in the regions to be separated from the Ottoman Empire. Of course, inasmuch as the United States had not declared war on Turkey, the European Allies would have to determine the means and manner of that control. David Lloyd George retorted that Great Britain was burdened in the Ottoman Empire with the support of approximately one million fighting men, of whom up to 300,000 were British, and it should therefore be clear that his country could not endure this great strain pending the final Turkish settlement or the functional establishment of the League of Nations. President Wilson had no need to pose technical obstacles to American participation in the mandate system, Lloyd George concluded, for the Turks well knew that they were to lose Armenia and Syria and would certainly prefer the presence of the United States in Armenia to that of any other power. Wilson was doubtful whether the American public would accept any obligations in Asia, but if it was expected of him to urge them to do so, the entire mandate question would have to be tabled until he could explain the situation to them.[75]

Having rendered the Turkish settlement even more remote by this condition, Wilson seemed to complicate the matter further by diluting his cautious formal pronouncements with frequent personal expressions of hope that the United States would accept the mandate. During the opening session of the League of Nations Commission on February 3, 1919, for example, he mentioned American opposition to involvement in European affairs, yet sources close to the President let it be known that he would be disposed to ask the country to make an exception in the case of Armenia.[76] To muster grass roots support for the League of Nations Covenant, Wilson undertook a whirlwind journey, sailing to the United States in mid-February, speaking along the eastern seaboard from Boston to Washington, and returning to Paris on March 14. This diversion kept the mandate issue in abeyance at the Peace Conference, but the President was constantly aware of its importance. Even while homeward bound upon the high seas, he searched for the right approach to coax a reluctant nation. The topic was broached on his first day ashore, February 24, as he addressed some 7,000 supporters in Boston, the backyard of his influential foe, Henry Cabot Lodge.[77] "Have

[75] Miller, *Documents*, XIV, 104–105. See also Charles T. Thompson, *The Peace Conference Day by Day* (New York [1920]), pp. 164–166.

[76] For a statement regarding this meeting of the League of Nations Commission, with reference to the Armenian question, see *New York Times*, Feb. 4, 1919, pp. 1–2.

[77] In January, White House Secretary Tumulty had urged Wilson to make an appearance in New England upon returning from Europe. Tumulty noted that the President had not been in that section of the country for some time and that an

you thought of the sufferings of Armenia?" Wilson exclaimed. "You poured out your money to help succor the Armenians after they suffered; now set up your strength so that they shall never suffer again." [78]

Two days later during a White House conference with members of the Foreign Relations Committees of the House and of the Senate, the President voiced his belief that the United States would want to shoulder the Armenian mandate.[79] Then on February 28 he told the Democratic National Committee that he had responded to Allied pressure to accept the obligation by stating that, although he was not sure the nation would agree, he was "perfectly willing to go home and stump the country and see if they will do it. . . ." Thereupon, he disclosed his sincere desire:

Now what I wanted to suggest is this: Personally, and just within the limits of this room, I can say very frankly that I think we ought to. I think there is a very promising beginning in regard to countries like Armenia. The whole heart of America has been engaged for Armenia. They know more about Armenia and its sufferings than they know about any other European area; we have colleges out there; we have great missionary enterprises, just as we have had Robert College in Constantinople. That is a part of the world where already American influence extends, a saving influence and an educating and an uplifting influence. . . . I am not without hope that the people of the United States would find it acceptable to go in and be the trustee of the interests of the Armenian people and see to it that the unspeakable Turk and the almost equally difficult Kurd had their necks sat on long enough to teach them manners and give the industrious and earnest people of Armenia time to develop a country which is naturally rich with possibilities.

Wilson urged all members of the National Committee to advocate publicly an American mandate over Armenia and the Constantinople-Straits region.[80]

Colonel House, the President's unofficial alternate in Paris, found it useful meanwhile to join in confidential discussions with Lloyd George, Clemenceau, and occasionally Orlando.[81] During one such tête à tête

---

enthusiastic demonstration of public support there would effectively undermine the position of Senator Lodge. See Joseph P. Tumulty, *Woodrow Wilson As I Know Him* ([Garden City, N.Y., 1921]), p. 517

[78] *New York Times*, Feb. 25, 1919, p. 1; *Current History*, X, pt. 1 (April, 1919), 87.

[79] *Christian Science Monitor*, Feb. 27, 1919, p. 1.

[80] Tumulty, *op. cit.*, pp. 376–377.

[81] In Wilson's absence, Secretary of State Lansing was the official ranking member of the American Commission to Negotiate Peace, but in fact it was House who acted for the President in matters requiring the attention of the Allied chiefs of state.

on March 7, he answered the European demand for American participation in the mandate system by divulging that he "thought the United
States would be willing when the proposal was brought before them." [82]
Lloyd George confirmed that in any distribution of mandates, France
would have jurisdiction over Syria, at which point Clemenceau quickly
interjected "and Cilicia." The old "Tiger" again reviewed the French
case for both Syria and Cilicia, but his American and British colleagues
rejected the pretensions to Cilicia, since this land "comprised the richest parts of the projected state of Armenia, and the United States might
take a mandate for it." [83] Colonel House confided to Lloyd George
that he had "no notion of allowing Armenia to be broken up without a
fight." [84] That same day he cabled the gist of this discussion to Wilson,
who, however, ignored the topic in his reply. House understood that it
would not be prudent to take up the question again. Consequently,
when on March 11 an agenda item on Turkey's future boundaries came
before an official session of the Peace Conference, Lloyd George dismissed the topic with the observation that no action was possible until
the President had returned to Paris with the American decision.[85] But
Wilson had by then arrived at the conclusion that it was "premature
and unwise" to launch a mandate campaign in the United States. Time
was needed, he told Acting Secretary of State Frank L. Polk, to prepare
American public opinion.[86] Senator Lodge, although a member of the
American Committee for the Independence of Armenia and an advocate of recognition and assistance to the Armenian republic, opposed
the League of Nations Covenant and its inclusive mandate scheme as
submitted by the President. The powerful Republican and chairman of
the Senate Foreign Relations Committee already had enough votes to
deny ratification unless his "reservations" were accepted by the Administration. Still, Woodrow Wilson believed that somehow he would bring
a sympathetic public to compel the Senate to yield.[87]

[82] Seymour, op. cit., pp. 358–359. Lloyd George, op. cit., I, 189, gives the following
account: "I asked Colonel House whether America would be prepared to accept a
mandatory in respect of the Turkish Empire, and I pressed him specially as to their
view for taking a mandate for Armenia and Constantinople. He replied that America was not in the least anxious to take these mandates, but that she felt she could
not shirk her share of the burden and he thought America would be prepared to
take the mandates for Armenia and Constantinople."
[83] Howard, op. cit., p. 32; Evans, op. cit., p. 133; Lloyd George, op. cit., I, 189–190.
[84] Gidney, op. cit., pp. 85–86.
[85] Paris Peace Conference, IV, 325–326; Miller, Documents, XV, 328.
[86] Tillman, op. cit., p. 368.
[87] On March 4, 1919, Senator Lodge produced the "Round Robin," signed by
thirty-seven Republican senators, four more than was needed to block ratification of
the peace treaty, should it include the League of Nations Covenant without the revi-

An Inter-Allied Commission and Cilicia

The intimate meetings between Colonel House and the European premiers having proved reasonably effective, the Council of Ten, with its chronic leakage of secret information, gave way to the Council of Four shortly after President Wilson rejoined his colleagues in Paris on March 14. Wilson, Clemenceau, Lloyd George, and Orlando thereafter decided when and if their foreign ministers (who with the Japanese delegate met separately as the Council of Five) were to attend.[88]

During the session of March 20 Near Eastern rivalries vaulted into the open, and, for the first time since the beginning of the Peace Conference, the secret wartime agreements were thoroughly aired. Stephen Pichon accused Angleterre of contriving to deny France her historic and just rights in Syria and Cilicia by stubbornly refusing to relinquish these regions, whereas Lloyd George minimized French participation in liberating the Levant and maintained that modifications in the secret Sykes-Picot agreement of 1916 were in order even though Great Britain had not the slightest interest in taking Syria for herself. President Wilson interjected that Cilicia connected Armenia with the Mediterranean and that there would be "a great danger of friction" if one mandatory (France) managed affairs in the south of Armenia and another (possibly the United States) in the north of Armenia. As for the dispute over Syria, the President suggested that an inter-Allied commission be sent to ascertain the needs and desires of the people themselves. This proposal, previously advanced by several of Wilson's advisers, displeased Lloyd George and Clemenceau, but caught off guard momentarily they could offer no substantial basis for objection. Clemenceau did stipulate, however, that the investigation should extend to the other areas to be severed from Turkey, such as Palestine, Mesopotamia, and Armenia. It was Foreign Secretary Balfour who cautioned that this course of action might delay the final treaty with Turkey. But Woodrow Wilson demurred: "For the purpose of peace, all that was necessary to tell Turkey

---

sions demanded by Lodge and his supporters. See Herbert Hoover, *The Ordeal of Woodrow Wilson* (New York, Toronto, and London, [1958]), pp. 187–188; John Morton Blum, *Woodrow Wilson and the Politics of Morality* (Boston, [1956]), pp. 170–172; Rayford W. Logan, *The Senate and the Versailles Mandate System* (Washington, D.C., 1945), pp. 34–38.

[88] The Council of Four met from March 20 through June 28, 1919, and, like the erstwhile Council of Ten, was known also as the Supreme Council. Some authors use the name Council of Three to denote those sessions from which Premier Orlando was absent. For a reliable account regarding the formation of the Council of Four, see Lord [Maurice] Hankey, *The Supreme Control at the Paris Peace Conference 1919* (London, [1963]), pp. 97–119.

was that she would have nothing." At a later date Turkey would be informed "who would be her next-door neighbor." [89]

The inter-Allied commission on Turkish mandates, according to the instructions drafted by the American delegation and adopted by the Council of Four, was to study the social, economic, and racial situation in the lands it visited and to report on the sentiments of the native populations regarding the future administration of these regions.[90] The decision to dispatch the mission was not welcomed by Avetis Aharonian, Boghos Nubar, and informed Armenian sympathizers. To await the completion of the investigation, they protested, would cause existing rivalries to be exacerbated and the agonizing uncertainties to be perpetuated. Even if the commission submitted findings favorable to Armenia, the effect of time lost in naming a mandatory power would heavily outweigh all potential advantages.[91] Of like mind, the American delegation's Western Asian Division advised that there already was ample information on which to base the Near Eastern settlement.[92] But President Wilson was not to be dissuaded from his project.

The inter-Allied commission did not, in fact, materialize. Clemenceau and Lloyd George soon resorted to obstructionism. The British eventually appointed envoys but withheld permission for them to depart until such time as the French would see fit to dispatch their own representatives. And while Clemenceau gave assurances that French commissioners would be named, he chided Lloyd George for not prodding Emir Feisal toward acceptance of a French mandate in Syria. Disregarding the original purpose of the inter-Allied delegation, Clemenceau insisted that the mandates in the Near East be apportioned to the interested powers before the fact-finding mission left Paris.[93]

[89] Baker, op. cit., III, 1–19; Paris Peace Conference, V, 1–14; Howard, op. cit., pp. 33–34. For the earlier suggestions to send a fact-finding team to the Near East, see Gidney, op. cit., pp. 136–140; Miller, Documents, XIV, 391–399; Evans, op. cit., pp. 104–105; Paris Peace Conference, III, 1015–1021.

[90] Paris Peace Conference, XII (1947), 745–747. See also Miller, Documents, XV, 505–508. For British papers relating to this mission, see FO 608/86, File 349/1/3.

[91] Rep. of Arm. Archives, File 103/2, H. H. Patvirakutiun, 1919 t.

[92] Howard, op. cit., pp. 47–48; Gidney, op. cit., p. 145; Evans, op. cit., p. 143; Paris Peace Conference, XI (1945), 155.

[93] Howard, op. cit., pp. 41–50 passim; Evans, op. cit., pp. 145–146. When news of this altercation reached London, Lord Curzon, who held the fixed belief that the Middle East formed the fulcrum of the world interests of Great Britain, deprecated the "divided councils and conflicting ambitions" that threatened to rob the Empire of the fruits of victory. In a memorandum penned on April 18, Curzon enjoined the British Empire Delegation to resolve the outstanding differences with France so that an early decision on the Eastern settlement could be realized. He was astounded by the venomous atmosphere weighing upon the Peace Conference, especially as the outlines of the postwar Middle East structure had previously been worked out by France

By the end of April the American commissioners, Henry Churchill King, President of Oberlin College, and Charles Richard Crane, an industrialist who had served as United States envoy extraordinary in Asia, were ready to abandon the undertaking, but Woodrow Wilson, in an intractable mood, announced that the American section would complete its assignment whether or not the other nations cooperated. Finally in late-May, after repeated delays and vain efforts to placate the bickering European governments, the American section, subsequently dubbed the King-Crane Commission,[94] set out for Constantinople. Thereupon Georges Clemenceau revealed that France would not participate until her right to Syria was recognized, and David Lloyd George reiterated Great Britain's inability to share in the project without the collaboration of France. Vittorio Orlando added garnish to the stalemate by declaring Italian noninvolvement in the "inter-Allied" venture. The "frocks" had put themselves and the issues into utter disarray.[95]

Meanwhile, Armenophiles, particularly officials of the American Committee for the Independence of Armenia, saturated Paris with admonitions and protests against the perversity of the French government in attempting to seize Cilicia by having it annexed to Syria. When in

and Great Britain. According to the overall plan, Armenia and possibly Cilicia were to be separated from the Ottoman Empire, but the rest of Asia Minor was to be left to the Turks as a residue of their former domains. But matters had now run afoul, as even Italy, "the most fantastic of all the aspirants," was establishing a chain of claims from Adalia to the Caucasus. Curzon stressed that Britain and France must resolve the Syrian question in private consultations and come to an understanding with the United States about the future of Cilicia. The "silly" project to dispatch an inter-Allied commission to the Levant should be abandoned immediately for "delay is the certain precursor, it has already been the main cause, of fresh outbreaks in the Eastern world." The Acting Undersecretary of State for Foreign Affairs warned that Allied rivalries were enabling the Ittihadists to continue their activities in the interior Ottoman provinces and were contributing to the coalescence of Muslim opposition sentiment. He chided the peacemakers with the following premonition: "The fate of Armenia is still not decided, and there is a good chance that, when it is, the difficulty will be, not to define Armenia, but to find the Armenians." When Curzon's memorandum was received in Paris, Lord Hardinge of Penshurst, the Permanent Undersecretary of State, attached to it the following observation: "Sitting in a comfortable armchair in Downing Street it is very easy to criticise, although there is much force to many of Lord Curzon's views, and he does not seem to realise that we cannot have entirely our own way or rather his way in a Conference with Powers with ambitions like France and Italy, or with an idealistic Power such as the United States." See Britain, FO 608/83, 342/8/4/7919/8514, and FO 406/41, no. 37.

[94] The King-Crane Commission will be discussed in the second volume of this history. The findings of the commission are in Paris Peace Conference, XII, 751-863, while the study by Harry N. Howard, cited in note 45 above, provides a detailed account of its organization, activities, and recommendations.

[95] Peace Conference, VI (1946), 132-133; Howard, op. cit., pp. 82-84. See also Britain, FO 406/41 passim.

February, 1919, an outburst of interracial hostilities in Adana and Aleppo left a number of Armenian refugees and repatriates dead, there were many who pointed the finger of guilt at Clemenceau's cabinet, in particular at Foreign Minister Pichon, an incontrovertible imperialist. French officers in Cilicia, it was asserted, were acting in collusion with Turkish leaders and had boasted that they would force Armenia to drop her claims to this fertile and strategic region. They had clamped excessive restrictions upon the Armenian Legion (previously the Légion d'Orient) and had even ordered the Armenian flag removed during a public function. Should Cilicia fall to any state but Armenia, exclaimed the outspoken Armenophiles, the Ittihadist policy of annihilation will have been crowned and shamefully rewarded.[96]

Former Secretary of State William Jennings Bryan again enumerated these contentions in a cable to President Wilson on March 18 and warned that to confine Armenia to an outlet on the Black Sea would in fact place the new country in a position more untenable than that of Serbia in 1914. The Allied nations must not drape this additional injustice upon the Armenian people. In a prompt reply Wilson noted that he was in full agreement with Bryan.[97] Not to be eclipsed as a crusader, James W. Gerard frequently exhorted the American Commission to Negotiate Peace to defend the Armenian lamb from the voracious wolves in the forest. In April he wired Colonel House the text of a protest he intended to dispatch to Pichon concerning French irregularities in Cilicia.[98] House was quick to advise against sending the blunt message, claiming that he had looked into the status of the Armenian question and found matters going very favorably. Acting Secretary of State Polk apparently joined House in dissuading Gerard from forwarding the wire that would certainly have outraged and scandalized the French Foreign Minister.[99]

The future status of Cilicia, House's assurances aside, became even more uncertain in May, as Italian troops struck out along the southern coastline of Asia Minor, while in Paris a small but significant current of official opinion began to jell in favor of a lenient settlement with

---

[96] For accounts of the bloodshed in Adana and Aleppo, see Le Temps, March 12, 1919, p. 4; Hairenik (daily), April 4, 12, 16, 17, 23, June 24-28, July 1-3, 23, 1919; Gidney, op. cit., p. 86. See also Britain, FO 371/3658, 47515/47516/512/58.

[97] Reprinted in Hairenik (daily), March 30, 1919, p. 3.

[98] Gidney, op. cit. p. 89; Hairenik (daily), April 30, 1919. p. 2.

[99] Hairenik (daily), May 4, 1919, p. 2. Gidney, op. cit., p. 89, shows Polk to be the author of the message to Gerard. While both House and Polk could conceivably have given the same advice, it is more likely that House's reply to Gerard was relayed via Polk's office at the Department of State.

Turkey.[100] Aroused by these unfavorable omens to yet more fervid activity, Gerard let loose a telegraphic barrage, reminding Wilson, House, Balfour, Clemenceau, Pichon, and Sonnino of specific statements and pledges each had made regarding the destiny of Armenia. Citing Wilson's response to Bryan, Gerard urged the President to uphold the boundaries outlined in the joint memorandum of Boghos Nubar and Aharonian. He demanded that should the Peace Conference contemplate any changes the American Committee for the Independence of Armenia at least be permitted to present its views in Paris. Gerard cautioned Foreign Secretary Balfour that any manipulation to deprive Armenia of her integral lands would prompt a sharp American reaction against the Peace Conference and against Europe in general. Public concern for the welfare of the Armenians, he said, was greater than it had ever been for any other people at any time. The ACIA chairman reminded Clemenceau and Pichon that the United States had risen to the defense of France when her rights had been violated. Should not the Third Republic now defend the just and inalienable rights of the Armenians? [101]

The fate of Cilicia, like that of Armenia as a whole, was not unlocked in 1919. Pichon and lesser French officials such as Jean Gout made it known privately that they would oppose an American mandate for Armenia were Cilicia included, but Clemenceau was more conciliatory. On April 14 he told Colonel House that France would acquiesce in the loss of Cilicia, excepting Alexandretta and its immediate hinterland, if the United States would take the mandate for Armenia.[102] Three days later Wilson reassured Aharonian and Nubar that Armenia stood foremost among any foreign obligations the United States might accept.[103] Still, even though his Near East advisers were now recommending American supervision from Cilicia to the Caucasus, the President slipped back into his fetters during formal sessions of the Peace Con-

[100] By mid-May, House himself was no longer so confident that all was well in regard to the Armenian question. He informed Gerard that it might be advisable for the ACIA to send someone to Paris. See US Archives, RG 256, 867B.00/122a.

[101] Releases of the Armenian Press Bureau, New York, in *Hairenik* (daily), May 22, 1919, pp. 2–3, and May 23, pp. 1–2. Gerard's cable to Balfour was filed in the Foreign Office with the following notation: "It is only irritating to receive this sort of thing from responsible Americans who must know well enough that the fate of Armenia lies in their own hands. If they would stir up their own foot instead of sending these futile appeals to us they might give some real help to the Armenian cause." An addendum reads: "I don't know why even ex-American ambassadors should apparently consider that we are all-powerful at the Conference." See Britain, FO 371/3658, 74847/512/58.

[102] Evans, *op. cit.*, pp. 149–150, n. 29.

[103] Aharonian, *Sardarapatits Sevr*, pp. 18–19.

ference. When on May 5 Lloyd George professed an eagerness to resolve the mandate question, Wilson interjected that "it could hardly be settled in 48 hours." [104]

Impulsive Mandate Schemes

In May of 1919, as Italian troops disembarked along the coast of Asia Minor and Allied destroyers steamed toward Smyrna to provide cover for the Greek divisions scheduled to go ashore, the Council of Four entertained in astounding succession one mandate scheme after another. The fluidity of the situation in the Near East was borne out by the floundering attempts of the Allied leaders to persuade the Italians to renounce their claims to the eastern Adriatic in return for compensation in Asia Minor.[105] Immediately after a private conference with Orlando and Sonnino on May 13, Lloyd George proposed to his French and American colleagues that room be made in Anatolia for an Italian mandate.[106] He glazed over this bribe by characterizing the Italians as an "extremely gifted race" of administrators. They could do much good in Asia Minor, which was in a "rut" just as Gaul and Britain had been before the Romans had come along. "It was curious," continued the loquacious Prime Minister, that the Italians had recently "developed some of the qualities for which the Romans had been famous." They were "vigorous and manly" and could deal with unruly populations and brigands. Thus, he now proposed placing Armenia under an American mandate, "Northern Anatolia" under France, "Southern Anatolia" under Italy, and Smyrna, with its environs and any other territories Venizelos had claimed, under Greece. Turkey as a separate sovereign state would cease to exist.[107]

The pie had been neatly cut by Lloyd George, but Wilson was compelled to reiterate that "he could not settle this question until he had returned to the United States and definitely ascertained whether the

[104] *Paris Peace Conference*, V, 472. American involvement in the mandate scheme was persistently opposed by Secretary of State Lansing. For his position and harsh criticism of Woodrow Wilson, see his account, *The Peace Negotiations: A Personal Narrative* (Boston and New York, 1921), pp. 149–161.

[105] For studies and documents of the Fiume-Adriatic controversy during Orlando's premiership, see Albrecht-Carrié, *op. cit.*, pp. 86–200, 364–525; Baker, *op. cit.*, II, 127–180, and III, 259–307; Thompson, *op. cit.*, pp. 317–341; Hankey, *op. cit.*, pp. 120–133, 162–166; Ivo J. Lederer, *Yugoslavia at the Paris Peace Conference* (New Haven and London, 1963).

[106] Harold Nicolson, *Peacemaking* (London, [1945]), pp. 272–273; Albrecht-Carrié, *op. cit.*, pp. 220–221.

[107] Mantoux, *op. cit.*, II, 57–58; *Paris Peace Conference*, V, 581–583. See also Baker, *op. cit.*, II, 186–187.

United States would accept a mandate." Clemenceau observed that America would have no easy time administering Armenia, "a state where massacre is a chronic malady," to which Wilson added that "he had at the present moment before him reports on affairs in Armenia of such an appalling nature that he found it difficult to read them." Many Armenians interned by the Turks were starving to death. Lloyd George concurred that "the Turk is a brute" and suggested it might be worthwhile to publicize these sad reports to augment American popular support for the mandate.[108]

Lloyd George's mandate plan was embodied in two resolutions submitted to the Council of Four, minus the still recalcitrant Orlando, the following afternoon.[109] The first of these affirmed that the President of the United States, *subject to the consent of the Senate,* would assume the mandate over the Constantinople-Straits region and "over the Province of Armenia as constituted within the frontiers to be agreed upon between the United States, British, French and Italian Delegations, whose recommendations, if unanimous, shall be accepted without further reference to the Council." The second resolution decreed an end to Ottoman rule in European Turkey, the Straits, and the Aegean coastal region from Smyrna to Aivali and reserved the remainder of Anatolia (but not the Armenian provinces) for French, Italian, and Greek mandates.[110]

Upon the Council's adoption of these complementary resolutions, President Wilson noted that the exact limits of several mandates had still to be determined and that certain discrepancies between the British and the American sketches of Armenia's future boundaries needed to be reconciled (see map 12). One important difference, for example, centered on the disposition of the port of Alexandretta, and Lloyd George observed a considerable variance in the western border near the Black Sea as he examined the large map in Wilson's antechamber. The two leaders agreed that further consultation with the regional experts was in order.[111] From the Armenian point of view it was significant that both the United States and Great Britain continued to act on the assumption that Armenia would extend to the Mediterranean Sea. Specifically, the second resolution adopted by the Council of Four reinforced

[108] Mantoux, *op. cit.,* II, p. 60. See also *Paris Peace Conference,* V, 585.

[109] Harold G. Nicolson, who had been given the responsibility of drafting the resolutions, termed them "terribly unreal." See his *Peacemaking,* p. 275.

[110] *Paris Peace Conference,* V, 614–616, 618–620, 622–623.

[111] *Ibid.,* p. 616. In the several alternative plans prepared by British advisers, Armenia's boundary invariably lay to the west of the Ordu-Sivas line. See Britain, FO 608/80, 342/1/13/7798/8483/8857.

this conclusion, for the proposed Italian mandate in southern Anatolia was to stretch along the seaboard "to the point where the suggested frontier for Armenia strikes the Mediterranean." [112]

Ray Stannard Baker subsequently termed the decision of the Council of Four as "one of the most remarkable episodes of the entire adventure of Paris, in which the Peace Conference set sail on the wings of Lloyd George's fervid imagination and remained aloft until the pilot himself lost his nerve and, as it were, took a nose-dive!" [113] That nose dive came with celerity as Lloyd George, seconded by Woodrow Wilson, executed a volte-face within the next few days. The two campaigners feared lest the Italians had acquired too many Roman qualities and aspired to the revivification of the Roman Empire. The Italian army, impervious to the schemes laid out in Paris and acting without the sanction of the Peace Conference, was landing more troops along the Anatolian coast and spreading its field of operations inland. Orlando's government wanted its way both in Asia Minor and in the eastern Adriatic region. The conviction that the Italians had become insatiable, coupled with the impact of worldwide Muslim opinion, was to prompt the Council of Four to a stunning reversal.

The British Cabinet was by no means united behind David Lloyd George. Men of influence in the War Office, the Admiralty, the Board of Trade, and the India Office voiced impatient criticism of the lately espoused policy overthrowing the traditional British stance toward Turkey. The conservatives, such as Secretary of State for India Sir Edwin Montagu and Chief of the Imperial General Staff Sir Henry Wilson, condemned the proceedings in Paris as disastrous to the vital world interests of Great Britain. On May 15 Montagu arrived in Paris to impress upon Lloyd George that the partition of Turkey would lead to "eternal war with the Mohammedan world." He was supported by Sir Henry, who quipped that "we don't want to increase our troubles by breaking up Turkey and dividing her amongst a lot of people— Greek, Italians, French and Americans—who can't even govern them-selves." [114] On the sixteenth Montagu took his protests to Colonel

---

[112] *Paris Peace Conference*, V, 623.

[113] Baker, *op. cit.*, II, 187.

[114] Callwell, *op. cit.*, II, 193. These views were shared by Rear Admiral Bristol, whose dispatches from Constantinople repeatedly advised against the partition of the Ottoman Empire. Rather than the creation of another "Balkan Question," Bristol advocated keeping the empire as a single unit and affording it the close supervision that would bring all its peoples the fruits of "civilization." The United States, he insisted, should take the "large point of view" and not be drawn into "a small question like Armenia through the self-interests of the European countries or by the sentimentalism of some of our missionaries and relief workers." Bristol

House, warning that the Muslim faithful were agitated by the unfavorable news regarding the Turkish Empire.[115] Foreign Secretary Balfour, who was not so immoderate in his disapproval of Lloyd George, prepared that day a memorandum advising a new approach to the Eastern question. That Turkey should lose her European possessions, the Arab-speaking population, and Armenia was right and just, but to partition the intrinsically Turkish heartlands of Anatolia in order to satisfy the whetted Italian appetite was not only unjust but fraught with extreme danger. In the absence of a more satisfactory solution, Balfour recommended that Anatolia be retained as an unmandated sovereign Turkish state and that the Italians be placated with certain economic concessions along that country's southern shoreline.[116]

Lloyd George circulated the memorandum to Wilson and Clemenceau on May 17 and took pains to emphasize that his previous proposals had been only suggestive in nature. Indeed, he now had grave misgivings as to their wisdom, for the entire Muslim world would be inflamed.[117] In the afternoon session of the Council of Four, with Orlando present, Montagu introduced the Agha Khan and other Indian notables who had come to plead for the integrity of Turkey and, in particular, for the retention of the Sultan-Caliph in Constantinople.[118] The

complained bitterly that the politicians who were taking actions favorable to the Greeks and the Armenians were not dealing with realities:

Without knowing these persecuted races, one naturally believes that they need only be set free from the Turkish yoke in order to correct all evils that they have been suffering from. A study of the subject demonstrates that these subjected races have many flaws and deficiencies of character that do not fit them for self-government. Still farther it is found that instead of there being certain districts which are inhabited by one race, as one is ordinarily led to believe by reading books and papers, it is found that the different races are intermingled throughout the country. Further, it is found that this is the desire of the people. The individual traits of the different races makes this living together a mutual benefit. The Turk has some individual traits of character that are so far superior to those of the other races that one is led to sympathize with the Turk, though you never forget the bad traits of his character that are illustrated by the acts committed against the subject races.

See Bristol Papers, Box 16, Report of May 25, 1919; Box 36, Correspondence of March 1 and May 18, 1919.

[115] Seymour, op. cit., p. 467.

[116] Paris Peace Conference, V, 664–672; Baker, op. cit., III, 303–307.

[117] Paris Peace Conference, V, 666–669.

[118] Baker, op. cit., II, 197–198, intimates that Lloyd George arranged for the Muslims to be brought in to provide him with some justification to reverse his previous position. Nicolson has postulated that Muslim world opinion was never vitally concerned with the fate of the Sultan Caliph or of the Ottoman Empire but that certain individuals created this specter to sway members of the British Cabinet. See Harold Nicolson, Curzon: The Last Phase, 1919–1925 (London, [1937]), pp. 98–103. Various petitions by Muslim spokesmen on this question are in Britain, FO 608/111, File 385/1/14.

31. BOGHOS NUBAR PASHA   32. MIKAYEL PAPADJANIAN

33. *Seated:* AVETIS AHARONIAN, ARMENAK BARSEGHIAN, HAKOB NEVRUZ *Standing:* HAMAZASP
OHANDJANIAN, MANUK HAMBARDZUMIAN, GAREGIN PASDERMADJIAN, ZATIK MATIKIAN

34. GENERAL GABRIEL KORGANIAN

35. MIKAYEL VARANDIAN

36. NIKOLAI CHKHEIDZE

37. IRAKLII TSERETELI

38. ELEUTHERIOS VENIZELOS

39. VISCOUNT JAMES BRYCE

40. GEORGES CLEMENCEAU, DAVID LLOYD GEORGE, VITTORIO ORLANDO

41. STEPEN PICHON

42. ARTHUR JAMES BALFOUR

43. BARON SIDNEY SONNINO

44. SIR HENRY HUGHES WILSON

45. WOODROW WILSON

46. EDWARD M. HOUSE

47. WILLIAM JENNINGS BRYAN AND ROBERT LANSING

48. HENRY CABOT LODGE

49. JAMES W. GERARD

50. V. I. LENIN

51. I. V. STALIN

52. STEPAN SHAHUMIAN

53. ARSHAVIR MELIKIAN

54. VARLAAM AVANESOV

55. ANASTAS MIKOYAN

56. HAKOB ZAVRIEV

57. LIPARIT NAZARIANTS

58. ANTON I. DENIKIN

59. ALEKSANDR V. KOLCHAK

60 – 62. TIFLIS, BAKU, AND EREVAN IN 1919

63. DELEGATES TO THE ARMENIAN NATIONAL CONGRESS, PARIS, FEBRUARY-APRIL, 1919
Seated: HAKOB NEVRUZ, PROFESSOR ABRAHAM TER-HAKOBIAN, VAHAN TEKEYAN,
GABRIEL NORADOUNGIAN, ARCHBISHOP EGHISHE TURIAN, BOGHOS NUBAR, ARSHAK CHOBANIAN

64. FIRST ANNIVERSARY OF THE ARMENIAN REPUBLIC, EREVAN, MAY 28, 1919

Agha Khan, claiming to express the sentiment of all Indians, both Muslim and Hindu, implored the Peace Conference to leave to the Turkish race its homeland of "centuries and centuries," above all Constantinople and Anatolia, and to guarantee in the region called Armenia equality for all races, all religions, and all peoples. Another Muslim spokesman, petitioning that Constantinople be preserved as the seat of the revered Sultanate-Caliphate, recited verbatim the war aims of Wilson and Lloyd George, who had specifically disclaimed any intention of depriving Turkey of her capital and Anatolian heartlands. Before withdrawing, the Indian Muslim leaders beseeched the peacemakers to uphold the principle of self-determination and to prove to the communicants of Islam that justice would prevail. Lloyd George was visibly moved by the presentation and confided to his colleagues that neither Great Britain nor France, as "Great Moslem Powers," nor even the United States, if she took a mandate, could afford the turmoil which would arise were the Sultan ejected from Constantinople. Would it not be possible to leave the Sultan where he was, but under an American mandate? [119]

The issue was of such vital importance to Great Britain that most of the Cabinet arrived in Paris on May 18 to consult with and advise Lloyd George.[120] On the nineteenth both Lloyd George and President Wilson dwelled on their being deeply impressed by the Muslim entreaties, especially by hearing their own pledges cited. The integrity of Anatolia should be preserved, Lloyd George now counseled, and Italy must be excluded. Reversing his opinion of the previous week, he no longer regarded the Italians as an "extremely gifted race" of "vigorous and manly" individuals. Their presence in Asia Minor, he warned, would foment grievous unrest because they were "absolutely despised" by the Turks. And they would indubitably aggravate problems in neighboring Armenia. Wilson admitted that the Muslim appeal to religious sentiment was forceful and that he therefore thought it might be possible to deprive the Turks of Constantinople yet leave the Sultan-Caliph there in circumstances analogous to the Pope's residency in Rome.[121]

[119] *Paris Peace Conference*, V, 690–701; Mantoux, *op. cit.*, II, 98–104. It is curious that the Agha Khan's previous like appeals, publicized as early as January, 1919, and repeated periodically, seem to have made no impression upon Lloyd George. The Agha Khan had stated in relation to Armenia, "We beg respectfully to urge that, whatever may be the ultimate settlement of the Armenian question, the rights and interests of the large Muhammedan population inhabiting that Province should be safeguarded; and that they should be protected from persecution." See *Christian Science Monitor*, Jan. 22, 1919, p. 2, and, for a subsequent appeal, May 15, 1919, p. 6.

[120] Nicolson, *Peacemaking*, p. 281.

[121] *Paris Peace Conference*, V, 707–711; Mantoux, *op. cit.*, II, 110–112. See also Baker, *op. cit.*, II, 199–200.

The precipitant succession of mandate schemes reached a climax on May 21 when Lloyd George reminded the Council of Four that Great Britain had some seventy million Muslim subjects in India and several million more in Egypt and the Sudan. During the World War, Muslims had constituted the largest single group in the Imperial divisions operating against the Ottoman Empire, but these soldiers had not fought to destroy the Turkish nation. He added that the Cabinet, now convinced that the Muslims would be wrought up by the partition of Anatolia, had gone on record advocating the territorial integrity of that region. "The Allies had a perfect right to say that the Turks should not rule over alien races like the Greeks, Armenians, and Arabs, whom they had always misgoverned," but this was not the case for the Turkish-populated lands of Anatolia. The Italians must have nothing there and the French too should forego the previously suggested mandate for "Northern Anatolia." Lloyd George thus posed the following revised solution:

1. Armenia, Mesopotamia, and Syria should be governed by powers other than Turkey.

2. The United States should accept the mandate for Armenia and Constantinople as well as a "light mandate" (administrative guidance) for Anatolia, west of the new Armenia.

3. Should the United States be unable to assume the light mandate over Anatolia, no mandate would exist there.

4. The United States should also supervise Russian Armenia and the Caucasus pending the settlement of the Russian question.

5. The Italians and French should, in the best interests of world peace, be turned away from Anatolia (Cilicia included).[122]

The dizzying British deviations and combinations provoked Georges Clemenceau to a vituperative exposé. Yesterday, he protested, the British were inviting France to take control of all Anatolia, while today they had put France in a class with Italy, telling her to think no more of Asia Minor. How long could these injustices be endured! France had compromised on one issue after another. She had consented to an extension of the British sphere to include Mosul and Palestine, and she had shown a willingness to waive her fast rights in much of Cilicia if the United States would accept the Armenian mandate. Lloyd George's newest plot, his insulting bad faith, were apparently the reward for the moderation and conciliation displayed by France.[123] Ray Stannard

---

[122] Carrié-Albrecht, op. cit., pp. 224–225; Paris Peace Conference, V, 756–758, 770–771. See also Mantoux, op. cit., II, 133–136.

[123] Mantoux, op. cit., II, 137–138; Paris Peace Conference, V, 760–765.

Baker derisively observed: "At Paris, throughout the Conference, the French were always more direct and outspoken than the British. If they believed a thing they said it. One knew where Clemenceau stood and what he intended to do; one never knew where Lloyd George stood: he never stood twice in the same place." [124]

The burgeoning manifestations of disharmony led President Wilson to urge postponement of further deliberation, but only after he had made it clear that the United States could not, in any case, be expected to serve as mandatory in western Anatolia: "It was difficult for her to take a mandate even for Armenia, where she had permanent interests of long standing, and where a good deal of money had been spent by Americans for the relief of the Armenian people." [125] At this juncture in the conference proceedings the King-Crane Commission set out for the Near East, and the Council of Four, shelving the mandate question, turned back to pressing matters in Europe.

Even though Avetis Aharonian and Boghos Nubar Pasha bemoaned the subsequent unavoidable suspension of their case, there was still some basis for consolation. In every fresh combination of mandates proposed in the Council of Four and in the sundry private caucuses, Armenia's right to complete separation from the Ottoman Empire had never been challenged. Anatolia had been cut into a number of different patterns during the discussions and debates in Paris, but Armenia proper had not been touched. At most, there existed the question of how much of the Cilician coastline Armenia should have. Furthermore, Wilson privately gave Nubar and Aharonian encouragement regarding the prospect of an American mandate over their country. The President was obviously sincere, for in mid-May, he even contemplated the appointment of Herbert Hoover as governor of the Constantinople and Armenian mandate. When Hoover learned of the intent, he warily advised that at least 150,000 troops would be needed to defend Armenia from hostile neighbors and that the mandatory standing to profit from the riches of Mesopotamia (Great Britain) should also assume the responsibilities for disadvantaged Armenia.[126] Still, on May 22 Woodrow Wilson confided to his Near East experts that he now believed the Senate would assent to the mandate for Armenia.[127]

[124] Baker, op. cit., I, 269–270.

[125] Paris Peace Conference, V, 765–766; Mantoux, op. cit., II, 141–143.

[126] Hoover, op. cit., pp. 228–229. As early as April 16, Hoover was mentioned as the probable choice for governor of Constantinople. See Thompson, op. cit., pp. 310–311.

[127] US Archives, RG 256, 185.5136/31. Throughout this period, Admiral Bristol, like a number of other American officials, warned against the "European plan to entangle the United States in a mandate scheme that would award the lucrative

Presentation of the Ottoman Case

The Council of Four, in its session of May 30, entertained the request of the Grand Vizier of the Ottoman Empire to be granted an audience by the Peace Conference. President Wilson frowned upon the petition, observing that Germany had received no such privilege, but Lloyd George, under pressure from several members of the Cabinet, maintained that German and Turk need not be treated exactly alike. Wilson cautioned against establishing an unwelcome precedent and of providing the Turks the opportunity to harangue about the Allied operations at Smyrna. Lloyd George received support from Clemenceau and Orlando, and it was finally decided that the Turks would be heard in Paris "and that is all." They would not be accorded the right of discussion.[128]

To create an awesome aura of formality, the Council of Ten was resuscitated for a single day to hear the Turkish case.[129] Facing this august body on June 17, 1919, Grand Vizier Damad Ferid Pasha admitted that the world had been shocked by crimes allegedly committed by the Turks. He did not deny that there had occurred "misdeeds which are such as to

---

provinces of the Near East to the Continental Powers and saddle the United States with Armenia, "a territory practically desolate, without natural resources and with practically no railroad communications or real seaports." Uncle Sam would be left holding the "little end of the horn" and "the lemon." The Caucasus, Bristol advised, had already become another Balkans and clearly indicated what would occur if the Ottoman Empire were partitioned. Reporting on a tour of Batum, Tiflis, and Baku in June, he stated that he could not find language adequate enough to describe his feelings: "It is that these so-called Republics in the Caucasus (Azerbaijan, Georgia and Armenia) are a perfect farce. The members of the Governments do not represent the people but are hands of secret societies that have been drilled by years of intrigue and deceit. With very few exceptions they are not straight and generally use their office for what they can get out of it. This condition in the Caucasus is a glaring example of what would happen in the rest of Turkey if it is split up into small countries."

See Bristol Papers, Box 36, Correspondence of May 20, June 3, and June 25, 1919.

[128] Mantoux, *op. cit.*, II, 257. See also *Paris Peace Conference*, VI, 116, 134. In apprising the Ottoman government of the decision to allow a Turkish delegation to proceed to Paris, the French High Commissioner at Constantinople (Albert deFrance) apparently let it be understood that the French government was the source of this consideration, thus precipitating a tempest in the Council of Four. See *Paris Peace Conference*, VI, 215–216, 217–218, 222, 232–233; Britain, FO 406/41, no. 58.

[129] For descriptions of the Turkish delegates and their journey to Paris, see Britain, FO 608/117, File 385/3/5, and Cab 29/25, M 280. In its session of June 13 the Council of Four had decided to receive the Ottoman representatives "in a formal manner in one of the large rooms of the Quai d'Orsay." See *Paris Peace Conference*, VI, 370. An account in the *Christian Science Monitor*, June 13, 1919, p. 1, tells of the extremely unceremonious manner in which Damad Ferid's twelve-man delegation arrived in Paris on the morning of June 12.

make the conscience of mankind shudder with horror forever." The blame, however, rested not with the Turkish people, but with the actual culprits, the German government of Wilhelm II and the Young Turk (Ittihad ve Terakki) party, which had seized dictatorial control in 1913. That band of criminals had not only annihilated countless Christians, but it had also pronounced death upon three million Muslims. "Asia Minor is today nothing but a vast heap of ruins," he exclaimed. This tragedy should not, however, be ascribed to racial or religious intolerance; the responsibility lay solely with Ittihad ve Terakki, the victimizer of the Turkish people.

Damad Ferid then pleaded for the rehabilitation of the Ottoman Empire. He could only lament the recent Greek occupation of Smyrna and "the most deplorable excesses which have been committed to the hurt of the defenceless Moslem population." The single basis for a just peace, he continued, was the status quo ante bellum. At the outbreak of the war the Ottoman Empire had already been reduced to its least possible bounds; the integrity of these remaining provinces was predicated on Wilsonian principles, which Turkey had invoked in suing for an armistice. It was true that the lands from the Taurus Mountains to the Arabian Sea were of different language, but they were nonetheless linked to Constantinople by sentiments which ran far deeper than nationality. The brother-in-law of Sultan Mehmed VI ended his appeal by emphasizing that the supreme interests of more than three hundred million Muslims around the earth lay in the balance: "The conscience of the world could only approve conditions of peace which are compatible with right, with the aspirations of people and with immanent justice." [130]

As president of the Peace Conference, Georges Clemenceau announced that an official reply would be forthcoming after the Ottoman communication had been duly considered. And when the Ottoman delegation requested permission to submit an additional memorandum, he consented to defer the reply until that statement too had been received.[131] The second Turkish memorandum, dated June 23, 1919, reiterated the contention that the Ottoman Empire had been drawn into the fatal war against the will of the people and that the vicious leadership of Ittihad ve Terakki was entirely to blame. Hence, the Ottoman Empire should not be judged by the "sad episode" of the preceding several years, for its history had been characterized by "a wise and toler-

---

[130] Britain, FO 608/115, File 385/3/5; *Paris Peace Conference*, IV, 509–511; Miller, *Documents*, XVI, 419–422.

[131] *Paris Peace Conference*, IV, 511–512; Miller, *Documents*, XVI, 422–423.

ant administration." The territorial integrity of the domain must be preserved, it being understood that the Arabs would receive broad autonomy and that the future status of Egypt and Cyprus was negotiable with Great Britain. The Ottoman people could not "accept the dismemberment of the Empire or its division under different mandates." Avoiding direct reference to Armenian claims to the eastern vilayets and Cilicia, the memorandum stated: "In Asia the Turkish lands are bounded on the north by the Black Sea, on the East by the Turco-Russian and the Turco-Persian frontiers as they were before the war." Yet, historically Ottoman diplomats had rarely stated their maximum concessions at the outset, and in Damad Ferid's choice of words one could discern that certain adjustments with Armenia were not out of the question:

If the Armenian republic established at Erivan is recognised by the Powers of the Entente, the Ottoman Delegation will consent to discuss *ad referendum* the frontier line which is to separate the new republic from the Ottoman State. The Imperial Government would grant to the Armenians who wish to expatriate themselves in order to establish themselves in the new republic all facilities in its power. As regards those who might wish to remain in Turkey and who are scattered in Thrace, the Caucasus and elsewhere, they would enjoy, like the other minorities, free cultural, moral and economic development.[132]

Even though Clemenceau had agreed to postpone a reply until receipt of this additional memorandum, the Council of Ten took action on June 17, immediately after Damad Ferid Pasha had withdrawn from the chamber. Secretary of State Lansing suggested that the Turks be asked to submit a more precise exposé, and President Wilson described the Turkish presentation as having "absolutely no value." He was annoyed that the Turks had attempted to absolve themselves by holding a tyrannical political group to blame. Every defeated country could make the same defense; the Peace Conference had allowed no such discussion in relation to Germany. Lloyd George and Clemenceau contributed lesser barbs before it was decided that Balfour should prepare the answer to the Ottoman declaration.[133]

On June 21 the Allied leaders, once again sitting as the Council of

[132] *British Documents*, IV, 647–651. *Paris Peace Conference*, VI, 691–694; Miller, *Documents*, XVI, 479–484. In a separate memorandum on June 19, Damad Ferid had protested the Greek landings and excesses at Smyrna. The role of the Allied Powers in this action was, he stated, not in the "spirit" of the Mudros Armistice. See Miller, XVIII, 514–518.
[133] Mantoux, *op. cit.*, II, 445–446.

Four, were presented the draft reply, which President Wilson termed "excellent." Balfour noted that Lloyd George, who was absent from the session, had not seen the document but that Edwin Montagu was vehemently opposed on grounds that it would rouse the Muslims of India.[134] Balfour did not share this view nor did Clemenceau, Wilson, or Baron Sonnino,[135] who were pleased that, while the Ottoman government had been taken to task, there was nothing derogatory concerning the Muslim faith and faithful. Still, because the nature of the matter was so delicate, the Council decided that Lloyd George should approve the final draft before its delivery to the Ottoman delegation.[136] On the twenty-third, in dictating minor revisions, Lloyd George announced his assent, and two days later, during the very session that the Turkish additional memorandum was first brought to the attention of the Council of Four, Clemenceau signed the official reply.[137]

In that declaration the Allied and Associated Powers showed themselves not kindly disposed to the Ottoman case as presented. Turkey had admitted "that she [had] acted as the subservient tool of Germany; that the war, begun without excuse, and conducted without mercy, was accompanied by massacres whose calculated atrocity equals or exceeds anything in recorded history." The assertions that the Turkish people were not responsible and that these crimes were "entirely out of harmony with the Turkish tradition" could not be accepted. The delayed Turkish denunciation of the terrible atrocities notwithstanding, "a nation must be judged by the Government which rules it, which directs its foreign policy, which controls its armies."

Regarding the plea to spare the Ottoman Empire, the Allied Powers, while wishing the Turkish people well and admiring their excellent qualities, could not find amongst those qualities the capacity to rule over alien races: "The experiment has been tried too long and too often for there to be the least doubt as to its results. . . . Neither among the Christians of Europe, nor among the Moslems of Syria, Arabia, and Africa, has the Turk done other than destroy whatever he has conquered; never has he shown himself able to develop in peace what he has won by war. Not in this direction do his talents lie."

[134] Montagu's specific objections and Balfour's rejoinders, placed in two parallel columns, are in Britain, FO 608/115, 385/3/5, and Cab 29/26, M 301.

[135] Baron Sonnino sometimes represented Italy in the Council of Four during Orlando's frequent absences in May and June. Unable to extricate himself from the Italian economic and parliamentary crisis, Orlando had tendered his resignation at the time that this session of the Council of Four took place.

[136] Mantoux, *op. cit.*, II, 473. For Balfour's draft reply, see Britain, Cab 29/25, M 295; *Paris Peace Conference*, VI, 577–580.

[137] *Paris Peace Conference*, VI, 617, 678.

It was, moreover, fallacious to base the case for Ottoman territorial integrity on the religious sentiment of peoples who had never felt the Turkish yoke or who had forgotten "how heavily it weighs on those compelled to bear it." Religious fervor, it had been shown, had not figured in the recent war: "The only flavour of deliberate fanaticism perceptible in these transactions was the massacre of Christian Armenians by order of the Turkish Government." Assuredly, thinking Muslims throughout the world could feel no pride in the modern history of the regime enthroned at Constantinople, where the Ottoman Turk was attempting a task for which he had little aptitude. The Turk, the humiliating declaration concluded, should be placed in surroundings more congenial to his talents and under conditions "less complicated and difficult." [138]

An unusual spirit of militancy and unbending resolve to dismember the Ottoman Empire pervaded the document.[139] The *New York Times* declared that the answer "makes clear to all that the Empire is at an end" and that it had dispelled the fear the Peace Conference might be moved by "powerful interests which advocated leaving the Turk pretty much as he is." [140] To the Armenian, the inexorable disposition of the victors in war was for once gratifying, giving fresh hopes that a favorable settlement was in the wind. But for the dishonored Turk it was a clear indication that there was little to be gained from looking to Paris for sympathy and moderation. It was time to turn to the East.

Deferral of the Turkish Treaty

By mid-June the peace treaty with Germany had been fully prepared and delivered to envoys from Weimar. The strain upon the drafting committee had been so intense in producing the voluminous document that on May 13 the Council of Four had concurred that work on the subsequent treaty with Turkey "should not be put in hand just yet." [141] The peacemakers next touched upon the subject on June 17, immedi-

---

[138] *British Documents*, IV, 645–647; Miller, *Documents*, XVI, 475–479; *Paris Peace Conference*, VI, 688–691. The Turkish memorandum of June 17 and the Allied reply were both made public on June 26, 1919.

[139] Lloyd George subsequently described the reply as the most powerful writing penned by Balfour and observed: "What adds force and a poignant interest to Mr. Balfour's indictment is the fact that he was present, as Lord Salisbury's secretary, at the Berlin Congress of 1878, when the British Government insisted upon placing the emancipated Armenians once more under Turkish rule, after they had been liberated by the Russian arms." See Lloyd George, *op. cit.*, II, 657.

[140] *New York Times*, June 28, 1919, p. 8.

[141] *Paris Peace Conference*, V, 588.

ately after Damad Ferid Pasha had stated the Turkish case. Lloyd George questioned whether the Ottoman representatives should be advised to turn back to Constantinople or to remain in Paris to begin negotiations. Clemenceau suggested that they be directed to stay, whereas Foreign Secretary Balfour felt that they should be sent away because Paris, he said, had become a virulent center of all sorts of propaganda. Lloyd George recommended that the Turkish spokesmen be informed that, with the German treaty still not signed and the Austrian draft treaty not yet completed, they could either return to their country or continue on in Paris "if they have the time to spare." The Council pursued the issue no further during that session.[142]

On June 25, the day Clemenceau signed the official Allied reply to the Ottoman delegation, the Council of Four again reflected upon the Turkish settlement. Lloyd George held that, in light of President Wilson's impending departure for America, it would be "unreasonable to maintain a state of war with Turkey for the next two months." He hoped the Council might agree to "put Turkey out of her misery" by outlining the new boundaries of that state while deferring the ultimate disposition of the detached territories until it was known whether the United States would act as a mandatory. To await the decision of the United States Senate before negotiating peace would not be prudent. President Wilson, too, deemed it ill-advised to delay the treaty and proposed that, as had been the procedure in the case of Austria, Turkey simply be told what lands she was not to have. The Allies could say, "Armenia, Mesopotamia, Smyrna, Syria, etc. shall belong to you no longer" and then keep these regions under occupation until a final settlement could be reached. The latter point prompted Lloyd George to remind Wilson that, with no Allied military forces in Turkish Armenia, the mistimed withdrawal of the Ottoman troops, who were in some way responsible for order in that area, would cast the surviving Armenians upon the mercy of the ferocious Kurds. Apparently unimpressed, Wilson repeated that these lands should be immediately detached and that the Ottoman government be required to accept "any condition with regard to over-sight or direction the Allied and Associated Governments might agree to." Clemenceau considered the plan highly unrealistic, yet Wilson continued to expound his views. There should be a firm hand, but no mandate, over Turkey, and the Sultan should be expelled from Constantinople. Wilson "had studied the question of the Turks in Europe for a long time, and every year confirmed his opinion that they

[142] Mantoux, *op. cit.*, II, 445–446.

ought to be cleared out." [143] The words of Woodrow Wilson were potent, but his actions were not. To Lloyd George's suggestion that "a short, sharp peace with Turkey" be formulated at once, he would give no positive response, and when the Prime Minister again made reference to the distribution of mandates, Wilson requested time "to read the question up." [144]

The status of the Ottoman delegation was again considered the next day, June 26. Wilson wanted to hand the Turks their traveling papers: "They had exhibited complete absence of common sense and a total misunderstanding of the West. They had imagined that the Conference knew no history and was ready to swallow enormous falsehoods." Lloyd George quipped that such were the attributes of traditional Turkish diplomacy, yet, contradicting his own suggestion of the previous day, he questioned the feasibility of Wilson's proposal to coerce Turkey into accepting any future decisions the Allies might make. Clemenceau insisted that the entire Eastern problem be settled at one time; piecemeal arrangements would not work. Italian and Greek maneuvers in Asia Minor had complicated matters, he said, and furthermore certain fundamental issues divided the French and British. These, however, he did not wish to raise until the European treaties had been completed. The three world leaders terminated the session, not by making a decision on the Turkish peace treaty, but by roundly denouncing the unabated Italian advances both in Anatolia and the Adriatic. The repeated display of impulsiveness and vacillation bode ill for Armenia.[145]

On the twenty-seventh, amidst the fluster and flurry that preceded the formalities concluding the treaty of peace with Germany, the Council of Four finally divested itself of the Turkish settlement by approving the following proposals:

1. That the further consideration of the Treaty of Peace with Turkey should be suspended until such time as the Government of the United States of America could state whether they are able to accept a mandate for a portion of the territory of the former Turkish Empire.
2. That the Turkish Delegation should be thanked for the statement they have made to the Peace Conference, and that a suggestion should be conveyed to them that they might return to their own country.[146]

---

[143] *British Documents*, IV, 643–645; Miller, *Documents*, XVI, 549–561; *Paris Peace Conference*, VI, 675–676.

[144] *Paris Peace Conference*, VI, 678; Miller, *Documents*, XVI, 463, 464.

[145] Mantoux, *op. cit.*, II, 530–531; *Paris Peace Conference*, VI, 711–712.

[146] *British Documents*, IV, 652; *Paris Peace Conference*, VI, 729; US Archives, RG 256, 867.014/4. Thompson, *op. cit.*, p. 406, relates that President Wilson told a number of correspondents on June 27 that although he had made no promises regarding

Arthur Balfour drafted an appropriate letter to the Ottoman delegation and Georges Clemenceau dispatched it on June 28, 1919, just after the Allied and Associated Powers had gathered in plenary session to thrust the Treaty of Versailles upon Germany.[147] With the brief signing ceremony in the Hall of Mirrors, the first phase of the Peace Conference had come to an end as had the three-month rendezvous of the Council of Four. President Wilson and Premier Lloyd George immediately sailed for home, whereas their colorful colleague, Vittorio Orlando, a few days earlier had been turned out by the Italian Chamber and replaced by Francesco Saverio Nitti.[148]

The Council of Four had expressed concern about the negative effects of deferring the Turkish treaty for two months, but in fact that settlement was to be delayed for more than a year. The President and the Congress of the United States of America jointly figured as a major factor in that critical postponement. Soon after Woodrow Wilson returned to Washington, the American delegation in Paris informed the Peace Conference that the President now advised that a decision regarding mandates would not be forthcoming for some time, and he wondered, in view of this unfortunate circumstance, what the Allied attitude toward Turkey would be in the interim. The only attitude the Allies could take, snapped Clemenceau, was one of "expectancy." France would not be prepared to discuss Turkish affairs or accept any commitments until the Peace Conference had attended to all other pending questions. President Wilson, concluded Clemenceau, was clearly aware of the intrinsic difficulties in the Near East. Balfour, now in the role of chief British spokesman, concurred that no definite response could be given Wilson, but he softened Clemenceau's jibe by expressing regret that the American Constitution prevented the President from taking action "for the time being." [149] Here the matter rested, as the Peace Conference turned its attention to the treaties with Austria, Hungary, and Bulgaria.

---

the Armenian mandate, "I am inclined to think that our people would consider it favorably, for they have always shown much interest in Armenia."

[147] *Paris Peace Conference*, VI, 757-758; *British Documents*, IV, 653-654. The difficulties the Ottoman delegation encountered on its return journey to Constantinople were described by the accompanying British officer, Lieutenant Colonel William Frederick Blaker. See Britain, FO 608/117, 385/3/4/17859. See also Gidney, *op. cit.*, pp. 131-133.

[148] Nitti assumed the premiership after the fall of Orlando's cabinet on June 19, 1919. He selected Tommaso Tittoni to replace Baron Sonnino as foreign minister and to lead a new Italian delegation to Paris. Shortly thereafter Nitti reversed Orlando's decision to supplant the British force in the Caucasus with Italian regiments and ordered all such preparations halted.

[149] *Paris Peace Conference*, VII, 193; Evans, *op. cit.*, pp. 197-198.

A Resident Commissioner in Armenia

Having failed to resolve the future of Armenia, the Peace Conference adopted Herbert Hoover's recommendation that a joint mission be sent to Armenia. Hoover held basic reservations about American involvement in mandates, but, like Henry Cabot Lodge and others of Woodrow Wilson's adversaries, he consistently advocated greater moral and material assistance to Armenia. While in Paris as the Director General of Relief, Hoover became concerned over the despairing reports emanating from his field staff in Armenia and the Caucasus, and he occasionally discussed the plight of the Armenians with President Wilson and such interested parties as former ambassador to Turkey, Henry Morgenthau. On June 27, a day before the scheduled signing ceremonies at Versailles, he suggested that the Allied chiefs of state appoint a temporary resident commissioner in Armenia to act as their joint representative and to offer administrative counsel to the de facto government at Erevan. Hoover advised that the commissioner's field of operation should include both Russian Armenia and Turkish Armenia and that, pending a final political settlement, the appointee would take charge of all matters relating to relief and repatriation. Hoover recommended General James G. Harbord of the American Expeditionary Force as the "ideal man for this position," adding that should Harbord be unavailable another official be selected in consultation with the commander of the Expeditionary Force, General John J. Pershing.[150] Late in the afternoon of the twenty-eighth, the Council of Four accepted the proposal, but upon the observation of Sir Maurice Hankey, the British secretary, that considerable administrative detail needed to be arranged, the Allied leaders, impatient to depart from Paris, transferred to their alternates the responsibility of implementing the plan.[151]

As it happened, the principal body at the Peace Conference following the Treaty of Versailles became the Council of Five, known also as the Heads of Delegations and normally composed of the foreign ministers of the United States, Great Britain, France, Italy, and Japan. On July 5, 1919, the Council of Five adopted the following resolution introduced by Secretary of State Robert Lansing:

Colonel W. N. Haskell, U.S.A., is appointed by this Council to act as High Commissioner in Armenia on behalf of the United States,

---

[150] Hoover, op. cit., p. 144; Paris Peace Conference, VI, 743–744; Britain, FO 371/3659, 98469/512/58.

[151] US Archives, RG 256, 180.03411/97/99, 181.94/1, and 867B.00/156; Paris Peace Conference, VI, 741, 756, and VII, 30–31.

British, French and Italian Governments, it being understood that
Colonel Haskell will be coincidentally appointed to take full charge
of all relief measures in Armenia by the various relief organisations
operating there. All representatives of the United States, British,
French, and Italian Governments in Armenia, Georgia, Azerbaijan
and Constantinople are to be at once instructed to co-operate with and
give support to Colonel Haskell.[152]

William Nafew Haskell, formerly Hoover's chief of relief operations
in Rumania, had been selected in lieu of General Harbord, who was
now being recommended to lead a military fact-finding mission to Asia
Minor and Armenia.[153] Thus the Peace Conference, instead of granting
Armenia a mandatory power, a definite boundary, and a guaranteed
future, had provided a resident commissioner to advise, supervise, and
console.[154] Haskell's appointment was a virtual admission by the Allies
that their assorted procedures to settle the long-standing Armenian
question had miscarried and that the prospect of a "short, sharp peace"
to put Turkey "out of her misery" had vanished.

In midyear, 1919, Avetis Aharonian and Boghos Nubar Pasha stood
at the threshold of a new phase of the Peace Conference. They had
helplessly watched Armenia's golden opportunity slip away. The Allied
heads of government were never again to join together as a single official body, and no longer would it be possible for the Armenian envoys
to concentrate their efforts upon Paris alone. Rather, they would have
to follow the world leaders over mountains, channels, and oceans. The
Allied response to Armenian petitions had been disheartening. Armenia
remained unrecognized as a belligerent state or as a de facto government, and she had been denied a formal place at the Peace Conference.
None of the major powers had shown a willingness to occupy Turkish
Armenia or even to provide the requisite cadre and matériel for the Armenian army to do so. A trenchant editorial comment published in the
Christian Science Monitor in June expressed the disillusion of many:
"The diplomats never have yet done anything for Armenia, and, until
the driving force of Principle becomes sufficiently strong, they never

[152] US Archives, RG 256, 180.03502/- and 184.94/10a; Paris Peace Conference, VII,
28.
[153] Hoover, op. cit., pp. 144–145. On July 3 Hoover suggested to Secretary of State
Lansing that Haskell be appointed and, in a cable signed also by delegation aide
John Foster Dulles, urged President Wilson to put Harbord on detail to Armenia.
The Harbord mission will be discussed in the second volume of this history.
[154] For the organization and personnel of Haskell's mission, see US Archives, RG
256, 181.94/1–33; Britain, FO 608/80, File 342/1/14. Le Petit Parisien announced
that Haskell departed for Armenia on Sunday, July 13, 1919.

will. A generation of massacres, while the diplomats were writing notes, ought to have convinced the Armenians of that." [155]

But the Armenians dared not be convinced. Instead, they searched desperately for signs of hope. They could perhaps be consoled in that the Allied and Associated Powers continued to plan for the inclusion of the Turkish Armenian provinces and at least a part of Cilicia in the new Armenian state. The fixing of the exact boundaries was largely dependent upon whether a mandatory could be found and, if so, whether that nation would be the United States of America. A rapid and firm American commitment would assure Armenia the broadest territories possible. Woodrow Wilson hoped to assume the mandate under the auspices of the League of Nations and had incorporated the Covenant in the Treaty of Versailles. If he could bring the Senate to ratify that treaty, the way to an American mandate over Armenia would be relatively clear. Pending the outcome of the anticipated struggle in Washington, however, the Turkish settlement was to be held in abeyance. And all the while the Ottoman armies remained mobilized in the eastern vilayets and the Turkish resistance movement spread vertically and horizontally. Allied rivalries, American vacillations, and Asiatic upheavals were to lead the Armenian delegates in Paris down the road to frustration.

[155] *Christian Science Monitor*, June 11, 1919, p. 22.

11

Caucasian Diplomacy and
the White Armies

The unceasing labors of Avetis Aharonian and Boghos Nubar to bring
to reality an Armenia from sea to sea were paralleled by the modest
efforts of the de facto Armenian republic to regularize relations with
its Transcaucasian neighbors. Its strategy to attain the maximum possible security pending a final settlement by the world powers required
unusual flexibility. Thus, the Republic joined with Georgia both in
opposing the "South-West Caucasus Provisional Government" at a
time when that Muslim administration was being tolerated by the
British command and in rejecting Azerbaijan's pretensions to much
of the Kars and Batum oblasts. Yet the Armenian government assiduously circumvented Georgian and Azerbaijani suggestions that the
mutually enervating territorial disputes be resolved through regional
negotiations and arbitration. It clung instead to the belief that, if only
Armenia could persevere, the Paris Peace Conference would certainly
render a decision more favorable than any that might be forthcoming
from a gathering of Transcaucasian delegations. Meanwhile, in the
presence of Lieutenant General Denikin, Admiral Kolchak, and Russian diplomats in Western Europe, Armenian spokesmen uttered
Russophile declarations, hoping thereby to procure grain, weapons,
and recognition from the widely divergent anti-Bolshevik leadership.
But this calculated tactic stirred the ire of both Georgia and Azerbaijan, whose territories and very existence were jeopardized by General Denikin's Volunteer Army. By the end of its first year the Armenian republic had made considerable progress in foreign relations, yet
it had not significantly attenuated the deep-seated suspicions of Georgia or the unflagging animosity of Azerbaijan.

The Consolidation of Georgian Power

The tenor of Armeno-Georgian relations in 1919 was conditioned by the determination of Zhordania's government to restore Georgian predominance in the Tiflis guberniia, especially in the city of Tiflis, where the Georgians had become a minority. During the first year of Georgian independence the collective power of the 400,000 Armenians of the Tiflis guberniia was sharply diminished. The most pointed blow fell upon the bourgeoisie, the masters of magnificent Golovinskii (Rustaveli) Prospect, with its stately mansions and imposing commercial centers. One after another these buildings were expropriated, assertedly to house government agencies, embassies and consulates, military and economic missions. Moreover, the complicated question of citizenship threatened to relegate all Armenians of Georgia to the status of second-class subjects. Were these people the citizens of Georgia, of Armenia, of Russia, or might they hold dual or even triple citizenship? Bilateral Armeno-Georgian discussions failed to resolve the issue, for understandably Georgia could not tolerate divided loyalties and steadfastly insisted that only those who registered as Georgian citizens would be entitled to the rights and privileges incumbent therein.[1]

By the beginning of 1919 most Armenian officials, militiamen, and municipal employees in Tiflis had been erased from the payrolls, and the Georgians gained control of the local administration by monopolizing an election held in January, shortly after the Armeno-Georgian war.[2] In February the Georgians tightened their grip over the entire country through elections to a constituent assembly. As had been the case in the Tiflis municipal elections, the sizable Russian and Armenian elements either excluded themselves or were disqualified by intimidation or revised franchise requirements.[3] Indicative of the primary area of Georgian power, more than 70 percent of the registered voters in rural Georgia went to the polls as opposed to some 50 percent in urban Georgia. The Menshevik ticket, according to published results, received 350,000 of the 433,000 rural votes and 58,000 of the

---

[1] Mikayel Varandian, *Le conflit arméno-géorgien et la guerre du Caucase* (Paris, 1919), p. 97; Djamalian, "Hai-vratsakan knjire" (Oct., 1928), pp. 127–128, 131. See also Noi Zhordaniia, *Moia Zhizn'* (Stanford, 1968), p. 97.

[2] P. G. La Chesnais, *Les peuples de la Transcaucasie pendant la guerre et devant la paix* (Paris, 1921), pp. 154–155; Djamalian, "Hai-vratsakan knjire" (April, 1929), pp. 145–146.

[3] Rep. of Arm. Archives, File 66/2. Scarcely half the eligible voters participated in the election according to V. B. Stankevich, *Sud'by narodov Rossii* (Berlin, 1921), p. 250.

81,000 urban votes.[4] Apropos of the popular mandate, 109 seats were awarded to Mensheviks, with the remaining 21 being distributed to 8 Georgian National Democrats, 8 Georgian Social Federalists, and 5 Social Revolutionaries. Whereas in 1917 Dashnaktsutiun had polled thousands of votes in Tiflis in elections to the Russian Constituent Assembly and in 1918 the party had been represented in the Georgian Parliament by a small faction, not a single member of the foremost Armenian political society was to be seated in the Georgian Constituent Assembly when it convened in 1919. The four Armenians who entered the new legislature did so as deputies of the Social Democrat (Menshevik) Labor Party of Georgia.[5]

On March 12, 1919, Sylvester Vissarionovich Djibladze, a veteran Marxist and one of the founders of the Georgian Social Democratic movement, opened the Constituent Assembly, which elected Nikolai Semenovich Chkheidze, then already in Paris, as its permanent chair-

[4] Wladimir Woytinsky, *La démocratie géorgienne* (Paris, 1921), pp. 193–194. This source shows that there were 156,000 registered voters in the cities and 614,000 in the rural areas. According to G. I. Uratadze, *Obrazovanie i konsolidatsiia Gruzinskoi Demokraticheskoi Respubliki* (Munich, 1956), p. 88, up to 80 percent of those registered exercised their right to vote. Using statistics supplied him by the Georgian government, the international Menshevik leader Kautsky, who visited the Republic in late autumn, 1920, wrote that "the Social-Democrats received eighty-two per cent of all votes cast in the country, on a total poll of seventy-six per cent," while "in the towns, they received seventy-two per cent on a total poll of only fifty-two per cent." See Karl Kautsky, *Georgia: A Social-Democratic Peasant Republic*, trans. H. J. Stenning (London, [1921]), p. 36. See also Zhordaniia, *op. cit.*, pp. 97–98.

[5] Rep. of Arm. Archives, File 66a/3, Information Bulletin, March 11, 1919. According to Woytinsky, *op. cit.*, p. 194, of the fifteen parties or groups for which votes were cast, the following received a total of more than 2,000: Social Democrat, 408,451; Social Federalist, 33,630; National Democrat, 30,128; Social Revolutionary, 21,453; Radical, 3,107; Dashnaktsutiun, 2,353. Slightly different figures are cited by Uratadze, *op. cit.*, p. 88. The ballots cast for Dashnaktsutiun were apparently write-in votes, since all Armenian parties boycotted the election. Woytinsky states that in 1920 the Constituent Assembly was reorganized somewhat, reducing the number of Social Democrats to 103 and increasing the number of seats allotted the 5 "small fractions" combined to 27. During the summer of 1919 additional elections to the Constituent Assembly were conducted in areas where conditions earlier had not allowed. The organ of Dashnaktsutiun in Tiflis, *Ashkhatavor*, engaged in a running feud with the Menshevik organ *Bor'ba* over the legality of Georgia's conducting elections in such disputed districts as Akhalkalak and parts of Borchalu. On August 19 *Bor'ba* announced that of 25,000 eligible voters in Akhalkalak 22,000 had taken part in the election and that the Menshevik slate had received 13,000 votes as against only 7,000 for Dashnaktsutiun. Of the 44,000 eligible voters in Borchalu, 22,000 were reported to have voted, with the Menshevik slate receiving 12,000. On September 20, 1919, *Bor'ba* announced that, as the result of the additional elections, three Dashnakists, Zori Zorian, Tigran Avetisian, and Davit Davitkhanian, one Georgian Social Federalist, Samson Dadiani, and one Nationalist, Grigorii Veshapeli, had been seated in the Constituent Assembly. Veshapeli had bolted the National Democrats and campaigned as the organizer of the even more chauvinistic Georgian National Political party.

man.[6] During its second session the Assembly entrusted Zhordania with the formation of a new cabinet and determined that as premier he would also act as the president of the Republic.[7] The resulting centralized, monolithic Menshevik cabinet (as abbreviated as Armenia's inaugural cabinet in mid-1918) would require immense versatility from each of its members:[8]

PREMIER-PRESIDENT	Noi Nikolaevich Zhordania
VICE-PREMIER, MINISTER OF FOREIGN AFFAIRS, AND MINISTER OF JUSTICE	Evgenii Petrovich Gegechkori
MINISTER OF INTERNAL AFFAIRS, MINISTER OF MILITARY AFFAIRS, AND MINISTER OF PUBLIC INSTRUCTION	Noi Vissarionovich Ramishvili
MINISTER OF FINANCE, MINISTER OF COMMERCE, AND MINISTER OF INDUSTRY	Konstantin Platonovich Kandelaki
MINISTER OF AGRICULTURE, MINISTER OF COMMUNICATION, AND MINISTER OF LABOR	Noi Georgievich Khomeriki

The Georgians had thus become firmly established in both town and country, while the Menshevik party had become entrenched even more firmly in all Georgia. Not a few Armenians in Georgia began considering an ultimate move to Armenia. For Georgia such an eventuality promised greater ethnic solidarity and stronger native commercial-professional classes, while for Armenia it could serve to repopulate the vast, desolated plateau of Turkish Armenia, which hope-

[6] For an account of the formal opening of the Constituent Assembly, as compiled from Tiflis newspapers, see Parti Ouvrier Social-Démocrate de Géorgie, *La Géorgie Indépendante* ([Geneva, 1919]), pp. 18–19, cited hereafter only by title. The full names and the political affiliation of the 130 members of the Assembly were published in *Bor'ba*, March 12, 1919, p. 2. Congratulatory messages from the governments and legislatures of Armenia, Azerbaijan, and the Mountaineer Confederation are in the issue of March 20.

[7] Uratadze, *op. cit.*, pp. 89–90.

[8] Rep. of Arm. Archives, File 66*a*/3; *La Géorgie Indépendante*, p. 19. Woytinsky, *op. cit.*, p. 196, states that Georgii Pavlovich Eradze held the post of Minister of Labor, but according to *Bor'ba*, March 26, 1919, p. 1, Eradze was named Assistant Minister of Labor. Other appointments announced simultaneously by the Georgian organ included Konstantin Bezhanovich Sabakhtarashvili, Assistant Foreign Minister; Major General A. K. Gedevanishvili (Gedevanov), Assistant Minister of Military Affairs; and Aleksandr Spiridonovich Lomtatidze, Chairman Pro Tem of the Constituent Assembly.

fully was to be redeemed by the Republic. In anticipation of such a transfer Armenian commercial magnates in Georgia sought the right to shift their belongings and capital assets to Erevan, but Georgia made it grievously clear that she would not permit such a tremendous drain on her resources. The Armenians of Georgia were welcome to depart, but without their accumulated wealth.[9]

Preliminary Armeno-Georgian Conventions

These ponderous obstacles to amity notwithstanding, both Armenia and Georgia realized that recourse to warfare had failed to resolve their fundamental differences. Diplomats thus found the mood propitious to begin mending the rifts so glaringly exposed during the recent military confrontation. The Armenian delegation that had arrived in Tiflis at the beginning of 1919 not only consented to a provisional plan for pacification, which included the creation of the neutral zone in Lori, but it also initiated pourparlers for the restoration and normalization of relations between the sister republics.[10] The delegation, now led by Stepan G. Mamikonian, met intermittently throughout January and February with the Georgian representatives, E. P. Gegechkori, N. V. Ramishvili, K. B. Sabakhtarashvili, and A. K. Gedevanov. These informal discussions centered upon mutual recognition, diplomatic relations, problems of communication and transportation, transit privileges, and the need for a post-telegraph convention. In addition, the spokesmen from Erevan asked that Georgia return all matériel belonging to the Armenian military corps, formerly based at Tiflis, and lift its freeze on 13 million rubles banked in Tiflis by the Armenian government. With much to gain from the regulation of these nonterritorial issues, Armenia pressed for immediate action. Conversely, Georgia adopted a policy of procrastination. The economic

[9] Djamalian, "Hai-vratsakan knjire" (Oct., 1928), pp. 127, 135, and (April, 1929), p. 148. The Georgian government also turned aside Armenian attempts to gain a share of the assets of the former Transcaucasian Federative Republic. When Chargé d'affaires Arshak Djamalian appealed for desks and other school supplies in the warehouses of Tiflis, Zhordania's cabinet rejected the bid on grounds that Georgia would have to give account to "democratic Russia." Djamalian reported the incident with scathing sarcasm: "As if this future Russia were going to hang them if a few school supplies had been begrudged to Armenia." Paradoxically, the Georgians exhibited no qualms about making generous use themselves of these properties of the erstwhile Romanov Empire. See Djamalian (Oct., 1928), pp. 124–125.

[10] See pp. 120–121 above. Prisoners of war were exchanged on January 23, 1919, and many Armenian civilians interned in Georgia, including five members of the former Georgian Parliament, were released on January 26. See Rep. of Arm. Archives, File 66a/3; Hairenik (daily), April 15, 1919, p. 2.

lever that could keep Armenia vulnerable, perhaps even prod her to concessions on substantive questions, was not a weapon Georgia could afford to forfeit freely.[11]

The Georgian tactic was countered on February 10 by a cable from Foreign Minister Sirakan F. Tigranian instructing Stepan G. Mamikonian to conclude all delegation business promptly and return to Erevan by the beginning of March. Once apprised of the communiqué, the Georgian leaders showed themselves amenable to more constructive negotiations.[12] This change in attitude was undoubtedly influenced by the Muslim insurrections then flaring in Akhalkalak and Akhaltsikh. With Azerbaijan laying claim to both districts and extending sympathy and support to the Muslim shura at Kars, a common enemy of Georgia and Armenia, the advisability of closer bonds between Tiflis and Erevan became even more evident.

From the middle of February, 1919, the two sides met regularly in private informal sessions so that when the Armeno-Georgian conference officially reconvened on the twenty-eighth positive results were soon forthcoming. Within a week, agreement was reached on the resumption of diplomatic relations, mutual recognition, a post-telegraph convention, and a transit treaty. On March 4 normal railway service between Erevan and Tiflis began; Armenia's road to Europe lay open once again.[13] Diplomatic ties were formally restored on March 8 with the appointment of Prince Mikhail G. Tumanov (Mikayel Tumanian) as Armenia's minister plenipotentiary to Georgia and, shortly thereafter, of Leon G. Evangulov (Levon Evanghulian) as chargé d'affaires.[14] Also on March 8, Georgian Foreign Minister Gegechkori cabled Erevan the welcome news that "my government has commissioned me to impart to the government of Armenia that it [the Georgian government], standing squarely on the principle of the right of peoples to self-determination, recognizes the Republic of Armenia as a sovereign independent nation." [15] This announcement was followed by the lifting of martial law, which had been in effect in Tiflis since December of 1918, and permission for the Armenian inhabitants of Shulaver

[11] Rep. of Arm. Archives, File 66a/3, Foreign Ministry reports.

[12] Vratzian, *Hanrapetutiun*, p. 212.

[13] Uratadze, *op. cit.*, p. 88; Vratzian, *Hanrapetutiun*, pp. 212–213. The post-telegraph convention of March 1 was ratified by the Armenian legislature on March 11 according to dispatches printed in *Hairenik* (daily), May 20, 1919, p. 2, and May 21, p. 2.

[14] US Archives, RG 84, Tiflis Consulate, 1919, pt. 4, File 710, Communiqué of March 15, 1919; *Mshak* (Tiflis), March 9, 1919.

[15] The full text of the Georgian declaration is in *Hairenik* (daily), May 28, 1919, p. 2.

and Bolnis-Khachen, who had fled their villages during the Armeno-Georgian war and the subsequent punitive missions, to return home.[16] The Georgian press, accentuating the fact that the preliminary agreements benefited Armenia far more than Georgia, nonetheless warmly congratulated the two states for making friendship the basis of their reciprocal relations. The Menshevik organs expressed satisfaction that the Armenian government had at last directed its primary interest where it should have been from the outset—to Kars and Turkish Armenia. Zhordania's cabinet was further gratified by the recent success of the Georgian army in quelling Muslim upheavals in parts of the Tiflis guberniia and in restoring Georgian suzerainty over Akhaltsikh.[17]

In Armenia, the cabinet, legislature, and press hailed the arrangements with Georgia as steps toward stable neighborly bonds. On March 14 the government promptly accepted the proposal of Acting Brigadier General Alan Brough, the British 27th Division's chief transportation officer, to form a Transcaucasian joint railway commission and appointed two representatives to collaborate in the project. Premier Hovhannes Kachaznuni, who was in Tiflis awaiting Allied authorization to begin his travels abroad, informed Noi Zhordania on March 15 that Minister of Finance Artashes Enfiadjian and Minister of Justice Samson Harutiunian would soon arrive to confer on economic questions, in particular the implementation of a common Transcaucasian monetary system.[18] And on March 24 Evgenii Gegechkori received from Sirakan Tigranian a note of appreciation for Georgia's formal recognition of Armenia:

The government of Armenia, profoundly aware that the republics formed on the soil of Transcaucasia share a community and a unity of interests on a number of issues having a fundamental bearing upon their existence and secure development, is pleased to regard the action of the Georgian government as evidence of harmony and of sharing this point of view.

[16] Rep. of Arm. Archives, File 66a/3, Information Bulletin, March 10, 1919; *Hairenik* (daily), May 21, 1919, p. 2. A number of Armenians arrested during the Armeno-Georgian war apparently remained interned for a time longer. On April 15, 1919, *Bor'ba*, p. 3, reported that the Armenian National Council of Georgia had petitioned the Minister of Interior to release the prisoners and that the Minister (Ramishvili), according the deputation a "very cordial" reception, had promised to urge the Constituent Assembly to consider the enactment of an amnesty.

[17] Rep. of Arm. Archives, File 66a/3, Press clippings.

[18] *Ibid.*, Press release of March 14, 1919. See also Kadishev, *Interventsiia v Zakavkaz'e*, p. 175; *Hairenik* (daily), June 12, 1919, p. 1. Reports and materials on the Armenian and Transcaucasian railways are in US Archives, RG 256, File 867B.77.

On its part, the government of Armenia has the honor of confirming to your government that it has recognized and does continue to recognize the Georgian Democratic Republic as an independent and sovereign state.[19]

Caucasian Boundaries and the Second International

Despite such encouraging affirmations, territorial questions continued to bar the way to actual harmony in Transcaucasia. The rivalry between Armenia and Azerbaijan would allow not even preliminary agreements. It seemed that as long as Karabagh, Zangezur, and much of the Erevan guberniia lay in contention the two republics would be bound by mutual animosity alone. Although somewhat less acute, the Armeno-Georgian dispute was only temporarily eased by the delimitation of a neutral zone in the Borchalu uezd. Before long the Erevan government resumed protests over what it termed a Georgian military occupation of Akhalkalak. Foreign Minister Tigranian asserted that all votes cast in Akhalkalak in the elections to the Georgian Constituent Assembly were void, for the county was "integrally Armenian." The Tiflis government, on the other hand, reiterated historic, strategic, and economic rights to the district and announced with relish that all Akhalkalak, except for the town itself, had voted the Menshevik ticket.[20] But Georgia was far from content in other directions. Not only did the Borchalu neutral zone, together with the southern reaches of the Lori uchastok, remain beyond its jurisdiction, but the British command had compelled Georgian companies to quit northern Ardahan at a time when Armenian units were being allowed to occupy most of the Kars oblast, including the southern half of the Ardahan okrug.

As the ruling parties of both Georgia and Armenia held membership in the Socialist (Second) International, their representatives in Europe placed the territorial problem before the first postwar gathering of that organization. Armenia may have taken this step as another tactical maneuver pending positive action by the Paris Peace Conference, for nothing more than moral pronouncements could be expected from the International. The socialist-laborite movement had been badly splintered and enervated during the war, with most groups having adopted a "defensist" position, placing national security before class

[19] Vratzian, *Hanrapetutiun*, p. 213.
[20] Rep. of Arm. Archives, File 66a/3, Bulletin no. 118.

warfare. It was to begin the difficult task of mending fences and charting a new campaign for legal parliamentary victory that the International was summoned to convene in Switzerland. Most of the approximately one hundred delegates, representing more than twenty
countries, reflected moderate or rightist opinion during the Berne
Conference, February 3-10, 1919, and either castigated the Bolshevik
regime in Russia or expressed dire misgivings about its methods. The
Georgian Mensheviks and Armenian Dashnakists could feel quite at
home in such company.[21]

The decision of Armenia to present her case to the Berne Conference might have appeared ill-calculated, for the Georgian Menshevik leaders numbered among the great names of the Russian Social
Democratic movement and had long enjoyed prominence in laborite
circles. But there were other factors to be considered. The Armenian
catastrophe had elicited profound sympathy in the socialist world, and
the delegates at Berne were uncomfortably aware that the tragedy had
occurred during the great war the International had been incapable
of forestalling. Perhaps the intangible factor of conscience weighed
in favor of Armenia. Furthermore, Dashnakist ideologue Mikayel
Varandian had cultivated intimate bonds with members of the laborite
pantheon, including Albert Thomas, Camille Huysmans, Pierre
Renaudel, and Arthur Henderson.[22] Thus the Dashnakist representatives at Berne, Hamazasp Ohandjanian and Avetik Isahakian, were

---

[21] For useful materials and accounts of the preliminaries and proceedings of the
Berne Conference, see Arno J. Mayer, *Politics and Diplomacy of Peacemaking* (New
York, 1967), pp. 373-409; C. D. H. Cole, *A History of Socialist Thought*, Vol. IV,
pt. 1: *Communism and Social Democracy, 1914-1931* (London, 1958), pp. 287-298;
Pierre Renaudel, *L'Internationale à Berne* (Paris, 1919); John De Kay, *The Spirit of
the International* ([New York], 1919). See also Patricia van der Esch, *La deuxième
internationale, 1889-1923* (Paris, 1957), pp. 144-147; Julius Braunthal, *Geschichte der
Internationale*, Vol. II (Hannover, [1963]), pp. 167-173. The sources are not in agreement on the number of delegates present and parties represented at the Berne Conference. Braunthal states there were 102 delegates from 23 countries; Mayer shows
97 delegates from 26 countries; and Richard Fester, *Die Internationale 1914-1919*
(Halle, 1919), p. 29, gives 80 delegates from 21 "lands." Renaudel, *op. cit.*, pp. 24-26,
explains that the conference opened with 80 delegates representing 21 countries and
that before its adjournment the number of delegates had increased to 97, representing 26 countries. He lists the membership of 24 delegations: Alsace-Lorraine, Argen-
tina, Armenia, Bohemia, Bulgaria, Canada, Denmark, Estonia, Finland, France,
Georgia, German Austria, Germany, Great Britain, Holland, Hungary, Italy, Latvia,
Norway, Poland, Russia (Social Democrat and Social Revolutionary delegations),
Spain, and Sweden.
[22] Albert Thomas presented his views on the Armeno-Georgian dispute in an introduction to the treatise by Varandian, *op. cit.*, pp. 5-15.

confident that they could counterbalance the Georgian delegation, led by Akakii Chkhenkeli.[23]

In his report to the International, Ohandjanian described the Armenian crucifixion of 1915 and resurrection of 1918. Like Avetis Aharonian he too had come to espouse the maximum Armenian goal, calling upon the labor movement to aid in the creation of a united republic encompassing Caucasian Armenia, Turkish Armenia, and Cilicia. The Second International, he insisted, must add its voice to the chorus of indignation that had arisen because Armenia, despite tremendous sufferings and the massacre of a million innocent victims, had not been given a place at the Paris Peace Conference. The gathering at Berne readily responded with a resolution demanding that Armenia be liberated once and for all from foreign domination, recognized as a free and independent nation, seated at the Peace Conference, and awarded the Armenian districts of Transcaucasia and the ethnic boundaries within the Ottoman Empire as they had existed prior to the decades of Hamidian and Young Turk persecutions, that is, the six Turkish Armenian vilayets and Cilicia.[24]

Through its Commission on Territorial Questions, the Berne Conference heard both sides of the Armeno-Georgian controversy and ruled that the ethnic principle alone should be applied in fixing boundaries. Meeting in plenary session, the Conference adopted the Territorial Commission's draft resolution advocating a strict application of the right of national self-determination, with recourse to plebiscite or referendum in instances of disagreement, and rejecting, among

[23] Varandian, who was a member of the Bureau of the Socialist International, asked Ohandjanian to head the Armenian delegation to Berne. As the only Russian Armenian on Nubar Pasha's National Delegation, Varandian felt that it was especially important that he remain in Paris, where the major postwar decisions were being made. He cautioned Ohandjanian not to level a direct attack on the Georgians because of the high repute Menshevik champion Iraklii Tsereteli enjoyed in socialist company. For pertinent correspondence, see Ohandjanian's papers in Rep. of Arm. Archives, File 101/2. Akakii Chkhenkeli, in 1918 the premier of the Transcaucasian Federative Republic and the first foreign minister of the Georgian republic, had been instrumental in securing German protection for his people. After the war he was stranded in Switzerland for several months because the French authorities, regarding him as a German collaborator, repeatedly denied him the required visa to move on to Paris, where he hoped to join his colleagues advancing the Georgian cause. Chkhenkeli eventually reached Paris in the spring of 1919, after the Quai d'Orsay had granted permission for the official Georgian delegates, I. G. Tsereteli and N. S. Chkheidze, to proceed to France from Constantinople.

[24] The text of the Armenian memorandum and of the Conference resolution are in Rep. of Arm. Archives, File 101/2. See also *Hairenik* (daily), March 30, April 23, and Sept. 3, 1919, p. 1 in each. The Conference also affirmed the right of Georgia to independence. See London *Times*, Feb. 10, 1919, p. 7.

other tactics, "the fixing of frontiers according to military or strategical interests; forced or veiled annexations claimed on the ground of so-called historic rights and so-called economic necessity; [and] the creation of 'faits accomplis' by the military occupation of disputed territories." [25] Thereupon, Chkhenkeli and Ohandjanian issued a conciliatory joint statement: "The delegations of the Social-Democrat Party of Georgia and the Armenian Revolutionary Federation [Dashnaktsutiun] of Armenia are agreed to settle territorial questions on the basis stipulated in the resolution of the International Socialist Conference at Berne." [26]

The Armenians claimed to have displayed magnanimity in consenting to plebiscites in districts that, according to population statistics and earlier admissions of the Menshevik leaders themselves, were Armenian. This "concession" did not diminish the satisfaction of the Dashnakist delegation or efface the fact that Ohandjanian had played his role well. A fairly conducted plebiscite or referendum could not but result in Armenia's incorporation of both Lori and Akhalkalak. The highly principled declarations of the International did not, however, cast a magic spell. In Tiflis, Armenian negotiators Stepan Mamikonian and Smbat Khachatrian failed, despite their adroitness, to persuade the Georgian government to countenance either plebiscite or referendum. The Berne Conference had negated the validity of economic and strategic claims, yet these were the very factors on which the Georgians rested their case. [27]

Transcaucasian matters were touched upon once again by the Second International during a gathering of its permanent commission in Amsterdam, April 26–29, 1919. [28] Although the cardinal agenda item

[25] De Kay, op. cit., pp. 85–87; Renaudel, op. cit., pp. 88–90. See also Mayer, op. cit., p. 397; Braunthal, op. cit., p. 172.

[26] Rep. of Arm. Archives, File 101/2. See also Varandian, op. cit., p. 141; Djamalian, "Hai-vratsakan knjire" (April, 1928), pp. 97–98; Z. Avalov, Nezavisimost' Gruzii v mezhdunarodnoi politike, 1918–1921 g.g. (Paris, 1924), pp. 212–213n.

[27] The texts of the resolutions adopted at the Berne Conference did not reach Tiflis until June of 1919. See Bor'ba, June 4, 1919, p. 1.

[28] Before adjourning, the Berne Conference had organized several bodies to carry on its work. A three-man executive, Arthur Henderson, Camille Huysmans, and Hjalmar Branting, was established to "supervise the execution of the resolutions of this conference, convoke the conference again when the decisions of the Paris [Peace] Conference make it necessary, prepare the agenda of such a conference and take whatever steps may be considered necessary for the early reorganization of the International." See Renaudel, op. cit., pp. 142–143; De Kay, op. cit., p. 99. The Berne Conference also created a permanent commission, on which all affiliated parties were granted representation. During its first meeting on February 10, 1919, the permanent commission selected a seven-man action committee for the purpose of impressing the Paris Peace Conference with the views of the world socialist-laborite movement. The

during the four-day meeting was what the socialist leadership regarded as the insidious proceedings at the Paris Peace Conference, the permanent commission found occasion to affirm that the independence of Georgia was founded on the right of self-determination and to demand that the Armenian people be indemnified for the abominable Turkish massacres. The Amsterdam conference, also addressing itself to the numerous territorial feuds around the world and making specific reference to the Armeno-Georgian frontier, called for "a rigorous application of self-determination through plebiscites." It then heard a gratifying announcement by the Georgian spokesman Tsereteli that the Tiflis and Erevan governments had resolved their differences. It was after this revelation that Camille Huysmans informed the press of a conference resolution "declaring that the two Labor groups in Georgia and Armenia had arrived at an agreement regarding points of conflict between the two countries," and expressing satisfaction "in the fact that the Georgian and Armenian delegates had agreed that the territorial questions pending between the two countries must be arranged on the basis formulated in the general resolution of the conference at Berne." [29]

Although it was not apparent from the press releases, no Dashnakist representative attended the Amsterdam conference. Correspondence between Mikayel Varandian and Hamo Ohandjanian indicates that the self-imposed absence was calculated to inspire greater confidence and popular support among the basically antisocialist Turkish Armenians, particularly Boghos Nubar's National Delegation, and to create around the dominant party of the Armenian republic an aura of moderation at a time when the future of the country depended much more upon the actions of nonsocialist Allied leaders in Paris than upon the resolutions of weaponless socialist comrades in Amsterdam.[30] But when the Menshevik delegate's assertion regarding an Armeno-Georgian accord became known, the Dashnakist envoys in Europe burst forth with a storm of protest and put aside, at least temporarily,

---

failure of the action committee (the three members of the executive plus Ramsay MacDonald, Pierre Renaudel, Jean Longuet, and George Stuart-Bunning) to influence the decisions made in Paris was one of the immediate causes for the Amsterdam conference, at which seventeen member parties participated. See Mayer, *op. cit.*, pp. 853–855; Cole, *op. cit.*, p. 322; Braunthal, *op. cit.*, pp. 173–174. The composition of the permanent committee as constituted at Berne is given by Renaudel, pp. 144–145.

[29] *Christian Science Monitor*, June 20, 1919, p. 8, and June 21, p. 7. See also Varandian, *op. cit.*, p. 142; Djamalian, "Hai-vratsakan knjire" (April, 1928), p. 98; Rep. of Arm. Archives, File 66a/3, Bulletin no. 123.

[30] The relevant correspondence is in Rep. of Arm. Archives, File 101/2.

their strategy of maintaining an aloofness from the International. On May 5, 1919, Mikayel Varandian denounced the Georgian maneuver to Albert Thomas and Camille Huysmans, charging the Mensheviks with callous misrepresentation in an attempt to renege upon the pledge made at Berne so that they could keep control over Armenian lands—Akhalkalak and much of Borchalu.[31]

The controversy reached scandalous proportions and was finally aired by the Second International's directors, who assembled in Paris on May 10. Even Avetis Aharonian abandoned his judicious policy of disassociation and appeared along with Ohandjanian and Varandian in order "to rip the shroud of deception" from the Georgian Mensheviks, among whose delegation were Iraklii Tsereteli, Nikolai Chkheidze, and Akakii Chkhenkeli. For two days Varandian and Tsereteli matched their powers of rhetoric before the august socialist tribunal—Arthur Henderson, Ramsay MacDonald, Pierre Renaudel, Jean Longuet, Camille Huysmans, and George Stuart-Bunning.[32] In an impassioned appeal for self-determination, Varandian berated the Georgian Social Democrats for having defiled their solemn declarations. Not to be outdone, Tsereteli argued the modified Menshevik tactic, proposing arbitration rather than referendum in drawing the Armeno-Georgian boundary. The Georgian government had apparently come to believe that a referendum might leave it empty-handed but that through arbitration, in which the aspirations of the inhabitants need not be the single determining factor, a sizable share of the contested territory might be secured. When Varandian re-sounded the case for a popular verdict, Tsereteli retaliated by inquiring whether the Armenian delegation would be willing to accept a referendum in Turkish Armenia. Keenly sensitive about the recent massacres and deportations that had left Turkish Armenia without Armenians, Varandian vilified Tsereteli's insinuation as shameless immorality. British Laborite Henderson,

[31] Varandian, op. cit., pp. 142–143; Rep. of Arm. Archives, File 1687/18, H. H. D.: Erkrord Midjazgaynakan, 1919.

[32] Cole, op. cit., p. 298, states that during the Amsterdam conference the permanent commission added MacDonald, Renaudel, Longuet, and Stuart-Bunning to the executive committee, which would have made the composition of the latter body identical with that of the action committee. The group conducting the hearings in Paris in May, 1919, has been erroneously identified by Avalov, op. cit., p. 212, and several other authors as the Bureau of the International. A contemporary account, Fester, op. cit., p. 31, states that the action committee would be meeting in Paris on May 10, 1919, thus providing grounds to assume that technically it was the action committee that presided. Mayer, op. cit., pp. 855–856, also shows that the action committee met on May 10–11, and he identifies the members of the committee as the same six men who sat as arbiters in the Armeno-Georgian dispute.

the chairman of the hearing, also chided the Georgian delegation, reminding Tsereteli that the question under consideration was not
Turkish Armenia but a Transcaucasian boundary.[33]

In rendering a decision, the members of the tribunal, bound by
their own formulas, echoed the Berne resolution calling for referendum or plebiscite. Tsereteli himself had advocated this solution for
lands disputed in other parts of the world and now finally consented
in principle to its application in Transcaucasia. He added with an
air of confidence that, in view of recent agrarian reforms inaugurated
by the Tiflis government, the Armenian population of Akhalkalak
and Lori would certainly opt for permanent union with the Republic
of Georgia. Apparently not satisfied with Tsereteli's concession, the
Armenian spokesmen struck a disagreeable note by demanding that
all Georgian officials and troops in the two districts be withdrawn for
the duration of the referendum as a guarantee against coercion. The
Menshevik representatives seized the opportunity to counterclaim that
the Armenians, by their own words, had exposed their total insincerity.
The socialist tribunal now scolded the Dashnakist leaders and admonished them to have faith in the international commission that
would be established to conduct the referendum.[34] No evidence has
been discovered, however, to indicate that steps to form such a body
were ever taken.

The issue lapsed once again until the permanent commission of the
International gathered in Lucerne in August to assess the difficulties
and failures in reviving the world organization. Mikayel Varandian
urged the commission to turn its attention to events in the East and to
the desperate struggle of small peoples to enforce the right of self-determination. In the name of Dashnaktsutiun, Varandian pleaded for
vigorous action rather than "ritualistic resolutions." The socialist leaders responded with a ritualistic resolution on the sanctity of plebiscite
and referendum.[35] Here the International allowed the matter to rest.

[33] Djamalian, "Hai-vratsakan knjire" (April, 1928), pp. 98–100; Varandian, op. cit.,
pp. 143–144. Varandian gives additional information in his article, "Ramzey Mak-
Donald ev kovkasian khndirnere," Hairenik Amsagir, VII (Oct. 1929), 113–114.

[34] Avalov, op. cit., pp. 212–214; Varandian, Le conflit arméno-géorgien, pp. 144–145.

[35] The activities of the Lucerne conference are outlined by Mayer, op. cit., pp.
870–873; Braunthal, op. cit., pp. 174–176; Cole, op. cit., pp. 322–333. The full French
text of Varandian's memorandum is in Rep. of Arm. Archives, File 1688/19, H. H. D.:
Erkrord Midjazgaynakan, 1920. See also Hairenik (daily), Oct. 24, 1919, p. 1. The
Georgian Menshevik memorandum submitted to the conference was published as
La Géorgie Indépendante, cited in full in note 6 above. See also " 'Demokraticheskoe'
pravitel'stvo Gruzii i angliiskoe komandovanie," ed. Semen Sef, Krasnyi Arkhiv, XXI
(1927), 169–173, cited hereafter as "Gruziia i angliiskoe komandovanie."

But perhaps it made no difference, since the convocations in Berne, Amsterdam, Paris, and Lucerne were of little interest to the Georgian troops in Akhalkalak and northern Borchalu, to the Armenian patrols in southern Lori, or to the British commissioner general in the "neutral zone."

A Transcaucasian Conference

On February 21, 1919, Foreign Minister Gegechkori issued a circular to the republics of Armenia, Azerbaijan, and the Mountaineer Confederation of the North Caucasus and Daghestan stating that in the opinion of Georgia the welfare of all four states required the creation of an atmosphere of reciprocal trust and harmony founded upon mutual defense of the independence of each. Therefore, the Georgian government wished to ascertain if there was any objection to discussing such matters as transit, tariff, trade, and finance, particularly as agreements in these fields could lead to the solution of more substantive questions. Gegechkori solicited suggestions on the best means to treat these subjects, adding that his government considered a general Transcaucasian conference most appropriate.[36]

The inflection of the message contrasted sharply with the directive-like summons that had led to the stillborn Transcaucasian conference in the autumn of 1918 and had further aggravated Armeno-Georgian relations. The time, structure, and agenda of this meeting were to be determined by consultation and mutual consent. The anomalous Mountaineer Republic readily accepted the invitation to confer with the relatively secure and established states to the south, and Azerbaijan suggested that the agenda be expanded to include basic issues such as the formation of a united Transcaucasian front at the Paris Peace Conference, the disentanglement of territorial questions, and the preparation of a regional defense plan against any and all external forces. Azerbaijani Premier and Foreign Minister Fathali Khan Khoiskii felt Baku was the most suitable site for the gathering but stated that he would not oppose its being held in Tiflis, preferably sometime in March. He did insist that the South-West Caucasus Republic at Kars, then still in existence, be included, terming its participation "desirable and necessary." [37]

[36] US Archives, RG 84, Tiflis Consulate, 1919, pt. 4, File 710; Rep. of Arm. Archives, File 3/3. See also Woytinsky, *op. cit.*, p. 285.
[37] US Archives, RG 84, Tiflis Consulate, pt. 4, File 710; Rep. of Arm. Archives, File 66/2, Report of May 6, 1919, and File 9/9, Foreign Minister to Aharonian, May 6, 1919.

Chargé d'affaires Leon Evangulov informed Gegechkori of Armenia's willingness to join in conference on condition that the boundary problem be resolved bilaterally and not by a four-nation panel.[38] Armenia continued to fear the specter of a power bloc in which she would stand alone against the combined votes of Georgia, Azerbaijan, and the Mountaineer Confederation. In reality, however, Georgia's relations with her neighboring Muslim republics were not without serious strain. Several districts lay in contention, and Georgia regarded Azerbaijan's support of the South-West Caucasus Republic as an act of provocation. Thus, while the ultranationalist Georgian press warned against trusting the Armenian "wolves in sheep's clothing," at least until a final territorial settlement had been reached,[39] Zhordania's government closed ranks with Armenia to resist the extension of an invitation to the local administration at Kars. In a devious tactic, the two Christian countries consented to an advisory voice for the South-West Caucasus Provisional Government only on condition that Azerbaijan assent to like representation for Mountainous Karabagh.[40] Azerbaijan naturally could not jeopardize her tenuous hold over the Armenian-populated highland by acquiescing in such a proposition. The overthrow of the South-West Caucasus Republic in mid-April and the Armenian occupation of Kars seem to have obviated that aspect of the issue. Azerbaijan no longer pressed for inclusion of delegates from Kars, and Armenia tacitly accepted the impracticability of gaining a rostrum for Mountainous Karabagh.

These preliminary arrangements having taken weeks, the first official Transcaucasian conference opened on April 25, 1919, with each republic represented by three authoritative spokesmen: Sirakan Tigranian, Samson Harutiunian, Stepan Mamikonian for Armenia; Evgenii Gegechkori, Noi Ramishvili, Konstantin Kandelaki for Georgia; Fathali Khan Khoiskii, Mohammed Iusuf Jafarov, Khalil Bek Khas-Mamedov for Azerbaijan; and Ali Khan Kantemirov, Bugaev, and Panguraev for the Mountaineer Confederation.[41] For

[38] Rep. of Arm. Archives, File 66a/3, Report of March 31, 1919.

[39] *Gruziia*, March 12, 1919.

[40] Rep. of Arm. Archives, File 9/9, Foreign Minister to Aharonian, May 6, 1919, and File 66a/3, Press release, April 15, 1919.

[41] Rep. of Arm. Archives, File 3/3, Foreign Minister to Aharonian, May 6 and May 10, 1919. Woytinsky, *op. cit.*, p. 285, erroneously states that the conference took place at the end of May. The inaccurate date is repeated by Haidar-Bammate, *Le Caucase et la révolution russe* (Paris, 1929), p. 41. It is quite possible that both authors used as their source of information the memorandum submitted to the International's permanent commission at Lucerne by Georgian officials in Europe who did not yet have details on the conference in Tiflis. According to contemporary accounts the

more than six weeks the delegates discussed a variety of economic and fiscal problems, the plight of Armenian and Muslim refugees, the proceedings at the Paris Peace Conference, and the mutual relations of the Caucasian republics.[42] Although few plenary sessions took place, a constant dialogue was maintained through several special commissions and through informal meetings involving two or more of the delegations.[43] The political combinations, however arranged, and the prolonged interviews produced meager results, if indeed results were anticipated or desired. Rivalry flared on nearly every topic. Azerbaijan demanded additional summer pasturage in the mountains of Armenia and the repatriation of all Muslim refugees who had fled in the face of Armenian bands led by such guerrilla fighters as Andranik. Armenia called for unhindered transit privileges throughout Transcaucasia and the withdrawal of Azerbaijani military forces from Karabagh. Georgia insisted that her neighbors not mix in her "internal affairs." And the Mountaineers exhorted all to defend the Terek and Daghestan from the intrusions of Russian Reds, Russian Whites, Cossacks, and assorted warlords.[44]

Both the Georgian and the Azerbaijani delegations urged that the territorial conflicts be aired in full, but the Armenians continued

---

opening ceremony took place on April 25 in the chamber of the President of the Georgian republic, and the first plenary session was held in the Georgian Foreign Ministry on April 27. The Mountaineer delegation apparently did not join the conference until the second plenary session, which met on May 3. See *Bor'ba*, April 26, 1919, p. 3, April 29, p. 2, and May 6, p. 1.

[42] Reports on and partial minutes of the Transcaucasian conference are included in Rep. of Arm. Archives, File 3/3 and File 4/4; *Bor'ba*, April–June, 1919, *passim*. Plenary sessions were held on April 27, May 3, May 21, and June 9.

[43] On the recommendation of the conference presidium, composed of Gegechkori, Kantemirov, Khan Khoiskii, and Tigranian, seven working commissions were organized: railway, finance, political, legal (including the citizenship question), refugee, nomad, and territorial principles. The commissions, each having an equal number of representatives from the participating republics, included aides of the accredited delegates. See *Bor'ba*, May 6, 1919, p. 1.

[44] The conference did reach some agreement on general principles. The railway commission, for example, was unanimous in recommending an integrated Transcaucasian railroad system but was not in accord on the form of unification. Moreover, the Armenian representatives proposed that the rolling stock of the Caucasus be divided among the republics in proportion to the total distance of railway in each state, whereas the Georgian and Azerbaijani spokesmen demurred, insisting that each republic should retain whatever rolling stock had fallen within its boundaries as of May 26, 1918, the day the former Transcaucasian Federative Republic had dissolved. Such a settlement would have continued to deprive Armenia of all but a few locomotives and coaches. Of the other subgroups, the finance commission advocated, in principle, the adoption of a common currency for the entire Caucasus and the removal of trade and transit barriers. See *Bor'ba*, May 22, 1919, p. 2, and May 24, p. 1.

evasive. Azerbaijani representative Khas-Mamedov argued that the regulation of secondary issues would be meaningless unless the frontiers of the neighboring republics had been clearly delineated. Not so unequivocal, Georgian spokesman Ramishvili expressed the general prevailing opinion that the unravelment of the boundaries, while highly desirable, was not an absolute prerequisite to improved mutual relations. Agreement on less controversial matters might well point the way to the establishment of firm, respected borders.[45]

The territorial question was actually discussed repeatedly in a commission charged with the formulation of principles and in private bilateral talks between the delegations. In their meetings with the Georgian conferees, Tigranian, Harutiunian, and Mamikonian indicated Armenia's readiness to make a concession in Akhalkalak in return for like action by Georgia in the Borchalu neutral zone, and, in their sessions with the Azerbaijanis, they pressed for concessions in Mountainous Karabagh but had little except goodwill to offer as compensation. The weakness of the Armenian footing was noted in Tigranian's accounting to his government: "The two other countries enjoyed a position of dominance because they are in occupation of the lands at issue and because our routes of transportation must pass through their territories."[46] The ultimate accomplished by the conference to settle the overlapping claims was the acceptance of a three-point statement of principles:

1. The internal boundaries of Transcaucasia were to be drawn in conformity with the right of peoples to determine their own destiny.

2. Only border districts were to be subject to litigation or partition.

3. The partition of borderlands was to result from mutual agreement of the interested republics or, failing this, from arbitration.[47]

On the topic of Transcaucasia's relations with Russia, Armenia stood apart from her neighbors. Even as the conference in Tiflis engaged in deliberations, General Denikin's Volunteer Army was challenging Georgia for control of the Black Sea coastal region between Sochi and Sukhum, invading the Mountaineer Republic, and making no secret of its designs toward strategic, oil-rich Baku, of late the Azerbaijani capital. Hence, in private meetings the Georgian representatives urged Foreign Minister Tigranian to align Armenia in a regional defense pact against Denikin or at least to denounce the

[45] Bor'ba, May 6, 1919, pp. 1–2.
[46] Rep. of Arm. Archives, File 4/4, Foreign Minister to Cabinet, June 12, 1919.
[47] Bor'ba, May 24, 1919, p. 1; Rep. of Arm. Archives, File 3/3 and File 4/4; La Géorgie Indépendante, p. 22. See also Adil Khan Ziatkhan, Aperçu sur l'histoire, la littérature et la politique de l'Azerbeidjan (Baku, 1919), pp. 88–89.

aggression of the Volunteer Army and maintain benevolent neutrality. The common good, the Georgians insisted, demanded that Transcaucasia present a united front against external intervention. Tigranian seized the opportunity to exert some little pressure of his own, contending that Armenia could not hope for sufficient stability to join such an alliance or be of measurable assistance until the debilitating boundary disputes had been resolved. Had Tigranian believed that Georgia would relinquish Lori and Akhalkalak and that Azerbaijan would give up Mountainous Karabagh as the price of Armenia's cooperation, he would have been astonishingly naïve. This was, of course, not his expectation. Rather, Tigranian's tactic was intended to avoid even paper agreements directed against the military forces of South Russia.[48]

Unable to secure Armenian assent through these unofficial discussions, the Georgian and Azerbaijani delegations altered their strategy and brought the matter to a plenary session of the conference. On June 9, 1919, with the Terek and much of Daghestan overpowered by the Volunteer Army, Gegechkori and Khan Khoiskii introduced a formal proposal to create a Transcaucasian defense system against Denikin. Although the affair was now in the open, Tigranian maneuvered to avoid a commitment by suggesting that simply a note condemning external aggression in Transcaucasia be relayed to the Paris Peace Conference. The advantages of preserving cordial relations with the White Armies were too substantial to allow Armenia any other stand. Veiled Georgian and Azerbaijani threats failed to shake the Armenian decision to endorse a vague declaration and nothing more.[49] The Transcaucasian conference ground to a halt on this issue. The Mountaineer Republic now scarcely figured in the proceedings, and neither Georgia nor Azerbaijan could afford to temporize any longer.[50] The two countries had already initiated the necessary preliminaries for a bilateral pact.

The Transcaucasian conference thus adjourned during the second week of June with almost no formality and certainly no ceremony. As the Armenian delegation entrained for Erevan, an air of excitement hovered about the Tiflis railway depot. A military band stood in formation on the platform. It had come, not to bid adieu to Tigranian, but to welcome General Samed Bek Mehmandarov, Azerbaijan's Min-

[48] Rep. of Arm. Archives, File 4/4, Report of Foreign Minister, June 12, 1919.

[49] Rep. of Arm. Archives, File 66/2, Diplomatic Representative of Armenia in Georgia to Aharonian, June 23, 1919. See also Bammate, *op. cit.*, pp. 42–43.

[50] For a description of the concluding activities of the conference, see *Bor'ba*, June 11, 1919, p. 1.

ister of War.[51] Georgia and Azerbaijan had been drawn together by the approaching menace of the Volunteer Army. Moreover, the two republics found it difficult not to perceive a certain unwelcome community of interest between that powerful aggressor from the north and their small sister republic to the south. Armenia had again become isolated.

The White Armies and Armenia

Throughout 1919 the Republic of Armenia shared no common boundary with Russia nor was it directly linked with the Volunteer Army, yet both were integral to its foreign policy. Armenia had taken the road to independence, but she hoped that a benevolent Russia would (1) relieve the severe pressures exerted by Georgia and Azerbaijan, (2) neutralize the ever constant threat of a rejuvenated Turkey, (3) safeguard the thousands of Armenian refugees in Russia and authorize the established Armenian communities there to send material aid to Erevan, and (4) accept the separation of the Russian Armenian provinces in advocacy of their unification with Turkish Armenia and the formation of a free, independent, and viable nation-state.

There were, of course, enormous difficulties in grappling with the Russian problem. To which Russia should Armenia turn—the Sovnarkom at Moscow, the Volunteer and Cossack center at Ekaterinodar, Kolchak's regime in Siberia, or perhaps the anti-Bolshevik administrations and armies of the Baltic and the Arctic? Any one or combination of these could conceivably emerge as the final victor in Russia. Armenia cautiously attempted, therefore, to win the sympathy and recognition of all. Announcing neutrality in the raging Russian civil war, the Erevan government made it known that Armenia would stand as a trusted friend and neighbor of any Russia as long as that Russia would respect the independence of the Republic.[52] Semiofficial Armenian representatives traveled to Moscow, Ekaterinodar, Rostov-on-Don, Murmansk, Omsk, Irkutsk, and other headquarters of the several Russias of 1918–1919. Still, considerations of geographic proximity and potential aid led Armenia to concentrate her efforts upon the Command of the Armed Forces of South Russia.

As early as the summer of 1918 Simon Vratzian, a member of the

[51] Vratzian, *Hanrapetutiun*, p. 316; Rep. of Arm. Archives, File 4/4, Report of Foreign Minister, June 12, 1919.
[52] Rep. of Arm. Archives, File 66a/3, Bulletin no. 109. See also Denikin, *Ocherki smuty*, IV, 176.

Armenian National Council and of the supreme Bureau of Dashnak-tsutiun, journeyed to the Sarmatian plains to appeal for food and military supplies at a time when the Armenian government was preparing to transfer from Tiflis to the disaster-ridden capital at Erevan. General Mikhail V. Alekseev, a masterful organizer of the Volunteer Army, received Vratzian cordially and granted the necessary authorization for Russian officers in Armenia to remain there as cadre for the army of the new state. In addition he allocated to Armenia several thousand tons of grain, but little, if any, of this foodstuff actually reached its destination.[53]

The primary liaison between the Volunteer Army and Armenia passed through military channels. Many Armenian officers had come up through tsarist military academies where they had been imbued with attitudes that now bound their sympathies to colleagues who directed the White Armies. In the autumn of 1918 the Armenian General Staff dispatched Colonel Vlasiev, a Russian officer, to enlist the cooperation of the Volunteer Army in facilitating the transfer to Erevan of many Armenian prisoners of war who, along with countless other soldiers of the former tsarist armies, were being released in Germany and Austria-Hungary. Vlasiev also repeated Vratzian's earlier pleas for bread and matériel. The leadership of the Volunteer Army promised its support and sent to Erevan a representative of its own, Colonel Lesley (Lesli), to gather information and to arrange for the exchange of permanent missions.[54] In the Armenian capital, Lesley gave assurances that the success of the Volunteer Army would not lead to the restoration of the old order and that the future relations of Russia with Armenia would be predicated upon friendship and alliance.[55] According to General A. I. Denikin, chief of the Volunteer Army after Alekseev's death, the Armenian government now reacted with extreme reticence, asserting that Colonel Vlasiev had really not been an official spokesman but only a military scout. In Denikin's estimation, Armenia was fearful that a public display of camaraderie

[53] Vratzian, *Ughinerov*, II, (1960), 106–108, and his *Hin tghter nor patmutian hamar* (Beirut, 1962), pp. 266–267, Report of Oct. 19, 1918. Georgian restrictions and interference in the movement of goods to Armenia are reported in US Archives, RG 59, 861.00/4017/5583; RG 84, Tiflis Consulate, 1919, pt. 3, File 360; RG 256, 184.021/4 and 867B.4016/32. See also London *Times*, Jan. 22, 1919, p. 7; *Hairenik* (daily), March 18, 1919, p. 1.

[54] Denikin, *Ocherki smuty*, IV, 136 n. 2, 176. See also A. M. Elchibekian *Velikaia Oktiabr'skaia sotsialisticheskaia revoliutsiia i pobeda Sovetskoi vlasti v Armenii* (Erevan, 1957), p. 86.

[55] Rep. of Arm. Archives, File 3/3, Foreign Minister to President of Peace Delegation (Aharonian), Jan. 13, 1919.

might compromise her claims to independence at a stage when the victorious Allies seemed sure to name for Armenia a mandatory power other than Russia.[56]

While Denikin's interpretation was certainly not groundless and Armenia did reveal a determination to preserve her independence from Russia, Kachaznuni's cabinet nonetheless found it expedient in 1919 to appoint an envoy, Hovhannes (Ivan) Saghatelian, to the Volunteer Army and the Cossack-dominated government of the Kuban. From these two sometimes discordant organizations, Armenia sought political recognition, food, military equipment, permission to recruit volunteers, and immunity for the many thousands of Armenians scattered throughout the steppelands of Russia.[57] In Rostov-on-Don, meanwhile, Grigor Chalkhushian acted as Armenia's spokesman in attempts to procure grain from the Don Cossacks.[58] That the Volunteer Army looked upon the Armenians with some partiality was evidenced in the fact that, while Denikin's divisions struck pitilessly at several minority groups and all suspected enemies, the Armenians of South Russia were spared from the pogroms. Denikin even authorized the local Armenian communities to gather supplies for the Republic and to outfit men headed for volunteer military service in Erevan.[59]

Armenian relief organizations in many Crimean, South Russian, and Ukrainian centers operated freely during periods of Volunteer Army control. In the Cossack regions, a longtime civic leader, Iakov (Hakob) Tadevosian, coordinated the activities intended to succor more than 70,000 destitute Turkish Armenian refugees. By the spring of 1919, with the World War at an end and with Russia paralyzed by political

[56] Denikin, *Ocherki smuty*, IV, 176.

[57] For materials about Saghatelian and his activities in South Russia, see Rep. of Arm. Archives, File 20/20, *Hayastani Hanrapetutiun, 1920*, and File 71, *H. H. Nerkayatsutsich Haravayin Rusastani Zinial Uzheri Mot, 1919 t.–1920/21 t.* See also *Hairenik* (daily), June 22, 1919, p. 2, and Aug. 9, p. 5. Denikin, *Ocherki smuty*, IV, 176–177, states that Saghatelian acted as the official Armenian representative to the Kuban government and as the unofficial and secret agent to the Volunteer Army. Vratzian, *Hanrapetutiun*, p. 225, states that Saghatelian was appointed Armenia's envoy to the Volunteer Army in January, 1919, and that in April the scope of his jurisdiction was extended to include the Kuban government at Ekaterinodar. On September 27, 1919, *Bor'ba* reprinted an article from *Obnovlenie*, another Tiflis journal, stating that Saghatelian, who until that time had been the Armenian envoy to the Kuban, had just been commissioned to enter into special conferences with the Commander of the Armed Forces of South Russia.

[58] Rep. of Arm. Archives, File 66a/3, Report of March, 1919; *Hairenik* (daily), March 9, 1919, p. 2.

[59] S. Vartanian, *Pobeda Sovetskoi vlasti v Armenii* (Erevan, 1959), p. 175. See also Rep. of Arm. Archives, File 65/1 and File 71; Ruben [Ter-Minasian], *Hai heghapokhakani me hishataknere*, Vol. VII (Los Angeles, 1952), pp. 258–259; *Hairenik* (daily), Nov . 25, 1919, p. 1.

upheavals, the refugees sought means to move to Erevan on the first leg of a trek that hopefully would culminate in their return to Erzerum, Van, Mush, and other Turkish Armenian provinces. Every surviving Armenian counted heavily in the plan to repopulate those lands, yet the Armenian government cautioned Saghatelian and Tadevosian that, in view of the Republic's intense economic crisis and the political uncertainty regarding Turkish Armenia, the refugees should not set out unless they had an ample supply of food and clothing. This requirement was the subject of discussions in Ekaterinodar between the Armenian representatives and the head men of the Kuban. By the arrangement adopted in May of 1919, every repatriate would be provisioned with 2 pouds (just over 72 pounds) each of flour, bread, and potatoes.[60]

Despite the goodwill generated by such consideration, genuine cordiality between Armenia and the Volunteer Army was circumscribed by ideological and logistical factors. Armenia had become independent, whereas the White Armies, their professed sympathy for the Armenians aside, were fighting not only to overthrow the Bolshevik regime but also to reconstitute an integral Russian empire. At most they might concede that some future constituent assembly of all Russia would one day pass on the status and degree of autonomy of the border regions. This objective prompted misgivings among Armenian political leaders, who flatly rejected any formula tinged with the possibility of Russian reabsorption of the Armenian provinces. Even if the entire former empire were reunited, Armenia, they insisted, must be an exception. It was upon the independence of a combined Russian Armenia and Turkish Armenia that the future of the nation rested. Although Denikin claimed to understand the aspiration of the Armenians to conjoin their historic lands, he never spoke out in favor of Armenian independence, this despite the guarantees recited in Erevan by Colonel Lesley. The willingness of anti-Bolshevik Russia to sanction the disengagement of Armenia was by no means ensured.

Logistically, Armenia and the Volunteer Army were separated by a solid block of hostile republics: Georgia, Azerbaijan, and the Mountaineer Confederation of the North Caucasus and Daghestan. The three states, suspecting collusion between Ekaterinodar and Erevan, impeded communication and transportation between these distant centers. Provisions destined for Armenia were frequently turned back or seized at the northern borders of Georgia and Azerbaijan. On occasion transit privileges were granted, but for exorbitant fees, making the

[60] Rep. of Arm. Archives, File 20/20, Report of Tadevosian, May 10, 1919.

transactions impractical. Furthermore, when General Denikin learned that aid to Erevan might in fact benefit the regimes in Tiflis and Baku, he suspended all consignments.

The limited nature of Armeno-Russian relations can also be attributed to the dualistic, yet explicable, strategy of Great Britain. The government of David Lloyd George participated, though reluctantly and inconsistently, in the French project to spin a *cordon sanitaire* around Bolshevik Russia, and it intervened in the civil war by supplying the White Armies with advisers and officers and money and matériel. In keeping with this policy, the military establishment in London required that Denikin and his fellow commanders concentrate their energies upon the Bolshevik threat. For the time being at least the border regions, the Caucasus included, should be allowed to maintain their separation from Russia.[61]

There was, however, another, unstated factor in the policy emanating from the combined councils of ranking members of the War Office, the India Office, and the Foreign Office. The Russian civil war had caused a major breakthrough in the long-standing Russo-British competition for predominance in Asia. Influential men with imperial visions still aglow deemed the situation most propitious to neutralize the impact of any future Russian empire. At the end of 1918 Foreign Secretary Arthur J. Balfour stated that "no one could wish that Russia's boundaries should be the same as before" in such regions as Finland, the Baltic, Transcaucasia, and Turkestan.[62] A noted historian of the period has made the following appraisal:

From the point of view of this traditional Anglo-Russian rivalry in the Balkans, the Near East, and the Middle East, England could only welcome Russia's collapse. Britain was conveniently released from the wartime secret treaties; she could stake out her claims to the Turkish legacy without worrying about Russia's claims or her collusion with France; and she was freed from pressures along the northwest frontier as she faced the unrest of postwar India. Some superrealists were not satisfied with these benefits of an endogenous nature. They wanted England to take advantage of Russia's plight to roll back her borders, especially in the Caucasus, Finland, and the Baltic provinces. Of course, whereas certain old Foreign Office hands pushed self-determination for border

---

[61] Denikin, *Ocherki smuty*, IV, 128–136, 139–146, 172–174, 177–179, presents his appraisal of British policy.

[62] Mayer, *op. cit.*, p. 309. For a discussion of the vicissitudes in British policy toward the Caucasus, based on the records of the War Cabinet's ad hoc Eastern Committee and of the Imperial War Cabinet, see Richard H. Ullman, *Anglo-Soviet Relations, 1917–1921*, Vol. II: *Britain and the Russian Civil War, November 1918– December 1920* (Princeton, 1968), pp. 64–68, 220–231. For the primary papers, see the files for 1918–1919 in Britain, Cab 23, Cab 24, and Cab 27.

minorities primarily in order to bring them under British influence, latter-day Gladstonians and a large array of Wilsonians advocated it primarily in obedience to their high principles, thereby unintentionally providing the government with a welcome ideological cover.[63]

The purpose of Great Britain in occupying the Caucasus in 1918–1919 was not, according to this valid interpretation, to exploit the natural resources of the region but "to close the ring around the Bolsheviks" by denying them desperately needed resources and also to establish provisional control in an area "from which they meant to exclude first the French and then the Russians." [64] The acceptance by the United States of a mandate for part or all of Transcaucasia would conveniently serve British designs.

Hence, while the British strategists supported Denikin against the Bolsheviks, they could not condone his thrusts to the south. The White Armies should liquidate Bolshevism before displaying active concern over the situation in the border provinces—first things first. Although some British military tacticians, headed by Secretary of State for War Winston S. Churchill, upheld Denikin's goal of reunifying Russia, most officers of the Imperial Army—nearly all in the Caucasus—were imbued with the traditional English skepticism and antipathy toward Russia. This paradox placed the Armenian government in difficult straits. In its opposition to Bolshevism, Lloyd George's cabinet might bolster General Denikin and the Volunteer Army, but should Armenia develop too genial a relationship with the Russian center at Ekaterinodar, many responsible British officials would come to regard the Republic with deep suspicion. There was abundant evidence that the Imperial command in Transcaucasia already considered the Muslim population a much more trustworthy anti-Russian element. Consequently, in her dealings with the north, Armenia had to steer a hazardous course. The continuum of harmony with Russia was a cornerstone of her policy, but the immediate need to gain the confidence of the British generals stationed in Tiflis and Baku was of at least equal significance.

The Volunteer Army and Transcaucasia

Of the separatist states in the Caucasus, only Armenia received professions of friendship from Anton Ivanovich Denikin, Commander of

---

[63] Mayer, op. cit., p. 308.

[64] Ibid., p. 315. For primary Cabinet and War Office records substantiating this evaluation, see Britain, Cab 23/8, Cab 27/24, and Cab 27/36-38, and WO 95/4958-4959.

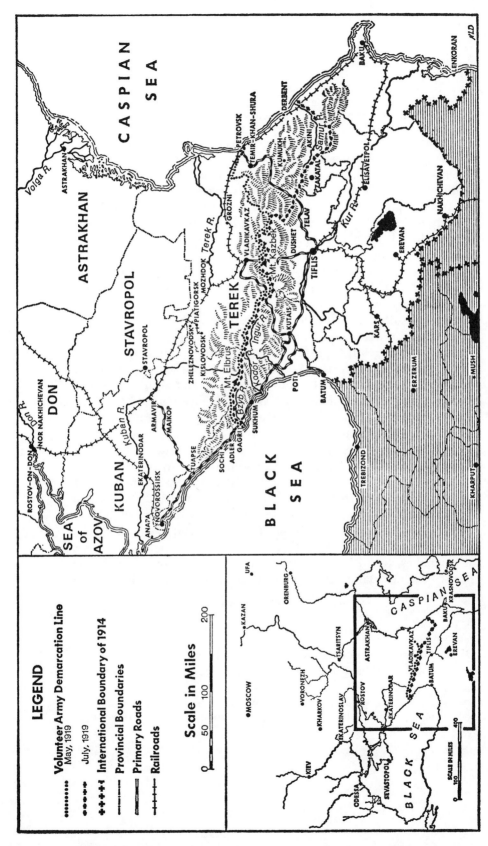

14. THE CAUCASUS AND RUSSIA, 1919

the Armed Forces of South Russia. He was appreciative of the freedoms enjoyed by Russians in Armenia, in sharp contrast with the shameful discrimination assertedly prevailing in Georgia and Azerbaijan.[65] But Denikin's hostility toward the Tiflis and Baku regimes was based on factors more consequential than the mistreatment of Russian subjects. The unity of the Russian Empire lay in the balance. And while Denikin was compelled to tolerate, at least temporarily, the existence of the self-constituted governments of Georgia and Azerbaijan, he was resolved to shatter their pretensions to lands north of the Kutais, Tiflis, and Baku guberniias. As for the Mountaineer Confederation of the North Caucasus and Daghestan, the Volunteer commander would accept no compromise whatever. This strategic mountain fastness had become, in his view, a den of Pan-Turanic and Bolshevik sedition. It had to be subjugated, he claimed, to safeguard the southern flank of the loyal, anti-Soviet forces of Russia.

The immediate dispute with the Georgian republic focused upon the Black Sea littoral, with the major towns of Tuapse, Sochi, Adler, Gagri, and Sukhum (see map 14). This region, much of which formed the historic land of Abkhazia, had in tsarist days comprised the province of Chernomorie (Black Sea) and the county of Sukhum, both multinational in population but with a definite Russian and Cossack preponderance in the former.[66] Supported by Germany in 1918, Georgia had established nominal control over the districts, and the Volun-

---

[65] Denikin, *Ocherki smuty*, III, 54; Rep. of Arm. Archives, File 62/2, Report of June 23, 1919. See also US Archives, RG 59, 861.00/5467. Zhordaniia, *op. cit.*, p. 103, states that his government threatened retaliation against the Russian population of the Georgian republic only after General Denikin had taken preliminary measures to expel all Georgians in territories occupied by the Volunteer Army.

[66] According to Russian statistics for 1916, the ethnic complexion of the Sukhum okrug and the Chernomorskaia oblast, the latter divided into the okrugs of Novorossiisk, Tuapse, and Sochi, was as follows:

| | Sukhum | Chernomorie | | |
		Novorossiisk	Tuapse	Sochi
Russian	25,400	72,400	26,800	31,800
Other European	6,600	—	1,900	9,300
Georgian	50,400	—	—	6,000
Armenian	20,700	1,000	2,800	14,200
Circassian and Abkhazian	103,200	—	5,300	—
Mountaineer	400			
Shi'a Muslim	—	300	500	800
Jew	600	1,600	—	—

See US Archives, RG 256, 867B.00/10. The Armenian population of the coastal region from Sukhum to Novorossiisk had increased considerably by 1919, as this expanse had become the major center for refugees from Trebizond and Ordu, on the southern shore of the Black Sea.

teer Army had not dared to initiate countermeasures. Negotiations in September, 1918, between the Georgian republic and the Volunteer Army and Kuban government failed to produce an understanding, and the subsequent defeat of the Central Powers deprived Georgia of the restraining influences Berlin had imposed upon the generals in South Russia.[67] In December of that year the Volunteers advanced into Sochi where they found an indigenous ally in the Armenian inhabitants, who, without exception, preferred the Russian eagle to the red banner of Georgia. At the time, Premier Noi Zhordania had charged that the Volunteer invasion along the Black Sea had been prearranged to coincide with the Armenian march into Lori in a scheme to subvert the independence of the Georgian republic. Indeed, a number of Georgian army units had been hurriedly transferred from the coastal garrisons to meet the piercing blow of Dro's troops.[68] And while Zhordania's contention could not be substantiated, Major General G. T. Forestier-Walker had been sufficiently impressed to warn Foreign Minister Tigranian that Great Britain would come to the defense of Georgia should the Armenians join the Volunteer Army in aggression against her.[69]

Throughout the first quarter of 1919 there was no significant change in London's strategy to keep the Caucasus apart from Russia, even though sundry generals in the field were profuse in their criticisms of the Tiflis and Baku governments. British-drawn demarcation lines in the Caucasus repeatedly denied Denikin control of Abkhazia and of Daghestan, including the vital Vladikavkaz-Petrovsk railway.[70] And in

[67] *Dokumenty i materialy*, pp. 391–414; Ia. Shafir, *Grazhdanskaia voina v Rossii i men'shevistskaia Gruziia* (Moscow, 1921), pp. 40–45; Britain, FO 371/3662, 102003/1015/58. See also *Bor'ba*, April 3, 1919, pp. 2–3; Woytinsky, *op. cit.*, pp. 175–177; Kazemzadeh, *Transcaucasia*, pp. 234–236; George A. Brinkley, *The Volunteer Army and Allied Intervention in South Russia, 1917–1921* (Notre Dame, 1966), pp. 145–148. Avalov, *op. cit.*, p. 197, criticized his Georgian Social Democrat compatriots for embroiling the Republic in the dispute over Tuapse and Sochi, districts in which Georgia "had no business."

[68] Brinkley, *op. cit.*, p. 153; Denikin, *Ocherki smuty*, IV, 154. See also *La Géorgie Indépendante*, pp. 16–17; "Gruziia i angliiskoe komandovanie," p. 163.

[69] Denikin, *Ocherki smuty*, IV, 154. See also Kazemzadeh, *Transcaucasia*, pp. 181, 237–238.

[70] For documents relative to British policy and to conditions in the North Caucasus and along the Black Sea littoral during the first months of 1919, see Britain, WO 32/3678, 33/365, 95/4958, and FO 371/3661, File 1015/58, and 371/3667, File 5890/58, and 371/3963, File 93/38; US Archives, RG 59, 861.00/6583, and RG 256, 184.01602/23 and 861G.00/103. See also Brinkley, *op. cit.*, pp. 148–157; George Stewart, *The White Armies of Russia* (New York, 1933), pp. 158–162; "Gruziia i angliiskoe komandovanie," pp. 127–131; "Gorskaia kontrrevoliutsiia i interventy," ed. A. Ivanov, *Krasnyi Arkhiv*, LXVIII (1935), 136–153; Denikin, *Ocherki smuty*, IV, 106–136 *passim*; A. Raevskii, *Angliiskaia interventsiia i Musavatskoe pravitel'stvo* (Baku, 1927), pp. 92–119; V. I.

a rash of anti-Volunteer activity the British commanders expelled Denikin's agents from Transcaucasia. In January, 1919, Colonel Lazar F. Bicherakhov, the partisan leader closely linked to the Volunteer Army, was "invited" to journey to London to receive the commendation of King George V for services rendered in the British war effort, and most of his Cossack troops were pressed to leave Azerbaijan. Then on February 28 Major General W. M. Thomson bluntly ordered Bicherakhov's successor, General M. A. Przhevalskii, and the remaining force to quit Baku and all Azerbaijan within twenty-four hours.[71] Equally indicative of the disposition of the British military authorities was the disarming of the highly opportunistic non-Bolshevik Russian Caspian flotilla, anchored off Baku. British gunboats successfully neutralized the fleet but to Denikin's chagrin did not place it under the jurisdiction of the Volunteer Army.[72] The views of Russophobe officers such as Forestier-Walker, Thomson, and Shuttleworth were reflected in a War Office communiqué of March 11 telling General Denikin in no uncertain terms that the British would protect the southern flank of the Volunteer Army and that hereafter the security of the Caspian Sea would be the sole responsibility of the western Allies. With little effort to couch the ultimatum in diplomatic terminology, the War Office warned the Volunteer Army to direct its activity exclusively northward and cease all hostility toward the Caucasian states or else risk a suspension of military aid.[73]

Adamiia, *Iz istorii angliiskoi interventsii v Gruzii (1918–1921 gg.)* (Sukhumi, 1961), pp. 77–80.

[71] Britain, FO 371/3661, 41025/1015/58, FO 371/3669, 21677/21677/58, and WO 95/4880, 27th Division War Diary; US Archives, RG 59, 861.00/6583; Raevskii, *op. cit.*, pp. 94–95; *Bor'ba v Gruzii*, p. 369; La Chesnais, *op. cit.*, pp. 116–117; Kadishev, *Interventsiia v Zakavkaz'e*, p. 168; Kazemzadeh, *Transcaucasia*, p. 242. Przhevalskii's force moved northward to Petrovsk, where it remained from March to May, 1919.

[72] Denikin, *Ocherki smuty*, IV, 128–130; F. J. F. French, *From Whitehall to the Caspian* (London, 1920), pp. 170–180; Stewart, *op. cit.*, p. 166; Kazemzadeh, *Transcaucasia*, p. 224; Brinkley, *op. cit.*, pp. 168–169; US Archives, RG 59, 861.00/6583. For documents on Great Britain's Caspian policy during the first half of 1919, see Britain, FO 371/3667, File 11067/58, and FO 608/83, File 342/8/4.

[73] Denikin, *Ocherki smuty*, IV, 132–133; Britain, WO 33/365, no. 3749. See also Brinkley, *op. cit.*, pp. 158–159; Kadishev, *Interventsiia v Zakavkaz'e*, p. 168, Britain, FO 371/3661, 25757/32483/41025/1015/58. The Azerbaijani government was most gratified by the direction of British policy. This sentiment was reinforced on March 31, when the British command transferred the responsibility for maintaining order in Baku from the Allied police force to Azerbaijani militiamen. On April 5 the headquarters and general staff of the Azerbaijani army returned to Baku after a six-month banishment in Ganja. The government arranged for a festive reception of the Azerbaijani units led by General Ali Agha Ismail oghli Shikhlinskii as they marched into the capital. See Ziatkhan, *op. cit.*, p. 81; [Republic of Azerbaijan], *Le 28 Mai 1919* ([Baku, 1919]), p. 18; Britain, WO 95/4880, 27th Division War Diary. According to Mehmet-Zade Mirza-Bala, *Milli Azerbaycan hareketi: Milli Az. "Müsavat" halk*

The Russian threat to the Mountaineer Confederation, Georgia, and Azerbaijan could not have had a beneficent effect on their relations with Armenia, a sister republic that consistently refused to condemn the counterrevolutionary White Armies. But despite the suspicions of her neighbors Armenia was not wholly committed to Russia in 1919. While the Volunteer Army did ease some of the Georgian and Azerbaijani pressure on Armenia, the Erevan government grew increasingly apprehensive about the ultimate intentions of Denikin and men of like persuasion. At a time when Avetis Aharonian and Boghos Nubar were attempting to convince the Peace Conference that only as an independent and united state could Armenia develop and prosper, rumors were circulating that Denikin regarded the Armenian army as one of his divisions. In addition, the Armenians were embittered by the British decision to ship large quantities of military matériel from Kars to South Russia. And in April, 1919, when the Armenian army finally received authorization to occupy Kars, Denikin allegedly claimed that the great fortress was being taken in the name of integral Russia. Impatient with such statements, Foreign Minister Tigranian ordered Saghatelian to lay the matter before the Russian generals in Ekaterinodar and to leave no doubt about the permanent independent status of the Republic of Armenia. The British, he complained in a report to Aharonian, persisted in distrusting the Armenians for their supposed devotion to Russia. What advantages the reputation of being Russophile might bring Armenia in the future Tigranian could not predict, but that in the past and at present it contributed to the Armenian tragedy he knew all too well. Still, Armenia could not afford to provoke the White Armies.[74]

During the second quarter of 1919 British policy toward Denikin and the Caucasus underwent significant modification. The White Armies having gained the initiative on every front, the overthrow of Bolshevism seemed at hand, a prospect that excited even the Russophobe British officers. Furthermore, the British command in Tiflis

---

fırkası tarihi ([Berlin], 1938), p. 170, the Azerbaijani army returned to Baku in June, 1919.

[74] Rep. of Arm. Archives, File 8/8, Foreign Minister to President of Peace Delegation. See also File 66/2, Report of May 10, 1919. Major A. Ranald McDonell, who was with the Imperial forces in the Caucasus and who had previously served as vice-consul at Baku, reported to the War Office in February that there appeared to be some kind of understanding between the Volunteer Army and Armenia. Several observers, he wrote, believed a formal alliance existed, but he was of the opinion that some type of private arrangement had been concluded between General Denikin and the dominant party in Armenia, Dashnaktsutiun. See Britain, FO 371/3661, 34957/1015/58.

had become troubled by the stubborn Bolshevik partisan activity in the North Caucasus and the recrudescence of Pan-Islamic and Pan-Turanic movements on both sides of the Caucasus range. British tolerance for local regimes such as the South-West Caucasus Republic had apparently only nourished defiance and arrogance among the Muslim peoples. These interrelated factors, as it has been established, influenced the eventual British decision to sanction the extension of Armenia's jurisdiction to both Kars and Nakhichevan.

As Admiral Aleksandr V. Kolchak launched his sweeping spring offensive against the Bolshevik strongholds of Russia, Denikin directed his regiments deeper into the Mountaineer Republic, again approaching districts claimed by Georgia and Azerbaijan.[75] In London the determination to restrain the Volunteers dipped to a low threshold as a growing number of officials conceded that General Denikin was entitled to at least partial satisfaction in the Caucasus. This view was repeated even more emphatically in a succession of newspaper editorials and articles. A correspondent for the London *Times* wrote:

Russia, or rather the incorruptible part of her as represented in the Volunteer Army, is still our Ally. These gallant troops have been true to the Entente all along, scorning the offer of a separate peace and refusing any compromise with Bolshevism. And the heavier their burden, the greater our obligation; yet instead of sending Russia aid, our concern seems to be with the states which have fallen away from her. . . . Anyone who has had experience of conditions in Georgia or Azerbaijan since the Russian revolution will understand that their independence would be a positive menace to the peace of the world.

The case of Armenia is different. Her national destiny, whatever degree of capacity she may have for self-administration, will be with the new Armenian State to be retrieved from Turkey, which will be sufficiently protected. I have reason to believe that a certain section of Russian opinion admits the justice of this. But to pledge ourselves to the separation of Georgia and Azerbaijan as a permanent disposition and to undertake to bolster them up against a potential organized Russia would be as wrong as it would be impolitic.[76]

[75] The governments of Georgia and Azerbaijan repeatedly protested the Volunteer invasion of the North Caucasus. See especially the Tiflis newspaper *Bor'ba* and the Baku organ *Azerbaidzhan*, March–June, 1919. According to *Bor'ba*, March 28, 1919, p. 3, and May 23, p. 2, the hard-pressed Mountaineer cabinet was reorganized between March 22–25, with Pshemakho Kotsev serving as premier and foreign minister. Unable to withstand the turbulence for long, Kotsev's cabinet fell on May 12, and General Khalilov, a collaborator of Denikin, formed a new government on a platform of concluding an immediate understanding with the Volunteer Army. See also Britain, WO 95/4950, Army of the Black Sea War Diary.

[76] London *Times*, April 14, 1919, p. 10. Articles in a similar vein are in the issues of April 25, p. 12, and May 9, p. 16.

In May of 1919 Lieutenant General Charles James Briggs, chief of the British military mission with the Volunteer Army, appeared in Tiflis to cajole Georgia to forego her claims to Sochi and much of Abkhazia. Despite the repeated refusals and protestations of Zhordania's government, the Georgian army, under mounting pressure from British officials and Volunteer regiments, was eventually constrained to withdraw from much of the disputed territory.[77] Moreover, through the good offices of General Briggs and his supporters in the War Office, preparations were made to entrust Denikin with control of the Caspian flotilla.[78] With the boundaries of Georgia and Azerbaijan seemingly about to crumble, the British intervened once again in May to draw a new demarcation line. Starting at the mouth of the Bzyb River on the Black Sea, it passed inland along the northern administrative boundaries of the Sukhum okrug and the Kutais and Tiflis guberniias, proceeded along the northern boundary of the Daghestan oblast to a point 5 miles from the Vladikavkaz-Petrovsk railway, then ran parallel to that railway, through the northern reaches of Daghestan, until it struck the Caspian Sea 5 miles south of Petrovsk (see map 14). The Volunteer Army had thus been awarded the Sochi-Gagri district and most of the North Caucasus, with its vital communication and transportation routes and the port of Petrovsk. Relaying this information to the Georgian and Azerbaijani governments on June 11, the commander of the 27th Division, General G. N. Cory, warned the Transcaucasian states not to violate the border as defined or engage in hostile actions against the Volunteer Army. Failure to

---

[77] Britain, WO 32/5678 and /5694; US Archives, RG 59, 861.00/6583, and RG 256, 861G.00/103; Uratadze, *op. cit.*, pp. 92–100; Brinkley, *op. cit.*, pp. 161–162; Kazemzadeh, *Transcaucasia*, pp. 239–240; "Gruziia i angliiskoe komandovanie," XXI, 141–153, and XXV (1927), 104–109. See also D. Enukidze, *Krakh imperialisticheskoi interventsii v Zakavkaz'e* (Tbilisi, 1954), pp. 156–159. General Briggs had consistently championed the right of Denikin to control the entire Caucasus region. In a message to the War Office in March, he deprecated the existing British policy that was allowing a "petty temporary" republic such as Azerbaijan to annex "Russian territory." See Britain, WO 33/365, no. 3844. In his antipathy toward the Georgians, Briggs was joined by General Milne. The General Officer Commanding, Army of the Black Sea, advised the War Office at the beginning of May that the Georgian government "contains all the worst elements of Bolshevism" and was "truculent and hostile" in its attitude toward Great Britain. He requested that he be empowered to inform Zhordania's cabinet that His Majesty's Government no longer looked with sympathy upon the creation of an independent Georgia. He further suggested that expulsion of the Georgian envoys at Paris and London would have a "sobering effect" upon the Tiflis government. See FO 371/3661, 55933/1015/58.

[78] For documents relating to the transfer of the Caspian fleet to Denikin and the implications this action held for the Caucasus, see Britain, FO 371/3667–3668, File 11067/58.

comply, Cory continued, would adversely affect the British attitude toward the independent republics and would make it impossible for His Majesty's Government to restrain Denikin should he attempt to advance south of the demarcation line.[79]

The Volunteer Army had in fact already thrust beyond that line. British officials chided Denikin about his obsession with the Caucasus, but they did nothing to prevent his march over Daghestan, the only remaining province of the Mountaineer Republic. In mid-July the British War Office and Foreign Office concurred that Denikin should have all Daghestan, with the strategic port of Derbent as his major southern outpost on the Caspian Sea.[80] This capitulation came after the cabinet of Francesco Nitti had intimated to London that it would not implement Orlando's decision to dispatch Italian troops to replace the British division scheduled to withdraw from the Caucasus.[81] Under the circumstances it was considered "dangerous" to exclude Denikin from any part of the North Caucasus. Hence, while Armenia spurned a general Caucasian pact against Denikin, the Mountaineer Republic was being sacrificed and the malefic threat of invasion hovered over both Georgia and Azerbaijan.

The Russian Political Conference vis-à-vis Armenia

The government of the Armenian republic deemed it prudent to cultivate the sympathies of Russian leaders, not only at the several military headquarters in Russia, but also in Paris where a full array of anti-Bolshevik spokesmen had gathered. The most pervasive of the various groups that assertedly represented "democratic Russia" was the so-called Political Conference, the membership of which reflected a broad spectrum ranging from former tsarist ministers and ambassadors to seasoned revolutionaries and radical socialists. Prince Georgii E. Lvov, the first premier of the Russian Provisional Government, chaired the Political Conference and publicized its views through a steering

[79] Bor'ba v Azerbaidzhane, pp. 168–169; Britain, WO 33/974, no. 4657, WO 95/4958, FO 371/3662, 80442/1015/58, and FO 608/83, 342/8/4/18010. Denikin, Ocherki smuty, IV, 134–135. The War Office had cabled the text of this communiqué to Cory via General Headquarters, Constantinople, on June 6. Georgia's protests regarding the arbitrary arrangement are in Britain, FO 608/88, File 356/2/2.

[80] British Documents, III, 451 n. 2; Britain, WO 33/974, FO 371/3662, 100552/105271/1015/58, and FO 608/88, 356/2/2/15988. Bor'ba v Azerbaidzhane, p. 427, shows that this decision was made known to the Azerbaijani government on August 4, 1919.

[81] Britain, WO 32/5691; British Documents, III, 452–453, and IV, 10–12. See also Ullman, op. cit., pp. 229–230.

committee in which he was joined by Ambassador to France Vasilii A. Maklakov, former Foreign Minister Sergei D. Sazonov, and the socialist chief of the Murmansk-based government of North Russia, Nikolai V. Chaikovskii.[82]

Although the complexities of the Russian situation prompted the organizers of the Paris Peace Conference to defer and ultimately to deny the seating of any and all delegations claiming to speak for the people of Russia, the anti-Bolshevik leaders in Paris pooled their diplomatic skill and resources in an effort to influence the Allied and Associated Powers to preserve the unity and integrity of the Russian Empire. To placate the border nationalities and the crusaders for popular rights, the Russian Political Conference set forth a platform of regional self-government, agrarian and economic reform, democratic electoral processes, and various other evolutionary measures. Its profusion of liberal pronouncements, however, failed to mask the conservative hue of the Political Conference even though it was disdained by the ultraroyalists who relied upon Admiral Kolchak to restore the old Russia with its traditional institutions.[83] In a petition of March 9, 1919, the steering committee urged the Peace Conference to acknowledge that "all questions concerning territories of the Russian Empire within the limits of 1914, with the exception of Poland, also questions relative to the future status of nationalities included in these limits, cannot be solved outside of and without taking the consent of the Russian people." Answers to these problems would have to be postponed until the people of Russia could express their will and participate in formulating acceptable solutions.[84]

It was clear to Avetis Aharonian that Armenia's cause would be strengthened were the Russian Political Conference to recognize the independence of the Armenian republic. The case of Armenia was so exceptional, argued Aharonian, that, even if the Russian leaders should insist upon the territorial integrity of the onetime empire, Russia's

[82] In an aftermath of the Bolshevik Revolution, members of the Russian diplomatic corps abroad formed the Conference of Ambassadors to defend the "true" interests of Russia. It was from the Conference of Ambassadors that the Russian Political Conference evolved, primarily on the initiative of B. A. Bakhmetev and V. A. Maklakov. For additional information on the establishment and activities of the Political Conference, see John M. Thompson, *Russia, Bolshevism, and the Versailles Peace* (Princeton, 1967), pp. 65–78.

[83] Thompson, *op. cit.*, pp. 77–81.

[84] Miller, *Documents*, XVII, 174. Sazonov, who served in Paris as the spokesman for both Denikin and Kolchak, was in receipt of instructions to press for the status quo ante bellum in Russia, Poland excepted, and "to oppose any compromise of Russia's territorial integrity or political unity for the sake of popularity in the Allied countries." See Brinkley, *op. cit.*, p. 106.

interests would best be served by the separation of the nonvital Caucasian Armenian provinces and their unification with Turkish Armenia. Aharonian's approach to the Political Conference was channeled
through Chaikovskii, Maklakov, Ambassador Boris A. Bakhmetov, Ambassador Michael de Giers, and André N. Mandelstam, the outspoken
Armenophile who before the World War had served as dragoman of
the Russian embassy at Constantinople.[85] All professed sympathy for
and endorsed in private the concept of an Armenian state extending
from the Caucasus to the Mediterranean. They frankly admitted to
other than strictly humanitarian motives. The Mediterranean had long
been the unattained goal of Russia. Through the formation of a
friendly, perhaps allied Armenia, indirect access to this important wa-
terway could be gained. This consideration alone would account for
the intensity with which Russian representatives followed the debates
in Paris regarding the future of Cilicia. It would be to Russia's distinct
advantage if control of this Mediterranean-swept land passed to a
"small friendly nation" rather than to Great Britain, France, or Italy.
The non-Bolshevik Russian attitude toward Armenia should be evaluated in this light, making more comprehensible the pledge made to
Aharonian: "Thus, while we will not agree, under any condition, to
the separation of, for example, an Azerbaijan or a Georgia, we respect
the resolute desire of the Caucasian Armenians to join with Turkish
Armenia, and, in one way or another, to become independent—particularly since we believe that such a united Armenia will be our friend
and even ally in the East. This is the basic view of the All-Russian
Political Conference in Paris." [86]

Aharonian's gratification at such affirmations was dampened by the
reluctance of the Russian spokesmen to make their position public.
They claimed that regretfully such action would be exploited by other
ethnic groups whose disengagement and independence Russia could
never tolerate: "If we are now silent, it is only in order not to provide
grounds for all the little governments formed around Russia to demand the same. Except for consenting to the unification and independence of Armenia, we will compromise with no others—yes, we
mean the various Azerbaijans." A further complication arose from the
Political Conference's stand that only a future all-Russian constituent
assembly could determine the fate of the border regions. The Russian

[85] Papers on the relationship between the Russian Political Conference and the
Delegation of the Republic of Armenia are in Rep. of Arm. Archives, File 373, *H. H.
Patvirakutiun ev Rusakan Nakhkin Nerkayatsutsichner, 1919–1922.*

[86] Aharonian, *Sardarapatits Sevr*, pp. 21–22. See also Britain, FO 371/3659, 97452/
512/58, and FO 608/78, 242/1/1/13031.

liaisons explained to Aharonian that this public policy, coupled with Russia's exclusion from the Paris Peace Conference, would probably compel the Political Conference to lodge a face-saving protest when the peacemakers drew the boundaries of Armenia to include a part of the Caucasus. They hastened to add that this mere formality should not be taken as opposition to Armenian aspirations. On the contrary, they advised Avetis Aharonian that he was quite at liberty to inform the Allied leaders of the true sentiments of a sizable segment of the Russian Political Conference. All forward-looking Russians, they maintained, would foster cordial and firm bonds between the new Armenia and the new Russia.[87]

On July 5, 1919, Lvov, Sazonov, and Maklakov submitted to the Peace Conference the views of the Russian Political Conference on the Turkish settlement. The memorandum began: "The new Russia greets with satisfaction the deliverance of Armenia from the Turkish yoke." Russia's endeavors on behalf of the Armenians dated back to the lamented Treaty of San Stefano in 1878 and were demonstrated more recently in the successful negotiations for reforms in Turkish Armenia. It was tragic that the World War had resulted in the nullification of those reforms and in the horrendous massacres that followed, but it was fortunate that through force of Russian arms the population of several districts had been spared and granted asylum on Russian soil. Democratic Russia now insisted that those guilty of organizing or perpetrating the massacres be brought to justice. As for the future of Armenia, it was clear that, according to the Covenant of the League of Nations, this state constituted one of the former Ottoman communities whose independence could be provisionally recognized, subject to advice and assistance of a mandatory power. Under other circumstances, Russia would willingly have assumed the Armenian mandate, but that obligation must now devolve upon another country, which, however, should act in conformity with the political and economic interests of Armenia and lead the state to total independence as soon as possible.[88] The memorandum made no specific mention of Russian Armenia, but it was understood that the mandate would surely extend over Turkish Armenia and Russian Armenia combined.

In his efforts to secure even unofficial Russian support, Avetis Aharonian took extreme care to avoid any action that might antagonize the Political Conference or the envoys of the White Armies. This tactic

---

[87] Aharonian, *Sardarapatits Sevr*, pp. 22–23, 26–27. See also Rep. of Arm. Archives, File 381/3, Pasdermadjian to Lansing, Nov. 3, 1919.

[88] *British Documents*, IV, 673; Rep. of Arm. Archives, File 381/3.

was conspicuously manifested in the wake of the Allied decision to grant quasi recognition to the government headed by Admiral Kolchak. Acknowledged as the supreme commander by the several far-flung White Armies, Kolchak launched a blistering offensive in the spring of 1919. His initial dramatic success aroused concern among some Allied "democrats" that a Kolchak victory over Soviet Russia might pave the way to the restoration of the ancien régime, a prospect no less frightful than Bolshevism. Still, the White Admiral had many partisans in Paris, particularly among French and British military circles, and on May 26, after considerable vacillation, the Allied chiefs of state offered to assist Kolchak and his "associates" in establishing themselves as the government of all Russia if a number of conditions were accepted.[89] Among other things Kolchak was to summon a constituent assembly as soon as he captured Moscow, recognize the independence of Poland and Finland, and make "no attempt to reintroduce the régime which the revolution has destroyed." The border regions were dealt with in the following condition:

Fifthly, that if a solution of the relations between Esthonia, Latvia, Lithuania and the Caucasian and Transcaspian territories and Russia is not speedily reached by agreement the settlement will be made in consultation and co-operation with the League of Nations, and that until such settlement is made the Government of Russia agrees to recognize these territories as autonomous and to confirm the relations which may exist between their *de facto* Governments and the Allied and Associated Governments.[90]

After an exchange of correspondence between Paris and Omsk, the Council of Four expressed satisfaction with the "tone" of Kolchak's discreet and astute reply, a reply that could be generously and variably interpreted, and announced on June 12 that the Allied and Associated Powers would now abide by their original offer. Kolchak's regime was recognized indirectly as the government of all Russia.[91]

[89] For materials on this subject, see Britain, FO 608/188, File 582/2/1; Mayer, *op. cit.*, pp. 813–826; Thompson, *op. cit.*, pp. 277–308; US Archives, RG 84, Tiflis Consulate, 1919, pt. 4, File 710; Ullman, *op. cit.*, pp. 162–170.

[90] *Paris Peace Conference*, VI, 73–75.

[91] *Ibid.*, pp. 321–323, 356; *British Documents*, III, 361–364. The fifth point made by the Allied leaders was answered by the fourth point of Kolchak's reply:

We are fully disposed at once to prepare for the solution of the questions concerning the fate of the national groups in Esthonia, Latvia, Lithuania, and of the Caucasian and Transcaspian countries, and we have every reason to believe that a prompt settlement will be made, seeing that the Government is assuring as from the present time, the autonomy of the various nationalities. It goes with-

Alarmed by this turn of events, the envoys of several nations that had declared independence from Russia drew together in denunciation of Kolchak and in protest against the ill-advised action of the Allied Powers. On June 17, 1919, the combined delegations proclaimed that their respective governments had been established by the "free will of the peoples of these states," which no longer were subject to the jurisdiction of Russia. Henceforth, they insisted, relations with Russia must be conducted on the basis of equality, sovereignty, and independence, but unfortunately the correspondence between the Allies and Kolchak "can be interpreted as the negation of such a right." [92] The delegations of White Russia (Belorussia), the Ukraine, Latvia, Estonia, the North Caucasus, Georgia, and Azerbaijan affixed their signatures to this declaration. The name of Armenia was missing. What Kolchak represented, Armenian politicians did not like, but Kolchak had now gained the support of the Russian Political Conference, the leaders of which had given full assurances that the new Russia would not oppose the separation of Russian Armenia and the independence of united Armenia. Aharonian therefore considered it impolitic, simply for the sake of harmony, to range Armenia alongside the governments toward which Russia maintained an uncompromising attitude. Indeed, Armenia prized her unique status—or rather a status that then seemed to be unique.

The same strategy branded Armenia as the spoiler in several subsequent displays of regional unity. On June 20, 1919, Nikolai Chkheidze, Ali Mardan Topchibashev, and Abdul Medjid Chermoev, presidents of the Georgian, Azerbaijani, and North Caucasus delegations in Paris, issued a joint declaration reasserting the right of their countries to independence. The Caucasian republics, they exclaimed, would never bow to reabsorption by Russia. More specifically the trio excoriated the Volunteer Army's aggression against the Mountaineer Confederation and implored the Allies to compel Denikin to clear the North Caucasus and respect the integrity of the independent republics.[93]

---

out saying that the limits and conditions of these autonomous institutions will be settled as regards each of the nationalities concerned.

And even in case difficulties should arise in regard to the solution of these various questions, the Government is ready to have recourse to the collaboration and good offices of the League of Nations with a view to arriving at a satisfactory settlement.

See also *Current History*, X, pt. 2 (July, 1919), 90–93.

[92] Rep. of Arm. Archives, File 72/a, *Hayastani Hanrapetutian Nerkayatsutschutiun Parizum ev Ukrainiayi Parizi Nerkayatsutschutiune, 1919–1921 t.t.;* US Archives, RG 256, 861K.00/84; *La Géorgie Indépendante*, pp. 21–22.

[93] US Archives, RG 256, 861K.00/78; Britain, FO 371/3662, 97451/1015/58; Rep. of Arm. Archives, File 66a/3, Bulletin no. 127; *La Géorgie Indépendante*, pp. 20–21.

Again Aharonian withheld his signature, although he made guarded verbal professions of sympathy and explained Armenia's abstention on grounds that his delegation, no longer representing Russian Armenia alone, was obliged to abide by the unanimous Turkish Armenian sentiment against embroilment in the general Russian problem.[94]

The Tiflis-Baku Axis

The Armenian tactic, as planned and measured in Erevan and Paris, was comprehensible and logical, but equally understandable was the charge of improbity leveled at Armenia by her neighbors. Actually most Armenian politicians were not at all distressed by the impending demise of the Mountaineer Republic, regarded as the creation of Turkey and the forces of Pan-Islam. It was to Armenia's advantage that Russia reabsorb the North Caucasus and array herself along the borders of Georgia and Azerbaijan.

As the Volunteer Army filtered through the Caucasian passes, the governments of Georgia and Azerbaijan labored frantically to gird against the northern colossus. Remonstrating before the Allied missions and the entire world, they deprecated the brazen imperialism of the reactionary White General. The two republics provided the Mountaineers with military matériel, but neither this aid nor cautious British intercession were of consequence in the end result.[95] The Volunteers penetrated the Caspian coastline as far as Derbent on May 23 and moved into Temir-Khan-Shura, the administrative capital of Daghestan, on June 3, expelling Azerbaijani Chargé d'affaires Hakhverdov. The Mountaineers had been subdued.[96]

[94] Rep. of Arm. Archives, File 231/130, Aharonian to Albert Thomas, July 7, 1919. For other like protests of the successionist states of Russia, see US Archives, RG 256, 861K.00/56/59/85 and 184.611/1201; United States, Department of State, *Papers Relating to the Foreign Relations of the United States, 1919: Russia* (Washington, D.C., 1937), pp. 766–767; Britain, FO 608/195, File 602/1/3, and FO 608/201, File 608/1/3. In September, 1919, Admiral Kolchak sent his "respects" to the Armenian government through an unofficial Armenian envoy and gave assurances that he would do all possible to safeguard those Armenians then located in Siberia. See Rep. of Arm. Archives, File 66a/3, Bulletin no. 190.

[95] Kazemzadeh, *Transcaucasia*, pp. 242–243; Zhordaniia, *op. cit.*, p. 103. Raevskii, *op. cit.*, pp. 98–104, discusses Azerbaijani pretensions to Daghestan.

[96] Gotthard Jäschke, "Die Republik Aserbeidschan," *Die Welt des Islams*, XXIII, 1–2 (1941), 63; Brinkley, *op. cit.*, p. 160. Numerous discrepancies exist regarding exact dates. A report in US Archives, RG 256, 184.01602/93, states, for example, that Derbent and Temir-Khan-Shura were taken on June 10. A communiqué originating from Denikin's headquarters on June 22, 1919, announced that General D. P. Dratsenko occupied Derbent on May 23 and that on June 7, after General I. G. Erdeli had taken Temir-Khan-Shura, a friendly "Government of Daghestan" was organized

Outraged and terrified, the Azerbaijani Parliament created the Committee for State Defense on June 5, vesting it with sweeping authority and extralegal prerogatives. The Committee for State Defense, unable to dismiss the possibility of collusion between the Volunteer Army and Armenia, laid plans for mobilization on two fronts.[97] Significantly, it was during this crisis that in Mountainous Karabagh blood was shed and a number of Armenian villages were razed by bands closely linked to Governor-General Khosrov Bek Sultanov. It was at this time, too, that Khan Tekinskii, the Azerbaijani envoy in Erevan, advised his government that the Volunteer offensive was being greeted with elation in Armenia, despite Acting Premier Khatisian's emphatic denials. In case of war between Azerbaijan and the Volunteer Army, Khan Tekinskii premonished, Armenia would cast off her chameleon-like cloak and openly embrace Denikin. Baku should take preventive measures by concentrating troops on Armenia's borders and fomenting insurrection in the Muslim centers south of Erevan.[98]

Meanwhile a saber-rattling atmosphere pervaded the legislature, political societies, and soviets of Georgia. An endless flow of resolutions called the nation to rise in defense of the Republic: "Everything for the revolutionary front against the reactionary front of the army of

---

under General Khalilov. Brinkley shows that Khalilov was confirmed in office by General Erdeli but also that Erdeli did not arrive in Daghestan until June 13. Contemporary accounts in *Bor'ba*, May 29, 1919, p. 2, and June 7, p. 2, date the fall of Petrovsk as May 21; Derbent, May 23; and Temir-Khan-Shura, June 3. It was reported that likewise on June 3 the Mountaineer cabinet resigned, the legislature dispersed, and Khalilov formed a Denikinist-dominated provisional government. British officers in the field warned the Mountaineer leaders not to resist Denikin. For the protest of the Paris-based Mountaineer Foreign Minister, Haidar Bammat, to Foreign Secretary Balfour, see Bammat's *Le Caucase*, pp. 48–49. The official protest of Azerbaijani Foreign Minister M. Iu. Jafarov to the British commander in the Caucasus (Cory) is reprinted in *Eastern Europe*, I (Oct. 1, 1919), 93–94. See also *Bulletin d'Informations de l'Azerbaïdjan*, no. 3 (Oct. 13, 1919), p. 6.

[97] Raevskii, *op. cit.*, p. 107; *Bor'ba*, June 7, 1919, p. 2. The creation of the committee is dated June 11 in documents cited in *Bor'ba v Azerbaidzhane*, p. 527 n. 143; and in *Istoriia gosudarstva i prava Azerbaidzhanskoi SSR: Velikaia Oktiabr'skaia sotsialisticheskaia revoliutsiia i sozdanie Sovetskoi gosudarstvennosti v Azerbaidzhane*, publ. of Akademiia Nauk Azerbaidzhanskoi SSR, Sektor Filosofii (Baku, 1964), p. 294. Members of the three-man committee were Nasib Bek Usubbekov, Khudadat Bek Melik-Aslanov, and Aslan Bek Safikurdskii. The committee placed all Azerbaijan under martial law on June 11 and listed numerous crimes that would be tried by summary court martial. The Governor-General of Karabagh was specifically charged with enforcing the committee's decree in the counties under his jurisdiction and with conducting the necessary "administrative searches." Without further recourse he could impose fines up to 10,000 rubles and mete out prison sentences of up to three months. See *Bor'ba v Azerbaidzhane*, pp. 166–168.

[98] Republic of Armenia, Ministry of Foreign Affairs, *Gaghtni pastatghtere: Adrbedjani davadrakan gordsuneutiunits mi edj* (Erevan, 1920), no. 130, p. 27.

Denikin!" On June 1 Foreign Minister Gegechkori stirred the Constituent Assembly with a description of the death throes of the Mountaineer Republic. The counterrevolution had enveloped Petrovsk and Derbent and had spread to the borders of both Azerbaijan and Georgia. Recent negotiations with representatives of the Volunteer Army, he continued, had proved beyond the shadow of a doubt that Denikin was not interested in this or that boundary but was instead determined "to crush with finality the workers' revolution and to annihilate democracy and the Republic of Georgia." Despair, however, was not to be the prevailing emotion in Georgia. The Republic had, during its first year, grown in solidarity, in prestige, and in self-confidence. It had established bonds with the nations of Europe and now stood prepared to safeguard its independence and sovereignty. This undaunted spirit, Gegechkori exclaimed, was buttressed by the knowledge that "the Republic of Azerbaijan is with us, that its troops have set out to ensure the defense of the frontiers." Uplifted by this oratory, the Constituent Assembly pronounced anathema upon the armies "directed by partisans of old imperialistic Russia whose aim it is to subjugate the small nations and strike down democracy" and also voiced confidence that the Transcaucasian republics "will act in solidarity by combining all their forces against the common menace." [99]

Despite their rhetorical value, resolutions could not of themselves forge a united front. With the failure to obtain a commitment from Armenia at the Transcaucasian conference in Tiflis, Georgia and Azerbaijan absolved themselves from responsibility for any "unfortunate consequences." For Armenia the matter was clear. Driven to a choice between military alliance against Denikin or renewed and intensified isolation, Armenia would risk the latter. But on the other side the focus was just as sharp: Georgia and Azerbaijan joined hands just a few days after Sirakan Tigranian departed from and Samed Bek Mehmandarov arrived in Tiflis.

The Georgian-Azerbaijani mutual defense pact was sealed on June 16, 1919, by General I. Z. Odishelidze, General A. K. Gedevanov, Foreign Minister E. P. Gegechkori, and Minister of War N. V. Ramishvili for Georgia, and by Foreign Minister M. Iu. Jafarov, Chief of Staff General S. Sulkevich,[100] and Minister of War S. B. Mehmandarov for

[99] *La Géorgie Indépendante*, pp. 6–11.
[100] Suleiman Sulkevich was a Lithuanian-born Muslim who had made common cause with the German military command in 1918 and had led a collaborationist government in the Crimea. After the war he escaped to Azerbaijan, there becoming Chief of Staff. See Richard Pipes, *The Formation of the Soviet Union* (rev. ed.; Cambridge, Mass., 1964), pp. 187, 207.

Azerbaijan. Each republic undertook for a period of three years to defend the independence and territorial integrity of the other and to refrain from concluding military conventions with other governments or initiating military action without the knowledge and consent of its ally. On the diplomatic front, the two states pledged themselves to strive for unity of purpose and the solution of existing disputes through either mutual agreement or arbitration. The tenth clause of the pact extended to Armenia a final opportunity to repent: "A period of fifteen days, beginning with the official communication of this convention, is accorded Armenia, the third Caucasian Republic, in order that she may be able to express her willingness to adhere to this convention." By her silence, however, Armenia spurned the gesture and remained apart.[101]

The defense alliance was acclaimed in Baku and Tiflis. The journal *Azerbaidzhan* announced:

The period of isolation of the new political organisms, based on race, was logically and historically inevitable; now this is coming to an end. A new phase is beginning in the life of the Transcaucasian democracies. The period of separation gives way to a period of federation.

It is evident that the alliance between the two Transcaucasian republics is not aggressive in character and that it has no goal other than the defense of the territorial integrity of Transcaucasia. The contracting parties have attempted to bring about the adherence of the third nation of Transcaucasia: Armenia. Unfortunately their efforts have been in vain. The treaty of alliance was signed only by the representatives of Azerbaijan and Georgia. A special clause of the treaty gives Armenia the possibility to join the alliance later; this fact is sufficient evidence that there was no intent to isolate Armenia. . . .[102]

The Tiflis newspaper *Gruziia* described the convention as "one of most particular importance for the future orientation of the political

[101] The text of this pact, with English and French translations, is included in US Archives, RG 256, 184.01602/68, 184.021/26, 861G.00/88; *Bulletin d'Informations de l'Azerbaïdjan*, no. 1 (Sept. 1, 1919), pp. 1–2; Rep. of Arm. Archives, File 70/2. See also "Treaty Signed between Georgia and Azerbaijan," *Eastern Europe*, I (Oct. 16, 1919), 156–158. According to a report in US Archives, RG 84, Tiflis Consulate, 1919, pt. 4, File 711, the Georgian Constituent Assembly ratified the pact on June 22. Azerbaijani ratification apparently followed on June 27. Milne informed the War Office that Premier Khatisian had accounted for Armenia's nonadherence on grounds that the pact was directed against Russia, whereas Khatisian felt it was essential "to keep on the right side of Denikin and Koltchak" and "to steer clear of all entanglements as he hopes [the] Great Powers will put Armenia on her legs again." See Britain, WO 33/974, no. 4761.

[102] *Azerbaidzhan*, June 21, 1919, in *Bulletin d'Informations de l'Azerbaïdjan*, no. 1, p. 3.

life of the Caucasus," and then echoed impatience with the Armenian strategy:

Another people, historically less attached to our country, has, after five hundred years of slavery, seen the birth of its national liberty on the territory of the Caucasus. These are the Armenians. But Armenia rejects systematically and obstinately the hand of friendship extended by her neighbors. To the detriment of the general interests of the country, she does not want to renounce her principle: the policy of isolation. The alliance between Georgia and Azerbaijan will bring to light with finality the politics of the leading circles of Armenia. Armenia will be forced to answer the query: will you unite with the peoples of the Caucasus or will you range yourself against them? In the latter event she will have to consider herself erased from the family of Caucasian peoples, quit the land entirely, and search for another field to implement her policies, devoid of sincerity and hostile to her neighbors.[103]

Had Armenia made the correct choice? Considering the aspirations and the contingencies of the times, perhaps she had, but that choice drove a deeper wedge between Erevan and the axis extending between Tiflis and Baku. In retrospect, the validity of the belief that Denikin would ultimately acquiesce in the independence of Armenia can be seriously challenged. In the summer of 1919 the commander of the Volunteer Army instructed his ranking envoy to the Caucasus, General Nikolai N. Baratov, to lay the groundwork for the region's "painless reunion" with "one and undivided Russia." Meanwhile, upon acceptance of certain conditions, Denikin would tolerate the interim governments in Georgia and Azerbaijan. As for Armenia, he noted:

[103] *Gruziia*, June 22, 1919, in *Bulletin d'Informations de l'Azerbaïdjan*, no. 1, p. 4. See also La Chesnais, *op. cit.*, pp. 185–186. When the provisions of the pact were received in the British Foreign Office, Professor J. Y. Simpson of the Russian Division noted in the ledger: "The Georgians and Azerbaijanis have at any rate the courage of their convictions and their determination. The Armenians expect the U.S.A. to do it all for them and at the same time themselves still maintain amicable relations with the Russians." See Britain, FO 608/115, 385/3/6/13477. In September, 1919, an official of the United States embassy in London called at the Foreign Office to relay information received by the Department of State concerning the Georgian-Azerbaijani pact. A Russian source "thought worthy of consideration" had reported that the arrangement included several secret clauses providing that the two contracting parties agreed to keep the Russians out of Transcaucasia, to join with the Bolsheviks and the Young Turks against the Entente in order to exclude the Entente from the Caucasus, to regard Armenia as a common enemy, and to have Georgia block all communications with Armenia in case of war between that recalcitrant republic and Azerbaijan. The Foreign Office assessed the unsubstantiated information as "the old Russian system of provocation." See Britain, FO 371/3671, 129487/129487/58.

Completely sympathizing with the strivings of the Armenian people to unite within their ethnographic borders and considering the Armenians closely bound in their historic and economic interests to One, Indivisible Russia, within whose limits the more prosperous part of Armenia falls, the Chief Command of the Armed Forces of South Russia accedes, until the final reestablishment of the all-Russian governmental order, to a temporary separate administration in the Armenian provinces. It harbors no aggressive design toward Armenia, but at the same time it stands unalterably in defense of a united Russian governmental structure.[104]

In what way, except for empathic expressions, did this guideline differ from the sternly worded policy toward Georgia and Azerbaijan? Denikin showed no proclivity to uphold the pledges given Aharonian by the Russian diplomats in Paris. Still, there were many strange and cloudy facets to this question, and Denikin's sympathy for the concept of a united Armenia might conceivably have been cultivated into eventual recognition of a free, independent, and united Republic of Armenia.

After one year of independence, the Transcaucasian republics had scarcely become adjusted to one another. In their mutual relations there remained much to be desired. Armenia stood alone once again. The issue of joint action against the Volunteer Army only served as a catalyst to accentuate basic underlying differences. Had the republics found a way to resolve their territorial disputes and dispel their distrust, a loose union might have evolved; but perhaps this was far too much to require of three newly independent and highly chaotic states. Moreover, the dissonant aspects of their relations were naturally more sharply pronounced than was the modest progress achieved in mutual accord. The mere fact that the Transcaucasian delegations were willing to sit together, to negotiate, and to disagree should be regarded as a forward step in the intricate art of international politics. And for Armenia there was the compensation that, although remaining aloof in mid-1919, she had gained in stature, extended her territories, concluded preliminary trade and consular agreements, and won professions of sympathy from the Volunteer Army and its many supporters abroad.

[104] Denikin, *Ocherki smuty*, IV, 137–138.

12

On Bolshevik
Horizons

In the vast expanse beyond the Caucasus, revolution and civil war had engulfed the peoples of Russia: White Armies had risen around the central heartlands to crush the budding Soviet regime in Moscow; British, French, Japanese, and American military expeditions had established bases on the empire's extremities; Allied advisers and matériel had been sent to bolster the anti-Bolshevik elements; thousands of Czech troops, former prisoners of war or deserters from the Austrian army, had seized long stretches of the Trans-Siberian Railway; and counterrevolutionary armies, successionist states, and foreign-sponsored hetmans had gained sway over most of Siberia, Central Asia, South Russia, the Ukraine, Poland and Finland, the Baltic provinces, and the White Sea–Arctic region. Several times during 1918 and 1919 it seemed that the destruction of the Soviet state was imminent.[1]

The Caucasus, too, had steeled itself against Bolshevism and the Council of People's Commissars, but the degree of opposition differed among its constituent peoples. The unmitigated hostility and cruelty of the Volunteer Army, coupled with factors of geography, provided

[1] Studies and materials on the Allied and American intervention in the Russian Civil War are extensive. Useful works in the English language include the following: Richard H. Ullman, *Anglo-Soviet Relations, 1917–1921,* Vol. I: *Intervention and the War* (Princeton, 1961), Vol. II: *Britain and the Russian Civil War, November 1918–December 1920* (Princeton, 1968); W. P. Coates and Zelda K. Coates, *Armed Intervention in Russia 1918–1922* (London, 1935); William Henry Chamberlin, *The Russian Revolution 1917–1921,* Vol. II (New York, 1935); George F. Kennan, *Soviet-American Relations, 1917–1920,* Vol. II: *The Decision to Intervene* (Princeton, 1958); Louis Fischer, *The Soviets in World Affairs,* Vol. I (Princeton, 1951); Leonid I. Stakhovsky, *Intervention at Archangel* (Princeton, 1944); John Bradley, *Allied Intervention in Russia* (London, [1968]); George A. Brinkley, *The Volunteer Army and Allied Intervention in South Russia, 1917–1921* (Notre Dame, 1966).

fertile grounds for recurrent Bolshevik partisan activity in the North Caucasus. Musavat-dominated Azerbaijan and Menshevik-dominated Georgia, solicitous of their redeemed independence, regarded all the rival forces of Russia with almost equal antipathy, whereas Dashnakist-dominated Armenia displayed considerable ambivalence. Not only did the Armenian government maintain informal bonds with the Volunteer Army and the Cossack chiefs of South Russia, but it was reluctant to rule out a modus vivendi with the Russian Soviet Federated Socialist Republic. Ideologically, Dashnaktsutiun was anti-Marxist and more decidedly anti-Bolshevik. Nonetheless, the Sovnarkom was a Russian government, a fact that encouraged some Armenian leaders to suggest that an understanding with Moscow was both feasible and imperative. Unofficial envoys therefore traveled to the Bolshevik centers to gain recognition or at least tacit acknowledgment of the independent Armenian republic.

Soviet Russia on Self-Determination

During the final campaigns of World War I the Bolsheviks and Dashnakists, despite political incompatibilities, were drawn together in face of the Turkish invasion of Transcaucasia. Individual members of Dashnaktsutiun's Bureau conferred secretly with prominent local Bolsheviks on plans for a coordinated defense. Formal agreement did not ensue, but the two parties did collaborate in Baku, where Dashnaktsutiun placed the Armenian national militia at the disposal of Stepan G. Shahumian, chairman of the Baku Commune, member of the Russian Bolshevik Central Committee, and the party's Extraordinary Commissar for the Caucasus.[2] Even after the Dashnakist-Bolshevik front disintegrated when Shahumian failed to prevent the Baku Soviet from calling for British military intervention against the Turkish onslaught, the Armenian spokesmen in Moscow, Hakob Zavriev, Liparit Nazariants, and Artashes Chilingarian (Ruben Darbinian), continued to petition the Sovnarkom for diplomatic and material assistance.[3]

[2] For accounts of negotiations and collaboration between Dashnakists and Bolsheviks in the Caucasus, see Hovannisian, *Road to Independence*, pp. 111–113, 170, 220–221; Ruben [Ter-Minasian], *Hai heghapokhakani me hishataknere*, Vol. VII (Los Angeles, 1952), pp. 139–144, 260–263; Kazemzadeh, *Transcaucasia*, pp. 69–76, 128–131 *passim*; Sergei Melik-Yolchian, "Bakvi herosamarte," *Hairenik Amsagir*, III (May, 1923), 105–126; St. Shahumian, *Erker*, publ. of Institut Marksizma-Leninizma pri TsK KPSS, Armianskii Filial—Institut Istorii Partii pri TsK KP Armenii, Vol. III (Erevan, 1958), pp. 124–126, 143–147.

[3] Reuben Darbinian, "A Mission to Moscow: Memoirs," *Armenian Review*, I

Throughout much of this initial period both Lenin and Trotsky voiced compassion for the victimized Armenians and even authorized Armenian organizations in Russia to send relief goods and armed volunteers to the Caucasus. Although Lenin opposed the establishment of independent border states and advocated instead a single, united Soviet republic with as many territories and peoples as possible, he was nevertheless pledged to the right of all peoples to self-determination up to and including total separation from Russia. Still, the principle of self-determination was a weapon that could be wielded with considerable flexibility. In January of 1918, for example, Lenin guided through the Sovnarkom the decree on Turkish Armenia, which, as previously described, granted the Armenians the right of self-determination but in fact justified the recall of all Russian divisions from the Turkish-Caucasus front, facilitated Soviet withdrawal from the World War, and spurred the Ottoman invasion of Turkish Armenia and Transcaucasia. Lip service to the principle of self-determination may have helped to soothe uneasy consciences.

Self-determination was also used by Lenin to allay the suspicions of peoples long oppressed by imperialism and "Great Russian chauvinism." The potential value of the colonial world in the struggle against the enemies of the Soviet system was inestimable. By the beginning of 1919 Lenin was insisting that a realistic policy must make allowance for the various stages of cultural and political development among given nationalities as well as the many peculiarities and "zigzags" in the passage of each people from feudalism to bourgeois-democracy and from bourgeois-democracy toward the proletarian society. Within the Romanov Empire, he maintained, all classes of the subject races had been held together by mutual fear, suspicion, and hatred of Great Russia. But with Soviet Russia now championing the right of self-determination, the artificial bonds would rapidly disintegrate and there would follow intensified class antagonism, the necessary prerequisite to the triumph of socialism.[4] This view Lenin defended before the VIII Congress of the Russian Communist Party in March,

(Spring, 1948), 23–26, 28–29; Ruben, *op. cit.*, p. 144; Gabriel Lazian, *Hayastan ev hai date (Vaveragrer)* (Cairo, 1946), pp. 214–216.

[4] For the development of Lenin's views on the nationality question, see Institut Marksizma-Leninizma pri TsK KPSS, *V. I. Lenin azgayin ev azgayin-gaghutayin hartsi masin* (Erevan, 1957), cited hereafter as *Lenin azgayin hartsi masin;* Richard Pipes, *The Formation of the Soviet Union* (rev. ed.; Cambridge, Mass., 1964), pp. 34–49, 108–113, 276–293; Alfred G. Meyer, *Leninism* (Cambridge, Mass., 1957), pp. 145–155. See also Lenin, *Sochineniia,* VII, 233–242, XII, 234–235, XXI, 121–156, XXII, 267–269, XXIII, 149–150, XXIV, 57–59, 113–150, 174–178, 223–229, 313–315, XXV, 16–18, 64–72, 85–86, 135–137, XXVII, 61–68, 252–266, XXX, 15–58, XXXI, 432–437, 439–440.

1919, despite vociferous denunciations by the theoreticians of the left, who equated self-determination, no less regional autonomy, to a tactless retreat from and a serious aberration of Marxist doctrines.[5] In contraposition to his prewar stand on the national question, Lenin now asserted that circumstances required a "federative union of soviet-type governments" which need not conform in all detail to the system adopted in Russia. "To cast aside the self-determination of nations and to advance only the self-determination of the workers is entirely incorrect, for this would fail to take into account the difficulties and devious routes leading to stratification within given nations." Soviet Russia must make every effort to avoid the semblance of compulsion. "This is why we must say to the other peoples that to the end we are thoroughly internationalist and strive for the voluntary alliance of the workers and peasants of all nations." With the motto of federalism and opposition to Great Russian chauvinism, Lenin, the Russian Communist Party, and the Sovnarkom had struck upon the formula for the reconstitution of a Russian empire.[6]

The Soviet leadership again invoked the principle of self-determination when it extended peace feelers to the Allied Powers during the weeks immediately preceding and following the end of the World War. Beset by acute domestic crises, a tightening cordon of counterrevolutionary armies, and foreign military intervention, Soviet Russia was in desperate need of a respite. The Sovnarkom, through Foreign Affairs Commissar Grigorii V. Chicherin, relayed messages to the West indicating a readiness to pay the price for the easing of external pressures.[7]

---

[5] Discussions and actions of the VIII Congress are in *Vos'moi s"ezd RKP/b/, mart 1919 goda: Protokoly*, in the series *Protokoly i stenograficheskie otchety s"ezdov i konferentsii Kommunisticheskoi partii Sovetskogo Soiuza*, publ. of Institut Marks-izma-Leninizma pri TsK KPSS (Moscow, 1959); and in Lenin, *Sochineniia*, XXXVIII, 125–215. See also Pipes, *op. cit.*, pp. 109–111.

[6] *Lenin azgayin hartsi masin*, pp. 637–649; Lenin, *Sochineniia*, XXXVIII, 159–160, 184; *Vos'moi s"ezd RKP/b/*, pp. 53–54, 108. For an analysis of Lenin's "dialectics of backwardness," see Meyer, *op. cit.*, pp. 257–273. See also *Lenin o druzhbe s narodami Vostoka*, ed. I. I. Kul'kov and intro. by V. Ia. Zevin (Moscow, 1961). Lenin's previous opposition to the principle of federalism as the solution to the nationality question is set forth in a letter to Stepan Shahumian in 1913. See *Lenin azgayin hartsi masin*, pp. 128–131; *St. Shahumian: Namakner, 1896–1918*, ed. Kh. Barseghian (Erevan, 1959), pp. 34–41; G. M. Mneyan, *Stepan Shahumiani partiakan ev petakan gordsuneutiune (1900–1918)* (Erevan, 1958), pp. 125–127. See also Pipes, *op. cit.*, pp. 36, 43–44; S. D. Dimanshtein, ed., *Revoliutsiia i natsional'nyi vopros*, Vol. III (Moscow, 1930), pp. xii–xxix, 3–40; Lenin, *Sochineniia*, VII, 102–106.

[7] John M. Thompson, *Russia, Bolshevism, and the Versailles Peace* (Princeton, 1966), pp. 88–89; Arno J. Mayer, *Politics and Diplomacy of Peacemaking* (New York, 1967), pp. 421–422; *Dokumenty SSSR*, I, 531–539, 549, 556, 593–595; Jane Degras, ed., *Soviet Documents on Foreign Policy*, Vol. I (London, New York, and Toronto, 1951), pp. 112–121.

Then in November, 1918, Deputy Foreign Affairs Commissar Maksim M. Litvinov, earlier the unofficial Soviet plenipotentiary in London, revealed in Stockholm his government's offer to suspend the civil war in Russia if the Allied stranglehold were lifted. In a communiqué addressed to President Wilson on Christmas Eve, December 24, Litvinov warned that a victory for the interventionist armies in Russia would result in a horrendous White Terror, a military dictatorship, and the restoration of tsarism with all its virulence. Appealing to the President's "sense of justice and impartiality," the Soviet agent pointed to similarities in the basic principles of the Sovnarkom and of the new Wilsonian diplomacy. The workers and peasants of Russia, he said, had been the first to condemn publicly and without reservation the evils of secret diplomacy.[8] Later the Bolshevik envoy added that the Sovnarkom would accept the application of self-determination in the various provinces of the empire on condition that obtrusions from abroad cease and the Allies not interfere in the class struggle being waged in those provinces.[9]

With the knowledge and full consent of President Wilson and Premier Lloyd George, William H. Buckler, a special assistant in the United States embassy in London and an adviser to the American Commission to Negotiate Peace, slipped quietly into the Swedish capital and met informally with Litvinov. Buckler was impressed by the frankness and apparent integrity of the Russian spokesman and subsequently informed his superiors that the Sovnarkom's bid for conciliation seemed genuine.[10] The Litvinov-Buckler dialogue gave impetus to a proposal endorsed by Wilson and Lloyd George, both sore at heart over their role in the armed intervention, to summon all rival factions in Russia to the conference table for the purpose of terminating hostilities, regulating mutual relations, and seeking a solution to the disastrous dilemma. This plan culminated in the Allied invitation of January 22, 1919, asking the several governments, major political parties, and all successionist states of Russia to send authorized negotiators to Prinkipo, one of the Princes Islands, in plain view of Allied-

---

[8] *Dokumenty SSSR*, I, 627–630; Thompson, *op. cit.*, pp. 89–91; Fischer, *op. cit.*, p. 158; *Soviet Union and Peace*, Intro. by Henri Barbuesse (New York, [1929]), pp. 58–60; Degras, *op. cit.*, pp. 129–132.

[9] Mayer, *op. cit.*, p. 423. For discussions of the British Imperial War Cabinet on the Soviet diplomatic feelers and a course of action regarding Litvinov, see Ullman, *op. cit.*, II, 87–95.

[10] United States, Department of State, *Papers Relating to the Foreign Relations of the United States, 1919: Russia* (Washington, D.C., 1937), pp. 1–3, 15–19, cited hereafter as *Russia, 1919;* and *Paris Peace Conference*, III, 643–646. See also Thompson, *op. cit.*, pp. 91–92; Mayer, *op. cit.*, pp. 424–427.

dominated Constantinople.[11] The site was selected in deference to French insistence that the Bolshevik envoys, that is, agents, not be afforded the opportunity to spread their malignant propaganda in Paris or any other city of Western Europe. But numerous complications, the most insurmountable of which were the intransigence of the French-nurtured anti-Bolshevik elements and a pervasive absence of sincerity, aborted the project. Significantly, the Soviet reply to the invitation from Paris, though considered devious by the Allied hosts, did reiterate the Sovnarkom's offer to tolerate the border states of Russia if the men and matériel of foreign powers were withdrawn from all territories of the erstwhile Romanov domains. In Lenin's estimation, a "breathing spell" such as that provided by the onerous Treaty of Brest-Litovsk was essential to the survival of the Soviet state. Just as that first humiliating document had eventually been voided, so too would any concessions the Sovnarkom might have to make to the Allies in order to gain time to consolidate the revolution.[12]

Discouraged by the Prinkipo fiasco, visionaries of the Wilson and Lloyd George stamp still groped for a way to bring about the cessation of the embarrassing and potentially cataclysmic intervention in Russia. When the two chiefs of state were away from Paris in February, 1919, their respective aides and confidants, Edward M. House and Sir Philip H. Kerr, arranged the details of a plan, hatched in the innermost chambers of the American and British delegations, to send a special fact-gathering mission to Russia. Kerr even wrote out several armistice terms that might be proposed to the Sovnarkom.[13] The outcome of this furtive activity was that William C. Bullitt, a young American liberal sympathetic to, or at least open-minded toward, the Soviet experiment, was dispatched to Moscow.

On this assignment, kept secret from all but a tight circle of British and American officials, Bullitt met with a number of Soviet ministers, including Litvinov, Chicherin, and Lenin himself. All openly affirmed Russia's preparedness to endure tremendous sacrifices in return for the relaxation of Allied pressures. Shortly after Bullitt's arrival in Moscow during the second week of March, 1919, Foreign Affairs

---

[11] *Dokumenty SSSR*, II, 45–46; *Paris Peace Conference*, III, 676–677, 691–692. The invitation was beamed to Russia by radio on January 23.

[12] For studies and documents relating to the Prinkipo project, see *Russia, 1919*, pp. 1–74 *passim; Dokumenty SSSR*, II, 42–48, 52, 54–55, 57–60, 84–87; B. E. Shtein, *"Russkii vopros" na parizhskoi mirnoi konferentsii (1919–1920 gg.)* ([Moscow], 1949), pp. 94–139; Mayer, *op. cit.*, pp. 427–449; Thompson, *op. cit.*, pp. 105–130; Fischer, *op. cit.*, pp. 166–171; Ullman, *op. cit.*, II, 99–117; Degras, *op. cit.*, pp. 137–139.

[13] *British Documents*, III, 425–429. See also Ullman, *op. cit.*, II, 145–147.

Commissar Chicherin submitted a draft proposal which he indicated the Sovnarkom would accept if it were proffered by the Allied Powers. Sanctioned by Lenin and the Central Committee of the Russian Communist Party, this plan would inaugurate a two-week armistice followed by a peace conference based on seven principles, among which were a few of the terms listed by Philip Kerr.[14] Briefly, the principles, as modified and supplemented by the Bolshevik leadership, included an end to the Allied economic blockade, the resumption of trade, the right of unrestricted transit privileges for Soviet Russia, the inviolability of Soviet citizens in Allied countries and in all parts of Russia and vice versa, a reciprocal amnesty for political foes, and the joint assumption of Russia's public debt by the Soviet and all other governments on territory of the onetime empire.[15]

For Armenia and other successionist states two additional points were of paramount importance and, taken together, embodied a double-edged sword. The first of these was in a conciliatory vein: "All existing *de facto* Governments which have been set up on the territory of the former Russian Empire and Finland [are] to remain in full control of the territories which they occupy at the moment when the armistice becomes effective, except insofar as the conference may agree upon the transfer of territories; until the peoples inhabiting the territories controlled by these *de facto* Governments shall themselves determine to change their Governments." Soviet Russia, on the one hand, and the governments operating against her, including the Allied Powers and "Finland, Poland, Galicia, Roumania, Armenia, Azerbaijan and Afghanistan," on the other, were to agree "not to attempt to upset by force the existing *de facto* Governments which have been set up on the territory of the former Russian Empire and the other governments signatory to this agreement." Lenin would consent to this compromise, but at the same time he forged the other edge of the sword into a provision not to be found in the original terms Bullitt had carried to Moscow: "Immediately after the signing of this agreement, all troops of the Allied and Associated Governments and other non-Russian Governments [are] to be withdrawn from Russia and

[14] For documents and discussions relating to the Bullitt mission, see *Russia, 1919*, pp. 74–98; *The Bullitt Mission to Russia: Testimony before the Committee on Foreign Relations, United States Senate, of William C. Bullitt* (New York, [1919]); Mayer, *op. cit.*, pp. 463–470; Thompson, *op. cit.*, pp. 149–177; Shtein, *op. cit.*, pp. 140–164; Ullman, *op. cit.*, II, 144–152.

[15] *Russia, 1919*, pp. 78–80. In this source, Bullitt reported that the proposals were handed him by Chicherin on March 14, whereas the date given in *Dokumenty SSSR*, II, 91–95, is March 12, 1919. See also Degras, *op. cit.*, pp. 147–150.

military assistance [is] to cease to be given to anti-Soviet Governments which have been set up on the territory of the former Russian Empire." [16]

The Bolshevik tactic was clear. Hard pressed, Soviet Russia would permit the temporary existence of the border states on condition that all foreign arms be withdrawn and further military assistance be withheld from those separatist regimes. Lenin also knew that no "bits of paper" could ink away the impact of Bolshevik propaganda and sedition. The conciliatory point itself had obvious loopholes, for changes, not barring those spawned of violence, could be dictated by "the peoples inhabiting the territories controlled by these *de facto* Governments." The dedicated directors of revolutionary Russia were convinced that the marchlands, deprived of active Allied support, would eventually and inevitably swing into the Soviet orbit.

The exploratory dialogue and proposals in Moscow failed to relieve the crisis in Russia. By the time William Bullitt returned to Paris at the end of March, events on the world scene had reinforced the implacable foes of Bolshevism and had cast the Supreme Allied Council into an uncompromising mood.[17] The spread of the Communist menace to Germany and Hungary roused the militarists to demand a grand crusade against the Bolshevik ogre, a crusade that Admiral Kolchak would launch as soon as the winter snows of Russia had thawed. For Armenia the relevance of Lenin's peace offensive lay in the fact that Soviet Russia, while still far removed from Transcaucasia, intimated a hypothetical willingness to tolerate the de facto Erevan government. It was equally germane, however, that the exigencies of Soviet strategy were predicated on the need for a breathing spell before expanding, through provocation and subversion, to the unprotected borderlands. Moreover, the Soviet proposals bore witness to the failure of the Armenian envoys in Moscow to ensure Russian benevolence, or

[16] *Russia, 1919*, pp. 78–79. See also *The Bullitt Mission to Russia*, pp. 39–43.

[17] Bullitt cabled the terms of the proposal to Paris from Helsinki on March 16, and concluded, "There is no doubt whatever of the desire of the Soviet Government for a just and reasonable peace, or of the sincerity of this proposal, and I pray you will consider it with the deepest seriousness." In his subsequent reports Bullitt expressed the belief that only a socialist government could prevail in Russia without the coercive support of foreign bayonets. Any such foreign-sponsored government, he maintained, would fall as soon as its artificial props had been withdrawn. Bullitt urged that every effort be made to take advantage of a unique opportunity to make peace "with the revolution," especially as the "Lenin wing of the Communist Party is today as moderate as any Socialist Government which can control Russia." The American agent also stated his favorable impressions of the improved educational system, the social development, and the high public morale in Russia. See Miller, *Documents*, VI (1924), 445–450, and VII (1924), 444–462; *Russia, 1919*, pp. 81–84.

at least nonmalevolence, toward the Republic of Armenia. The draft submitted to Bullitt by Chicherin had ranked Armenia among the states "operating against Soviet Russia."

The Armenian Affairs Commissariat

As the Sovnarkom maneuvered to attenuate Allied belligerence, the chasm between the Communist party and Dashnaktsutiun and between Moscow and Erevan grew progressively broader and deeper. All moves toward a rapprochement were effectively wrecked by the People's Commissariat for Nationalities (Narkomnats), directed by I. V. Stalin. The Georgian-born Bolshevik burned with enmity toward the ruling parties in Transcaucasia and displayed none of the pendulation, sympathy, or tolerance that could be read into the declarations of Lenin and Trotsky.[18] Supported by a number of like-minded Armenian Bolsheviks, Stalin charred every proposal for a modus vivendi between Soviet Russia and the Republic of Armenia. Beginning in December, 1917, the Commissariat for Nationalities created several subsectors, among which was the Armenian Affairs Commissariat (Komissariat po armianskim delam), headed by V. A. Avanesov, the secretary of the Central Executive Committee of the Soviet of All Russia.[19] The men who clustered around this subsector were convinced that the Armenian masses, ignorant of the promises of Marxism, lay tangled in the "claws of nationalism." This small circle of Armenian Bolsheviks labored under extreme difficulties to emancipate their people from a "bourgeois-nationalist" mentality, to spread the gospel of communism, particularly among the refugee population, to martial spirits against the forces of counterrevolution, and to offer, through the aegis of Soviet Russia, salvation to Armenia. These themes filled the pages of the irregularly published weekly newspaper, *Komunist*, which commenced in June, 1918, under an editorial board directed by Avanesov. The paper was soon suspended because of technical and internal political troubles, but a new organ, *Karmir droshak* ("Red

[18] For examples of Stalin's views on the nationality question, see *I. V. Stalin: Sochineniia*, publ. of Institut Marksa-Engel'sa-Lenina pri TsK VKP(b) (13 vols.; Moscow, 1946–1949), I, 32–55; II, 285–367 *passim*; IV, 3–4, 25–26, 31–32, 33–35, 51–73, 155–167, 225–229, 351–363, 370–373; V, 15–59. See also Pipes, *op. cit.*, pp. 37–40, 109–110.

[19] Varlaam Aleksandrovich Avanesov was a native of Kaghisman in the Kars oblast. He dropped his legal name, Suren K. Martirosian, in 1907 when he used the passport of a certain Avanesiants to slip abroad. For a résumé of his activities in the Russian revolutionary movement and Communist party, see S. T. Alikhanian, "V. Avanesovi hamategh ashkhatanke Lenini het," *Patma-banasirakan handes*, I (1970), 79–94.

Banner"), emerged for a time in 1919 under the editorship of Artashes B. Karinian (Gabrielian). In addition, a rather prolific literature in tracts and pamphlets rolled off the confiscated Armenian presses of Petrograd and Moscow. Titles such as "A Message to the Armenian Refugees," "What Does Lenin Say to the Peasants?" "On the National Question," "Imperialism and Armenia," indicate the genre of these treatises.[20]

In areas beyond the Soviet capital, branches or individual agents of the Armenian Affairs Commissariat were established in cities of central and southern Russia, the Ukraine, and the North Caucasus. The effectiveness of these local groups was sharply diminished, however, by the lack of coordination among them and by the counter-measures of more pervasive non-Bolshevik organizations. In regions falling under the control of the White Armies, the branches were crushed or driven far underground. Enemy seizure of more than 6 million rubles the Commissariat had forwarded to Astrakhan and Piatigorsk for work among the Turkish Armenian refugees was only an isolated example of the difficulties encountered. The Sovnarkom subsequently reallocated the money, but there is no convincing evidence that it was used for the original purpose.[21] With few exceptions Soviet historians, while extolling the contributions of the Armenian Commissariat, nonetheless confirm, some more obliquely than others, that the activities of this subsector were circumscribed and unbalanced. Channels to relay propaganda to Transcaucasia were constricted or absent and, especially demoralizing, the organization became infested with "opportunists" and "adventurers." Still, the core of Armenian converts dedicated itself to an eventual Communist victory and,

[20] For materials on the Armenian Affairs Commissariat, see the following Soviet publications: S. T. Alikhanian, *Haikakan Gordseri Komisariati gordsuneutiune (1917–1921)* (Erevan, 1958), cited hereafter as *Haikakan Komisariat,* and his *Sovetakan Rusastani dere hai zhoghovrdi azatagrakan gordsum (1917–1921)* (Erevan, 1966), pp. 55–88, cited hereafter as *Rusastani dere;* A. M. Elchibekian, *Velikaia Oktiabr'skaia sotsialisticheskaia revoliutsiia i pobeda Sovetskoi vlasti v Armenii* (Erevan, 1957), pp. 49–52; B. H. Lalabekian, *V. I. Lenine ev Sovetakan kargeri hastatumn u amrapndumn Andrkovkasum* (Erevan, 1961), pp. 197–205; Kh. A. Barsegian [Kh. H. Barseghian], *Istoriia armianskoi bol'shevistskoi periodicheskoi pechati* (Erevan, 1958), pp. 236–252, cited hereafter as *Istoriia armianskoi pechati.* The Commissariat's résumé of its activities is reprinted in *Velikaia Oktiabr'skaia revoliutsiia,* pp. 242–249 (not to be confused with Elchibekian's work in this note; see abbreviated titles).

[21] *Velikaia Oktiabr'skaia revoliutsiia,* pp. 221–222; H. Sahakian, *Meds Hoktembere ev azgayin hartsi ludsume Andrkovkasum* (Erevan, 1967), p. 30; Ds. Aghayan, *Hoktemberian revoliutsian ev hai zhoghovrdi azatagrume* (Erevan, 1957), pp. 142–144, cited hereafter as *Hai zhoghovrdi azatagrume;* Alikhanian, *Haikakan Komisariat,* pp. 37–48, 91–95.

equating Dashnaktsutiun to enslavement of the Armenian people, strove to destroy this "terrible creature of chauvinism." The attempts of less militant Bolsheviks such as Sahak M. Ter-Gabrielian to gain acceptance of a tempered policy acknowledging the benefits of at least a short-term Armeno-Soviet accord were fruitless. The meetings Ter-Gabrielian arranged between Bolsheviks Trotsky, Kamenev, and Karakhan and Dashnakists Zavriev, Nazariants, and Chilingarian were skillfully sabotaged by the Commissar for Nationalities and his Armenian associates.[22]

The inviolability, however precarious, of the Dashnakist envoys in Moscow evaporated during the latter half of 1918 as the result of a series of unnerving episodes. In July Russian Social Revolutionary conspirators assassinated German Ambassador Count Wilhelm von Mirbach in a plot to shatter the Treaty of Brest-Litovsk. In August they wounded Lenin in an assassination attempt, while in the Caucasus the non-Bolshevik majority of the Baku Soviet precipitated the fall of the Baku Commune. In September the Ottoman armies captured Baku, and anti-Soviet Russian authorities in Transcaspia, in probable collusion with at least one British officer, executed Stepan Shahumian and twenty-five other commissars of the former Commune. Stung by this rash of treachery, the Sovnarkom retaliated by proscribing the political activities of all groups save Bolshevik organizations. The Red Terror extended over the land, filling prisons with actual and suspected agents of counterrevolution. Invigorated by the new wave of militancy, the Armenian Affairs Commissariat redoubled its vilification of Dashnaktsutiun, charging that party with complicity in the fall of Baku and the massacre of the twenty-six commissars. The Armenian Bolsheviks, channeling their petitions through Stalin, urged the Soviet leadership to heed their admonitions against Dashnakist perfidy.[23]

The Soviet reaction swept Zavriev, Nazariants, and many other Armenian nationalists into prison. Artashes Chilingarian was among the handful spared through the direct intervention of Vahan S. Terian (Ter-Grigorian), a talented poet serving as assistant director of the Armenian Affairs Commissariat. Because of a critical shortage of qualified Armenian Bolshevik intellectuals, Dashnakist rivals like Chilingarian were put to work translating into Armenian the very

[22] Darbinian, "Memoirs" (Spring, 1948), pp. 28–29, 33–34. See also Alikhanian, *Haikakan Komisariat*, pp. 70–71.

[23] S. T. Alikhanian, *Vahan Teriani petakan gordsuneutiune* (Erevan, 1956), pp. 174–175, cited hereafter as *Terian*; Darbinian, "Memoirs" (Summer, 1948), pp. 28–29, 35–36. See also *Velikaia Oktiabr'skaia revoliutsiia*, pp. 295–297; Ruben, *op. cit.*, p. 263.

literature they had long refuted and satirized.[24] The imprisoned Dashnakists, the Soviet authorities announced, would be held hostage until the family of Stepan Shahumian had been freed. Weeks passed before those authorities chose to believe that Dashnaktsutiun had never molested Ekaterina Shahumian or her four children. Even then, Varlam Avanesov declared that Zavriev and Nazariants would be liberated only in exchange for Bolshevik agents interned by the Allies.[25] When this became known in Paris, Avetis Aharonian appealed to British officials to include the pair on the roster being prepared for a possible Anglo-Soviet prisoner exchange. Since the British denied the request, Aharonian sought the intercession of the Danish Red Cross, whose representatives in Russia might hopefully be in a position to arrange the release of the captives or at least see that they received humane treatment.[26] The fate of the hostages remained in suspense until the spring of 1919 when, perhaps as an outgrowth of the Soviet overtures to the Allies, they and other Armenians were freed and all except Zavriev eventually reached safety abroad. Dr. Hakob Zavriev, one of Armenia's few experienced diplomats and a dedicated patriot long active in the national emancipatory struggle, was discharged from prison in extremely poor health and succumbed to typhus shortly thereafter.[27]

Meanwhile the People's Commissariat for Nationalities turned its attention to destruction of the broad network of Armenian benevolent, educational, religious, and auxiliary organizations in Russia. Bourgeois and nationalist, as viewed by confirmed Armenian Bolsheviks, nearly all these societies were affiliated with the Armenian National Council in Tiflis and, after mid-1918, with the Armenian republic. The Armenian Affairs Commissariat exhorted the Sovnarkom to liquidate the "counterrevolutionary centers" as a major step in squelching nationalism and breaking Dashnaktsutiun's powerful grip on thousands of Armenians in Russia. As early as March of 1918 the

[24] Darbinian, "Memoirs" (Spring, 1948), pp. 35–36, and (Summer, 1948), p. 27.

[25] Rep. of Arm. Archives, File 65/1, Tumanov (Tiflis) to Armenian mission (Constantinople), Sept. 27, 1918; Darbinian, "Memoirs" (Summer, 1948), pp. 28–36 passim; Alikhanian, Terian, pp. 174–175.

[26] Rep. of Arm. Archives, File 231/130, includes Aharonian's correspondence with Robert G. Vansittart of the British delegation and with officials of the Danish Red Cross. It was explained to Aharonian that "until all British subjects are released, the Foreign Office do not feel that they would be justified in agreeing to the exchange of adherents of the Soviet Government for Armenians." See Britain, FO 608/80, 342/1/15/14415/15204/18184.

[27] Darbinian, "Memoirs" (Summer, 1948), pp. 38–39, and (Autumn, 1948), p. 52; Rep. of Arm. Archives, File 231/130, Report of July 26, 1919; Gabriel Lazian, Heghapokhakan demker (mtavorakanner ev haidukner) (Cairo, 1945), p. 252.

Sovnarkom, acting on the advice of the Commissariat for Nationalities, dissolved and confiscated the assets of the Petrograd Armenian Military Defense Committee. That same month the Lazarian Institute (Jemaran) of Moscow, renowned for its role in the Armenian cultural renaissance, was expropriated and attached to the Armenian Affairs Commissariat. In June the governing board and most of the faculty were expelled and, under the supervision of Poghos N. Makintsian, the Institute was restructured in conformity with the principles and curriculum set forth by the People's Commissar of Enlightenment, Anatolii V. Lunacharskii.[28]

Prodded by Stalin's ministry the Sovnarkom on July 19, 1918, adopted a sweeping decree authorizing the liquidation of all non-Bolshevik Armenian organizations and the consignment of their goods and properties to branches of the Armenian Commissariat or, where such branches were nonexistent, to the local soviets of soldiers', workers', and peasants' deputies. Armed with this edict Varlaam Avanesov wired soviets throughout Russia to accelerate the eradication program, supervised from Moscow by a special commission headed by Vahan Terian. Among the first victims of the decree were the affluent Armenian Defense Committee of Moscow and the Armenian Circle of Petrograd. Thereafter, Armenian schools in many districts were closed or converted into Soviet-styled academies.[29] Despite this apparent success the Commissariat for Nationalities was disgruntled with the generally slow pace of liquidation and especially with the tenacity of many Armenian associations that continued to operate by means of "deception and intercession." Remonstrating with the Sovnarkom and the regional soviets, Stalin's assistants repeatedly "exposed" the true counterrevolutionary nature of all non-Bolshevik Armenian groups without exception. The zeal of the Commissariat for Nationalities was not shared, however, by many local officials who evaded forceful action. At the beginning of 1919, nearly a half year after the Sovnarkom's all-inclusive decree, the Armenian Commissariat was obliged to dispatch special envoys to enlighten provincial authorities who had been "tricked" into believing that the Armenian societies functioned sim-

---

[28] Aghayan, *Hai zhoghovrdi azatagrume*, pp. 139, 142; Alikhanian, *Haikakan Komisariat*, pp. 75–79, 142–143, and *Rusastani dere*, pp. 68–69. In 1920 the Lazarian Jemaran was converted into the Institute of Living Oriental Languages. See Elchibekian, *op. cit.*, p. 51n.

[29] A. N. Mnatsakanian, *V. I. Lenine ev hai zhoghovrdi azatagrakan paikare* (Erevan, 1963), pp. 242–245, cited hereafter as *V. I. Lenin;* Alikhanian, *Haikakan Komisariat*, pp. 81, 143–146; Elchibekian, *op. cit.*, p. 50. Alikhanian, *Terian*, pp. 153–155, states that Vahan Terian was the principal drafter of this decree.

ply to aid the refugee population and were in no way incompatible with the Soviet system.[30]

Although the network of Armenian organizations in central Russia was ultimately inactivated, many units in regions along the peripheries of Soviet rule reemerged whenever the Red Army was rolled back. Employing a far less stringent operational code with regard to Armenian associations, the White Armies and Cossack regimes of the south granted them general freedom of action and condoned their liaison with the Armenian republic. It was not unreasonable therefore that Moscow should give credence to rumors of an entente between Erevan and Ekaterinodar, particularly after the Armenian Bolsheviks, intent on substantiating the charge, released a barrage of slanderous reports. Hence, in one way or another, Soviet Russia came to look upon Armenia as the Transcaucasian state least amenable to some form of collaboration. This attitude was borne out in August of 1919 when Foreign Affairs Commissar Chicherin urged the Georgian and Azerbaijani governments to join with Soviet Russia against the mutually menacing Volunteer Army of General Anton Denikin.[31] It was not the result of oversight that Armenia received no such summons.

Renewed Bolshevik Activity in the Caucasus

During her first year of independence Armenia was in fact the only Transcaucasian republic to take a permissive stance toward native Bolsheviks, apparently in the hope that these men could pave the way to a rapprochement with Moscow. By contrast, Menshevik Georgia rigorously suppressed its Bolshevik activists. Mensheviks and Bolsheviks perhaps understood each other too well for there to have been any of the vacillation displayed in Erevan. In mid-1918 the Tiflis-based Bolshevik Caucasus Regional Committee (Kavkazskii kraevoi komitet) fled to safety in the North Caucasus, while those of the party faithful who remained in Georgia had to face the constant threat of exposure and imprisonment. Still, the Bolsheviks were not fully silenced. With financial aid from the north, they published intermittently the clandestine newspapers *Kavkazskaia pravda* ("Truth of the Caucasus") and the Georgian-language *Brdzola* ("Struggle"), and the

[30] Alikhanian, *Rusastani dere*, pp. 77-78.

[31] *Bor'ba v Gruzii*, pp. 467-469; Central State Archives of the October Revolution, Georgian SSR, Fund 11, work 11, p. 65, as cited in Lalabekian, *op. cit.*, pp. 151-152. For excerpts of this communiqué, translated into English, see Kazemzadeh, *Transcaucasia*, p. 248.

party's Tiflis Bureau, headed by Mikha G. Tskhakaia, attempted to hold together the badly undermined local organization.[32]

Despite the unrelenting persecution, a number of Bolshevik delegates, claiming to represent the entire membership in Transcaucasia, gathered in illegal conference just outside Tiflis in mid-November, 1918. The conference declared that the Armenian, Georgian, and Azerbaijani so-called republics had been created solely for the purpose of oppressing the workers and peasants and counteracting the international struggle for the triumph of socialism. The delegates adopted resolutions committing the Bolsheviks of Transcaucasia to escalate their organizational labors, to expose the true nature of the counter-revolutionary republics, and to awaken in the workers and peasants the will to take power and make the Caucasus a unit of the Russian Soviet Federated Socialist Republic. The Bolshevik membership would arm and prepare the masses to strike the death blow at the "Anglo-Russian counterrevolutionary bands" and liquidate once and for all the "counterrevolutionary lairs in Transcaucasia." [33] During the Armeno-Georgian war, which burst forth one month after the illegal conference, the underground Bolshevik cells distributed leaflets condemning the fratricidal bloodshed spawned by the divide-and-rule policies of the imperialist powers and their Transcaucasian "lackeys," the Menshevik and Dashnakist governments of Georgia and Armenia.[34]

To revitalize the crippled Regional Committee, the Russian Communist Party summoned the Second Congress of Caucasian Bolshevik organizations to meet in Vladikavkaz in January, 1919.[35] In its invitation-appeal the committee in charge of arrangements deprecated the

[32] *Istoriia Kompartii Gruzii*, pp. 331–332. For a description of the extreme difficulties under which the Bolsheviks had to operate in the Caucasus, see G. Devdariani, ed., *Dni gospodstva men'shevikov v Gruzii (dokumenty i materialy)* ([Tiflis], 1931), pp. 414–421.

[33] *Velikaia Oktiabr'skaia revoliutsiia*, pp. 238–241; *Hayastani Komkusi patmutiun*, pp. 272–273; G. Zhvaniia, *Velikii Oktiabr' i bor'ba Bol'shevikov Zakavkaz'ia za Sovetskuiu vlast'* (Tbilisi, 1967), pp. 196–198.

[34] Spartak, *Vinovniki armiano-gruzinskago stolknoveniia* ([Tiflis, 1918]); H. N. Karapetian, *Hayastani komeritmiutian dsnunde* (Erevan, 1956), p. 92; G. B. Gharibdjanian, *Hayastani komunistakan kazmakerputiunnere Sovetakan ishkhanutian haghtanaki hamar mghvads paikarum* (Erevan, 1955), p. 256; *Istorii Kompartii Gruzii*, p. 633; *Revoliutsion kocher*, pp. 496–497.

[35] The Caucasus Regional Committee of the Russian Social Democrat Labor Party (bolshevik) was elected by the First Congress of Caucasian Bolshevik organizations, held at Tiflis in October of 1917. See Hovannisian, *Road to Independence*, pp 85–86; R. Movsisian, *Kovkasian bolshevikian kazmakerputiunneri Erkrayin aradjin hamagumare ev Stepan Shahumian* (Erevan, 1955); K. B. Udumian, RSDBK(b) Kovkasian kazmakerputiunneri erkrayin aradjin hamagumare," *Lraber hasarakakan gitutiunneri*, 11 (1967), 76–88; Zhvaniia, *op. cit.*, pp. 83–102; Dimanshtein, *op. cit.*, pp. 408–412.

currents that had splintered the Caucasus and declared that now, more than ever, the Bolshevik party must draw together all the workers and peasants regardless of their ethnic origins and historic differences.[36] Because of the widespread harassment of Bolsheviks, however, the Second Congress convened with representatives from the North Caucasus but none from Transcaucasia.[37] Nevertheless, under the direction of G. K. (Sergo) Ordzhonikidze,[38] the meeting resolved to intensify party activity and reinforced the membership of the Caucasus Regional Committee, known generally by the abbreviated title of Kraikom. But the relative security the Bolsheviks had found in the North Caucasus was short-lived. As the Voluteer Army advanced over the Terek, the Kraikom again went underground and eventually, after crossing the towering mountain range, sifted into Tiflis and Baku.[39]

The Bolshevik fabric in Baku had been worn extremely thin by the collapse of the Commune in August, 1918, the general exodus toward Astrakhan and the massacre of the twenty-six commissars in September, and the subsequent foreign occupation, first Turkish, then British. Still, by the beginning of 1919, a few Bolshevik organizers had slipped back into the city with the throngs of returning refugees. Reviving the local cells, they formed a temporary party bureau,[40] which established bonds with the Hummet (Energy) and Adalet (Justice) Muslim Marxist groups, both of which gravitated increasingly toward a Bolshevik orientation.[41] The strategic, economic, and political importance of

[36] *Bor'ba v Gruzii*, pp. 361–363.

[37] The summons to the Second Congress was circulated on December 29, 1918, only four days before the opening session. Soviet historians have ascribed much importance to the meeting, but it is likely that, at the time, most Bolshevik organizations in the Caucasus were not even aware that the Congress was in progress.

[38] On July 11, 1918, the Russian Central Committee had named Ordzhonikidze as Commissar for South Russia and Vladikavkaz. See *Istoriia Kompartii Gruzii*, p. 332.

[39] *Bor'ba v Gruzii*, pp. xxiv–xxv; *Istoriia Kompartii Gruzii*, p. 363. Veteran Georgian Bolshevik Filipp Makharadze subsequently wrote that the unfavorable conditions in Georgia had caused party work in that country to be "all but absent" until the spring of 1919. See Devdariani, *op. cit.*, p. 445.

[40] The names of the bureau members are given in *Kompartiia Azerbaidzhana*, p. 294.

[41] *Istoriia Kompartii Azerbaidzhana*, pp. 317–318. The Hummet (Gummet) society split into right and left wings. The pro-Bolshevik leftists gained ascendency during a party conference in March, 1919, and then undertook to exclude the Menshevik-oriented element. The Adalet society was composed almost entirely of natives of Iranian Azerbaijan who had come to Baku for employment in the oil fields. For a discussion of the internal divisions among the Muslim Marxists and the eventual victory of the Bolshevik faction, see *Kompartiia Azerbaidzhana*, pp. 295–299. In July of 1919 the Orgburo and the Politburo of the Russian Communist Party ruled that there would be no objection to recognizing Hummet as one of its provincial organizations, and in August the Orgburo officially acknowledged Hummet as an affiliated unit. See *Bor'ba*

Baku having held the constant attention of the Russian Sovnarkom, the Commissariat for Nationalities created in January, 1919, a special subsector to deal with Transcaucasian Muslim affairs and dispatched via Astrakhan the first echelon of party professionals to direct the work in the most highly industrialized and proletarian city of the Caucasus.[42]

In the early stages of reorganization, the Bolshevik leadership of Baku clashed over an issue of momentous consequence. One faction upheld the goal of creating a Soviet Caucasus and guiding it into an integral union with Russia, whereas the other insisted that the only way to combat the pervasivenes of the local nationalist parties was to adopt the motto, "Independent Soviet Azerbaijan." Recent Soviet historians emphasize that prior to mid-1919 the Bolshevik hierarchy in the Caucasus failed to accord due recognition to national sentiment, thereby losing control of the masses and surrendering the initiative to the Mensheviks, Musavatists, and Dashnakists. And indeed, it was nearly a year after the partition of Transcaucasia into three independent states that a Communist regional gathering first pronounced in favor of distinct Azerbaijani, Georgian, and Armenian Soviet republics.[43]

The party functionaries in Baku pioneered the new approach. Anastas I. Mikoyan, who in late February, 1919, returned to the city and helped set up the Baku Bureau of the Caucasus Regional Committee, lent his support to the majority faction, which held that in order to woo the masses from the clutches of the dominant Musavat party the motto "Soviet Caucasus" must be altered to "Soviet Azerbaijan." [44] This obvious concession to nationalism outraged the Caucasus Regional Committee, which, having hailed the multinational structure

v Azerbaidzhane, pp. 257, 530 n. 178; M. S. Iskenderov, Iz istorii bor'by Kommunisticheskoi partii Azerbaidzhana za pobedu Sovetskoi vlasti (Baku, 1958), pp. 418–419.

[42] Kompartiia Azerbaidzhana, p. 300; Istoriia Kompartii Azerbaidzhana, pp. 320–321. For biographical sketches of prominent Bolsheviks active in Astrakhan and Azerbaijan, see Aktivnye bortsy za Sovetskuiu vlast' v Azerbaidzhane, publ. of Institut Istorii Partii pri TsK KP Azerbaidzhana–Filial Instituta Marksizma-Leninizma pri TsK KPSS (Baku, 1957).

[43] Hayastani Komkusi patmutiun, p. 282; Zhvaniia, op. cit., pp. 203–204; P. A. Azizbekova, V. I. Lenin i sotsialisticheskie preobrazovaniia v Azerbaidzhane (1920–1923 gg.) (Moscow, 1962), pp. 85–86; N. B. Makharadze, Pobeda sotsialisticheskoi revoliutsii v Gruzii (Tbilisi, 1965), pp. 304, 356–357; Kh. H. Barseghian, Hayastani Komunistakan partiayi kazmavorume (Erevan, 1965), pp. 259–262, cited hereafter as Hayastani Kompartiayi kazmavorume.

[44] Kompartiia Azerbaidzhana, p. 296; Barseghian, Hayastani Kompartiayi kazmavorume, pp. 258–259. Mikoyan arrived in Baku after having been released from imprisonment by the anti-Soviet forces in Transcaspia.

of its organization, was convinced that the comrades in Baku had sanctioned a serious blunder and were flirting with deviation and opportunism. Those same comrades, however, went a step further in May by calling for the formation of an Azerbaijani Communist party, thus stirring the Kraikom to even greater fury.[45]

As a result of the growing dissension, the dispute was placed before the Russian Central Committee.[46] A conclusive judgment was not rendered until the end of 1919, but in July the Political Bureau (Politburo) and the Organizational Bureau (Orgburo) of the Central Committee agreed to recognize in principle the concept of a future Soviet Azerbaijani state, and in August the Central Committee informed the Kraikom that in due time it might not be improper for Azerbaijan to declare herself a Soviet republic.[47] In December the Politburo ultimately authorized the establishment of a separate Communist party not only for Azerbaijan but, to the utter amazement and unqualified opposition of the Regional Committee and all other official Bolshevik agencies in the Caucasus, for Georgia and Armenia as well. The territorially structured parties were to merge at the level of the Kraikom and, through that body, were to be subject to the Russian Communist Party.[48] In order to become more effective in the national republics of the Caucasus, the Bolsheviks, too, would operate within a national framework. The Russian Communist Party had

[45] *Istoriia Kompartii Azerbaidzhana*, p. 328; *Hayastani Komkusi patmutiun*, p. 282; Barseghian, *Hayastani Kompartiayi kazmavorume*, pp. 233, 259–260; *Kompartiia Azerbaidzhana*, pp. 307–309; *Istoriia Azerbaidzhana*, ed. I. A. Guseinov et al., publ. of Akademiia Nauk Azerbaidzhanskoi SSR, Institut Istorii, Vol. III, pt. 1 (Baku, 1963), pp. 184–185. See also Pipes, *op. cit.*, pp. 218–220; Kazemzadeh, *Transcaucasia*, pp. 230–231. Makharadze, *op. cit.*, p. 356, explains that the Georgian members of the Kraikom were especially opposed to the formation of an Azerbaijani Communist party as it would establish a precedent that would logically lead to a separate Georgian organization, this at a time when the Georgian Bolsheviks were branding the Georgian Mensheviks as separatists and nationalists.

[46] In a letter to Lenin on May 22, 1919, Mikoyan stated his concern over the paucity of Muslims in the Communist party. The Muslim peoples stood aloof, he said, because they feared that the establishment of Communist rule in Azerbaijan would lead to domination by Russians. Mikoyan therefore urged the Soviet leadership to endorse the concept of an independent Soviet Azerbaijan bound closely with Soviet Russia in order to gain the trust of the Muslims. Such a motto, he said, would be popular and could serve to unite the working Muslims and spark an insurrection against the Musavat government. Although a conference of Transcaucasian party organizations on May 7–8 had rejected this approach, the Baku comrades resolved not to retreat on the issue. See *Bor'ba v Azerbaidzhane*, pp. 138–141.

[47] *Istoriia Kompartii Azerbaidzhana*, p. 328; *Hayastani Komkusi patmutiun*, p. 282; Azizbekova, *op. cit.*, p. 86; Zhvaniia, *op. cit.*, pp. 222–223; *Kompartiia Azerbaidzhana*, p. 309.

[48] Barseghian, *Hayastani Kompartiayi kazmavorume*, p. 261; *Hayastani Komkusi patmutiun*, p. 282; Iskenderov, *op. cit.*, p. 419.

thus set the precedent for the existence of Transcaucasian Soviet republics, bound individually or collectively to Moscow. At the beginning of 1920 the Politburo, in a resolution "About Communist Labors Pending in Armenia," reconfirmed this stand: "The creation of conditions favorable to combat local chauvinism and to propagate socialist revolution among the nationalities which have suffered under the yoke of Russian tsarism requires that Communist groups in the factually organized 'republics' within the bounds of the former Russian empire must operate as separate Communist organizations." [49]

Bolshevism in Armenia

Armenia, an agrarian land with almost no industrial development, lacked the conditions that, according to Marxist precepts, were conducive to class warfare and effective revolutionary agitation. The railway employees and the workers of several small factories constituted the full extent of Armenia's proletariat. And the few among this limited group who were attracted to Marxism were further splintered into Bolshevik, Menshevik, and "Specifist" factions. That Communist ideologies had failed to strike firm roots in Armenia is readily admitted by Soviet historians. Marxism developed as a radical fringe among Russian-educated intellectuals or else filtered through the Social Democrat Hnchakist party, composed primarily of Turkish Armenians and heavily permeated by nationalism. In the Caucasus the "Specifist" Social Democratic Workers Armenian Organization gained a small following in Baku and Tiflis, but it, too, was not bereft of the "nationalistic deviations" scorned by orthodox Marxists.[50]

[49] *Hayastani Komkusi patmutiun*, p. 283; Zhvaniia, *op. cit.*, p. 276. See also Mnatsakanian, *V. I. Lenin*, pp. 363–364.

[50] For materials on the introduction and development of Marxist ideologies among the Armenians and for accounts of Bolshevik operations in the Armenian provinces before the establishment of independent republics in the Caucasus, consult the following Soviet publications: Kh. G. Gulanian, *Marksistakan tntesakan mtki taradsume hai irakanutian medj, 1890–1920* (Erevan, 1959), and his *Marksistskaia mysl' v Armenii* (Erevan, 1967); Artashes Voskerchian, *Hai marksistakan knnadatutian himnadirnere: Stepan Shahumian, Suren Spandarian* (Erevan, 1962); Gr. Sargsian, *Suren Spandarian* (Erevan, 1960); L. A. Abrahamian, *Hayastanum marksizmi taradsman patmutiunits* (Erevan, 1959); M. V. Arzumanian, *Bolshevikneri gordsuneutiune ev revoliutsion sharzhumnere Hayastanum 1907–1917 tvakannerin* (Erevan, 1959); Barseghian, *Hayastani Kompartiayi kazmavorume*, pt. 1; *Hayastani Komkusi patmutiun*, pts. 1–3; *Hayastani Komunistakan partiayi patmutian urvagdser*, ed. by H. Kh. Margarian, A. N. Mnatsakanian, and Kh. H. Barseghian (Erevan, 1968), chaps. i–iii. The Armenian "Specifists" were sharply criticized by both Lenin and Stalin.

The Armenian disciples of Lenin shunned the several Marxist societies structured along ethnic lines and instead associated themselves with the Russian Communist Party and its multinational Caucasus Regional Committee. Armenian Bolsheviks were active in Tiflis, Batum, Baku, the cities of the North Caucasus, and Moscow, but significantly only a handful were to be found in the Armenian provinces. The latter circle, because of the paucity of its numbers, usually joined in a single organization with the Mensheviks, who were equally scarce in Armenia. When the Central Committee of the Russian party, acting upon Lenin's prepotent demand, ordered the formation of purely Bolshevik cells, the membership in Armenia was slow to comply, for, at the time, survival as a separate organization seemed absolutely impossible. At the end of 1918 the several Bolsheviks in Erevan did at long last announce complete disassociation from their Menshevik comrades and rivals, but in fact joint groups existed in Armenia as late as the summer of 1919, more than two years after the Russian Central Committee had dictated the disengagement.[51]

The Armenian government showed no great concern over the operations of the small cluster of Mensheviks and Bolsheviks. Kachazuni's cabinet believed that they might serve as effective couriers to Moscow and recognized that older Marxists such as Arshavir M. Melikian, the lone Bolshevik in the Armenian legislature, held certain revisionist attitudes attenuating the orthodox tactic of violent upheaval and accepting the possibility of Communist victory through legal action. While not in favor of full Armenian independence, such Bolsheviks nevertheless regarded the "bourgeois-nationalist" republic as the necessary forerunner of the proletarian state and on that basis justified their own participation in the government. In *Khosk* ("Word"), the legal Marxist newspaper he edited from September, 1918, to March, 1919, Melikian exhorted the peoples of the Caucasus to reunite with the Great Russians under the banner of the October Revolution. Moreover, the Armenian Marxists filled the columns of *Khosk* with condemnations of the chauvinism and interracial antagonism that racked the Caucasus and commented with sarcasm on the so-called independence of the Transcaucasian republics. Yet they did not call for the forceful overthrow of the existing regimes. Herein lay the "op-

[51] H. S. Karapetian, *Mayisian apstambutiune Hayastanum, 1920* (Erevan, 1961), p. 84n; Aghayan, *Hai zhoghovrdi azatagrume,* p. 215; Gharibdjanian, *op. cit.,* pp. 262–264; Barseghian, *Hayastani Kompartiayi kazmavorume,* pp. 256–257; *Hayastani Komkusi patmutiun,* pp. 277–280; H. Danielian, *Spartak Hayastanum* (Moscow, 1931), pp. 57, 61.

portunism" and "deviation" of which they were later charged by writers of the Stalinist era.[52]

Communist endeavors in Armenia during 1919 were concentrated on the creation of a loose network of cells. This goal was partially facilitated by the return of seasonal laborers from Baku, Tiflis, Batum, and the North Caucasus, where revolutionary currents unknown to most Armenian villagers had affected some of the workers. A few carried Bolshevik propaganda back to their homes and were among the first to enter the small cells that began to dot the land. Another important target of Bolshevik activity was the student youth. Under the impact of the extreme hardships then prevailing in Armenia, there were sensitive and keen young minds that recoiled against the horror and sought an answer to human suffering through a new, positivist doctrine. It is thus not inexplicable that most converts to communism in Armenia were young men who showed quick impatience with the old-guard Bolshevik of the Melikian type. They were bolder, more impetuous, and less compromising. The Communist-oriented students distributed clandestine handbills deprecating Dashnakist oppression and the shameful treatment of the Muslim population. They urged the villagers to defy military levies, and the soldiers to desert or to turn their weapons against the officer class.[53]

A vivid example of this emerging militant group was Ghukas H. Ghukasian, an executive member of the Marxist Student Union of Erevan.[54] At the end of March and beginning of April, 1919, he was

[52] For materials on Melikian's activities in Armenia and on the newspaper *Khosk*, see *Hayastani Komkusi patmutiun*, pp. 275–280; Barsegian, *Istoriia armianskoi pechati*, pp. 415–421; Gharibdjanian, *op. cit.*, pp. 264–266. In recent years Arshavir Melikian has been rehabilitated in Soviet literature. In 1969, on the occasion of the ninetieth anniversary of Melikian's birth, a number of tributes appeared in the newspapers and scholarly journals of Soviet Armenia. See, for example, K. Melik-Ohandjanian, "Akanavor Komunist Arshavir Melikiani masin (1912–1920 tt.),", *Lraber hasarakakan gitutiunneri*, 3 (1969), 82–87; and the articles of Ds. P. Aghayan: "Arshavir Melikian (dsnndian 90-amiaki artiv)," *Patma-banasirakan handes*, 1 (1969), 139–146; "Arshavir Melikiane V. I. Lenini ashkhatutiunneri masin," *Banber Hayastani arkhivneri*, 1 (1969), 95–99; and "Leninian gaghaparneri annkun propagandiste ev khoshor tesabane (Arshavir Melikiani dsnndian 90-amiakin)," *Lraber hasarakakan gitutiunneri*, 1 (1969), 21–39.

[53] Aghayan, *Hai zhoghovrdi azatagrume*, pp. 219–220; Gharibdjanian, *op. cit.*, pp. 285–286; Danielian, *op. cit.*, pp. 65–66, 72–74; *Revoliutsion kocher*, pp. 498–499. For a collection of articles and memoirs by men who participated in these activities, see *Spartak, 1917–1920: Husher ev vaveragrer*, publ. of Institut Istorii Partii pri TsK KP(b)A—Sektsiia Istmoa (Erevan, 1935).

[54] A society known as the Marxist Internationalist Student Circle had been formed in Erevan in April, 1917, and attempted to undermine the Dashnakist youth organization, Miutiun, which had a broad network throughout the Caucasus. In December of that year the Student Circle was renamed the Marxist Student Union, under the

in Tiflis participating in a conference of the Organization of Young Internationalists "Spartak" and there joined the faction that excluded most Menshevik delegates.[55] The conference strengthened its bonds with the regular Communist establishment by changing the society's name to Organization of Young Communists "Spartak," and, in a multilingual proclamation, summoned the youth of Transcaucasia to the Communist banner and the struggle against counterrevolution.[56] But Ghukasian's enthusiasm with the policies set down in Tiflis did not sway most of his Marxist student colleagues in Erevan. The non-Bolshevik majority of the Erevan chapter refused to sanction the realignment of the society and voted to uphold its original standard.[57] Undaunted, Ghukasian and his few supporters labored feverishly to publish a newspaper for distribution on May 1, the international labor holiday. Presently acclaimed by Soviet historians as the first, albeit somewhat unorthodox, organ of Armenia's revolutionary youth, the one and only issue of *Spartak* excoriated the nationality policy of the Erevan government and exhorted progressive young people to battle the "mauserist bandits" lurking under the cloak of officialdom. The vibrant articles never reached the youth of Armenia, however, for the Ministry of Interior, finally aroused to action, seized the entire printing. Nonetheless, punitive measures did not follow, and Ghukasian, turning once again to organizational matters, skillfully maneuvered the "Menshevik-oriented" members out of the Marxist student association and triumphantly emerged as the chairman of the Organiza-

---

presidency of Ghukas Ghukasian. The numerical weakness of the Marxist youth was demonstrated in the spring of 1918 when their resolution condemning the Armenian parties that recognized the Transcaucasian Commissariat and demanding the union of the Caucasus with the "people's democracy of Russia" was defeated by the All-Armenian Student Congress by a vote of 162 to 8. For a study of the organization and activities of the Erevan Marxist student groups during 1917 and 1918, see G. A. Avetisian, *Komsomol Zakavkaz'ia v bor'be za pobedu i uprochnenie Sovetskoi vlasti (1917-1921)* (Erevan, 1964), pp. 24-141.

[55] Tiflis and Baku were the centers of the student Marxists in the Caucasus. The Socialist Internationalist "Spartak" group had been organized in September, 1917, with an initial membership of from 15 to 25. The society was reactivated in November, 1918, with 13 persons attending the meeting. At the time of the Tiflis conference, the organization claimed a membership of from 90 to 150. Many members of the Tiflis cells were Armenian. See Avetisian, *op. cit.*, pp. 53-60, 83-86, 150, 458 n. 3.

[56] Danielian, *op. cit.*, pp. 44-47; Gharibdjanian, *op. cit.*, pp. 286-287; H. N. Karapetian, *op. cit.*, pp. 94-96; Avetisian, *op. cit.*, pp. 149-159. See also *Istoriia Kompartii Gruzii*, pp. 340-341.

[57] In an apparent compromise move to prevent an irreparable breach, the group did adopt the name Organization of Young Socialist-Internationalists "Spartak," the title used by the Tiflis Marxist circle when it had included both Mensheviks and Bolsheviks. See Avetisian, *op. cit.*, pp. 159-161; *Hayastani Komkusi patmutiun*, p. 281.

tion of Young Communists "Spartak," the first Communist youth group in Armenia.[58]

Despite the intensification of Bolshevik agitation and antagonism, the Armenian government continued to function throughout 1918–1919 as if the native Communists posed no serious threat. When Georgian and Azerbaijani security forces penetrated the underground Bolshevik centers and began a new wave of arrests, many Armenian Communists were shielded by Dashnakist groups in Baku and Tiflis and directed to sanctuary in Armenia. Among the first to benefit from this policy was Bagrat B. Gharibdjanian, a young but experienced party organizer who had been imprisoned during the Armeno-Georgian war and then expelled from the Georgian republic. In Alexandropol, Armenia's strategic railway juncture, Gharibdjanian revived the local cell and created new units in the railway depot and garages.[59] In March, 1919, the British command in Tiflis informed Premier Kachaznuni that a Communist circle in Alexandropol was spreading malicious propaganda and complained that the government, although earlier apprised of the situation through authorities in Alexandropol, had initiated no countermeasures. The British now demanded swift action to weed out the provocateurs. The order was ignored.[60] Three months later Gharibdjanian coordinated an illegal conference of the combined Bolshevik cells of Alexandropol. He described to the membership the program and tactic of the Russian Communist Party, but like Arshavir Melikian he said nothing to encourage an immediate armed uprising. The land was so backward and the work to be done so prodigious, he explained, that all energies must be martialed merely to enlighten the masses and to instill in them an awareness of the dangers posed by the enemies of the Soviet system.[61]

The influx of Communists was not only the result of oppression in neighboring lands. Having resolved to increase the tempo of party

[58] Barsegian, *Istoriia armianskoi pechati*, pp. 422–425; Elchibekian, *op. cit.*, p. 111; H. N. Karapetian, *op. cit.*, pp. 96–105; Danielian, *op. cit.*, pp. 59–68. Armenak Budaghian served as vice-president and Aghasi Khanjian acted as secretary of the Erevan Spartak organization, whose membership roster apparently numbered less than twenty in mid-1919. See Avetisian, *op. cit.*, pp. 161–162.

[59] See S. H. Melkonian, *Bagrat Gharibdjanian (1890–1920)* ([Erevan], 1954), pp. 125–128.

[60] *Velikaia Oktiabr'skaia revoliutsiia*, p. 263; Kadishev, *Interventsiia v Zakavkaz'e*, p. 174; Elchibekian, *op. cit.*, p. 95. The French representative in Armenia, Captain Antoine Poidebard, issued similar warnings to the Erevan government in January, 1919, according to Elchibekian, and to Gharibdjanian, *op. cit.*, pp. 268–269.

[61] Melkonian, *op. cit.*, pp. 128–130. See also B. Ohandjanian, *Egor Sevian* (Erevan, 1955), pp. 40–41; G. Galoyan, *Mayisian herosakan apstambutiune* (Erevan, 1960), p. 38; Gharibdjanian, *op. cit.*, p. 271.

activity throughout Transcaucasia, the Russian Central Committee and its Caucasus Regional Committee directed a number of veteran Bolsheviks to transfer to Armenia. This initial move of Communist agents was climaxed in July, 1919, with the arrival of two representatives of the Kraikom, Sargis H. [I.] Kasian and Askanaz A. Mravian. It was their assignment to tighten the party network in the Republic and to coordinate the labors of the scattered cells, which hitherto had largely been left to fend for themselves.[62]

With amazing indiscretion the Erevan government provided employment for many of the newcomers, some of whom were former Dashnakists or classmates of the Republic's leaders, and required in return only their pledge not to engage in subversive activity. The Kachaznuni and Khatisian cabinets permitted these unusual liberties in the hope that the Sovnarkom would reciprocate with a more tolerant attitude toward the Armenian national organizations still surviving in Russia and perhaps with the eventual acceptance of a non-Communist independent Armenian republic.[63] Although Armenia absorbed a steady trickle of Bolsheviks throughout the spring and summer of 1919, the party's membership remained distressingly thin. Soviet studies indicate that at most four hundred Communists, some non-Armenian, were operating in the Republic of Armenia in September.[64] A cadre existed; there remained the challenge to recruit and train a rank and file.

The "Armenian Communist Party"

Not until the summer of 1920 was the official Communist Party of Armenia formed, but there was as early as 1918 a group that claimed

[62] Aghayan, Hai zhoghovrdi azatagrume, pp. 217–218; H. S. Karapetian, op. cit., p. 85; Hayastani Komkusi patmutiun, pp. 280–281; Barseghian, Hayastani Kompartiayi kazmavorume, p. 263. For an account of Bolshevik activities in Armenia during the spring and early summer of 1919, see Gharibdjanian, op. cit., pp. 266–284. Avetisian, op. cit., pp. 166–235, describes the activities of the Spartakist youth, the future Komsomol, in the major centers of Transcaucasia in 1919.

[63] Ruben, op. cit., pp. 319–321; Shahan, Tiurkizm Angoraen Baku ev trkakan orientatsion (Athens, 1928), pp. 69–70; S. Vratzian, Hayastane bolshevikian murji ev trkakan sali midjev (Beirut, 1953), pp. 46–47.

[64] Gharibdjanian, op. cit., p. 300. Writing to Lenin, A. I. Mikoyan confirmed the frailty of revolutionary labors in Armenia. See the archival references in Lalabekian, op. cit., pp. 308–309. Soviet historians are not agreed on the question of whether a Bolshevik coup in Transcaucasia was feasible in 1919. For an introduction to the dispute, see P. S. Kol'tsov, P. A. Rodionov, S. V. Kharmandarian, and M. V. Tsertsvadze, "Iz istorii kommunisticheskikh organizatsii Zakavkaz'ia," Voprosy istorii KPSS, 6 (1962), 56–73.

the title. The historic role of this organization has elicited heated controversy among contemporary Soviet scholars. Attacked and discredited by the Communist hierarchy during the 1920's and largely ignored throughout the subsequent years of the Stalinist era, the so-called "Armenian Communist Party" (Hayastani Komunistakan Kusaktsutiun) was in the 1960's given belated recognition in histories of Soviet Armenia. The new generation Armenian historian, while faithfully enumerating the defects, errors, and opportunism of the "Armenian Communist Party," has come to assume a more measured view and now acknowledges its service, particularly in the dissemination of Marxist ideology among the Turkish Armenian refugee population.[65]

The "Armenian Communist Party" was an extraterritorial organization composed almost exclusively of Turkish Armenian intellectuals, some of whom held concurrent membership in the Russian Social Democrat Bolshevik (subsequently Russian Communist) party. At the beginning of 1918 in Tiflis, this circle of Marxists, exhilarated by the Sovnarkom's decree advocating freedom and self-determination for Turkish Armenia, announced the creation of the "Armenian Communist Party." The primary goal of the association was to assist in the implementation of the decree on Turkish Armenia and to safeguard the future of the surviving Armenian population by closing ranks with the world proletariat and Soviet Russia. Gurgen Haikuni, a central figure among these Turkish Armenian "Communists," appeared before the Russian Bolshevik Central Committee, then still in Petrograd, and secured quasi recognition for his party. The manifesto of the organization indicated that its field of operation would lie beyond the prewar Russo-Turkish border, in the eastern vilayets of the Ottoman Empire. The term "Armenia," as understood at the beginning of 1918, referred to Turkish Armenia; no separate Armenian state in Transcaucasia had yet been established. This factor might account for the decision of the Russian Central Committee to authorize the "Armenian Communist Party" to function independently of the Caucasus Regional Committee, much to the chagrin of the latter.[66]

During its brief existence in Tiflis the "Armenian Communist Party" campaigned to reveal to the Armenian masses the promises of Marx-

[65] The most useful study to date of the "Armenian Communist Party" is that of Barseghian, *Hayastani Kompartiayi kazmavorume*, especially pp. 195-247. A bibliographical note on the controversy relating to this subject is given by Barseghian, p. 197.

[66] *Hayastani Komkusi patmutiun*, pp. 261-262; Barseghian, *Hayastani Kompartiayi kazmavorume*, pp. 210-216; B. A. Borian, *Armeniia, mezhdunarodnaia diplomatiia i SSSR*, Vol. II (Moscow and Leningrad, 1929), pp. 94-95.

ism and to enlist converts to the cause. An official organ, *Karmir orer* ("Red Days"), was published in March, 1918, and although soon suppressed by the Mensheviks reappeared in April as *Karmir droshak* ("Red Banner").[67] Nevertheless, efforts to swell the ranks of the party proved disappointing; its records show a membership of less than one hundred. In May of 1918 the group was subjected to direct persecution and had to scatter into the North Caucasus, thus bringing organizational activity temporarily to a halt.[68]

By the beginning of 1919 most of the party's leaders had moved on to Moscow, where they found employment in the Armenian Affairs Commissariat. Befriended and encouraged by Varlam Avanesov, Gurgen Haikuni eventually replaced Vahan Terian as assistant director of the Commissariat[69] and succeeded in persuading the Russian Central Committee that the "Armenian Communist Party" had unlimited potential, including the means to extend revolutionary propaganda into the heartlands of Turkey. He claimed that a number of cells were already operating in South Russia and the North Caucasus. Haikuni's critics have charged that these and subsequent reports were deliberately falsified, that the party was a paper organization, and that its principal spokesman was an "opportunist," seeking personal glory and gain.[70]

These accusations notwithstanding, Haikuni enjoyed the singular honor of attending the inaugural congress of the Third International, the Comintern, as delegate of the Armenian party.[71] Moreover, like

[67] Barsegian, *Istoriia armianskoi pechati*, pp. 253–254.

[68] Barseghian, *Hayastani Kompartiayi kazmavorume*, pp. 220–221. In his memoirs, the Armenian partisan leader Sebouh describes his encounters with Gurgen Haikuni while both were in the North Caucasus in 1919. See Sebouh, *Edjer im husheren*, Vol. II (Boston, 1929), pp. 259–292 *passim*.

[69] Terian was embittered by what he characterized as an invasion of opportunists into the Armenian Affairs Commissariat. In May of 1919 he wrote the Central Committee of the "Armenian Communist Party," announcing his resignation from both the party and the central committee and berating the "*chinovnik*-bureaucratic ways" the party leadership had adopted. He protested his being cast aside at "personal whims" to make room for adventurers such as Gurgen Haikuni—men, he said, who knew no language other than Armenian and who had absolutely no Marxist preparation. See Barseghian, *Hayastani Kompartiayi kazmavorume*, p. 221.

[70] See, for example, A. Mravian, *Erb ev inchpes e himnvel Hayastani Komunistakan (bolsh.) Kusaktsutiune?* (Erevan, 1928); Borian, *op. cit.*, pp. 24–26, 94–95. See also Barseghian, *Hayastani Kompartiayi kazmavorume*, pp. 197–203.

[71] For materials on the establishment of the Third International, see James Hulse, *The Formation of the Communist International* (Stanford, 1964); Leon Trotsky, *The First Five Years of the Communist International*, Vol. I (New York, [1945]), pp. 1–30; F. Borkenau, *The Communist International* (London, 1938); Edward Hallett Carr, *The Bolshevik Revolution, 1917–1923*, Vol. III (London, 1953), pp. 116–126, 567–570; Julius Braunthal, *Geschichte der Internationale*, Vol. II (Hannover, [1963]), pp. 180–

the delegates from established parties abroad, he was given full voting privileges in contrast with the advisory, nonvoting capacity in which the Georgian, Azerbaijani, and several other representatives participated. At a time when the Paris Peace Conference was disposed to unify Turkish Armenia and Russian Armenia under a mandatory power, the Russian Communist strategists apparently considered it expedient to recognize the separate existence of the "Armenian Communist Party." [72] The agility of Haikuni in securing a creditable position for himself and his organization in the Communist International vexed his Bolshevik rivals and the regular party machinery in Transcaucasia, but current Soviet Armenian authors assign much significance to the inclusion of an Armenian Communist group in the historic congress.[73] They voice a certain pride that an Armenian society was one of the seventeen sponsoring parties whose names were affixed to the manifesto of the First Comintern Congress, a manifesto that has been widely publicized, translated, and quoted.[74]

The need for an international Communist body had been stressed by Lenin immediately after his return to Russia in 1917, but the direct impetus for its formation in March of 1919 seems to have been the attempt of non-Bolshevik socialist leaders to revive the Second Inter-

186; C. D. H. Cole, *A History of Socialist Thought,* Vol. IV, pt. 1: *Communism and Social Democracy, 1914–1931* (London, 1958), pp. 298–322; K. S. Trofimov, "Lenin i osnovanie Kommunisticheskogo internatsionala," *Voprosy istorii KPSS,* 4 (1957), 28–48.

[72] Partial records of the First Comintern Congress are in the following publications: *Der I. Kongress der Kommunistischen Internationale: Protokoll der Verhandlungen in Moskau vom 2. bis zum 19. März 1919* (Hamburg, 1920); *Manifest, Richtlinien, Beschlüsse des Ersten Kongresses: Aufrufe und offene Schreiben des Exekutivkomitees bis zum Zweiten Kongress* (Hamburg, 1920), pp. 3–73; *Pervyi kongress Kominterna, mart 1919 g.,* ed. E. Korotkov, B. Kun, and O. Piatnitskov, publ. of Institut Marksa-Engel'sa-Lenina (Moscow, 1933). The roster of delegates, both those with full voting privileges and those with consultive voice only, is given in *Der I. Kongress,* pp. 4–5, and in *Pervyi kongress,* pp. 250–251. Unlike the Armenian delegate, the Georgian and Azerbaijani representatives were placed under the Comintern's Central Bureau of Eastern Peoples.

[73] Former Premier Nikita S. Khrushchev officially sanctioned this trend in 1961 when, on the occasion of the fortieth anniversary of the Sovietization of Armenia, he declared in Erevan: "The Armenian people can be proud of the fact that Armenian Communists participated in the creation of the Communist International." See N. S. Khrushchev, *Jar Erevan kaghakum teghi unetsads handisavor nistum, nvirvads Hayastanum Sovetakan ishkhanutian hastatman ev Hayastani Komunistakan partiayi kazmavorman 40-amiakin* (Erevan, 1961), pp. 6–7.

[74] For an English translation of the manifesto, see Jane Degras, ed., *The Communist International, 1919–1943: Documents,* Vol. I (London, New York, and Toronto, 1956), pp. 38–47. The manifesto is carefully analyzed by Cole, *op. cit.,* pp. 305–318. For the original German publication of the document, see *Manifest, Richtlinien, Beschlüsse des Ersten Kongresses,* pp. 3–18.

national. Indeed, the Third International convened in Moscow just one month after the socialist-laborite Berne Conference had adjourned.[75] The First Congress of the Comintern, besides laying the foundations for worldwide Communist collaboration, heard reports from the various delegations on party activities in their respective lands (although many delegates attending the Congress lived in Russia as exiles from those lands). When his turn arrived, Gurgen Haikuni relishing the role of orator vented forth the vitriolic epithets so characteristic of the early brazen style of many crusading Communists. The bourgeois-nationalist parties of Transcaucasia, cried Haikuni, were "sons of bitches" and "procurers" who warped the principle of self-determination in their schemes to splinter the world and forestall the class struggle by turning one people against another. "National independence," he maintained, was the latest perfidy of the counterrevolutionaries, who would embrace anyone, "the devil included," to destroy Bolshevism. The Armenian bourgeoisie and the Tatar Musavatist beks, "sucking the blood of the peasantry," plotted together to further their policy of divide and rule. They were snakes who had groveled at the feet of the Turkish and German imperialists. And what of Dashnaktsutiun? That rabble had flung itself into whoredom. "Dashnaktsutiun is a beggar and its organ, *Haradj*, licks the crumbs of the Armenian bourgeoisie in an attempt to save 800,000 Armenians from starvation." The Armenian nationalist coterie represented in the "Berne yellow so-called socialist international" was guilty of dipping its hands in the blood of thousands of workers, but it was a depraved general without soldiers. And what of the "Republic of Armenia?" It was a "mocking insult to the workers and villagers," a land where the bourgeoisie and the clergy determined what was self-determination. "The Armenian government is a pack of bandits; the ministers have risen from the dregs of society. We will rid ourselves of all these foul dogs!" The "Armenian Communist Party," the single true representative of the peasants and workers, would struggle, Haikuni promised, until Armenia had been freed, the bourgeoisie extirpated, and the imperialist-interventionists expelled.[76]

[75] See pp. 348–352, above.

[76] *Hayastani Komunistakan kusaktsutian nerkayatsutsichi zekutsume errord Komunistakan Internatsionalin* (Moscow, 1919). A considerably less colorful version of Haikuni's speech was published in *Pravda*, March 11, 1919, pp. 1–2; and in *Pervyi kongress Kominterna*, pp. 235–241. Immediately after the First Comintern Congress, Haikuni and Terian attended the VIII Congress of the Russian Communist Party, there intimating that they represented 10,000 members of the "Armenian Communist Party." See *Vos'moi s"ezd RKP/b/*, pp. 457, 472; *Hayastani Komkusi patmutiun*, p. 262.

The existence of an extraterritorial organization claiming jurisdiction over an undetermined number of Armenian Bolsheviks in Russia and the Caucasus was greeted with utmost hostility by the Caucasus Regional Committee and the advocates of a multinational party structure. To rising young leaders such as Anastas Mikoyan, the "Armenian Communist Party" smacked of nationalist deviation (although Mikoyan himself subsequently advocated national-territorial Communist parties). In May of 1918 the Caucasus Regional Committee, Kraikom, laid its complaints before Lenin, indicting Haikuni's group for spreading confusion among the Armenian Bolsheviks. Operating with free rein and without regard to or respect for the Kraikom, the "Armenian Communist Party" was fostering division and undoing the long, painful labors to create a pan-Caucasian organization. The Armenian workers, the Kraikom warned, were being dangerously drawn into isolation from the Russian Social Democrat Labor (Bolshevik) Party.[77]

The dispute flared anew and with greater intensity in 1919. The Regional Committee heaped derision upon Haikuni and demanded a clarification of the relationship between the "Armenian Communist Party" on the one hand and the Kraikom and the Russian Communist Party on the other. But Haikuni had garnered the patronage of influential Armenian Bolsheviks in Moscow. The Armenian Affairs Commissariat stressed the need for agitation among the refugee population and declared that the "Armenian Communist Party" was best equipped for that assignment.[78] This endorsement was sufficient to convince the Russian Central Committee to allocate large sums of money to Haikuni for concentrated activity in the Armenian refugee centers in Russia. In August of 1919 Elena D. Stasova, the secretary of the Russian Central Committee, wrote the Caucasus Kraikom that the "Armenian Communist Party" had been authorized to send agents to Armenia to expand the struggle against Dashnaktsutiun [79] This news indicated that the extraterritorial organization had digressed radically from its original purpose of working in Turkish Armenia and was entering a realm that logically should belong to the Kraikom.

By the middle of 1920, however, the original "Armenian Communist Party" had fallen into disrepute and inactivity and the Russian mother organization had come to depend on a new group, the Communist

[77] Barseghian, *Hayastani Kompartiayi kazmavorume*, pp. 230–232.

[78] For an account of Haikuni's role in the Armenian Affairs Commissariat and the strife within that sector of the Commissariat for Nationalities, see Darbinian, "Memoirs" (Summer, 1948), pp. 40–41.

[79] *Bor'ba v Azerbaidzhane*, pp. 257–258; Zhvaniia, *op. cit.*, p. 223; Barseghian, *Hayastani Kompartiayi kazmavorume*, pp. 232–237.

Party of Armenia. The circumstances surrounding the demise of Haĭkuni's faction are a source of disagreement and contradiction. According to earlier accounts the Orgburo of the Russian Central Committee decreed in July, 1919, that the "Armenian Communist Party" must submit to the jurisdiction of its bitter rival, the Caucasus Regional Committee. In September there followed a directive for the "Party" to terminate its extraterritorial status by transferring and confining its activities to the "so-called Armenian republic." The command was tantamount to a death sentence, since whatever influence the "Armenian Communist Party" might have had was limited to Russia and the North Caucasus.[80] The "Party" proved incapable of establishing a base of operation in Transcaucasia and, with the formation and recognition of the regular Communist Party of Armenia, faded from the scene.[81]

The fullest study to date shows that the lot of the "Armenian Communist Party" was not settled quite so decisively and that even as late as 1920 the Russian Communist ruling bodies were beset by ambivalence. When the Caucasus Kraikom dispatched Anastas Mikoyan to Moscow in October, 1919, to expose the incalculable damage wrought by the existence of the "Armenian Communist Party," the Central Committee saw fit to grant a hearing to Haikuni and his ardent supporter, Varlam Avanesov. Throughout November and December of 1919 the Orgburo and the Politburo, individually and in joint session, grappled with the problem. Finally on December 20 the Politburo adjudged it imperative that a Communist party subject to the Caucasus Regional Committee operate as a territorial organization within the Armenian republic. Even though this decision undermined the "Armenian Communist Party," the Politburo, over the vociferous protests of the Kraikom, allowed Haikuni to present his draft plan for a party structure in Armenia, and the Orgburo, in confirming a new central committee of Haikuni's faction, thereby continued to grant it recognition.[82]

The top echelon of the Communist hierarchy continued to create loopholes and from the available records of the correspondence exchanged among the several involved bodies during the first half of 1920 it would appear that the issue was never resolved with finality. In that interim the Caucasus Regional Committee and the "Armenian

[80] See, for example, Mnatsakanian, *V. I. Lenin*, pp. 363–364.

[81] The formation of the Communist Party of Armenia will be discussed in the second volume of this history.

[82] Barseghian, *Hayastani Kompartiayi kazmavorume*, pp. 237–243. See also Mnatsakanian, *V. I. Lenin*, pp. 363–364.

Communist Party" lashed out at each other with acerbic denunciations and vied for the favor of the Russian Central Committee. The latest evidence gives grounds to conclude that the "Armenian Communist Party" was never pointedly ordered to dissolve. As late as July, 1920, the mother organization consented to take under advisement certain proposals put forward by Haikuni, although it did again instruct his group to submit to the Kraikom as long as that regional body existed.[83] Meanwhile, the Communist cadre in Armenia struck out on a distinct path and filled the void which Haikuni could do only on paper. It was to the men on the spot that the reins of Armenian government would ultimately fall. Thus, in whatever way, the original "Armenian Communist Party" passed into history, its ghost destined to emerge in the post-Stalinist era to challenge and to tempt the new-generation Soviet scholar.

By mid-1919 it should have been clear to the Armenian government that hopes for a working arrangement with Soviet Russia and with the Communist party were illusive. The Armenian envoys to Moscow had failed in attempts to gain Soviet recognition of the Armenian republic or to bridge the chasm separating Dashnaktsutiun and Bolshevism. On the contrary, relations had progressively deteriorated. The Sovnarkom imprisoned Armenian leaders and suppressed Armenian national societies, their assets forever lost. Spurring the discord between Moscow and Erevan were the Commissar for Nationalities and his Armenian deputies. The Armenian Bolsheviks were determined that, with the aid and intervention of Soviet Russia, they would one day rise supreme in Erevan.

[83] Barseghian, *Hayastani Kompartiayi kazmavorume*, pp. 237–243. According to *Hayastani Komkusi patmutiun*, p. 283, the "Armenian Communist Party" ceased to function after the Politburo approved, in January, 1920, the formation of distinct party units in the Transcaucasian states. The evidence presented by Barseghian is, however, more convincing.

13

On Anatolian
Highlands

The creation of an independent Armenian state on the borders of the Ottoman Empire raised many new questions regarding the future of Armeno-Turkish relations. The Armenian government undoubtedly recognized the need to dispel the intense hatred and bitterness directed toward the masters of more than four hundred years. The perpetuation of old grievances could in no way serve the Republic. Turks and Armenians, Muslims and Christians were destined to live as neighbors, whether as friends or as enemies. Yet, Armenia would not be able to rise above the past until recompense had been made and the great plateau of eastern Anatolia restored to her. The lasting tragedy of the situation, however, was that the leaders of the Turkish resistance deemed the eastern vilayets equally vital to the future of their people. The nascent Turkish Nationalist movement took root in the heart of Turkish Armenia and was nurtured by the sheer determination to entomb all Armenian pretensions to the lands extending from Sivas and Erzerum to Mush and Van and from Trebizond and Alashkert to Kharput and Diarbekir. The realization of that goal was in part contingent upon the support of an audacious external power. The Turkish partisans discovered Soviet Russia to be that force.

Turkey and Armenia

Defeated, demoralized, and partially occupied, Turkey in 1919 still aroused deep fears in Armenia. Even in a crippled condition, the Ottoman Empire was far more formidable and organized than the Republic of Armenia. In 1918 Enver Pasha had directed his finest divisions toward Caucasia, and thousands of these soldiers remained mobilized in the eastern vilayets after the war. Moreover, the lure of Turkey and the influence of Turkish officials and agents were strongly felt in Azerbaijan, in the North Caucasus, and among the Muslim inhabitants of the Armenian republic itself. In retrospect, it is clear that Armenia should have probed every available avenue for an understanding with her bruised neighbor to the west; but in reality the obstacles were too many and too great. Not only was the Turk despised as the historic oppressor and of late the butcher of half the nation but, on a more objective plane, the Armenian question had become an international issue, its solution seemingly dependent more on decisions reached in Europe than in either Constantinople or Erevan. The Allied Powers, having occupied the forts of the Dardanelles and the strategic coastal points from the Bosporus to the Caucasus, had repeatedly indicated that Russian Armenia and Turkish Armenia, perhaps Cilicia too, would be combined into a separate, self-governing state. Thus, even if bilateral Armeno-Turkish negotiations had been feasible in 1919, Erevan could not but have viewed them as superfluous and most untimely.

Those historians who have criticized the Armenian government for not having attempted a direct settlement with Turkey have failed to consider another factor. With which Turkey was it that Armenia was to negotiate—the Sultan's cabinet in Constantinople or the emerging Nationalist organization in Anatolia? Had Armenia been so farsighted as to have sought an agreement with the latter, would not such action have been a betrayal of the very Allied Powers that had defeated Turkey and pledged themselves to guarantee the future of the Armenians? As evidenced by the many desperate appeals to Paris in 1919, Armenia was immediately alert to the menace posed by the resistance movement in Turkey, but no one could at that time believe that the Nationalist groups would humble the Allies and bring them to sacrifice Armenia. On the other hand, if Armenia had entered into parleys with the Sultan's tottering regime in Constantinople, could the resistance leaders have been expected to accept a settlement thus achieved? The fact is that an accord between Constantinople and Erevan would have prompted the Nationalists to greater belligerence unless, of course, Armenia had been willing to abandon her claims to the eastern vilayets and possibly even to the province of Kars. But above all, Armenia in 1919 could trust neither Sultanate Turkey nor Nationalist Turkey. The near-mortal wounds inflicted by the massacres of 1915–1916, the Ottoman violation of the Erzinjan truce of 1917, and the invasion of Transcaucasia in 1918 were fresh and unhealed. It was not blind faith in the Allies but political exigency that led the Armenian government to avoid direct relations with Turkey. In Constantinople, Chargé d'affaires Ferdinand Tahtadjian acted as an envoy, not to Turkey, but to the Allied High Commissioners and military authorities ensconced in the Ottoman capital.

Only a handful of Armenian leaders, among them Dashnakist Ruben Ter-Minasian and Social Revolutionary Vahan Minakhorian, argued in favor of a bilateral settlement, but by their own admission it was instinct rather than logic that moved them. Turkey, they hoped, might assent to the expansion of the Armenian republic to include the easternmost vilayets of Turkish Armenia. Such a homeland, though modest in size, would allow for the rapid establishment of an Armenian majority and would seal the potential arteries of collusion between Turkey and Azerbaijan.[1] Minakhorian further asserted that the major source of Armeno-Turkish antipathy had sprung from the machinations of imperialist powers; the Ottoman Empire had reacted to the threat of domination by Europe with oppression and massacres of the Armenians. Now, however, the time had come for Armenia to cry out against the dismemberment of Turkey and to shatter the fantasy of the vast Armenian state to which Boghos Nubar Pasha and his associates aspired. Every true socialist, Minakhorian insisted, should strive for the creation of an Armenia embracing Russian Armenia and only the three eastern vilayets—Erzerum, Bitlis, and Van. This limited Armenia should then federate with the peoples of a "free and democratic Russia."[2] Given the hopes and illusions of 1919, the Armenian leadership and public alike viewed the solution posited by Minakhorian as absurd and senseless abnegation. No one seemed to consider the possibility that this very solution might be regarded as preposterous fatuity by the commanders in Turkey.

With the signing of the Mudros Armistice, the dispirited official Turkish government realized that the Ottoman Empire would suffer many losses and that concessions to the Armenians would be required. Yet, in an attempt to absolve the Turkish nation from responsibility for the Armenian massacres, the Ottoman Parliament pointed the finger of blame at the Committee of Union and Progress, in particular those Ittihadists who had already fled the country. And on December 6, 1918, Sultan Mehmed VI (Vahiddedin) added that he mourned the sufferings inflicted upon the Armenian people by "certain political committees in Turkey." The brother of Abdul-Hamid II continued: "Such misdeeds

[1] Ruben [Ter-Minasian], *Hai heghapokhakani me hishataknere*, Vol. VII (Los Angeles, 1952), pp. 250–254.
[2] Vahan Minakhorian, *Tragediia Turtsii* ([Baku], 1919).

and the mutual slaughter of sons of the same fatherland have broken my heart. I ordered an inquiry as soon as I came to the throne so that the fomenters might be severely punished, but various factors prevented my orders from being carried out. The matter is now being thoroughly investigated. Justice will soon be done and we will never have a repetition of these ugly events." [3]

At the end of 1918, after the Allied fleet had cast anchor in the Golden Horn, the Sultan called for a probe into the Armenian massacres, and the new Ottoman Council of Ministers created ten regional teams to take on-the-spot depositions. Legal proceedings against accused criminals were to be undertaken by the Ministry of Interior and the Ministry of Justice.[4] Warrants were issued for the arrest of the Ittihadist leaders, but most had already escaped to Germany, the Caucasus, Russia, or the remoter Anatolian provinces. A rather large number of lesser party officials were apprehended, as were the pashas who had commanded on the eastern front: Mehmed Vehib, Ali Ihsan, Halil, and subsequently Yakub Shevki and Nuri.[5] Mehmed Ali Pasha, the envoy to Armenia from June to December, 1918, committed suicide.[6]

After repeated delays the Ottoman military tribunals began hearings and legal action against the indicted offenders, but few were convicted. Allied civilian and military representatives in Constantinople and Armenian organizations abroad loudly protested that the whole affair was a sham, that punishment would not be forthcoming, and that the Ottoman tactic was clearly one of evasion and procrastination.[7] American Commissioner Lewis Heck characterized the litigation as progressing in

[3] *Current History*, IX, pt. 2 (Jan., 1919), 92–93; M. Tayyib Gökbilgin, *Millî mücadele başlarken: Mondros mütarakesinden Sivas Kongresine*, Vol. I (Ankara, 1959), p. 15.

[4] Cemal Kutay, *Millî mücadelede öncekiler ve sonrakiler* (Istanbul, [1963]), p. 58; Gökbilgin, *op. cit.*, pp. 15–16, 40; *Hairenik* (daily), March 6, 1919, p. 2, and April 4, p. 3.

[5] US Archives, RG 256, 867.00/76; London *Times*, Jan. 23, 1919, p. 10, and May 3, p. 11; *Le Temps*, Feb. 15, 1919, p. 2; *Hairenik* (daily), March 21, 1919, p. 3, and May 20, p. 3; Gökbilgin, *op. cit.*, pp. 36–40. For a list and description of the military commanders arrested in 1919, see Tevfik Bıyıklıoğlu, *Atatürk Anadolu'da (1919–1921)*, Vol. I (Ankara, 1959), pp. 33–34; and Hüsameddin Ertürk, *İki devrin perde arkası*, comp. by Samih Nafiz Tansu (Instanbul, 1964), pp. 202–203, 205–207, 323, 325–328.

[6] *Hairenik* (daily), April 22, 1919, p. 2.

[7] London *Times*, Jan. 13, 1919, p. 7, Feb. 10, p. 8, and May 11, p. 11; *Hairenik* (daily), Feb. 14, 1919, p. 3, and April 19, p. 4; US Archives, RG 256, 867.00/59; Laurence Evans, *United States Policy and the Partition of Turkey, 1914–1924* (Baltimore, [1965]), p. 171. Numerous documents relating to the organization of the Armenian massacres, the role of specific Turkish officials in executing the orders to deport and to massacre, and the postwar charges and proceedings against those officials are deposited in the British archives. See especially FO 371/4172–4173, File

a "characteristically dilatory Turkish fashion." [8] In April of 1919, under strong inter-Allied pressure, several prominent Ittihadists were at last arraigned, but the results were disappointing and in May the British military authorities transferred them and other Young Turk prisoners to Malta "owing to the delay in the judicial proceedings begun against them." [9] Eventually, Enver Pasha, Talaat Pasha, and Jemal Pasha, the Ittihadist triumvirate of World War I, were put on trial and in mid-July sentenced to death in absentia.[10] They had, however, slipped beyond the jurisdiction of Damad Ferid's cabinet, which made no serious effort to have them or other convicted Ittihadists extradited from their European sanctuaries. Few of those who had plotted the Armenian genocide or carried the project to near total fulfillment were meted justice. Enforcement of the verdict against the principal Young Turk criminals was left to the hand of individual revenge-driven Armenians.[11]

1270/44; FO 608/109, File 385/1/4; FO 608/113, File 385/1/18; and FO 608/247, File 1809/1/1.

[8] US Archives, RG 256, 867.00/81 and 867.4016/8.

[9] *Christian Science Monitor*, June 10, 1919, p. 1. See also Gotthard Jäschke, "Beiträge zur Geschichte des Kampfes der Türkei um ihre Unabhängigkeit," *Die Welt des Islams*, n.s., V, 1–2 (1957), 17, cited hereafter as "Beiträge."

[10] *Current History*, X, pt. 2 (Aug., 1919), 247, gives July 14 as the date of the sentencing. Cemal Kutay, *Atatürk-Enver Paşa hadiseleri* (Istanbul, [1956]), p. 24, states that the Ittihadist leaders were condemned on July 13. According to Jäschke, "Beiträge," p. 17, and A. A. Cruickshank, "The Young Turk Challenge in Postwar Turkey," *Middle East Journal*, XXII (Winter, 1968), 17n, the "principal culprits" were sentenced on July 5. Enver Pasha and Jemal Pasha had been courtmartialed and dismissed from the Ottoman army on January 1, 1919. See Bernard Lewis, *The Emergence of Modern Turkey* (London, New York, and Toronto, 1961), p. 235; Gotthard Jäschke and Erich Pritsch, "Die Türkei seit dem Weltkriege: Geschichtskalender 1918–1928," *Die Welt des Islams*, X (1927/1929), 10; Britain, FO 608/113, File 385/1/17.

[11] The Ittihadist triumvirate as well as several fellow members of the erstwhile Ittihadist central committee met a violent death before the end of 1922. On March 15, 1921, Talaat Pasha was assassinated on the streets of Berlin by Soghomon Tehlirian. On December 6 of that year, former Ottoman Foreign Minister Said Halim was struck down in Rome by Arshavir Shirakian. On April 17, 1922, Dr. Behaeddin Shakir and Jemal Azmi were felled in Berlin by Aram Erkanian and Arshavir Shirakian. On July 25 of the same year, Jemal Pasha was killed in front of Cheka headquarters in Tiflis by Petros Ter-Poghosian and Artashes Gevorgian. Less than two weeks later, on August 4, 1922, Enver Pasha, having become estranged from the Moscow government and now leading the Muslim Basmachis of Central Asia against the Red Army, was caught in ambush and killed. There have been highly speculative reports that the Soviet agent who fired the fatal shot was an Armenian. The trial of Soghomon Tehlirian in Berlin drew worldwide attention in mid-1921. The counsel for the defense submitted documents establishing Talaat as a prime author of the Armenian massacres and entered into the record the testimony of numerous European eyewitnesses to those sad events. Tehlirian's acquittal by the German jury was hailed throughout the Western world.

Memoranda

During the months following the end of the World War, both official and unofficial Turkish circles in Constantinople and several European cities invoked Wilsonian principles to plead for the unity and integrity of the Ottoman Empire. In a rash of pamphlet literature and memoranda, these groups, operating under a variety of party and organizational names, claimed that for centuries the predominant ethnic-religious element in the eastern provinces had been Muslim. They insisted that at the turn of the century fewer than 650,000 Armenians had inhabited those lands as compared with more than 3,000,000 Turks and Kurds.[12] The Ottoman rulers, one of the tracts asserted, had treated the Armenian minority charitably until Russia and the other European Powers had become involved in the domestic affairs of the empire. The Armenians had then fallen under the accursed spell of the revolutionary Hnchakist and Dashnakist political committees and had schemed as a man to reestablish an independent state: "The Armenian people had been welded by its leaders into a compact mass unanimously resolved upon profiting by the first favorable concourse of circumstances to establish for the benefit of their race an independent Armenia in the Eastern Anatolia which they stubbornly claimed as their patrimony in spite of the flat contradictions of history and statistics." It was true, the treatise continued, that Abdul-Hamid and the Young Turks had responded with lamentable, repressive measures, but "the exigencies of war know no law," and although the Ittihadist authorities who had exceeded all bounds in perpetrating the massacres of the Armenians could not be exonerated, the world should not forget that "today there are as many Turkish widows and orphans thrown helpless and starving on the world as Armenian; as many grief-stricken hearths; as many victims of outrage and cruelty—mostly the result of Armenian savagery!"[13]

The Sublime Porte presented its own views on the Armenian question in a memorandum of February 12, 1919, informing the American, British, French, and Italian Commissioners in Constantinople that nearly 80 percent of the inhabitants in the six eastern vilayets were Muslims, "the Armenians being everywhere in a small minority." The

---

[12] Gökbilgen, op. cit., pp. 28–29. See also US Archives, RG 256, 867.00/8/18; Les Turcs et les revendications arméniennes (Paris, 1919); Kara Schemsi [R. S. Atabinen], Turcs et Arméniens devant l'histoire (Geneva, 1919); Ahmet Cevat Emre, İki neslin tarihi: Mustafa Kemal neler yaptı ([Istanbul], 1960), pp. 225–226.

[13] [Millî Kongre], The Turco-Armenian Question: The Turkish Point of View (Constantinople, 1919).

memorandum revealed the government's intent to prosecute those Turks guilty of wartime crimes, but it also urged that an international tribunal be formed to judge the responsibility of the Armenian bands that "massacred more than one million Mohammedans previous to the measure of deportation and especially after the Eastern provinces had been overrun by the armies of the Tzar." The solution of the so-called Armenian question, the Turkish document continued, did not lie in the creation of an Armenian state extending from the Caucasus to Cilicia, for this would subjugate more than five million Muslims to a few hundred thousand Armenians and would with the utmost certainty unleash bloody strife. At a time when it seemed definite that the eastern vilayets would be severed from the Ottoman Empire, the Sublime Porte proposed two compromise arrangements:

1. To leave the entire region under Ottoman sovereignty, with permission for Armenian refugees to return to their homes in the assurance that their rights would be fully guaranteed.

2. To expand the boundaries of the existing Armenian republic enough to settle the Armenian refugees who were in the Caucasus and the sanjak of Zor (Syria), with an international commission to determine the number of survivors and the measure of land to be awarded the Armenian republic.[14]

The Sublime Porte apparently reasoned that the adoption of either alternative would keep territorial losses at a minimum, for even if the borders were drawn according to the number of surviving refugees, the resultant Armenian state would at most extend only into the easternmost districts of the Van and Erzerum vilayets. It was some four months after the publication of the Ottoman memorandum that Grand Vizier Damad Ferid Pasha was permitted to address the Council of Ten in Paris, and, while he was ostensibly no longer willing to suggest a cession of territory to Armenia, he did make a tangential reference to a readjustment of the frontier. In view of the scathing rebuttal issued by the Peace Conference, it is not surprising that the Armenian government should have scoffed at any "compromise" that would fix the boundary by counting refugees.[15]

The Armenian exposition on the Ottoman statement of February 12 was equally grandiloquent. Only the Turks, it began, could be so

[14] *Memorandum of the Sublime Porte Communicated to the American, British, French and Italian High Commissioners on the 12th February 1919* (Constantinople, 1919). See also Sabahattin Selek, *Milli mücadele: Anadolu ihtilâli* (2 vols.; Istanbul, 1963–1965), I, 50–52; Esat Uras, *Tarihte Ermeniler ve Ermeni Meselesi* (Ankara, 1960), pp. 677–684. Britain, FO 608/110, 385/1/8/6346.
[15] See pp. 330–334 above.

shameless as to term the massacre of more than a million Armenians "regrettable incidents" committed by "certain Moslem agents." The traditional, cunning modus operandi had once again been brandished in a maneuver to deceive the West. The Turkish population statistics were incomplete, inaccurate, and falsified, for in truth an Armeno-Christian majority had prevailed in the eastern vilayets until the Turks had embarked on a policy of extermination under cover of the World War. The bitterest irony of the Ottoman memorandum, however, was the impudence with which the Sublime Porte accused the Armenians, after all that had happened, of sedition and the annihilation of a million Muslims. Who else but the Turks could so contrive to obscure their crimes by ascribing them to their victims! The Armenian reply expressed confidence that the Allies would not reward with inaction the odious Ottoman transgressions against mankind and concluded by declaring that Armenia would never remain within the Ottoman Empire and by demanding that the Armenian patrimony not be diminished as the result of Turkish barbarity.[16]

The Armenian reaction to the Ottoman memorandum has been cited by at least one scholar as evidence that "the Dashnaks were not really interested in settling their conflict with Turkey. . . ."[17] This appraisal unfortunately fails to take into account the status of the Armenian question in 1919 and the inability of Armenia to regard the Turkish tactic as anything but a desperate attempt to retain as much of Turkish Armenia as possible. On the other hand, it assumes, in spite of the fact that the memorandum of February 12 called for continued Ottoman suzerainty even in the Arab provinces, that the Ottoman gesture was motivated by a certain bona fide desire to reach an equitable settlement. To represent the memorandum as a Turkish peace overture that was spurned by a disingenuous Armenian leadership is to render a harsh and untenable judgment.

The Genesis of Resistance and Kiazim Karabekir Pasha

Soon after the Mudros Armistice, Turkish nationalists, faced with the likelihood of an end to Ottoman domination in the Arab provinces, Cilicia, the eastern vilayets, the Aegean coastal regions, and perhaps even Constantinople and the Straits, began an irregular—later well

[16] *Réponse au mémoire de la Sublime-Porte en date 12 février 1919* (Constantinople, 1919).
[17] Kazemzadeh, *Transcaucasia*, p. 214.

coordinated—campaign to preserve the integrity of the empire. The initial stirrings came from the administrative and military bureaucracy, which at the same time feigned subservience to the Allied Commissioners in Constantinople. In December of 1918, members of the Ottoman General Staff and Foreign Ministry were instrumental in the formation of the Association for the Defense of the Rights of the Eastern Vilayets, and the government channeled to it 50,000 liras for propaganda purposes, in particular to convince the Allied Powers that so-called Turkish Armenia was not and had never been an Armenian population center.[18] A leader of the Association, Suleiman Nazif Bey, declared that the fundamental rights of the Muslim majority as well as of the non-Armenian Christians would be brazenly profaned should a mere 600,000 Armenians be allowed to rule over the eastern vilayets. Nazif Bey castigated those Turkish officials who favored conciliation, and he urged immediate retraction of all innuendoes of a concession. The maximum Ottoman sacrifice, he insisted, should entail an exchange of Armenians in Turkey for Muslims in the Caucasian Armenian republic.[19]

Under the surveillance of Allied control officers in Constantinople, the Association encountered operational difficulties and lacked vitality. Several leaders, in the belief that the road to success lay in a grassroots movement, soon left for the interior provinces, where indigenous, unrelated leagues for self-defense had begun to emerge. The Muslim notables in the eastern vilayets, many of whom had been adjuncts of the Ittihadist regime and had good reason to fear for the loss of their lands and status, clustered around the Association's Erzerum branch, organized by Jevad Dursunoghlu (Dursunbeyzade), a member of the Ottoman Parliament.[20] In its initial manifesto of March 10, 1919, the Erzerum group proclaimed that the mosques and minarets gilding the land bespoke its intrinsically Muslim character. The Armenians could find no historic identity, the manifesto asserted, for their claims to culture and civilization were based upon a feudal system in a feudal period. The eastern provinces had always been Muslim and Turk, whereas the Armenian had ever been a minority. It was unfortunate

<hr />

[18] Selck, op. cit., p. 82; Ertürk, op. cit., pp. 220–226.

[19] Gökbilgen, op. cit., pp. 114–115. See also Cevat Dursunoğlu, Milli mücadelede Erzurum (Ankara, 1946), pp. 19–20; Britain, FO 371/3658, 52432/512/58.

[20] Gotthard Jäschke, "Mustafa Kemals Sendung nach Anatolien," in Aus der Geschichte des Islamischen Orients (Tübingen, 1949), p. 19, cited hereafter as "Sendung"; Tarik Z. Tunaya, Türkiyede siyasi partiler, 1859–1952 (Istanbul, 1952), p. 490. See also Mustafa Kemal, A Speech Delivered by Ghazi Mustafa Kemal (Leipzig, 1929), pp. 10–12, cited hereafter as Speech; Yavus Abadan, Inkılâp tarihine giriş (Ankara, 1962), pp. 46–48.

that the Armenian provocation of the last half century had necessitated countermeasures; the Christian population, however, had invariably committed the initial outrage. The manifesto, issued on the eve of the first anniversary of the Turkish reoccupation of Erzerum, pledged that the Armenians would never be permitted to take possession of these Turco-Muslim cradlelands.[21]

Meanwhile the Ottoman General Staff and Ministry of War abetted the spirit of defiance by evading or delaying the general demobilization demanded by the Allies. Through the calculated tactics of these departments, the regiments in Turkish Armenia remained armed and were reinforced in February of 1919 by General Yakub Shevki's divisions. Despite the severe winter and demoralization in the ranks, Shevki Pasha had succeeded in preserving the basic unity of the shabby but experienced Ninth Army during its withdrawal from Kars. Once in Erzerum, however, he declined the call to lead the resistance and, pleading illness and loss of sight, complied with orders to relinquish his command and proceed to Constantinople.[22] Not long thereafter Erzerum welcomed its hero and liberator. Once again in time of boundless distress Major General Kiazim Karabekir had returned.

On the Caucasus front in 1918 Karabekir Pasha had commanded the divisions that captured Erzerum and Kars and participated in the invasion of the Erevan guberniia.[23] Stationed in North Persia when World War I came to an end, Karabekir was recalled to Constantinople, where he served briefly on the General Staff before taking charge of the XIV Army Corps in Thrace. But impatient to return to Anatolia he managed in March of 1919 to obtain command of the XV Corps, encamped in the vilayets of Van, Erzerum, and Trebizond. By this time Karabekir had become convinced that the preservation of the Ottoman fatherland required a military organization in the interior and the facing up to the Armenian threat; he so informed Mustafa Kemal and other officers in Constantinople. According to Karabekir, Kemal conceded that the idea was generally valid but did not commit himself further. Disappointed, Karabekir retorted that the plan was not an "idea" but a goal he would achieve by inspiring the soldiers and populace of the eastern vilayets.[24]

[21] Gökbilgen, op. cit., p. 74; Dursunoğlu, op. cit., pp. 33–34, 143–144.

[22] Bıyıklıoğlu, op. cit., p. 47; Selek, op. cit., p. 154; Gökbilgen, op. cit., p. 74. Ertürk, op. cit., p. 209, states that Ittihadist leaders in Erzerum kept Yakub Shevki a virtual prisoner for a month before allowing him to depart for the capital.

[23] For a résumé of Karabekir's military operations in 1918, see Kandemir, Karabekir, pp. 142–158; Karabekir, Esasları, pp. 24–31.

[24] Karabekir, İstiklâl Harbimiz, pp. 2–9, 16–17, and Esasları, pp. 36–37; Kandemir,

Certain that there was nothing more to be gained by marking time in Constantinople, Karabekir sailed out of the Bosporus on April 12, 1919, taking with him promises of support and collaboration from prominent officials in the Ministry of War.[25] Upon his disembarkation at Trebizond, Karabekir exhorted the Muslim inhabitants to defend against all aliens. Only Greeks and Armenians would have to be dealt with, he promised, for the Europeans were weary of war and would not intervene. He admonished loyal Turks not to waste their energies on appeals to the Allied Powers but instead to organize and follow him. Arriving in Erzerum on May 3 Karabekir solemnly vowed that, as long as a handful of Turkish soil remained free, he would carry the struggle forward. The Ottoman Empire would retrieve the three sanjaks of Kars, Ardahan, and Batum, and also occupy Armenia. The French and British, he again presaged, would send not a single soldier to assist the Greeks and Armenians.[26] Meeting furtively on May 4 with the Association for the Defense of the Rights of the Eastern Vilayets, Karabekir urged defiance of British control officers who had come to remove the breechblocks from the artillery pieces and transport arms and ammunition to Allied military stations along the Black Sea and in Transcaucasia. He roused the Muslim notables with visions of first liberating the eastern plateau and then spearheading the battle for freedom in the imperiled western sector of the country, adding: "I shall take Armenia as a pawn. This is the key to securing for ourselves the favorable peace settlement we desire." [27]

When Karabekir assumed command of the XV Corps the 18,000 men of its four divisions constituted nearly 40 percent of what was left of the Ottoman Army. Operating along the borders of Russian Armenia, the 3d Division was headquartered at Trebizond, the 9th at Erzerum, the 11th at Bayazit, and the 12th east of Hasankale.[28] To keep the units

---

Karabekir, pp. 160–161, and *Kemal*, p. 15. For a different account, see Gökbilgen, *op. cit.*, p. 79.

[25] Enver Behnan Şapolyo, *Kemâl Atatürk ve milli mücadele tarihi* (Istanbul, [1958]), pp. 285–287; Bıyıklıoğlu, *op. cit.*, p. 47; Karabekir, *Esaları*, p. 38.

[26] Karabekir, *İstiklâl Harbimiz*, pp. 19–23; Bıyıklıoğlu, *op. cit.*, p. 47.

[27] Jäschke, "Beiträge," pp. 25–26; Karabekir, *İstiklâl Harbimiz*, p. 23.

[28] Şapolyo, *op. cit.*, p. 310; Jäschke, "Sendung," p. 22; Karabekir, *Esaları*, p. 47. Selek, *op. cit.*, pp. 88–89, gives Tortom as the headquarters of the 3d Division. Belen, *Türk Harbi*, V, 237, shows the following distribution: 3d Caucasus Division, Trebizond; 9th Caucasus Division, Erzerum; 11th Caucasus Division, Van; 12th Infantry Division, Khorasan. According to Elaine Smith, *Turkey: Origins of the Kemalist Movement and the Government of the Grand National Assembly (1919–1923)* (Washington, D.C., 1959), p. 16, Karabekir had some 10,000 troops under his command.

combat ready, Karabekir knew he had to gain control of the large stores of war matériel that the few Allied officials were preparing to transfer. Outwardly cooperating with the senior British inspector, Lieutenant Colonel Alfred Rawlinson, Karabekir gave secret instructions for his men to sever the rails and for "bandit groups" to attack the weapon convoys and raid the storage depots. The loot in arms and ammunition was to be stashed away in caches and held in reserve for the 50,000-man force Karabekir considered requisite to effective control in the vilayets bordering and coveted by the Republic of Armenia.[29]

The Turkish leader soon learned from the Ministry of War that the British had overturned the Muslim administration at Kars and installed an Armenian governor and that Armenian officers had been observed advancing into Olti and Kaghisman, just beyond the old Russo-Turkish frontier. The disconcerting news was attenuated, however, by the additional information that the British garrison at Kars was departing.[30] In the tense and heavy atmosphere pressing upon the Muslims of the eastern vilayets, burgeoning rumors reverberated from district to district. The reported sighting of an Armenian detachment near the border gave rise to whispers of 10,000 Armenians standing poised in the heights between Kars and Sarikamish. Andranik, the bête noire of the Muslims, was said to be marching upon Van with an army of 30,000. Kiazim Karabekir did his utmost to calm the terrified population by dismissing the rumors on the premise that the Armenians could never scrounge enough food and supplies to sustain 30,000 troops and that Andranik would find it impossible to muster even 10,000 "beggar Armenians." The despicable Armenians were too engrossed in the struggle for physical survival to dare risk an attack.[31] Karabekir was right. Armenia could not have undertaken the occupation of the eastern vilayets without the active collaboration of the Allied Powers, the endless pleas for which went unanswered.

[29] Kandemir, *Karabekir*, pp. 161–162. See Rawlinson's own descriptions in his memoirs, *Adventures in the Near East, 1918–1922* (London and New York, 1923), pp. 163–234. See also Dursunoğlu, *op. cit.*, pp. 61, 73–74; London *Times*, Aug. 5, 1919, p. 10; Lord [John P. D. B.] Kinross, *Atatürk: The Rebirth of a Nation* (London, [1964]), p. 175.

[30] Karabekir, *İstiklâl Harbimiz*, pp. 25–26.

[31] *Ibid.*, pp. 37–38. According to Karabekir, *Esasları*, p. 53, Kemal disseminated this rumor while he was at Havza, en route to the Anatolian interior. Karabekir apparently relayed the information to Constantinople in the hope of stirring the Ottoman government to action. The Ministry of War responded by instructing Karabekir to take whatever precautions were necessary, but also made it clear that the government could shoulder no responsibility for the consequences. See Gökbilgen, *op. cit.*, pp. 132–133.

Karabekir claimed to hold no fear of an invasion from the east, but he was incensed over the Armenian expansion to Kars and Nakhichevan. During the World War he had become especially alert to the strategic importance of these districts, both in rendering Erevan perpetually vulnerable and in serving as a vital bridge to Muslim Azerbaijan and the lands beyond. Although constrained to withdraw his troops from the Erevan guberniia in late 1918, Karabekir nevertheless left a number of officers in Nakhichevan to assist the Muslim population, and in the summer of 1919 he dispatched additional agents from the XV Corps, taking care, however, to disavow any connection with them and to list them as army deserters.[32]

At the end of May, 1919, General Karabekir and the Association for the Defense of the Rights of the Eastern Vilayets denounced the proclivity of Grand Vizier Damad Ferid Pasha to acquiesce in certain concessions to the Armenians. They pledged unrelenting opposition to this treachery and called upon all officials in the eastern provinces to rally to the resistance and to cultivate the sympathies of the Kurdish tribesmen. Their forces combined, the two proud Muslim peoples would smother the insidious Armenian conspiracy. As Grand Vizier Damad Ferid Pasha prepared to depart for Paris in June, Karabekir urged him to uphold the interests of the nation, warning that the least inkling to endure interference in the affairs of the Ottoman Empire, by Armenia or any other foreign power, would be tantamount to perfidy. What was the meaning of such pronouncements from Constantinople as "the Armenians will have the opportunity to attain their just rights," the XV Corps commander queried. In one of several similar communiqués, Karabekir exclaimed that the eastern vilayets had been the wellspring of the Osmanlis. "There is nothing of Armenians here—the ruins of a few churches and nothing more." Let Europe rant and rave, but "there can not and there will not be an Armenian government here, and this you must make explicit when you arrive [in Paris]."[33] Karabekir's admonition was reiterated by apprehensive and resentful local groups throughout Turkey. Furthermore, the congealing Nationalist movement was about to gain a new champion. Kiazim Karabekir was joined by a dynamic ally and keen competitor. Mustafa Kemal appeared in Anatolia.

[32] Karabekir, *Istiklâl Harbimiz*, pp. 31, 48, 65, 78. See also Gökbilgen, *op. cit.*, p. 187. For an account of the activities engaged in by Karabekir's agents in Nakhichevan, see Veysel Ünüvar, *Istiklâl harbinde Bolşeviklerele sekiz ay 1920–1921* (Istanbul, 1948).

[33] Karabekir, *Istiklâl Harbimiz*, pp. 40, 42, 44–45.

Mustafa Kemal as Inspector General

Mustafa Kemal, a hero of the Gallipoli campaign who had risen to lead an entire army, weathered the World War without having sustained a major defeat. He was recalled from the Syrian front in November of 1918, and, after making an unsuccessful bid for a cabinet post, began to weigh the possibilities of challenging the Allied decision to partition the Ottoman Empire.[34] Cautiously ascertaining the sentiments of key individuals in official circles, he received encouragement from several quarters, in particular the Ministry of War and the General Staff, both of which subsequently publicly reviled Kemal but managed nevertheless to serve him and his cause. In an almost unbelievable saga of shrewd manipulation and prodigious good fortune, Mustafa Kemal on April 30, 1919, was commissioned Inspector General of the Ninth Army, formerly commanded by Yakub Shevki Pasha. The inspectorate, one of three created by the General Staff, was designed to encompass much of central and eastern Anatolia and to be based at Samson on the Black Sea.[35] In documents issued at the beginning of May the Ottoman government enjoined Kemal to maintain law and order, stockpile arms and munitions in military depots, and suppress the emergent bands attempting to incite the population. To discharge these responsibilities Kemal was vested with broad jurisdiction, not only over the Ninth Army, which had been restructured into the XV Corps at Erzerum and the III Corps at Sivas, but also over the civil functionaries in the corresponding regions. In addition, the Inspector General was empowered to require the cooperation of the authorities in the contiguous provinces of Bitlis, Diarbekir, Mamuret-ul-Aziz (Kharput), Angora (Ankara), and Kastamuni.[36] Kemal

---

[34] Dankwart A. Rustow, "The Army and the Founding of the Turkish Republic," *World Politics*, XI (July, 1959), 537–538; Kinross, *op. cit.*, pp. 125–126, 129, 136–137.

[35] Numerous documents relating to the Turkish resistance movement and the role of Mustafa Kemal have been published by the historical section of the Turkish General Staff under the title *Harb Tarihi Vesikaları Dergisi*, appearing periodically since 1952. Kemal's appointment of April 30 appears as the first document in that series. He was commissioned to head the Third Inspectorate, with jurisdiction over the III and XV Army Corps. The First Inspectorate, headquartered at Constantinople, had jurisdiction over the I, XIV, XVII, and XXV corps, while the Second Inspectorate, at Konia, was responsible for the XII and XX corps. The XIII Army Corps at Diarbekir operated independently. In June of 1919 the Ninth Army was reorganized and redesignated as the Third Army. See *Harb Tarihi Vesikaları Dergisi* (April, 1953), no. 74; Bıyıklıoğlu, *op. cit.*, pp. 47–48; Jäschke, "Sendung," pp. 21–22.

[36] *Harb Tarihi Vesikaları Dergisi* (Sept., 1952), nos. 3–6. See also Bıyıklıoğlu, *op. cit.*, pp. 42, 46; Selek, *op. cit.*, pp. 172–180; Gökbilgen, *op. cit.*, pp. 79–81; Şapolyo, *op. cit.*, pp. 289–290; Jäschke, "Sendung," pp. 28–29.

and his sympathizers in Constantinople had laid the basis for a pervasive organization far removed from sight and range of Allied battleships.

The circumstances surrounding Kemal's appointment have elicited divers interpretations and considerable disagreement.[37] Some historians and Kemal himself have maintained that the Ottoman government did not comprehend the precise scope of the prerogatives granted the Inspector General. Several scholars have adopted the view that high-ranking officials in Constantinople distrusted Kemal Pasha and therefore favored his mission to the interior as a path to oblivion. A pivotal factor in the case was the demeanor of the Sultan. Perhaps he, too, was wary of Kemal and would have been relieved to have him away from the capital, but, on the other hand, the two men had experienced a rather cordial past association. Mehmed VI may have looked to the war hero to strengthen the position of the throne by stemming the chaos in Anatolia. The Sultan feared and hated Enver Pasha and the Ittihadist party, the adherents of which still waxed powerful in the interior provinces. There were ominous rumors that these unbridled elements were awaiting the arrival of a Muslim army from the Caucasus, organized and led by Enver himself. As continued Ittihadist foment in Anatolia might induce the Allied Powers to occupy the entire region and thus render inevitable the establishment of a large Armenia and a separate Kurdistan, the Sultan conceivably relied on Kemal to exert a firm hand. This interpretation would explain the concentration of such extensive authority in the post of inspector general. Less conjectural and now substantiated is the analysis that Turkish officials who themselves lacked the courage to flout the directives of the Allied military commanders centered their unspoken hopes on Kemal and therefore aided him in reaching the interior to launch the war of national restitution. The Chief of General Staff, for example, not only knew of Kemal's intentions but pledged the maximum support within the limits of discretion. He furnished Kemal with a cipher code unknown to the Allied controllers, who moreover were not informed of the scope of the Inspector General's jurisdiction until Kemal had already sailed from Constantinople.[38] Whatever the circumstances of his

[37] The literature on Mustafa Kemal and on the Turkish Nationalist movement is both voluminous and controversial. For useful studies on Kemal in English, see, in addition to the cited works of Kinross, Lewis, and Smith, H. C. Armstrong, *Grey Wolf: Mustafa Kemal* (London, 1937); Hanns Froembgen, *Kemal Atatürk: A Biography* (New York, 1937); Irfan Orga and Margaret Orga, *Atatürk* (London, [1962]).

[38] Kandemir, *Kemal*, pp. 9–13, 17–18; Ertürk, *op. cit.*, pp. 330–333; Jäschke, "Sendung," pp. 22–25; Bıyıklıoğlu, *op. cit.*, p. 43; Kinross, *op. cit.*, pp. 149–153, 156–157;

appointment, Kemal had been provided the all-important momentum toward etching his name in history.

Mustafa Kemal's departure for Samson on May 16 came just one day after thousands of Greek troops, under cover of an inter-Allied naval squadron, had begun disembarking at Smyrna. The "Greek invasion," which, as noted, had been sanctioned by Woodrow Wilson, Georges Clemenceau, and David Lloyd George, was ultimately to haunt the dreams of Eleutherios Venizelos and to augur ill for Armenia. Mustafa Kemal Pasha was the Turkish man of the moment, the ghazi around whom the loosely structured opposition groups could rally. The nation had been given a strong-willed, ruthless, and dedicated commander who possessed the *élan* necessary to inspirit the hitherto passive and fatalistic Turkish masses.

Kemal arrived in Samson on May 19 and promptly appealed to the civil and military authorities in his inspectorate to conjure up a storm of protest against the pernicious occupation of Smyrna.[39] In a separate cipher telegram to Kiazim Karabekir, he urged immediate joint action on behalf of the fatherland. The reply was gratifying, for Karabekir revealed that nearly 18,000 troops stood armed on the eastern plateau and that in spite of the endeavors of the English control officers the weapons of his corps had not been surrendered.[40] Then on May 29, as Kemal traveled inland through the Pontic Mountains, he wrote Karabekir that under no circumstances would they "swallow" the concept of an Armenian state. The army regulars would hurl back all opponents approaching from the west, while in the east guerrilla bands would deal with the Georgians and the Armenians, should they be foolhardly enough to advance. In another message that day Kemal told Karabekir and Ali Fuad Pasha, commander of the Angora-based XX Corps, that the Sultan's government was floundering helplessly as the enemy plotted to usurp the eastern vilayets and incited the Greek inhabitants along the Black Sea. In view of this threat, Kemal continued, it was imperative that local militias be organized to defend the nation through guerrilla tactics until an effective regular force could be consolidated. He insisted that arms and matériel in coastal areas be moved inland and carefully hidden. Above all, Kemal prescribed absolute secrecy during this preparatory period.[41] On the thirtieth the Inspector General wired

---

Orga and Orga, *op. cit.*, p. 141. In confirming Kemal's commission the Ottoman Ministry of War advised the Inspector General to leave immediately for his post. See *Harb Tarihi Vesikaları Dergisi* (Sept., 1952), no. 6.

[39] Kemal, *Speech*, pp. 24–25; Smith, *op. cit.*, p. 13.

[40] Kandemir, *Kemal*, pp. 35–36.

[41] Karabekir, *İstiklâl Harbimiz*, pp. 35–36; Kandemir, *Kemal*, pp. 37–38. See also

Karabekir yet again to caution that the Allies would contrive to use the Armenians in seizing the eastern homelands just as they had already manipulated the Greeks along the Aegean. The Sublime Porte had become a plaything of the Entente, said Kemal, and was incapable of thwarting the stratagems of the enemy. The call to duty thus weighed upon Anatolia.[42] On June 3 Kemal appealed to the governors and commanders of his inspectorate to denounce the obvious propensity of Grand Vizier Damad Ferid Pasha to accede to the formation of an autonomous Armenia, as such a concession would subvert Turkish independence and violate the principle of majority rule.[43]

The blunder of allowing Mustafa Kemal to slip away, vested with comprehensive and flexible powers, was belatedly recognized by Allied officials in Constantinople. On May 19, upon his return from an inspection circuit of the Caucasus, General George F. Milne of the British Army of the Black Sea asked the Ottoman government to account for Kemal's mission, and three weeks later he followed with the demand that Kemal be recalled.[44] The order dispatched in compliance with Milne's directive gave rise to a month-long exchange between Kemal and the several involved departments in the capital. Both the General Staff and the Ministry of War played upon words so that the Inspector General would understand that the writs they relayed were issued under duress and that they hoped he would not obey. The secret code that the General Staff had provided Kemal prior to his departure was put to good use.[45]

On June 23, as the pressures exerted by the British commanders mounted, Minister of Interior Ali Kemal Bey wired instructions to all civil authorities in Anatolia, relieving them of obligations to Mustafa Kemal and forbidding henceforth any communication with him. Three days later the same officials were directed to prevent by whatever means necessary unauthorized military conscription, cases of which had been

---

Nutuk, Kemal Atatürk, Vol. III, *Vesikalar*, publ. of Türk Devrim Tarihi Enstitüsü (Istanbul, [1960]), p. 901, cited hereafter as *Nutuk*. On May 28 Kemal instructed the military commanders of his inspectorate to be prepared for a "small war" in case of an attempted foreign occupation of the eastern vilayets. See Jäschke, "Beiträge," p. 34n.

[42] Kandemir, *Kemal*, p. 39.

[43] Kemal, *Speech*, pp. 28–30.

[44] *British Documents*, IV, 688–689; *Harb Tarihi Vesikaları Dergisi* (Sept., 1952), nos. 15–19; Gotthard Jäschke, "General Milne zur Entsendung Mustafa Kemals nach Anatolien," *Die Welt des Islams*, n.s., II, 4 (1953), 267–268; Şapolyo, *op. cit.*, p. 324.

[45] *Harb Tarihi Vesikaları Dergisi* (Sept., 1952), nos. 20–22; Kandemir, *Kemal*, p. 13; Rustow, *op. cit.*, p. 539; Şapolyo, *op. cit.*, p. 325. For British materials on the early stages of the Turkish Nationalist movement, see WO 32/5377, and FO 608/111–112, File 385/1/14.

reported from various districts in the interior.[46] Yet, vacillation and procrastination still prevailed among Ottoman ruling circles. Commander of the British Mediterranean fleet Vice Admiral Gough-Calthorpe became sufficiently galled by the Sublime Porte's heedless attitude to threaten that unless Milne's order was effectuated post haste he would gain compliance through armed intervention.[47] Finally, on July 8, 1919, the weeks of indecision and apparent collusion ended with an Imperial irade stripping Kemal of his commission.[48] That same day, however, Sultan Mehmed VI made it known to Calthorpe that the Greek encroachments at Smyrna, together with rumors of an imminent Armenian attack toward Erzerum, were causing matters to slip from his control. The Ottoman Foreign Ministry repeated a similar admonition on July 10, adding that statements about extending the Armenian republic as far west as Sivas only served to nurture the truculent Ittihadist partisans.[49]

Throughout this period Kemal acted with icy calculating resolve. He exhorted local Muslim leaders wherever he traveled not to despair but to stand in defense of the *vatan*—the fatherland. In a prearranged rendezvous in the city of Amasia, he also met with men who were to become integral to the history of Nationalist Turkey. Husein Rauf Bey, former Minister of the Marine and the senior Ottoman delegate during the Trebizond conference and the Mudros negotiations in 1918, General Ali Fuad Pasha, commander of the XX Corps, and Colonel Refet Bey, Commander of the III Corps, joined with Kemal on the night of June 21–22, 1919, in signing the Amasia Protocol, to which Karabekir Pasha and Mersinli Jemal Pasha, the head of the Second Army Inspectorate at Konia, soon subscribed. The document stated that, because Allied restrictions had disabled the central government, a "national committee" should be organized to coordinate defense efforts and that the military leaders should disregard directives to vacate their posts or surrender their equipment and should not tolerate foreign occupation under any guise whatsoever. In order to implement these decisions, the protocol continued, a national congress was being summoned to meet in Sivas, considered one of the safest sites in Anatolia.[50]

[46] Kemal, *Speech*, pp. 34–35; Orga and Orga, *op. cit.*, p. 145; Kandemir, *Kemal*, pp. 77–79; Emre, *op. cit.*, pp. 231–232.

[47] *British Documents*, IV, 688–689.

[48] *Harb Tarihi Vesikaları Dergisi* (Oct., 1952), no. 30; Emre, *op. cit.*, p. 236; Kandemir, *Kemal*, p. 63.

[49] *British Documents*, IV, 668, 689–690.

[50] Kemal, *Speech*, pp. 30–34, and *Nutuk*, III, 915–916; Şapolyo, *op. cit.*, pp. 318–

The Erzerum Conference

In Erzerum, meanwhile, the Association for the Defense of the Rights of the Eastern Vilayets (Eastern Anatolia) became increasingly troubled by reports of Armenian troop concentrations and impending assault. In June, under the Association's sponsorship, a five-day provincial conference of civic and religious notables attempted to strike on an effective plan to shield the region. Jevad Dursunoghlu drew particular attention to the harmful impact of Armenian and Kurdish separatist propaganda and to the aim of certain prominent Armenians led by former Ottoman Foreign Minister Gabriel Noradoungian to divide the Kurds and Turks by alleging that Kurds and Armenians had sprung from a common racial origin. No means should be spared, exclaimed Dursunoghlu, to crush this intrigue and to ensure the perpetuation of the centuries-long bond between Muslim Kurd and Muslim Turk.[51] In its resolutions the vilayet conference decried the fact that, while President Wilson had proclaimed the basis of his peace program to be majority rule, a carefully organized plot had been hatched to expel the Turkish majority from the eastern vilayets and Cilicia in advocacy of an independent Armenian state. The delegates vowed that the heroic provinces of eastern Anatolia would resist each and every act of Armenian aggression and guard to the last man their right to remain within the Ottoman Empire. To prepare for a general, coordinated defense the Muslim leaders of Erzerum called for a broader congress with representatives from the six adjoining provinces of Van, Bitlis, Kharput, Diarbekir, Sivas, and Trebizond.[52]

The Association for the Defense of the Rights of the Eastern Vilayets had in fact already summoned such a congress, instructing it "to stand steadfast against Armenian incursions and, with this in mind, to organize a militia in the provinces." [53] Mustafa Kemal, regarding this assemblage as an important precursor to the national convention he had invited to Sivas, decided to attend and, at the same time, to inspect the headquarters of the XV Corps. Arriving in Erzerum on July 3, 1919, he discussed the perils from both east and west with General Karabekir,

---

319; Kandemir, *Kemal*, pp. 69–72; Ali Fuat Cebesoy, *Milli mücadele hâtıraları* (Istanbul, 1953), p. 123.

[51] Dursunoğlu, *op. cit.*, pp. 63–69, 151–154. Although the Kurds had become Muslims, they indeed did share a common Indo-European origin with the Armenians. There is evidence moreover, that a number of Kurdish tribes in the eastern vilayets descended directly from onetime Christian Armenians.

[52] *Ibid.*, pp. 49–63, 155–157.

[53] Jäschke, "Beiträge," pp. 25–26.

who told of the persistent attempts of British Colonel Rawlinson to sequester the military stockpiles in order to assist the Greeks and the Armenians "in clasping one another's blood-soaked hands across the Kizilirmak [Red—the historic Halys—River], which they want to turn veritably red with Turkish blood." The XV Corps commander disclosed that he had taken precautionary measures against Armenian border violations and had contravened the Interior Ministry's decree outlawing the formation of local armed detachments. In Karabekir's estimation, the time was ripe for an invasion of Armenia; the entire operation should take no longer than a month or two and Turkey could thus acquire a valuable hostage.[54]

It was five days after his appearance in Erzerum that Kemal was divested of all formal authority by the Imperial irade. Not to be intimidated, Kemal immediately reciprocated by resigning the commission that the Sultan had just rescinded, declaring to the government in Constantinople and to the people of Erzerum that his action had been prompted by a call to serve the nation free of the fetters and shackles of officialdom. Kemal promised to prevail against the partition of the sacred homeland and to spare it from being forfeited to the Greeks and the Armenians.[55] As the rift between Constantinople and Anatolia widened, Sultan Mehmed VI signed the papers for the arrest of the former inspector general, and the Ministry of War instructed Kiazim Karabekir to apprehend Kemal and Refet Bey, giving him to understand that his reward for compliance would be the now vacant inspectorate. But Karabekir, subsequently one of Kemal's bitterest political foes, spurned the opportunity and circumvented the order.[56]

After several delays the Erzerum Congress convened on July 23, 1919,

---

[54] Karabekir, *İstiklâl Harbimiz*, pp. 68, 78. See also Kandemir, *Kemal*, pp. 88–89. Dursunoğlu, *op. cit.*, pp. 87–95, gives an account of Kemal's activities in Erzerum during the period before the opening of the congress.

[55] Gökbilgen, *op. cit.*, p. 153; Selek, *op. cit.*, p. 222; Cebesoy, *Milli mücadele*, pp. 97–98; Ertürk, *op. cit.*, pp. 252–253; Şapolyo, *op.cit.*, p. 326.

[56] *Harb Tarihi Vesikaları Dergisi* (March, 1953), no. 48; Emre, *op. cit.*, p. 236; Kandemir, *Karabekir*, p. 164; Şapolyo, *op. cit.*, pp. 325–326; Kemal, *Speech*, pp. 62–63. Several authors, including Smith, *op. cit.*, p. 17; Kinross, *op. cit.*, pp. 180–181; and Cebesoy, *Milli mücadele*, pp. 119–120, state that the orders were for the arrest of Kemal and Rauf Bey (rather than Refet Bey). According to Orga and Orga, *op. cit.*, p. 145, the Ottoman government instructed Rauf Bey to take charge of the inspectorate after Kemal was dismissed, but document 35 in *Harb Tarihi Vesikaları Dergisi* shows that as early as July 20 the Ottoman government had designated the commander of the XV Corps (Karabekir) as the person who was to assume the functions of the Inspector General. Kemal's last link with officialdom was broken on August 9, 1919, when he was expelled altogether from the Ottoman army. See Jäschke and Pritsch, *op. cit.*, p. 19.

ironically in what had been the Sanasarian Academy, the foremost institution of Armenian culture and education in the eastern provinces during the decades preceding World War I.[57] Karabekir Pasha welcomed the some fifty delegates, all but five of whom came from Erzerum, Sivas, and Trebizond, and enjoined them to direct their energies toward "smothering the lust of the Armenians and the Greeks to our land and crushing their hopes forever." [58] Logically, the presidency of the Erzerum Congress belonged to Karabekir, but in fact the honor was accorded Mustafa Kemal, who put his powers of manipulation and force of character to a successful test. In his address Kemal pledged that, despite the Greek threat from the west and the Armenian threat from the east and the south, the Turkish people would unite, persevere, strike, and triumph.[59]

During the fortnight the Erzerum Congress was in session, it laid a cornerstone of the future National Pact by proclaiming the *vatan* an inviolable whole within the "natural frontiers," which safely ensheathed the vilayets of Trebizond, Erzerum, Sivas, Diarbekir, Kharput, Van, and Bitlis. The Turkish people would shred the grotesque blueprint to dismember the fatherland, and if, as it seemed, the central government proved incapable of directing the holy war, a provisional administration would stand forth. The Erzerum Congress further resolved to countenance neither foreign mandate nor protectorate for any part of the country and to allow no privileges whatever to the Greek and Armenian Christian elements, as that would compromise the political rights and the social equilibrium of the Muslim majority.[60] Prior to adjournment on August 7, 1919, the delegates selected a "Representative Committee" (Heyet-i-temsiliye) to provide continuity and leadership pending the decisions of the nationwide assembly to be held shortly in Sivas.[61] Thus, less than a year after their admission of defeat

[57] For materials on the Erzerum Congress, see a collection of articles in *Erzurum Kongresi ve Mustafa Kemâl Atatürk* (n.p., n.d.). See also Tunaya, *op. cit.*, pp. 489–491; Kemal, *Speech*, pp. 57–62; Dursunoğlu, *op. cit.*, pp. 107–120, 160–170; Şapolyo, *op. cit.*, pp. 226–230; Maurice Pernot, *La question turque* (Paris, 1923), pp. 68–70, 282–295.

[58] Selek, *op. cit.*, p. 228, states that there were 54 delegates, of whom 23 were from the Erzerum vilayet, 16 from Trebizond, 10 from Sivas, 3 from Bitlis, and 2 from Van. Dursunoğlu, *op. cit.*, pp. 109–112, lists the names, occupations, and native districts of the participants.

[59] Kemal, *Nutuk*, III, 926–931; Uras, *op. cit.*, pp. 704–705; Türk İnkılâp Tarihi Enstitüsü, *Atatürk soylev ve demeçleri*, Vol. I (Istanbul, 1945), pp. 3–6.

[60] Pernot, *op. cit.*, pp. 296–300; Emre, *op. cit.*, pp. 239–240; Karabekir, *Esasları*, pp. 89–91; Dursunoğlu, *op. cit.*, pp. 168–170.

[61] For the composition of the Representative Committee, see Şapolyo, *op. cit.*, p. 329; Kandemir, *Kemal*, p. 105; Cebesoy, *Milli mücadele*, p. 122; Kemal, *Nutuk*, III,

at Mudros, the Turks had begun to surge in a current of resistance that moved the swiftest on the Anatolian plateau.

Soviet Russia and the Turkish Resistance

From the very outset of the long, stubborn struggle for national revival, the pioneers of the Turkish resistance discerned the potential benefits of Russian friendship and collaboration. Both Russia and Turkey suffered the anguish of foreign intervention, deep domestic fissures, and insurgent or secessionist provinces. With the capitalist powers of Europe as a common enemy, Soviet Russia and Nationalist Turkey, each skeptical of the ideologies and motivations of the other, were drawn toward mutual dependence and cooperation.[62] News of the Bolshevik revolution in Russia and of the Sovnarkom's initial proclamations denouncing traditional tsarist foreign policy had been greeted with guarded optimism in the Ottoman Empire. Earlier still, in the spring of 1917, Lenin had deprecated the flagitious hold on Turkish Armenia by the regimes of Tsar Nicholas and the Provisional Government, and he assailed the Entente pacts that would have "'robbed" Turkey of her Armenian provinces. On assuming power the Sovnarkom created a worldwide sensation by repudiating those secret treaties and making public their terms.[63] Ripples of enthusiasm spread across Muslim-populated lands over this apparent demonstration of good faith. Among the ulema, the learned men of Islam, there were those who discovered parallels between Lenin and Mohammed and between the tenets of communism and those of the true faith. The mutual ap-

---

934. British intelligence reports and other documents on the Erzerum and Sivas congresses are in Britain, FO 371/4159, File 521/44, and FO 608/112, File 385/1/15.

[62] For useful works on Soviet-Turkish relations, particularly during the period 1918–1921, see the following: S. I. Kuznetsova, *Ustanovlenie sovetsko-turetskikh otnoshenii* (Moscow, 1961); A. M. Shamsutdinov, *Natsional'no-osvoboditel'naia bor'ba v Turtsii, 1918–1923 gg.* (Moscow, 1966); P. Moiseev and Iu. Rozaliev, *K istorii sovetsko-turetskikh otnoshenii* (Moscow, 1958), pp. 8–36; A. N. Kheifets, *Sovetskaia Rossiia i sopredel'nye strany Vostoka v gody grazhdanskoi voiny (1918–1920)* (Moscow, 1964), pp. 77–171; Ali Fuat Cebesoy, *Moskova hâtıraları (21/11/1920–2/6/1922)* (Istanbul, 1955); Gotthard Jäschke, "Kommunismus und Islam im türkischen Befreiungskriege," cited hereafter as "Kommunismus," and his "Der Weg zur russisch-türkischen Freundschaft im Lichte Moskaus," both in *Die Welt des Islams*, XX (1938), 110–117, and 118–134; W. "Les relations russo-turques depuis l'avènement du Bolchevisme," in pt. 2 of "Le Bolchevisme et l'Islam," *Revue du monde musulman*, LII (Dec., 1922), 181–217; Zarevand, *Miatsial ankakh Turania* ([Boston], 1926), pp. 157–220 *passim*; S. Vratzian, *Hayastane bolshevikian murji ev trkakan sali midjev* (2d ed.; Beirut, 1953).

[63] Hovannisian, *Road to Independence*, pp. 97–98; Lenin, *Sochineniia*, XXXI, 347–348, and XXXII, p. 16.

peal to internationalism seemed to place the opposing currents of Bolshevism and Islamism into a single mainstream.

In its "Appeal to the Muslims of Russia and the East" in December, 1917, the Sovnarkom promised unhindered cultural and religious freedom to the Muslim peoples formerly subjected to the evils of Great Russian chauvinism. Moreover, Soviet Russia disclaimed any intent to annex new lands: "Constantinople must remain in the hands of the Muslims. . . . We declare that the treaty on the partition of Persia is null and void. . . . We declare that the treaty on the partition of Turkey and the wresting of Armenia from her is null and void." The historic document, bearing the signatures of Lenin and Stalin, concluded: "Muslims of Russia! Muslims of the East! On this road to the renovation of the world, we anticipate from you sympathy and support." [64] Significantly, the decree on Turkish Armenia followed a month later, providing the desired justification to recall the Russian armies from the Armenian plateau and Transcaucasia. The need to gain the confidence of the peoples of Asia in order to foster national-colonial upheavals against the imperialist nations of the West became a fundamental plank in early Bolshevik strategy.

Communists of Muslim origin were put in action to enhance the Soviet-Turkish rapprochement. Most of these men came from among the 100,000 Ottoman subjects living in Russia and the more than 50,000 Turkish captives taken during the World War.[65] In January of 1918, soon after the Bolshevik coup, a Muslim subsector of the Commissariat for Nationalities was established and, like its Armenian counterpart, became engaged in propagandism and agitation. A central figure in the Muslim Affairs Commissariat was Mustafa Subhi (Mevlevizade), a native of Kerasund (Gerisun), Trebizond vilayet, who in the wake of the October/November Revolution was freed from Russian imprisonment. In the spring of 1918 Subhi began publication of *Yeni Dünya* ("New World"), regarded as the first Turkish-language Communist newspaper, and directed a program to inculcate the spirit of Bolshevism into the thousands of Ottoman prisoners of war.[66] In July of that year

[64] *Dokumenty SSSR*, I, 34–35. See also Ivar Spector, *The Soviet Union and the Muslim World, 1917–1958* (Seattle, 1959), pp. 33–35; Jane Degras, ed., *Soviet Documents on Foreign Policy*, Vol. I (London, New York, and Toronto, 1951), pp. 15–17; Joseph Castagné, "Les organisations soviétiques de la Russie musulmane," as pt. 1 of "Le Bolchevisme et l'Islam," *Revue du monde musulman*, LI (Oct., 1922), 7–9.

[65] E. Ludshuveit, "Konferentsiia levykh turetskikh sotsialistov v Moskve letom 1918 goda," in *Vostokovedcheskii sbornik*, publ. of Akademiia Nauk Armianskoi SSR, Sektor Vostokovedeniia (Erevan, 1964), pp. 174–175.

[66] Shamsutdinov, *op. cit.*, pp. 154–159; Ludshuveit, *op. cit.*, pp. 178–180; Castagné, *op. cit.*, p. 10.

a small number of those men organized themselves into the Turetskii otriad, a volunteer unit in the Red Army. At about the same time some twenty Ottoman subjects gathered in Moscow as the conference of Turkish left-socialists, which, in addition to adopting the Soviet slogans then current, elected a standing executive, the Central Committee of Turkish Socialists-Communists.[67]

When Turkish war prisoners were gradually repatriated after the Treaty of Brest-Litovsk, many carried to their native Anatolian towns and villages translations of *The Communist Manifesto, Program of the Russian Communist Party, The Life of Lenin, The April Theses,* and other tracts distributed through the Commissariat for Nationalities and its Muslim subsector.[68] Radical literature and ideologies were also imported into Turkey by individual students and laborers from among the several thousand who returned from Germany and Austria following the war. These persons had been exposed to the social ferment in Europe and on arriving home tended to cluster together in a number of leftist leagues, nearly all of which were eventually absorbed into the Turkish nationalist movement.[69] A Communist association, the first in Turkey, was founded in Constantinople at the end of the war but collapsed within three months, its leaders either having been arrested or having fled to Anatolia.[70]

In Russia meanwhile the Communist party drew the scattered Muslim Bolshevik units under its direct control. In November, 1918, the Central Committee of the Turkish Socialists-Communists was reconstructed as the Central Bureau of Muslim Organizations of the Russian Communist Party and was placed under the close supervision of I. V. Stalin and such faithful aides as Mustafa Subhi.[71] Based in Moscow

[67] R. P. Kornienko, *Rabochee dvizhenie v Turtsii, 1918–1963 gg.* (Moscow, 1965), pp. 11–12; Ludshuveit, *op. cit.*, pp. 184–191; E. K. Sargsian [Sarkisian], *Velikaia Oktiabr'skaia sotsialisticheskaia revoliutsiia i natsional'no-osvoboditel'naia bor'ba v Turtsii (1918–1922)* (Erevan, 1958), p. 46. See also Jäschke, "Kommunismus," p. 110.

[68] George S. Harris, *The Origins of Communism in Turkey* (Stanford, 1967), pp. 53–55; A. Novichev, "Antikrest'ianskaia politika kemalistov v 1919–1922 godakh," *Voprosy istorii* (Sept., 1951), p. 60; Kheifets, *op. cit.*, pp. 87–88; Shamsutdinov, *op. cit.*, pp. 48–49.

[69] Harris, *op. cit.*, pp. 35–36; Shamsutdinov, *op. cit.*, p. 50.

[70] Kornienko, *op. cit.*, p. 16; Shamsutdinov, *op. cit.*, p. 151.

[71] The reorganization took place during the first congress of Muslim Communists of Russia. The spokesmen who advocated a separate Muslim Communist party with its own central committee were roundly denounced by those oriented toward Moscow. For contemporary accounts of the proceedings and the "adventurism" of the participants demanding a distinct Muslim party, see *Bor'ba v Azerbaidzhane*, pp. 19–25, 512 n. 10. See also Richard Pipes, *The Formation of the Soviet Union* (rev. ed.; Cambridge, Mass., 1964), p. 160; Harris, *op. cit.*, p. 55; *Istoriia Kompartii Azerbaidzhana*, pp. 299–300.

until the spring of 1919, Subhi attended the First Congress of the Communist International, there expounding the thesis that the world in the East held the key to the elimination of the antagonist powers in the West.[72] Having won the trust of the Soviet leadership, Subhi was then named to head the Central Bureau of Communist Organizations of the Peoples of the East, a new coordinating board taking in non-Muslim elements as well and functioning under the auspices of the Comintern. This realignment was apparently a move by the Russian Communist Party to structure its associated groups along regional-geographic rather than religious-ethnic lines.[73]

Soviet strategists sustained unflagging interest in the postwar situation in Turkey. Even as early as April, 1919, a month before Mustafa Kemal went ashore at Samson, *Izvestiia* acclaimed the growing unrest in Anatolia and the zealous opposition to dismemberment of the Ottoman Empire as the "first Soviet revolution in Asia" and demanded the restoration of the Straits to the "toiling Turkish masses." The front-page article pointed to the many ramifications of the Turkish revolution. First and foremost was its impact upon the Caucasus, where counterrevolutionary "governments" had been set up by the German and then by the Anglo-French imperialists. Those hostile states were standing between the "Russian and Turkish Soviet Republics, which are inspired by mutual sentiments." The Turkish revolution would guarantee that those counterrevolutionary creations would no longer discomfort "either of the Soviet Republics." Moreover, it would eventually deprive the Entente Powers of the bases from which they were directing their campaign against Soviet Russia. The ripples the revolution had stirred would send waves into the Balkans, Central Europe, Africa, and, in particular, all Asia, where the oppressed peoples were at last awakening from the torpor and apathy of centuries. "The Turkish revolution has given us an important ally," concluded the article in the Sovnarkom's organ.[74] In its May Day manifesto the Executive Committee of the Third International, hailing the beginning of the Turkish revolution, called upon the Turkish workers, soldiers, and peasants to form their own Red army and soviets in order to ensure the success of the movement. The Executive Committee then delivered a denunci-

[72] Subhi's address to the founding Comintern congress has been reprinted in *Pervyi kongress Kominterna, mart 1919 g.*, ed. E. Korotkov, B. Kun, and O. Piatnitskov (Moscow, 1933), pp. 244–246.

[73] Pipes, *op. cit.*, p. 161. See also *Istoriia Kompartii Azerbaidzhana*, p. 300.

[74] *Izvestiia*, April 23, 1919, p. 1. See also *Pravda*, April 23, 1919, p. 1; Spector, *op. cit.*, p. 64; Alfred L. P. Dennis, *The Foreign Policies of Soviet Russia* (New York, 1924), p. 217.

ation of the Peace Conference at Versailles and all its intrigue.[75] That same month the journal of the Commissariat for Nationalities, *Zhizn' natsional'nostei* ("Life of the Nationalities") declared: "The revolution is moving to the south, and if in Turkey the government actually passes to the workers, then the fate of the Caucasus can be regarded as predetermined." [76]

The role of Mustafa Kemal's avowed political enemies, the chiefs of the deposed Committee of Union and Progress (Ittihad ve Terakki), in preparing the groundwork for a Soviet-Turkish alliance has been the subject of interesting speculation. Many authors have pointed to the irreconcilable difference between Kemal and the Young Turks and have ascribed reports of early widespread Ittihadist support for Kemal to inaccurate information and mistaken identities. Recent studies and the memoirs of several Nationalist commanders reveal, however, that there was considerable continuity from the Enver-Talaat era into the Kemalist period. The Ittihadist organization, even after its dissolution in November, 1918, was the only effective force in Anatolia, providing the first leaders of the resistance. Moreover, like many other members of the military hierarchy, Kemal, too, had been an Ittihadist.[77] And while he may have regarded Enver Pasha as a dangerous and hated rival, Kemal certainly possessed the political astuteness to welcome whatever aid the former rulers of Turkey might bring his cause. Several months before the initial communication between Kemal and Soviet envoys, Bolshevik agents and Ittihadist émigrés in Germany had already come together to stir the waters of conspiracy.

Abandoning Constantinople during the last days of World War I, most members of the Ittihadist central committee took circuitous paths to exile and hiding in Germany.[78] Their rumored presence in several cities of central Europe was soon confirmed by Allied intelligence offi-

[75] *Manifest, Richtlinien, Beschlüsse des Ersten Kongresses: Aufrufe und offene Schreiben des Exekutivkomitees bis zum Zweiten Kongress* (Hamburg, 1920), pp. 81–99. See also Jane Degras, ed., *The Communist International, 1919–1943: Documents,* Vol. I (London, New York, and Toronto, 1956), pp. 54–58; *Izvestiia,* May 1, 1919, p. 1.

[76] *Zhizn' natsional'nostei,* May 18, 1919. See also *Bor'ba v Azerbaidzhane,* pp. 135–137.

[77] See, for example, Rustow, *op. cit.,* pp. 520–536, 541–543; Ertürk, *op. cit.,* pp. 211, 328–329; Dursunoğlu, *op. cit.,* pp. 58–59; Cruickshank, *op. cit.,* pp. 18–20. For useful and revealing details given by European contemporaries of Kemal, see Pernot, *op. cit.,* pp. 44–47, 68–69, 99–100; E. Nicol, *Angora et la France* (Paris, 1922), pp. 20–24.

[78] The worldwide Armenian press was quick to report the activities of Turkish Ittihadist leaders in Germany. See, in addition to nearly every Armenian newspaper printed in 1919, the following sources: Britain, FO 608/110, File 385/1/8; Rep. of Arm. Archives, File 353, Communiqués of the Armenian plenipotentiary in Germany; London *Times,* Feb. 14, 1919, p. 8; Omer Kiazim, *L'aventure kémaliste* (Paris, 1921), pp. 168–172, and his *Angora et Berlin* (Paris, 1922), pp. 93–96, 105.

cers. Beginning in February, 1919, for example, Samuel Edelman, American Vice-Consul at Geneva and an intelligence expert, frequently warned his superiors that Ittihadists and Bolsheviks had definitely established contact in Germany. The past Turkish dictators apparently hoped that the Communists would throw the world into upheaval and that the waves of revolution in Europe would sweep them back to their palaces along the Bosporus. On its part the Bolshevik regime, in Edelman's estimation, was seeking the collaboration of the notorious Turkish pashas as a means of bringing the Muslims of Russia to accept the Soviet system.[79] This was not an isolated appraisal. Diplomatic and military personnel throughout Europe and the Ottoman Empire filed reports of collusion between Bolsheviks and Ittihadists and imputed much of the turmoil in Anatolia to the Committee of Union and Progress.[80]

Although these dispatches were not free of imprecise and erroneous data, the Ittihadist triumvirate, Enver, Talaat, and Jemal, had indeed taken refuge in Germany and were soon invited by Karl Radek and other Bolshevik agents to continue their patriotic endeavors in Moscow, immune from exposure and arrest.[81] Late in 1919 Talaat Pasha wrote Mustafa Kemal that Radek had pledged active Soviet support for the Anatolian movement and that Enver and Jemal were among those who had already departed for Russia. The Ittihadists, Talaat insisted, were striving toward a goal in no way incongruous with the aims of Kemal and would apply all their available resources to engender a foreign opinion favorable to the Turkish revolution. The wartime Grand Vizier now offered to bow to Kemal's direction. Mustafa Kemal not only acknowledged receipt of the letter but also thanked Talaat Pasha unsparingly for his patriotic labors.[82] Further evidence of the early bonds between the Ittihadists and Nationalists becomes apparent in the revelation that during the summer of 1919, on instructions from Talaat Pasha, secondary Ittihadist officers who had remained in Turkey to

[79] US Archives, RG 256, 867.00/87/89/149.

[80] Britain, FO 608/110, 385/1/8/5968/6424/6910, and FO 608/115, File 385/1/25; Evans, op. cit., pp. 171–172, 174–175, 176; US Archives, 867.00/64/135/476, 867.00B/1/2/3, and 867B.00/116; London Times, Jan. 1, 1919, p. 7, April 14, p. 11, April 19, p. 1. See also Cebesoy, Milli mücadele, pp. 138–140.

[81] Cruickshank, op. cit., p. 22; Mir-Yacoub, Le problème du Caucase (Paris, 1933), pp. 143–145; Vratzian, op. cit., pp. 20–28; Kiazim, Angora et Berlin, pp. 158–162; Zarevand, op. cit., pp. 165–166. See also Cebesoy, Milli mücadele, p. 42, and Moskova hâtıraları, pp. 157–159, 220–222, 231–235; Galip Kemali Söylemezoğlu, Başımıza gelenler: Yakin bir mazinin hâtıraları, Mondrosdan-Mudanyaya, 1918–1922 (Istanbul, 1939), pp. 166–167.

[82] Cebesoy, Milli mücadele, pp. 42–43. See also Söylemezoğlu, op. cit., p. 171; Kiazim, Angora et Berlin, pp. 158–160.

perpetuate the party under the cloak of offshoot societies recognized Kemal as the head of the resistance.[83]

Toward a Nationalist-Soviet Entente

The first direct channel of communication between Soviet Russia and the oppositional elements in Turkey seems to have been passed through the Crimean Peninsula, which came under the occupation of the Red Army in the spring of 1919. Mustafa Subhi and several comrades transferred to the Crimea, there resuming publication of *Yeni Dünya* and establishing the Muslim Central Bureau to enlighten the unsympathetic Tatar population.[84] According to Soviet historians the appearance of the Red Army on the northern shores of the Black Sea had an immeasurable impact on the rate of ferment in Turkey. Mustafa Kemal could take heart in the knowledge that a potential major ally was now accessible, the intervening British and French installations and battleships notwithstanding.[85]

Actually, General Denikin soon expelled the Red Army and Soviet administration from the Crimea, but the Muslim Central Bureau continued to function and successfully dispatched an agent to Constantinople to seek out the organizers of the Turkish resistance. Once in the Ottoman capital the envoy was placed in liaison with the Karakol society, one of the Ittihadist successor groups. The Karakol, with conduits into several government ministries, lent assistance to the Nationalists by relaying invaluable information to Mustafa Kemal and directing fresh converts and supplies toward the Anatolian hinterland.[86] The Muslim Bolshevik emissary, in discussions with Karakol chief Kara Vasif, advocated the evolvement of a democratic regime in Turkey and offered Soviet aid in expelling the Allied interventionists, in ministering to the poor, and in defending the interests of the Turkish workers and peasants. The Sovnarkom, he said, was prepared to furnish gold, silver, and military matériel; Turkish negotiators should be sent to Russia to work out the details of the entente. Kara Vasif endorsed the proposal in principle but made clear that the ultimate decision to ac-

---

[83] Ertürk, *op. cit.*, pp. 343–346; Emre, *op. cit.*, pp. 242–243. See also Britain, FO 608/115, File 385/1/25.

[84] Pipes, *op. cit.*, pp. 184–189; Harris, *op. cit.*, pp. 55–56; Novichev, *op. cit.*, p. 60.

[85] See, for example, the works of Kheifets and of Sargsian, cited above.

[86] Harris, *op. cit.*, p. 47; Rustow, *op. cit.*, p. 540; Tunaya, *op. cit.*, pp. 520–523; Cruickshank, *op. cit.*, pp. 18–19. See also Gotthard Jäschke, "Neues zur russisch-türkischen Freundschaft von 1919–1939," *Die Welt des Islams*, n.s., VI, 3–4 (1961), 204, cited hereafter as "Freundschaft"; and Kheifets, *op. cit.*, pp. 96–98.

cept or reject any Soviet-Turkish agreement rested with the leaders in Anatolia.[87]

Meanwhile, Mustafa Kemal showed himself receptive to other feelers sent out from Moscow. Several sources corroborate an account that during his stay in Havza, May 25–June 12, 1919, Kemal conferred secretly with Colonel Semen M. Budenny of subsequent Soviet military fame. Traveling incognito on a fact-finding mission, Budenny broached the possibility of achieving Soviet-Turkish collaboration vis-à-vis the Allied Powers and the states in the Caucasus. An air of mystery still shrouds the particulars of the meeting, the authenticity of which has been challenged. Yet it becomes increasingly clear that such an exchange would have conformed to the strategy then espoused by both Mustafa Kemal and the Sovnarkom.[88] According to the most detailed available description of the rendezvous, Colonel Budenny gave assurances that Soviet Russia would stand with Turkey against all schemes to carve from the Ottoman Empire separate Armenian, Kurdish, and Pontic states. The Armenians in particular, said Budenny, had become troublemakers; their Hnchakist and Dashnakist parties were opportunist, serving as lackeys of whatever power happened to be ascendant. He pledged money, weapons, ammunition, and even armed forces in return for Turkish defiance of the common enemies in the West. But the envoy also made innuendoes about the establishment of a Soviet-type system in Turkey and the abolition of the Sultanate and Caliphate. Alert to the implications, Kemal evasively replied that Turkey would naturally choose a route similar to that of Soviet Russia. The Sultanate, he observed, was tottering, but the Caliphate presented a more complicated problem since it involved the sentiments of the Muslim world, whose support was essential in putting the British in their place. The same consideration, Kemal asserted, prevented him from declaring forthwith in favor of communism. Only with the success of the national struggle and the end of foreign intervention would Turkey be able to turn serious attention to Soviet principles. During their consultations Kemal and Budenny are said to have developed a cordial relationship and the Russian officer, departing from Havza with a sense of accomplishment,

[87] Karabekir, İstiklâl Harbimiz, p. 74; Cebesoy, Millî mücadele, pp. 94–95. For accounts of other early contacts between Bolshevik agents and Turkish leaders, see Selek, op. cit., II, 56; Ertürk, op. cit., pp. 217, 244–245; Zarevand, op. cit., p. 165. Bolshevik agents were reportedly instrumental in the establishment of the short-lived leftist newspapers in Trebizond, the Greek-language Epokhi ("Epoch") and the Turkish-language Selamet ("Security"). See Pernot, op. cit., p. 84.

[88] See Harris, op. cit., pp. 47, 57; Şapolyo, op. cit., p. 505; Ertürk, op. cit., pp. 294, 324, 338–342, 431, 436. Bıyıklıoğlu, op. cit., p. 64, apparently rejects the evidence of a rendezvous between Kemal and Budenny, stating that Soviet Russia and Nationalist Turkey were unable to enter into direct relations until 1920.

submitted a gratifying report to his government and urged an active program of assistance to Nationalist Turkey. Mustafa Kemal had proved the shrewder of the two, however, for he won offers of material aid and pocketed a flexible political weapon. In case of dire need, he could call upon Soviet reinforcements. Kemal confided to an associate that the nation must cross one bridge at a time and that all means were honorable in attaining the opposite shore.[89]

On June 7 one of Kemal's aides wrote General Karabekir from Havza that there was much to be gained from an accord with the Bolsheviks provided, of course, that they made no attempt to tamper with Turkish traditions or the Islamic faith. Karabekir readily agreed and recommended that steps be taken to determine precisely what the Bolsheviks expected.[90] In a detailed cipher telegram from Amasia on June 23, Kemal personally revealed his views to Karabekir. He suggested that Bolshevism in itself was not necessarily incompatible with custom and religion, as had been demonstrated in the Russian Muslim regions of the Crimea, Kazan, and Orenburg, but that it should nevertheless not be allowed to spill over the borders into Turkey. By sending a few trusted men to negotiate with the Bolsheviks, Kemal went on, a large-scale Soviet military operation could be averted. The Turkish envoys should seal a pact for weapons, equipment, currency, and, only when and if requested, for active armed intervention. Such an arrangement could then be thrust before the Allied Powers to coerce them to evacuate Ottoman lands and forego their plans for partition. They would be given the choice of restoring complete independence to Turkey or else watching the Bolsheviks patrol the shores of the Mediterranean and the Straits.[91]

It was after these exchanges that the Nationalists elected not to rely on Kara Vasif's Karakol society or the reputed Bolshevik agent in Constantinople but rather to deal directly with the Soviet authorities through handpicked emissaries sent from Anatolia to the Caucasus and Russia. Once again the cardinal importance of the passageway over Nakhichevan, Zangezur, and Karabagh loomed to the fore.[92] While in Erzerum, Mustafa Kemal, Husein Rauf, and Kiazim Karabekir con-

---

[89] Ertürk, *op. cit.*, pp. 338–342.

[90] Jäschke, "Freundschaft," p. 204.

[91] Kandemir, *Kemal*, pp. 74–75; Karabekir, *Esaları*, p. 64, and *İstiklâl Harbimiz*, pp. 57–58.

[92] Cebesoy, *Moskova hâtıraları*, pp. 128–135. According to Yanus Nadi, former Ittihadist journalist, newspaper editor, and a member of the "eastern-oriented" wing in the Nationalist movement, the Turkish resistance leaders also planned to send agents over an alternate route via the Black Sea on motor launches to Odessa and the Crimea. See Kheifets, *op. cit.*, p. 94; S. I. Aralov, *Vospominaniia sovetskogo diplomata, 1922–1923* (Moscow, 1960), p, 20.

curred that Bolshevism was not the path their movement would follow but that Soviet Russia must be pressed into the service of Turkey. This basic strategy required the subjugation of Armenia, the neutrality of Georgia, and the inclusion of Azerbaijan within the Soviet sphere. Azerbaijan would form the link to Moscow. Karabekir Pasha, declaring that the Turkish cause was hopeless unless this tactic succeeded, assumed personal responsibility for ensuring the safe passage of the envoys over the southern highlands of the Armenian republic.[93] Indeed, the secret negotiators were soon to be welcomed by the Bolshevik underground in Baku and put into communication with the Caucasus Regional Committee of the Russian Communist Party.[94]

Meanwhile, rumors circulating throughout the eastern vilayets placed the Red Army in the Caucasus. The Armenians were purportedly evacuating Sarikamish and Kars, and the British and Italian troops (the latter nonexistent) abandoning the Caucasus. Perhaps to bolster the morale of his men General Karabekir, and at times Kemal, too, gave currency to such hearsay. Karabekir even suggested that the so-called Bolshevik partisans in the Caucasus were actually led by Enver Pasha and that the Pan-Islamic hero would soon reach the Arpachai (Akhurian) River, the western boundary of the Erevan guberniia.[95] At the end of June, 1919, XV Corps Commader Karabekir informed all division heads that the combined forces of Enver and the Bolsheviks, having overpowered the Armenians of Karabagh, were marching upon Zangezur, and he ordered that couriers be sent to Nakhichevan, the district bordering Zangezur, to encourage the Muslim inhabitants resisting the Armenians not to lay down their arms.[96] In a dispatch to General Ali Fuad Pasha a few days later, Karabekir contended that only

[93] Kandemir, Kemal, pp. 88–89. According to unconfirmed rumors Bolshevik agents were present at the Erzerum Congress. See Pernot, op. cit., p. 84. During his address to the Erzerum Congress Mustafa Kemal extolled the struggle of the Russian people for their national freedom, a struggle from which the Turkish people could take heart in confronting all enemies. See Kemal, Nutuk, III, 927; B. Dantsig, Turtsiia (Moscow, 1949), p. 85. Earlier, on July 4–5, 1919, XX Corps Commander Ali Fuad Pasha received information from Kemal that Karabekir was attempting to establish contact with the Bolsheviks and that progress toward that goal was quite satisfactory. See Cebesoy, Millî mücadele, p. 95.

[94] The Soviet-Turkish negotiations will be treated in the subsequent volumes of this history.

[95] Karabekir, İstiklâl Harbimiz, pp. 46, 52–53, and Esasları, p. 69.

[96] Karabekir, İstiklâl Harbimiz, pp. 64–65. The bloodshed in Karabagh at the beginning of June, 1919, (see pp. 175–177 above) apparently gave rise to Karabekir's reports on the subjugation of Karabagh by the Muslim-Bolshevik army. The information was not totally unfounded, for the Azerbaijani governor-general of Karabagh, Khosrov Bek Sultanov, was an ardent Ittihadist sympathizer and could readily have maintained liaison with Ittihadist agents and Enver's couriers in the Caucasus.

the Dashnakists continued to fight in the Caucasus, for all other elements had made common cause with the Bolsheviks. The Armenians, he continued, were morally and materially bankrupt and their government's last hope, the military might of Great Britain, was rapidly evaporating. What better time was there for Turkey to excise this annoying growth to the east! [97] Karabekir's communiqués were highly colored, but they indicate the weight Bolshevism and Soviet Russia carried in the minds and actions of the Turkish commanders in 1919.

Even as Kiazim Karabekir was embellishing the countless rumors, intelligence agents and the General Staff of the Armenian army reported the presence of Turkish regulars in Alashkert, Olti, and Sarikamish. Turkish emissaries, too, had been observed in the Kars oblast, spurring the Muslim villages to challenge the Erevan government and heralding the participation of the Red Army in the campaign against the Armenians.[98] It was upon the receipt of this portentous news that Avetis Aharonian warned the Peace Conference and the Allied Powers that the forces of Pan-Turan and Pan-Islam on the one hand and Soviet Russia and Bolshevism on the other had resolved to embrace over the prostrate body of Armenia. Aharonian's premonitions and admonitions could bring no action to bear on the imminent bond between Soviet Russia and Nationalist Turkey.

Within a few months of the Mudros Armistice, the abased Turkish nation had shown signs of fierce pride and a determination to hold fast to all Anatolia. The retention of mobilized divisions in the eastern vilayets, the inability and the reluctance of the Allies to enforce the Armistice, the humiliating Greek occupation of Smyrna, and the diligence of certain ranking Turkish officials in Constantinople had together provided the elements necessary for the rise of Kiazim Karabekir and Mustafa Kemal on the interior plateau. Neither the Erevan government nor the Turkish resistance organization indicated a readiness to initiate a dialogue, yet each clearly understood the essence of the other. The attitudes prevailing on both sides of the old Russo-Turkish border left little if any possibility for a modus vivendi. The Armenian leadership was convinced that without Turkish Armenia the Republic could achieve neither security nor viability, while the new Turkish leadership was equally certain that national integrity was inconceivable without the eastern Anatolian highlands—Turkish Armenia. The arena was thus prepared for mortal combat.

[97] Karabekir, İstiklâl Harbimiz, p. 71. See also Cebesoy, Milli mücadele, p. 96.
[98] US Archives, RG 256, 184.611/889; Rep. of Arm. Archives, File 8/8 and File 319/1, no. P.0176.

14

Toward
the Second Year

The Republic of Armenia, having persevered through months of domestic and international turbulence, observed its first anniversary on May 28, 1919. Conditions were far from stable; food shortages, lawlessness, and deep internal fissures still racked the land. Progress toward fusing the two halves of the Armenian people was slow and the initial results were disappointing. Yet many dedicated citizens were striving to forge an organized state, and the belief prevailed that, once the final boundaries had been drawn in Paris, it would be possible to overcome the obstacles—dialects, customs, alien influences, and mutual suspicions—separating Russian Armenian and Turkish Armenian.

Within its limited means the Armenian government attempted further internal renovation during the spring of 1919. One of the foremost experts on Transcaucasian water resources was brought to Erevan to head a large team of engineers and geologists in charting plans for electrification and an improved irrigation network.[1] Generous allocations were made for the construction and restoration of schools, and a special committee was formed to prepare the groundwork for a state university.[2] The first conference of the nation's governors took steps to

[1] Vratzian, *Ughinerov*, V, 71–72. The team was led by S. Zavalishin. Financial contributions from Armenian communities around the world began to reach Erevan at this time. The community of Rostov-Nakhichevan in the Don basin of South Russia contributed a million rubles and organized a detachment of young volunteers to move to Erevan to assist in the government's campaign against infectious diseases. This information was reported by Armenia's quasi-official plenipotentiary in Rostov, Grigor K. Chalkhushian. See *Hairenik* (daily), June 22, 1919, p. 2. On March 27 *Bor'ba* announced the arrival in Tiflis of seventy of these youths.

[2] Rep. of Arm. Archives, File 66a/3, Bulletin no. 110. The university planning committee, headed by Professor Stepan Ghambarian, recommended that Armenia's first

upgrade the quality of the militia by providing it uniforms and higher pay and by petitioning the Ministry of Interior to establish training academies. The conference also rectified certain unnatural variants in the administrative boundaries separating the ten existing provinces: Erevan, Etchmiadzin, Surmalu, Daralagiaz, Zangezur, Novo-Bayazit, Dilijan, Karakilisa, Alexandropol, and Kars.[3] The Ministry of Justice announced corresponding legal reforms, including the creation of ten provincial courts, a court of appeals, and a senate—the supreme court of Armenia.[4] But most important in mid-1919, the typhus epidemic and freezing blizzards, having reaped their toll, had run their course and the intensity of the vengeful famine had eased.

It is perhaps natural that, with the relative amelioration of internal physical conditions, ideological rivalries among the several parties should have become more pronounced. The minor parties now considered themselves absolved of the self-imposed moral restrictions which had induced them to temper their attacks upon the government. Within the coalition cabinet itself, division along partisan lines became common, although a show of unity was maintained as late as April, 1919, when Dashnakist Premier Kachaznuni and Populist Finance Minister Enfiadjian embarked on a joint mission to Europe and America. In the legislature bombastic oratory eclipsed constructive labor, and, with the defection of several Populist deputies to the opposition benches, political stalemate resulted. Dashnakist leaders, angered by the "obstructionist" tactics of the parties that had been granted representation heavily out of proportion to their popular base, apparently resolved to neutralize the legislature. On April 27 the Khorhurd adopted a Dashnakist-sponsored motion to recess for a month, during which all legislative prerogatives were to be vested in the cabinet.[5] This action threatened

---

institution of higher learning begin operations with the faculties (departments) of jurisprudence and history-philology. See the dispatches in *Hairenik* (daily), Aug. 16, 1919, p. 3, Aug. 30, p. 1, Oct. 31, p. 4, and Nov. 25, p. 1; *Bor'ba*, May 22, 1919, p. 2, and May 25, p. 2.

[3] Vratzian, *Hanrapetutiun*, pp. 320–321. The governors or their representatives at the conference were Levon Amirkhanian, Erevan; Sedrak Djalalian, Etchmiadzin; Iusuf Bek Temurian (a Yezidi), Surmalu; Nupar Hakobian, Daralagiaz; Nikolai Hovsepian, Zangezur; Beno Nalchadjian, Novo-Bayazit, Mesrop Saratikian, Dilijan; Sigo Ter-Sargsian, Karakilisa; Talanian, Alexandropol; Stepan Korganian, Kars. In May, Gevorg Varshamian was added as governor of Nakhichevan and in the same month the towns of Khamarlu, Vagharshapat (Etchmiadzin), Ashtarak, Igdir, Kulp (Goghb), Karakilisa, and Jalal-oghli were elevated to city status. See Rep. of Arm. Archives, File 66a/3, Bulletin no. 85.

[4] Rep. of Arm. Archives, File 8/8; Vratzian, *Hanrapetutiun*, p. 320.

[5] Rep. of Arm. Archives, File 66a/3; Vratzian, *Hanrapetutiun*, p. 227. See also pp. 152–154 above.

the parliamentary experiment, removing as it did the sole official podium of the Social Democrats and the Social Revolutionaries.

Of concern to all political factions were questions relating specifically to the Turkish Armenian refugees. These prime victims of hunger, disease, and exposure regarded the Republic of Armenia as neither a haven nor a permanent home. Inculcated with a strong sense of national awareness, the Turkish Armenians found repugnant the "Russianism" of the Erevan republic and its native inhabitants. It seemed incongruous, at the very least, that Armenia should have reemerged as a nation-state, not in the great central plateau of historic Armenia, the focal point of the emancipatory struggle, but in a peripheral province bearing the stamp of things Russian. To the half million Turkish Armenians in the Caucasus, the government and capital of liberated Armenia should be located in Karin (Erzerum), Van, or even a major center in Cilicia, but certainly not in Erevan. With mounting impatience they awaited the opportunity to turn homeward, to lands extending into the western horizon. Consequently, the refugee population persisted in maintaining its distinct militia, clustering around compatriotic societies bearing the names of Western Armenian districts, and evading, whenever possible, the obligations of citizenship in the Erevan republic. The political and intellectual leaders of the Turkish Armenians shared some of these popular misgivings, but they also perceived the tragic consequences of a lasting internal division. Thus, as the Armenian government initiated a program of its own to heal the deep rift, two Turkish Armenian congresses, one in Erevan and the other in Paris, attempted to define a policy with regard to the Armenian republic and the coalescence of the Eastern (Russian) and Western (Turkish) Armenians.

The Second Congress of Western Armenians

In the spring of 1917 a congress of Turkish Armenian representatives had created several committees to guide, aid, and safeguard the refugee masses until circumstances permitted them to reclaim their homes.[6] No one would then have believed that during the ensuing year civil war would engulf Russia, the Russian army would abandon the Caucasus front, and Transcaucasia would be set adrift and broken jaggedly into

[6] For a brief description of the First Congress of Western Armenians, see Hovannisian, *Road to Independence*, pp. 78–79. See also A. Terzipashian, *Nupar* (Paris, 1939), pp. 145–154; G. Sassuni, *Tajkahayastane rusakan tirapetutian tak (1914–1918)* (Boston, 1927), pp. 136–140; Vahan Papazian, *Im hushere*, Vol. II (Beirut, 1952), pp. 438–441.

three separate republics. These upheavals crippled and disorganized the responsible Turkish Armenian bodies and rendered ineffective their efforts to protect the displaced population. In view of the drastic political changes in the Caucasus and the aggravated plight of the refugees, an interparty council of Turkish Armenians named a special commission in December, 1918, to arrange for a second general conference of Turkish Armenian leaders. The commission proposed as major agenda items (1) the political goals of the Western Armenians, (2) the problems associated with repatriation, (3) the selection of new executive organs and the liquidation of all other boards still in existence.[7]

The Second Congress of Western Armenians met in Erevan, February 6–13, 1919, in the chamber of the Khorhurd. The participants included some fifty delegates from the various refugee centers in the Republic, the editors of the Turkish Armenian newspapers *Ashkhatank* ("Labor") and *Van-Tosp*, representatives of benevolent-compatriotic societies, and members of the government. It was hoped that General Andranik, too, would attend, but he was still in Zangezur and would not, in any case, have condescended to appear in Erevan. The presidium and various committees were appointed during preliminary caucuses on February 4–5, and several addresses made up the agenda of the first official session on the sixth.[8] After Catholicos Gevorg V had blessed the gathering, Premier Hovhannes Kachaznuni welcomed the delegates, inviting all to join in the campaign against regional particularism and internal rivalry: "I am filled with the hope that this Congress will be the last to convene in the name of one part of the Armenian people. I believe the day shall come when no longer will there be mention of Western Armenian or any other kind of Armenian and that instead there shall stand forth the single and fully integrated will of united Armenia." Kachaznuni reminded the delegates that a generation of Russian Armenian leaders had dedicated itself to the cause of an emancipated Turkish Armenia, and he called upon them to express the combined aspirations and demands of the nation, "for no more can there be an ours and a yours, since what is ours is yours and what is yours is ours." [9]

In its working sessions the Congress evaluated the critical problems facing the refugee population, terminated the powers of all local Turk-

[7] Vratzian, *Hanrapetutiun*, p. 229.

[8] *Miatsial ev Ankakh Hayastan*, publ. of H. H. Dashnaktsutiun (Constantinople, 1919), pp. 64–66; Vratzian, *Hanrapetutiun*, pp. 229–230.

[9] For the text of Kachaznuni's address and an account of the opening session of the Congress, see *Hairenik* (daily), May 3, 1919, p. 1, as reprinted from *Jakatamart* (Constantinople).

ish Armenian administrative organs, and enjoined a new permanent Executive Body to coordinate efforts for the earliest possible repatriation and to plan for the protection and sustenance of the refugees during that mass movement.[10] Heated controversy flared on the draft resolution proposed by the political affairs committee, necessitating long private caucuses and several modifications before its adoption on February 12, a day before adjournment. The text of the document revealed the incertitude and confusion besetting many Turkish Armenian leaders. Inhabitants, albeit temporary, of the Armenian republic and advocates of the merger of Western and Eastern Armenia, they nonetheless looked for guidance to the National Delegation in Paris. The compromise resolution read as follows:

The Second Congress of Western Armenians, having studied the current situation of the Armenian people:
1. sincerely hails and extols the independence of Free and United Armenia;
2. expresses confidence in His Excellency Boghos Nubar Pasha's first cabinet of Free and United Armenia [it was then rumored that Nubar had formed a government in Paris];
3. proclaims its firm determination and will to have one political and governmental entity through the confluence of the lands and people of all Armenia;
4. charges the elected "Executive Body" to communicate immediately with the council of ministers [of Boghos Nubar], having as a goal the fulfillment of all political and governmental measures necessary for the creation of Free and United Armenia;
5. directs the elected "Executive Body" to work actively, at the same time, with the cabinet and the legislature of the Araratian [Erevan] Republic to declare the independence of United, Free Armenia and, in order to effect the all-national union, to participate in the administrative and legislative institutions [of that republic];[11]

[10] A résumé of the Congress proceedings was printed in *Hamarot teghekagir Arevmtahai Erkrord Hamagumari, 1919 t.*, publ. of the Western Armenian Executive Body (Tiflis, 1919).

[11] Five delegates, all members of the Ramkavar party, left the session as an expression of protest and opposition to this point. The Sahmanadir or Sahmanadrakan Ramkavar (Constitutional Democrat) party was organized in 1908 by the merger of three preexisting Turkish Armenian groups. Although including an element that supported the Armenian resistance movement, the party operated legally until the first year of the World War, advocating a platform of Ottoman constitutional reforms as the solution to the Armenian question. It gained considerable popularity among the Armenian communities of Egypt, Cilicia, Constantinople, Europe, and America. In the eastern Ottoman vilayets, the Sahmanadir Ramkavars centered their activities at Van, where in 1915 they participated in the general Armenian defense against the Turkish army until the Russian divisions and Armenian volunteer corps from the Caucasus relieved the city and the Armenian population of the

6. requests the Allied governments to guarantee the sovereign existence of free and United Armenia through political, economic, and
democratic aid and cooperation;
7. demands the punishment, by military court-martial, of the authors
and culpable creatures of the Great Armenian Atrocity—[Kaiser] Wilhelm, Enver, Talaat, Jemal, Nazim, Behaeddin Shakir, and their fellow
governors, administrators, and chiefs;
8. demands total indemnification by the Ottoman government for
the losses sustained by the Armenian people.[12]

The Western Armenian Congress, many if not most of its delegates
Dashnakist sympathizers, regarded Boghos Nubar (the sole national
leader mentioned in the resolution) as the man best qualified to advance Armenian interests. Yet, in its ambivalence, the Congress had instructed its Executive Body to collaborate with and participate in the
ruling organs of the "Araratian Republic" in order to hasten the realization of a free and united land. The resolution, combining two not
entirely congruous points of view, wavered between Erevan and Paris.
The dualism was also reflected in the greetings addressed to Boghos
Nubar and to Hovhannes Kachaznuni. The telegram to Paris read:

The Second Congress of Western Armenians relays its heartfelt felicitations to Your Excellency and expresses boundless confidence that
through Your competent and efficient activity the foundations of government for the native Armenian land will be shaped with finality and
that the incessantly tormented Armenian people will be afforded the
opportunity to labor and re-create its native home. The Congress, holding You to be the truest spokesman of its desires and aspirations, believes that You will strive to accomplish its political and national goals,
the unification of the artificially separated segments of the Armenian
people and the creation of a single governmental-political organism.[13]

The above profession notwithstanding, the message to Premier Kachaznuni urged the Erevan government to initiate decisive measures:

---

province took refuge in Russian Armenia. In 1921 the Sahmanadrakan Ramkavar
party was to become the Ramkavar Azatakan Kusaktsutiun (Democratic Liberal
party) through a dual merger with the Armenakan society, which had been founded
in 1885, and with the Verakazmial Hnchakian (Reformed Hnchakist) faction, which
had separated from the Marxist Hnchakian party in 1896 and, casting aside the
socialist program, had concentrated solely on the emancipation of the Turkish
Armenians. For a concise account of these groups and their ultimate unification, see
the brochure of the Ramkavar Azatakan Kusaktsutiun, *Mer gaghaparn u gordse:
Ramkavar Azatakan Kusaktsutian miutian eresnamiakin aritov* (Fresno, Calif., 1952).
[12] Rep. of Arm. Archives, File 9/9. An English translation of the resolution is in
US Archives, RG 256, 184.021/6.
[13] Vratzian, *Hanrapetutiun*, p. 232.

The Second Congress of Western Armenians, hailing the government of one part of the Armenian people, is hopeful that the government will add its voice to the decision of the Western Armenian Congress to have a single fatherland and a single united, free Armenian state structure.

The Congress, deeming this issue to be of historic importance to the Armenian people, is convinced that the government of the Ararat Republic will hasten to declare without delay the independence of United, Free Armenia and will take active steps to effect that unification.[14]

The nine-man Executive Body, elected during the final session, was instructed to implement the decisions of the Congress and to function until the creation of a combined government of united Armenia.[15] In pursuance of this goal the Executive Body soon petitioned Kachaznuni's cabinet to declare the two sectors of the nation officially conjoined. The coalition government approved the proposal on February 25, 1919, and directed Foreign Minister Tigranian to draft relevant reports and documents for submission to the legislature.[16] The outcome of these measures was to be a historic act proclaimed on the first anniversary of the Republic of Armenia.

The Armenian National Congress in Paris

Even as the Western Armenian Congress met in Erevan, Vahan Papazian (Dashnakist) and Avetis Terzipashian (Ramkavar) were en route to Paris to participate, as representatives of the refugees in the Caucasus, in another assembly, the Armenian National Congress.[17] The gathering had been summoned by Boghos Nubar in October, 1918, for the purpose of reorganizing the National Delegation and deliberating vital issues affecting the future of Armenia.[18] As general elections were then out of the question for Armenians in most parts of the world, nearly all the delegates were appointed by existing national bodies. In the United States, however, a spirited popular campaign was conducted to secure the votes of all Armenian men and women. In an intensely partisan and controversial election, the American-Armenian commu-

[14] *Miatsial Ankakh Hayastan*, p. 68.
[15] The Executive consisted of Smbat Baroyan, Khachatur Bonapartian, Armen Sassuni, Grigor Bulgaratsi, Varazdat Teroyan, Ruben Drambian, Vahagn Krmoyan, Vagharshak Hokhikian, and Arsen Kitur.
[16] Vratzian, *Hanrapetutiun*, p. 234.
[17] In their memoirs the two Turkish Armenian leaders give accounts of their journey from the Caucasus to Paris. See Papazian, *op. cit.*, III (Cairo, 1957), pp. 19–33; and Terzipashian, *op. cit.*, pp. 227–228. A memorandum the pair submitted to the British High Commissioner at Constantinople was forwarded to the Foreign Office on February 13, 1919. See Britain, FO 371/3657, 38707/512/58.
[18] See *Hairenik* (daily), Feb. 4, 1919, p. 1.

nity of almost 100,000 chose four delegates (three Dashnakists and one Ramkavar).[19] This exception aside, representation in the National Congress was highly disproportionate. The Persian Armenian community of 100,000, for example, received only two seats, whereas the small circle of merchants who constituted the Armenian colony in England was also granted two places. The handful of Armenians in Switzerland and in Italy each sent one delegate as did the Rumanian Armenian community of more than 30,000. Nevertheless, nearly every population center of Turkish Armenians was represented.[20]

A published summary of the proceedings of the National Congress shows that the credentials of thirty-eight delegates were confirmed and that Avetis Aharonian and Hamo Ohandjanian of the Delegation of the Republic of Armenia attended in an advisory capacity. The roster of delegates also reveals the participation of distinguished national leaders, including Archbishop Eghishe Turian, scholar and erstwhile Patriarch of Constantinople; Gabriel Noradoungian and Grigor Sinapian, former members of the Ottoman Council of Ministers; Hovhannes Khan Massehian, onetime ambassador of Persia to Great Britain and to Germany; and noted men of letters Levon Shant, Arshak Chobanian, and Vahan Tekeyan. Boghos Nubar Pasha spoke both as the representative of the Armenians of Java and India and as the chairman of the National Delegation. By political affiliation the delegates divided into roughly equal groupings of Ramkavars, Dashnakists, and nonpartisans, the latter gravitating toward the conservative or constitutional-evolutionary platform of the Ramkavar party.[21]

[19] The election was conducted by the Armenian National Union of America. Slates were put up by the Armenian Apostolic Church, the Armenian Protestant churches, Hai Heghapokhakan Dashnaktsutiun, the Verakazmial Hnchakian party, the Sahmanadrakan-Ramkavar party, and the Armenian General Benevolent Union. For articles and accounts of the campaign, see the issues of *Hairenik* (Dashnaktsutiun), *Pahak* (Verakazmial Hnchakian), and *Azg* (Sahmanadrakan-Ramkavar), Jan.–Feb., 1919. See also Manuk G. Jizmejian, *Patmutiun amerikahai kaghakakan kusaktsutiants, 1890–1925* (Fresno, Calif. 1930), pp. 366–370; Rep. of Arm. Archives, File 1407a/27a, *H. H. D. Amerikayi Kedronakan Komite, 1919.* The four delegates attending the Paris gathering as representatives of the Armenian-American community were Ervand Aghaton (Ramkavar) and Manuk Hambardzumian, Arsen Mikayelian, and Zatik Matikian (Dashnakists).

[20] Vratzian, *Hanrapetutiun*, pp. 241–242, is critical of the unbalanced representation, whereas Papazian, *op. cit.,* III, 48, shows that the system used in selecting the delegates was, under the circumstances, the best possible and that the results were basically democratic.

[21] See *Ampopum hai azgayin hamagumari ashkhatutiants ev voroshmants (petrvar 24en minchev april 22),* cited hereafter as *Azgayin hamagumar.* The delegation roster and a description of the delegates are also given by Papazian, *op. cit.,* III, 38–44; and Terzipashian, *op. cit.,* pp. 245–253. See also *Hairenik* (daily), Feb. 2, 1919, p. 1, and

The Armenian National Congress met in formal session from February 24 to April 22, 1919, amidst the tension and suspense that then gripped Paris. The nations of the world had converged on the capital of Europe either to challenge or to defend. The Armenians had come to do both: to challenge the territorial integrity of the Ottoman Empire and to defend Armenia's right to statehood and independence. The National Congress unanimously endorsed the official memorandum that Boghos Nubar and Avetis Aharonian had submitted to the Peace Conference on February 12 and 26.[22] Among its other varied activities, the Congress resolved to dispatch medical teams to the major refugee centers, to assist the famine-stricken population in Eastern Armenia, and to protest the most recent Muslim outrages against Armenians in Aleppo, Cilicia, and western Anatolia.[23]

The delegates also confirmed for submission to the Peace Conference a separate memorandum on reparations and indemnities "to be borne by the Ottoman government for the losses the Armenian nation sustained in Turkey and the Caucasus during this war as the result of massacre, deportation, and other atrocities." The memorandum stated that, of the two million Armenians in the Ottoman Empire in 1914, 1,800,000 had been either slain, deported, or compelled to flee into the Caucasus. The attached schedules detailed the losses in human life, movable and immovable property, implements and livestock, and capital assets. The total injury, as shown in monetary terms, came to more than 19 billion French francs: 14.6 billion in Western Armenia and 4.5 billion in Eastern Armenia.[24] The memorandum was subsequently considered by the Peace Conference's Commission on the Reparation of Damage through a special committee dealing with nations not represented on the Commission.[25] In its final report of April 14, 1919, the

Feb. 6, p. 1; Rep. of Arm. Archives, File 231/130 (showing the local addresses in Paris of all delegates); Britain, FO 608/97, 375/1/1/1466/1484/2347, and FO 371/3657, 30411/512/58.

[22] See pp. 277–281 above.

[23] In addition to the summary of the proceedings published after the adjournment of the Congress, frequent accounts and observations appeared in the Armenian-American newspapers *Pahak, Azg, Hairenik,* and *Eritasard Hayastan* (Social Democrat Hnchakian), March through June, 1919. See also Terzipashian, *op. cit.,* pp. 254–279. For descriptions of the unrest in Aleppo and Adana, see *Le Temps,* March 12, 1919, p. 4, and pp. 320–321 above.

[24] *Tableau approximatif des réparations et indemnités pour les dommages subis par la nation arménienne en Arménie de Turquie et dans la République Arménienne du Caucase* (Paris, 1919). See also *Hairenik* (daily), April 8, 1919, p. 2.

[25] Philip Mason Burnett, *Reparations at the Paris Peace Conference: From the Standpoint of the American Delegation* (2 vols.; New York, 1940), I, 35–36, 943–945, II, 580–593. The special committee was responsible to the Reparation Commission's First Subcommittee (Valuation of Damage).

three-man special committee[26] classified into several general categories the claims of the seventeen peoples having come within its purview. The Armenian claims were listed as follows:[27]

Category	French Francs	[Equivalent in Dollars]
I. Damage to Physical Property, Requisitions, Fines, Taxes, etc.	11,317,632,000	2,184,871,042
II. Losses of Revenue, Support of Civilians, Repatriation of Refugees, etc.	1,080,000,000	208,494,208
III. Compensation for Civilian Injuries and Deaths	6,108,350,000	1,179,218,146
IV. Compensation for Military Injuries and Deaths	625,000,000	120,656,370
V. Other War Costs	—	—
VI. Total Claim	19,130,982,000	3,693,239,766

There is no evidence to indicate that any action on these claims was taken by the Commission on the Reparation of Damage, which was preoccupied with the European settlement and the imposition of a crushing financial liability upon Germany.

Partisan and particularist sentiments in the Armenian National Congress were exposed most blatantly during the sessions that focused on relations between the National Delegation on the one hand and the government and representatives of the Republic of Armenia on the other. A considerable number of non-Dashnakists in this basically Turkish Armenian assemblage opposed Aharonian's presence in Paris. The existence of a second delegation could be interpreted as a sign of internal Armenian discord at a time when a display of national solidarity was imperative. There was also the apprehension that the Russian Armenian leaders were scheming to thrust their will upon the Turkish Armenians and that Dashnaktsutiun, by virtue of its dominance in the Erevan republic, hoped to determine policies affecting all Armenians. Some delegates did not regard kindly the Republic itself. They feared that the peacemakers might decrease the size of the Armenian region to be separated from the Ottoman Empire on grounds that a state with modest territories had already emerged in the Caucasus. Furthermore, they were convinced that to safeguard Armenia's future the national

[26] Members of this committee were Brigadier General Charles H. McKinstry (United States), Colonel Sidney C. Peel (Great Britain), and Inspecteur des finances Georges Jouasset (France).

[27] Burnett, op. cit., II, 583-585, 590.

leaders should make every effort to avoid the danger of involvement in the hopelessly gnarled Russian question. This would not be possible if former Romanov subjects, the Russian Armenians, and former Romanov lands, Russian Armenia, should be regarded as the core of the redeemed homeland.[28]

Although this skepticism was shared in varying degrees by many of the delegates in Paris, most nonetheless believed that the Caucasian Armenian republic had a positive significance for the nation as a whole. The mere fact that Russian Armenia had already achieved independence need not in itself, they felt, affect the extent of the Turkish Armenian territories. With the eventual unification of the two sectors, the larger, western region would naturally regain its proper leverage. In this atmosphere the National Congress rejected, by a three-vote margin, a Dashnakist-sponsored motion to acknowledge the Republic as the nucleus of united Armenia. Rather, the emphasis being shifted, the National Delegation was simply instructed "to do its utmost to bring about the creation of a united Armenia." [29]

In anticipation of that elusive day the National Congress formed several committees for such specific purposes as determining the most suitable system of government and drafting the compact to be entered into with the mandatory power, hopefully the United States of America. The committees were to submit their findings during the second sitting of the Armenian National Congress, to be summoned by Boghos Nubar after the Peace Conference had taken substantive action on resolving the Armenian question. The committee on government, functioning throughout the spring and summer of 1919, studied an array of national constitutions and, drawing heavily upon the statutes of Switzerland and the United States, came to advocate a provisional distribution of power among a president, a council of ministers, and a parliament until such time as a constituent assembly of United Armenia would convene and settle upon a permanent ruling system.[30]

On April 2, 1919, the National Congress named a new National Delegation, led once again by Boghos Nubar Pasha and composed of the three major currents: Arshak Chobanian and Vahan Tekeyan (Ramkavars), Garegin Pasdermadjian and Hakob Nevruz (Dashnakists), Pro-

[28] Papazian, op. cit., III, 44–45; Jizmejian, op. cit., pp. 397–398.

[29] Rep. of Arm. Archives, File 1407a/27a, Report of M. Hambardzumian and Z. Matikian. Jizmejian, op. cit., pp. 394–395, states that the National Delegation was directed "to work in harmony with the representatives of the Republic of Armenia on all national questions.

[30] Papazian, op. cit., III, 45–48, 316–329.

fessor Abraham Ter-Hakobian and Boghos Nubar (nonpartisans).[31] There were some who felt that the inclusion of the Dashnakists would foster closer bonds between the two delegations in Paris, especially as Pasdermadjian (Armen Garo), a member of the Bureau of Dashnaktsutiun and the Republic's unofficial emissary in the United States, had collaborated with Nubar before. The ultimate merger of the delegations did not seem unrealistic, for Avetis Aharonian and Boghos Nubar had already joined on numerous occasions to speak in the name of L'Arménie Intégrale.

During its final session on April 22 the National Congress, in addition to addressing appropriate messages to President Wilson and Premiers Clemenceau, Lloyd George, and Orlando, issued a public appeal to the Allied nations in order to emphasize once more "the determination of the Armenian people to have a free fatherland with all its lands" and to urge the citizens of the world powers "to join your voices with ours in demanding of the Peace Conference a swift settlement of the Armenian question." [32] In another direction the National Congress "felt the obligation to send warm brotherly felicitations to the Republic of Armenia, seeing in it the joy-inspiring embodiment of renascent Armenian independence for the first time in six hundred years." The actual cable to Erevan read: "The Armenian Congress, assembled in Paris, relays, on the occasion of the end of its first sitting, its heartfelt fraternal greetings to the Republic of Armenia. We earnestly desire that the formation of the United Armenian Republic will be realized once and forever, and we are filled with the hope that through your and our combined efforts our mutual aspirations will be crowned, at the signing of the general peace, with total victory for the national cause." [33] With these words the Armenian National Congress recessed in the belief that it would convene yet another time when the day of justice had become manifest.

The Act of United Armenia

As the Turkish Armenian convocations in Erevan and Paris arrived at various policy decisions, the cabinet of Alexandre Khatisian, introducing measures of its own, prepared to proclaim the official unification of Armenia on the first anniversary of the Republic. The chair-

[31] *Azgayin hamagumar*, pp. 2–3. See also *Hairenik* (daily), April 6, 1919, p. 1.
[32] *Azgayin hamagumar*, pp. 4–5; Rep. of Arm. Archives, File 1283/26, *H. H. D. Areumtian Evropayi Kedronakan Komite, 1919.*
[33] *Miatsial ev Ankakh Hayastan*, p. 70; *Azgayin hamagumar*, pp. 4, 5.

man of the committee on arrangements, Gevorg Melik-Karageozian, appealed to the citizenry to make the celebration an unforgettable reminder that after centuries of martyrdom the Armenian nation had finally witnessed the rebirth of independence, May 28, 1918. Striking emotional chords the Populist Minister of Public Instruction continued:

> Passing before you were the Turkish hordes, which enveloped your fields, devastated your villages and cities, slaughtered your parents and children, carried away your brothers and sisters. With its exhausted forces the Armenian people, bled white by countless wounds and left unaided, armed only with faith in its sacred cause and with strength of soul, bravely withstood the infamous enemy and brought glory to the nation at the battles of Sardarabad, Bash-Abaran, and Karakilisa. . . . Let the day of May 28 be a memorial to our martyrs, but let it also be an all-national day of rejoicing, day of the creation of a new government around biblical Ararat, day of triumph of noble Armenian aspirations and of international justice! [34]

While Erevan made ready for its first festive event since independence, the cabinet, invoking the powers entrusted to it by the legislature's resolution of April 27, confirmed two momentous decisions. On May 26 it adopted by a vote of five to one, with one abstention, the text of the declaration on Armenia's unification. The abstaining Populist minister favored the act in principle but insisted that the responsibility for approving it rested not with the cabinet but with the legislature. The cabinet was unanimous, however, in accepting Melik-Karageozian's proposal to solemnize the celebration of independence and national unification by (1) the construction of a monument "in tribute to the heroes who have fallen in the emancipatory struggle," (2) the publication of a history of the final phases of that long crusade, and (3) the striking of an honorary medal with "For Services Rendered the Fatherland" inscribed thereon. The related second major cabinet decision, following on May 27, authorized the Executive Body of the Western Armenians to select twelve deputies to sit in the legislature of united Armenia.[35]

On the morning of May 28, 1919, the streets of Erevan, particularly the central square facing City Hall, were overflowing with an excited citizenry and formations of students, scouts, wards of the orphanages, and soldiers. At ten o'clock Commander in Chief General Tovmas Nazarbekian and Acting Interior Minister Sargis Manasian escorted

---

[34] *Miatsial ev Ankakh Hayastan*, pp. 75–76.
[35] *Ibid.*, pp. 81–82, 96; Vratzian, *Hanrapetutiun*, p. 235.

Catholicos Gevorg V to the portals of City Hall, where the Supreme Patriarch said an open-air requiem for the heroes of Armenian independence. Acting Premier Khatisian then stepped before the sharpest contingents the army could muster and led a parade down Astafiev (Abovian) Boulevard. The crowds, still bearing the grim marks of the preceding winter, were treated to an unprecedented spectacle as a band, several marching units, and, above all, two floats mounted on automobiles advanced along the thoroughfare. The first of these, strewn with flowers, carried a woman clothed and veiled in black. Above her flew black banners bearing the names of Mush, Sassun, Shabin-Karahisar, Tigranakert, Sis, and other Turkish Armenian centers—the tragedy and devastation of Armenia. Upon the second float stood the image of new Armenia, a woman in white proudly resting her hands upon a child on either side. The youths, one in the raiment of a Turkish Armenian and the other of a Russian Armenian, joined hands in the symbolic gesture of emancipation and unification.[36]

The procession drew up at the Khorhurd. Within had assembled the leaders of the Republic and numerous guests, including the Catholicos, the envoys of Persia, Azerbaijan, and Georgia, British Brigadier General K. M. Davie, and representatives of the American relief agencies. Gevorg Melik-Karageozian presided at the ceremonies, which began with the national hymn, Mer Hairenik ("Our Fatherland"), and a moment of silent tribute to those who had fallen on Armenia's road to independence. Alexandre Khatisian then moved to the rostrum for the eagerly awaited reading of the Act of United Armenia:[37]

To restore the integrality of Armenia and to secure the complete freedom and prosperity of her people, the Government of Armenia, abiding by the solid will and desire of the entire Armenian people, declares that from this day forward the divided parts of Armenia are everlastingly combined as an independent political entity.

Exactly one year ago the Armenian National Council, which was elected by the Congress of Russian Armenians, declared itself the supreme authority in the Armenian provinces of Transcaucasia. The government formed by the National Council, after officially apprising the representatives of the nations of that political act, has during the course of this one year established in fact its authority over the Armenian provinces of Transcaucasia.

[36] Miatsial ev Ankakh Hayastan, pp. 77–79; Vratzian, Hanrapetutiun, pp. 235–236; Hairenik (daily), Aug. 13, 1919, p. 1.

[37] Khatisian, Hanrapetutian zargatsume, pp. 129–130; Miatsial ev Ankakh Hayastan, pp. 80, 86–87. Freely translated English and French versions are in US Archives, RG 84, Tiflis Consulate, 1919, pt. 4, File 801, and RG 256, 867B.00/136, Jenkins (Tiflis) to Ammission (Paris) and to Department of State, June 14, 1919.

The Second Congress of Western Armenians, which met in Erevan during February, 1919, has solemnly declared that it regards Armenia united and independent.

Now, in promulgating this act of unification and independence of the ancestral Armenian lands located in Transcaucasia and the Ottoman Empire, the Government of Armenia declares that the political system of United Armenia is a democratic republic and that it has become the Government of this United Republic of Armenia.

Thus, the people of Armenia are henceforth the supreme lord and master of their consolidated fatherland, and the Parliament and Government of Armenia stand as the supreme legislative and executive authority conjoining the free people of united Armenia.

The Government of Armenia publishes this act under the special powers vested in it by the decision of the legislature on April 27, 1919.

ACTING PRESIDENT OF THE COUNCIL OF MINISTERS AND MINISTER OF FOREIGN AFFAIRS	Al. Khatisian
ACTING MINISTER OF INTERIOR	S. Manasian
MINISTER OF MILITARY AFFAIRS, MAJOR GENERAL	K. Araratian
ACTING MINISTER OF JUSTICE	H. Chmshkian
MINISTER OF WELFARE	S. Torosian
MINISTER OF PUBLIC INSTRUCTION	G. Melik-Karageozian
MINISTER OF PROVISIONS	K. Vermishian
ACTING MINISTER OF FINANCE	G. Djaghetian
DIRECTOR OF THE CHANCELLERY	G. Khatisian

Done in the City of Erevan on May 28, 1919.

When the thunderous applause that followed the reading of the Act had abated, Khatisian invited the twelve newly designated Turkish Armenian deputies to take their places in the rows reserved for members of the legislature. Speaking on behalf of the twelve, Vahagn Krmoyan pledged active Western Armenian participation in the Republic's governing bodies to enhance the ideal of independent Armenia, one and united.[38] The enthusiasm of the audience grew with each oration. Avetik Sahakian, the popular President of the Khorhurd, depicted May 28 as the greatest of Armenian holidays. The Armenian people, he declared, had after endless suffering finally dropped anchor and had legislated out of existence the artificial barrier dividing the nation into Eastern and Western, Russian and Turkish: "To us there now remains the mission to rebuild, to construct a stable governmental system drawing upon all the peoples of Armenia, to defend our father-

---

[38] The twelve Turkish Armenian deputies were Vahagn Krmoyan, Hmayak Manukian, Zaven Korkotian, Vagharshak Hokhikian, Van-Push, Vardan Arakelian, Armenak Maksapetian, Artashes Mirzayan, Arsen Kitur, Haik Kosoyan, Armen Sassuni, and Hairapet Hairapetian.

land with our blood, and to ensure its good fortune and destiny." [39]

Catholicos Gevorg was eloquent in his blessing of "United and Independent Armenia." The nation, he cautioned, dared not rely on foreign powers for security: "Now when, like a magnet, Masis [Ararat] has drawn together and merged the two halves of the Armenian people, when United Armenia has been forged, now we must summon forth all our national aptitudes in order to safeguard and train our people for the glory of its free fatherland." After the representatives of Georgia and Azerbaijan, Mountainous Karabagh, the Armenians of America, and many others had offered congratulations, Khatisian proceeded to the balcony of the Khorhurd where he again proclaimed the Act of May 28 for the benefit of the throngs below. A thirty-gun salute sounded in response. Long into the night Erevan celebrated the unification of Armenia, even though the actual jurisdiction of the government did not reach beyond the Russo-Turkish frontier of 1914 nor even into many districts within the Republic of Armenia itself.[40]

The first anniversary of independence was observed over the breadth of the country, in Azerbaijan and in Georgia, in Cilicia and in Constantinople, on the Atlantic and Pacific shores of the United States, and in many capitals of Europe. The program in Paris, held in La Salle des Ingénieurs Civils de France, included an unparalleled array of European Armenophiles and Armenian intellectuals of diverse political persuasions. Avetis Aharonian, this time the poet and romanticist rather than the civic leader and delegation president, rhapsodized in stirring tones: "Let the world witness today that all Armenian elements are now united. We are one!" The Armenian people had defied misery and death to roughhew a republic on a small bit of the mother soil. Russian Armenia, the little brother, had taken that step and now had come forward to embrace the great sister, Turkish Armenia. "Glory to the departed heroes, the Vahagns of our race,[41] whom we hold not in mourning but in admiration. I mourn those, not who found the death of heroes, but who perished in the carnage without knowing why and for what they died." The sufferings of these innocent demanded requital. "Every tear and every drop of blood," concluded Aharonian, "will enrich the soil from which the Law of Justice shall blossom forth." [42]

[39] *Miatsial ev Ankakh Hayastan*, pp. 82–83.

[40] *Ibid.*, pp. 84–85; Vratzian, *Hanrapetutiun*, pp. 237–238.

[41] Vahagn was the pre-Christian Armenian sun god, the god of courage and of war, the dragon slayer, and the progeny of heaven, earth, and sea who had issued forth from fire. Although related to other early Indo-European deities, Vahagn has been looked upon as the all-Armenian god and the personification of Armenian ideals.

[42] *Miatsial ev Ankakh Hayastan*, pp. 107–108; *Hairenik* (daily), June 29, 1919, p. 1.

Boghos Nubar, speaking in French, recounted the valiant wartime deeds of "our brothers in the Caucasus," who had struggled on despite unimaginable privation, the treachery of neighboring peoples, and abandonment by all friends. "To our compatriots in the Caucasus belongs the honor of creating the first Armenian republic—small in size but vast in the principle that it embodies. The republic is the pith, the first manifestation of the resurrection of Armenia in her entirety." That republic, he observed with satisfaction, would merge one day soon with a liberated Turkish Armenia, and the Armenian nation would, as in centuries past, once again assume her historic role of spreading light and progress in the world of the East. Vilifying the heinous crimes of the Envers and Talaats who had plotted "with still unknown means" to annihilate the Armenian race, Boghos Nubar ended on an optimistic note: "It is my fervent desire to be amongst you when the hour has come, hopefully soon, for me to summon you to exalt in a patriotic celebration the birth of United Independent Armenia, the One and Indivisible New Armenian Nation." [43]

The Populist Reaction

The worldwide observances of independence day seemed to indicate growing Turkish Armenian enthusiasm and support for the Republic of Armenia. Yet the Act of May 28, 1919, precipitated tumultuous repercussions. The proclamation that had been intended as an expression of unity actually aggravated the discord between Russian Armenian and Turkish Armenian and between Dashnakist and anti-Dashnakist leaders. A startling about-face by the Populist party in the days following the celebration in Erevan administered the coup de grace to the coalition cabinet.

A number of related factors might explain the Populist reversal. Since November, 1918, the party had shared authority in the coalition government, but its central committee remained in Tiflis, distant from the daily occurrences and frequent crises in Armenia. In time a rift developed between the party leadership in Tiflis and the rank and file in Erevan, the latter group tending to identify more closely with the Republic and to regard it as the nucleus of united Armenia. The Erevan Populists had apparently endorsed the Act of May 28 without the consent of the central committee, which on its part questioned ever

[43] *Miatsial ev Ankakh Hayastan*, pp. 109–112. In Constantinople, the Republic's first anniversary was celebrated in several mass meetings on both shores of the Bosporus. For a description of these programs in the Ottoman capital and the leading participants, see *Hairenik* (daily), July 2, 1919, p. 2.

more seriously the wisdom of continued participation in the coalition. The results of partnership with Dashnaktsutiun had proved bitterly disappointing to the Armenian liberal-constitutionalists. One Populist minister after another had found excuse to quit Erevan and return to Tiflis. Even as the Act of May 28 was being drafted, approved, and proclaimed, the most influential Populist in the cabinet, Samson Harutiunian, was away on one of his prolonged stays in the Georgian capital.

The Russian Armenian Populists, the approximate ideological counterparts of the Turkish Armenian Ramkavars, steadily gravitated toward the stewardship of Boghos Nubar and the guidelines set down by the National Congress in Paris. The Act of May 28 included certain passages that either ignored or contradicted the views of the Armenian leaders abroad. Thus, when the text of the Act reached Tiflis, the Populist center became embroiled in a brief, trenchant internal struggle that ended in victory and vindication for the Tiflis-Paris orientation. At the beginning of June, 1919, Samson Harutiunian carried to Erevan the central committee's decision to reject the legality of the declaration symbolically uniting Armenia.

The Populists now contended that the Act of May 28 had been promulgated unilaterally, that Boghos Nubar had neither sanctioned nor even known of the intent to issue the decree, and that it was not commensurate with the realities affecting the Armenian question. They therefore regarded the document null and void. In defense of the government Alexandre Khatisian replied that the Act had been drafted and proclaimed with due consideration to legalities, the Populist ministers had signed it of their free will, and, for that matter, a Populist minister had even presided during the historic public ceremony. Khatisian held the objections to be thoroughly unfounded and warned the Populist party that its reversal could gravely injure the prestige and future of Armenia. But the Populist central committee, having at last adopted a clear-cut, though sadly timed stand, remained intractable.[44]

The Populist volte-face was mirrored in the Erevan newspaper, Zhoghovurd ("People"), which, having acclaimed the unification of Armenia on May 28, followed with a retraction shortly thereafter. In its editorial of June 4 the Populist organ declared that the principle of united Armenia was noble and most laudable but the manner in which it had been applied was intolerable. Only the legislature had the authority to pass on issues of such fundamental bearing and with

[44] Vratzian, Hanrapetutiun, p. 239.

such far-reaching implications. Furthermore, the cabinet in Erevan had neither the right nor the mandate to vest itself with jurisdiction over all Armenia. Instead, a provisional government, to be formed in collaboration with the national bodies in Paris, should summon a constituent assembly to determine the lines of authority and responsibility. According to *Zhoghovurd,* any other alternative would prove unworkable inasmuch as Russian Armenia and Turkish Armenia "have existed under disparate political and economic circumstances and have passed through dissimilar cultural stages." [45]

When the legislature reassembled on June 4, for the first time since April 27, all twelve Turkish Armenian deputies took seats with the Dashnakist faction, thus giving it a clear majority in the Khorhurd. The Populist, Social Revolutionary, and Social Democrat factions protested this arrangement by walking out and leaving the chamber to the Dashnakists alone. Addressing the legislature that day, Acting Premier Khatisian attempted to justify the measure that had stirred the controversy and prompted the crisis:

1. The Republic had now expanded to the prewar frontiers, and the refugee population was surging homeward. As nothing could stop this unbridled movement, the establishment of a government of all Armenia could be delayed no longer.

2. The immediacy of the need had been demonstrated recently when Allied officials questioned the legal jurisdiction of the Erevan government in making representations for the repatriation and indemnification of the Western Armenians.

3. The Act of May 28 not only furnished the Republic with the technical authority to defend the interests of all Armenia, but it also struck at the skepticism prevailing in some circles that the government did not aspire to full independence and was loath to separate from Russia.

4. A strong, organized army was essential to protect the expanding borders, but the Western Armenians, uncertain about the resolve of the Eastern Armenians to stand independent, had generally evaded military service. The Act would help to surmount this obstacle and engender an effective, unified military force.

5. The Allied Powers had at long last consented to repatriation toward the Turkish Armenian border districts of old Bayazit and Alashkert. However, the refugees should under no conditions return to their homeland as Ottoman subjects or as aliens. The Act provided

---

[45] *Ibid.,* pp. 239–240.

them the legitimate premises to reclaim their lands as citizens of independent Armenia.

6. The Khorhurd had been created under extraordinary circumstances and must soon give way to a democratically elected parliament. It was most important that the Western Armenians in the Republic participate in the election; the Act made this possible, even though the cabinet had realized that the small political circles tending toward Russia (Social Democrat and Social Revolutionary) would protest.

7. International political considerations rendered the Act of May 28 absolutely indispensable. As for the twelve Turkish Armenian deputies who had been seated, the cabinet had taken no part in their selection, and, in any case, their inclusion in the Khorhurd was merely symbolic, since the legislature was scheduled to meet only once more before the general parliamentary elections.

8. The cabinet was fully aware of and responsible for its actions.[46]

These arguments failed to placate the Populist party or to alter the decision of its central committee. The Populist ministers resigned from the cabinet en masse, although Harutiun Chmshkian, incensed by his party's stand, shed the Populist label in order to remain at his post.[47] The Dashnakist-Populist coalition of eight months was no more. Pending the general elections and the formation of a new cabinet, Khatisian patched together an interim government:[48]

PREMIER-PRESIDENT (ABROAD)	Hovhannes Kachaznuni
ACTING PREMIER AND FOREIGN AFFAIRS	Alexandre Khatisian
INTERNAL AFFAIRS	Sargis Manasian
WELFARE	Sahak Torosian
PUBLIC INSTRUCTION	Sirakan Tigranian
JUSTICE	Harutiun Chmshkian
MILITARY AFFAIRS	General Kristapor Araratian

Benjamin B. Moore, a member of the Tiflis section of the American Field Mission to South Russia, informed the United States delegation

[46] US Archives, RG 256, 184.01602/89, Moore (Tiflis) to Tyler (Paris), July 16, 1919; Rep. of Arm. Archives, File 3/3. See also *Miatsial ev Ankakh Hayastan*, pp. 93–96; and *Hairenik* (daily), Aug. 15, 1919, p. 1.

[47] Vratzian, *Hanrapetutiun*, p. 240. According to a report in *Hairenik* (daily), Aug. 14, 1919, p. 3, Melik-Karageozian also left the Populist party, but no further evidence has been discovered to confirm this news.

[48] *Miatsial ev Ankakh Hayastan*, p. 50. The Assistant Minister of Interior was a Western Armenian Ramkavar. See Rep. of Arm. Archives, File 66a/3, Bulletin no. 109. Arshak Alboyajian, "Ankakh Hayastan," in *Amenun Taretsuitse*, XV (Constantinople, 1921), 126, states that Khatisian continued on as foreign minister, that Torosian served also as minister of labor and minister of provisions, and that Papetian acted as minister of finance. Vratzian, *Hanrapetutiun*, p. 240, shows Djaghetian to have been the minister of finance.

in Paris that Khatisian's explanations were valid and logical. Yet, accurately citing the objections of the Populist party, he adjudged Dashnaktsutiun at least partly responsible for the intrigues leading to the cabinet crisis. Moore nonetheless believed that the dissolution of the coalition government by the Populists was extremely ill-advised and most regrettable.[49] Many veteran Dashnakists did not share that regret. Even though Dashnaktsutiun held sway among the Armenian masses, it had frequently been obliged to compromise with the Populists, as its faction in the Khorhurd could be outvoted by a combined front of the lesser parties. The forthcoming parliamentary elections would, they felt, set the matter right.

The Reaction in Paris

Boghos Nubar Pasha learned of the Act of May 28 several days after he had participated in the program celebrating the Republic's first anniversary. Though he did not obtain a verbatim copy of the document for some time, the information relayed from Tiflis was sufficient to lead him to the conclusion that a coup d'etat had been staged in Erevan. This conviction was strengthened by the reports of Mikayel Papadjanian, the third official member of the Delegation of the Republic of Armenia, who had left Erevan in December, 1918, and arrived tardily in Paris during the first half of June, 1919. Papadjanian, a member of the Populist central committee, repeatedly cabled his colleagues in Tiflis, urging them to stand firm against the proclivity of some party officials to center their aspirations for the nation on the Erevan government.[50]

Nubar Pasha was so offended by the astounding revelations that he planned to lodge a formal protest with the Allied Powers to expose the illegal maneuvers and bad faith of the ruling clique in Erevan. Both the Dashnakists and the Ramkavars of the National Delegation recognized the grim consequences inherent in such a move and implored Nubar to desist. The disputes of the Armenians, they maintained, must be kept within their own house and there resolved. Yielding at last to the admonition and persuasion of his entire delegation, Boghos Nubar consented to direct his remonstrances to the Erevan government alone.[51]

[49] US Archives, RG 256, 184.01602/89.
[50] Jizmejian, op. cit., pp. 401–403, includes a report by Aharonian concerning Papadjanian's contrary actions in Paris.
[51] Rep. of Arm. Archives, File 1407a/27a, Report of M. Hambardzumian and Z. Matikian. The friction generated in the Armenian-American community by the Act

Avetis Aharonian, himself a long-time advocate of a declaration formally uniting Armenia, was equally distressed by the negative reaction to the Act of May 28. He therefore supported the efforts of intermediaries to pacify Nubar and to arrange for the resumption of preliminary discussions on a united Armenian government and a single delegation in Paris. During the unofficial consultations that ensued during June and July, 1919, Boghos Nubar proffered the following guidelines for a compromise agreement with the de facto government of the Armenian republic:

1. A united parliament should be constituted with an equal number of Eastern Armenian and Western Armenian deputies.

2. A united provisional cabinet should be formed on the same basis.

3. The Turkish Armenian cabinet members would be selected by the National Delegation, and the Russian Armenian members by the current Erevan administration.

4. The ministerial portfolios would be distributed by mutual consent, with the exception that Boghos Nubar must be tendered both the premiership (with residence abroad) and the presidency of the delegation in Paris.

5. The ministers of foreign affairs and military affairs must not be members of Dashnaktsutiun.

6. Upon formation of a united provisional cabinet, the legislature in Erevan should be recessed forthwith and a united parliament convoked.

7. The delegation in Paris would be composed of an equal number of Turkish Armenians and Russian Armenians, the former appointed by Boghos Nubar and the latter by the Erevan government. Since Nubar's appointees were to be permanent, the provisional united cabinet could not require their resignation, either individually or collectively, at least until the Armenian question had been settled in full.

8. As the president of the united delegation, Boghos Nubar would possess extraordinary powers.[52]

Aharonian accepted the first three points without reservation, consenting further that the minister of military affairs be entrusted to a nonpartisan and that Nubar Pasha lead the united delegation and

---

of May 28 is described by Jizmejian, *op. cit.*, pp. 389-391, and was reflected in the issues of the ideologically opposed newspapers, *Pahak, Eritasard Hayastan, Azg,* and *Hairenik,* during the the latter half of 1919.

[52] The project in its French original and its Armenian translation, together with other materials on the negotiations between the two sides, is included in Rep. of Arm. Archives, File 296/3, *H. H. Patvirakutiun—Azgayin Patvirakutiun, 1919.*

appoint its Turkish Armenian members. He rejected, however, the stipulation that Dashnakists be barred ipso facto from the foreign affairs post. Moreover, to Nubar's intense dissatisfaction, Aharonian insisted that the premier, whoever he might be or whatever other capacity he might have, should reside in Armenia. The united delegation, he continued, must at all times be responsible to the provisional cabinet and, to assure maximum efficiency, should be small, preferably composed of Boghos Nubar, one other non-Dashnakist, and one Dashnakist.[53] The differences and reservations, though not inconsequential, seemed negotiable, and in July Aharonian and Nubar wired Erevan requesting that the planned reorganization of government and the official ratification of the Act of May 28 be postponed.[54] Deference in this matter would allow a pair of conferees already en route to Erevan to begin direct deliberations for a united cabinet, a united parliament, and a united delegation of united Armenia.[55]

In another conciliatory gesture Avetis Aharonian apparently acquiesced in affixing his signature to a joint public communiqué drafted by Nubar. The document stated that the National Delegation, which had been called into being long before the emergence of the Armenian republic, regarded that new political entity in the Caucasus as the hope and symbol of reunited Armenia. Nevertheless, sight should not be lost of the fact that the National Delegation had proclaimed Armenian unity and independence as early as November, 1918. Moreover, the National Congress in Paris had rejected a motion to acknowledge the Erevan government as the sole legal authority for "Integral Armenia" since there were no Turkish Armenians in that government and the issues relating to the former Ottoman and Romanov territories were notably different. Thus, not until the Allies had imposed a final settlement upon Turkey could Russian Armenia and Turkish Armenia unite in reality. The National Delegation did not oppose a general declaration of Armenian oneness, the first part of the Act of May 28, but felt compelled to challenge Erevan's right to claim jurisdiction over all Armenia. The National Delegation and the Delegation of the Republic, the message concluded, were issuing this communication to clarify the situation and to make known their close collabora-

[53] Rep. of Arm. Archives, File 296/3. See also excerpts of Aharonian's reports to the Erevan government in Jizmejian, *op. cit.*, pp. 399–403.

[54] Rep. of Arm. Archives, File 140/39, and File 231/130, Communiqué of July 18, 1919; Britain, FO 608/78, 342/1/15853.

[55] The envoys, both members of the Ramkavar party, were Vahan Tekeyan and Nshan Ter-Stepanian. The negotiations they entered into in Erevan will be discussed in the second volume of this study.

tion in the goal of bringing to ultimate fruition a united government of Integral Armenia.[56]

Parliamentary Elections in the Republic

The crisis surrounding the Act of May 28 was paralleled by a brisk political campaign in what was to be the first parliamentary election in Armenian history. The Statute for Elections to the Parliament of Armenia, a modified version of the procedures used in 1917 for elections to the All-Russian Constituent Assembly, was adopted by the government on March 12, 1919. It enfranchised, without regard to sex, religion, or race, all adult citizens who registered, including the Turkish Armenian refugee-residents. The principle of general, equal, direct, and proportional elections, with the entire country as a single electoral district, was to be applied in selecting the eighty members of Parliament.[57] The Central Election Bureau, appointed by the Khorhurd to supervise the campaign, operated through a hierarchy of provincial, county, village, and precinct committees.[58] Its registration drive, launched in late April, enfranchised just over 365,000 citizens.[59] A published timetable fixed the election dates as June 21–23, 1919, and established a series of deadlines throughout May and June for such formalities as the final announcement of party slates, the combination or merger of slates, and the posting of electoral lists.[60]

At the very outset, in an explicit policy decision, the Armenian Social Democrats announced that they would boycott the election. The flavor of separatism and nationalism in Armenia had become much too sharp for the Marxist palate. Moreover, under the existing arrange-

[56] US Archives, RG 256, 183.9 *Armenia*/16. See also *Hairenik* (daily), Aug. 13, 1919, p. 1; Britain, FO 608/97, 351/1/18094.

[57] Vratzian, *Ughinerov*, V, 87, and *Hanrapetutiun*, p. 249.

[58] The Central Election Bureau was headed by Khorhurd member Smbat Khachatrian. See *Hairenik* (daily), June 6, 1919, pp. 1–2, and June 7, p. 2; *Bor'ba*, April 3, 1919, p. 3.

[59] Rep. of Arm. Archives, File 66a/3. This figure does not include any citizens who might have registered in Kars and Sharur-Nakhichevan. A statistical report in *Hairenik* (daily), Aug. 16, 1919, p. 3, shows considerably fewer citizens enfranchized, but it does not include figures from Zangezur and a few other districts:

City of Erevan	29,932	Igdir (city and county)	20,984
City of Alexandropol	9,530	Etchmiadzin	68,288
City of Novo-Bayazit	5,959	Dilijan	29,638
Erevan county (uezd)	44,000	Karakilisa	3,000 [sic]
Alexandropol county	40,000	Daralagiaz	12,941
Novo-Bayazit county	26,391		

[60] Rep. of Arm. Archives, File 66a/3.

ment, the Social Democrats held six seats in the Khorhurd, whereas the forthcoming popular election would likely exclude them from the new legislature. It was perhaps preferable to boycott than to admit lack of public support. The groups that submitted preliminary slates included Dashnaktsutiun, 120 candidates; the Populist party, 65; the Social Revolutionary party, 35; the Assyrians, 3; and the Kurds, 2.[61] Only a small fraction of the Muslim population of Armenia chose to register, if indeed the Central Election Bureau expended any energy toward that end. With rare exception, the Muslims remained totally impervious to campaign and election.

Troubled and torn by the Act of May 28, the Populist party finally withdrew its slate of candidates and announced a boycott on June 20.[62] Significantly, this move on the eve of the election came after an urgent radiogram from Boghos Nubar had been received in Armenia. The message, dated June 13 and addressed to Catholicos Gevorg V, acknowledged the right of the Erevan government to conduct local and regional elections but rejected the validity of parliamentary elections in the name of all Armenia. Through the Supreme Patriarch, Boghos Nubar advised the Turkish Armenian residents of the Republic that their participation in the election would be "untimely" and that they should refrain from voting.[63] It is quite possible that Nubar's opposition to general elections in Armenia was instrumental in the belated Populist decision to drop out of the campaign. Had the Populist party seen the election through, its slate of candidates would undoubtedly have polled no more than a few thousand votes. This fact did not, however, temper the blow the boycott dealt the prestige of the Republic. The Populists had put forward the only nonsocialist Armenian slate, which logically should have become the rallying standard of the nascent liberal, evolutionary middle-class elements. However honorable may have seemed their motives and however justified their tactics, the Populists had denied the electorate this point of concentration. It was ironic and unfortunate that the party that had shared the reins of government for eight months would have not a single spokesman in the Parliament of Armenia.

Having turned its back upon the campaign, the Populist party nonetheless swiftly proclaimed unflinching dedication to the ideals of Armenian independence and unity, taking pains to disassociate itself

[61] Vratzian, *Hanrapetutiun*, p. 250.

[62] Rep. of Arm. Archives, File 66a/3, Bulletin no. 123. Kristapor Vermishian publicly criticized his party for resorting to a boycott of the election.

[63] Rep. of Arm. Archives, File 380/2, Letter of June 13, 1919, and File 66a/3, Bulletin no. 71. See also *Hairenik* (daily), July 13, 1919, p. 1.

from the other boycotters, the Social Democrats, in particular the Bolshevik faction, which scorned and belittled the very principles on which the Armenian constitutional group was founded. The Bolshevik "Spartak" youth of Erevan, for example, distributed and posted fliers cautioning the masses not to be deceived by enemies who extolled the terms "independence" and "parliament." That the exploiting classes should glorify these warped phrases was natural, declared the Spartakists, for such mottoes were the weapons currently used by the bourgeois oppressors. The toiling masses could find salvation, not in the bane of "parliamentarianism," but in unification with Soviet Russia.[64]

The rhetoric of the Communist youth and the boycott of the Populist and the Social Democrat parties notwithstanding, the election was conducted as scheduled, with nearly 260,000 votes cast. While certain irregularities and possibly even some intimidation may have impaired the election, the completion of a nationwide campaign did represent a landmark in the history of the Armenian republic. As unprepared as the population was for republican institutions and democratic processes, they had been afforded a modicum of practical experience. The ballots tallied, the Central Election Bureau announced the following not unexpected results:[65]

Party or group	Votes	Percentage	Seat in Parliament
Dashnaktsutiun	230,772	88.95	72
Social Revolutionary[66]	13,289	5.12	4
Tatar	9,187	3.54	3
Independent Peasants Union	4,224	1.30	1
Kurd	1,305	.50	—
Populist	481	.19	—
Assyrian	173	.007	—

It was regrettable that Dashnaktsutiun had gained a near monopoly in Parliament, for the virtual absence of an effective legal opposition

[64] Revoliutsion kocher, pp. 508–511; H. N. Karapetian, Hayastani Komeritmiutian dsnunde (Erevan, 1956), pp. 122–124.

[65] Rep. of Arm. Archives, File 66a/3, Bulletin no. 90. Later, more complete returns, with results in from Zangezur, showed that approximately 280,000 votes had been cast. See also US Archives, RG 256, 184.016/81. Apparently by the time Parliament convened an additional seat was awarded Dashnaktsutiun.

[66] The Social Revolutionaries campaigned on a platform of federation with Russia and of antinationalism, stressing that only when the governments of the Caucasus had removed the barriers between themselves and Russia would they find a solution to the prevailing chaotic conditions. See Bor'ba, May 23, 1919, p. 1.

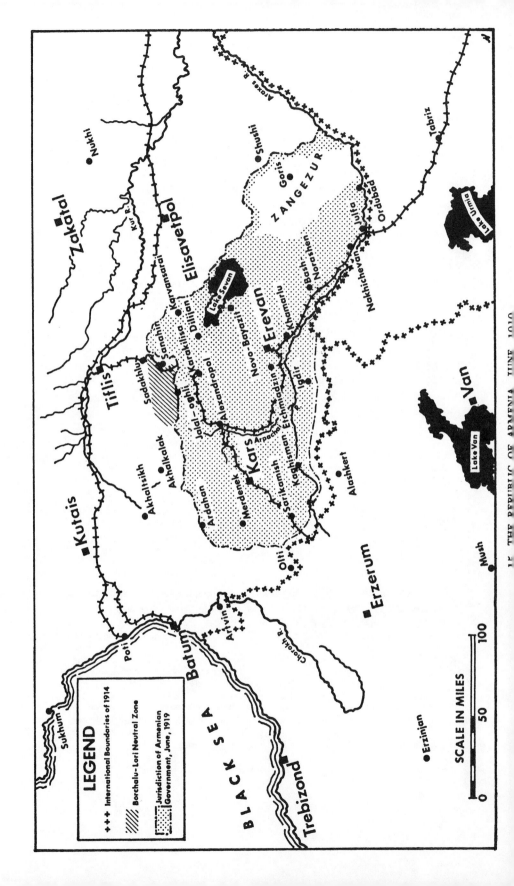

15. THE REPUBLIC OF ARMENIA, JUNE, 1919

LEGEND

+++ International Boundaries of 1914

▨ Borchalu–Lori Neutral Zone

⬚ Jurisdiction of Armenian
 Government, June, 1919

SCALE IN MILES

0   50   100

BLACK SEA

Sukhum

Kutais

Poti

Batum

Trebizond

Chorokh R.

Artvin

Erzinjan

Erzerum

Mush

Lake Van

■Van

Lake Urmia

Tabriz

Zakatal

Nukhi

Kur R.

Tiflis

Elisavetpol

Zangezur

Shushi

Goris

Ordubad

Julfa

Nakhichevan

Bash
Norashen

Karvansarai

Sadakhlu

Sanahin

Jalal-oghli

Karaklisa

Dilijan

Lake Sevan

Novo-Bayazit

Erevan

Khamerlu

Igdir

Etchmiadzin

Arpacha

Koghisman

Akhaltsikh

Akhalkalak

Ardahan

Merdenek

Kars

Sarikamish

Olti

Alashkert

Aloxes R.

Alexandropol

would be sorely felt and would narrow further the base of government. There arose the possibility that the cabinet would be controlled by Parliament, the Parliament by the Dashnakist faction, and the faction by the Bureau of Dashnaktsutiun. The unhealthy prospect that government and party might become synonymous hung over Armenia. Eventually, in September of 1919, the Ninth General Congress of Dashnaktsutiun was to grapple with the dilemma and to rule emphatically that a clear distinction between party and government must under all circumstances be maintained.[67]

Prior to the scheduled opening of Parliament, the newly designated Dashnakist deputies met in frequent caucus to determine what relationship should exist between their legislative faction on the one hand and the party hierarchy and official government on the other. They also selected their whips and their candidates for the presidium of the legislature and for the post of prime minister. Alexandre Khatisian, it was decided, would henceforth become the head of government, not only in fact, as during the preceding months, but also in name.[68] There were, however, individual members of the party Bureau who believed that this arrangement should be temporary and that Garegin Pasdermadjian should be called home from Washington, D.C., to assume the premiership. Pasdermadjian seemed to possess the rare qualities needed to bridge the existing internal cleavages. His reputation had been solidly established among both Russian Armenians and Turkish Armenians. He had served as the Catholicos's special envoy to the United States, was a member of Nubar's National Delegation, and, above all, was a native Turkish Armenian leader. In addition, Pasdermadjian was the revolutionary figure Armen Garo, had actively participated in Russian Armenian affairs, and, as the aureole of his other impressive credentials, was a member of the Bureau of Dashnaktsutiun. Pasdermadjian was a man of many parts, perhaps the ideal compromise candidate, who, as premier, could guide the Turkish Armenian masses to closer identification with the Republic of Armenia. Yet, in the summer of 1919, Pasdermadjian's response to the private summons of his comrades had still to be received in Erevan.[69]

[67] The world gathering of Dashnaktsutiun will be discussed in the second volume of this study.

[68] Vratzian, Hanrapetutiun, p. 251. For the membership of Parliament, see Alboyajian, op. cit., pp. 123–124. Of the 80 deputies selected, 1 was Yezidi, 2 were Muslim, and 77 were Armenian. Of the Armenian representatives, 64 were of Russian Armenian origin and 13 of Turkish Armenian. It is noteworthy, particularly for the year 1919, that 3 of the deputies were women.

[69] Rep. of Arm. Archives, File 380/2; S. Vratzian, Hin tghter nor patmutian hamar (Beirut, 1962), pp. 292–298, and Ughinerov, V, 89–91.

The Opening Session

The Parliament of Armenia convened on August 1, 1919, a year to the day after the inaugural session of the Khorhurd. The changes that had taken place during the intervening twelve months were staggering. The World War had ended and the Turkish stranglehold had been relaxed, a deadly winter had come and gone, the wheels of government had begun to turn, and, most important of all, the Republic, defying enormous odds, had managed to survive. Once again it was Avetik Sahakian who called the legislature to order. His faith in the Armenian people and their fledgling state remained inexhaustible:

Citizens, representatives of United Armenia, exactly one year ago on August 1, our country was surrounded by the iron chain of the Turkish forces, the enemy's sword hung over our head, our fatherland had become a prison. In the capacity of President of the Khorhurd, I declared during that first historic session my invincible trust and profound conviction that the narrow horizons of our Republic, which was suffocating within its limits, must expand and that our heroic and martyred people must become the master of its ever-cherished fatherland. Today I am overjoyed to confirm that not only did my prediction become an established fact and reality but that the sacred will of our people has solidly united the two halves of the Armenian nation and has proclaimed one, united, independent, and free Armenia, in whose defense we have sworn to sacrifice our lives and to fight to our last breath. We take pride in our infant state; it is weak, far from perfect, but it draws together all its territory. The people revere their young Republic, they have become imbued with the ideal of independence, and they shall never compromise this ideal. It is true that beyond the sealed frontiers of Turkish Armenia our enemy continues to spin diabolic plots and to extend its intrigues to this side of the border. But I have no doubt that we, aided by our Great Allies, shall shatter that door and take possession of our homeland, which has been irrigated with the blood of countless martyrs and heroes.[70]

Then the Parliament turned to the business at hand, thus introducing a new phase in the political history of the Republic of Armenia.

[70] Rep. of Arm. Archives, File 66a/3. See also *Hairenik* (daily), Sept. 21, 1919, p. 1, and Sept. 23, p. 1.

Transliteration Key

The Library of Congress system of transliteration has been used, but without diacritical marks and ligatures. The transliteration of several proper names varies slightly from this system—thus *Kerensky*, not *Kerenskii*.

А а	a		*Р р*	r
Б б	b		*С с*	s
В в	v		*Т т*	t
Г г	g		*У у*	u
Д д	d		*Ф ф*	f
Е е	e		*Х х*	kh
Ё ё	e		*Ц ц*	ts
Ж ж	zh		*Ч ч*	ch
З з	z		*Ш ш*	sh
И и	i		*Щ щ*	shch
I i	i		*Ъ ъ*	"
Й й	i		*Ы ы*	y
К к	k		*Ь ь*	'
Л л	l		*Ѣ ѣ*	e
М м	m		*Э э*	e
Н н	n		*Ю ю*	iu
О о	o		*Я я*	ia
П п	p			

Armenian

The transliteration system is based on the phonetic values of Classical and Eastern Armenian. Diacritical marks are not used. The transliteration of several proper names varies slightly from this system—thus *Kachaznuni,* not *Kadjaznuni,* and *Alexandropol* not *Aleksandropol.*

Ա ա	a		Ծ ծ	ds		Ջ ջ	dj
Բ բ	b		Կ կ	k		Ռ ռ	r
Գ գ	g		Հ հ	h		Ս ս	s
Դ դ	d		Ձ ձ	dz		Վ վ	v
Ե ե	e		Ղ ղ	gh		Տ տ	t
Զ զ	z		Ճ ճ	j		Ր ր	r
Է է	e		Մ մ	m		Ց ց	ts
Ը ը	e		Յ յ	h[1], y *or* —[2]		Ւ ւ	v
Թ թ	t		Ն ն	n		Փ փ	p
Ժ ժ	zh		Շ շ	sh		Ք ք	k
Ի ի	i		Ո ո	vo[1] *or* o		Օ օ	o
Լ լ	l		Չ չ	ch		Ֆ ֆ	f
Խ խ	kh		Պ պ	p			

Diphthongs

ու	—u, v[3]		յու	—iu[4]
ոյ	—ui, oy[3] *or* o[2]		եա	—ia *or* ya[5]
այ	—ai, ay[3] *or* a[2]		յա	—ia[4] *or* ya[4, 5]
իւ	—iu			

[1] In initial position only.
[2] The letter յ is not transliterated in final position.
[3] When followed by a vowel.
[4] In Soviet Armenian orthography only.
[5] When preceded by a vowel.

Bibliography

Archival Materials

Republic of Armenia. Archives of the Delegation to the Conference of Peace. (Now integrated into the Archives of Dashnaktsutiun, Boston, Massachusetts.)

File 1/1. *Hayastani Hanrapetutiun, 1918 t.* [Republic of Armenia, 1918].
File 2/2. *Hayastani Hanrapetutiun, 1918 t.* [Republic of Armenia, 1918].
File 3/3. *Hayastani Hanrapetutiun, 1919 t.* [Republic of Armenia, 1919].
File 4/4. *Hayastani Hanrapetutiun, 1919 t.* [Republic of Armenia, 1919].
File 5/5. *Hayastani Hanrapetutiun, 1919 t.* [Republic of Armenia, 1919].
File 6/6. *Hayastani Hanrapetutiun, 1919 t.* [Republic of Armenia, 1919].
File 7/7. *Hayastani Hanrapetutiun, 1919 t.* [Republic of Armenia, 1919].
File 8/8. *Hayastani Hanrapetutiun, 1919 t.* [Republic of Armenia, 1919].
File 8/8a. *Hayastani Hanrapetutiun, 1919 t.* [Republic of Armenia, 1919].
File 9/9. *Hayastani Hanrapetutiun, 1919 t.* [Republic of Armenia, 1919].
File 11/11. *Hayastani Hanrapetutiun, 1920 t.* [Republic of Armenia, 1920].
File 13/13. *Hayastani Hanrapetutiun, 1920 t.* [Republic of Armenia, 1920].
File 16/16. *Hayastani Hanrapetutiun, 1920 t.* [Republic of Armenia, 1920].
File 20/20. *Hayastani Hanrapetutiun, 1920 t.* [Republic of Armenia, 1920].
File 22/22. *Hayastani Hanrapetutiun, 1920 t.* [Republic of Armenia, 1920].
File 25/25. *Zinvorakan Nakhararutian Hramanner, 1920 t.* [Commands of the Military Ministry, 1920].
File 65/1. *Vrastani Divanagitakan Nerkayatsutsich ev Vrastani Karavarutiun, 1918* [Diplomatic Representative in Georgia and the Government of Georgia, 1918].
File 66/2. *Vrastani Divanagitakan Nerkayatsutsich ev Vrastani Karavarutiun, 1919* [Diplomatic Representative in Georgia and the Government of Georgia, 1919].
File 66a/3. *H. H. Vrastani Divanagitaken Nerkayatsutschutiun ev Vrastani Karavarutiun, 1919–1920: Teghekatu, 1919* [R. (Republic) of A. (Armenia) Diplomatic Mission in Georgia and the Government of Georgia, 1919–1920: Bulletins, 1919].
File 69/1. *H. H. Adrbedjani Divanagitakan Nerkayatsutsich ev Adrbedjani*

479

Karavarutiun, 1918 t. [R. (Republic) of A. (Armenia) Diplomatic Representative in Azerbaijan and the Government of Azerbaijan, 1918].

File 69a/1a. *H. H. Adrbedjani Divanagitakan Nerkayatsutsich ev Adrbedjani Karavarutiun, 1919 t.* [R. (Republic) of A. (Armenia) Diplomatic Representative in Azerbaijan and the Government of Azerbaijan, 1919].

File 70/2. *H. H. Adrbedjani Divanagitakan Nerkayatsutsich ev Adrbedjani Karavarutiun, 1920 t.* [R. (Republic) of A. (Armenia) Diplomatic Representative in Azerbaijan and the Government of Azerbaijan, 1920].

File 71. *H. H. Nerkayatsutsich Haravayin Rusastani Zinial Uzheri Mot, 1919 t.–1920/21 t.* [R. (Republic) of A. (Armenia) Representative with the Military Forces of South Russia, 1919–1920/21].

File 72. *H. H. Nerkayatsutschutiun Ukrayinayum, 1918–1928 t.t.* [R. (Republic) of A. (Armenia) Mission in the Ukraine, 1918–1928].

File 72/a. *Hayastani Hanrapetutian Nerkayatsutschutiun Parizum ev Ukrainiayi Parizi Nerkayatsutschutiune, 1919–1921 t.t.* [Republic of Armenia Mission in Paris and the Paris Mission of the Ukraine, 1919–1921].

File 74/1. *H. H. Patvirakutiun ev Divanagitakan Nerkayatsutschutiun Tajkastanum, 1914–1918 t.t.* [R. (Republic) of A. (Armenia) Delegation and Diplomatic Mission in Turkey, 1914–1918].

File 100/1. *H. H. Patvirakutiun, 1918: H. Ohandjaniani Tghtere* [R. (Republic) of A. (Armenia) Delegation, 1918: H. Ohandjanian's Papers].

File 101/2. *H. H. Patvirakutiun, 1919: H. Ohandjaniani Tghtere* [R. (Republic) of A. (Armenia) Delegation, 1919: H. Ohandjanian's Papers].

File 102/1. *H. H. Patvirakutiun, 1919 t.* [R. (Republic) of A. (Armenia) Delegation, 1919].

File 103/2. *H. H. Patvirakutiun, 1919 t.* [R. (Republic) of A. (Armenia) Delegation, 1919].

File 104/3. *H. H. Patvirakutiun, 1919 t.: Hashtutian Konferens* [R. (Republic) of A. (Armenia) Delegation, 1919: Peace Conference].

File 104a/3a. *H. H. Patvirakutiun, 1919 t.* [R. (Republic) of A. (Armenia) Delegation, 1919].

File 105/4. *H. H. Patvirakutiun, 1919: Hushagrer* [R. (Republic) of A. (Armenia) Delegation, 1919: Memoranda].

File 107/6. *H. H. Patvirakutiun, 1919 t.* [R. (Republic) of A. (Armenia) Delegation, 1919].

File 108/7. *H. H. Patvirakutiun, 1919* [R. (Republic) of A. (Armenia) Delegation, 1919].

File 111/10. *H. H. Patvirakutiun, 1919* [R. (Republic) of A. (Armenia) Delegation, 1919].

File 115/14. *H. H. Patvirakutiun, 1920* [R. (Republic) of A. (Armenia) Delegation, 1920].

File 116/15. *H. H. Patvirakutiun, 1920* [R. (Republic) of A. (Armenia) Delegation, 1920].

File 118/17. *H. H. Patvirakutiun, 1920: Hashtutian Konferens* [R. (Republic) of A. (Armenia) Delegation, 1920: Peace Conference].

File 132/31. *H. H. Patvirakutiun, 1920 t.* [R. (Republic) of A. (Armenia) Delegation, 1920].

File 144/43. *H. H. Patvirakutiun: Tntesakan Hartser* [R. (Republic) of A. (Armenia) Delegation: Economic Questions].

File 157/56. *H. H. Pat., 1921* [R. (Republic) of A. (Armenia) Del. (Delegation), 1921].

File 230/129. *H. H. Patvirakutiun, 1919* [R. (Republic) of A. (Armenia) Delegation, 1919].

File 231/130. *H. H. Patvirakutiun, 1919* [R. (Republic) of A. (Armenia) Delegation, 1919].

File 241/140. *H. H. Patvirakutiun: Azgayin Patvirakutiun* [R. (Republic) of A. (Armenia) Delegation: National Delegation].

File 283/182. *H. H. Pat.: Hayaserner* [R. (Republic) of A. (Armenia) Del. (Delegation).: Armenophiles].

File 295/2. *H. H. P.—Azgayin Patvirakutiun, 1918* [R. (Republic) of A. (Armenia) D. (Delegation)—National Delegation, 1918].

File 296/3. *H. H. Patvirakutiun—Azgayin Patvirakutiun, 1919* [R. (Republic) of A. (Armenia) Delegation—National Delegation, 1919].

File 319/1. *H. H. Patvirakutiun ev Fransiakan Karavarutiune, 1919* [R. (Republic) of A. (Armenia) Delegation and the French Government, 1919].

File 331/1. *H. H. Londoni Nerkayatsutschutiun ev Britanakan Karavarutiune, 1917* [R. (Republic) of A. (Armenia) London Mission and the British Government, 1917].

File 333/3. *H. H. Londoni Nerkayatsutschutiun ev Britanakan Karavarutiune, 1919* [R. (Republic) of A. (Armenia) London Mission and the British Government, 1919].

File 344/1. *H. H. Hromi Nerkayatsutschutiun ev Italakan Karavarutiune, 1918* [R. (Republic) of A. (Armenia) Rome Mission and the Italian Government, 1918].

File 353. *H. H. Berlini Nerkayatsutschutiun, 1918–1919* [R. (Republic) of A. (Armenia) Berlin Mission, 1918–1919].

File 373. *H. H. Patvirakutiun ev Rusakan Nakhkin Nerkayatsutsichner, 1919–1922* [R. (Republic) of A. (Armenia) Delegation and the Former Representatives of Russia, 1919–1922].

File 379/1. *H. H. Vashingtoni Nerkayatsutsich ev H. Amerikian Karavarutiune, 1917–1918* [R. (Republic) of A. (Armenia) Washington Representative and the N. (North) American Government, 1917–1918].

File 380/2. *H. H. Vashingtoni Nerkayatsutsich ev H. Amerikayi Karavarutiune, 1919* [R. (Republic) of A. (Armenia) Washington Representative and the Government of N. (North) America, 1919].

File 381/3. *H. H. Vashingtoni Nerkayatsutsich ev H. Amerikian Karavarutiune, 1919* [R. (Republic) of A. (Armenia) Washington Representative and the N. (North) American Government, 1919].

File 421/1. *H. H. Hai Teghekagir Biuro Parizum, 1919 t.* [R. (Republic) of A. (Armenia) Armenian Information Bureau in Paris, 1919].

File 503. *Kamavorakan Gnder, 1914–1918* [Volunteer Units, 1914–1918].

File 504. *Azgayin Miutiun Kilikio ev Siurio, 1919–1924* [The National Union of Cilicia and Syria, 1919–1924].

(The files that follow are part of the original archives of Dashnaktsutiun.)

File 1283/26. *H. H. D. Arevmtian Evropayi Kedronakan Komite, 1919* [A. (Armenian) R. (Revolutionary) F. (Federation) Central Committee of Western Europe, 1919].

File 1378/9. *H. H. D.: Germania, 1916–1920* [A. (Armenian) R. (Revolutionary) F. (Federation): Germany, 1916–1920].

File 1406a/26a. *H. H. D. Amerikayi Kedronakan Komite, 1918* [A. (Armenian) R. (Revolutionary) F. (Federation) Central Committee of America, 1918].

File 1407a/27a. *H. H. D. Amerikayi Kedronakan Komite, 1919* [A. (Armenian) R. (Revolutionary) F. (Federation) Central Committee of America, 1919].

File 1649. *H. H. D.: Gharabagh* [A. (Armenian) R. (Revolutionary) F. (Federation): Karabagh].

File 1687/18. *H. H. D.: Erkrord Midjazgaynakan, 1919* [A. (Armenian) R. (Revolutionary) F. (Federation): Second International, 1919].

File 1688/19. *H. H. D.: Erkrord Midjazgaynakan, 1920* [A. (Armenian) R. (Revolutionary) F. (Federation): Second International, 1920].

Great Britain

Cabinet Office Archives. Public Record Office (London).

Class 23. *Cabinet Minutes.* (1916–1939).

Class 24. *Cabinet Memoranda.* (1915–1939).

Class 25. *Supreme War Council.* (1917–1919).

Class 27. *Cabinet Committees: General Series.* (1915–1939).

Class 28. *Allied War Conferences.* (1915–1920).

Class 29. *International Conferences.* (1916–1939).

Class 32. *Imperial Conferences.* (1917–1937).

Class 44. *Cabinet Office Historical Section. Official War Histories: Compilations.*

Class 45. *Cabinet Office Historical Section. Official War Histories: Correspondence and Papers*

Foreign Office Archives. Public Record Office.

Class 371. *General Correspondence: Political.*

Class 406. *Confidential Print: Eastern Affairs, 1812–1946.*

Class 418. *Russia and the Soviet Union, 1821–1954.*

Class 424. *Turkey, 1841–1951.*

Class 608. *Peace Conference, 1919–1920: Correspondence.*

Class 800. *Private Collections: Ministers and Officials.*

War Office Archives. Public Record Office.

Class 32. *Registered Papers: General Series.*

Class 33. *Reports and Miscellaneous Papers (1853–1939).*

Class 95. *War Diaries, 1914–1922.*

Class 106. *Directorates of Military Operations and Intelligence, 1870–1925.*

United States of America

Library of Congress. Manuscript Division (Washington, D.C.).

The Papers of Mark L. Bristol.

The Papers of Woodrow Wilson.

The National Archives (Washington, D.C.).

Record Group 59. *General Records of the Department of State.*

Record Group 84. *Foreign Service Posts of the Department of State.*

Record Group 256. *Records of the American Commission to Negotiate Peace.*

Official Publications

Armenia [Republic of]

Hayastani Khorhrdi hastatads orenknere, 1918–1919 t. [The Laws Enacted by the Legislature of Armenia, 1918–1919]. Erevan, 1919.

Delegation to the Conference of Peace. *The Armenian Question before the Peace Conference.* [London, 1919].

———. *L'Arménie transcaucasienne: Territoires, frontières, ethnographie, statistique.* Paris, 1919.

———. *Données statistiques des populations de la Transcaucasie.* Paris, 1920.

———. *Réponse au mémoire de la Sublime-Porte en date 12 février 1919.* Constantinople, 1919.

———. *La République Arménienne et ses Voisins: Questions territoriales.* Paris, 1919.

———. *Tableau approximatif des réparations et indemnités pour les dommages subis par la nation arménienne en Arménie de Turquie et dans la République Arménienne du Caucase.* Paris, 1919.

Ministry of Foreign Affairs. *Gaghtni pastatghtere: Adrbedjani davadrakan gordsuneutiunits mi edj* [Secret Documents: A Page from the Conspiratorial Activity of Azerbaijan]. Erevan, 1920.

Armenian Revolutionary Federation [Hai Heghapokhakan Dashnaktsutiun]

Arame [Aram (Manukian)]. [Beirut], 1969.

Dsragir [Program]. Geneva, [1908].

Miatsial ev Ankakh Hayastan: Patmakan Kaile [United and Independent Armenia: The Historic Step]. Constantinople, 1919.

Programma armianskoi revoliutsionnoi i sotsialisticheskoi partii Dashnaktsutiun [Program of the Armenian Revolutionary and Socialist Party Dashnaktsutiun]. Geneva, 1908.

The Bureau. *Hushapatum H. H. Dashnaktsutian, 1890–1950* [Commemorative Volume of the A. (Armenian) R. (Revolutionary) Federation, 1890–1950]. Boston, 1950.

Central Committee of America. *Divan H. H. Dashnaktsutian* [Archives of the A. (Armenian) R. (Revolutionary) Federation]. Boston, 1934–1938. 2 vols.

———. *H. H. D. Vatsunamiak (1890–1950)* [Sixtieth Anniversary of the A. (Armenian) R. (Revolutionary) F. (Federation), 1890–1950]. Ed. by S. Vratzian. Boston, 1950.

Azerbaijan [Republic of]

Le 28 Mai 1919. [Baku, 1919].

Délégation Azerbaidjanienne à la Conférence de la Paix. *L'Azerbaïdjan en chiffres.* [Paris, 1919].

———. *Bulletin d'Informations de l'Azerbaïdjan.* Paris, 1919–1920. 12 issues.

———. *Carte de la République de l'Azerbaïdjan.* [Paris, 1919].

———. *Claims of the Peace Delegation of Caucasian Azerbaijan Presented to the Peace Conference in Paris.* Paris, 1919.

———.*Composition anthropologique et ethnique de la population de l'Azerbaïdjan du Caucase.* Paris, 1919.

——. *Economic and Financial Situation of Caucasian Azerbaijan.* Paris, 1919.

——. *La République de l'Azerbaïdjan du Caucase.* Paris, 1919.

——. *Revendications de la Délégation de Paix de la République de l'Azerbaïdjan du Caucase présentées à la Conférence de la Paix à Paris, 1919.* [Paris, 1919].

Communist International

Der I. *Kongress der Kommunistischen Internationale: Protokoll der Verhandlungen in Moskau vom 2. bis zum 19. März 1919.* Hamburg, 1921.

Manifest, Richtlinien, Beschlüsse des Ersten Kongresses: Aufrufe und offene Schreiben des Exekutivkomitees bis zum Zweiten Kongress. Hamburg, 1920.

Pervyi kongress Kominterna, mart 1919 g. [The First Congress of the Comintern, March, 1919]. Ed. by E. Korotkov, B. Kun, and O. Piatnitskov. Moscow, 1933.

France

Ministère des Affaires Étrangères. *Documents diplomatiques: Affaires arméniennes: Projets de réformes dans l'empire Ottoman, 1893–1897.* Paris, 1897.

——. ——. *(Supplément) 1895–1896.* Paris, 1897.

——. Commission de Publication des Documents Relatifs aux Origines de la Guerre de 1914. *Documents diplomatiques français (1871–1914).* Ire sér. *(1871–1900).* Paris, 1929–1954. 16 vols.

Georgia [Republic of]

Dokumenty i materialy po vneshnei politike Zakavkaz'ia i Gruzii [Documents and Materials on the Foreign Policy of Transcaucasia and Georgia]. Tiflis, 1919.

Iz istorii armiano-gruzinskikh otnoshenii, 1918 god: Pogranichnye konflikty, peregovory, voina, soglashenie [From the History of Armeno-Georgian Relations, 1918: Boundary Conflicts, Negotiations, War, Agreement]. Tiflis, 1919.

Délégation Géorgienne a la Conférence de la Paix. *Mémoire présenté à la Conférence de la Paix.* Paris, 1919.

Parti Ouvrier Social-Démocrate de Géorgie. *La Géorgie Indépendante.* [Geneva, 1919].

Germany

Auswärtiges Amt. *Die deutschen Dokumente zum Kriegsausbruch 1914.* Berlin, 1919. 4 vols.

——. *Die grosse Politik der europäischen Kabinette, 1871–1914.* Berlin, 1922–1927. 40 vols.

Reichsarchiv. *Der Weltkrieg 1914 bis 1918.* Berlin, 1925–1956. 14 vols.

Great Britain

Committee of Imperial Defence. Historical Section. *Military Operations: Macedonia.* Comp. by Cyril Falls and A. F. Becke. London, 1933–1935. 2 vols. In the series *History of the Great War.*

——. ——. *Naval Operations.* Comp. by Julian S. Corbett and Henry Newbolt. London, 1920–1931. 5 vols. In the series *History of the Great War.*

——. ——. *Order of Battle of Divisions.* Comp. by A. F. Becke. London, 1935–1945. 4 pts. in 7 vols. In the series *History of the Great War*. Part 4 is entitled *Order of Battle: The Army Council, G.H.Q.s, Armies, and Corps 1914–1918*.

——. ——. *The Campaign in Mesopotamia, 1914–1918*. Comp. by F. J. Moberly. London, 1923–1927. 4 vols. In the series *History of the Great War*.

Foreign Office. *British Documents on the Origins of the War: 1898–1914*. Ed. by G. P. Gooch and Harold Temperley. London, 1926–1938. 11 vols.

——. *Documents on British Foreign Policy, 1919–1939*, 1st series. Ed. by W. L. Woodward, Rohan Butler, J. P. T. Bury, *et al.* London, 1947–1970. 17 vols. to date.

——. *The Treatment of the Armenians in the Ottoman Empire*. Miscellaneous no. 31 (1916). London, 1916.

——. Historical Section. *Peace Handbooks*. Vol. IX, *The Russian Empire:* No. 54, *Caucasia*. London, 1920.

——. ——. *Peace Handbooks*. Vol. XI, *Turkey in Asia:* No. 62, *Armenia and Kurdistan*. London, 1920.

Parliament. House of Commons. *Sessional Papers (Accounts and Papers)*, 1890–1919.

——. ——. *The Parliamentary Debates*. 5th ser., 1917–1919.

——. House of Lords. *The Parliamentary Debates*. 5th ser., 1918–1919.

Persia [Iran]
Claims of Persia before the Conference of the Preliminaries of Peace at Paris, March, 1919. [Paris, 1919].

Russia [Imperial]
Kavkazskii kalendar' [Caucasian Calendar]. Tiflis, 1846–1916.

Kavkazskaia Arkheograficheskaia Kommissiia. *Akty sobrannye Kavkazskoiu Arkheograficheskoiu Kommissieiu* [Acts Collected by the Caucasian Archaeographic Commission]. Tiflis, 1866–1904. 12 vols. From the Archives of the Viceroy for the Caucasus.

——. Ministerstvo Inostrannykh Del. *Sbornik diplomaticheskikh dokumentov: Reformy v Armenii, 26 noiabria 1912 goda—10 maia 1914 goda* [Collection of Diplomatic Documents: Reforms in Armenia, November 26, 1912–May 10, 1914]. Petrograd, 1915.

Turkey
Aspirations et agissements révolutionnaires des comités arméniens avant et après la proclamation de la constitution ottomane. Constantinople, 1917.

Memorandum of the Sublime Porte Communicated to the American, British, French and Italian High Commissioners on the 12th February 1919. Constantinople, 1919.

Genelkurmay Başkanlığı. *Birinci Cihan Harbinde Türk Harbi*. [The Turkish War in the First World War]. Prepared by General Fahri Belen. Ankara, 1964–1967. 5 vols.

——. Harb Tarihi Dairesi. *Harb Tarihi Vesikaları Dergisi* [Journal of War History Documents]. Ankara. Sept., 1952——. The form *Harp* is used in several issues.

——. ——. *Türk İstiklâl Harbi* [The War of Turkish Liberation]. Vols. I–II. Ankara, 1962–1963.

Türk Devrim Tarihi Enstitüsü. *Atatürk'ün söylev ve demeçleri* [Ataturk's Speeches and Statements]. Ankara, 1952–1961. 2 vols.

———. *Nutuk, Kemâl Atatürk* [Speech of Kemal Ataturk]. Istanbul, [1960]. 3 vols. Documents referred to in Kemal's speech are in Vol. III, *Vesikalar* [Documents].

Türk İnkilâp Tarihi Enstitüsü. *Atatürk'ün söylev ve demeçleri* [Ataturk's Speeches and Statements]. Vol. I. Istanbul, 1945. Also 2d ed. Ankara, 1959–1961. 3 vols.

———. *Atatürk'ün tamim, telgraf ve beyannameleri* [Ataturk's Circulars, Telegrams, and Declarations]. Vol. IV. *1917–1938*. Ankara, 1964.

Union of Soviet Socialist Republics

Akademiia Nauk Armianskoi SSR. Institut Ekonomiki. *Sovetakan Hayastani tntesakan zargatsume, 1920–1960* [The Economic Development of Soviet Armenia, 1920–1960]. Erevan, 1960.

———. Institut Istorii—Armianskii Filial Instituta Marksizma-Leninizma pri TsK KPSS—Arkhivnoe Upravlenie MVD Armianskoi SSR. *Hoktemberian sotsialistakan meds revoliutsian ev Sovetakan ishkhanutian haghtanake Hayastanum: Pastatghteri ev niuteri zhoghovadsu* [The Great October Revolution and the Victory of Soviet Order in Armenia: Collection of Documents and Materials]. Ed. by A. N. Mnatsakanian *et al.* Erevan, 1960.

Akademiia Nauk Azerbaidzhanskoi SSR. Institut Istorii. *Istoriia Azerbaidzhana* [History of Azerbaijan]. Ed. by I. A. Guseinov *et al.* Baku, 1958–1963. 3 vols. in 4 pts.

———. Sektor Filosofii, *Istoriia gosudarstva i prava Azerbaidzhanskoi SSR: Velikaia Oktiabr'skaia sotsialisticheskaia revoliutsiia i sozdanie Sovetskoi gosudarstvennosti v Azerbaidzhane* [The History of Government and Law of the Azerbaijani SSR: The Great October Socialist Revolution and the Creation of the Soviet Form of Government in Azerbaijan]. Baku, 1964.

Akademiia Nauk Gruzinskoi SSR—Gruzinskii Filial Instituta Marksizma-Leninizma pri TsK KPSS—Arkhivnoe Upravlenie Gruzinskoi SSR. *Bor'ba za pobedu Sovetskoi vlasti v Gruzii: Dokumenty i materialy (1917–1921 gg.)* [Struggle for the Victory of Soviet Order in Georgia: Documents and Materials (1917–1921)]. Comp. by S. D. Beridze, A. M. Iovidze, S. V. Maglakelidze, and Sh. K. Chkhetiia. Tbilisi, 1958.

Akademiia Nauk SSSR—Glavnoe Arkhivnoe Upravlenie. *Velikaia Oktiabr'skaia sotsialisticheskaia revoliutsiia: Dokumenty i materialy* [The Great October Socialist Revolution: Documents and Materials]. Ed. by A. L. Sidorov *et al.* Vol. II. Moscow, 1963.

Armianskii Filial IML pri TsK KPSS—Institut Istorii Akademii Nauk Arm. SSR—Arkhivnyi otdel MVD Arm. SSR. *Velikaia Oktiabr'skaia revoliutsiia i pobeda Sovetskoi vlasti v Armenii (Sbornik dokumentov)* [The Great October Revolution and the Victory of Soviet Order in Armenia (Collection of Documents)]. Ed. by A. N. Mnatsakanian, A. M. Akopian, and G. M. Dallakian. Erevan, 1957.

Institut Istorii Partii pri TsK KP Armenii—Armianskii Filial Instituta Marksizma-Leninizma pri TsK KPSS. *Hayastani Komunistakan kusaktsu-*

tian patmutian urvagdser [Historical Outlines of the Communist Party of Armenia]. Ed. by Ds. P. Aghayan *et al.* Erevan, 1967.

————. *Revoliutsion kocher ev trutsikner, 1902–1921* [Revolutionary Appeals and Circulars, 1902–1921]. Erevan, 1960.

————. Sektsiia Istmoa. *Spartak, 1917–1920: Husher ev vaveragrer* [Spartak, 1917–1920: Memoirs and Documents]. Erevan, 1935.

Institut Istorii Partii pri TsK KP Azerbaidzhana—Filial Instituta Marksizma-Leninizma pri TsK KPSS. *Aktivnye bortsy za Sovetskuiu vlast' v Azerbaidzhane* [Active Fighters for Soviet Order in Azerbaijan]. Baku. 1957.

————. *Bol'sheviki v bor'be za pobedu sotsialisticheskoi revoliutsii v Azerbaidzhane: Dokumenty i materialy, 1917–1918 gg.* [Bolsheviks in the Struggle for the Victory of the Socialist Revolution in Azerbaijan: Documents and Materials, 1917–1918]. Ed. by Z. I. Ibragimov and M. S. Iskenderov. Baku, 1957.

————. *Istoriia Kommunisticheskoi partii Azerbaidzhana* [History of the Communist Party of Azerbaijan]. Vol. I. Baku, 1958.

————. *Ocherki Istorii Kommunisticheskoi partii Azerbaidzhana* [Sketches of the History of the Communist Party of Azerbaijan]. Ed. by M. S. Iskenderov *et al.* Baku, 1963.

————. *V. I. Lenin ob Azerbaidzhane* [V. I. Lenin about Azerbaijan]. Comp. by Dzh. B. Kultsev, E. A. Nalbandian, and S. M. Samebova. Baku, 1959.

————. Institut Istorii AN Azerbaidzhanskoi SSR—Arkhivnoe Upravlenie pri Sovete Ministrov Azerbaidzhanskoi SSR. *Bor'ba za pobedu Sovetskoi vlasti v Azerbaidzhane, 1918–1920: Dokumenty i materialy* [Struggle for the Victory of Soviet Order in Azerbaijan, 1918–1920: Documents and Materials]. Baku, 1967.

Institut Istorii Partii pri TsK KP Gruzii—Filial Instituta Marksizma-Leninizma pri TsK KPSS. *Ocherki istorii Kommunisticheskoi partii Gruzii* [Sketches of the History of the Communist Party of Georgia]. Ed. by V. G. Esaishvili. Pt. 1. Tiflis, 1957.

Institut Marksizma-Leninizma pri TsK KPSS [Formerly Institut Marksa-Engel'sa-Lenina-Stalina pri Tsk VKP(b)]. *I. V. Stalin: Sochineniia* [Works]. Moscow, 1946–1949. 13 vols.

————. *Protokoly i stenograficheskie otchety s"ezdov i konferentsii Kommunisticheskoi partii Sovetskogo Soiuza: Shestoi s"ezd RSDRP (bol'shevikov), Avgust 1917 goda: Protokoly* [Protocols and Stenographic Records of the Congresses and Conferences of the Communist Party of the Soviet Union: The Sixth Congress of the Russian Social Democrat Labor Party (Bolshevik), August, 1917: Protocols]. Moscow, 1958.

————. ————. *Vos'moi s"ezd RKP/b/, mart 1919 goda: Protokoly* [The Eighth Congress of the Russian Communist Party/Bolshevik/, March, 1919: Protocols]. Moscow, 1959.

————. *V. I. Lenin azgayin ev azgayin-gaghutayin hartsi masin* [V. I. Lenin on the National and the National-Colonial Question]. Erevan, 1957.

————. *V. I. Lenin: Polnoe sobranie sochinenii* [V. I. Lenin: Complete Collected Works]. 5th ed. Moscow, 1958–1965. 55 vols.

Ministerstvo Inostrannykh Del. *Dokumenty vneshnei politiki SSSR* [Documents on the Foreign Policy of the USSR]. Moscow, 1957–1967. 13 vols. to date.

―――. *Konstantinopol' i Prolivy po sekretnym dokumentam b. ministerstva inostrannykh del* [Constantinople and the Straits According to the Secret Documents of the F. (Former) Ministry of Foreign Affairs]. Ed. by E. A. Adamov. Moscow, 1925–1926. 2 vols.

―――. *Razdel Aziatskoi Turtsii po sekretnym dokumentam b. ministerstva inostrannykh del* [The Partition of Asiatic Turkey According to the Secret Documents of the F. (Former) Ministry of Foreign Affairs]. Ed. by E. A. Adamov. Moscow, 1924.

―――. Institut Istorii Akademii Nauk SSSR. *Dekrety Sovetskoi vlasti* [Decrees of the Soviet Government]. Vols. I–II. Moscow, 1957–1959.

United States of America

American Relief Administration. *Bulletin.* 22 issues. 1919.

Congress. *Congressional Record.* 65th Cong., 2d sess. Washington, D.C. Vol. LVI, pt. 11 (1918). 3d sess. Vol. LVII, pt. 1 (1918). 66th Cong., 1st sess. Vol. LVIII, pt. 1 (1919).

―――. Senate. *Journal.* 65th Cong., 3d sess. Washington, D.C. (1919).

Department of State. *Papers Relating to the Foreign Relations of the United States. 1917.* Supplement 2. *The World War.* Washington, D.C., 1932. 2 vols.

―――. ―――. *1918.* Washington, D.C., 1931. 3 vols.

―――. ―――. *1918: Russia.* Washington, D.C., 1931–1932. 3 vols.

―――. ―――. *1918.* Supplement 1. *The World War.* Washington, D.C., 1933. 2 vols.

―――. ―――. *1919.* Washington, D.C., 1934. 2 vols.

―――. ―――. *1919: The Paris Peace Conference.* Washington, D.C., 1942–1947. 13 vols.

―――. ―――. *1919: Russia.* Washington, D.C., 1937.

Newspapers

Ashkhatavor ["Laborer"]. Tiflis, 1918–1919.

Azerbaidzhan ["Azerbaijan"]. Russian ed. Baku, 1919.

Azg ["Nation"]. Boston, 1918–1919.

Bor'ba ["Struggle"]. Tiflis, 1918–1920.

Christian Science Monitor. Boston, 1917–1919.

Droshak ["Banner"]. Geneva, 1914–1915.

Eritasard Hayastan ["Young Armenia"]. Providence, 1918–1919.

Ertoba ["Labor"]. Tiflis, 1918–1919.

Gruziia ["Georgia"]. Tiflis, 1919.

Hairenik ["Fatherland"]. Boston, 1914–1920.

Horizon ["Horizon"]. Tiflis, 1917–1918.

Izvestiia ["News"]. Petrograd and Moscow, 1918–1919.

Jakatamart ["Battle"]. Constantinople, 1919.

Kavkazskoe slovo ["Word of the Caucasus"]. Tiflis, 1918–1919.

Mshak ["Worker"]. Tiflis, 1919

New York Times. 1915–1920.
Pahak ["Sentry"]. Boston, 1918–1919.
Pravda ["Truth"]. Moscow, 1919–1920.
Sakartvelos Respublika ["Georgian Republic"]. Tiflis, 1919.
Slovo ["Word"]. Tiflis, 1919.
Le Temps. Paris, 1917–1919.
Times. London, 1916–1919.
Zhizn' natsional'nostei ["Life of the Peoples"]. Moscow, 1919.
Zhoghovurd ["People"]. Erevan, 1919.

Published Documents, Memoirs, and Studies

Abadan, Yavus. *Inkilâp tarihine giriş* [Beginning of the History of the Revolution]. Ankara, 1962.
Abeghian, Art. "Menk ev mer harevannere—Azgayin kaghakakanutian klhndirner" [We and Our Neighbors—Problems of National Policy], *Hairenik Amsagir,* VI (Dec., 1927–Oct., 1928), and VII (Nov., 1928–Jan., 1929).
Abov, G. *Dashnaktsutiunn antsialum ev aizhm* [Dashnaktsutiun in the Past and Present] 2d ptg. Erevan, 1930.
Abrahamian, L. A. *Hayastanum marksizmi taradsman patmutiunits* [Material from the History of the Spread of Marxism in Armenia]. Erevan, 1969.
Adamiia, V. I. *Iz istorii angliiskoi interventsii v Gruzii (1918–1921 gg.)* [From the History of English Intervention in Georgia (1918–1921)]. Sukhumi, 1961.
Adonts, M. H. *Hayastani zhoghovrdakan tntesutiune ev hai tntesagitakan mitke XX dari skzbin* [The Popular Economy of Armenia and Armenian Economic Thought at the Beginning of the Twentieth Century]. Erevan, 1968.
Agababian, Grigor. "The Economic Situation of the Armenian Republic," *Asiatic Review,* XVI (April, 1920), 308–315.
Agadzhanov, M. *Ordzhonikidze v bor'be za osushchestvlenie natsional'noi politiki Kommunisticheskoi partii v Zakavkaz'e* [Ordzhonikidze in the Struggle for the Realization of the Nationality Policy of the Communist Party in Transcaucasia]. Tbilisi, 1960.
Aghayan, Ds. P. "Arshavir Melikian (dsnndian 90-amiaki artiv)" [Arshavir Melikian (On the 90th Anniversary of His Birth)], *Patma-banasirakan handes,* 1 (1969), 139–146.
———. "Arshavir Melikiane V. I. Lenini ashkhatutiunneri masin" [Arshavir Melikian on the Works of V. I. Lenin], *Banber Hayastani arkhivneri,* 1 (1969), 95–99.
———. *Hai ev adrbedjanakan zhoghovrdneri darevor barekamutiune* [The Centuries-Long Friendship of the Armenian and Azerbaijani Peoples]. Erevan, 1961.
———. *Hoktemberian revoliutsian ev hai zhoghovrdi azatagrume* [The October Revolution and the Liberation of the Armenian People]. Erevan, 1957.
———. "Leninian gaghaparneri annkun propagandiste ev khoshor tesabane (Arshavir Melikiani dsnndian 90-amiakin)" [The Invincible Propagandist and Ideologue of Leninist Concepts (On the 90th Anniversary of the Birth of Arshavir Melikian], *Lraber hasarakakan gitutiunneri,* 1 (1969), 21–39.

————. *Velikii oktiabr' i bor'ba trudiashchikhsia Armenii za pobedu Sovetskoi vlasti* [Great October and the Struggle of the Workers of Armenia for the Victory of Soviet Order]. Erevan, 1962.

Aharonian, Avetis. "Mi kani jshdumner" [A Few Corrections], *Hairenik Amsagir*, I (Oct., 1923), 79–82.

————. *Sardarapatits minchev Sevr ev Lozan (kaghakakan oragir)* [From Sardarabad to Sèvres and Lausanne (Political Diary)]. Boston, 1943.

Aharonian, Gersam, ed. *Hushamatian Meds Egherni, 1915–1965* [Memorial Volume of the Great Atrocity, 1915–1965]. Beirut, 1965.

Aharonian, Vardges [Vartkes]. *Andranik, marde ev razmike* [Andranik, the Man and the Warrior]. Boston, 1957.

Ahmad, Feroz. *The Young Turks: The Committee of Union and Progress in Turkish Politics, 1908–1914.* Oxford, 1969.

Akopian, S. M. *See* Hakobian, S. M.

Akşin, Aptülahat. *Atatürk'ün dış politika ilkeleri ve diplomasi* [Ataturk's Foreign Policy Principles and Diplomacy]. Pt. 2. Istanbul, [1964].

Albertini, Luigi. *The Origins of the War of 1914.* Trans. Isabella M. Massey. London, 1952–1957. 3 vols.

Alboyajian, Arshak. "Ankakh Hayastan" [Independent Armenia], in *Amenun Taretsuitse* [Constantinople], XV (1921), 107–129.

————. *Patmakan Hayastani sahmannere* [The Boundaries of Historic Armenia]. Cairo, 1950.

Albrecht-Carrié, René. *Italy at the Paris Peace Conference.* New York, 1938.

Alekseev, M. V., and M. A. Kerimov. *Vneshniaia politika Turtsii* [The Foreign Policy of Turkey]. Moscow, 1961.

Alikhanian, S. T. *Haikakan Gordseri Komisariati gordsuneutiune (1917–1921)* [Activity of the Commissariat of Armenian Affairs (1917–1921)]. Erevan, 1958.

————. *Sovetakan Rusastani dere hai zhoghovrdi azatagrman gordsum (1917–1921 t.t.)* [The Role of Soviet Russia in the Work of Liberating the Armenian People (1917–1921)]. Erevan, 1966.

————. *Vahan Teriani petakan gordsuneutiune* [The Governmental Activities of Vahan Terian]. Erevan, 1956.

————. "V. Avanesovi hamategh ashkhatanke Lenini het" [V. Avanesov's Teamwork with Lenin], *Patma-banasirakan handes*, 1 (1970), 79–94.

Allen, W. E. D. *A History of the Georgian People.* London, 1932.

Allen, W. E. D., and Paul Muratoff. *Caucasian Battlefields: A History of the Wars on the Turco-Caucasian Border, 1828–1921.* Cambridge, 1953.

Ambarian, A. S. *See* Hambarian, A. S.

American Committee for the Independence of Armenia. *A Report of the Activities: The American Committee for the Independence of Armenia, 1918–1922.* New York, 1922.

Amirkhanian, Aram. *Rus ev turk zinadadare: Patmakan antsker, 1917–1918* [The Russo-Turkish Cease-Fire: Historical Events, 1917–1918]. Fresno, Calif., 1921.

Ampopum hai azgayin hamagumari ashkhatutiants ev voroshmants (petrvar 24en minchev april 22) [Résumé of the Activities and Decisions of the Armenian National Congress (February 24 to April 22)]. [Paris, 1919].

Ananun, D. *Rusahayeri hasarakakan zargatsume* [The Social Development of the Russian Armenians]. Vol. III. *1901–1918*. Venice, 1926.

Andonian, Aram, ed. *Documents officiels concernant les massacres arméniens*. Paris, 1920.

Aralov, S. I. *Vospominaniia sovetskogo diplomata, 1922–1923* [Memoirs of a Soviet Diplomat, 1922–1923]. Moscow, 1960.

Aramayis. *Mi kani glukh hai-trkakan endharumnerits* [A Few Chapters from the Armeno-Turkish Clashes]. Tiflis, 1907. 2 pts.

Arkomed, S.T. *Materialy po istorii otpadeniia Zakavkaz'ia ot Rossii* [Materials on the History of the Separation of Transcaucasia from Russia]. Tiflis, 1923.

Armen Garo. *See* Pasdermadjian, G.

"Armenia and the American Mandate," *Current History*, X, pt. 1 (April, 1919), 71–72.

[Armenian National Council of Baku] Bakinskii Armianskii Natsional'nyi Sovet. *Armiano-gruzinskii vooruzhennyi konflikt: Na osnovanii fakticheskikh dannykh i podlinnykh dokumentov* [The Armeno-Georgian Armed Conflict: On the Basis of Factual Data and Authentic Documents]. Baku, 1919.

Armenian National Union of America. *The Case of Armenia*. [New York, 1919].

———. *Teghekagir Hai Azgayin Miutian Amerikayi, 1917–1921* [Report of the Armenian National Union of America, 1917–1921]. Boston, 1922.

Armenian SSR. Akademiia Nauk. Institut Literatury. *Hai nor grakanutian patmutiun* [History of Modern Armenian Literature]. Vols. I–III. Erevan, 1962–1964.

Armenia's Charter. An Appreciation of the Services of Armenians to the Allied Cause by the Rt. Hon. David Llyod George, M. Georges Clemenceau, the Rt. Hon. A. J. Balfour, the Rt. Hon. Lord Robert Cecil, the Rt. Hon. Viscount Bryce, General Sir Edmund Allenby. London, 1918.

Armstrong, H. C. *Grey Wolf: Mustafa Kemal*. London, 1937.

Armstrong, Harold. *Turkey in Travail: The Birth of a New Nation*. London, 1925.

Arzumanian, M. V. *Bolshevikneri gordsuneutiune ev revoliutsion sharzhumnere Hayastanum 1907–1917 tvakanin* [Bolshevik Activity and the Revolutionary Movements in Armenia, 1907–1917]. Erevan, 1959.

———. *Hayastan, 1914–1917* [Armenia, 1914–1917]. Erevan, 1969.

———. "Leninskii 'Dekret o Turetskoi Armenii'" [The Leninist "Decree About Turkish Armenia"], *Vestnik obshchestvennykh nauk* [*Lraber hasarakakan gitutiunneri*], 1 (1968), 23–32.

Ash, Bernard. *The Lost Dictator: A Biography of Field-Marshal Sir Henry Wilson*. London, [1968].

Astakhov, G. *Ot sultanata k demokraticheskoi Turtsii: Ocherki iz istorii kemalizma* [From Sultanate to Democratic Turkey: Sketches from the History of Kemalism]. Moscow and Leningrad, 1926.

Astvadsatrian, Arshaluis. "Arame" [Aram (Manukian)], *Vem*, II, 6 (1934), 23–35, and III, 1 (1935), 57–71.

Avagian, V. L. "Anglo-Amerikian interventneri gishatich kaghakakanutiune

Andrkovkasum 1919–1921" [The Predatory Policy of the Anglo-American Interventionists in Transcaucasia, 1919–1921], *Teghekagir: Hasarakakan gitutiunner,* 1 (1964), 3–4.

————. *Edjer Andrkovkasum otarerkria interventsiayi patmutiunits (1918 t)* [Pages from the History of Foreign Intervention in Trancaucasia (1918)]. Erevan, 1957.

Avalov [Avalashvili], Z. *Nezavisimost' Gruzii v mezhdunarodnoi politike, 1918–1921 g.g.: Vospominaniia: Ocherki* [The Independence of Georgia in International Politics, 1918–1921: Memoirs: Sketches]. Paris, 1924.

Avetian, M. *Hai azatagrakan azgayin hisnamia (1870–1920) hushamatian ev Zor. Andranik* [Commemorative Tome of Fifty Years of the Armenian National Liberation Movement, 1870–1920, and Gen. Andranik]. Paris, 1954.

Avetisian, G[H]. A. *Komsomol Zakavkaz'ia v bor'be za pobedu i uprochnenie Sovetskoi vlasti (1917–1921)* [The Komsomol of Transcaucasia in the Struggle for the Victory and Strengthening of Soviet Order (1917–1921)]. Erevan, 1964.

————. "Razvitie molodezhnogo dvizheniia i vozniknovenie Komsomola Zakavkaz'ia (1917–1919 gg.)" [The Development of the Youth Movement and the Evolvement of the Komsomol in Transcaucasia (1917–1919)], *Lraber hasarakakan gitutiunneri,* 11 (1967), 89–101.

Azizbekova, P.A. *V. I. Lenin i sotsialisticheskie preobrazovaniia v Azerbaidzhane 1920–1923 gg.* [V. I. Lenin and the Socialist Transformations in Azerbaijan, 1920–1923]. Moscow, 1962.

Babalian, A. *Edjer Hayastani ankakhutian patmutiunits* [Pages from the History of Armenia's Independence]. Cairo, 1959.

Babayan, L. H. *Hayastani sotsial-tntesakan ev kaghakakan patmutiune XIII–XIV darerum* [The Socioeconomic and Political History of Armenia during the 13th and 14th Centuries]. Erevan, 1964.

Badalian, Kh. H. *Germana-turkakan okupantnere Hayastanum 1918 tvakanin* [The Germano-Turkish Occupants in Armenia in 1918]. Erevan, 1962.

Baghdasarian, T. "Hayastani Hanrapetutian verdjaluisin" [At the Sunset of the Republic of Armenia], in *Edjer mer azatagrakan patmutenen* [Pages from the History of Our Liberation Movement]. Paris, 1937. Pp. 193–280.

Bagirov, Iu. A. *Iz istorii sovetsko-turetskikh otnoshenii v 1920–1922 gg. (po materialam Azerbaidzhanskoi SSR)* [From the History of Soviet-Turkish Relations in 1920–1922 (Based on Materials of the Azerbaijani SSR)]. Baku, 1965.

Baikov, B. "Vospominaniia o revoliutsii v Zakavkaz'i (1917–1920 g.g.)" [Memoirs of the Revolution in Transcaucasia (1917–1920)], *Arkhiv Russkoi Revoliutsii* [Berlin], IX (1923), 91–194.

Bailey, Thomas A. *Woodrow Wilson and the Lost Peace.* New York, 1947.

Baker, Ray Stannard, ed. *Woodrow Wilson: Life and Letters.* Vol. VIII. New York, 1939.

————. *Woodrow Wilson and the World Settlement: Written from His Unpublished and Personal Material.* Garden City, N.Y., 1923. 3 vols.

Balasanian, T. A. "Mankatnere Hayastanum 1917–1920 tt." [The Orphanages in Armenia, 1917–1920], *Banber Erevani Hamalsarani,* 2 (1968), 217–220.

Bammate, Haidar. *Le Caucase et la révolution russe.* Paris, 1929.

——. "The Caucasus during the War," *Current History,* X, pt. 1 (April, 1919), 122–127.

Bane, Suda Lorena, and Ralph Haswell Lutz. *Organization of American Relief in Europe 1918–1919.* Stanford, 1934.

Barbusse, Henri. *Voici ce qu'on a fait de la Géorgie.* Paris, 1929.

Barby, Henry. . . . *Le débâcle russe: Les extravagances bolcheviques et l'épopée arménienne.* Paris, 1919.

Barseghian, Kh. H. *Hayastani Komunistakan partiayi Kazmavorume* [The Formation of the Communist Party of Armenia]. Erevan, 1965.

—— [Barsegian, Kh. A.]. *Istoriia armianskoi bol'shevistskoi periodicheskoi pechati* [History of the Armenian Bolshevik Periodic Press]. Erevan, 1958.

——. *Stepan Shahumian: Kianki ev gordsuneutian vaveragrakan taregrutiun, 1878–1918* [Stepan Shahumian: Documentary Chronicle of His Life and Activities, 1878–1918]. Intro. by A. I. Mikoyan. Erevan, 1968.

Barsegian, Kh. A. *See* Barseghian Kh. H.

Barton, James L. *Story of Near East Relief (1915–1930).* New York, 1930.

Baumgart, Winfried. "Das 'Kaspi-Unternehmen'—Grössenwahn Ludendorffs oder Routineplanung des deutschen Generalstabs?" *Jahrbücher für Geschichte Osteuropas,* n.s., XVIII, 1 (March, 1970), 47–122, and 2 (June, 1970), 231–278.

Bayur, Yusuf Hikmet. *Atatürk, hayeti ve eseri* [Ataturk, Life and Works]. Vol. I. *Doğumundan Samsun'a çıgışına kadar* [From His Birth to His Landing at Samson]. Ankara, 1963.

——. *Türk İnkilâbi tarihi* [History of the Turkish Revolution]. Vol. III. *1914–1918 genel savaşı* [The 1914–1918 World War]. Pts. 3–4. Ankara, 1957–1967.

——. *Türkiye devletinin dış siyaseti* [The Foreign Policy of the Turkish State]. Istanbul, 1942.

Baziiants, A. P. *Zakhvatnicheskaia politika anglo-amerikanskogo imperializma v Baku i Azerbaidzhane (noiabr' 1918 g.–aprel' 1920 g.)* [The Annexationist Policy of Anglo-American Imperialism in Baku and Azerbaidjan (November, 1918–April, 1920)]. Moscow, 1950.

Bechhofer-[Roberts], C. E. *In Denikin's Russia and the Caucasus, 1919–1920.* London, [1921].

Beers, Henry P. *U.S. Naval Detachment in Turkish Waters, 1919–1924.* Washington, D.C., 1943.

Bıyıklıoğlu, Tevfik. *Atatürk Anadolu'da (1919–1921)* [Ataturk in Anatolia (1919–1921)]. Vol. I. Ankara, 1959.

——. "Mondros mütarekenamesinde Elviyei Selâse ile ilgili yeni vesikalar" [New Documents Relating to the Three Sanjaks in the Mudros Armistice], *Belleten,* XXI (Oct., 1957), 567–580.

——. *Trakya'da milli mücadele* [The National Struggle in Thrace]. Ankara, 1955–1956. 2 vols.

Blum, John Morton. *Woodrow Wilson and the Politics of Morality.* Boston, [1956].

Bonsal, Stephen. *Suitors and Suppliants: The Little Nations at Versailles.* New York, 1946.

————. *Unfinished Business*. Garden City, N.Y., 1944.
Borian, B. A. *Armeniia, mezhdunarodnaia diplomatiia i SSSR* [Armenia, International Diplomacy and the USSR]. Moscow and Leningrad, 1928–1929. 2 vols.
Borkenau, F. *The Communist International*. London, 1938.
Boyajian, Tigran. *Haikakan Legeone* [The Armenian Legion]. Boston, 1965.
Bradley, John. *Allied Intervention in Russia*. London, [1968].
Braunthal, Julius. *Geschichte der Internationale*. Hannover, [1961–1963]. 2 vols.
Brémond, E. *La Cilicie en 1919–1920*. Paris, 1921.
Brinkley, George A. *The Volunteer Army and Allied Intervention in South Russia, 1917–1921*. Notre Dame, 1966.
Buchan, John, ed. *The Baltic and Caucasian States: The Nations of Today*. Boston and New York, [1923].
The Bullitt Mission to Russia: Testimony before the Committee on Foreign Relations, United States Senate, of William C. Bullitt. New York, 1919.
Buniatov, Ziia. *Azerbaidzhan v VII–IX vv.* [Azerbaijan in the 7th–9th Centuries]. Baku, 1965.
Bunyan, James. *Intervention, Civil War and Communism in Russia, April–December, 1918*. Baltimore, 1936.
Bunyan, James, and H. H. Fisher. *The Bolshevik Revolution, 1917–1918: Documents and Materials*. Stanford, 1934.
Burnett, Philip Mason. *Reparations at the Paris Peace Conference: From the Standpoint of the American Delegation*. New York, 1940. 2 vols.

Callwell, C. E. *Field-Marshal Sir Henry Wilson*. London, [1927]. 2 vols.
Carnegie Endowment for International Peace. *Official Statements of War Aims and Peace Proposals, December 1916 to November 1918*. Prepared under supervision of James Brown Scott. Washington, D.C., 1921.
Carr, Edward Hallett. *The Bolshevik Revolution, 1917–1923*. London, 1950–1953. 3 vols.
Castagné, Joseph. "Les organisations soviétiques de la Russie musulmane," as pt. 1 of "Le Bolchevisme et l'Islam," in *Revue du monde musulman*, Vol. LI (Oct., 1922). Part 2 of "Le Bolchevisme et l'Islam" is in Vol. LII (Dec., 1922), and consists of several individual articles.
Cebesoy, Ali Fuat. *Millî mücadele hâtıraları* [Memoirs of the National Struggle]. Istanbul, 1953.
————. *Moskova hâtıraları (21/11/1920–2/6/1922)* [Moscow Memoirs (November 21, 1920–June 2, 1922)]. Istanbul, 1955.
Çelik, Fahrettin. "Kars eli tarihi" [History of the Province of Kars], in *Kars*. Ed. by Kemal Çilingiroglu *et al.* Instanbul, 1943. Pp. 19–45.
Chalkhushian, G. *Inch er ev inch piti lini mer ughin?* [What Was and What Shall Be Our Path?]. [Vienna], 1923.
Chamberlin, William Henry. *The Russian Revolution, 1917–1921*. New York, 1935. 2 vols.
Chater, Melville. "The Land of the Stalking Death," *National Geographic Magazine*, XXXVI, 5 (Nov., 1919), 393–420.
Chicherin, G. V. *Stat'i i rechi po voprosam mezhdunarodnoi politiki* [Articles and Speeches on Questions of International Politics]. Moscow, 1961.

Choburian, Edvard. *Meds paterazme ev hai zhoghovurde* [The Great War and the Armenian People]. Constantinople, 1920.

Churchill, Winston, S. *The Aftermath.* New York, 1929. Vol. V in the series *The World Crisis.*

Clemenceau, Georges. *Grandeurs et misères d'une victoire.* Paris, [1930].

Coates, W. P., and Zelda K. Coates. *Armed Intervention in Russia, 1918–1922.* London, 1935.

Cole, C. D. H. *A History of Socialist Thought.* Vol. IV. *Communism and Social Democracy, 1914–1931.* London, 1958. 2 pts.

Collier, Basil. *Brasshat: A Biography of Field-Marshal Sir Henry Wilson.* London [1961].

Conker, Orhon. Turk-Rus savaşları [Turco-Russian Wars]. Ankara, 1942.

Craig, Gordon A., and Filix Gilbert, eds. *The Diplomats 1919–1939.* Princeton, 1953.

Cruickshank, A. A. "The Young Turk Challenge in Postwar Turkey," *Middle Eastern Journal,* XXII (Winter, 1968), 17–28.

Cumming, Henry H. *Franco-British Rivalry in the Post-War Near East: The Decline of French Influence.* London, 1938.

Daniel, Robert L. "The Armenian Question and American-Turkish Relations, 1914–1927," *Mississippi Valley Historical Review,* XLVI (Sept., 1959), 252–275.

Danielian, H. *Spartak Hayastanum* [Spartak in Armenia]. Moscow, 1931.

Daniels, Emil. "England und Russland in Armenien und Persien," *Preussische Jahrbücher,* CLXIX (July/Sept., 1917), 237–267.

Dantsig, B. *Turtsiia* [Turkey]. Moscow, 1949.

Darbinian, Reuben. "A Mission to Moscow: Memoirs," *Armenian Review,* I (Spring, 1948), 23–37, (Summer, 1948), 27–41, (Autumn, 1948), 44–61, and II (Spring, 1949), 89–103, (Summer, 1949), 76–88.

Dasuurançi [Daskhurantsi], Movses. *The History of the Caucasian Albanians.* Trans. C. J. F. Dowsett. London, 1961.

Davison, Roderic H. "The Armenian Crisis, 1912–1914," *American Historical Review,* LIII (April, 1948), 481–505.

Degras, Jane, ed. *The Communist International, 1919–1943: Documents.* London, New York, and Toronto, 1956–1960. 2 vols.

———. *Soviet Documents on Foreign Policy.* Vol. I. *1917–1924.* London, New York, and Toronto, 1951.

De Kay, John. *The Spirit of the International.* [New York], 1919.

" 'Demokraticheskoe' pravitel'stvo Gruzii i angliiskoe komandovanie" [The "Democratic" Government of Georgia and the English Command], Comp. by Semen Sef, *Krasnyi Arkhiv,* XXI (1927), 122–173, and XXV (1927), 96–110.

Denikin, A. I. *Ocherki russkoi smuty* [Sketches of the Troubled Era of Russia]. Paris and Berlin, [1921–1926]. 5 vols.

Dennis, Alfred L. P. *The Foreign Policies of Soviet Russia.* New York, 1924.

DeNovo, John A. *American Interests and Policies in the Middle East 1900–1939.* Minneapolis, [1963].

Devdariani, Gaioz, ed. *Dni gospodstva men'shevikov v Gruzii (dokumenty, materialy*) [In the Days of Menshevik Rule in Georgia (Documents, Materials)]. [Tiflis], 1931.

Dillon, E. J. *The Inside Story of the Peace Conference.* New York and London, [1920].

Dimanshtein, S. D., ed. *Revoliutsiia i natsional'nyi vopros* [Revolution and the National Question]. Vol. III. Moscow, 1930.

Djamalian, Arshak. "Hai-vratsakan knjire" [The Armeno-Georgian Entanglement], *Hairenik Amsagir*, Vol. VI (April, 1928–Oct., 1928), and Vol. VII (Nov., 1928–April, 1929).

Djanachian, Mesrop. *Patmutiun ardi hai grakanutian* [History of Modern Armenian Literature]. Venice, 1953.

Djemal Pasha. *Memories of a Turkish Statesman, 1913–1919.* New York, 1922.

"Dnevnik Ministerstva Inostrannykh Del za 1915–1916 g.g." [Journal of the Ministry of Foreign Affairs for 1915–1916], *Krasnyi Arkhiv*, XXXI (1928), 3–50, and XXXII (1929), 3–87.

Dubner, A. *Bakinskii proletariat v gody revoliutsii (1917–1920)* [The Baku Proletariat in the Years of the Revolution (1917–1920)]. Baku, 1931.

Duguet, Raymond. *Moscou et la Géorgie martyre.* Paris. [1927].

Dunsterville, L. C. *The Adventures of Dunsterforce.* London, 1920.

Dursunoğlu, Cevat. "Erzurum Kongresi sırasında Atatürk'ün düşünceleri" [Ataturk's Thoughts during the Erzerum Congress], *Belleten*, XXVII (Sept., 1953), 633–639.

———. *Milli mücadelede Erzurum* [Erzerum in the National Struggle]. Ankara, 1946.

D. Z. T. "La première République musulmane: L'Azerbaidjan," *Revue du monde musulman*, XXXVI (1918/1919), 229–265.

Edib, Halidé. *Turkey Faces West: A Turkish View of Recent Changes and Their Origin.* New Haven, 1930.

———. *The Turkish Ordeal.* New York, 1928.

Egan, Eleanor Franklin. "This To Be Said for the Turk," *Saturday Evening Post*, CXCII (Dec. 20, 1919), 14–15, 71–77.

Eghiazarian, A. M. "Andrkovkasi hai bnakchutian sotsialakan kazmi masin" [About the Social Structure of the Armenian Inhabitants of Transcaucasia], *Teghekagir: Hasarakakan gitutiunner*, 9 (1961), 61–68.

Elchibekian, Ambartsum [Hambardzum] M. *Armeniia nakanune Velikogo Oktiabria* (fevral'-oktiabr' 1917 goda) [Armenia on the Eve of Great October (February–October, 1917)]. Erevan, 1963.

———. "Gharakilisayi jakatamarte 1918 tvi mayisin" [The Battle of Karakilisa in May, 1918], *Teghekagir: Hasarakakan gitutiunner*, 8 (1947), 51–63.

———. "Sovetakan ishkhanutian haghtanake Hayastanum" [The Victory of Soviet Order in Armenia], *Teghekagir: Hasarakakan gitutiunner*, 1–2 (1950), 3–54.

———. *Velikaia Oktiabr'skaia sotsialisticheskaia revoliutsiia i pobeda Sovetskoi vlasti v Armenii* [The Great October Socialist Revolution and the Victory of Soviet Order in Armenia]. Erevan, 1963.

Elchibekian, Hambardzum, and A. M. Hakobian. *Urvagdser Sovetakan Hayastani patmutian* [Outlines of the History of Soviet Armenia]. Pt. 1. Erevan, 1954.

Elder, John. "Memories of the Armenian Republic," *Armenian Review*, VI (Spring, 1953), 3–27.

Emin, Ahmed. *Turkey in the World War*. New Haven, 1930.

Emirov, N. *Ustanovlenie Sovetskoi vlasti v Dagestane i bor'ba s germano-turetskimi interventami* [The Establishment of Soviet Order in Daghestan and the Struggle against the German-Turkish Interventionists]. Moscow, 1949.

Emre, Ahmet Cevat. *İki neslin tarihi: Mustafa Kemal neler yaptı* [History of Two Generations: What Mustafa Kemal Did]. [Istanbul], 1960.

Engoyan, P. I. *Hayastani Kompartiayi paikare respublikayi industriatsman hamar* [The Struggle of the Communist Party of Armenia for the Industrialization of the Republic]. Erevan, 1965.

Enukidze, D. *Krakh imperialisticheskoi interventsii v Zakavkaz'e* [The Downfall of Imperialist Intervention in Transcaucasia]. Tbilisi, 1954.

Ertürk, Hüsameddin. *İki devrin perde arkası* [Behind the Curtains of Two Eras]. Comp. by Samih Nafiz Tansu. Istanbul, 1964.

Erzurum Kongresi ve Mustafa Kemâl Atatürk [The Erzerum Congress and Mustafa Kemal Ataturk]. N.p. N.d. A collection of articles.

Esadze, P. *Istoricheskaia zapiska ob upravlenii Kavkazom* [Historical Record on the Administration of the Caucasus]. Vol. I. Tiflis, 1907.

Esmer, Ahmet Şükrü. *Siyasi tarih, 1919–1939* [Diplomatic History, 1919–1939]. Ankara, 1953.

Eudin, Xenia Joukoff, and Robert C. North. *Soviet Russia and the East, 1920–1927: A Documentary Survey*. Stanford, 1957.

Evans, Lawrence. *United States Policy and the Partition of Turkey, 1914–1924*. Baltimore, [1965].

Ezov, G. A., ed. *Snosheniia Petra Velikago s armianskim narodom: Dokumenty* [The Relations of Peter the Great with the Armenian People: Documents]. St. Petersburg, 1898.

Faradjian, Peter. "A Scholar Examines Our Paris Delegates," *Armenian Review*, IX (Spring, 1956), 79–84.

Feldmann, Wilhelm. *Kriegstage in Konstantinopel*. Strassburg, 1913.

Fester, Richard. *Die Internationale 1914–1919*. Halle, 1919.

Field, Wm. O., Jr. "The International Struggle for Transcaucasia," *American Quarterly on the Soviet Union*, II (July/Oct., 1939), 21–41.

Fischer, Fritz. *Griff nach der Weltmacht*. 3d ptg. Düsseldorf, 1964.

Fischer, Louis. *Oil Imperialism*. New York, 1926.

———. *The Soviets in World Affairs: A History of the Relations between the Soviet Union and the Rest of the World, 1917–1929*. 2d ed. Princeton, 1951. 2 vols.

Footman, David. *Civil War in Russia*. London, [1961].

French, F. J. F. *From Whitehall to the Caspian*. London, 1920.

Froembgen, Hanns. *Kemal Ataturk: A Biography*. Trans. Kenneth Kirkness. New York, 1937.

Furaev, V. K. *Sovetsko-amerikanskie otnosheniia 1917–1934* [Soviet-American Relations, 1917–1934]. Moscow, 1964.

Gafurov, B. S. "Sovetskaia Rossiia i natsional'no-osvoboditel'naia bor'ba narodov Srednego i Blizhnego Vostoka" [Soviet Russia and the National-Liberation Struggle of the Peoples of the Middle and the Near East], *Voprosy istorii,* XLI (Oct., 1967), 37–53.

Galoyan, G. A. *Bor'ba za Sovetskuiu vlast' v Armenii* [Struggle for the Soviet Order in Armenia]. Moscow, 1957.

———. *Mayisian herosakan apstambutiune* [The Heroic May Rebellion]. Erevan, 1960.

———. *Sotsialisticheskaia revoliutsiia v Zakavkaz'e v osveshchenii burzhuaznoi istoriografii* [The Socialist Revolution in Transcaucasia in the Interpretation of Bourgeois Historiography]. Moscow, 1960.

Gambashidze, Givi. *Iz istorii politiki S Sh A v otnoshenii Gruzii, 1917–1920.* [From the History of the Policy of the USA toward Georgia, 1917–1920]. Tbilisi, 1960.

Gates, Caleb. *Not to Me Only.* Princeton, 1940.

Gelfand, Lawrence E. *The Inquiry: American Preparations for Peace, 1917–1919.* New Haven and London, 1963.

General Andranik: Haikakan Arandzin Harvadsogh Zoramase [General Andranik: The Armenian Special Striking Division]. Transcribed by Eghishe Kadjuni. Boston, 1921.

Gentizon, Paul. *La résurrection géorgienne.* Paris, 1921.

Gerard, James W. *England and France in Armenia.* [New York, 1920].

Gharibian, I. "Lori kaghake matenagrutian medj" [The City of Lori in Historical Literature], *Banber Erevani Hamalsarani,* 1 (1968), 209–214.

Gharibdjanian, G. B. "Aleksandropoli bolshevikian kazmakerputiune 1917–1918 t.t." [The Bolshevik Organization in Alexandropol in 1917–1918], *Teghekagir: Hasarakakan gitutiunner,* 7 (1948), 3–37.

———. *Hayastani komunistakan kazmakerputiunnere Sovetakan ishkhanutian haghtanaki hamar mghvads paikarum* [The Communist Organizations of Armenia in the Struggle for the Victory of Soviet Order]. Erevan, 1955.

———. "V. I. Lenine Andrkovkasi zhoghovurdneri heghapokhakan sharzhman sotsial-kaghakakan paimanneri masin" [V. I. Lenin on the Sociopolitical Conditions of the Revolutionary Movement of the Transcaucasian Peoples], *Lraber hasarakakan gitutiunneri,* 1 (1969), 10–20.

———. *V. I. Lenine ev Andrkovkasi zhoghovurdneri azatagrume* [V. I. Lenin and the Liberation of the Peoples of Transcaucasia]. Erevan, 1960.

———. *V. I. Lenin i bol'shevistskie organizatsii Zakavkaz'ia (1893–1924)* [V. I. Lenin and the Bolshevik Organizations of Transcaucasia (1893–1924)]. Erevan, 1967.

Ghazarian, Haik. *Arevmtahayeri sotsial-tntesakan ev kaghakakan katsutiune 1800–1870 tt.* [The Socioeconomic and Political Condition of the Western Armenians, 1800–1870]. Erevan, 1967.

Gidney, James B. *A Mandate for Armenia.* Kent, Ohio, [1967].

Giulkhandanian, A. "Bakvi herosamarte" [The Heroic Battle of Baku], *Hairenik Amsagir,* XIX (July, 1941), 89–102, (Aug., 1941), 101–115, and (Sept./Oct., 1941), 81–92.

———. *Hai-tatarakan endharumnere* [The Armeno-Tatar Clashes]. Tiflis, 1907.

———. *Hai-trkakan endharumnere* [The Armeno-Turkic Clashes]. Vol. I. Paris, 1933.

Gökbilgin, M. Tayyib. *Milli mücadele başlarken: Mondros mütarekesinden Sivas Kongresine* [Beginnings of the National Struggle: From the Mudros Armistice to the Sivas Congress]. Vol. 1. Ankara, 1959.

Gologlu, Mahmut. *Erzurum Kongresi* [The Erzerum Congress]. [Ankara, 1968].

Gönlübol, Mehmet, and Cem Sar. *Atatürk ve Turkiyenin dış politikası (1919–1938)* [Ataturk and the Foreign Policies of Turkey (1919–1938)]. Istanbul, 1963.

Gontaut-Biron, R. de. *Comment la France s'est installée en Syrie (1918–1919)*. Paris, 1922.

"Gorskaia kontrrevoliutsiia i interventy" [The Mountaineer Counterrevolution and the Interventionists], comp. by A. Ivanov, *Krasnyi Arkhiv*, LXVIII (1935), 125–153.

Gulanian, Kh. G. *Marksistakan tntesagitakan mtki taradsume hai irakanutian medj, 1890–1920* [The Spread of Marxist Economic Thought on the Armenian Scene, 1890–1920]. Erevan, 1961.

———. *Marksistskaia mysl' v Armenii* [Marxist Thought in Armenia]. Erevan, 1967.

———. *Uruagdser hai tntesagitakan mtki patmutian* [Outlines of the History of Armenian Economic Thought]. Erevan, 1959.

Guliev, Dzh. B. *V. I. Lenin ob Azerbaidzhane* [V. I. Lenin about Azerbaijan]. Baku, 1966.

Gurko-Kriazhin, V. A. "Angliiskaia interventsiia 1918–1919 gg. v Zakaspii i Zakavkaz'e" [English Intervention in Transcaspia and Transcaucasia in 1918–1919], *Istorik marksist*, 2 (1926), 115–139.

———. *Istoriia revoliutsii v Turtsii* [History of the Revolution in Turkey]. Moscow, 1923.

Guse, Felix. *Die Kaukasusfront im Weltkrieg bis zum Frieden von Brest*. Leipzig, [1940].

Guseinov, Geidar [Huseinov, Haidar]. *Ob istoricheskom sodruzhestve russkogo i azerbaidzhanskogo narodov* [Concerning the Historical Friendship of the Russian and Azerbaijani Peoples]. Baku, 1946.

Guseinov [Huseinov], Mirza-Davud. *Tiurkskaia Demokraticheskaia Partiia Federalistov "Musavat" v proshlom i nastoiashchem* [The Turkic Democratic Federalist Party "Musavat" in the Past and at Present]. [Tiflis], 1927.

Guseinov [Huseinov], T. *Oktiabr' v Azerbaidzhane* [October in Azerbaijan]. Baku, 1927.

Haikakan Hartse Khaghaghutian Zhoghovin Ardjev [The Armenian Question before the Peace Conference]. [Boston, 1919].

Hakobian, St. M. "Arevmtian Hayastane Fransiakan Imperialistneri planerum" [Western Armenia in the Plans of the French Imperialists], *Teghekagir: Hasarakakan gitutiunner*, 5 (1964), 29–39.

———. *Zapadnaia Armeniia v planakh imperialisticheskikh derzhav v period pervoi mirovoi voiny* [Western Armenia in the Plans of the Imperialist Powers in the Period of the First World War]. Erevan, 1967.

Hakobian, T. Kh. *Erevani patmutiune* [The History of Erevan]. Erevan, 1959–1963. 2 vols.

———. *Siuniki tagavorutiune* [The Kingdom of Siunik]. Erevan, 1966.

————. *Urvagdser Hayastani patmakan ashkharhagrutian* [Outlines of Armenia's Historical Geography]. Erevan, 1960.

Hamarot teghekagir Arevmtahai Erkrord Hamagumari, 1919 t. [Concise Report of the Second Congress of Western Armenians, 1919]. Tiflis, 1919.

Hambarian, A. S. *Agrarayin haraberutiunnere Arevmtian Hayastanum (1856–1914)* [Agrarian Relationships in Western Armenia (1856–1914)]. Erevan, 1965.

————. "Arevelian Hayastani tntesakan zargatsume Rusastanin miatsumits heto" [The Economic Development of Eastern Armenia after Its Union with Russia], *Lraber hasarakakan gitutiunneri*, 11 (1968), 20–29.

————. "Fabrika-gordsaranayin artadrutian zargatsume nakhasovetakan Hayastanum" [The Development of Factory Production in Pre-Soviet Armenia], *Teghekagir: Hasarakakan gitutiunner*, 11 (1957), 3–20.

————. *Razvitie kapitalisticheskikh otnoshenii v armianskoi derevne (1860–1920)* [The Development of Capitalistic Relationships in the Armenian Village (1860–1920)]. Erevan, 1959.

Hamo. "Hayastani Hanrapetutian erkamia kiankn u gordsuneutiune" [The Two-Year Existence and Activity of the Republic of Armenia], in *Hairenik: Batsarik tiv nvirvads Hayastani Hanrapetutian 2rd taredardzin* (Special issue on the second anniversary of the Armenian republic). Boston, 1920. Pp. 35–42.

Hankey, Lord Maurice P. A.]. *The Supreme Command, 1914–1918.* London, [1961]. 2 vols.

————. *The Supreme Control at the Paris Peace Conference, 1919.* London, [1963].

Harris, George S. *The Origins of Communism in Turkey.* Stanford, 1967.

Harutiunian, Ashot. "Sarighamishi jakatamarti dere Kovkase turkakan nerkhuzhman vtangits prkelu gordsum (1914 t. dektember)" [The Role of the Battle of Sarikamish in Delivering the Caucasus from the Threat of Turkish Invasion (December, 1914)], *Banber Hayastani arkhivneri*, 2 (1967), 89–109.

Harutiunian, B. "Siuniats tagavorutian himnadrman taretive" [The Founding Date of the Kingdom of Siunik], *Banber Erevani Hamalsarani*, 1 (1969), 145–153.

Harutiunian, G. *Revoliutsion sharzhumnere ev Bolshevikneri gordsuneutiune Andrkovkasum 1910–1912 tvakannerin* [The Revolutionary Movements and the Activity of the Bolsheviks in Transcaucasia, 1910–1912]. Erevan, 1959.

"Hayastani Khorhrdi ardzanagrutiunnere" [The Minutes of the Legislature of Armenia], *Vem*, II (1934), no. 4, pp. 113–123, no. 5, pp. 92–104, no. 6, 87–95, and III (1935), no. 1, pp. 72–83, no. 2, pp. 89–96, no. 3, pp. 84–88.

Hayastani Komunistakan kusaktsutian nerkayatsutsichi zekutsume errord Komunistakan Internatsionalin [Report of the Representative of the Armenian Communist Party to the Third Communist International]. Moscow, 1919.

Hin Bolshevikneri hishoghutiunner [Memoirs of Veteran Bolsheviks]. Publ. of Armianskii Filial Instituta Marksizma-Leninizma pri TsK KPSS—Institut Istorii Partii pri TsK KP Armenii. Erevan, 1958–1961. 2 vols.

Hippeau, Edmond. *Les républiques du Caucase: Géorgie—Azerbaidjan.* Paris, 1920.

Hodgetts, E. A. Brayley. "The Strategic Position of Armenia," *Asiatic Review,* XVI (July, 1920), 385–394.

[Hoover, Herbert]. *The Memoirs of Herbert Hoover.* New York, 1952. 3 vols.

———. *The Ordeal of Woodrow Wilson.* New York, Toronto, and London, [1958].

House, Edward M., and Charles Seymour, eds. *What Really Happened at Paris: The Story of the Peace Conference, 1918–1919, by American Delegates.* New York, 1921.

Hovannisian, Richard G. "The Allies and Armenia, 1915–18," *Journal of Contemporary History,* III (Jan., 1968), 145–168.

———. "The Armenian Republic," *Armenian Review,* XVII (Winter, 1964), 20–39.

———. *Armenia on the Road to Independence, 1918.* Berkeley and Los Angeles, 1967.

Hovhannisian, Ashot. *Drvagner hai azatagrakan mtki patmutian* [Episodes from the History of Armenian Liberation Thought]. Erevan, 1957–1959. 2 vols.

———. *Hayastani avtonomian ev Antantan: Vaveragrer imperialistakan paterazmi shrdjanits* [Armenia's Autonomy and the Entente: Documents from the Period of the Imperialistic War]. Erevan, 1926.

Hovhannisian, G. A. "Msmnayi jakatamarte" [The Battle of Msmna], *Banber Erevani Hamalsarani,* 3 (1968), 150–153.

Hovhannisian [Varandian], Mikayel. *Dashnaktsutiun ev nra hakarakordnere* [Dashnaktsutiun and Its Opponents]. Tiflis, 1907.

———. *Kovkasian Vandean (turk-haikakan endharumnere: Nrants patjarnere)* [The Caucasian Vendée (The Turco-Armenian Clashes: Their Causes)]. Tiflis, 1907.

Hovsepian, H. A. "Petutian dzeveri hartse St. Shahumiani ashkhatutiunnerum" [The Question of the Forms of State in the Works of St. Shahumian], *Lraber hasarakakan gitutiunneri,* 10 (1969), 3–16.

Howard, Harry N. *The King-Crane Commission: An American Inquiry in the Middle East.* Beirut, 1963.

———. *The Partition of Turkey: A Diplomatic History, 1913–1923.* Norman, Okla., 1931.

Hulse, James. *The Formation of the Communist International.* Stanford, 1964.

Hurewitz, J. C. *Diplomacy in the Near and Middle East: A Documentary Record.* Princeton, [1956]. 2 vols.

Ishkhanian, B. *Kontr-revoliutsiia v Zakavkaz'e* [Counterrevolution in Transcaucasia]. Baku, 1919.

———. *Narodnosti Kavkaza* [The Nationalities of the Caucasus]. Petrograd, 1916.

———. *Velikie uzhasy v gor. Baku: Anketnoe issledovanie sentiabr'skikh sobytii 1918 g.* [Great Horrors in the City of Baku: A Documentary Investigation of the September Events, 1918]. Tiflis, 1920.

Ishkhanian, E. "Depkere Gharabaghum: Jshdumner ev ditoghutiunner" [The Events in Karabagh: Corrections and Observations], *Hairenik Amsagir,* XI (Sept., 1933), 85–93, and (Oct., 1933), 111–127.

Iskenderov, M. S. *Iz istorii bor'by Kommunisticheskoi partii Azerbaidzhana za pobedu Sovetskoi vlasti* [From the History of the Struggle of the Communist Party of Azerbaijan for the Victory of Soviet Order]. Baku, 1958.

Jackh, Ernest. *The Rising Crescent: Turkey Yesterday, Today and Tomorrow.* New York and Toronto, [1944].

Jäschke, Gotthard. "Beiträge zur Geschichte des Kampfes der Türkei um ihre Unabhängigkeit," *Die Welt des Islams*, n.s., V, 1–2 (1957), 1–64.

———. "Entwurf zu einem Friedens- und Freundschaftsvertrag zwischen dem Osmanischen Reich und der Föderativen Transkaukasischen Republik," *Die Welt des Islams*, XXIII, 3–4 (1941), 170–174.

———. "Der Freiheitskampf des türkischen Volkes," *Die Welt des Islams*, XIV (1932), 6–21.

———. "General Milne zur Entsendung Mustafa Kemals nach Anatolien," *Die Welt des Islams*, n.s., II, 4 (1953), 267–269.

———. "Kommunismus und Islam im türkischen Befreiungskriege," *Die Welt des Islams*, XX (1938), 110–117.

———. "Mondros'a giden yol" [The Road to Mudros], *Belleten*, XXVIII (Jan., 1964), 141–152.

———. "Mustafa Kemals Sendung nach Anatolien," in *Aus der Geschichte des Islamischen Orients*. Tübingen, 1949. Pp. 17–40.

———. "Neues zur russisch-türkischen Freundschaft von 1919–1939," *Die Welt des Islams*, n.s., VI, 3–4 (1961), 203–222.

———. "Die Republik Aserbeidschan," *Die Welt des Islams*, XXIII, 1–2 (1941), 55–69.

———. "Die Südwestkaukasische Regierung von Kars," *Die Welt des Islams*, n.s., II, 1 (1952), 47–51.

———. "Der Turanismus der Jungtürken: Zur osmanischen Aussenpolitik im Weltkriege," *Die Welt des Islams*, XXIII, 1–2 (1941), 1–54.

———. "Der Weg zur russisch-türkischen Freundschaft im Lichte Moskaus," *Die Welt des Islams*, XX (1938), 118–134.

Jäschke, Gotthard, and Erich Pritsch. "Die Türkei seit dem Weltkriege: Geschichtskalender 1918–1928," *Die Welt des Islams*, X (1927/1929), 1–129.

Jewett, Frank. "Why We Did Not Declare War on Turkey," *Current History*, XIV (1921), 989–991.

Jizmejian, Manuk G. *Patmutiun amerikahai kaghakakan kusaktsutiants, 1890–1925* [History of the Armenian-American Political Parties, 1890–1925]. Fresno, Calif., 1930.

Kachaznuni, H. *H. H. Dashnaktsutiune anelik chuni ailevs* [The A. (Armenian) R. (Revolutionary) Federation Has Nothing More To Do]. Vienna, 1923.

Kadishev, A. B. *Interventsiia i grazhdanskaia voina v Zakavkaz'e* [Intervention and Civil War in Transcaucasia]. Moscow, 1960.

Kaikhanidi, A. E. *Leninskaia teoriia i programma po natsional'nomu voprosu* [The Leninist Theory and Program on the National Question]. Minsk, 1962.

Kandemir, Feridun. *Atatürk'ün kurduğu Türkiye Komunist Partisi ve sonrası*

[The Communist Party Formed by Ataturk and Thereafter]. Istanbul, [1965]

———. *Hatıraları ve söyleyemedikleri ile: Rauf Orbay* [Memoirs and What Was Not Said: Rauf Orbay]. Istanbul, [1965].

———. *Kâzım Karabekir*. Istanbul, 1948.

———. *Kâzım Karabekir'in yakılan hâtıraları meselesinin içyüzü* [The Inside Story of the Question of Kiazim Karabekir's Burned Memoirs]. Istanbul, [1964].

———. *Milli mücadele başlangıcında Mustafa Kemâl, arkadaşları ve karşısındakiler* [Mustafa Kemal, His Friends and Opponents, at the Beginning of the National Struggle]. Istanbul, [1964].

Karabekir, Kâzım. *İstiklâl Harbimiz* [Our War of Independence]. Istanbul, [1960].

———. *İstiklâl Harbimizin esasları* [The Principles of Our War of Independence]. Istanbul, 1951.

Karaev, A. G. *Iz nedavnogo proshlogo (materialy k istorii Azerbaidzhanskoi Kommunisticheskoi partii (bol'shevikov)* [From the Recent Past (Materials for the History of the Communist Party (Bolshevik) of Azerbaijan)]. Baku, 1926.

Karal, Ziya Karal. *Türkiye Cumhuriyeti tarihi (1918–1960)* [History of the Turkish Republic (1918–1960)]. Istanbul, 1960.

Karaman, Sami Sabit. *İstiklâl mücadelesi ve Enver Pasha* [The National Struggle and Enver Pasha]. Izmit, 1949.

Karapetian, H. N. *Hayastani Komeritmiutian dsnunde* [The Birth of the Komsomol of Armenia]. Erevan, 1956.

Karapetian, H. S. *Mayisian apstambutiune Hayastanum, 1920* [The May Rebellion in Armenia, 1920]. Erevan, 1961.

Karapetian, S. Kh. *Kommunisticheskaia partiia v bor'be za pobedu Oktiabr'skoi revoliutsii v Armenii* [The Communist Party in the Struggle for the Victory of the October Revolution in Armenia]. Erevan, 1956.

———. *Zinvads apstambutiune Lorum 1921 tvakanin* [The Armed Rebellion in Lori, 1921]. Erevan, 1955.

Kara-Schemsi [Atabinin, R. S.]. *Turcs et Arméniens devant l'histoire*. Geneva, 1919.

Kautsky, Karl. *Georgia: A Social-Democratic Peasant Republic*. Trans. H. J. Stenning. London, [1921].

Kazemzadeh, Firuz. *The Struggle for Transcaucasia (1917–1921)*. New York and Oxford, [1951].

Kemal, Mustafa [Ataturk]. *A Speech Delivered by Ghazi Mustapha Kemal, President of the Turkish Republic, October 1927*. Leipzig, 1927.

Kennan, George F. *Soviet-American Relations, 1917–1920*. Vol. II. *The Decision to Intervene*. Princeton, 1958.

Kévork-Mesrob. *L'Arménie au point de vue géographique, historique, statistique et cultural*. Constantinople, 1919.

Khachapuridze, G. *Bol'sheviki Gruzii v boiakh za pobedu Sovetskoi vlasti* [Bolsheviks of Georgia in the Battles for the Victory of Soviet Order]. 2d ed. [Moscow], 1951.

———. *Bor'ba gruzinskogo naroda za ustanovlenie Sovetskoi vlasti* [The

504   BIBLIOGRAPHY

Struggle of the Georgian People for the Establishment of Soviet Order].
    3d ptg. Moscow, 1956.
Khachatrian, A. *Armianskie voiski v XVIII veke: Iz istorii armiano-russkogo
    voennogo sodruzhestva* [Armenian Forces in the 18th Century: From the
    History of Armeno-Russian Military Collaboration]. Erevan, 1968.
Khaleyan, E. "St. Shahumiani handipumnere V. I. Lenini het ev nrants
    namakagrutiune 1903–1918 t.t." [St. (Stepan) Shahumian's Meetings with
    V. I. Lenin and Their Correspondence, 1903–1918], *Teghekagir: Hasara-
    kakan gitutiunner*, 11 (1953), 3–22.
Khatisian, Al. "Batumi Dashnagire" [The Treaty of Batum], in *Mayis 28*
    [May 28]. Paris, 1926. Pp. 35–43.
———. *Hayastani Hanrapetutian dsagumn u zargatsume* [The Creation and
    Development of the Republic of Armenia]. Athens, 1930.
———. "Kaghakapeti me hishataknere" [The Memoirs of a Mayor], *Hairenik
    Amsagir*, X (May, 1932–Oct., 1932), and XI (Nov., 1932–March, 1933).
Kheifets, A. N. *Sovetskaia Rossiia i sopredel'nye strany Vostoka v gody
    grazhdanskoi voiny (1918–1920)* [Soviet Russia and the Contiguous Coun-
    tries of the East in the Years of the Civil War (1918–1920)]. Moscow, 1964.
Khondkarian, Arsham. "Opozitsian Hanrapetakan Hayastanum" [The Op-
    position in Republican Armenia], *Vem*, I (1933), no. 1, pp. 63–82, no. 2,
    pp. 68–79, and II (1934), no. 1, pp. 76–97, no. 3, 42–60, no. 4, 73–95.
———. "Tsarakan Rusastane ev Kovkasahayutiune" [Tsarist Russia and the
    Caucasian Armenians], *Hairenik Amsagir*, VIII (March, 1930), 80–91, and
    (April, 1930), 143–155.
———. "Varantsov-Dashkovi namaknere Tsarin" [Vorontsov-Dashkov's Let-
    ters to the Tsar], *Hairenik Amsagir*, VII (May, 1929), 81–98.
Khrushchev, N. S. *Jar Erevan kaghakum teghi unetsads handisavor nistum,
    nvirvads Hayastanum Sovetakan ishkhanutian hastatman ev Hayastani
    Komunistakan partiayi kazmavorman 40-amiakin* [Speech at the Ceremoni-
    ous Session in the City of Erevan, Dedicated to the 40th Anniversary of
    the Establishment of Soviet Order in Armenia and the Formation of the
    Communist Party of Armenia]. Erevan, 1961.
Khurshudian, L. A. *Stepan Shahumian: Petakan ev partiakan gordsuneutiune
    1917–1918 tvakannerin* [Stepan Shahumian: Governmental and Party Ac-
    tivity in 1917–1918]. Erevan, 1959.
Kiazim, Omer. *Angora et Berlin*. Paris, 1922.
———. *L'aventure kémaliste*. Paris, 1921.
Kinross Lord [John P. D. B.]. *Atatürk: The Rebirth of a Nation*. London,
    [1964].
Kirakosian, Dj. S. *Aradjin hamashkharhayin paterazme ev Arevmtahayutiune,
    1914–1916 t.t.* [The First World War and the Western Armenians, 1914–
    1916]. Erevan, 1965.
———. "Hisun tari aradj (Sardarapati herosamarti aritov)" [Fifty Years Ago
    (On the Occasion of the Heroic Battle of Sardarabad)], *Banber Erevani
    Hamalsarani*, 2 (1968), 36–53.
———. 'Midjazgayin imperializme ev Arevmtahayutian bnadjndjman turka-
    kan kaghakakanutiune [International Imperialism and the Turkish Policy
    of Annihilating the Western Armenians], *Teghekagir: Hasarakakan gitu-
    tiunner*, 4 (1965), 81–99.

Kirov, S. M. *Stat'i, rechi, dokumenty* [Articles, Speeches, Documents]. Vol. I. Moscow, 1935.

Kliuchnikov, Iu. V., and A. Sabanin, eds. *Mezhdunarodnaia politika noveishego vremeni v dogovorakh, notakh i deklaratsiiakh* [International Politics of Recent Times in Treaties, Notes, and Declarations]. Moscow, 1925–1929. 3 vols. in 4 pts.

Koças, Sadi. *Tarih boyunca Ermeniler ve Türk-Ermeni iliskileri* [The Armenians Throughout History and Turkish-Armenian Relations]. Ankara, 1967.

Kol'tsov, P. S, P. A. Rodionov, S. V. Kharmandarian, and M. V. Tsertsvadze. "Iz istorii kommunisticheskikh organizatsii Zakavkaz'ia" [From the History of the Communist Organizations of Transcaucasia], *Voprosy istorii KPSS*, 6 (1962), 56–73.

Korganoff, G. *La participation des Arméniens à la guerre mondiale sur le front du Caucase, 1914–1918*. Paris, 1927.

Korienko, R. P. *Rabochee dvizhenie v Turtsii, 1918–1963 gg.* [The Workers Movement in Turkey, 1918–1963]. Moscow, 1965.

Korkud, Refik. *Marxisme karşı Atatürk* [Ataturk against Marxism]. Ankara, 1967.

———. *Son üç asırda Türkiye ile ilgili Rus politikası* [Turkey in Russian Policy for the Last Three Centuries]. Ankara, [1966].

Korsun, N. G. *Pervaia mirovaia voina na Kavkazskom fronte: Operativnostrategicheskii ocherk* [The First World War on the Caucasus Front: Operational-Strategical Sketch]. Moscow, 1946.

———. *Sarykamyshskaia operatsiia na Kavkazskom fronte mirovoi voiny v 1914–1915 godu* [The Sarikamish Operation on the Caucasus Front during the World War in 1914–1915]. Moscow, 1937.

Kostiaeff, F. "Intervention des puissances étrangères en Russie méridionale et dans les régions du Caucase et du Turkestan de 1918 à 1920," in *Les Alliés contre la Russie avant, pendant et après la guerre mondiale (faits et documents)*. Paris, [1926]. Pp. 249–303.

Kurat, Akdes Nimet. "Brest-Litovsk müzakereleri ve barışı (20 aralık 1917–3 mart 1918)" [The Brest-Litovsk Negotiations and Peace (December 20, 1917–March 3, 1918)], *Belleten*, XXXI (July, 1967), 375–413.

Kutay, Cemal. *Atatürk-Enver Paşa hadiseleri* [The Ataturk-Enver Pasha Incidents]. Istanbul, [1956].

———. *Milli mücadelede öncekiler ve sonrakiler* [Those Who Came Before and After in the National Struggle]. Istanbul, [1963].

———. *Türkiye'de ilk Komunistler* [The First Communists in Turkey]. Istanbul, [1956].

———. *Üç paşalar kavgası* [The Quarrels of the Three Pashas]. Istanbul, [1964].

Kuznetsova, S. I. *Ustanovlenie sovetsko-turetskikh otnoshenii* [The Establishment of Soviet-Turkish Relations]. Moscow, 1961.

La Chesnais, P. G. *Les peuples de la Transcaucasie pendant la guerre et devant la paix*. Paris, 1921.

Lalabekian, B. H. *V. I. Lenine ev Sovetakan kargeri hastatumn u amrapn-*

dumn Andrkovkasum [V. I. Lenin and the Establishment and Strengthening of Soviet Order in Transcaucasia]. Erevan, 1961.

Lalayan, Ervand. "Borchalu gavare" [The County of Borchalu], *Azgagrakan handes* (Tiflis), VI (1901), 271–437, VII (1902), 197–262, and VIII (1903), 112–268.

———. "Djavakhk" [Jàvakhk (Akhalkalak)], *Azgagrakan handes* (Shushi), I (1895), 117–380.

———. "Sisian" [Sisian (A district of Zangezur)], *Azgagrakan handes* (Tiflis), III, 1 (1898), 102–272.

———. "Varanda" [Varanda (A district of Mountainous Karabagh)], *Azgagrakan handes* (Tiflis), II (1897), 4–244.

———. "Zangezur," *Azgagrakan handes* (Tiflis), III, 2 (1898), 7–116.

———. "Zangezuri gavar" [The County of Zangezur], *Azgagrakan handes* (Tiflis), IX (1905), 175–202.

Lang, David Marshall. *The Last Years of the Georgian Monarchy, 1658–1832.* New York, 1957.

Langer, William L. *The Diplomacy of Imperialism, 1890–1902.* 2d ed. New York, 1951.

Lansing, Robert. *The Peace Negotiations: A Personal Narrative.* Boston and New York, [1921].

Larcher, M. *La guerre turque dans la guerre mondiale.* Paris, 1926.

Lazian, Gabriel. *Demker hai azatagrakan sharzhumen* [Personalities of the Armenian Liberation Movement]. Cairo, 1949.

———. *Hayastan ev hai date: Hai-ev-rus haraberutiunneru luisin tak* [Armenia and the Armenian Question: In the Light of Armeno-Russian Relations]. Cairo, 1957.

———. *Hayastan ev hai date (Vaveragrer)* [Armenia and the Armenian Question (Documents)]. Cairo, 1946.

———. *Heghapokhakan demker (mtavorakanner ev haidukner)* [Revolutionary Figures (Intellectuals and Guerrillas)]. Cairo, 1945.

Lederer, Ivo J. *Yugoslavia at the Paris Peace Conference.* New Haven and London, 1963.

Lenczowski, George. *The Middle East in World Affairs.* Ithica, 1952.

Lenin o druzhbe s narodami Vostoka [Lenin on Friendship with the Peoples of the East]. Ed. by I. Kul'kov and intro. by V. Ia. Zevin. Moscow, 1961.

Leo [Babakhanian, Arakel]. *Hayots hartsi vaveragrere* [The Documents on the Armenian Question]. Tiflis, 1915.

———. *Hayots patmutiun* [History of the Armenians]. Vol. I, Tiflis, 1917; Vols. II and III, Erevan, 1946 and 1947. 3 vols.

———. *Tiurkahai heghapokhutian gaghaparabanutiune* [The Ideology of the Turkish Armenian Revolution]. Paris, 1934–1935. 2 vols.

Lepsius, Johannes. *Armenia and Europe: An Indictment.* London, 1897.

———. "The Armenian Question," *Muslim World,* X (1920), 341–355.

———. *Der Todesgang des Armenischen Volkes.* 4th ed. Potsdam, 1930.

———, ed. *Deutschland und Armenien, 1914–1918: Sammlung diplomatischer Aktenstücke.* Potsdam, 1919.

Lewis, Bernard. *The Emergence of Modern Turkey.* London, 1961.

Lewis, Geoffrey. *Turkey.* London, [1960].

Lifshits, L. M. *Geroicheskii podvig bakinskikh bol'shevikov: Iz istorii bor'by*

za pobedu sotsialisticheskoi revoliutsii v Azerbaidzhane v 1917–1918 gg.
[The Heroic Feat of the Baku Bolsheviks: From the History of the Struggle
for the Victory of the Socialist Revolution in Azerbaijan in 1917–1918].
Baku, 1964.

Liloyan, G. Ts. *Natsional'nyi vopros v armianskoi bol'shevistskoi publitsistike
(1904–1914 gg.)* [The National Question in Armenian Bolshevik Journal-
ism (1904–1914)]. Erevan, 1967.

Lisitsian, Stepan. *Zangezuri hayere* [The Armenians of Zangezur]. Erevan,
1969.

Lloyd George, David. *Memoirs of the Peace Conference.* New Haven, 1939.
2 vols.

———. *War Memoirs.* Boston, 1933–1937. 6 vols.

Logan, Rayford W. *The Senate and the Versailles Mandate System.* Washington, D.C., 1945.

Loris-Melicof, Jean. *La révolution russe et les nouvelles républiques trans-
caucasiennes: Bolchevisme et antibolchevisme.* Paris, 1920.

Ludendorff, Erich. *Meine Kriegserinnerungen, 1914–1918.* Berlin, 1919.

Ludshuveit, E. F. "Konferentsiia levykh turetskikh sotsialistov v Moskve letom
1918 goda" [Conference of Turkish Left Socialists in Moscow in the Summer of 1918], in *Vostokovedcheskii sbornik* [Orientology Collection], publ.
of Akademiia Nauk Armianskoi SSR, Sektor Vostokovedeniia. Erevan, 1964.
Pp. 174–192.

———. *Turtsiia v gody pervoi mirovoi voiny 1914–1918 gg.: Voenno-politicheskii ocherk* [Turkey in the Years of the First World War, 1914–1918: A
Military-Political Sketch]. Moscow, 1966.

Luke, Harry. *The Making of Modern Turkey: From Byzantium to Angora.*
London, 1936.

Lybyer, A. H. "Turkey under the Armistice," *Journal of International Relations,* XII, 2 (1922), 447–473.

Lynch, H. F. B. *Armenia: Travels and Studies.* London, 1901. 2 vols.

MacDonell, Ranald. ". . . *And Nothing Long.*" London, [1938].

Magnes, Judah L. *Russia and Germany at Brest-Litovsk: A Documentary
History of the Peace Negotiations.* New York, [1919].

Makharadze, Filipp. *Diktatura men'shevistskoi partii v Gruzii* [The Dictatorship of the Menshevik Party in Georgia]. Moscow, 1921.

———. *Ocherki revoliutsionnogo dvizheniia v Zakavkaz'e* [Outlines of the
Revolutionary Movement in Transcaucasia]. Tiflis, 1927.

———. *Sovety i bor'ba za Sovetskuiu vlast' v Gruzii* [The Soviets and the
Struggle for Soviet Order in Georgia]. Tiflis, 1922.

Makharadze, N. B. *Pobeda sotsialisticheskoi revoliutsii v Gruzii* [Victory of
the Socialist Revolution in Georgia]. Tbilisi, 1965.

Mandelstam, André. *La Société des Nations et les Puissances devant le
Problème Arménien.* Paris, 1926.

———. *Le sort de l'empire Ottoman.* Paris and Lausanne, 1917.

Mantoux, Paul. *Les délibérations du Conseil des Quatre (24 mars–28 juin
1919): Notes de l'officier interprète.* Paris, 1955. 2 vols.

Manvelichvili, Alexandre. *Histoire de la Géorgie.* Paris, [1951].

Margarian, Hr., A. Mnatsakanian, and Kh. Barseghian, eds. *Hayastani Komu-*

nistakan partiayi patmutian urvagdser [Outlines of the History of the Communist Party of Armenia]. Erevan, 1958.

Marmarian, Arsen. *Zor. Andranik ev ir paterazmnere* [Gen. Andranik and His Wars]. Constantinople, 1920.

Marriot, H. A. R. *The Eastern Question: A Historical Study in European Diplomacy.* 4th ed. Oxford, 1951.

Martirosian, Martin. "Sardarapati jakatamarte" [The Battle of Sardarabad], *Banber Hayastani arkhivneri,* 1 (1969), 151–166.

Maslovskii, E. V. *Mirovaia voina na Kavkazskom fronte, 1914–1917 g.* [The World War on the Caucasus Front, 1914–1917]. Paris, [1933].

Masurian, S. "Rusahayots Azgayin Hamagumare" [The National Congress of Russian Armenians], in *Mayis 28* [May 28]. Paris, 1926. Pp. 4–22.

Mauclair, Camille, ed. *Pour l'Arménie libre.* Paris, 1919.

Maurice, Frederick. *The Armistice of 1918.* London, 1943.

Mayer, Arno J. *Political Origins of the New Diplomacy, 1917–1918.* New Haven, 1959.

———. *Politics and Diplomacy of Peacemaking.* New York, 1967.

Mears, Eliot Grinnell. *Modern Turkey: A Politico-Economic Interpretation, 1908–1923.* New York, 1924.

Mécérian, Jean. *Le génocide du peuple arménien.* Beirut, 1965.

Melikian, Hovakim. "Arian janaparhov" [On the Bloody Path], *Hairenik Amsagir,* III (Nov., 1924), 72–86, (Dec., 1924), 91–99, (Jan., 1925), 119–124, (Feb., 1925), 84–88, (April, 1925), 128–135, (May, 1925), 71–78, (July, 1925), 94–101.

Melikian, M. A. *K voprosu o formirovanii armianskoi natsii i ee sotsialisticheskogo preobrazovaniia* [On the Question about the Formation of the Armenian Nation and Its Socialistic Reorganization]. Erevan, 1957.

Melik-Ohandjanian, K. "Akanavor Komunist Arshavir Melikiani masin (1912–1920 tt." [On the Noted Communist Arshavir Melikian (1912–1920)], *Lraber hasarakakan gitutiunneri,* 3 (1969), 82–87.

Melik-Yolchian, Sergei. "Bakvi herosamarte" [The Heroic Battle of Baku], *Hairenik Amsagir,* III (May, 1925), 105–128, (June, 1925), 104–118, (July, 1925), 68–74, (Aug., 1925), 97–113, (Sept., 1925), 68–78, (Oct., 1925), 123–129.

Melkonian, S. H. *Bagrat Gharibdjanian, 1890–1920.* [Erevan], 1954.

Merkviladze, V. N. *V. I. Lenin i stroitel'stvo osnov Sovetskoi natsional'noi gosudarstvennosti.* [V. I. Lenin and the Construction of the Foundations of the Soviet Governmental System]. Tbilisi, 1959.

Mermeix [Terrail, Gabriel]. *Le combat des trois: Notes et documents sur la conférence de la paix.* 5th ed. Paris, 1922.

Meyer, Alfred G. *Leninism.* Cambridge, Mass., 1957.

Mikayelian, Arsen, "Gharabaghi verdjin depkere" [The Final Events in Karabagh], *Hairenik Amsagir,* I (May, 1923), 156–167, (June, 1923), 110–122, (July, 1923), 115–121, (Sept., 1923), 110–119, (Oct., 1923), 118–127.

Mikayelian, V. A. *Hayastani giughatsiutiune Sovetakan ishkhanutian hamar mghvads paikari zhamanakashrdjanum (1917–1920 tt.)* [The Peasantry of Armenia in the Period of Struggle for the Victory of Soviet Order (1917–1920)]. Erevan, 1960.

Miliukov, Paul. "The Balkanization of Transcaucasia," *New Russia*, II (June 24, 1920), 236–241, (July 1, 1920), 269–274, and (July 8, 1920), 299–303.

Miller, A. F. *Ocherki noveishei istorii Turtsii* [Sketches of the Recent History of Turkey]. Moscow and Leningrad, 1948.

Miller, David Hunter. *The Drafting of the Covenant*. New York, 1928. 2 vols.

———. *My Diary at the Conference of Paris: With Documents* [New York, 1924–1926]. 22 vols.

Miller, William. *The Ottoman Empire and Its Successors, 1801–1922*. Cambridge. 1923.

[Millî Kongre]. *The Turco-Armenian Question: The Turkish Point of View*. Constantinople, 1919.

Mil'man, A. Sh. *Politicheskii stroi Azerbaidzhana v XIX–nachala XX vekov* [The Political System in Azerbaijan in the 19th and the Beginning of the 20th Centuries]. Baku, 1966.

Minakhorian, Vahan. "Andjatakannere" [The Secessionists], *Vem*, I (1933), no. 1, pp. 100–111, no. 2, pp. 90–107.

———. "Batumi Khorhrdazhoghove" [The Batum Conference], *Hairenik Amsagir*, XIV (March, 1936), 91–99, (April, 1936), 123–131, and (May, 1936), 112–120.

———. "Karsi ankume" [The Fall of Kars], *Hairenik Amsagir*, XIII (Aug., 1935), 79–87, (Sept., 1935), 83–96, (Oct., 1935), 79–92, and XIV (Dec., 1935), 133–139, (Jan., 1936), 145–152.

———. *Tragediia Turtsii* [The Tragedy of Turkey]. [Baku], 1919.

Minasian, O. "Vneshniaia politika zakavkazskoi kontrrevoliutsii v pervoi polovine 1918 goda" [The External Policy of the Transcaucasian Counterrevolution in the First Half of 1918], *Istorik marksist*, 6 (1938), 53–86.

Mir-Yacoub [Mehtiev]. *Le problème due Caucase*. Paris, 1933.

Mirza-Bala, Mehmet-Zade. *Millî Azerbaycan hareketi: Millî Az. "Müsavat" halk fırkası tarihi*. [The National Azerbaijan Movement: History of the National Az. (Azerbaijani) "Musavat" People's Party]. [Berlin], 1938.

Mkhitarian, On. *Vani herosamarte* [The Heroic Battle of Van]. Sofia, 1930.

Mnatsakanian, A. N. *Amerikian agresorneri ev nrants gordsakalneri dem mghads paikari patmutiunits* [From the History of the Struggle Waged against the American Aggressors and Their Agents]. Erevan, 1953.

———. *Hai zhoghovrdi voghbergutiune: Rus ev hamashkharhayin hasarakakan mtki gnahatmamb* [The Tragedy of the Armenian People: As Appraised by Russian and Worldwide Public Opinion]. Erevan, 1965.

———. *Poslantsy Sovetskoi Rossii v Armenii* [Envoys of Soviet Russia to Armenia]. Erevan, 1959.

———. *Revoliutsian Andrkovkasum ev Rusastani patviraknere, 1917–1921* [The Revolution in Transcaucasia and the Envoys of Russia, 1917–1921]. Erevan, 1961.

———. *V. I. Lenine ev hai zhoghovrdi azatagrakan paikare* [V. I. Lenin and the Armenian People's Struggle for Freedom]. Erevan, 1963.

Mneyan, G. M. *Stepan Shahumiani partiakan ev petakan gordsuneutiune (1900–1918)* [Stepan Shahumian's Party and Governmental Activity (1900–1918)]. Erevan, 1963.

Moiseev, P., and Iu. Rozaliev. *K istorii sovetsko-turetskikh otnoshenii* [On the History of Soviet-Turkish Relations]. Moscow, 1968.

Morgenthau, Henry. *Ambassador Morgenthau's Story.* Garden City, N.Y., 1919.

Moschopoulos, N. *Les Turcs jugés par leur histoire: Une réponse à Damad Férid Pacha.* Paris, 1920.

Movsesian, Lewond. "Histoire des rois Kurikian de Lori," trans. Frédéric Macler, *Revue des études arméniennes,* VII, pt. 2 (1927), 209–265.

Movsisian, R. *Kovkasian bolshevikian kazmakerputiunneri Erkrayin aradjin hamagumare ev Stepan Shahumian* [The First Regional Conference of Caucasian Bolshevik Organizations and Stepan Shahumian]. Erevan, 1955.

Mravian, A. *Erb ev inchpes e himnvel Hayastani Komunistakan (bolsh.) Kusaktsutiune?* [When and How Was the Armenian Communist (Bolshevik) Party Founded?]. Erevan, 1928.

Mühlmann, Carl. *Das deutsch-türkische Waffenbündnis im Weltkrieg.* Leipzig, [1940].

Nadzhafov, Adil. *Formirovanie i razvitie azerbaidzhanskoi sotsialisticheskoi natsii* [The Formation and Development of the Azerbaijani Socialist Nation]. Baku, 1955.

Nalbandian, Louise. *The Armenian Revolutionary Movement: The Development of Armenian Political Parties through the Nineteenth Century.* Berkeley and Los Angeles, 1963.

Narimanov, N. *Stat'i i pis'ma* [Articles and Letters]. Moscow, 1925.

Naslian, Jean. *Les Mémoires de Mgr. Jean Naslian Évêque de Trebizonde sur les événements politico-religieux en Proche-Orient de 1914 à 1928.* Vienna, [1955]. 2 vols.

Navasardian, Vahan. *Bolshevizme ev Dashnaktsutiune* [Bolshevism and Dashnaktsutiun]. Cairo, 1949.

———. *Inch cher ev inch piti chlini mer ughin* [What Was Not and What Shall Not Be Our Path]. Cairo, 1923. A response to Chalkhoushian's work, listed above.

Nerkararian, V. N. *Hayastani Kompartian zhoghovrdakan tntesutian verakangnman zhamanakashrdjanum (1921–1925 tt.)* [The Communist Party of Armenia during the Restoration Period of the People's Economy (1921–1925)]. Erevan, 1956.

Nersisian, A. N. *Arevmtahayeri tntesakan u kaghakakan vijake ev nrants rusakan orientatsian XIX dari aradjin kesin* [The Economic and Political Condition of the Western Armenians and Their Russian Orientation in the First Half of the 19th Century]. Erevan, 1962.

Nersisian, M. G., ed. *Genotsid armian v Osmanskoi imperii: Sbornik dokumentov i materialov* [Genocide of the Armenians in the Ottoman Empire: Collection of Documents and Materials]. Erevan, 1965.

Nicol, E. *Angora et la France.* Paris, 1922.

Nicolson, Harold. *Curzon: The Last Phase 1919–1925: A Study in Post-War Diplomacy.* London, [1937].

———. *Peacemaking.* London, [1945].

Nikogosian [Nikoghosian], M. G. "Iz istorii Sovetov Armenii v period dvoevlastiia" [From the History of the Soviets in Armenia during the Period of Dual Rule], *Teghekagir: Hasarakakan gitutiunner,* 1 (1960), 3–16.

Nippold, O. *La Géorgie du point de vue du droit international.* Berne, 1920.

Novichev, A. "Antikrest'ianskaia politika kemalistov v 1919–1922 godakh" [The Anti-Peasant Policy of the Kemalists in 1919–1922], *Voprosy istorii*, 9 (1951), 56–75.

"Nubar Pasha," *Encyclopaedia of Islam*, Vol. III (Leiden, 1936), pp. 946–948.

"Nupar Pasha, 1825–1899," in *Hishatakaran*, comp. by Vahan G. Zardarian. Vol. II (Constantinople, 1911), pp. 278–294, and n.s., Vol. III, 2–3 (Cairo, 1934), pp. 48–67.

Ohandjanian, B. *Egor Sevian*. Erevan, 1955.

Ordzhonikidze, G. K. *Izbrannye stat'i i rechi, 1911–1937* [Selected Articles and Speeches, 1911–1937]. [Moscow], 1939.

Orga, Irfan. *Phoenix Ascendant: The Rise of Modern Turkey*. London, [1958].

Orga, Irfan, and Margaret Orga. *Atatürk*. London, [1962].

Otian, Ervand. *Poghos Pasha Nupar* [Boghos Nubar Pasha]. Constantinople, 1913.

Paillarès, Michel. *Le Kémalisme devant les Alliés*. Paris, 1922.

Papazian, Vahan. *Im hushere* [*My Memoirs*]. Vol. I, Boston, 1950; Vol. II, Beirut, 1952; Vol. III, Cairo, 1957. 3 vols.

Parsamian, V. A. *Hai azatagrakan sharzhumneri patmutiunits: Usumnasirutiun ev pastatghter* [From the History of the Armenian Liberation Movements: Study and Documents]. Erevan, 1958.

Pasdermadjian, G. *Aprvads orer* [Bygone Days]. Boston, 1948.

——. *Why Armenia Should Be Free*. Boston, 1918.

Pavlovich, Mikh. [Vel'tman, M.]. *Revoliutsionnaia Turtsiia* [Revolutionary Turkey]. [Moscow], 1921.

Pech, Edgar. *Les Alliés et la Turquie*. Paris, 1925.

Pernot, Maurice. *La question turque*. Paris, 1923.

Pipes, Richard. *The Formation of the Soviet Union: Communism and Nationalism 1917–1923*. Rev. ed. Cambridge, Mass., 1964.

Poghosian, A. M. *Sotsial-tntesakan haraberutiunnere Karsi marzum, 1878–1920* [The Socioeconomic Relations in the Province of Kars, 1878–1920]. Erevan, 1961.

"Poghos Pasha Nupar, 1851–1930," in *Hishatakaran*, comp. by Vahan G. Zardarian, n.s., Vol. III, 3 (Cairo, 1934), pp. 69–81.

Poidebard, A. "Rôle militaire des Arméniens sur le front du Caucase après la défection de l'armée russe (décembre 1917–novembre 1918)," *Revue des études arméniennes*, I, pt. 2 (1920), 143–161.

——. "Le Transcaucase et la République d'Arménie dans les textes diplomatiques du Traité de Brest-Litovsk au Traité de Kars, 1918–1921," *Revue des études arméniennes*, III (1923), 64–78, and IV, pt. 1 (1924), 31–103.

——. *Voyages: Au carrefour des routes de Perse*. Paris, 1923.

Pomiankowski, Joseph. *Der Zusammenbruch des Ottomanischen Reiches: Erinnerungen an die Türkei aus der Zeit des Weltkrieges*. Leipzig, 1928.

Popov, A. L. "Iz istorii revoliutsii v Vostochnom Zakavkaz'e (1917–1918 g.g.)" [From the History of the Revolution in Eastern Transcaucasia (1917–1918)], *Proletarskaia revoliutsiia*, 5 (May, 1924), 13–35; 7 (July, 1924), 110–143; 8–9 (Aug./Sept., 1924), 99–116; 11 (Nov., 1924), 137–161.

Price, Clair. *The Rebirth of Turkey*. New York, 1923.

Price, M. Philips. *War and Revolution in Asiatic Turkey.* New York, [1918].
"Provisional Accord between the Armenians of Karabagh and the Government of Azerbaijan," *Eastern Europe,* I (Oct. 16, 1919), 158–160.

Radkey, Oliver Henry. *The Election to the Russian Constituent Assembly of 1917.* Cambridge, Mass., 1950.
Raevskii, A. *Angliiskaia interventsiia i Musavatskoe pravitel'stvo* [English Intervention and the Musavatist Government]. Baku, 1927.
——. *Angliiskie "druz'ia" i Musavatskie "patrioty"* [English "Friends" and Musavat "Patriots"]. Baku, 1927.
——. *Partiia Musavat i ee kontrrevoliutsionnaia rabota* [The Musavat Party and Its Counterrevolutionary Work]. Baku, 1929.
Ramkavar Azatakan Kusaktsutiun [Democratic Liberal Party]. *Mer gaghaparn u gordse: Ramkavar Azatakan Kusaktsutian miutian eresnamiakin aritov* [Our Ideology and Work: On the Occasion of the Thirtieth Anniversary of the Merger of the (Armenian) Democratic Liberal Party]. [Fresno, Calif.], 1952.
Ramsaur, Ernest E. *The Young Turks: Prelude to the Revolution of 1908.* Princeton, 1957.
Rassoul-Zadé, M. E. *L'Azerbaidjan en lutte pour l'Indépendance.* Paris, 1930.
—— [Rasulzade]. "The Meaning of a Certain Historical Act," *United Caucasus,* 3–4 (1953), 7–10.
Ratgauzer, Ia. *Revoliutsiia i grazhdanskaia voina v Baku* [Revolution and Civil War in Baku]. Pt. 1. *1917–1918 g.g.* Baku, 1927.
Rawlinson, A. *Adventures in the Near East, 1918–1922.* London and New York, 1923.
Renaudel, Pierre. *L'Internationale à Berne: Faits et documents.* Paris, 1919.
"The Republic of North Caucasia," *Eastern Europe,* I (Oct. 1, 1919), 85–87.
Rifat, Mevlanzade. *Türkiye inkilabının içyüzü* [The Inner Aspects of the Turkish Revolution]. Aleppo, 1929.
Rihbany, Abraham Mitrie. *Wise Men from the East and from the West.* Boston and New York, [1922].
Ross, Frank A., C. Luther Fry, and Elbridge Sibley. *The Near East and American Philanthropy: A Survey Conducted under the Guidance of the General Committee of the Near East Survey.* New York, 1929.
Ruben [Ter-Minasian]. "Gandzak-Gharabaghi veje" [The Dispute over Gandzak and Karabagh], *Droshak,* XXVI, 2 (1926), 46–52.
——. *Hai heghapokhakani me hishataknere* [The Memoirs of an Armenian Revolutionary]. Los Angeles, 1951–1952. 7 vols.
Rudin, Harry R. *Armistice, 1918.* New Haven, 1944.
Rustem Bey, Ahmed. *La guerre mondiale et la question turco-arménienne.* Berne, 1918.
Rustow, Dankwart A. "The Army and the Founding of the Turkish Republic," *World Politics,* XI (July, 1959), 515–552.

Sachar, Howard M. *The Emergence of the Middle East: 1914–1924.* New York, 1969.
Sahakian, H. *Meds Hoktembere ev azgayin hartsi ludsume Andrkovkasum*

[Great October and the Solution to the National Question in Transcaucasia]. Erevan, 1967.

Sahakian, Hovhannes. "Erku tari haikakan banakin medj" [Two Years in the Armenian Army], in *Edjer mer azatagrakan patmutenen* [Pages from the History of Our Liberation Movement]. Paris, 1937. Pp. 7–191.

Sahakian, T .M. "Siuniats tagavorutian himnume ev nra kaghakakan dere XI darum" [The Founding of the Kingdom of Siunik and Its Potitical Role in the 11th Century], *Patma-banasirakan handes*, 3 (1966), 220–228.

Samson. "Depker hai-parskakan sahmani vra" [Incidents on the Armeno-Persian Boundary], *Vem*, III, 4 (1935), 1–13.

Şapolyo, Enver Behnan. *Atatürk'ün hayatı* [The Life of Ataturk]. Ankara, 1954.

———. *İnkilâp tarihi* [History of the Revolution]. Ankara, 1961.

———. *Kemâl Atatürk ve millî mücadele tarihi* [Kemal Ataturk and the History of the National Struggle]. Istanbul, [1958].

———. *Kuvayi Milliye tarihi* [History of the National Forces]. Ankara, [1957].

Sargsian [Sarkisian], E. Gh [K]. "Anglo-amerikian interventsian Andrkovkasum 1918–20 tvakannerin ev Andrkovkasi zhoghovurdneri paikare irents azatutian hamar" [Anglo-American Intervention in Transcaucasia in 1918–20 and the Struggle of the Peoples of Transcaucasia for their Freedom], *Teghekagir: Hasarakakan gitutiunner*, 3 (1953), 35–48.

———. *Ekspansionistskaia politika Osmanskoi imperii v Zakavkaz'e nakanune i v gody pervoi mirovoi voiny* [The Ottoman Empire's Expansionist Policy in Transcaucasia on the Eve and during the Years of the First World War]. Erevan, 1962.

———. "Iz istorii turetskoi interventsii v Zakavkaz'e v 1918 g." [From the History of the Turkish Intervention in Transcaucasia in 1918], *Teghekagir: Hasarakakan gitutiunner*, 7 (1958), 24–41.

———. *Velikaia Oktiabr'skaia sotsialisticheskaia revoliutsiia i natsional'no-osvoboditel'naia bor'ba v Turtsii (1918–1922)* [The Great October Socialist Revolution and the National Liberation Struggle in Turkey (1918–1922)]. Erevan, 1958.

Sargsian, Gr. *Suren Spandarian*. Erevan, 1960.

Sarkissian, A. O. *History of the Armenian Question to 1885*. Urbana, Ill., 1938.

Sarur [Asur]. "Gharabaghi ktsume Adrbedjani" [The Annexation of Karabagh to Azerbaijan], *Hairenik Amsagir*, VII (June, 1929), 128–146.

Sassuni, G. *Tajkahayastane rusakan tirapetutian tak (1914–1918)* [Turkish Armenia under Russian Domination (1914–1918)]. Boston, 1927. The 2d ed. rev. is published under the title *Trkahayastane I Ashkharhamarti entatskin (1914–1918)* [Turkish Armenia during World War I (1914–1918)]. Beirut, 1966.

Schmitt, Bernadotte E. *The Coming of the War, 1914*. New York and London, 1930. 2 vols.

Schopoff, A. *Les réformes et la protection des Chrétiens en Turquie, 1673–1904*. Paris, 1904.

Sebouh [Nersesian, Arshak]. *Edjer im husheren* [Pages from My Memoirs]. Boston, 1925-1929. 2 vols.

Sef, S. E. *Revoliutsiia 1917 goda v Zakavkaz'i (dokumenty, materialy)* [The Revolution of 1917 in Transcaucasia (Documents, Materials)]. [Tiflis], 1927.

Selek, Sabahattin. *Milli mücadele: Anadolu ihtilâli* [The National Struggle: Anatolian Revolution]. Istanbul, 1963–1965. 2 vols.

Seymour, Charles. *Letters from the Paris Peace Conference.* Ed. by Harold B. Whiteman, Jr. New Haven and London, 1965.

Seymour, Charles, ed. *The Intimate Papers of Colonel House.* Boston and New York, [1926–1928]. 4 vols.

Shabanov, F. Sh. *Razvitie Sovetskoi gosudarstvennosti v Azerbaidzhane* [The Development of the Soviet Governmental System in Azerbaijan]. Moscow, 1959.

Shafir, Ia. M. *Grazhdanskaia voina v Rossii i men'shevistskaia Gruziia* [The Civil War in Russia and Menshevik Georgia]. Moscow, 1921.

Shahan. *Tiurkism Angoraen Baku ev trkakan orientatsion* [Turkism from Angora to Baku and the Turkish Orientation]. Athens, 1928.

Shahinian, G. "Herosakan shabate" [The Week of Heroism], in *Miatsial ev Ankakh Hayastan.* Constantinople, 1920. Pp. 23–25.

Shahumian, St. *Erker* [Works]. Erevan, 1955–1958. 3 vols.

Shakhatuni, A. *Administrativnyi peredel Zakavkazskago kraia* [Administrative Divisions of the Transcaucasian Region]. Tiflis, 1918.

Shamsutdinov, A. M. *Natsional'no-osvoboditel'naia bor'ba v Turtsii, 1918–1923 gg.* [The National-Liberation Struggle in Turkey, 1918–1923]. Moscow, 1966.

Shpil'kova, V. I. *Imperialisticheskaia politika SShA v otnoshenii Turtsii (1914–1920 gg.)* [The Imperialist Policy of the USA in Relation to Turkey (1914–1920)]. Moscow, 1960.

Shtein, B. E. *"Russkii vopros" na parizhskoi mirnoi konferentsii 1919–1920 gg.)* [The "Russian Question" at the Paris Peace Conference (1919–1920)]. [Moscow], 1949.

Smith, Elaine. *Turkey: Origins of the Kemalist Movement and the Government of the Grand National Assembly (1919–1923).* Washington, D.C., 1959.

Soghomonian, A. G. *Kaghakatsiakan krivnere Zangezurum* [The Civil War Battles in Zangezur]. Erevan, 1968.

Soghomonian, M. S. "Artsakh-Gharabaghi patmutiunits" [From the History of Artsakh-Karabagh], *Banber Hayastani arkhivneri,* 1 (1969), 127–150.

Soviet Union and Peace. Intro. by Henri Barbuesse. New York, [1929].

Söylemezoğlu, Galip Kemalî. *Başımıza gelenler: Yakın bir mazinin hâtiraları, Mondrosdan-Mudanyaya, 1918–1922* [The Tribulations We Faced: Memoirs of the Recent Past, from Mudros to Mudanya, 1918–1922]. Istanbul, 1939.

Spartak. *Vinovniki armiano-gruzinskago stolknoveniia* [The Culprits Responsible for the Armeno-Georgian Collision]. [Tiflis, 1918].

Spector, Ivar. *The Soviet Union and the Muslim World, 1917–1958.* Seattle, 1959.

Stakhovsky, Leonid I. *Intervention at Archangel.* Princeton, 1944.

Stankevich, V. B. *Sud'by narodov Rossii* [The Fates of the Peoples of Russia]. Berlin, 1921.

Stavrovskii, Al. *Zakavkaz'e posle Oktiabria: Vzaimo-otnosheniia s Turtsiei v pervoi polovine 1918 goda* [Transcaucasia after October: Mutual Relations with Turkey in the First Half of 1918]. Moscow and Leningrad, [1925].

Stepanian, Hovak. "Andranike Siuniats erkrum" [Andranik in the Land of Siunik (Zangezur)], *Vem*, IV (1936), no. 3, pp. 70–80, no. 4, pp. 59–71, no. 5, pp. 50–69.

Stewart, George. *The White Armies of Russia: A Chronicle of Counterrevolution and Allied Intervention.* New York, 1933.

Stuermer, Harry. *Two War Years in Constantinople: Sketches of German and Young Turkish Ethics and Politics.* New York, [1917].

Surface, Frank M., and Raymond L. Bland. *American Food in the World War and Reconstruction Period.* Stanford, 1931.

Taeschner, Franz, and Gotthard Jäschke. *Aus der Geschichte des islamischen Orients.* Tübingen, 1949.

[Talaat]. "Posthumous Memoirs of Talaat Pasha," *Current History*, XV (Nov., 1921), 287–295.

————. *Talât Paşa'nın hâtıraları* [The Memoirs of Talaat Pasha]. Istanbul, 1946.

Tansel, Selâhattin. *Atatürk ve kurtuluş savaşı* [Ataturk and the Wars of Deliverance]. Ankara, 1965.

Tchalkhouchian, Gr. *Le livre rouge.* Paris, 1919.

Temperley, H. W. V., ed. *A History of the Peace Conference of Paris.* London, 1920–1926. 6 vols.

Ter-Gasparian, R. H. "Shushu bnakchutiune 18-rd darits minchev mer orere" [The Population of Shushi from the 18th Century to Our Times], *Teghekagir: Hasarakakan gitutiunner*, 9 (1963), 67–76.

Ter-Karapetian, Gegham. *Hoghayin hartse hayabnak nahangneru medj* [The Agrarian Question in the Armenian-Populated Provinces]. Constantinople, 1911.

Ter-Minasian, Ruben. *See* Ruben.

Terzipashian, A. *Nupar* [(Boghos) Nubar]. Paris, 1939.

Tevetoğlu, Fethi. *Türkiye'de sosyalist ve komunist faaliyetler, 1910–1960* [Socialist and Communist Activities in Turkey, 1910–1960]. Ankara, 1967.

Thompson, Charles T. *The Peace Conference Day by Day.* New York, [1920].

Thompson, John M. *Russia, Bolshevism, and the Versailles Peace.* Princeton, 1967.

Tillman, Seth P. *Anglo-American Relations at the Peace Conference of 1919.* Princeton, 1961.

The Times History of the War. London, [1914]–1921. 22 vols.

Tiutiunjian, Levon. *H. H. Dashnaktsutiune ibrev petakan gordson: Paster ev iroghutiunner (1918–1920)* [The A. (Armenian) R. (Revolutionary) Federation as a Governmental Element: Facts and Realities (1918–1920)]. Constantinople, 1921.

Tokarzhevskii, E. A. *Iz istorii inostrannoi interventsii i grazhdanskoi voiny v Azerbaidzhane* [From the History of Foreign Intervention and Civil War in Azerbaijan]. Baku, 1957.

Tonapetian, A. "Angliiskaia interventsiia v Zakavkaz'e" [English Intervention in Transcaucasia], *Istoricheskii zhurnal*, 10th yr., 2 (1940), 47–53.

Torgomian, Vahram H. "Hushatetres" [From My Diary], *Vem*, IV (1936), no. 2, pp. 12–16, no. 3, pp. 20–24, no. 4, pp. 54–58, V (1937), no. 1, pp. 31–50, no. 2, pp. 44–57, and VI (1938), no. 1, pp. 57–74, no. 2, 29–47.

Tovmasian, S. H. *Sovetakan Hayastane Hoktemberi dsnundn e* [Soviet Armenia Is the Progeny of October]. Erevan, 1967.

Toynbee, Arnold J. *Armenian Atrocities: The Murder of a Nation.* London, 1915.

Traité conclu en 1783 entre Catherine II, impératrice de Russie, et Irakly II, roi de Géorgie. Pref. by Paul Moriaud and commentaries by A. Okoumeli. Geneva, 1919.

"Traité de Paix et d'Amitié entre le Gouvernement Impérial Ottoman et le Gouvernement de l'Union des Montagnards du Caucase," *Die Welt des Islams,* n.s., V, 3–4 (1958), 259–262.

"Treaty Signed between Georgia and Azerbaijan," *Eastern Europe,* I (Oct. 16, 1919), 156–158.

Trofimov, K. S. "Lenin i osnovanie Kommunisticheskogo Internatsionala" [Lenin and the Founding of the Communist International], *Voprosy istorii KPSS,* 4 (1957), 28–48.

Trotsky, Leon. *The First Five Years of the Communist International.* New York, [1945–1953]. 2 vols.

Tsérételli, Irakly. *Séparation de la Transcaucasie et de la Russie et indépendance de la Géorgie: Discours prononcés à la Diète transcaucasienne.* Paris, 1919.

Trukhanovskii, V. G., ed. *Istoriia mezhdunarodnykh otnoshenii i vneshnei politiki SSSR, 1917–1939 gg.* [History of the International Relations and Foreign Policy of the USSR, 1917–1939]. Vol. I. Moscow, 1961.

Trumpener, Ulrich. *Germany and the Ottoman Empire, 1914–1918.* Princeton, 1968.

Tumanov, Cyril. *Studies in Christian Caucasian History.* [Washington, D.C., 1963].

Tumanov, G. M. *K vvedeniiu na Kavkaz zemskago samoupravleniia* [On the Introduction of the Zemstvo Self-Administration into the Caucasus]. Tiflis, 1905.

Tumulty, Joseph P. *Woodrow Wilson As I Know Him* [Garden City, N.Y., 1921].

Tunaya, Tarik Z. *Türkiyede siyasî partiler, 1859–1952* [Political Parties in Turkey, 1859–1952]. Istanbul, 1952.

Les Turcs et les revendications arméniennes. Paris, 1919.

Türkgeldi, Alî. *Moudros ve Mudanya mütarekelerinin tarihi* [History of the Mudros and Mudania Armistices]. Ankara, 1948.

Turshian, H. G. *Sardarapati herosamarte* [The Heroic Battle of Sardarabad]. Erevan, 1965.

Udumian, K. B. "RSDBK(b) Kovkasian kazmakerputiunneri erkrayin aradjin hamagumare" [The First Regional Congress of the Caucasian Organizations of the RSDLPb (Russian Social Democrat Labor Party Bolshevik)], *Lraber hasarakakan gitutiunneri,* 11 (1967), 76–88.

Ullman, Richard H. *Anglo-Soviet Relations, 1917–1921.* Vol. I. *Intervention and the War.* Princeton, 1961. Vol. II. *Britain and the Russian Civil War, November 1918–December 1920.* Princeton, 1968.

Ünüvar, Veysel. *İstiklâl harbinde Bolşeviklerle sekiz ay 1920–1921* [Eight

Months with the Bolsheviks in the War of Liberation, 1920–1921]. Istanbul, 1948.

Uras, Esat. *Tarihte Ermeniler ve Ermeni Meselesi* [The Armenians in History and the Armenian Question]. Ankara, 1950.

Uratadze, G. I. *Obrazovanie i konsolidatsiia Gruzinskoi Demokraticheskoi Respubliki* [The Creation and Consolidation of the Georgian Democratic Republic]. Munich, 1956.

———. *Vospominaniia Gruzinskogo Sotsial-Demokrata* [Memoirs of a Georgian Social Democrat]. Stanford, 1968.

Van der Esch, Patricia. *La deuxième internationale, 1889–1923.* Paris, 1957.

Varandian, Mikayel. *Le conflit arméno-géorgien et la guerre du Caucase.* Paris, 1919.

———. *H. H. Dashnaktsutian patmutiun* [History of the A. (Armenian) R. (Revolutionary) Federation]. Paris and Cairo, 1932–1950. 2 vols.

———. "Ramzey MakDonald ev kovkasian khndirnere" [Ramsay MacDonald and the Caucasian Affairs], *Hairenik Amsagir,* VII (Oct., 1929), 107–117, and VIII (Nov., 1929), 94–105.

Vardanian, H. "Dashnaktsutiune vorpes imperializmi ev rusakan kontrrevoliutsiayi gordsakale 1918–1920 t.t." [Dashnaktsutiun as the Agent of Imperialism and Russian Counterrevolution, 1918–1920], *Teghekagir: Hasarakakan gitutiunner,* 7 (1949), 9–16.

Vardanian, H. G. "Arevmtahayeri sotsialakan ev azgayin jnshman uzheghatsume Berlini Kongresits heto" [Intensification of the Social and National Oppression of the Western Armenians after the Congress of Berlin], *Patmabanasirakan handes,* 3 (1964), 69–78.

Vartanian [Vardanian], S. *Pobeda Sovetskoi vlasti v Armenii* [Victory of Soviet Order in Armenia]. Erevan, 1959.

Villari, Luigi. *Fire and Sword in the Caucasus.* London, 1906.

Voskerchian, Artashes. *Hai marksistakan knnadatutian himnadirnere: Stepan Shahumian, Suren Spandarian* [Founders of Armenian Marxist Criticism: Stepan Shahumian and Suren Spandarian]. Erevan, 1962.

Voskerchian, P. T. *Sovetakan Hayastani ardiunaberutiune 1920–1940* [Soviet Armenia's Industry, 1920–1940]. Erevan, 1966.

Vratzian, Simon. *Hayastane bolshevikian murji ev trkakan sali midjev* [Armenia between the Bolshevik Hammer and the Turkish Anvil]. Beirut, 1953.

———. *Hayastani Hanrapetutiun* [Republic of Armenia]. Paris, 1928. 2d ed. rev., Beirut, 1958.

———. *Hin tghter nor patmutian hamar* [Old Papers for New History]. Beirut, 1962.

———. *Kharkhapumner* [Gropings]. Boston, 1924. Written in response to Kachaznuni's work, listed above.

———. *Kianki ughinerov: Depker, demker, aprumner* [Along Life's Ways: Episodes, Profiles, Experiences]. Vol. I, Cairo, Vols. II–VI, Beirut, 1955–1967. 6 vols.

W. "Les relations russo-turques depuis l'avènement du Bolchevisme," in pt. 2 of "Le Bolchevisme et l'Islam," *Revue du monde musulman,* LII (Dec., 1922), 181–206.

Wheeler-Bennett, John W. *Brest-Litovsk: The Forgotten Peace, March 1918.* London, 1938.

Williams, Talcott. "The Disposition of the Turkish Empire," *Annals of the American Academy of Political and Social Science,* LXXXIV (July, 1919), 41–50.

[Wilson, Woodrow]. *The Messages and Papers of Woodrow Wilson.* New York, 1924. 2 vols.

———. *War and Peace: Presidential Messages, Addresses, and Public Papers (1917–1924).* New York and London, [1927]. 2 vols. Issued as Vols. V–VI in the series *The Public Papers of Woodrow Wilson,* ed. Ray Stannard Baker and William E. Dodd.

Woytinsky, Wladimir. *La démocratie géorgienne.* Paris, 1921.

———. *Stormy Passage.* New York, [1961].

Yale, William. *The Near East: A Modern History.* Ann Arbor, 1958.

Yanus Nadi. *Mustafa Kemal Paşa Samsun'da* [Mustafa Kemal at Samsun]. Istanbul, [1955].

Zarevand. *Miatsial ankakh Turania* [United Independent Turan]. [Boston], 1926.

Zavriev, D. S. *K noveishei istorii severo-vostochnykh vilaetov Turtsii* [On the Most Recent History of the Northeastern Vilayets of Turkey]. Tbilisi, 1947.

Zhordaniia, N. *Moia Zhizn'* [My Life]. Stanford, 1968.

———. *Za dva goda* [During Two Years]. Tiflis, 1919.

Zhvaniia, G. *Velikii Oktiabr' i bor'ba Bol'shevikov Zakavkaz'ia za Sovetskuiu vlast'* [Great October and the Struggle of the Bolsheviks of Transcaucasia for the Soviet Order]. Tbilisi, 1967.

Ziatkhan, Adil Khan. *Aperçu sur l'histoire, la littérature, et la politique de l'Azerbeidjan.* Baku, 1919.

Ziemke, Kurt. *Die neue Türkei: Politische Entwicklung, 1914–1929.* Stuttgart, Berlin, and Leipzig, 1930.

Glossary of Place Names

Nearly all place names in the text appear in the form most widely used prior to 1920, as listed in the column on the left. Sites that have since been renamed or given already existing alternate forms are listed in the column on the right.

Former Name	*Current Name*
Adalia	Antalya, Turkey
Akhta	Hrazdan (Razdan), Armenia
Alashkert	Eleşkirt, Turkey
Alexandretta	Iskenderun, Turkey
Alexandropol	Leninakan, Armenia
Alexandrovka	Maksim Gorki, Armenia
Angora	Ankara, Turkey
Baouk Vedi	Vedi, Armenia
Bash-Abaran	Aparan, Armenia
Bash-Garni	Garni, Armenia
Bayazit	Doğubayazit, Turkey
Belyi-Kliuch	Tetri-Tskaro, Georgia
Bolnis-Khachen	Bolnisi, Georgia
Constantinople	Istanbul, Turkey
Davalu	Ararat, Armenia
Dorpat	Tartu, Estonia
Dsegh	Tumanian, Armenia
Ekaterinenfeld	Liuksemburg (Luxemburg), Georgia
Ekaterinodar	Krasnodar, Russian S.F.S.R.
Ekaterinoslav	Dnepropetrovsk, Ukraine
Elenovka	Sevan, Armenia

Former Name	*Current Name*
Elisavetpol	Kirovabad, Azerbaijan
Enzeli	Bandar-e-Pahlavi, Iran
Gandzak	Kirovabad, Azerbaijan
Ganja	Kirovabad, Azerbaijan
Gerger (Russian part)	Pushkino, Armenia
Gerusy	Goris, Armenia
Hamamlu	Spitak, Armenia
Hasankale	Pasinler, Turkey
Jalal-oghli	Stepanavan, Armenia
Karakilisa	Kirovakan, Armenia
Kariagin	Fizuli, Azerbaijan
Karvansarai	Idjevan, Armenia
Keshishkend	Eghegnadzor, Armenia
Khamarlu	Artashat, Armenia
Khankend	Stepanakert, Azerbaijan
Kharput	Elâziz, Turkey
Kolageran	Antaramut, Armenia
Krkejan	Now incorporated into Stepanakert, Azerbaijan
Kulp	Tuzluça, Turkey
Nikolaevka	Kirov, Armenia
Novo-Bayazit	Kamo, Armenia
Novo-Pokrovka	Kuibyshev, Armenia
Pahliul	Now incorporated into Stepanakert, Azerbaijan
Petrograd	Leningrad, Russian S.F.S.R.
Petrovsk	Makhachkala, Russian S.F.S.R.
St. Petersburg	Leningrad, Russian S.F.S.R.
Sardarabad	Hoktemberian (Oktemberian), Armenia
Shahali	Vahagni, Armenia
Shulaver	Shahumiani (Shaumiani), Georgia
Smyrna	Izmir, Turkey
Temir-Khan-Shura	Buinaksk, Russian S.F.S.R.
Tiflis	Tbilisi, Georgia
Tsaritsyn	Volgograd, Russian S.F.S.R.
Vladikavkaz	Ordzhonikidze, Russian S.F.S.R.
Vorontsovka	Kalinino, Armenia
Ulukhanlu	Masis, Armenia
Zeitun	Süleymanli, Turkey

Index

Abbas Quli Khan. *See* Nakhichevanskii, Abbas Quli Khan
Abdul-Hamid II, Sultan, 10, 418, 421
Abdul Kerim Pasha, 101
Abkhazia and Abkhazians, 92, 367–368, 372
Action committee. *See* International, Socialist (Second)
Adalet, Muslim Marxist society, 400
Adalia *vilayet:* Italian claims in, 306 n. 49, 319–320 n. 93
Adams, Captain Percy Tidswell: at Nakhichevan, 236 n. 24
Adana, city and *vilayet:* future status of, 265, 278, 279; interracial hostilities in, 275, 321
Adjaria, 205
Adler, Sochi *okrug*, 367
Adriatic region: Italian pretensions to, 306, 323, 336
Aegean Sea: naval forces in, 57 n. 47; coastal regions of, 324, 423
Afghanistan, 241, 391
Africa, 302 n. 34, 333, 440
Agamemnon, H.M.S.: Mudros Armistice signed on, 56, 57 n. 47
Agarak, Lori *uchastok*, 105
Aghaev, Ahmed (Agha oghlu Ahmed), 288–289 n. 115
Agha Khan: at Paris Peace Conference, 326, 327
Aghaton, Ervand, 455 n. 19
Aghbaba, Kars *oblast*, 226
Aghbalian, Nikol: on National Council, 18 n. 34
Aharonian, Avetis, 341, 350, 396, 463; on National Council, 18 n. 34; on mission

to Constantinople, 52–55; as president of Republic Delegation to Paris, 105–106, 251–339 *passim*, 370, 447; and Second International, 353; and Russian Political Conference (Paris), 373–379 *passim*, 384; and Armenian National Congress (Paris), 455, 456, 457; and Act of United Armenia, 469–471
Ahmed Izzet Pasha. *See* Izzet Pasha, Ahmed
Aivali, 324
Akhalkalak *uezd*, Tiflis *guberniia:* maps of, 6, 26, 36, 74, 198; Turkish occupation of, 28, 132 n. 16; Armenian refugees from, 49 n. 24, 68, 100; conflicting claims to, 70–73, 92, 99–100, 125, 265, 278, 358, 359; Georgian occupation of, 100–102, 355; Turkish evacuation of, 101–102; British intercession in, 114, 115, 116, 121, 213, 215 n. 48, 218, 231 n. 12, 235, 247 n. 57, 267; Muslim unrest in, 121 n. 88, 211, 220, 346, 347; elections in, 343 n. 5, 348; decisions of Second International regarding, 351, 353, 354
Akhaltsikh *uezd*, Tiflis *guberniia*, 92, 235, 265, 267; maps of, 6, 26, 36, 198; Turkish occupation and evacuation of, 28, 70, 100, 101–102; Muslim unrest in, 102, 121 n. 88, 211, 220, 346
Akhova, Lori *uchastok*, 111
Akhta, Novo-Bayazit *uezd:* refugees in, 127, 129
Akhtala, Lori *uchastok*, 74, 112, 113
Akhurian River. *See* Arpachai
Akhverdov. *See* Hakhverdov; Hakhverdian

521